THE GREAT AGRARIAN CONQUEST

NEELADRI BHATTACHARYA

The Great Agrarian Conquest

❧

THE COLONIAL RESHAPING
OF A RURAL WORLD

The Great Agrarian Conquest: The Colonial Reshaping of a Rural World by Neeladri Bhattacharya was first published by Permanent Black, D-28 Oxford Apts, 11 IP Extension, Delhi 110092 INDIA, for the territory of SOUTH ASIA.

Not for sale in South Asia

Cover: "The Past Comes in Fragments," ceramic installation by Manisha Bhattacharya
Cover design by Anuradha Roy

Published by State University of New York Press, Albany

For information, contact State University of New York Press, Albany, NY
www.sunypress.edu

Library of Congress Cataloging-in-Publication Data

Names: Bhattacharya, Neeladri, author
Title: The great agrarian conquest: the Colonial reshaping of a rural world
Description: Albany : State University of New York Press, 2019 | Includes bibliographical references.
Identifiers: ISBN 9781438477398 (hardcover : alk. paper) | ISBN 9781438477411 (e-book) | ISBN 9781438477404 (pbk.: alk. paper)
Further information is available at the Library of Congress.

10 9 8 7 6 5 4 3 2 1

for

Isha

and

J.N.U.
as it was

Contents

FIGURES AND MAPS

Acknowledgements

A BOOK THAT TAKES SHAPE over many years rests on a bedrock of support from people and institutions. Threads of ideas at conferences, incitement to thought in conversations, comments on presentations at seminars, and discussions with colleagues, peers, and students have all helped shape my work. It is difficult often to disentangle the imprint of all these others in many of the arguments and analyses I offer here.

I owe most to the institution where I have taught for years, Jawaharlal Nehru University (J.N.U.), which has been a wonderfully stimulating place – politically alive and intellectually energising. To the many students I have taught and mentored I owe more than they know. Discussions in classrooms and with research groups help students, certainly, but they also help teachers clarify ideas, pose new questions, and think up fresh ways of reflecting on issues.

The Centre for Historical Studies at J.N.U. has provided a supportive milieu for research and teaching, and I have been fortunate to have had great colleagues. Sabyasachi Bhattacharya nurtured me over my early years as a historian and has continued to offer intellectual advice. S. Gopal, Bipan Chandra, Satish Saberwal, and K.N. Panikkar offered encouragement that mattered. Discussions with Romila Thapar and Muzaffar Alam opened up for me the many deep layers of pre-modern histories; Kunal Chakrabarti and Kumkum Roy have never tired of dialogues across the chronological divisions that separate our specialisations; Radhika Singha, Janaki Nair and M.S.S. Pandian readily engaged with many of my conceptual concerns; Indivar Kamtekar and Sangeeta Dasgupta have been generous with their intellectual friendship.

E.P. Thompson encouraged me to explore the world of customary relations, sparking my early ideas in this terrain. Tanika Sarkar and

Sumit Sarkar have been enthusiastic about this project since I first discussed it with them over dinner many years ago and have provided incisive comments on whatever I have given them to read. With Prabhu Mohapatra and Bodhisattva Kar I have debated many ideas that appear in this book. Conversations with Dipesh Chakrabarty are invariably intellectually stimulating; and discussions with David Ludden, K. Sivaramakrishnan, Gyan Prakash, and Ramachandra Guha – with whom I share many academic concerns – have always been productive. With Jairus Banaji I have reflected for long on the conceptual problems of agrarian history. From Rajeev Bhargava I have learnt the value of analytically separating out the different strands of a seemingly singular argument.

Various chapters of this book have in earlier forms been presented at the Center for South Asian Languages and Civilizations at the University of Chicago, the Center for South Asian Studies at Yale, the Centre for Modern Indian Studies at Göttingen, and at the Agrarian Studies Colloquium, Yale. Discussions in all these places have helped me think through my ideas and frame my arguments. I would like to thank in particular Ravi Ahuja, Tariq Thachil, and Aditya Sarkar for their thoughtful comments.

Officials at several libraries have helped my research: in Delhi, the Jawaharlal Nehru University Library, the Centre for Historical Studies DSA Library, the Nehru Memorial Museum and Library, the Ratan Tata Library, the Central Secretariat Library, the Supreme Court Judges Library, and the National Archives of India; in Chandigarh the Punjab State Archives, the Punjab Secretariat Library, the Haryana State Archives, and the Financial Commissioner's Record Room; in Patiala the Punjab State Archives; in the UK the British Library in London, the Centre of South Asian Studies Library in Cambridge, the Bodleian Library in Oxford, and the National Archives of Scotland in Edinburgh. I thank them all.

Shalini has been my sounding board: she read many versions of each chapter, offered perceptive comments, and helped me keep away from convoluted arguments and stilted language. With Madhu, Dilip, Ania, Suvir, Rana, Ben, Suvritta, Sudipta, Tani, Pankaj, Nillofer, Rashmi, Bharat, Sunita, Prita, Mukul, Ravi, Sikha, Radha, Achin, Pamela,

Ajoy, Arati, Kamal, Anu, Shahid, Phil, Indrani, Sumit, Rudrangshu, Shobita, Jayati, Chandru, Anuradha, Andreas, and Indra I have had long discussions on many different issues over alcohol and good food. Many others have offered friendship and intellectual support: Amit and Ira, who made my early research trips to Chandigarh enjoyable; Rana (Sen), Praful, and Robi – three friends no longer there – whose passion for ideas was infectious; Indu, with whom I have made many research trips and shared my love for the Punjab countryside; Abhi, who helped me procure material from the Supreme Court Judges Library; Maitreyee, Sunita, Kannu, Alika, and Googsie Khosla, who were always affectionate. Keya has always understood my vagaries, and she and Andrew made their home my own during my research trips to London. The support of my brothers – Amitabh and Gautam – has been critical in my life; and I will always miss the friendship and love of my sister, Manisha, and my Ma, who had a blind faith in the infallibility of her children. Chitra has witnessed the conceptual turns in my work, shared my excitement for history, and commented on the chapters with care, pointing out many problematic formulations. Isha, my daughter, has been a wonderful presence through the writing of the book: responding to queries about syntax, empathising with my states of mind, and feeding me delicious cakes and coffee while I read proofs.

Satish Maurya has carefully redrawn old maps and produced the charts. Parth and Charu helped me access material from the Cambridge South Asian Studies Library; and Paulami carefully cross-checked my footnotes during the last stages of publication. Shyama has read the proofs as meticulously as ever, Anuradha has designed the jacket as beautifully as always, and Rukun has been, as usual, an editor beyond compare: both his close reading and his frequently irate comments have improved this book. The flaws, he has declared, are all mine.

Abbreviations

Agr. Rev. & Com.	Agriculture, Revenue, and Commerce (Departmental Proceedings)
App.	Appendix
ASBI	*Agricultural Statistics of British India*
BEIP	The Board of Economic Inquiry, Punjab
Com.	Commerce
Comm.	Commissioner
CRSS	*Correspondence Relating to the Settlement of Sirsa*
CSAL	Cambridge South Asia Library
DG	District Gazetteer
Div.	Division
Div. Rec.	Divisional Records
For.	Foreign
GOI	Government of India
GOP	Government of Punjab
HOCPP	*House of Commons Parliamentary Papers*
IOR	India Office Record
IDR	*Irrigation Department Report*
Irr.	Irrigation
LSBI	*The Land Systems of British India* (Baden-Powell)
NAI	National Archives of India
NS	New Series
Offg	Officiating

PCC   *Principles of the Civil Code* (Bentham)

PCL   *Punjab Customary Law* (Tupper)

PLR   *Punjab Law Reporter*

PP   Parliamentary Papers

PR   *Punjab Record*

PRFAP   *Progress Report of the Forest Administration of the Punjab*

PTECR   *The Punjab Tenancy Enquiry Committee Report and Correspondence*

Punjab For.   Punjab, Foreign Department Proceedings

RAP   *Report on the Administration of the Punjab and Its Dependencies*

RCGWCC   *Report on the Colonisation of the Government Waste on the Chenab Canal*

Rev.   Revenue

Rev. Agr. &   Revenue, Agriculture, and Commerce
   Com.   (Department Proceedings)

RFCO   Records of the Financial Commissioner's Office

RLRAP   *Report of the Land Revenue Administration of the Punjab*

RLBDCC   *Report of the Lower Bari Doab Canal Colony*

RNNP   *Report of the Native Newspapers of the Punjab*

RRIDP   *Revenue Report of the Irrigation Department, Punjab*

SAPP   *Selected Agricultural Proverbs of the Punjab* (R. Maconachie)

Sec.   Secretary

SPCAAP   *Selections from the Public Correspondence of the Administration for the Affairs of the Punjab*

SRFCP   *Selections from the Records of the Financial Commissioner, Punjab*

SRFCP, NS	*Selections from the Records of the Financial Commissioner, Punjab, New Series*
SRGNWP	*Selections from the Records of the Government of the North-West Provinces*
SRGOI	*Selections from the Records of Government of India*
SRGOP	*Selections from the Records of the Government of Punjab*
SRGOP, NS	*Selections from the Records of the Government of Punjab, New Series*
SRGPD	*Selections from the Records of the Government of the Punjab and Its Dependencies*
SRGPD, NS	*Selections from the Records of the Government of the Punjab and Its Dependencies, New Series*
Sup.	Superintendent
STD	*Selections from Thomason's Despatches*
V.S.	*Village Survey*

The Great Agrarian Conquest

THIS BOOK IS BUILT on the premise that the notion of the
agrarian we take for granted has a history that we need to
explore. It traces the processes through which – in colonial
India – the agrarian was naturalised as the universal rural, and the
landscape of settled peasant agriculture was projected as normative.
It seeks to unpack the organising concepts of the agrarian economy
whose legitimacy we so often unquestioningly accept. Agrarian colonisation could not possibly have proceeded without the creation of
spaces that conformed with the needs of such colonisation, nor without the establishment of a regime of appropriate categories – tenancies,
tenures, properties, habitations – and the framework of customs and
laws that made such colonisation possible.

Agrarian colonisation was in this sense a deep conquest. It did
not simply happen through some inexorable economic process that
displaced earlier forms of livelihood and work. It proceeded by developing a new and enabling imaginary whereby the rural universe could
be made afresh: revisualised, reordered, reworked, and altogether
transformed. The process entailed refiguring the terms used for
describing social relations and for the ties that bound communities
together. It altered perceptions of space and time, of the legal and
the permissible, the ideal and the normal. It defined the telos towards which rural history was to move; it produced specific notions of
development and growth; it made the repression of certain practices
and subsistence forms appear necessary and desirable; it celebrated
specific patterns of life and devalued others. By naturalising this new
framework, it shaped the way the rural could be imagined. In positing

1

settled peasant agriculture as the norm within the rural – creating the "normative rural" – it denied the legitimacy of other forms of rural livelihood and landscape. The changes brought about were, at the same time, cultural, discursive, legal, linguistic, spatial, social, and economic. So, to understand the several layers of meaning compacted within the term "agrarian", we need to analyse this great conquest and the seemingly silent and unobtrusive way in which it was brought about.

To focus on imaginaries is, at one level, to discuss ideas and discourses, their constitutive structure, the intellectual resources they are built on, and the ways in which they are appropriated, reworked, and deployed. But imaginaries are neither just ideas, nor come into being simply at the level of ideas. They are formed through material processes and embodied in material things: records, manuals, settlement papers, cadastral maps, village boundaries. They are encoded in laws – property acts, codes of custom, rules of inheritance, the rights of tenants. They are embedded in and fashioned through practices of mapping, writing, classifying, categorising, demarcating individual fields, bounding villages, adjudicating conflicts, planning irrigation, introducing crop varieties, planting trees, clearing scrubs, and restricting access to the commons. If imaginaries, in this sense, are constituted by history, they are also constitutive of history.[1] This is the sense in which I talk of the making of an agrarian imaginary.

My primary focus is neither on the grand schemes of state engineering nor the dramatic programmes of high modernisation.[2] These are important, and I do discuss through one case study how they might unfold in the colonial context. But my central concern is to understand how a new taken-for-granted world comes into being under colonialism, refiguring the old and normalising the colonial modern. I focus on the seemingly routine, the undramatic,

---

[1] Castoriadis, *The Imaginary Institution of Society*.

[2] In some ways my concerns in this book resonate with those of James C. Scott in *Seeing Like a State*. But Scott's focus is primarily on the grand projects of state engineering, the high modernist schemes that have often failed. My primary focus is on small projects of social engineering by the colonial state that produced the colonial agrarian order.

the everyday, on acts that organise life and institutionalise practices, integrating people and things into a new order of the normative within the rural. What I discuss was a conquest of phenomenal proportions. But the deep and profound is not always grand and dramatic.

This conquest was not driven by a unitary vision. There was no pre-scripted plan of social engineering that the colonial state put into effect, no definite scheme of colonial reordering that British officials unquestioningly endorsed. Henry Lawrence, John Lawrence, the Marquess of Dalhousie, and James Wilson – some of the individuals this book focuses on – were all colonial officials who affirmed the logic of colonialism; but they acted in dissimilar ways, imagined power diversely, and often played out their differences – privately and publicly – with great polemical vigour. And these differences mattered. They tell us about the elasticity and even contradictions in imaginings of the colonial agrarian, the formulation of policy, and the nature of governance. It is important to scrutinise this heterogeneity within officialdom, the diversity of voices and specificity of each, and the inner tensions within official minds. In this search for the heterogeneous, however, it is equally important not to ignore the overarching unity which, with all its constitutive inner differences, is recognisable as unity nevertheless. Dissonance does not mean paralysing discord, ambiguities do not freeze decisions, and conflicts of opinion do not block the possibility of confident action. I try and explore how such differences are articulated, negotiated, and transcended, how the authority of imperium is expressed.[3]

The mere assertion of an authoritative voice, however, does not necessarily make it effective. The sovereign can command a norm which may be subverted by his subjects. There is a distinction between intent and effect, between desire and its realisation. How did people come to accept the colonial regime of laws and categories, its redefinition of what was normal and permissible? How was the

---

[3] Bhabha's productive comments about ambivalence and ambiguity in "Of Mimicry" (and elsewhere in *The Location of Culture*) have often been fetishised into meaningless concepts, dissolving the notion of imperial command. See Cooper and Stoler, ed., *Tensions of Empire*, for creative explorations of ambivalence in colonial discourse and the anxieties of rule.

new habitus constituted and naturalised? What, indeed, signifies a general acceptance and normalisation? In exploring such questions, I build on Bourdieu's concept of "habitus" but rework his formulation. For Bourdieu, habitus is the taken-for-granted world within which subjects live; it defines the way people act spontaneously without being conscious of the social norms that regulate their behaviour, their dispositions. Bourdieu's notion is, however, underpinned by a structural determinism, regardless of the fact that one of the intentions of his oeuvre is to transcend the opposition between structure and practice, objectivism and subjectivism. Within his frame, the habitus produces unquestioning and spontaneous action, endorsing the sanctity of a pre-given and pre-scripted normative world – the one within which individuals are located.[4] My idea of habitus, on the other hand, shows the prefigured taken-for-granted world as continuously reworked by human beings and classes through everyday actions; the norm is undercut by its persistent transgression.[5] So, apart from arguing that colonial power was never able to create a regulatory regime that seamlessly incorporated the subjects within it – in other words that the subjects subsumed within the disciplinary order were always capable of defining their distance from it – I try to show that the operations of the state and practices of power created spaces of conflict and negotiation that people refigured. By manoeuvring, transgressing, and negotiating, people questioned the meaning of new norms and reworked their implications. The order that acquired legitimacy came into being through such refigurations. The normative is constituted through the working of this dialectic between the norm and its transgression, the code and its subversion. There is no taken-for-granted world that does not bear the imprint of those who inhabit

---

[4] See Bourdieu, *Outline of a Theory of Practice*; idem, *The Logic of Practice*. For a critique, see de Certeau, "Foucault and Bourdieu"; Bouveresse, "Rules, Dispositions, and the Habitus".

[5] My ideas here are close to those of Michel de Certeau though he tends to separate disciplinary and transgressive spaces too sharply. Such a separation becomes difficult if we explore their mutual entanglement and the way each space redefines the other. See de Certeau, *The Practice of Everyday Life*; idem, *Heterologies*.

that world.[6] My object is to explore the agrarian vision as well as its reworkings, and the constitutive connection that tied the two together.

∾

To argue this is to question the very frame within which I myself began understanding agrarian studies. In the mid 1970s, New Delhi's Jawaharlal Nehru University, where I was a student, was an enchanted place. It buzzed with political activity, intense intellectual discussion, polemic, and theoretical debate. All forms of radical thought wafted through its corridors, capturing the imagination of students, shaping the questions they posed. Intellectual activity, even historical writing, it was widely felt, had to be socially relevant and politically meaningful; they ought to help social transformation. The Emergency of 1975–7 managed to prevent public discussions but not silence thought. Inspired by the ideals of socialism and the dreams of a better future, many at the Centre for Historical Studies, including myself, began researching the histories of peasants and workers, and the agrarian and industrial economies within which they were located.

The agrarian question – always central to the nationalist and socialist imaginary – had become an obsession in the decades after Independence. The troubles of the rural sector and the problems of backwardness, it was widely agreed, could not be addressed without resolving the agrarian problem. While the state pursued its project of high industrialisation and the green revolution, economists spoke of the social barriers to development and the constraints on agrarian growth. To know these barriers, Marxist economists argued, it was essential to study the internal structure of the agrarian economy and identify the modes of production in agriculture.[7] Within the

---

[6] In this sense, E.P. Thompson's use of the productive notion of "moral economy" remains problematic. He conceives moral codes as pre-constituted, as inherited tradition: they shape crowd action but are not refigured through that action. See Thompson, "The Moral Economy".

[7] The important contributions to the debate are now collated in Patnaik, *Agrarian Relations and Accumulation*; see also Banaji, "Mode of Production in Indian Agriculture"; idem, "Capitalist Domination and the Small Peasantry".

debate, the problems of conceptual definition and the question of characterisation were never resolved, and differences persisted, but the antagonists shared one assumption – that to discuss the mode of production was to focus on the agrarian, not spaces beyond the bounds of settled agriculture. However the rural was characterised – feudal, semi-feudal, capitalist – the object of analysis was the settled peasant economy.

The categories deployed in these debates became part of the intellectual habitus of the time, providing the frame within which other discussions unfolded. Many of us, who saw ourselves as critical Marxists, felt the need to define a dialogic relationship with the debates of the time. But there was no getting away from the mode of production debate. The narratives of transition – from feudalism to capitalism – shaped our vision, even as we resisted the power of this frame. Moving away from an exclusive focus on the post-Independence decades, we were keen on a *longue durée* examination of the agrarian economy. To explore the colonial agrarian, we began mapping forms of labour, looking at the logic of tenancy cultivation, the interlinkages of different markets, the movements of prices and rents, and the consequent transformations they reflected.[8] We questioned unilinear teleologies as well as the mechanical application of terms drawn out of Western debates, but still focused on transformations within the agrarian, not beyond it.

In doing agrarian history we saw ourselves as engaged in making a radical shift from the revenue histories of earlier decades and from nationalist readings of the agrarian crisis.[9] Levels of revenue extraction had no doubt affected peasant lives, but a singular focus on revenue appeared myopic. It could not tell us all that was worth knowing about

[8] Bhattacharya, "The Logic of Tenancy Cultivation"; idem, "Agricultural Labour and Production"; Guha, "Commodity and Credit in Upland Maharashtra"; idem, *The Agrarian Economy of the Bombay Deccan*; Mohapatra, "Land and Credit Market in Chota Nagpur".

[9] Some of the finest senior historians of the time had worked on British revenue policies in India, and it was widely assumed that the study of the colonial agrarian had to be a study of revenue policy in its diverse incarnations. Stokes, *The English Utilitarians and India*; Guha, *A Rule of Property for Bengal*.

the working of the colonial agrarian economy. Moving away from the nationalist idea of a homogeneous agrarian – uniformly ravaged by colonial expropriation – we were looking for variations – between and within regions. The colonising process had to operate within different social contexts, confront embedded structures that were diverse, and environmental regimes that were dissimilar. From the homogeneous colonial there was thus a turn to the heterogeneous agrarian.[10] Elsewhere too, agrarian historians were conceptualising such variations, operating with different frames, ending up with diverse answers. The distinctions between wet and dry zones, eastern and western India, Bengal and Punjab, were being carefully examined.[11] But the focus of all this research was on the inner working of the colonial agrarian economy. The search for heterogeneity remained bounded within the agrarian frontier.

By the mid 1980s, it was evident that there were problems with this focus on the agrarian. It was exclusionary. It blocked the historian's vision in many ways. It provided a frame within which only peasants – poor, middle, rich – mattered. The rural, it was assumed, was synonymous with the agrarian. There were others outside the space of the urban who did not figure in this focus. Whatever, for instance, happened to pastoralists, forest dwellers, food gatherers, and itinerant cultivators who refused to settle? Why did their stories and lives stay outside the frame of our concern, excluded from the subjects that interested us? Why did they not appear in the pages of our histories?

Part of the problem lay with the way longer-term transformations had been identified in India's pre-colonial past. Within the accepted *longue durée* narrative of the time – one that is widely shared even today – historians tracked a transition from tribal to settled peasant society in the later-Vedic period, when pastoralists settled down, took to the iron plough, developed the agrarian economy, and expanded

[10] Bhattacharya, ed., *Essays on the Agrarian History of Colonial India.*
[11] Ludden, *Peasant History in South India*; Bose, *Agrarian Bengal*; Charlesworth, *Peasants and Imperial Rule*; Washbrook, "Economic Development and Social Stratification in Rural Madras"; Islam, *Bengal Agriculture, 1920–1946.*

the agrarian frontier.[12] Subsequent history was mostly read as the gradual unfolding of this agrarian economy in different forms and historical contexts, with its ups and downs, its phases of expansion and contraction. As settled agriculture expanded on the fertile plains, surpluses were produced which could finance the state and sustain social groups – the upper castes – that did not work on the land. Keen on tracking the transitions within settled peasant agriculture, historians ignored the non-agrarian within this rural realm. It was as if forest dwellers and pastoralists were fading figures within a bygone past and thus, ironically, not worth the while of historians – who needed to focus on trajectories that presaged the future.

Within this transition narrative of the Indian rural, history moves inexorably towards a settled peasant society. This teleology is assumed to be normative, as if it referred to a natural and inevitable process. The focus of this history was the alluvial tracts and the fertile settled peasant belts, not so much the dry zones, the scrublands, the forests, and the pastures.[13] The extraction of *agrarian* surpluses – land revenue and rent – was foregrounded, while overlooking the significance of other forms of exactions that related to non-agrarian rural spaces. A natural corollary was for the village to be seen as the universal rural, to the exclusion of other habitations and settlements. To talk of the rural was to focus on the village. Caste – the social order of the alluvial agrarian tracts – was consequently considered a universal institution. This was an agrarian-centric, state-centric, peasant-centric framework for looking at the past. As always, the limits of the frame inevitably structured the nature of the occlusions.

Dissatisfied with such erasures, some historians of India turned their gaze to forests and pastures, to the history of "tribals" and pastoralists, food gathering and shifting agriculture. They tracked the way the colonial state extended its control over forest resources, established a new regime of "scientific" forestry, and integrated forest

---

[12] See Sharma, *Material Culture and Social Formation*; Thapar, *From Lineage to State*. On iron technology and agrarian change, see the collection of essays in Sahu, ed., *Iron and Social Change in India*.

[13] For the turn to pastures and forests in studies of pre-colonial India, see Ratnagar, ed., *On Pastoralism*; Thapar, "Perceiving the Forest".

economies with the structures of colonial exploitation.[14] Others explored the implication of state policies on pastoralists and pastoral economies.[15] As environmental history acquired intellectual prestige, forests and pastures slowly displaced the peasant's field as the object of historical concern.[16]

This turn away from the agrarian was, at one level, immensely productive, opening up many new arenas of research. Historians began exploring the history of shifting agriculture and scientific forestry, rivers and mountains, animals and insects, dams and canals, minerals and plants.[17] But in the process, something was lost. Now, agrarian history was seen as antiquated, the remnant of a bygone time. Constituted as a distinct field and defined in opposition to the agrarian, environmental history sought, at least in its early articulations, to recover a state of nature untouched by the settled agrarian. Nor did it query the agrarian, look at the way its life and history were shaped by its connection with what was seen as non-agrarian. The intimate and troubled history of these interconnections remained unexplored.[18]

[14] In India two books pioneered the shift in focus: Guha, *Unquiet Woods*, and Grove, *Green Imperialism*. More internationally, Worster's *Ends of the Earth* and Crosby's *Ecological Imperialism* became the foundational texts of environmental history. See also Cronon, *Changes in the Land*.

[15] Bhattacharya, "Pastoralists in a Colonial World"; Singh, *Natural Premises*.

[16] The fecundity of the new field of environmental studies in India can be seen in the many collections that were published in the 1990s: Arnold and Guha, *Nature, Culture, Imperialism*; Grove, Damodaran, and Sangwan, *Nature and the Orient*. See also Rangarajan, *Fencing the Forest*; Prasad, "The Political Ecology of Swidden Cultivation"; Skaria, *Hybrid Histories*; Rajan, *Modernizing Nature*.

[17] See the essays in Arnold and Guha, *Nature, Culture, Imperialism*; Grove, Damodaran, and Sangwan, *Nature and the Orient*. A large selection of essays published over the years is now collected in Rangarajan and Sivaramakrishnan, *India's Environmental History*, 2 vols. For a sweeping transnational environmental history of the early modern world, see Richards, *The Unending Frontier*.

[18] This frame came under question in the 1990s. See Agrawal and Sivaramakrishnan, *Agrarian Environments*; also Bhattacharya, ed., *Forests, Fields and Farms*. See also Prasad, "Forests and Subsistence in Colonial India".

It is not enough, however, to explore these interconnections. It is not enough to look at the way different livelihoods, spaces, and histories intermesh, constituting their mutual forms. We need to push the argument further. The important point is to explore how the agrarian came into being as the universal rural. The very idea of the agrarian, I emphasise, has itself to be problematised and historicised.

~

In developing my arguments I am also arguing against two orthodoxies. When I began research, doing economic and social history was exciting. "Economic" and "social" were seen as foundational categories. It was as if their materiality was pre-constituted, only their working had to be grasped. We were critical of schematic Marxism and reductive explanations, but did not probe the constituted nature of the categories we operated with. We were aware of the need to be sensitive to questions of culture, but did not adequately reconceptualise the object of our study – the economy – to take account of cultural mediation.[19]

As the discursive turn swept through academia in the late 1980s and '90s, the seduction of economic history faded rapidly. Historians turned to the study of discourses and texts, signs and symbols, images and representations.[20] What followed was a radical rethinking of

---

For fine examples of subsequent works that look at these connections, see Guha, *Environment and Ethnicity in India, 1200–1991*; D'Souza, *Drowned and Dammed*; Cederlof, *Landscapes and the Law*; Kar, "Framing Assam"; Goswami, "Rivers in History".

[19] While Thompson's *Making of the English Working Class* had an immediate and powerful influence on studies of the working class, it did not have the same transformative effect on the study of the "economy". Thompson himself moved increasingly towards the study of popular cultural practices and rituals, law, and custom. See Thompson, *Customs in Common*. In his great series on the modern age, Hobsbawm wrote separate chapters on culture, economy, and politics without exploring their mutual mediations. See Hobsbawm, *The Age of Empire*; idem, *The Age of Capital*.

[20] In India, the essays published in *Subaltern Studies* – especially after the first four volumes – express this shift most clearly.

the idea of the archive, critical explorations of the notions of truth and history, and an opening up of new arenas of research. Disturbed by this cultural turn, many economic historians pleaded for a return to old economic history. They saw in the intellectual currents of the time the dissolution of all they valued.

In a sense both these trends shared something in common. The discursive and cultural turn moved away from the realm of the economic, as though the study of the economy itself did not have to be rethought, as if the domain that economic historians had focused on earlier was irrevocably sullied. It was as if to talk of the agrarian was to return to something archaic. On the other hand, the desperate plea of economic historians to return to economic history was not simple hostility against the discursive turn. It assumed that the domain of the economic could and should be studied only in the way it had been before, untainted by the critical and discursive turn.

This book is a product of my effort to negotiate these oppositions.[21] I do not believe that opening oneself to the discursive turn means renouncing the agrarian as a subject of study. Nor do I feel that a study of what was earlier seen as the sphere of the economic can, and ought to, be through a revival of economic history as it was practised earlier. To rethink the agrarian we need to unpack it as a category and subject it to critical scrutiny. We can do this, I think, through a productive and dialogic engagement with insights provided by the discursive turn.

∽

The site of my enquiry is Punjab, though the arguments I offer have a much wider valence. As a historian, I develop my arguments through a dialogue with records and sources, so the archive does define certain spatial limits to my enquiry, as it does for other historians. But my effort is to move beyond the parochial limits of the local, to

---

[21] I have for long emphasised the need to reconcile these oppositions in some of my general conceptual essays. See Bhattacharya, "Rethinking Marxist History", and idem, "Lineages of Capital". For a similar emphasis on the need to rethink the category "economy", see Mitchell, *Rule of Experts*.

connect – as is often said – the local to the global. One could turn the argument around to make the opposite point. The global can exist historically only through the many locals. Capital, for instance, can be conceptualised as a universal category, but it operates in local contexts, confronts embedded structures, is refigured through historically specific processes, and personified in "real" human beings. As a universal category, capital is an abstraction, but historically it exists in concrete forms, as specific capitals. There is no understanding the abstract universal in its historical forms without looking carefully at its concrete articulations. Similarly, the history of colonisation forces us to reflect on a seemingly universalising process; but colonialism operates in different forms, is articulated in dissimilar ways at diverse sites, and is refigured by local histories. Only the local can imbue the abstract universal with density and thickness, fashion its distinctive forms. My narrative focuses on one such local history that can also tell us about wider processes of agrarian colonisation.

The book is organised in four parts. I begin in Part I with a discussion of the specific style of colonial governance that took shape in nineteenth-century Punjab. What developed there, I suggest, was masculine paternalism as an ideal of governance. This ideal emerged through an embattled negotiation with an alternative utilitarian vision of rule, and its contours were shaped by these conflicting ideals. Masculine paternalism defined the vision within which the agrarian society of Punjab was imagined and its framing categories developed. Without an understanding of the constituent elements of this vision, I argue, we cannot explore the way the agrarian came into being.

In Part II, my effort is to explore the agrarian imaginary as it evolved in Punjab. Over four chapters, I track the lineage of a set of categories and institutions that provided the grand frame of agrarian reordering. These became the basis of a dramatic reorganisation of the rural landscape, a radical reworking of how social groups were perceived and the forms in which relations between people and things were legally constituted. I unpack the category "village" to show how villages were consecrated as the universal form of rural settlement. By mapping villages over the entire landscape, the British displaced alternative forms of habitation and livelihood. The whole terrain was taken over and bounded as a space within which the agrarian frontier would be expanded, pastoralists and nomadic communities displaced, and settled agriculture established. Marking village boundaries became an act of agrarian conquest, an act of enclosure on a massive scale.

I then look at the remaking of customs, the constitution of tenures, and the production of categories through which social relations in the countryside were ordered and the landscape made legible. My effort is to look at the inner logic of these processes of remaking – the conceptual resources they drew upon, the inner tensions within the discourses of property, customs, tenures, and tenancies, and the implications of the establishment of this codifying regime.

However, the desire for legibility does not necessarily create a legible world; projects of simplification often end up in classificatory convolutions. What we need to see are the ways in which schemes and plans work on the ground, the manner in which visions are concretised, laws read, notifications received. So, in Part III I shift from the exploration of models to strategies, from codes to practices, from discourses of power to the activities of everyday life. These were neither hard binaries nor absolute oppositions. We cannot understand the making of a code without looking at the way it is reordered through practices; we cannot explore discourses of power without probing the discursive practices within which they are embedded, without examining the ways in which they are interpreted, questioned, and refigured in everyday life. But the central focus of analysis can shift. If in Parts I and II I touched on practices while keeping my central focus on the making of the ideals of governance and the colonial agrarian vision, in Part III I look more closely at the working of the codifying regime on the ground – the everyday practices which are both shaped by and which reshape the regime of rules, codes, laws, and categories.

I look next at the ways in which the redefinition of rights was perceived by the peasants who cleared the commons and settled the land, expecting that their rights would be undisturbed, as had been the custom in the countryside. Through the verses of a peasant poet and the protests that unfolded in one part of Punjab, I reflect on how peasants experienced the process of colonisation. A new regime of rights does not simply become part of the habitus once rules are legally codified. People understand and react to the new codes in their own ways, drawing upon notions and ideals they are familiar with, thus creating spaces of conflict and negotiation. I look at the troubled history of such encounters that mediated the constitution of this new regime of rights and customs.

If codes seek to fix the meaning of customs and rights, battles in courts reveal the ambiguities in their definition. And so the book moves to the courtroom. It was here, through the judicial process and struggles over interpretation, that notions of rights unravelled and were remade. Practices of inheritance, rules of adoption and gift, and notions of patriliny and primogeniture were persistently re-formulated and re-specified through litigation. The new property regime that came into being was a product of such histories. Tenants and landlords, fathers and sons, mothers and daughters, did not operate within a pre-scripted legal habitus whose scripts they had to unquestioningly follow. In contesting the codes, they both affirmed its power and subverted its fixity.

Beyond the court, in everyday life, codes are negotiated in a variety of ways. No rule has predictable consequences. Historically, we see individuals and groups in different contexts, confronting rules creatively, refiguring their implications. I proceed to look at the ways in which peasants negotiated the implications of primogeniture, confounding official perceptions. Drawing on the experience in England, colonial officials deprecated the custom of equitable male inheritance as an irrational practice that accounted for all the ills of the countryside: fragmentation of holdings, parcellisations of land, the proliferation of uneconomic plots that blocked all possibilities of improved agriculture. To reveal the colonial premises of these common assumptions, I track the history of individual holdings, explore the strategies deployed by landowners to consolidate their fields, and examine the logic of scatter.

In Parts II and III, thus, I examine the many different ways in which the agrarian was constituted through discursive, legal, and social processes. Everything was now supposed to happen through the terms established within this agrarian regime. In Part IV, I go on to explore a more dramatic form of agrarian conquest. By the late nineteenth century, the process of agrarian conquest had pushed beyond the limits of the old agrarian settlements in Central Punjab to transform the vast highland pastures further west.

In the colonial imagination, pastures and scrublands were unproductive wastes, empty spaces waiting to be settled and cultivated. They had to be surveyed, mapped, and bounded. The rights of commoners had to be restricted, the movements of mobile people regulated, pastoralists turned into peasants, large-scale farming established, canal irrigation introduced, and "scientific" agriculture encouraged. On the highlands in Punjab west of the River Sutlej, we see a new experiment in state engineering, a more aggressive form of agrarian colonisation. I now shift focus to the way these pasturelands of west Punjab – the bārs as they were called – were first taken over and then radically transformed. I look both at the colonisation project as it was imagined and initiated, as well as the ways in which peasant settlers and nomadic pastoralists experienced this process.

I conclude by distinguishing two distinct but related forms of agrarian conquest: one that operates from below, slowly and silently transforming the world of peasants, and another that is implanted more dramatically from above, forcibly displacing earlier life-worlds. The meaning of colonial violence differed within these two processes. My effort in the book is to understand that meaning.

1

Masculine Paternalism and
Colonial Governance

Colonial Riders

S OME YEARS BEFORE the British and Sikh forces confronted
each other in the decisive battle of Gujrat, a quieter encounter –
involving the two hostile nations, a horse, and cultural interpretation – was imagined as having taken place in Punjab.[1] In
Henry Lawrence's *Adventures of an Officer in the Punjaub* (1846), a
European traveller by the name of Bellasis is described as making his
way on horseback to the Sikh court at Lahore, riding his favourite
steed, Chanda.[2] Before he can reach his destination, Bellasis happens
to run into the region's monarch, Maharaja Ranjit Singh. Mounted
on a handsome horse himself, the maharaja is on his way back from
his morning ride. Surrounding him are his favourite sirdars and following him an impressive escort of five hundred cavalrymen.

Seeing a European, some of Ranjit Singh's horsemen draw within
sniffing distance, crowd around Bellasis, and begin sneering and jeer-
ing. One of the horsemen, Nand Singh, a keen and active equestrian,

---

[1] Defeated by the Sikhs in the Battle of Chillanwala (January 1849), the
British forces under Hugh Gough won the decisive battle of Gujrat (February
1849), leading to the annexation of Punjab.

[2] The book appeared in its second edition in 1846 with this title. Lawrence
had published the first edition in 1845 as *Adventures of an Officer in the Service of Runjeet Singh* (London: Henry Colburn, Publisher, 1845). By 1846
the British had defeated the Sikhs in the Battle of Aliwal. The 1845 title may
in 1846 have seemed servile to Lawrence.

and second in command of the newly raised cavalry corps of his chief's Khalsa Raj, circles threateningly near, chanting a ribald song and grazing Bellasis with his steel-clad shoulder. Stung by this slight, Bellasis touches the reins of his horse, makes it perform a quick half-turn, and pricks the animal's loins with a gentleness belied by the consequences: one tremendous kick, and Nand Singh goes flying off his horse.[3] Later, at the darbar, Bellasis first offers nazar, and then his services, to the maharaja. He is asked to hold his horses; first the maharaja will test his skills. Can he build a fort? Cast a gun? Cure a nagging disease? Mend a watch? Bellasis replies courteously to this volley, saying he can do as much as any mortal.[4] But the maharaja needs more than verbal claims: the skills have to be demonstrable. Can he show-jump his horse, an art the firangis are supposed to have mastered? Nand Singh, Ranjit Singh's most adept horseman, directs Bellasis to a fence that has been specifically positioned. Humiliated in his first encounter and eager now at this opportunity to recover his injured dignity, Nand Singh spurs his horse forward. But the horse is too tightly curbed; it fails the attempt to clear the hurdle, and Nand Singh comes tumbling down once more. Bellasis on the other hand nudges Chanda with his heel, springs across the barricade, and then, wheeling around, rubs salt on the wound by jumping over both the fence and the sprawling figure of Nand Singh. The maharaja is now sufficiently impressed. He presents Bellasis with khillat, appoints him a colonel, and asks him to train the lancers of the Khalsa Raj. (Subsequently, he sends him to Kangra, 270 km distant to the north-east, to look after the affairs of his state there.)

This framing scene in Henry Lawrence's narrative shapes the confrontation between Bellasis and Nand Singh as a martial trope. Mastery over the horse, in such tellings, is the supreme proof of masculinity and military prowess – an idea common to histories across cultures when writing up allegories of conquest and power, assertions of European male prowess,[5] and, by implicit comparison, proof of

---

[3] Lawrence, *Adventures*, vol. I, pp. 18–19.

[4] Ibid., p. 21.

[5] At one level tales of valorous horses are universal. Alexander's Bucephalus, Napoleon's Marengo, the mythical Greek horse Pegasus, and Chetak celebrated

native ineptitude. Bellasis, a European, knows how to ride a horse; Nand Singh, a Sikh chabuk sawar (expert rider), does not. "The Sikh are indubitably bad horsemen, however common report may say to the contrary," Bellasis tells us.[6] All through Lawrence's book, control of the horse comes to signify the capacity to command: a bad rider cannot be a good master. Bellasis loves to ride and rides tirelessly. His native companions need to rest, Bellasis does not. His authority over Chanda is wielded gently, a touch often sufficing as command. Bellasis can tame wild horses. The inferiority of native riders is made apparent from their not being able to remain on the saddle and rolling off even well-trained studs.[7] In Lawrence's imagination a skilful rider on a well-groomed horse is the quintessential masculine master.

In his book, Lawrence clearly draws from his own experiences and identifies with its hero, Bellasis. Yet *Adventures* is not simply experiential and autobiographical. Written partly as fiction, the narrative emancipates itself from the constraints of facticity to explore the realms of imperial fantasy and desire. Structured as the autobiography of a Western adventurer, it tells the story of a life as if it had really been lived.

Like the historical novels of Walter Scott that Lawrence loved reading, *Adventures* recognises the difficulty of representing the past, capturing its essence, suggesting its alterity.[8] Rooted in the Romantic

---

in the legends of Rana Pratap all suggest the war horse as valorous and, naturally, male. My interest, however, is not in universal symbolism. I wish to explore how the power to ride comes to characterise a cultural formation, and becomes a symbol of the colonial power to rule.

[6] Lawrence, *Adventures*, vol. I, p. 22.

[7] The theme recurs in the journals and diaries of many imperial travellers. Forster, *A Journey from Bengal to England,* vol. I (1798); Henty, *Through the Sikh War* (1894), p. 60. In these texts we also see a repressed though persistent imperial fear of falling off the horse, and the demeaning blow this deals to the the rider as master. See Eden, *Up the Country* (1866), pp. 194–5. In the late colonial period, Aurobindo Ghose's symbolic dissent against colonial rule is expressed as a refusal to join the Indian Civil Service because it means having to pass the horse riding test.

[8] In exploring the anxiety of "imperfect history", Ann Rigney suggests that our recognition of the elusive nature of historical knowledge is a legacy of

historicism of the early nineteenth century, Lawrence saw the poetic imagination as indispensable when representing the essence of the past, its complexity and richness, its sublime nature. *Adventures* claims to capture a profounder truth even as it frees itself from the tyranny of facts. Asking his readers to suspend disbelief, Bellasis says: "if all my facts are not found to be sober realities, take my word for it they have a deeper foundation in truth than the narratives of most travellers."[9] This narrative freedom allows Lawrence to play out his imperial fantasies while writing in a realist mould. The distinctions between fact and representation, reality and imagination, the historical and the fictive, dissolve within his text.

As the qualities of the hero unfold, the identity of the ideal imperial self is specified. Bellasis is bold, wise, and honest, taking tough measures when necessary, always ready for battle – which he inevitably wins. No native can ever challenge him, displace his authority, subvert his plans. Bellasis defies even Maharaja Ranjit Singh, refusing to implement his orders when he thinks them injudicious. Yet the maharaja does not punish him; on the contrary, he recognises the wisdom in Bellasis' disobedience. When Bellasis, during his tenure in Kangra, is impelled to take harsh measures, the maharaja is able to see these as necessary and just.

Bellasis is both desired and hated; he is the object of affection and the target of revenge. *Adventures* gives us a stockpile of stories about courtly intrigues and conspiracies, jealousy and malevolence. Envious officials at the court conspire to displace Bellasis, provoke the maharaja to act against him, plot to kill him, encourage his soldiers to rebel. Through his figure of equestrian supremacy, Lawrence expresses the imperial anxieties of survival in a hostile environment. Bellasis speaks of his life as being in "hourly peril", of his head being in the "lion's jaw", of adversaries baying for his blood, determined on his

---

Romantic historicism of the early-nineteenth century. Doubting the capacity of either fiction or history to comprehend the alterity of the past, Romantic historicism proposed a hybrid mode of representation that questioned the autonomy of these domains and their incompatibility. See Rigney, *Imperfect Histories*. See also Davies, *Romanticism, History, Historicism*.

   [9] Lawrence, *Adventures*, vol. I, p. 2.

ruin. But, like the heroes of all survival narratives, he overcomes all odds. His heroism is transparent: even as schemers at the court intrigue, the common folk come to like him. When he leaves Kangra, the populace mourns; traders and zamindars come to his tent at night, offering prayers and good-will. Through Bellasis, Lawrence takes pain to explain "how there could be real pain at parting, between the Governor and the Governed."[10] The unknown soldier at the beginning of the narrative soon comes to be widely known and celebrated for practising an ideal form of governance.

The will to power is validated through claims to knowledge. Bellasis is knowledgeable. A stranger to the land, he still knows his way to his destination; he knows the land and its history, its past and present, its terrain and resources;[11] he is keen to demonstrate that Punjab is no terra incognita for a wilayati.[12] Bellasis also knows the people of the region – their innate characteristics, their essential weaknesses and strengths, and their potential. He knows how to handle them, master them, "cultivate their better qualities and make the best of their defects"; he knows how to fashion them into disciplined subjects.[13] He knows above all how to transform a time of disorder, anarchy, and chaos into a time of linear progress; how to establish peace and order, law and governance, rules and principles, security of life and property; how to end oppression and injustice.

The allegory of masculine conquest is also elaborated upon through a story of sexual possession. Bellasis, the daring soldier, is desired

[10] Ibid., vol. II, p. 392.

[11] Ibid., vol. I, ch. 9.

[12] Ibid.

[13] Through Bellasis, Lawrence outlines his philosophy of paternal authoritarianism. Bellasis tells us: "The true philosophy is to cultivate their ('Orientals') better qualities, and make the best of their defects, treating them with what indulgence is possible, respecting their religious prejudices, but at the same time, obliging them to respect yours, and not to treat you as if you were an unclean animal; keeping them strictly to their duty, even though it be a matter of routine, mindful that though false alarms may deaden vigilance, dishabitude does so much more certainly, and that what men are not taught in ordinary times to do as matter of course, they may, in times of need, look on as hardship." Ibid., p. 252.

by Indian women. When he is grievously hurt, shot by Nand Singh's brother, he is nursed back to life by a woman called Mehtab, and her mother. The women care for him, talk to him, and tell him the tragedies of their lives – the sufferings and injustices they have endured; and finally, the young Mehtab professes love for him. The inner feminine space of the household, carefully guarded from the male gaze, is opened for Bellasis.[14] But, written before the conquest of Punjab, *Adventures* is haunted by the fear of loss, an anxiety about the stability of possession. The recognition of love and union is followed by forced separation; reunion and marriage are followed by Mehtab's death.

In *Adventures* the idea of the masculine self fuses with the image of the proficient rider to delineate the figure of the imperial hero: they become synonymous. Bellasis' masculinity – a defining element in imperial self-fashioning – is affirmed in Lawrence's inaugural scene through an upstanding man's control of his horse. This masculinity is subsequently reaffirmed in a variety of ways: he asserts his power over people, confronts the court, conquers women, and establishes his authority. Yet he is not one-dimensional: he is simultaneously masculine and sensitive, assertive and gentle, strong and vulnerable, daring and emotional. By painting a heroism that is multifaceted and complex, Lawrence seeks to elaborate – even before he himself is given charge of ruling Punjab – his own ideal of the paternal imperial figure, powerful yet caring.

Styles of Governance

The figure of the rider continued to obsess imperial officials. Horse-riding, in fact, became a fetish. Every official imagined himself a great

[14] Lawrence's story of sexual conquest distances itself from the long pornotropic tradition that associates Oriental women with erotic excess. Mehtab does not represent the lascivious East. She is the embodiment of innocence, unsullied nature, virginal and pure. On the discursive construction of this erotic excess, see McClintock, *Imperial Leather*; Gregory, "Writing Travel, Mapping Sexuality"; Bell and Gill, *Mapping Desire*; Kabbani, *Imperial Fictions*. On the desire of the alien male to penetrate the secluded interior of the household, see Teltscher, *India Inscribed*.

rider; official biographies and autobiographies returned repeatedly to the theme, seeking to demonstrate their hero's fascination for
and ability with a horse. Knowing about colts, taking care of them,
controlling and taming them became the defining attributes of the
officer-hero.

Henry Lawrence personified this ideology of the heroic rider as
the truly regal ruler. Trained at the Addiscombe military seminary as
an artilleryman, he began exercising at the cavalry school at Karnal
soon after reaching India in 1829.[15] He loved to ride horses that
were fierce and wild, to tame them, then nurture them. In a letter to
a friend he confessed with a touch of irony to an excessive concern for
his horse: "I take so much care of him that I suspect that he will die."[16]
As President of the Punjab Board of Administration he was known
to travel thirty or forty miles a day on horseback.[17] His brother John
Lawrence, one of the three members of the Punjab Board and later
the first Chief Commissioner of Punjab, who shared Henry's equestrian enthusiasm, was described as a "vehement, swift-riding man",[18]
and recognised for his knowledge of horses in India. During his
walks and rides, his friends had to often listen to his discourses on
different breeds, and his pronouncements on "their build, nourish-
ment and training, temperament and docility."[19] Richard Temple, the
second Secretary of the Punjab Board, had learnt to ride and fence
when young; on reaching Calcutta his first interest was in purchasing a riding horse. Through his years in the North West Provinces
(1848–51) and Punjab (1851–8), he enjoyed being on the saddle every
morning and evening.[20] In the province as a whole, the image of the

---

[15] At Karnal, we are told: "He was continuously on horseback, not only
because he loved the exercise but also because he had the foresight to equip
himself for the future. Unsparing of himself he was as good a horse master as
a horseman." Gibbon, *The Lawrences*, p. 22.

[16] Ibid., p. 23.

[17] Ibid., p. 169.

[18] Aitchison, *Lord Lawrence*, p. 39.

[19] Bosworth-Smith, *Life of Lord Lawrence*, vol. I, p. 442.

[20] Temple, *The Story of My Life*, vol. I, p. 46. W.S.R. Hodson (of "Hodson's Horse"), another of Henry Lawrence's trusted men at the frontier,

good officer could no longer be dissociated from that of the good rider, and well-appointed stables became part of the essential equipment of every official.[21]

Riding expressed symbolically the ideals of one style of imperial governance as elaborated in Punjab. Mastery of a horse, according to this doctrine, was inseparable from the desire to know, relate, and communicate, a way of establishing contact with the people, feeling their pulse, perceiving their problems. To control a horse was in some ways to control the world. As Henry Lawrence galloped around the countryside, he imagined himself in closer touch with rural folk than those sitting in a kutcherry.[22] When carrying on survey work, Richard Temple was inspired by the same ideal. "My method was then, as it has ever been," he tells us, "to ride all over the country in order to see and hear for myself. The peasant proprietors were to tell me all they knew, standing on their own ground, and in the presence of their fellows."[23]

More and more, in the early years of imperial consolidation, Henry Lawrence's band of soldier-officials celebrated and propagated restless energy on horseback. The dedicated official had to be seen as always on the move, ready for action, guarding the frontier, galloping twenty miles to be on the spot of a dispute, working at a phenomenal pace, surveying, mapping, and reordering the lives of people. Officers came to define their identity through the expectations that Henry Lawrence imposed on them, seeing themselves as men of

---

was emphatic about his ideal life-style: "I prefer the saddle to the desk, the frontier to a respectable wheel-going dinner-giving dressy life at the capital . . ." Letter dated 7 October 1852, written in Kussowlee (i.e. Kasauli), in Hodson, *Twelve Years of a Soldier's Life in India,* p. 180.

[21] Aitchison, *Lord Lawrence*, p. 62.

[22] Official biographies celebrated such ideals: "By his tours from the end to end of the land, the President of the Board learned still more of the conditions of his people – how his measures had affected the well being of the people, in what manner further improvements could best be made, and where it might be wise to ease the pressure of some too rigorous reform." Gibbon, *The Lawrences*, p. 169.

[23] Temple, *The Story of My Life*, p. 54.

prodigious energy. "I am daily and all day at work with compasses and chain, pen and pencil," wrote Hodson when he was a cavalry leader at the frontier, "following streams, diving into valleys, burrowing into hills, to complete my work . . . I should not be surprised if I am asked any day to build a ship, compose a code of laws or hold assizes."[24]

This masculine energy came to be constantly written about and valorised in colonial texts.[25] During his early years of apprenticeship under Thomason, Henry Lawrence earned the nickname "gunpowder" because of the "explosive force with which he shattered all obstacles".[26] His father had died, his mother was ill, and his love for his cousin, a woman called Honoria Marshall, was paralysing. Yet, we are told, he "threw himself into the survey work with redoubled energy to lift his thoughts above the ruin of his hopes."[27] Busy with his revenue surveys, classifying villages according to soil and extent of holding, investigating rights and drawing up maps, he had no time for familial distractions. Energetic and purposeful action was entirely a male prerogative. Biographers recounted tales of Lawrence's commitment to duty and Honoria's selfless devotion. In a letter to a friend, Honoria wrote: "though I cannot interrupt him by speaking, I can sit by him while he works at his maps and papers."[28]

[24] Hodson, Letter dated 29 January 1848, Camp Raje ke Bagh, reproduced in Hodson, *Twelve Years of a Soldier's Life*, p. 14. See also Trotter, *A Leader of Light Horse*, p. 24.

[25] Of Henry Lawrence, Richard Temple wrote: "his appearance betokened an impulsive disposition and restless energy . . . In the field or on horseback he was indefatigable, evincing much endurance in all vicissitudes of weather." Temple, *Men and Events*, p. 61. The appeal of this ideal of the great colonial official as indefatigable wanderer becomes, in fact, hegemonic, as is apparent from the canonical literature of British imperialism, from Kipling to Jim Corbett. Their heroes, like Lawrence's, cover vast swathes of territory every day, continuously looking out for those in dire need of their beneficence.

[26] Gibbon, *The Lawrences*, p. 46.

[27] Ibid., p. 47.

[28] Ibid., p. 52.

Speed and energy became a measure of efficiency. The speedy disposal of business required simple rules, minimal regulations, unencumbered structures. Men on the spot, unfettered by rules, were needed to take quick decisions. "Neither regulations nor decrees of the Governor General," it was felt, "could do as much as the personal influence of the small army of magistrates, collectors and similar officials, who had the heart and the brain, and the will to understand and sympathise with those under their charge."[29] A regime of personal rule was to be built on the basis of local customs and norms, discovered through local enquiry and implemented by men on the spot.

This style of governance came to be associated with a specific idea of masculine freedom. When Henry Lawrence became Resident of the Lahore Durbar in 1846, he gathered around him a brotherhood of soldier-officials: Herbert Edwards, John Nicholson, Edward Lake, Harry Lumsden, Reynell Taylor, James Abbot, Hugh James, Frederick Mackeson, George Macgregor.[30] Lawrence, it was said, sent them to rule with the instruction: "Settle the country; make the people happy, and take care there are no rows."[31] He wanted his disciples "to stand alone, fearing no responsibility, acting on their own initiative and adapting to diverse situations."[32] External controls that restricted freedom questioned the very morality of officialdom and its sense of responsibility.

As colonial power sought to consolidate itself, this dream of unrestrained initiative and unrepressed freedom was rudely shattered. Henry Lawrence, appointed Resident of the Lahore Durbar in 1846 and subsequently President of the Punjab Board of Administration in 1849, had left Punjab by 1853. The governor general of the day, James Andrew Broun Dalhousie, dissolved the Punjab Board,

[29] Ibid., p. 26.

[30] Temple, *Men and Events,* ch. 4.

[31] Gibbon, *The Lawrences,* p. 119.

[32] Ibid., p. 119. Hodson said that Henry Lawrence's answer to every question was "act on your judgement" and "do what you think is right." Trotter, *A Leader of Light* Horse, p. 54. For Henry's letters to all his subordinates, see Henry Lawrence Collection, Mss Eur. 85/6 (BL).

stripped Henry of all authority, and appointed John Lawrence as the first Chief Commissioner of Punjab. The transfer of power from Henry Lawrence to his brother was emblematic of a profound yet ambiguous shift in visions of governance.

The Fear of Ambiguity

If at the heart of colonial power is a deep anxiety about its own authority, it also seeks forever to transcend the premises of that crippling uncertainty. Henry Lawrence's vision of rule disturbed Dalhousie (who had replaced Henry Hardinge as governor general in 1848 and remained in power till 1856). From the moment of Punjab's annexation to the day of his departure from the province that he loved, Henry Lawrence was entangled in controversies. The nature and meaning of colonial power in Punjab came to be negotiated and defined through the events of these embattled early years. If Dalhousie's idea of power appeared harshly opposed to that of Henry Lawrence, John Lawrence came to symbolise a position in between.

For Dalhousie there could be no ambiguity about the identity of power or the rules of its recognition. It had to be made visible, demonstrated through action, established beyond doubt. Henry Lawrence was resistant to the idea of Punjab's annexation, nurturing a belief in British control within a friendly Sikh state. When the Sikhs were defeated in 1849, he was keen that power be asserted with seeming gentleness and sensitivity. It was necessary, he felt, not to destroy the popular authority of native chiefs – the sirdars and jagirdars. Once they accepted British suzerainty it was important to treat them with consideration, display gestures of paternal benevolence, and establish bonds through affective relationships. Dalhousie desired the opposite.[33] "The task before me," he announced, "is the

[33] As early as September 1849, Dalhousie referred to Henry as "unconsciously perhaps a Sikh". GG to Hobhouse, President BOC, 22 September 1849, Broughton Papers, Mss Eur., F 213/24, pp. 246–7 (BL). Deeply suspicious of Henry Lawrence's empathy for the Sikhs, Dalhousie wanted to watch every move he made. He told him: "every measure but those of the merest detail should have my sanction before any thing whatever was done upon it by the Board." In a letter to Hobhouse, his superior as well as friend, Dalhousie

utter destruction and frustration of the Sikh power, the subversion of its dynasty, the subjection of its people. This must be done promptly, fully and finally."[34] Power had to be authoritative and total; its signs were to be normalised, accepted without question. When the last resistance of the chiefs was crushed, Lawrence favoured clemency towards those not active in the rebellion. Dalhousie saw them as all equally implicated, uniformly guilty, unworthy of any consideration. Their property was to be confiscated, their movements put under surveillance. "If they run away," he declared, "our contract is void. If they are caught I will imprison them. And if they raise tumult again, I will hang them, as sure as they now live; and I live then."[35] To consolidate power and remove the ambiguity of authority, the colonised had to be made aware of the reality of subjection – through spectacle and theatricality when possible, and ruthless violence when necessary.[36]

Afflicted by the fear of ambiguity, Dalhousie was persistently irritated by Henry Lawrence's political moves. At the time of annexation, Lawrence drafted a proclamation and sent the text for approval. Dalhousie was livid.[37] The proclamation, he declared, was

---

confessed that he had set up the Board of Administration in Punjab only to counteract Henry Lawrence's softness for those who had been conquered. Ibid.

[34] Quoted in Diver, *Honoria Lawrence*, p. 355. On the need for merciless action against the Sikhs, see Dalhousie to Henry Lawrence, 3 February 1849, Lawrence Collection, Mss Eur. 85/45a (BL); Dalhousie to Henry Lawrence, 5 February 1849, Henry Lawrence Collection, Mss Eur. 85/45a (BL), and Dalhousie Papers, GD 45/6/97 (NAS).

[35] Quoted in Smith, *Life of Lord Lawrence*, vol. I, p. 272.

[36] Dalhousie's aggressive refusal to be considerate and understanding towards the colonised subjects came up for official criticism, particularly after the 1857 Mutiny. See Kaye, *A History of the Sepoy War in India*, vol. I, book III; and Temple, *The Story of My Life*. Justificatory narratives of his policies followed. See Lee-Warner, *The Life of the Marquis of Dalhousie*, 2 vols; Jackson, *A Vindication of the Marquis of Dalhousie*.

[37] Dalhousie to Henry Lawrence, 3 February 1849, Lawrence Collection, Mss Eur. 85/45a (BL). See also his letter to the President of the Board of Control, 21 February 1849, Broughton Papers, Mss Eur., F 213/24, 47 (BL), and to his friend George Couper, 5 February 1849, in Baird, ed., *Private Letters of the Marquess of Dalhousie*, p. 52.

Fig. 1: Henry Montgomery Lawrence, by John Robert Dicksee,
published by Henry Graves & Co. in 1866, mezzotint,
© National Portrait Gallery, London.

objectionable; it fostered in the minds of the vanquished false expectations of favourable terms and tended to project Henry Lawrence
as a conciliator, a peace-maker who had arrived to stand between
the Sikhs and the government: "this cannot be. There must be entire
identity between the Government and its agent, whoever it be. And
I see no reason whatever to depart from my opinion that the power
of the Sikh Government should not only be defeated, but subverted
and the dynasty abolished. No terms can be given but unconditional

Fig. 2: John Laird Mair Lawrence, by Maull & Polyblank, albumen print, published in June 1859, © National Portrait Gallery, London.

surrender."[38] For Dalhousie, power had a unitary centre, an unambiguous locus. It could not speak with conflicting voices, send inconsistent signals. The agent of the government had to articulate the mind of power, not act at variance with it.[39]

[38] Dalhousie to Henry Lawrence, 3 February, 1849, Henry Lawrence Collection, Mss Eur. 85/45 a (BL); Dalhousie Papers, GD 45/6/97 (NAS).
[39] Dalhousie to Hobhouse, President BOC, 20 August 1849, Broughton Papers, Mss Eur. F 213/24, pp. 233ff. (BL); Dalhousie to Hobhouse, President

Henry Lawrence's fantasy of the official as the strong man standing alone troubled Dalhousie,[40] for whom power had to operate only with an unambiguously defined unitary centre and an ordered hierarchy. Doubts about the locus of power, its valid centre, could not be tolerated. After one of his spats with Henry Lawrence, an irate Dalhousie wrote to a close friend: "Lawrence has been greatly praised and rewarded and petted, and no doubt naturally supposes himself a King of Punjab; but as I don't take the Brentford dynasty for a pattern, I object to sharing the chairs; and think it best to come to an understanding as to relative positions at once."[41] Infuriated by Henry's officers, who resisted official command and flaunted their autonomy, Dalhousie added:

> I further wish to repeat what I said before, that there are more than Major Edwardes in the Residency who appear to consider themselves nowadays as Governor Generals at least. The sooner you set about disenchanting their minds of their illusions the better for your comfort and their own . . . for my part, I will not stand it in quieter times for half-an-hour, and will come down unmistakably upon any one of them who may "try it on", from Major Edwardes, CB, down to the latest enlisted general-ensign-plenipotentiary on the establishment.[42]

BOC, 22 September 1849, Broughton Papers, Mss Eur. F 213/24, p. 246 (BL); see also Dalhousie to Hobhouse, President BOC, 25 May 1849, F 213/24, p. 182 (BL).

[40] See GG to Hobhouse, President BOC, 25 May 1849, Broughton Papers, Mss Eur. F 213/24, p. 182 (BL).

[41] Dalhousie to George Couper, Camp Ferozepore, 5 February 1849, in Baird, ed., *Private Letters of the Marquess of Dalhousie*, p. 52.

[42] Letter to Henry on 20 February 1849, Dalhousie Papers (NAS), GD 45/6/97. On another occasion, he told Henry about his men who saw themselves as strategists thinking out their moves on the war front: "what 'thought' the camp of the Commander-in-Chief has signifies little. The camp's business is to find fighting; I find thought; and such thought as the camp has hitherto found is of such d-d bad quality, that it does not induce me to forgo the exercise of my proper functions." Dalhousie to Henry Lawrence, 20 February 1849, Dalhousie Papers, GD 45/6/97 (NAS). On Dalhousie's comments on Henry Lawrence, see Dalhousie to Hobhouse, Broughton Papers, Mss Eur. F 213/24, 47 (BL). See also Dalhousie to Henry Lawrence, 17 August 1849,

Fig. 3: James Andrew Broun Ramsay Dalhousie,
by Sir John Watson-Gordon, oil on canvas, 1847,
© National Portrait Gallery, London.

This conflict between opposing visions of power continued to simmer through the early years of the Punjab administration. It was replayed within the board as a clash between the two Lawrence brothers. They worked together, shared many ideals, but differed in their thinking about styles of governance. John saw the need for rules

Henry Lawrence Collection, F 85/45b (BL); Dalhousie to Henry Lawrence, 25 February 1849, Henry Lawrence Collection, Mss Eur. F 90/16a (BL); also Dalhousie Papers, GD 45/6/97 (NAS).

and codes, accounts and procedures, hierarchies and controls. If Henry personified the ideology of the soldier-civilian, the official on horseback dispensing quick justice, John emphasised long hours in the kutcherry and the careful auditing of finance and revenue.[43] When Dalhousie, exasperated with Henry, decided to dissolve the Punjab Board, it was to John that he turned for establishing the necessary structures of administrative control.[44] In the years to come John Lawrence came to be known as Dalhousie's "Coachman John".[45]

The new ideal of power took time to evolve. Through the years of their close association, the relationship between the Lawrences was one of fraternal tension, oscillating between affection and hostility. Henry, fêted by his band of devoted frontier officers, came to imagine himself as the spirit of Punjab.[46] Patronising and domineering, he was certain he could feel the pulse of the people and knew how best to win their support and sympathy. Yet, sentimental and emotional, he was easily hurt, much troubled by the fear of being misunderstood and persecuted. John valued the bonds that tied him to his brother but was suffocated by the constraints of their intimacy, fearful of being dominated and silenced, of speaking his mind and expressing disagreements lest they offend his brother.[47] When John became

[43] Temple, *Men and Events*, p. 61.

[44] For a retrospective recounting of Dalhousie's calculations, see Dalhousie to George Couper Edinburgh, 22 March 1857, in Baird, *Private Letters of the Marquess of Dalhousie*, p. 378.

[45] Gibbon, *The Lawrences*, p. 208.

[46] Many later colonial reminiscences and biographies memorialise this early period as a heroic and stirring time, guided by the genius and imagination of Henry Lawrence: "It was a wonderfully real and happy life in those early days of the Old Residency at Lahore. Here was a band of strong and young and earnest men, all bent on doing good, with their minds clear and strong, and full of hope, and at their head was Henry Lawrence, a giant in the battle of life, fighting against evil and wrong, and guiding all, and quickening into life and usefulness all bright thoughts and schemes that came to any of that earnest band of friends." Edwardes, *Memorials of the Life and Letters of Sir Herbert Edwardes*, pp. 161–2.

[47] On his profound sense of hurt on being displaced from Punjab, see Henry Lawrence to Dalhousie, 19 January 1853. Edwardes & Merivale, *Life of Sir Henry Lawrence*, pp. 194–5. Even before joining the Board, John

a junior member of the Punjab Board, he persuaded Richard Temple to join as secretary to the Board so that the conflict between the two Lawrences did not paralyse the administration. Till he assumed the chief commissionership, John was hesitant about pushing ahead with his ideas.

Once Henry Lawrence moved to Rajasthan, John Lawrence proceeded to tighten control. Henry's frontier soldiers – "exuberant young men" – were all reined in. They were told to respect hierarchy, submit accounts, get their projects approved, and desist from independent action. Riding had yielded to writing. Power had now to be structured around rules, codes, memos, letters, estimates, explanations, proposals, sanctions, approvals, and reports.[48] Writing alone, it was felt, could render power accountable and secure, provide it with a stable basis and coherence; it alone could connect different levels within the hierarchy and convey the existence of a high command. In 1855, when Robert Napier, the Chief Engineer of Punjab, came under attack for an empty treasury and excessive expenditure on public works, John Lawrence proceeded to discipline him, spelling out the terms of official normative behaviour:

> I do not like the way in which things have gone on, and I have wished gradually but decidedly to work a change. This I have attempted by putting a *pench* (a twist of screw), as far as possible, on new undertakings when

---

Lawrence expressed apprehensions about working with his brother. He wrote to Dalhousie: "The views of my brother, a man far abler than I am, are, in many respects, opposed to mine. I can no more expect that, on organic changes, he will give way to me, than I can to him. He is my senior in age, and we have always been staunch friends. It pains me to be in a state of antagonism to him. A better man or more honourable man I do not know . . . but in matters of civil policy, we differ greatly." Dalhousie Papers, GD 45/4/94 (NAS).

[48] On the Utilitarian obsession with specifying, encoding, and producing records, see Postema, *Bentham and the Common Law Tradition*. On the eighteenth- and nineteenth-century fascination with facticity and precision, see Frängsmyr, *et al.*, eds, *The Quantifying Spirit in the 18th Century*; Poovey, *A History of the Modern Fact*; Wise, ed., *The Values of Precision*. On the increasing role of writing within the nineteenth-century bureaucratic culture in India, see Raman, *Document Raj*. On the power of records, see Smith, *Rule by Records*.

not absolutely necessary, and by calling for estimates and explanations when the work appears necessary, but the expenses doubtful. I see that this system chafes and distresses you; that it causes you, to use your own words "to eat your own heart". You had, as you say, formerly our full swing, and were allowed to do exactly as you liked. Now, you are brought up [short] at every turn.[49]

A few months later, John Lawrence wrote to Dalhousie: "He [Napier] is all for pushing on works or originating new ones. But he dislikes details and accounts of all kinds, and cannot find it in his heart to censure anyone under him . . . He had the most decided aversion to estimates of all kinds, and considers that they are nothing but 'snares to entrap the Engineers'."[50]

In short John Lawrence, though Henry's brother, was Dalhousie's man. His task was to implement the alternative to his sibling's vision, to impose a new regime of rules and codes, a colonial institutional infrastructure for the new province.

The New Paternalism

The new Punjab tradition as it evolved was, however, intimately tied to the old. Shaped by the intensity of conflict, the clash of egos and ideas, the break was significant but neither total nor radical. Divested of the romantic notion of independence and disdain of formality, paternalism now emerged strangely wedded to the Utilitarian ideology of governance.[51] If John Lawrence was distressed by his

[49] John Lawrence to Napier, Rawalpindi, 25 April 1855, reproduced in Bosworth-Smith, *Life of Lord Lawrence,* vol. I, p. 429. He told Napier that he had always been averse to a system that granted unregulated freedom to officials, and had endeavoured as a member of the Board to enforce some checks, but: "I found that my endeavours were fruitless, and only caused a row between Henry and myself. So I gave it up." Ibid., p. 429. See also his powerfully worded letter censuring Napier and disciplining him: Lawrence to Napier, Murrie, 28 August 1855, ibid., p. 430.

[50] Lawrence to Dalhousie, Murrie, 26 August 1855, reproduced in ibid., p. 430.

[51] For a discussion on the relationship between the paternalism, protectionism, and poor laws in Victorian England, see Roberts, *Paternalism in Early*

brother's dislike for systems and rules, he was equally uncomfortable with Dalhousie's aggressive Utilitarianism. His apprehensions over Henry's style went hand in hand with a silent and hidden attraction for his ideas. Within the new masculine paternalism that matured as the dominant discourse of colonial power in rural Punjab after the 1850s, many of the earlier ideals reappear – refigured and reoriented, but recognisable.

Beyond the fractures that regularly ripped apart this discourse of paternalism, we can perceive a certain coherence. First, there was the rhetoric of contact and empathy. Expressed in Henry Lawrence's ideology of riding, the paternalist discourse of personal contact gradually came to be institutionalised within the new regime under John Lawrence via an alternative: Shanks' Pony took over from the heroic horseman. The practice of the march, an annual official ritual, had now to be performed without fail. Through a romanticised picture of these marches, endlessly replicated and circulated through colonial texts, the district officer emerges as the paternal figure overlooking the pastoral charge under his care:

> Whenever the season is favourable, that is, the deluge of rain or the overpowering heat allow them to do so – he makes a progress through his dominions, pitching his tent, now here, now there, as best suits the purpose of this work. The people no longer have to go to see him, but what is much better, he goes to see them. He rides about redressing human wrongs. Divested of all state, and often quite alone, he visits each village contained in his care of souls, takes his seat under some immemorial tree or beside the village well, where the village elders soon cluster around him. He talks to them, listens to their stories and their grievances, discusses the weather and crops . . . He thus gets to know the people and to be known to them.[52]

Victorian England; Dunkley, "Paternalism, the Magistracy and Poor Relief in England, 1795–1834", pp. 317–97; Himmelfarb, *The Idea of Poverty*; Jones, *Outcast London*; Brundage and Eastwood, "The Making of the New Poor Law Redivivus", pp. 183–94; Lawes, *Paternalism and Politics*; Claeys, *Mill and Paternalism*.

[52] Bosworth-Smith, *Life of Lord Lawrence,* vol. I, p. 55.

The same images are to be found in the biographies of nearly every official. The district officer with his retinue, riding ten to fifteen miles a day, camping in tents, chatting with sturdy farmers, arguing with the native gentry, lounging in the shade of a spreading banyan or in the vestibule of his canopy, empathising, listening, seeing. The march became what the horse-ride had been: a signifier of the official's desire to know the people, be with them. As the distance between coloniser and colonised dissolved within such narratives, the ruler and the ruled were bathed in a mist of understanding: "Before long the chief men in his district would gather round the new sahib in the evening and unfold the stories of their lives, opening out with more and more confidence until he knew their virtues and vices and understood their ways of reasoning . . ."[53] In this paternalist ideal the good civil officer is one who establishes bonds of confidence in the imperial state via personal relations, expressing his empathy via direct contact.

Second, the discourse of empathy was linked to a theory of knowledge. Valid and authoritative knowledge, in this paternalist tradition, was derived not from a study of books but from direct experience and observation. Book-knowledge was derivative, an inappropriate guide to action, an unreliable basis of policy. This assumption became part of the Thomason School as it defined itself against the high academicism and classicism of the Bengal administrators. "It is not in the secretariat bureau alone, or in the private study that administrative capacity is to be gained . . . no study will supply the place of personal experience; and so long as an officer has not himself mixed with the people, and come into immediate contact with them, as their District Officer, his opinions cannot, properly speaking, be called his own, since they are grounded, not upon personal observation, but upon the reports of others."[54] Only after the appropriate district training could the civil officer join the secretariat, only after practical experience could he stand on his own, seeing and thinking for himself and being answerable for the results. No officer could be genuinely committed, Thomason argued, to ideas that flowed not from his own observations

---

[53] Gibbon, *The Lawrences,* p. 27.
[54] Muir, "The Hon. James Thomason".

but from the minds of others. Schooled under Thomason, and convinced of the innate superiority of experiential knowledge, the new generation of Punjab paternalists transformed district training and local knowledge into fetishised objects of desire.[55]

The identity of the colonial master was shaped by this vision. A master had, naturally, to be masterful; he had to possess intimate knowledge of the work of each department. Stories told of the careers of official heroes of the North Western Provinces and Punjab tend to be stereotypical. Of Thomason, for example, it was said:

> He would walk into the record room of a collectorate, take down a bundle of vernacular proceedings, detect at a glance if they had been properly arranged, and remark upon the orders passed by the collector. He would enter a medical dispensary, examine the book of cases, gladden the heart of the native surgeon by a few pertinent remarks, and perhaps set him thinking on the properties of a drug, procurable in the bazaar, and relied upon by Native physicians, but unknown to English physicians. He would question a revenue officer about the condition of his villages, and remark upon the effect of [the] hailstorm which had lately occurred in some village under his control. Every officer was aware that with him generalities were of no avail, that the Governor knew more of his district than he did himself . . .[56]

To repeatedly eulogise a practice and sanctify its practitioners is to create a hegemonic myth. In colonial biographies even the local people were made complicit in the production of such myths. The people of Delhi, we are told, said about their collector John Lawrence in the 1830s: "*Jan Larens sahib sab janta*" (John Lawrence knows everything).

Third, the language of empathy was premised on an implicit paternalist contract that specified the hierarchical reciprocity within a filial relationship. Paternal compassion and concern in the administrator

[55] Looking back on his years in the Punjab, Aitchison wrote in 1892: "It was an unwritten law that the civil officers should see things with their own eyes, do things with their own hands, and enquire into things for themselves. Thus they came to know the people, the people learned to know them." Aitchison, *Lord Lawrence*, p. 62.

[56] Temple, *James Thomason*, p. 191.

was the flip side of the deference and submission required of the populace. This dialectic of love and reprimand, the pen and the sword, was not new: it had been spelt out at the very time of Punjab's annexation by officials of the old paternalist school. Alarmed at the possible loss of power and wealth, the jagirdars and chiefs in Punjab had joined the Khalsa in opposing the British takeover of the region in 1848. Keen on fracturing the bonds between jagirdars and landowners, Robert Cust, Deputy Commissioner and Superintendent of the district of Hoshiarpur, wrote to the principal landowners in that same year:

> I expect, and am fully confident, that you are in your own villages, and have kept clean of any rebellion. If any of your relations have joined the rebels, write to them to come back before blood is shed; if they do so their faults will be forgiven. Consider that I have in person visited every one of your villages, and I know the position of every one of you: what is your injury I consider mine: what is gain to you, I consider my gain. The rule of the British is in favour of the agriculturists. If your lands are heavily assessed, tell me so, and I will relieve you: if you have any grievance, let me know it, and I will try to remove it: if you have any plans, let me know them, and I will give you my advice; if you will excite rebellions, as I live, I will severely punish you. I have ruled this district three years by the sole agency of the pen, and if necessary I will rule it by sword. God forbid that matters should come to that. This affects your families and your prosperity. The Rajas of the country get up the disturbance, but it is the landowners whose lands are plundered. Consider what I have said and talk it over with your relations, and bring all back from rebellion, and when my camp comes to your neighbourhood attend at once in person, and tell those who joined the rebellion to return to me, as children who have committed a fault return to their fathers, and their faults will be forgiven them.[57]

Paternal affection from above was conditional on submission and respect from below. Such filial reciprocity, enforced upon the weak by the powerful, always works within a framework defined by the father. Any effort at redefinition of the terms by the "children" is deemed insubordination, their demands for dignity and independence an insolence unacceptable within the bounds of the relationship.

[57] Quoted in Aitchison, *Lord Lawrence*, p. 45.

Defiance ruptures the bonds of paternal reciprocity, the terms of its implicit contract: it makes paternal love impossible, freeing the father from the obligation to love and depriving the children from any claim to love. Punishment then becomes necessary to re-establish the normal ties of affection. A breakdown of the imagined filial contract in the colonies, in fact, legitimates repression and ruthless violence, as the map of resistance begins to overlap in the imperial mind with those of native savagery and barbarism. This is what happened in 1857, when the collapse of paternal authority was no longer a lurking fear; it was palpable, haunting the minds of those in power and recurring as the disrupting nightmare that ruined confidence in the virtue of benevolent imperialism.

The imagery of the sword and the pen remained important in the politics of the new paternalism. Many years later, when Edgar Boehm presented a statue of Lord John Lawrence to the municipality of Lahore, Lawrence is shown offering people the choice between willing obedience and enforced submission: "By which will ye be governed – the pen or the sword?"[58] The patriarchal self-image centring on the figure of the father was forged in diverse ways, ceremonial as much as literary, as profoundly authoritarian and masculine. Within popular imperial literature this patriarchal masculinity was underlined via tales of daring, adventure, and courage. In them the civil official is fearless and powerful, and, like Bellasis, faces danger with a practised ease born of an instinct for power.

In his old age, as his children crowded around the fireplace and demanded their Sunday budget of stories of stirring times, John Lawrence recounted his youthful days at Panipat as an era of adventure,

---

[58] Sir Joseph Edgar Boehm (1830–1890), was a sculptor of Hungarian descent who settled in London and became close to the royal family. The statue of Lord John Lawrence was originally meant to stand at Waterloo Place in London. Boehm subsequently offered the completed statue – disliked by those who commissioned it – to the City of Lahore. During the upsurge of nationalism in the 1920s, the inscription at the bottom of the statue provoked anger and indignation, leading to a movement for removal of the statue. Damaged by attacks, the statue – showing both hands broken – was ultimately removed and sent back to London. See Israel, *Communication and Propaganda*.

when he often put his own life in "considerable peril" during the pursuit of his official duties.[59] Dramatised by Lawrence, recorded and embroidered by his wife, many of these stories circulated through popular print for an audience eager to consume every tale of colonial adventure and excitement.[60]

Reason and the Imagination

Layers of difference inevitably persisted – and were reconstituted – beneath the shared vision of paternalist rule. The two Lawrences, while expressing alternative conceptions of the self and the world, both wanted to empathise with rural people, see British policies through their eyes, and base colonial rule on their support; both spoke of the significance of local custom and opposed the simple transfer of Western ideals of law and notions of property; both talked of the need for a "non-regulation system". In developing these ideas, they drew on ideals both had absorbed at Addiscombe or Haileybury from the intellectual discourses of nineteenth-century Europe – Romanticism, Utilitarianism, Liberalism, Evangelism – and during their association

[59] Gibbon, *The Lawrences*, p. 27. John Lawrence, we are told, once saved an old lady trapped in her hut that was gutted by fire, unperturbed by the risk to his own life. On another occasion, on the way to arrest a robber, Lawrence and his policemen were halted by "a river, broad and rapid, across which the men refused to swim their horses." Exasperated, John Lawrence told his men: "Well you cowards may do what you like, but I am going." As the young magistrate of Delhi started across the river, the native officers followed. One man slipped, fell into the river, and disappeared under water. Lawrence swam back alone, saved the rassaldar, hastened to the village, caught the murderer, chasing him across rooftops, jumping from the roof to the ground, and seriously hurting his ankle in the process. These are imperial tales of dedication to duty, desire for justice, commitment to serve, as well as courage, grit, and determination. The attributes of the coloniser and the colonised are defined in opposition: the fearlessness of the former underscored by the cowardice of the latter. The myth of the masculine master, the valiant soldier official, is grounded on the myth of the faint-hearted native.

[60] See *The Gentleman's Magazine*, May 1883, pp. 513ff.; Bosworth-Smith, *Life of Lord Lawrence*, vol. I, p. 55.

with Thomason in the North Western Provinces. To be schooled within common traditions does not necessarily, though, produce a homogeneity of conceptions. Traditions provide a cultural resource that can be appropriated and developed in diverse and opposed ways. Inscribed in the new ideas are elements and traces of the old, but refigured within the framework of a new discursive structure. While the Lawrences accepted the ideas of personal rule, masculine paternalism, and a non-regulatory system, they interpreted them in distinct and at times divergent ways. Henry was inspired more by a conservative romantic imagination, John by Utilitarianism. But in neither do these ideals reappear untainted, uncorrupted.

For Henry Lawrence the hero, like all romantic heroes, is an alien in the world, standing on his own and, like his protagonist Bellasis, separated from his surroundings. *He* creates the world, orders it, overcomes loneliness, and is desired and loved by all. His isolation underlines the power of his masculine creativity. The world, like the one Bellasis inhabits, is inhospitable and hostile. It has to be made hospitable. The theme of conspiracy that runs through *Adventures* is one that pursued Henry through his life. He felt hounded, was always upset with criticism of his work, and childishly proud of any praise.[61] Dalhousie's last letter to him, discharging him as president of the Punjab Board, confirmed his darkest emotions: the paranoia of non-recognition, the feeling of betrayal. Not only had he been displaced, even his minimal competence had been brought under question.[62]

[61] In 1842 George Clerk wrote to Henry appreciating his actions: "all along the frontier praises are loud of your exertions, alacrity, and spirit . . . it is gratifying to know that you are everywhere thought of in the way that I well know is so much deserved." George Clerk to Henry Lawrence, 1842, extracted in Edwardes and Merivale, *Life of Sir Henry Lawrence*, vol. I, p. 364. An overwhelmed Henry wrote to his wife: "It is wonderful what soft snobs we are, and how we like butter better than bread." Henry Lawrence to Honoria Lawrence, 1842, quoted in Gibbon, *The Lawrences*, p. 77.

[62] To Henry Lawrence's admirers Dalhousie's words appeared astoundingly callous and ruthless in their very understatement. Dalhousie wrote to Henry Lawrence: "we do not think it expedient to commit the sole administrative charge of the administration of a kingdom to any other than to a thoroughly trained and experienced civil officer . . ." Dalhousie to Henry Lawrence, Govt

When leaving Punjab for Rajasthan, he was overcome by the feeling that often torments the romantic self – of annihilation, a sense that he could not realise the fulness of his potential, the grandeur of his imagination. He died a few years later, during the 1857 Mutiny, from a gunshot at the Residency in Lucknow, but for him and his friends his departure from Punjab was a symbolic death.

While Lawrence's admirers went on to reinvent him as the spirit of Punjab and concretised their hero's vision in edificatory flights within hagiographic narratives, they grudged John Lawrence any originality, tracing all the elements that come to characterise the Punjab tradition to Henry's inspiring vision. They canonised the early pioneering years as a time of intense, irrepressible creativity.[63] In casting Henry Lawrence as the romantic imperial hero they saw within him not only a "fire that could not be easily subdued" but also a passion and emotion that stirred everyone to action. By contrast, John Lawrence is full of sincerity and zeal but lacking in imagination and feeling. He is reticent, rough, brusque and unwilling to reveal his emotion. For him masculine individuality was to be fashioned not just through

House, 23 December 1852, reproduced in Edwards and Merivale, *Life of Sir Henry Lawrence*, vol. II, p. 192. Gibbon, *The Lawrences*, p. 196. See also, Letter of Henry Lawrence to Hardinge, 6 March 1853, reproduced in Edwardes, *Life of Sir Henry Lawrence*, vol. II, p. 200. See also Henry Lawrence Papers, Mss Eur. F 85.

[63] Even Temple, who was close to John Lawrence, deified Henry as "one of the most gifted men whom this generation has beheld in India." John had energy but no inspiration: "His career appealed in a lesser degree to the popular imagination. His genius did not manifest itself so quickly. The fire within him did not kindle so readily, and when excited, burnt slower . . ." Temple, *Men and Events*, p. 57. Henry's spirit, his inspirational presence, and the fire that burned within him, are themes that recur in all the hagiographic official biographies and recollections. Edwardes and Merivale, *Life of Sir Henry Lawrence*; Gibbon, *The Lawrences*. See also Kaye, *Sepoy War*, vol. I, pp. 8–9. In 1858, General Abbot wrote of Henry: "his was the spirit which inspired every act of local government, which touched the heart of all his subordinates with ardour to fill up each his own part in a system so honourable to the British name. All caught from him his sacred fire, his presence seemed all pervading . . ." Gibbon, *The Lawrences*, pp. 197–8.

the fantasy of autonomous action, but on diligent hard work within the framework of rules and norms, through the use of reason and calculation, not pure inspiration.[64]

These conflicting ideals shaped the ways in which notions of work and experience were interpreted in Punjab. Henry's valorisation of the emotive nature of experience was contradicted by John, for whom work had to be expressive of diligence and discipline, not pleasure. Pain was a necessary part of dedicated effort; it was constitutive of virtue. It dignified a person and his work, transforming the individual into a moral being, and his work into worth.

The language of drudgery rather than joy saturates this conception of work. Packed in official recollections and the biographies of Punjab officials are countless tales of the long hours the civil officer was expected to spend in the kutcherry, and the phenomenal range of activities they performed. Water tanks were to be constructed, rivers bridged, roads made, new dispensaries, hospitals, schools, and jails built, lands cleared or drained, primeval forests felled or new ones planted, new crops or new methods of cultivation introduced.[65] Tales of pain, suffering, and sacrifice dominate: "For many hours every day while the rain is descending in cataclysms and turning the world into a vapour bath, or again, while the sun is scorching it like a furnace and baking it till it is hard as iron, he sits patiently in his stifling cutcherry, listening, reproving, advising, consoling, condemning."[66]

This is a new image of India as a necessary hell – of deprivation and endless work – battling with the contrary idea of India as paradise – of picturesque mountains and mangroves, adventures and thrilling

[64] For a discussion of the differing notions of masculinity represented by Carlyle and Mill – the conservative romantic and the utilitarian rationalist – see Hall, "Competing Masculinities: Thomas Carlyle, John Stuart Mill and the Case of Governor Eyre", in Hall, *White Male and Middle-Class*.

[65] The collector, wrote Cust, had to be "publican, auctioneer, sheriff, road maker, timber dealer, recruiting sergeant, slayer of wild beasts, bookseller, cattle breeder, postmaster, vaccinator, *discounter* of bills, and registrar . . ." Cust, "Collector of Revenue in the North West Provinces of India", p. 150. For a valorisation of the duties of the collector, see also Gibbon, *The Lawrences*, p. 27; Bosworth-Smith, *Life of Lord Lawrence*, vol. I, p. 55.

[66] Bosworth-Smith, *Life of Lord Lawrence*, vol. I, p. 49.

experiences, pig-sticking and hunting, riding and summer balls. The pursuit of pleasure was publicly disavowed by harping on the image of an unedenic furnace.[67]

Drawing upon these differing cultural traditions, the two Lawrences defined their object of empathy differently. Who exactly were the "people" in their discourses of contact and understanding? Romantic conservatives imagined village communities in which the aristocracy and the people, patrons and clients, were tied by natural and immemorial bonds. Traditional hierarchies were not to be radically disturbed; the authority of the past was not to be dramatically subverted. Utilitarians and Liberals detested the aristocracy and searched for industrious yeomen as the founding figures of their agrarian imagination. Wary of John's anti-aristocratic impulse, Henry wrote to his brother just before leaving Punjab in 1853:

> As this is my last at Lahore, I venture to offer you a few words of advice, which I hope you will take in the spirit it is given in, and that you will believe that, if you preserve the peace of the country, and make the people high and low happy, I shall have no regrets that I vacated the field for you. It seems to me that you look on all questions affecting Jagheerdars and Mafeedars in a perfectly different light from all others; in fact, that you consider them as nuisance and as enemies. If anything like this be your feeling, how can you expect to do them justice, as between man and man? I am sure if you will put it to yourself in this light, you will be more disposed to take up questions affecting them in a kindly spirit. I think we are doubly bound to treat them kindly, because they are down, and because they and their hangers on have still some influence as affecting public peace and contentment. I will do to them as I would be done by.[68]

[67] Hutchins tends to suggest that this image of "necessary hell" encompassed and defined the entire experience of officials in India. See Hutchins, *The Illusion of Permanence*. Such a view does not recognise the plurality of experience and the different languages in which they are expressed. The language of pleasure and pain, paradise and hell, coexisted within the official imagination.

[68] Henry Lawrence to John Lawrence, 20 January 1853, Henry Lawrence Collection, Mss Eur. F85 (BL). This was widely reproduced. See Gibbon, *The Lawrences*, pp. 199–200; Edwardes and Merivale, *Life of Sir Henry Lawrence*, vol. II, p. 195.

For all this, the differences between the two brothers can be over-stated.[69] Drawing simultaneously upon the contrary impulses of Utilitarianism and Romanticism, dislike of the aristocracy and love of tradition, John Lawrence continued with a policy of cautious dispossession.[70] The rebel sardars and chiefs of the1840s lost their jagirs, but the loyal were rewarded, their grants being reconfirmed as revenue assignments.[71] Despite faithful chiefs losing their political, administrative, and judicial powers – even their forts were razed and their forces disbanded – they remained an important political presence. The total revenue assigned by the state to grantees fell dramatically, from about 35 per cent at the time of the Lahore darbar, to 12 per cent by the late nineteenth century;[72] in absolute terms, all the same, the value of the revenue they enjoyed increased over time.[73]

The patriarchal system as it evolved in Punjab came to be known as the non-regulation system. Originally in operation in the Delhi territory annexed in 1832, this non-regulation system was reworked in Punjab, in very different ways by the two Lawrences. Even after leaving charge of Punjab, Henry continued to scoff at the idea of ruling through regulations and records, celebrating instead his vision of paternalist rule, especially at the frontier:

[69] Henry Lawrence was acutely aware of his differences with John but also recognised their shared vision. See Henry Lawrence to Hardinge, 6 March 1853, Henry Lawrence Collection, Mss Eur. F 85 (BL).

[70] For Dalhousie's support of John Lawrence's policy of dispossession, see no. 481, 31 March 1849, Elliot to Board of Adm., Punjab, Foreign Secret Consultations, 28 April 1849, no. 73 (NAI).

[71] For details, see Foreign Political, 8 April 1853, no. 165 (NAI). For an estimate of the total value of these pensions, see Foreign Secret, 28 July 1849, no. 39 (NAI); Foreign Political, 3 April 1850, nos 227–9 (NAI). For the development of the policy of resumptions after 1852 see Foreign Political Consultations, 11 February 1853, nos 53–5 (NAI); Foreign Political Consultations, 12 March 1852, no. 95 (NAI); Foreign Consultations, 27 April 1854, no. 15 (NAI); Foreign Political, 5 September 1856, no. 111 (NAI), case no 5.

[72] Calculation based on figures in *RAP*, relevant years.

[73] For a comprehensive overview of the politics of assignments, see Major, *Return to Empire*, ch. 5.

We do not want antique generals, and brigadiers with antiquated notions, in such quarters; but energetic, active-minded men, with considerable discretionary power, civil and military. It is all non-sense, sticking to rules and formalities, and reporting on foolscap paper, when you ought to be upon the heels of a body of marauders, far within their own fastness, or riding into the villages and glens consoling, coaxing, or bullying, as may be, the wild inhabitants. Such men, in short, as Nicholson, Taylor, Edwardes, Lake, and Becher, are wanted; and with them, very little writing paper, still less pipeclay, with their accompaniment of redcoats, heavy muskets, and grey-headed, discontented commandments.[74]

For John, regulations, rules, accountability, and controls were all-important. Yet he saw himself as a pioneer of the non-regulation system. As it shaped under him, it came to mean three things: governance according to the essence of a rule rather than the letter; a union of administrative, executive, and judicial power, rather than their separation, within a regime of commissionership; and a demarcation of the territory into small divisions and districts within which the direct personal rule of the collector and the commissioner was possible.[75] Rules were to be imposed but within the structure of a personalised and patriarchal administration.[76]

The Return of the Despot

Though the colonial cult of the fearless male drew upon the cultural resources of eighteenth- and nineteenth-century Europe, nothing in the colony replicated developments in the metropolitan centre.[77] In Europe, a new cult of the individual had since the eighteenth century merged with a new ideal of masculinity to define a modern patriarchal notion of gentlemanliness, honour, and moral dignity. Patriarchalism, criticised as paternal despotism, was reaffirmed as male

[74] Edwardes and Merivale, *Life of Sir Henry Lawrence*, vol. II, p. 219.

[75] This was in contrast to the administration within the three presidencies – Bengal, Bombay, and Madras – where a set of administrative regulations were formulated, and the judiciary and executive were separated.

[76] For a general account of the policy, see Major, *Return to Empire*, ch. 5.

[77] Bhabha, "Of Mimicry and Man".

power. Within the anti-aristocratic spirit of the time, gentility was dissociated from land and wealth, and linked to moral seriousness, religious belief, and commitment to public life. It was independence and individuality – not lineage and ancestry – that expressed a man's identity. And the individual subject was one who, liberated from subjection to the will of others, constituted himself, was free to act, and acted on others. Purged from a life of idleness and indolence, the self was to be fashioned through hard work and moral commitment, for work was seen as ennobling, as being of public value.

The individual who thus fashioned himself and the world around him could not but be male. Constrained by the ideology of domesticity, excluded from an active role in the public sphere, the woman was confined to the interior of the household: she could be a good mother, a child bearer, a housekeeper upholding the moral foundation of society by training children into the virtues of hard work and obedience. The ideals of this masculine individuality, generalised through the pedagogic practices of public schools and consecrated in the canonical texts of the time, were glorified by intellectuals – among whom Kipling was later pre-eminent – and emulated by the middle classes struggling to free themselves from the *ancien regime* culture of paternalism and clientage. Over time, this ethos acquired hegemonic power within society. Thomas Arnold at Rugby set the trend for English public school education.[78] As physicality was linked to moral and intellectual growth within the public school system, athleticism and sportsmanship became symbols of manliness and individuality.[79] *Tom Brown's Schooldays* idealised the shaping power of these schools in the making of the new morality and masculine identity. The cult of athleticism also inspired a muscular Christianity that Christianised sports, re-emphasising the value of physicality in shaping men of action and disciplining the moral fibre of a society, creating healthy

[78] Bamford, *Rise of the Public Schools*; idem, "Thomas Arnold and the Victorian Ideal of Public Schools"; Simon and Bradley, eds, *The Victorian Public School.*

[79] Collini, *Public Moralists*. Colls, *et al.*, eds, *Englishness*; Wilkinson, *Gentlemanly Power*; Haley, *The Healthy Body and Victorian Culture*; Hutchins, *The Illusion of Permanence.*

minds and healthy bodies that could be mobilised to serve Nation and Empire.[80]

By the mid-nineteenth century the figure of the new Hero had firmly established itself in British popular imagination. Public intellectuals like Thomas Carlyle and John Stuart Mill – one a romantic conservative and the other a Utilitarian rationalist – differed in their specific conceptions of individuals, but both powerfully affirmed a shared faith in the efficacy of human action, the capacity of the individual subject to transform himself and the world. Both defined the Hero as strong and masculine.[81] For Carlyle the very essence of the new individuality and morality was embodied in the figure of the Hero: "He, such as he may be is the soul of all. What he teaches the whole world will do and make."[82] His exemplary life had to be celebrated, emulated, and installed in the memory of the nation.

In the colonies, these ideals could not be transplanted untransformed. The doctrine of individualism could not be extended to allow everyone, colonisers and the colonised, equal rights to masculine individuality. The colonised, as subjects and not citizens, came to be defined precisely by their lack of masculinity and spirit of independence.[83] Liberal ideals of freedom, liberty, and human dignity had to be radically reinterpreted when legitimising the idea of subjecthood.[84] The conceptual validation of this colonial disavowal was, I suggest, effected partly through the paternalist doctrine. Under pressure in Europe since the Enlightenment, questioned and decried by social contract theorists, paternalism was reinvented as a colonising ideal in the nineteenth century. While claiming male power over women,

[80] On muscular Christianity, see van der Veer, *Imperial Encounters*; Hall, ed., *Muscular Christianity*.

[81] On the contrast between Carlyle and Mill, see Hall, "Competing Masculinities".

[82] Carlyle, "The Hero as Man of Letters", p. 236.

[83] On colonial masculinity see, Nandy, *The Intimate Enemy*; Sinha, *Colonial Masculinity*; Fox, *Lions of the Punjab*.

[84] On the irony of the liberal defence of empire, see Mehta, *Liberalism and Empire*; Morefield, *Covenants Without Swords*. On the powerful liberal voices against empire, see Muthu, *Enlightenment Against Empire*; Pitts, *A Turn to Empire*.

anti-paternalist social contract theories of eighteenth-century Europe had denied the absolute right of the father to be despotic and freed the son from the bonds of filial servitude. In stories of social contract, the despotic father is symbolically killed by the son who transforms patriarchal rights into civil government, transferring political power to representatives of the state.[85] With the political defeat of the despotic father, patriarchy was no longer paternal: it was reconstituted by social contract theorists as fraternal patriarchy: boys subordinated to the despotic rule of the father were now to be seen as equal men within civil society, and their right over women was naturalised.[86] In the colonies the father returns, resurrected from death, to relive another long and traumatic life. And within the colonial versions, the two notions of patriarchal power – the father's right over children and the male's right over women – remained interconnected. Patriarchal power was manifestly male as well as paternal. White women may not have been entirely excluded from the ambit of power, but in the end they had little choice except to affirm the male's right. Happy in their domesticity, in the celebration of the masculine authority of husbands, travelling and writing about natives, observing and representing them, the memsahibs were in their own specifically subordinated and feminine ways complicit in reproducing masculine power.[87] This male power was also, as we shall see, to be established over feminised colonised bodies through the complicity of male natives – the village elders and chaudhris. The implicit masculine patriarchal contract between colonising white males and certain sections of colonised black males defined the ground on which the rights and customs of local society were then reworked.

[85] For a provocative discussion of the implicit sexual contract behind the social contract theories, see Pateman, *The Sexual Contract*. For a discussion of the seventeenth-century debate on patriarchal power, see Coward, *Patriarchal Precedents*; Schochet, *Patriarchalism in Political Thought*.

[86] Pateman, *The Sexual Contract*, particularly ch. 4.

[87] Indira Ghose and Sara Mills have underlined the active agency of women travellers in the making of colonial images of difference and consolidating masculinist assumptions. Ghose, *Women Travellers in Colonial India*; Mills, *Discourses of Difference*.

The return of the patriarchal idea meant a rehabilitation of the despot. In associating patriarchy with ancient society and the despotism of the father, anti-patriarchal social theory had since the eighteenth century projected patriarchy back into the past. It defined the European present as a time of individual freedom and liberation from patriarchal control within civil society. Yet the same theory also suggested that the ideals of individualism and freedom could not work in the colonies. If patriarchy was inappropriate within a modern civil society centred in individual freedom, the end of patriarchy could not even be imagined in colonised societies, which were seen as primitive and ancient. Here, patriarchal theory made the despotic rule of a masculine father a supposedly rational necessity. Having invented and critiqued the idea of Oriental Despotism – contrasting the despotic essence of the East with the commitment to freedom of the West – liberalism, in an ironic double bind, went on to deify the civil officer as a paternal despot. The despotism of the father was now seen as a necessary sign of his affection and love when entrusted with a society seen as peopled by infants – immature, not yet fully individuals or wholly human, not yet ready for the responsibilities of freedom. This idea of masculine despotism over an infantile society was passionately affirmed both by men like Dalhousie – imperious and arrogant in his refusal to listen to native voices – as well as the Lawrences, who spoke the language of paternal care.[88]

[88] John Kaye wrote of Dalhousie: "Dalhousie had no imagination. He had but one idea of the people among whom his lot was cast – an idea of a people habituated to the despotism of a dominant race . . . He could not see with other men's eyes, or think with other men's brains; or feel with other men's hearts." Kaye, *Sepoy War*, vol. I, book III, p. 356. For Dalhousie, despotism in India was an inescapable necessity. "We govern India now by a limited despotism," he wrote, "because India is wholly incapable of governing itself, and we are wise in doing so." Quoted in Lee-Warner, *The Life of the Marquis of Dalhousie*, vol. I, p. 124. But the caring civil officer who sat below the tree listening to the villagers also liked seeing himself as a paternal despot – sensitive and compassionate but despot nevertheless. Charles Raikes wrote about John Lawrence as a civil officer in charge of Panipat: "he led a life as *primus inter pares*, rather than a foreigner or a despot, among the people. Yet a despot he was, as any man soon discovered who was bold enough or silly enough to

But subjects do not always accept the terms in which masters define the social contract. They may publicly, and out of necessity, conform to rules and submit, but they are more than likely in private to mock and revile the instruments of their subordination. They may be obliged to listen to the language of command, but their own command of a language almost inevitably involves reworking intended meanings, subverting the original intent of the vocabularies of power.[89]

As patriarchal power consolidated itself over the nineteenth century, it was persistently troubled by voices that questioned its authority. When Malcolm Darling realised on his last ride through North India in the winter of 1946 that the colonised "children" were desperate to disown their colonial paternity and claim an alternative lineage for themselves, he was stung by a sense of betrayal. In an ironic realisation of the anti-patriarchal myth of the father's death, the colonised had asserted their freedom to be masculine. They claimed to be adults and demanded the right to be citizens, not subjects. They seemed to proclaim with chilling frankness: "Father you are dead."

Paternal Violence

Complicit in the project of colonialism, paternalism had a beleaguered life warped by tensions and dualities. It was driven forward, like all ideologies, neither through the unfolding of its inner coherence nor by a pre-formed logic embedded within its discourse, but by inner contradictions that tended to rip it apart, unsettling its assumptions and self-assurance, questioning the authenticity of its rhetoric. As the conflict between contrary ideas, norm and practice, was playing out, uncertain colonial officials sought to rework the meaning of their governing vision, searching for a new coherence in their thought that could sustain self-belief.

---

question his legitimate authority, a despot, but full of kindly feelings, and devoted heart and soul to duty and hard work." Gibbon, *Lawrences,* p. 29.

[89] On the intimate relationship between the visible and invisible transcripts, see Scott, *Domination and the Arts of Resistance.*

Paternalism provided a language and a framing ideal within which concrete policy measures could be thought out. But this process of concretisation was profoundly problematic. In terms of practical measures, the discourse of empathy was expressed in two key slogans: moderation and protection. The rhetoric of moderate revenue assessment, however, contradicted colonialism's restless desire for the maximisation of fiscal returns. The rule of a caring district officer was to be built on the gentle economy of low assessment, but the logic of this paternal compassion was repeatedly expressed in a language that reaffirmed the centrality of colonial interest. "Do not be hard on the zamindars," John Lawrence told Charles Raikes, his assistant in Panipat. Government revenue had to be collected, but gently: "the calf gets the milk which is left in the cow."[90] As a settlement officer at Jullunder, Lawrence wrote to George Christian: "Mind you assess low. If you don't I shall be your enemy for life, and indeed, what is worse, you will be your own."[91] An impoverished peasantry would yield no revenue, and a discontented peasantry might rebel. When Henry Lawrence argued for the need to retain the loyalties and support of the chiefs and sardars, his brother disagreed, again expressing his concern for the peasantry within a vocabulary of political self-interest: "It is a mistake to think that by making Rajas and Chiefs powerful you attach the country. One lakh given in the reduction of assessments and making the people comfortable and happy in their homes is better than three lakhs given to Rajas."[92] Colonial self-interest, misrecognised by the paternalist discourse of disinterested empathy and care, returned insistently to question the authenticity of this disavowal.

The fiscal history of the Delhi territory, where John Lawrence introduced the revenue settlement of the 1830s, shows the inner contradictions of this ideology of low assessment – the conflict between norm and practice. In the districts of Gurgaon, Karnal, Rohtak, Hissar, and Delhi, acquired in 1803, much before the acquisition of the Jullunder region in 1846 and the rest of Punjab in 1849, several

---

[90] Quoted in Aitchison, *Lord Lawrence*, p. 32.
[91] Quoted in ibid., pp. 32–3.
[92] Quoted in ibid., p. 44.

summary settlements were introduced at various points in the 1820s and 1830s. Subsequently, the First Regular Settlement was begun around 1837–8, partial revisions were carried out in the 1840s and 1850s; the Second Regular Settlement was made in the 1870s and revised in the first decade of the twentieth century. From the time of the earliest settlements, British officials in the high corridors of power regularly congratulated themselves for their moderation, contrasting the humanity of the British regime with the oppressiveness of the Sikh. Equally regularly, at the level of practical administration in the districts, revenue officials were forced to recognise the fragility of their claims, retract from their self-flattering rhetoric, and reduce the level of their revenue demand. In a rearguard effort to recuperate its self-image in the present, the discourse of paternal care critiqued the evidence of severe assessment as a mistake of past practice.

While moderation remained a founding principle from the very first settlement, the actual revenue demand was calculated in ways that magnified the limit that could be defined as moderate. In the early Summary Settlements of the 1820s and 1830s there were no regular surveys, no records of rights, no assessment of yields and returns from land.[93] Revenue had to be collected to maintain the frontier force and meet the fiscal needs of an expanding administrative structure. The assessing officer looked through old pre-British village papers, ascertained the revenue that the jagirdars had collected over a period of five years, considered that to be the revenue-yielding capacity of an estate, and fixed the British demand accordingly. The new demand, pitched lower than the pre-British level, was then projected as the sign of a new time of moderation; because of it, the productive energies of peasants would be released; they were being freed of the vicious and enervating fiscal system of the past. But on the ground the settlements tended to break down, arrears of unpaid revenue mounted, villages were deserted, and worried officials were

[93] "The only guide for the Assessing Officer was the amount collected from each village by our predecessors; and this was ascertained, so far as was possible for a period of five years from the old papers, statements of leading men, &C." Walker, *Ludhiana S.R., 1873–83*, p. 172. See also Purser, *Jullunder S.R., 1880–6*, p. 152.

jolted out of their self-delusion. The core reason was that the jagir-
dari demand early British officials had chosen to see as normative had
been particularly high. Engaged in continuous warfare over the late-
eighteenth century and a shrinking revenue resource base, the jagirdars
of that period had intensified the fiscal demand on villages under
their control. British calculations made on this basis were therefore
far from moderate: even subsequently reduced cash demands proved
ruinous, particularly when crops failed in the arid Delhi territory and
prices collapsed over a depression in the 1830s (they remained low
till the late 1840s). While John Lawrence served in the region in the
1830s, two terrible famines decimated the countryside (1833 and
1837). On his usual rides through the villages in 1833, he witnessed
only the melancholy signs of desolation and death. "As early as the
end of April," he wrote, "there was not a blade of grass to be seen for
miles, and the surrounding plains were covered with the carcass of
the cattle that had died from starvation."[94] The rains had failed, the
grass had withered; not an acre could be ploughed, thousands died
of disease and want; even the rich starved, for grain had become far
dearer than money. By the time the rains came the oxen were dead,
no animals remained to draw the plough. Emaciated women could
be seen pulling at ploughs in barren fields. Shaken by these images of
desolation, Lawrence reduced the revenue demand and emphasised
the virtues of moderation to his officers.

John Lawrence, however, dispensed lenience with parsimony. The
result was that settlements soon broke down, once again forcing the
imperial rhetoric of restraint to face what it construed as the peasant's
reluctance to pay even a reasonable demand. The fear of an empty
treasury and the pressure of escalating state expenditure also limited
the reductions that were actually granted. In Gurgaon, the jama fixed
at the Summary Settlement was Rs 14 lakhs. Realising that the district
was "terribly over-assessed", the demand was reduced to Rs 12 lakhs
at the First Regular Settlement of 1838. Soon, officials were admitting
that "even the reduced demand pressed heavily on the impoverished
landowners." By 1842 officials had to carry out another revision,

[94] Quoted in Aitchison, *Lord Lawrence*, p. 31.

entailing the sanctioning of further reductions. When at the Second Regular Settlement (1873–7) the assessment was again increased to Rs 12 lakhs, the system collapsed again, and yet another official, James Wilson, had to be called in to suggest revisions (1881–4).[95]

To the east of Gurgaon, in pargana Karnal, an official by the name of Gubbins carried out the First Regular Settlement. Like all settlement officers, he applauded himself for an assessment that he described as "exceedingly low".[96] Thirty miserable years later, Denzil Ibbetson, carrying out the Second Regular Settlement, recounted the sad history of Gubbins' magnanimous system.[97] When Gubbins' assessment was first announced, the villagers revolted, entering into "a covenant not to accept the terms offered." In a tract like the Karnal Nardak, where the assessed demand was Rs 30,763, uncollected balances mounted to Rs 65,000 within five years of the settlement (between 1847 and 1851). As peasant anger spread, a Mr Ross was rushed in to revise the settlement in 1852. Everywhere he went, Ross heard tales of despair and the complaints of despondent villagers against disastrous rates that would have seemed impossibly extortionate even in good years. Yet Ross saw no reason for any substantial reduction. The years between 1847 and 1851, he felt, had been exceptionally bad, and there was little likelihood of "such strain ever falling upon the pargana". So he proposed a prudent reduction of 4 per cent of the jama, and a payment of the earlier balances in two to four instalments. Village after village refused to accept the demand. Revenue officials looked desperately for lambardars who would contract to collect the revenue. But they could find no lambardars to engage for about half of the total assessment of Rs 100,901. As the years passed, Ross' expectation of good seasons was belied: three of six harvests after 1852 failed. An embarrassed Ross now confessed that most of the villages of the Nardak had "seriously deteriorated, even from their wretched condition in 1852 . . . it was

[95] See Lawrence, *Rewari Pargana S.R., 1838*; Wilson, *Gurgaon S.R., 1872–83*.

[96] No. 30, 14 February 1878, Ibbetson, Sett. Officer, Karnal, to Comm. & Sup. Delhi Div., Delhi Division Records, series I, basta 118, p. 92.

[97] Ibid. The quotations in this para are from this extremely rich report. See also Ibbetson, *Karnal S.R., 1872–73*.

surprising that the estates had not sunk altogether."[98] Recounting this dark past, Ibbetson in the 1880s presented his own settlement as the embodiment of moderation and flexibility – a claim dented by the history of fluctuating collections and accumulating balances through the early twentieth century.[99]

∿

This contradiction between rhetoric and practice, the ideal and the concrete, unsettled the self-assurance of paternalism. Torn by inner tensions, anxious and uncertain, a reshaped ideology of power struggled to present itself as coherent. A ceaseless search for certainty and inner coherence, I would argue, is in fact one of the defining logics of imperial power. A radical Humean anxiety about the self could not typify imperial practice; it would have paralysed authority. If the self were eternally confounded and forlorn, as Hume saw it, if it always appeared to be an "uncouth monster", if on all sides one could see nothing but dispute, contradiction, and doubt, if every step that one took was hesitant and every new reflection made one dread the error and absurdity of one's reasoning, then that self could guarantee nothing beyond an open-ended dialogue, a conversation tempered by humility.[100] Every trace of this radical uncertainty had to be transcended if imperial power was to be presented as omnipotent and absolute.

[98] No. 30, 14 February 1878, Ibbetson, Sett. Officer, Karnal, to Comm. & Sup. Delhi Div., Delhi Division Records, series I, basta 118.

[99] Every year of bad harvest saw the revenue collection dip dramatically in the insecure tracts of south-east Punjab. In tehsil Thanesar (Karnal district) revenue collection was 78 per cent of the demand in 1905–6 and 41 per cent in 1907–8; in tehsil Kaithal (Karnal district) the corresponding figures were 75 per cent and 65 per cent. In nearby Hissar district the proportion of collection to demand was 20 per cent in 1901–2, 34 per cent in 1902–3, and 63 per cent in 1905–6. *RLRAP*, relevant years; *Punjab DG*, 1912, vol. VI B, Statistical Tables (Karnal), Table 39.

[100] On the varied ways in which Hume and James Mill confronted the unfamiliar, see Mehta, *Liberalism and Empire*. On Hume's notion of the self, see Seigel, *The Idea of the Self*; Schwerin, *Hume's Labyrinth*; Pitson, *Hume's Philosophy of the Self*; Frasca-Spada, *Space and the Self in Hume's Treatise*.

How was this to be done? How could imperial power be both uncertain and self-confident, stricken with self-doubt yet self-possessed? How could it confront the opposition between norm and practice, between the ideal and the corporeal? In the troubled history of colonial power, this contradiction was negotiated through several strategies.

There was, first, a strategy of time distancing.[101] Violations of the normative ideal were recognised, but the self, situated in the living present, was distanced from the practice of this violation. A breakdown of norms was projected back into the past, presented as characteristic of another time, subsequently displaced by a more authentic practice. Exorcised from this disquieting past, the imperial self saw itself emerge sanitised and purified, untainted by the mistakes of predecessors. In imperial narratives from the late-nineteenth century, in the pages of settlement reports and official memos, we read candid accounts of harsh practices, especially during Company rule before 1833. Aitchison, who served in Punjab for many years, wrote of the early Company years in the Delhi territory:

> In those days the company's Government of the Delhi Territory was supposed to be patriarchal. But the revenue administration was thoroughly vicious and hardly less oppressive than in the worst Native States. The assessment of the land tax was fixed at a ruinous rate. The demand was never paid in full. Balances were always recurring. When the revenue of a village was overdue, horse and foot were quartered on the inhabitants till everything was squeezed out of all who could pay. One hundred and thirty-six horsemen were retained in Panipat for the collection of revenue, while twenty-two considered sufficient for the duties of the police! No wonder the revenue system broke down. An estate was considered fairly lucky if it escaped resettlements every five years. Almost all settlements Lawrence made were large reductions on the previous demand.[102]

In such strategic recountings, imperial practice is located, over and over again, within a discontinuous time. The contrast between the present and the past comes to stand for an opposition between good and bad time, a time of ideal practice and a time of the violation of

---

[101] On "time distancing", see Fabian, *Time and the Other*.
[102] Aitchison, *Lord Lawrence*, p. 32.

norms. Here John Lawrence is seen as breaking with an unacceptable past. Subsequently, in the 1880s, officials like Wilson and Ibbetson project themselves as making a more definitive move towards a realisation of the ideal of benevolently paternal rule.

Second, there was a strategy of the spatial segregation of practices and discourses – between private and public, internal and external. There was an attempt, never fully successful, to confine radical doubt to the interiorised realm of official circles, within secret and confidential memos, and to render uncertainty private. At each point in time, public policy was pronounced with astounding self-assurance as the distilled essence of official wisdom. It was as if, enriched by debate and discussions, modified by reflection on the problems of past practices, imperial policy had emerged with a rightful claim to supreme self-arrogance, embodying the authoritative voice of a master in control.

Third, there was the strategy of misrecognition and denial. Imperial officials often could not see evidence of any violation of norms, any breakdown of the paternalist ideal. Seeing was a question of visualising reality, defining what constitutes valid evidence of that reality, and deciding how it was to be read. Why was it necessary to interpret the impoverishment of peasants, their utter failure to pay the revenue demand, as evidence of a brutal settlement by an uncaring master? Could not the same evidence tell another story, one that might comfort the imperial mind? In official narratives, impoverishment was regularly traced to native laziness and harvest failure, to peasant profligacy and the moneylender's greed. Some felt, in fact, that impoverishment was a sign of prosperity rather than poverty: for it was the rich who borrowed more than the poor.[103] Famines and scarcities, in such accounts, do not question the foundation of agrarian paternalism, they reaffirm it. In such times of trouble, the Raj came forth to grant remissions of revenues, introduce relief, give work to the starving, and help the poor survive seasons of want. In the great famine of 1897 thousands died in the arid south-eastern tract of south Punjab. When relief measures were ultimately introduced, officials were keen to hear words of gratitude that would reaffirm their

[103] Darling, *Punjab Peasant in Prosperity and Debt.*

self-image as kind and compassionate. Reporting back on the effect of the relief measures, junior local officials produced the words that persons in authority were eager to hear. "This is the opinion of every officer in contact with the people," reported the deputy commissioner of Karnal, '*Sarkar ne Zilha ko basaya*' (the sarkar has settled the region) was on every tongue."[104] From another district it was reported: "The people are grateful to the Sarkar for the relief measures undertaken to help them . . . The people say that *sarkar* is their *ma bap* and is ready to help them in times of trouble."[105] Stories of famine thus become a part of narratives of imperial self-fashioning, tales in which the telos of a paternalist ideal unfolds with uncomplicated ease.

What the sarkar resisted hearing were other voices that disconcertingly said relief had come too late, that remissions were too meagre and the revenue burden too heavy. Listening, like seeing, is a question of judging, making sense, attributing meaning. How were officials to know that the complaints of the peasants were authentic? That their cries of pain and suffering were not fraudulent? That their starvation was real, not simulated? In official perception, paternal measures became necessary only when the real conditions had been properly investigated, the facts indisputably determined, when the famine was, in official reckoning, beyond doubt. Unwarranted and excessive kindness, officials felt, could be unproductive and debilitating. The distinction between "flexibility" and "laxity" was carefully spelt out in the *Land Administration Manual*: the former was essential, the latter "demoralising", since it nurtured idleness and apathy.[106] The sanctity of the settlement contract could be disturbed and remissions granted only in extraordinary circumstances: "in exceptional cases of calamity so severe as to justify and necessitate a relaxation of the settlement contract."[107] No relief was to be given for a failure of less than half the crop. Remissions were to be made only when balances of suspended revenue could not be collected over several years. Pressurised by the need for finances, officials were reluctant to see crop failure as

[104] Land Rev. & Agr. (Famine), April 1898, A 30–7, p. 28.
[105] Ibid.
[106] Douie, *Panjab Land Administration Manual*, ch. 16.
[107] Ibid., p. 310.

indisputable evidence of famine, and eager to visualise an optimistic future of clement weather and good harvests. Famine was officially acknowledged and relief works formally started only when the poor were willing to labour at test works on "starvation wages" – that is, at one-fourth the normal rate. But the ultimate test of a famine was often a sociological one. Famine was seen to have definitely arrived when Jat zamindars came out to work with Chamars at the relief works, crossing the social marks of their status and distinction.[108] Their social death was a precondition for judging their right to a biological life.

To test goings-on on the ground and uncover the truth of peasant conditions required cautious scepticism. In official imagination, the villagers' failure to pay revenue was often a sign of their "recusant" behaviour, their "intransigence", their unwillingness to submit to a rule of order. Apprehensive of being seen as soft and gullible, imperial officials tended to doubt the claims of villagers, suspected duplicity, and asserted the need to be stern and firm. Of the many tales told of John Lawrence in heroic colonial narratives, there is one in particular that reveals his profound fear of being seen as innocent and gullible, an image which he counters by adopting an attitude of cold severity.[109] One year, while John was master of the Delhi territory in the 1830s, the Gujars of the region failed to pay their revenue. The season was bad, they said, and the harvest poor. They had no reserves to draw upon and no crop to offer. Could the sarkar grant a remission? Uncertain of the truth of their claims, and suspicious of duplicity, John refused. He was, however, willing to grant them a little extra time to settle their dues. But the Gujars, pastoralists who had been forced to accept a revenue settlement, failed to pay up. Seeing them move out of their settlements with their cattle in search of pasture, John Lawrence marched with his sawars to surround the Gujar settlements and announced he would allow them no access to

[108] See *Punjab Famine Code*, 1884, 1896, 1906, 1930; Douie, *Panjab Land Administration Manual*. Also Land Rev. & Ag. (Famine), April 1898, A 30–7, file no. 59 of 1898, serial no. 1 (NAI), pp. xxix; *Report on the Punjab Famine of 1899–1900*, vol. 6.

[109] Gibbon, *The Lawrences*, pp. 29–30.

pasturage till they paid the government its dues. Within a few days, we are told, the villagers appeared with the money. An instance of virtual extortion during a particularly difficult time is here narrated as evidence of effective masculine authority. To be paternal as well as masculine, the official had to be considerate without being sentimental, caring yet firm, sympathetic without getting to the point of seeming malleable. Beneath this discourse of gentility lay practices of everyday violence and the peasant's experience of that violence – a severity made to appear necessary, legitimate, and acceptable within official discourse. This violence, subsumed by the voice of gentility, needs to be recognised for what it is – as does the language of gentility which fetishises such violence.

For all this, the ideology of paternalism remained important in defining the shape of agrarian society in North India. By the end of the nineteenth century, the idea of moderation, continuously violated in practice, came to define a certain barrier to relentless increases in revenue demand. In money terms, revenue demands continued to increase with price rises, but in real terms, expressed in produce, they declined: falling sharply during the price rise of the last decades of the nineteenth century and through the War boom after 1914, rising when prices collapsed during the Great Depression, and dropping again with the price rise of the 1940s.[110]

A commitment to the idea of moderation, deepened by the fear of revolt after 1857, was regularly emphasised through the twentieth century.[111] As Punjab's peasants swelled the ranks of the army and

[110] The levels of collection varied. In the wet zones, revenue was realised in full, but in the dry tracts over 50 per cent of the demand could not be collected during bad years. Rigidities of collection, official resistance to sanction remission – more important than the absolute burden of the revenue – weighed on the lives of peasants subjected to inflexible violence. The wet and dry zones emerged from this experience bearing the marks of distinct histories of insecurity and stability, impoverishment and accumulations, misery and well-being.

[111] At times the idea was stressed by local officials against their superiors in the provincial Board of Revenue; at times words of caution percolated down from the top. In 1909, for instance, R.W. Carlyle wrote to the Government

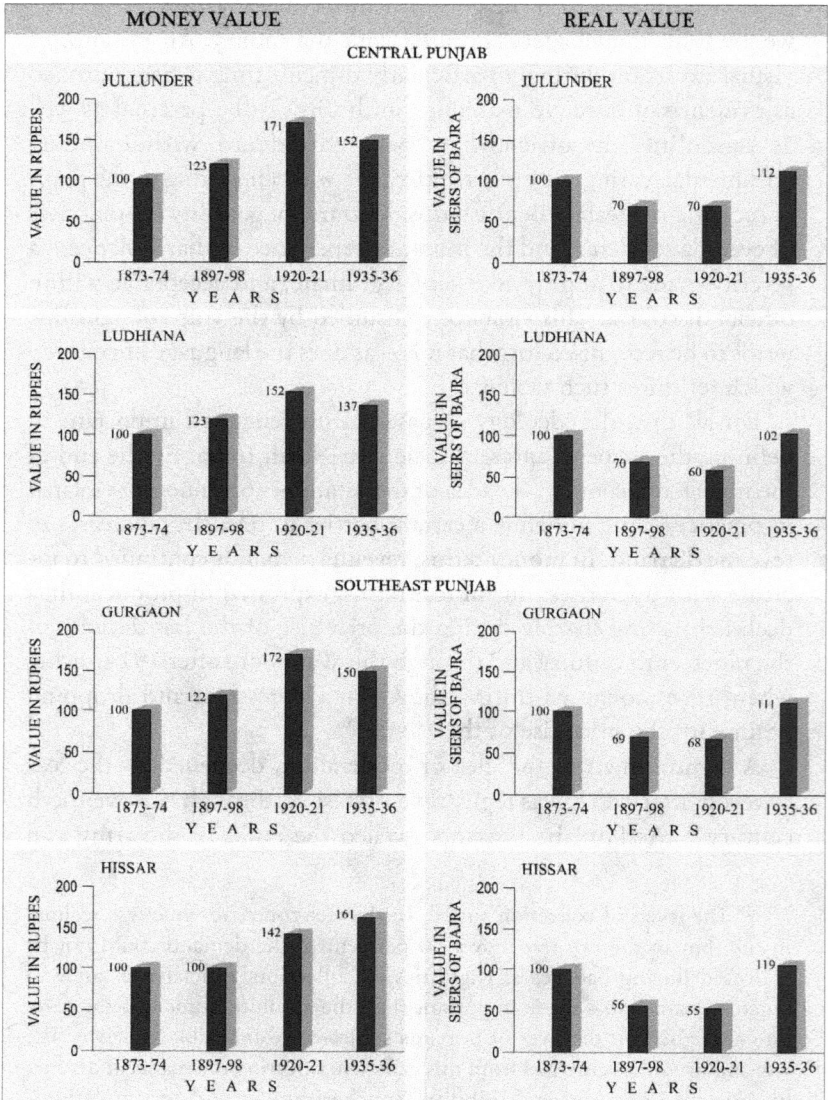

Fig. 4: Revenue per acre of cultivated area.

Source: *RAP* and *ASBI*, relevant years. Retail prices of bajra in Ludhiana have been used to calculate the real value of revenue demand (Column 2).

the dread of agrarian disturbance fused with the horror of mutiny, "protection" became a sacred official idea, a term through which policies were to be judged as good or bad, acceptable or unacceptable. Paternalist protection became the ordering rhetoric of agrarian conquest, the central idea that provided the rationale for official policy and its legitimacy. Peasants, within this agrarian imagination, were to be protected from the pain of unfair ejection; destitute landowners needed to be sheltered from the anguish of dispossession, local customs and institutions had to be preserved from the merciless dissolving power of time, and "ancient village communities" were to be consolidated as the foundation of the colonial agrarian regime.

To achieve so much, power had to confront and reduce the unfamiliar. It had to know about local practices and norms, understand peasant needs, listen to voices of despair and songs of joy. But what did it mean to listen, know and represent? What did it mean to protect peasant customs and rights? These, as we shall see, were problematic projects with profoundly consequential histories.

---

of Punjab expressing the opinion of the GOI: "It is noticed that in the order passed, the proposals of the Settlement Officers are frequently set aside by the higher authorities and the assessments raised on the strength of purely theoretical considerations. Much use is made by the Financial Commissioner of General arguments against undue leniency of assessment, while at the same time insufficient weight appears to be attached to considerations which tell in favour of the cultivator . . . Moderation has always been recognised as essential in the Punjab, and it is no less necessary in the present day than in the past." No. 1202–30, 3, Sec. GOI, to Chief Sec. GOP, 27 October 1909, GOI, Land Rev. & Ag. (Rev.), November 1909, A 11.

2

How Villages were Found

"India means her seven hundred thousand villages."

– M.K. Gandhi[1]

PERCEPTIONS OF THE Indian rural landscape are commonly filtered through a set of encapsulating terms. The rural is associated with the agrarian and the agrarian with the village, as though to speak of the rural landscape is to speak of village India. Most of India, we are repeatedly told, lives in its villages. This notion has been naturalised over time – reaffirmed by academics and political thinkers, circulated in the popular media and literature.

For a long while, social anthropology (or sociology) in India meant village studies.[2] In the 1930s and '40s anthropologists at Sriniketan pioneered such writings in Bengal, collecting information about the material conditions of village life.[3] In the post-War years, American anthropologists went around Indian villages, mapping social structure and change. Village societies, they showed, were not isolated entities, but embedded within wider social worlds: the "Little Traditions" within them were intimately tied to the "Greater Traditions" of Indian

---

[1] Letter to Professor Valji G. Desai, 27 July 1947, *CWMG*, vol. 96, pp. 154–5.

[2] See Béteille, "Peasant Studies and their Significance".

[3] Anthropologists associated with the Rural Research Department of Sriniketan at Visva Bharati University pioneered these village studies between 1931 and 1934. The same villages were re-surveyed in the 1950s. See Ali and Basu, *Then and Now, 1933–1958*. Also Ali and Basu, *Rice and Rural Reconstruction*.

society.[4] When caste became the central focus of the sociological imagination, studies still remained bounded by the spatial frame of the village,[5] seen as the site where castes seemed to exist and operate.

Historical writings consolidated this synecdoche: the village standing for the rural. When tracking the transition from nomadic to settled society, historians of ancient India showed how, with the coming of iron technology and iron ploughs, intensive cultivation became possible, enlarging the frontiers of settled agriculture. With the production of a surplus, villages came into being and state societies emerged.[6] It was as if the establishment of villages was the telos, the pre-designated end-point towards which the history of ancient India had been moving, with the formation of villages imbuing this teleology with meaning, thus allowing historians to track the stages through which agrarian history had unfolded. Within this frame, dominant till recently, spaces outside the settled agrarian had only transitional significance: they were waiting to disappear, to be eliminated by the march of history, transformed by new technology and advanced forms of surplus production.[7] Once settled agriculture appeared, non-agrarian forms could only survive as traces, vestiges of "earlier" modes, silhouettes in a landscape of outmoded and vanishing pasts.

When looking at agrarian change, historians of medieval India explored how village societies in India were organised, how rights and

---

[4] See in particular Marriott, *et al.*, *Village India*; Mayer, *Caste and Kinship in Central India*.

[5] See Srinivas, ed., *India's Villages*. For an early survey, see Dumont, and Pocock, eds, "Village Studies". Béteille, "Peasant Studies and their Significance".

[6] Kosambi, *An Introduction to the Study of Indian History*; Sharma, "Iron and Urbanization on the Gangetic Basin"; Sharma, *Material Culture and Social Formation*; Thapar, *From Lineage to State*, ch. 4. For critiques of the Kosambi–Sharma thesis, see Chakrabarti, "Beginning of Iron and Social Change in India", pp. 329–38; Ratnagar, "Archaeology and the State".

[7] Only recently have historians of ancient India seriously turned their gaze on pastoral tracts, forest regions, and semi-arid locations. See in particular Heredia and Ratnagar, ed., *Mobile and Marginalised Peoples*; Thapar, "Perceiving the Forest", pp. 1–16; Chattopadhyaya, *Aspects of Rural Settlements and Rural Society*.

obligations within villages were defined.[8] Reading the past over the post-colonial decades, historians began critiquing the problematic stereo-typing of Indian village society, but without unpacking the category "village" as a spatial unit. They argued that Indian villages were not self-sufficient entities insulated from the world outside, neither stagnant and backward nor internally homogeneous and self-repro-ducing. Rather, village societies were shown as internally differen-tiated, tied to the wider world through webs of social and economic relations, transformed continuously by many forces of change.[9] Even this critique, however, served basically to reaffirm the idea that rural India was village India, that rural society was peasant society.[10]

Within the nationalist imagination the village became the locus of tradition and culture, virtue and authenticity. If the city was the site of modernity, commerce, and industry, the village was where the "real" India lived, insulated from the seductions of the modern. For Gandhi, in particular, it was the locus of all creativity and goodness, morality and happiness, innocence and purity, beauty and genius, a place of nature to be protected from the corrupting and evil in-fluence of modernity. It had to be saved from the depredations of the city – cultural, moral, and economic.[11]

How did this category, "village", come to encapsulate the rural? How did the word acquire the status of a synecdoche and start substi-

---

[8] Habib, *The Agrarian System of Mughal India*, ch. 4. This remains the finest account of villages in Mughal India.

[9] See the early works of economic historians like Mukherjee, "Six Villages of Bengal"; idem, *The Dynamics of a Rural Society.*

[10] Even critics who set out to historicise the idea of the village end up repeating that India is essentially a land of villages. Surveying the works on Indian villages, A.R. Kulkarni emphasizsed in 1992: "India still remains a land of villages and 80% of its population lives in villages." Kulkarni, "The Indian Village". In this essay, as in most such essays, the idea that rural India is essentially village India is never questioned.

[11] At one level, Gandhi argued that villages were being economically suf-focated: "for the last 150 years the trend has been for cities to exist only to squeeze wealth out of the villages . . . Towns exist to exploit the villages." Speech at prayer meeting, New Delhi, 9 December 1947, *CWMG*, vol. 98, p. 20. At another level, he saw the village as being morally degraded, a consequence of the debasing influence of modernity.

tuting for the rural? Villages existed earlier, of course, but they had appeared in wet zones – in the riverine plains, in regions of intensive cultivation. There were vast stretches beyond the agrarian frontier where settled agriculture was not pervasive, nor were villages. In the 1870s no more than 40 per cent of the surveyed area of Punjab was cultivated.[12] In many regions it was less than 15 per cent. By the early 1890s, before the great era of canal extension, the agrarian frontier had extended, but about 54 per cent was still uncultivated.

As Fig. 5 shows, the proportion of area under cultivation varied widely over the landscape, as did the forest cover. By the 1870s, the proportion of cultivated area to the total was as high as 80 per cent in the central alluvial plains of Punjab.[13] Within this zone the most fertile tract was the Doab between the Beas and the Sutlej – the Bist Doab, also known as the Jullunder Doab. It was a seemingly continuous plain, unbroken by hill or valley, dotted with clusters of mud-roof houses, sparsely wooded, except near habitation sites and irrigation wells. This zone had a high population density, small peasant farms, and intensively cultivated double-cropped fields – a land of maize and wheat. The proportion of cultivated to total area was equally high in the riverine lands below the River Sutlej – the powadh, as it was called. The powadh of District Ludhiana was covered with intensively cultivated small holdings, producing fine crops of sugar, cotton, and maize. To the north of the Sutlej was the majha tract. The older settled parts of the majha – particularly around Amritsar and Lahore – were highly fertile, amply watered by the Beas and Ravi rivers, and for long the locus of political power in the region.

Beyond these fertile plains of Central Punjab the landscape was radically different. Down in the south-east was a semi-arid and sparsely populated region where dry cultivation coexisted with pastoral farming; here, two crops were difficult to produce, and kharif (the autumn crop) predominated over rabi (the spring crop). To the north-west, beyond the Ravi, was a vast pastoral tract – the bār – where the nomadism of the upland combined with cultivation in the low-lying riverine belts, the cultivated area in many places being less

---

[12] *RAP, 1871–2*, and subsequent years, Statement I.
[13] Calculations based on *RAP, 1893–94*, Statement I.

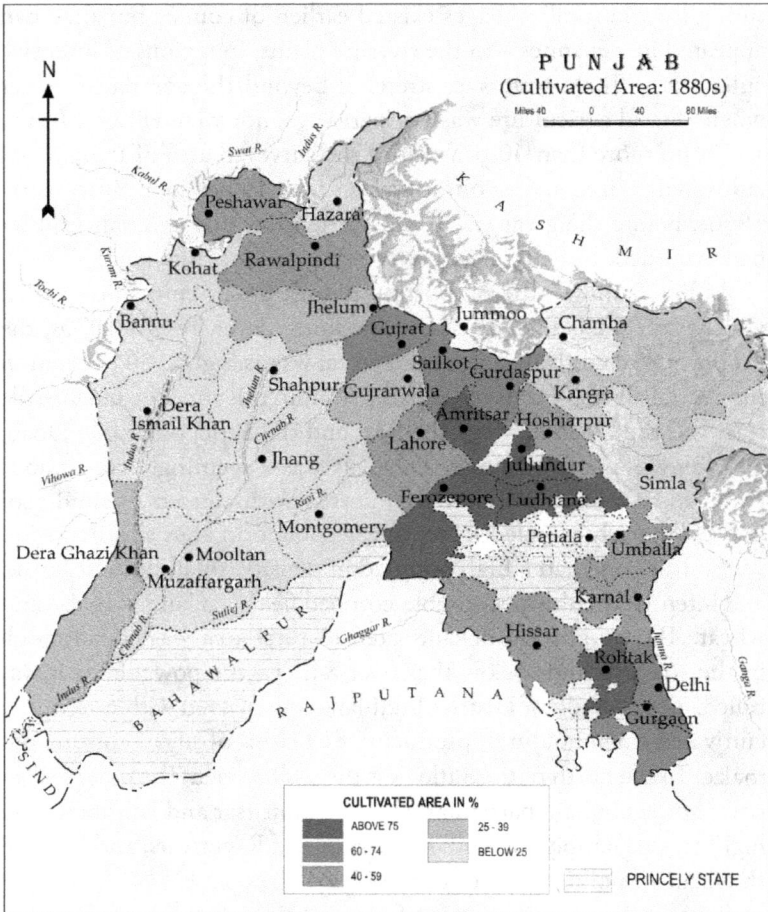

Fig. 5: The Limits of the Agrarian: Distribution of Cultivated and Uncultivated Land in Punjab, 1891–3. Calculations are based on village papers collated in *RAP 1892, 1893*.

than 15 per cent.[14] The southern part of the Bari Doab – the land between the Sutlej and the Ravi – was a similar pastoral tract with over 75 per cent of the area around Multan still uncultivated in the early 1890s.[15]

[14] Ibid.
[15] Ibid.

Further west, beyond the bãr, between the rivers Jhelum and Indus, was the Thal, a desert with only small pockets of cultivation and extensive grazing lands, the cultivated area in places being less than 10 per cent of the total.[16] Further to the north-west was a dry sub-montane tract around Rawalpindi, rocky and bare, the lower heights covered with scrub and the upper zones with *Pinus longifolia*, with patches of cultivation honeycombed in between, the proportion of cultivated area to the total nowhere more than 40 per cent. On the foothills around Hoshiarpur and Ambala, a tract known as kandi was dry and rocky, as distinct from the sirwal, the long strip bordering Jullunder that was fertile and carefully cultivated. Further up, in the mountain tracts – from Kullu to Kangra – rural life was sustained by an interdependent subsistence economy of pastoralism, terraced cultivation, and the utilisation of forest resources, a region that could produce commercially valuable timber – deodar, teak, sheesham.

Keen to convert all rural spaces into productive landscapes, colonial officials idealised an image of the peasants of central Punjab as a hardy lot busy cultivating their own farms. Settled agriculture was valorised as normative and desirable. When fixed to a piece of land, peasants became knowable and controllable; their lands could be surveyed, assessed, and taxed. Pastoralists were more difficult to control, govern, and extract revenue from. So they had to be settled, fixed to the land, bounded within delimited spaces, and turned into fiscal subjects of the state. Constituting rural spaces as villages was one way of creating such landscapes of settled agriculture. Survey officials went looking for villages everywhere and mapped villages on to the landscape even where there were none. The desired elements of the core agrarian regions were projected onto every variety of space; they provided the frame through which the rural was made intelligible, governable, and taxable.

What happened as a consequence is the conquest of an entire rural universe, a conquest in the strongest sense of the term. To visualise the rural as agrarian, and to imagine the village as the universal sign of the rural, can only be through a process of massive erasure, a refusal to see the legitimacy of other spaces, other habitations – the forests

[16] Ibid.

and the scrublands, the pastures and the meadows, the deserts and the dry tracts, the hilly regions and the mountains. To understand these erasures we need to see how villages came to be universalised as a spatial and institutional category, how they were seen, established, and normalised in the colonial period. "Villagisation" here was not a forced settlement of "tribals" and nomads into ordered villages, but a slower and deeper transformation – almost imperceptible – of the entire rural landscape.[17]

How Estate becomes Village

From the earliest days of Company rule, "estate" as a category returns incessantly in all reflections on the Indian agrarian order. It became a category taken for granted, a term that no-one seemed to question. Officials differed on who the proprietor of the soil was, and who was responsible for paying revenue. But they all assumed that "estate" was the term through which the rural was to be ordered. The meaning of the word, however, mutated, changing as Company rule spread north-west from Bengal in the nineteenth century. If we track the history of its mutation, we come to understand how the village was produced as the universal rural.

In the late eighteenth century, when the Permanent Settlement was imposed in Bengal, zamindaris were identified as estates, and zamindars were made liable for the revenue assessed on their estate.[18] The authority and power of the zamindar was both affirmed and subverted. Zamindars could no longer have their own armed regiments or their police force; their judicial prerogatives were restricted and their administration supervised by Company collectorates.[19] They still retained symbolic authority and power, but their "estates" – in the eyes of the Company – were essentially units of revenue administration. Translated into an indigenous term the estate was a mahal, a category

[17] On the Tanzanian efforts at forced villagization (1973–6) as part of Nyerere's high modernist project, see Scott, *Seeing Like a State*, ch. 7.

[18] Ray, *Change in Bengal Agrarian Society*. See also Islam, *The Permanent Settlement in Bengal*; Bose, *Peasant Labour and Colonial Capital*.

[19] Ray, *Change in Bengal Agrarian Society*.

that had been in use in revenue parlance since Mughal times. Within the estate could be many hundred villages, each officially anointed as a "mauza". In the early nineteenth century, mahal and mauza were thus distinct terms, the latter a spatial unit within the former.

The boundaries of the zamindari estates – the mahals – were ambiguous. The Permanent Settlement was not initially based on detailed measurements or records. There were no maps of the mahals, no cadastral surveys of fields within the mauzas (the villages), no classification of soils, no careful estimation of productivity and produce.[20] Keen to impose the settlement as quickly as possible and minimise costs of administration, the Company in 1793 (the year of the Permanent Settlement's formal inauguration) saw no need to conduct new enquiries: the revenue estimates made permanent were based on the records of decennial settlements that had been carried out in the 1780s.[21] By the second decade of the nineteenth century troubled officials were writing regular notes about the worrying fluidity of estate boundaries.[22] Some of the zamindari estates had dramatically expanded while others had broken up. The Burdwan Raj, after a difficult time in the 1890s, had acquired vast stretches, slowly nibbling away at other zamindaris, breaking up jungle land, and purchasing estates that had been auctioned for arrears of revenue payment. The Bishnupur Raj, on the other hand, had broken up: partly reorganised into several smaller estates, partly taken over by bigger zamindars such as those of the Raja of Burdwan.[23] Without records, how could Company officials have any precise idea of the measure of these changes? How were they to calculate what the zamindars had gained and what the Company thought it was losing by way of possible revenue? Frustrated with their own lack of knowledge, officials complained of usurpation and fraud by zamindars. The search for records only produced evidence of their absence. The Revenue Board reported in 1842: "In many Bengal districts the Collector's registers shew nothing more than the name of the estate (even the name is sometimes

[20] Phillimore, *Historical Records of the Survey of India*, vol. IV, pp. 179ff.
[21] Ray, *Change in Bengal Agrarian Society*.
[22] Phillimore, *Historical Records of the Survey of India*, vol. IV, pp. 177–8.
[23] Ibid.

incomplete and undefined), and the jumma paid for it. The villages, or portions of villages, of which it consists . . . frequently scattered in different pergunnahs . . . are known perhaps only to the proprietor or his agents."[24]

By the 1830s, surveys had been ordered in all the areas in eastern India where the Permanent Settlement had not been introduced.[25] When a wider survey was called for in 1842, worried zamindars began to protest. They feared the surveys were a prelude to revenue enhancement, a revocation of the promise of the Permanent Settlement. The Board of Revenue responded with reassuring words. The object of the survey, it declared, was only to prepare a correct map of the country, mark the boundaries of the mahals, and put an end to unnecessary disputes over the limits of the estates. The intent was not to map the mauzas or enhance revenue.[26]

As Company power moved north-west, colonial officials rethought the premises of the revenue settlement and the language of their administration. Unhappy with the rentier zamindars of Bengal, dismayed by stagnant revenue returns, and disturbed by the pace at which jungle lands were being swallowed up by the zamindaris with no financial return to the Company, officials dumped the idea of a permanent settlement in the newly acquired territories.[27] New theories

[24] From Revenue Board, Lower Provinces, Bengal Revenue Consultations, 24 October 1842 (11, 13). The Board of Revenue reported that the government often "found themselves in the predicament of purchasing nominal estates without the possibility of tracing the lands which should belong to it." Ibid.

[25] See the annual reports of the SOI revenue surveys in Bengal, Survey of India – Dehra Dun Records, Serial no. 484, Rev. 3; Serial no. 86, Rev. 11, 1861–2; Serial no. 87, Rev. 12, 1862–3. Also Phillimore, *Historical Records of the Survey of India*, vol. IV, ch. XI.

[26] The Board of Revenue clarified: "The present survey has not . . . any purpose of enhancing the rates of assessment, or disturbing . . . the rights and interests . . . of any zemindar holding his estate by virtue of decennial settlement . . .". Ibid., p. 179.

[27] Asiya Siddiqi, *Agrarian Change in a North Indian State*; Stokes, *The English Utilitarians*; Husain, *Land Revenue Policy in North India, 1801–33*; Gupta, "Retreat from Permanent Settlement".

of political economy offered fresh ways of looking at the relationship between rent and revenue, suggesting a new logic of taxation.
Increasing yield and rent from land, David Ricardo had pronounced,
had to be absorbed through enhanced taxation.[28] Surplus income,
beyond the average rate of profit, was likely to sustain unproductive
accumulation. Company officials readily heeded this advice. The arguments of Ricardian political economy made increases in taxation not
only possible but necessary. The logic was simple: to counter rentier
income and encourage landowners to invest in production, it was
essential to periodically revise the state revenue demand. Revenue
assessments were to be linked to the revenue-yielding capacity of each
village, calculated by estimating crop yields and rents on different
types of soil, and based on careful surveys and mapping. The village
was now to be the unit of revenue assessment. In Bengal the mahal
and the mauza were discrete categories, not overlapping. By the time
Thomason carried out his settlement of the North West Provinces in
the 1830s, the mahal became the mauza. The two terms were now
coterminous. The village – the mauza – thus became a fiscal unit. It
was defined as the revenue estate.[29] Constituted now as a fiscal category, the village became the object of careful scrutiny.

When settlement operations began in Punjab in the 1850s, Thomason's men came from the North West Provinces with ideas and
experience that had provided them the absolute conviction that the
village was the natural unit of revenue assessment. They saw themselves as paternal masters, moving from village to village, surveying,
mapping, and exploring the interior, listening to villagers and looking
after their needs. Knowing the village became an act of constituting
the village through records, establishing it as an entity with specific
boundaries, customs, peoples, soils, fields, rights, and obligations.
Each village was now to be endowed with a range of village records.
A register of holdings (jamabandi) was to specify the land held by
each owner in a village and the rent or revenue he was expected to

---

[28] See Stokes, *The English Utilitarians.*
[29] Thomason, *Directions for Revenue Officers*; Phillimore, *Historical Records
of the Survey of India*, vol. IV, ch. XI; *PP*, 1852–3, lxxv, pp. 5ff.

pay. A separate listing was done of all landowners and tenants with their holding numbers (khewat-khatauni); and a genealogical tree prepared of landowners (shajra nasb). The wajib-ul-arz was to record rights on common land, forests, and quarries, customs relating to village irrigation, rights in tanks, natural drainage, and streams, as well as the rights of all classes of cultivators, and dues paid to "village servants".[30] Attached to each set of revenue records was a history of the village. It was as if by exploring and recording the facticity of the village, its objective existence was being irrefutably established. To write its history was to endorse its lineage, validate its discrete life, and authorise its existence as a distinct spatial body. The village inscribed was the village historicised and naturalised.

Recording the Interior

Soon after Punjab's annexation in April 1849, Company officials were engaged in devising an elaborate system to survey and measure the land, classify soil types, and determine the ownership of each field within the bounds of each village.[31] In 1850 George Barnes, the deputy commissioner of Kangra, outlined a new method of field measurement, emphasising the urgency of adopting a clear scheme.[32] The proposal was developed and elaborated by E.A. Prinsep and R.H. Davies, who were given charge of the revenue settlement of the Rechna Doab.[33] By 1852 the Board of Administration was already asking for a full report on the new system of field measurement; officials were

[30] Douie, *Panjab Land Administration Manual*, 1908; idem, *Punjab Settlement Manual*, 1899.

[31] For some of the early recommendations about village marking, see note of Secretary to Governor General, 4 June 1850, Home Misc., Punjab, 1148.

[32] Barnes tried the system in Kangra. See Barnes, *Memorandum on the System of Measurement Pursued in the Kangra District*, SPCAAP, vol. I, no. 1 (3). Barnes' proposal of 1850 was prescribed by the board. See Barnes, Memorandum of 29 November 1850, and Board's Letter no. 68, 9 December 1850, in Barnes, *et al.*, *New System of Field Measurement in the Punjab* (1852), SPCAAP, vol. I, no. 3.

[33] Ibid.

assessing the difficulties of surveying villages and the problems of acquiring "desirable information regarding their interior economy, working and conditions . . ."[34]

This project of surveying proceeded with great speed. By 1854 John Lawrence, one of the minds that shaped the agrarian imagination of the British in Punjab, looked back with satisfaction at the survey work done by his officers. All villages within the province's ten districts had been surveyed, including those in the richest tracts. The area surveyed was no less than 14,000 sq. miles, the pace maintained being about 2000 sq. miles a season.[35] In this process the entire interior topography of each village was also mapped in intricate detail:

> What are termed interior details have been given for every estate (i.e. *mauza*, village), that is to say, not only have the boundaries of estates been sketched, but the surfaces of the ground have also been faithfully portrayed; every detail of cultivation, of forest, grove, brushwood, of sterile waste and sand, of hillock and ravine, of pool marsh, and rivulet, of road and path; of building habitation, and garden; have all been depicted and represented with coloured variations. The area of each description has also been ascertained, that is, the area under cultivation, or taken up by pathways, or covered with forest, or absorbed by streams, and so on. So that each map not only presents, with scientific precision the external boundary and area of each estate, but also its physical aspects and internal peculiarities; these maps, when fitted together on a small scale for entire districts, or Doabs, furnish the most complete topographical information that can be desired . . . The interior surveys of course added much to the expense of the work, but its topographical value is great; *it actually brings before the eye a perfect picture, or rather miniature, of the village* . . .[36]

It was as if a totalising gaze had absorbed within it the entire landscape. Not a patch of grass, not a plot of land remained hidden from this basilisk, its eye leaving nothing unmarked, unnumbered, unenquired, uncatalogued. Every possible knowable detail had been checked, classified, recorded, and mapped. A vast terrain which the eye

[34] Barnes, Comm. and Sup. Lahore Div., to P. Melvill, Sec. to the Board of Adm., Lahore, 13 December 1852, ibid.

[35] *SRGOI*, no. 6, p. 139.

[36] Ibid. Emphasis added.

could not encompass was grasped visually, the necessary information being condensed and compressed on sheets of paper.

The idea of visibility was important within the new regime of records and surveys. Visibility and transparency were essential not only for the exercise of colonial power, but for its very constitution. Invisibility created within the mind of the powerful a deep anxiety, a paralysing sense of powerlessness, the urge to penetrate that which was veiled.[37] Once the cartographic vision is naturalised and maps are seen as the normal way of looking at the landscape and knowing it, unmapped territory is simultaneously recognised as a domain hidden from the eye, an area that has escaped the exercise of power. Hence the urgency to map and survey every unknown colonial territory: surveying and mapping being acts of unveiling, of visual possession. The enormity of the project of surveying is continually emphasised and denied in official statements. Officials spoke of the difficulties of the task as well as the ease with which the British settlement officers carried it through. A thing seemingly impossible had been made possible by efficiency and planning. When Davies and Temple settled the Bari Doab and the Rechna Doab, the chief commissioner of Punjab detailed their achievements:

> They assessed after minute enquiry and on elaborate statistical data, about forty lakhs of revenue; not far short of half a million Sterling. They marked off the boundaries of about 7000 estates (i.e. *mauzas* – or villages). They measured and mapped 10,000 square miles, not village by village, but field by field – not only depicting each field, but recording every particular regarding it. They inquired into or otherwise disposed of, at least 80,000 petty rent-free tenures. They divided about two-thirds of the revenue they assessed among coparceners, assigning to each man his quota, defining all his rights and responsibilities and entering all his fields to his name. In the course of this operation they decided some 6000 suits to landed property or ancestral rights; all needing consideration and many involving difficult points of decision. They made a complete census of the population, distinguished into its various castes and classes; for the cities every grade of profession being shown; and in this manner

[37] On the anxiety about visual possession of the landscape, see McClintock, *Imperial Leather*; Hulme, "Polytropic Man"; Pratt, *Imperial Eyes*.

some three million of souls were enumerated. This census is not based on house averages, nor on an enumeration given on one given day, but on returns made for every house; and for this purpose each building, cottage and tenement, every street and alley, throughout the towns and villages, have been both mapped and numbered.[38]

The description piles detail upon detail, concretising its claims with quantitative measures and "hard facts", emphasising the size of the work, its all-encompassing nature. The completion of a difficult task served to affirm the worth of those in power.

The rhetoric of accuracy sought to authorise the records.[39] But every claim to "scientific enumeration" and mapping put under question similar claims made by earlier officials. Settlement officers and surveyors invariably criticised the technology of previous surveys in an effort to present their methods as unquestionably superior.[40] When the new system of field measurement was being elaborated in 1850, earlier field maps produced under Thomason's directions were condemned as inaccurate, as "nothing but a rough eye sketch laid down without rule, scale or compass."[41] The plane table system being devised was said to be "infinitely more valuable, because founded on correct and scientific principles."[42] By the late 1870s the plane table

[38] *SRGOI*, no. 6, p 138.

[39] This rhetoric drew upon a wider discourse of precision and quantification that was naturalised in nineteenth-century Europe. See Wise, *The Values of Precision*; Porter, *The Rise of Statistical Thinking*; Porter, *Trust in Numbers*; Hacking, *The Taming of Chance*.

[40] Survey of India officials claimed with monotonous zeal that their surveys were conducted with the utmost rigour and care. See Dehra Dun Records, SGO 16/3, 1850–60, Serial no. 666.

[41] New System of Field Measurement in the Punjab (1852), *SPCAAP*, vol. I, no. 1 (II), p. 130. See Survey of India reports from different regions of Punjab, Dehra Dun Records, Serial no. 483, Rev. 2, 1847–54; 582, SGO 319 – A, 1850–5; Serial no. 625, Rev./5, 1854–7.

[42] Ibid. p. 131. By the use of the plane table compass, the sighting rod, and a system of triangulation, maps were drawn to scale and fields plotted within them. Known as the Punjab system, this method of mapping was developed over the years and became popular in UP. See Smith, *Settlement Officer's Manual for North-Western Provinces*; and idem, *Manual of Land*

system was under attack and the square system introduced by Colonel Wace in 1883 was projected as both more accurate and simple than the process of triangulation that the earlier system required.[43]

The claims of accuracy meant that the competence of the surveying agency be continuously emphasised. Initially, in 1849, the colonial government employed professional surveyors, convinced of the need for technical expertise and critical of the capabilities of local village officials. But deterred by the expenses, it soon transferred the responsibility of mapping and surveying to village accountants – patwaris.[44] Now, with a volte face both remarkable

---

Measurement, Appendix I; Smyth and Thuillier, *Manual of Surveying for India*; Douie, *Panjab Settlement Manual*; Phillimore, *Historical Records of the Survey of India*, vol. III, ch. 15.

[43] For a criticism of the 1850s survey on the plane table method, see Markham, *Memoir*, ch. VIII. In the square system, for mapping a village, a baseline of 200 kadams (steps) was first marked on the open ground represented by a 5-inch line on the map, the scale adopted being 1 inch to 40 kadams. The area of the village was divided into squares of equal size, the skeleton traverse being built upon a square usually of 200 kadams drawn on the base line. The system is described at length in Francis, *Manual of Land Measurement for Patwaris*. See also "Translation of the Directions to Putwarees, or Village Accountants, Regarding the Conduct of Field Measurements in the Baree Doab, as Modified to the System Pursued in the Rechna Doab", in New System of Field Measurement in the Punjab (1852), *SPCAAP*, vol. 1, no. 1.

[44] The new system, according to official claims, cut costs by a third. When the Rechna Doab was being surveyed in 1851, officials estimated the cost of measuring 100 acres through the agency to be Rs 2–5 annas-9 paise per 100 acres, while the older system of surveying through the amins would have cost between Rs 4–11 annas to Rs 7 per 100 acres. The total cost of the Rechna Doab survey through the new system was an estimated Rs 36,589; a continuation of the earlier system would have raised the costs to Rs 93,060. New System of Field Measurement in the Punjab (1852), *SPCAAP*, vol. I, no. 1, p. 140. Officials tended to overstate the costs of the earlier measurement in an effort to demonstrate the benefits of the new. Since the cost of surveying was a persistent concern in the 1850s, officials dismissed khasra survey (plot by plot, cadastral survey) as "unnecessary": it required more time and money. See Sec. to GG, to Board of Administration, 6 January 1851, Home Misc., Punjab, 1089.

and understandably unremarked upon, officials discovered the hidden merits of these patwaris, their competence, their fund of local knowledge, and their commitment to the preparation of accurate records.[45] As familiar figures in the village, patwaris were expected to allay peasant apprehensions about colonial enquiries. The amins – officials who had been employed at first – were now seen as alien figures, visible representatives of the outside world, and hence objects of suspicion within the village. Facts that patwaris knew without enquiries were unknown to amins. So, surveys by amins, it was felt, were unnecessarily intrusive, provoked more hostility, and consumed more time and money.

The old patwari system could not, however, be taken over wholesale; it had to be modernised and made efficient. Village servants, carrying the imprint of tradition and a nomenclature that tied the present to the past with a seemingly unbroken thread of continuity, were now to be refigured as colonial servants, trained and supervised by their colonial masters. By the 1850s an elaborate system of selection and training had been set up. "Old hereditary servants," Prinsep reported, "are put to the test, and if found competent, are at once re-trained; inefficient hands are turned off; and new nominations are judiciously made."[46] Schools were started to train patwaris: in each institution there were a hundred patwaris and four teachers. Each patwari had to go through four grades, two lower and two higher, before being considered qualified to prepare village records.[47]

The authenticity and accuracy of patwari records were to be further ensured by a complicated method of scrutiny. The fallibility of individual observation and possible uncertainty of personalised

[45] Temple wrote: "I cannot doubt that our village accountants are a well-educated competent set. Many of them, indeed, are fully equal to professional ameens as draftsmen and surveyors. The majority also read and write Persian . . ." Richard Temple, Settlement Officer, Rechna Doab, to G.C. Barnes, Commissioner and Sup., Lahore Division, 25 September 1852. New System of Field Measurement in the Punjab (1852), *SPCAAP*, vol. I, no. 1 (11), p. 139.

[46] Ibid., p. 146.

[47] New System of Field Measurement in the Punjab (1852), *SPCAAP*, vol. 1, no. 1 (II).

understanding were to be overcome by a system of double-checking. The shajra nasb, the khataunis, and the jamabandis prepared by patwaris were first to be checked and attested by the kanungo, then by the naib-tahsildar, and finally by the tahsildar. Before attesting them, the naib-tahsildar was directed to re-measure 20 per cent of the entries.[48] Only when the settlement officer attested the authenticity of the jamabandi, after the correction of all errors and omissions, could the record become part of the Standing Record to be used by revenue officials. This discourse of measurement and re-measurement, of scrutiny and verification, of corrections and attestations, was a discourse of authenticity. Evidence verified and attested had a greater claim to truth.

Within a decade of the introduction of the new system, the working of the patwari agency perturbed revenue officials. Enthused by the prospect of cutting costs, the Punjab government had declared in the early 1850s that patwaris and chowkidars, being village servants, were to be paid by the community: their income was to be a specified portion of the harvest. The government saved money thereby, but discovered soon that the system "in practice is very difficult to work".[49] The earnings of patwaris fluctuated with the harvest and varied between villages in relation to the level and nature of production. Seen as an imposition by the state, the additional charge was resisted by landholders, who refused to pay "often for a year or 18 months at a time".[50] In times of scarcity there was no hope of any income: after the famine of 1868, revenue officials were forced to recognise that the conditions of these "wretched men . . . are much to be pitied".[51] Hungry souls tended not to share the great love for authentic records among their well-fed superiors. Fearing the collapse of their recording agency, anxious officials debated the need for reform.[52]

[48] Douie, *Panjab Settlement Manual*, pp. 156–9.

[49] Perkins, Deputy Comm., Hoshiarpur, to T.D. Forsyth, Commissioner and Sup., Jullunder Division, no. 463, 5 December 1868, *Pay of Village Chowkidars and Patwaris*, SRFCP, no. 30 (1869).

[50] *Pay of Village Chowkidars and Patwaris*, SRFCP, no. 30 (1869).

[51] Ibid.

[52] In the 1880s uniform scales of pay were fixed for patwaris and chowkidars, but the payment remained a responsibility of the landholders. Fixed

The great famine of 1877 confirmed their fears. The Famine Commission criticised village records, recommended a revamping of the patwari and kanungo agencies, and proposed a centralised supervision over the surveying, mapping, and compiling of village statistics.[53] Colonel Wace was appointed Director of Agriculture in 1882, a Director of Land Records was appointed in 1885, and new directions were embodied in the Punjab Land Revenue Act of 1887.[54] The existing system of patwari training was now deemed "useless" and new plans were made to train patwaris.[55] To prepare accurate records, they were to be taught arithmetic and mensuration; they were to learn how to do plane table surveys and prepare village and survey papers. Fresh claims were now made about the reliability of the new records produced under the supervision of the Directorate of Land Records. Questionings never entirely subverted the rhetoric of authenticity, they only relaid its basis.[56]

Information had to be gathered with care and efficiently processed. The power and significance of the records depended on the ease

---

scales did not ensure prompt payments. Patwaris, according to reports, continued to be at the mercy of landowners. By the Revenue Act of 1907, finally, the government agreed to pay patwaris for sustaining the elaborate regime of records.

[53] *The Report of the Indian Famine Commission*, 1880; Proposal for the Systematisation of Future Survey Operations in the Punjab, *SRFCP*, 26.

[54] Recent Papers on Leading Questions Relating to Settlement and Land Revenue Administrations, 1885, *SRFCP*, *NS*, no. 1.

[55] "Memorandum by the Director of Settlements and Revenue Records on Patwaris' School in the Punjab", Punjab Rev. and Agr., March 1886, A 3. See also Punjab Rev. and Agr. (Rev.), April 1886, A 6.

[56] Improvement of records and their better preservation became an official obsession. For the 1880s debate on the reliability of the patwari maps and the reaction of Punjab revenue officials to the Survey of India suggestions for improving mapping procedures, see Punjab Rev. and Agr., September 1884, A 7. On the rejection of the Survey of India proposals, see in particular Senior Sec. to Financial Comm. Punjab, no. 835, 24 July 1884, paragraphs 4 and 5; and Joint Note by Surveyor General and Settlement Commissioner, 27 June 1884, paragraphs 4 and 11; Punjab Rev. and Agr., September 1884, A 7; for subsequent discussions, see Punjab Home (Gen.), August 1893, A 1–3; Punjab Home (Gen.), July 1904, A 98–145.

and speed with which they could be marshalled. When the khewat-khatauni papers finally reached the Record Room, they were said to be "so arranged that they can be traced and referred to with the utmost facility."

> The villages in each subdivision of a district are catalogued alphabetically, and have their places assigned to them in the record-rack according to this order. All the fiscal papers then for each village, are grouped together, and are then classified into separate bundles according to their separate descriptions. To the larger bundle of each village is attached an abstract list, showing the smaller bundles contained therein, and to each smaller bundle is attached a detailed list of the papers which it may contain. If the system be properly carried out, there ought not to be a paper, in the whole mass of voluminous and multifarious records which could not be traced in the space of a few minutes . . . The importance of such a system can be readily understood, when it is remembered that in these offices are filed the papers which are virtually the title-deeds of all the landed property in a district, of which the most minute and even fractional details are authoritatively fixed.[57]

This is the self-confident and contented voice of control. It seemed possible to assert that the minutest detail of village economy had been "authoritatively" captured in records collated, classified, organised, indexed, and accessible. It was as if the Record Room expressed colonial power's sense of order and rationality.

To forge this order, information had to be hierarchised and the relation between different types of reports had to be clearly specified. Each department produced its own annual reports and detailed surveys after collecting all the information it considered necessary. This information was then collated and condensed into reports that allowed a bird's-eye view, a totalising picture that could relate parts to the whole and transform fragments into a meaningful totality. First the information of the different branches of each department was synthesised from separate reports into a single annual departmental report. Then the departmental reports in each province were condensed into an annual administration report. Beyond this there

----

[57] Statement of John Lawrence, Chief Comm. for the Punjab, *SRGOI*, no. 6, p. 140.

were gazetteers, which sought to present the distilled essence of information available in other surveys. The authority of all these texts was based not on claims of authenticity through direct observation and enquiry, but on the synthesis they offered. Looking down from an elevated vantage point, these texts aimed to define the Archimedean point from which to observe the colonial world. Signed by the supreme authority within the provincial administration, Administration Reports were related to Departmental Reports in a way that replicated the hierarchy within the administration. As you moved down the hierarchy, the level of detail became denser, the picture more specialised; as you moved towards the top, the details disappeared, the view became more panoramic, seemingly more total.

Maps were similarly hierarchically ordered. Different types of maps offered specific pictures of the landscape. From the 1880s the revenue survey department produced three types of maps: the topographical map, the mauza map (the revenue map), and the cadastral map.[58] The topographical surveys used the one-inch scale by the method of plane tabling to capture the general features of the ground, the positions of principal towns and villages, and the courses of rivers – indicating only the provincial boundaries, and not those of villages. The mauza survey in Punjab was on a four-inch scale, again through plane tabling, but done by carrying out traverses with theodolites and chains around the boundaries of villages, instead of on a triangulated basis, marking village boundaries and broad details of types of land – cultivated, fallow, or waste.[59] Cadastral surveys were on a sixteen-inch scale, based on traversed village boundaries to plot the limits of each field. The

[58] See Black, *A Memoir of the Indian Surveys: 1875–1890*, ch. V. For the earlier period, see Phillimore, *Historical Records of the Survey of India*, vols I–IV.

[59] Traversing is a method of survey in which a number of connected survey lines form the network, and the directions and lengths of the survey lines are measured with the help of an angle-measuring instrument (like the theodolite) and a tape or chain. Traverse networks involve placing survey stations along a line or path of travel, and then using the previously surveyed points as a base for observing the next point. The theodolite is a precision instrument used in surveying that can measure angles in the horizontal as well as vertical planes. For a description of these methods for mid-nineteenth-century surveyors in India, see Smyth and Thuillier, *A Manual of Surveying for India*.

interior detail of each village was captured on the basis of "systematic chaining", which was then entered in the field books. As you moved up the cartographic hierarchy – from the cadastral to the mauza to the topographical – there was a reduction in detail. The topographical map gave a view from, as it were, the mountain top, uncluttered by the specificities of soil types and field boundaries, a panorama spanning the entire terrain. The wide-angle lens of the topographical survey was discarded as the focus shifted to the villages, and then to fields. The close-up lens of the cadastral survey was to reveal the interior picture of the village in all its minutiae. Command over the land-scape required overview as well as detail, both enabled by maps on these three separate scales.

Another level of hierarchy was between the trigonometric and revenue surveys. For the surveyors involved in the Trigonometric Survey of India, the distinction between the two was simple: one was classed as "scientific", the other as "native". The two forms of survey were always distinct: they were expected to complement each other, but their relationship remained intensely problematic. The topographical survey of a region was to proceed on the basis of traverse points defined through triangulation. But in many regions the imperatives of revenue collection and the urgency of completing the surveys meant that these were carried out before the triangulation had been done. For the "scientific surveyors", maps that had not been plotted within the triangulated grid were useless.[60] While the North West Provinces' surveys were condemned on this ground, in Punjab the topographical maps were constructed on the basis of patwari maps since they were said to be based on "a scientific framework comprising all the trijunction points of the villages."[61]

[60] See Markham's comments on the revenue surveys of the North West Provinces; Markham, *Memoir*.

[61] See Wilson's strong defence of the system of mapping deployed by the patwaris, no. 1179, 30 November 1885; J. Wilson, Senior Sec. to Financial Comm., Punjab, to the Officiating Junior Sec. to GOP, Punjab Land Rev. Agr. (Rev.), A 1, January 1886. See also Black, *A Memoir of Indian Surveys*, pp. 105–6. After the 1831 Allahabad conference Mertins Bird and James Thomason pushed ahead with the survey at an enormous speed, expecting

The project of appropriating, ordering, and dominating the landscape, however, remained rooted in a profoundly conflict-ridden
process. At every stage, the imperial vision, with its dream of reshaping reality, its desire to mark every space with its name, its confidence
in its power to conquer nature and subject it to the will of rational
man, came up against barriers and resistance. At every stage, hidden
beneath colonial certitude was a sense of doubt about the authenticity
of what was recorded, about the very capacity to know and reorder
local society – an anxiety the regime sought to overcome with ever-
louder assertions of authenticity and more ambitious claims about the
certainty of complete surveys and total mapping.[62] So, how exactly
did British revenue maps manage to produce village-scapes?

The Cartographic Truth

The first set of village maps in Punjab had been produced by the
1850s. Within the next two decades, thousands of Revenue Survey
maps were drawn by cartographers at the Survey of India. The entire
rural landscape was thereby visually encapsulated as village space.
Bounded and demarcated, villages became cartographic truths, each
with a name and delimited territory.

Enclosed within a grid of firm lines and clear boundaries, unknown
landscapes now appeared legible and capable of being grasped. Delimited spaces are reassuring to those in power: they create a sense of
comfort, nurture a vision of control. These revenue maps did not
record only the pre-existing boundaries – those congealed in history, already marked and fixed. Hand in hand with the mapping
went the business of enclosing. Revenue officials were expected to

---

surveyors to cover 1000 sq. miles per annum, a limit that was increased to
3000 sq. miles per annum. Many criticised this obsession with speed and
the sacrifice of accuracy. See Bedford's criticism of these surveys, Phillimore,
Survey, vol. IV, ch. VIII. Markham rejected these early surveys as "useless".
Markham, *Memoir*, p. 181.

[62] In chapter 9 I explore this dialectic between the ideal and the possible,
the fantasy of total grasp and the reality of persistent slippages.

Fig. 6: Mapping Villages: Congregated Village Map of Jullunder Tahsil, 1847–8.

This is a fragment of a rough map locating all the villages, produced for the summary settlement after Jullunder was acquired in 1846. These early village maps were not based on careful surveys of the interior landscape.

Source: Survey of India, Dehra Dun Records.

Courtesy: National Archives of India.

work with the Survey of India, first to mark village boundaries and then to map them.[63] Mapping was not only the act of bounding: it re-spatialised the terrain: diverse kinds of space, with all their heterogeneity and difference, their histories and lived pasts, were transformed into abstract and uniform space that could then be divided into homogeneous units.

In the vast pastoral lands that stretched to the west of the River Sutlej, British officials searched in vain for the villages of their imagination. What they found was an arid tract over which camels, sheep, and goats grazed, moving from place to place in search of pasture. Outside the river valleys, on the elevated scrubland of the bār, water was scarce and wells difficult to dig, the water table lying 140 feet below ground. People lived around wells, in little hamlets, cultivating small patches and pasturing their livestock.[64] Habitations were scattered, seemingly cut off from each other, and often temporary. Community relations were mostly formed around rights in wells and ownership of animals rather than land. Pastoral groups moved when the wells dried; they searched for new pastures if a tract was overgrazed. To the British, seemingly fluid landscapes and shifting habitations connoted anarchy, a lack of even the premises of order. The hamlets that dotted the open spaces appeared beyond the reach of the state, its bureaucratic grip and enumerative machinery. They seemed difficult, unidentifiable, unnameable.

Keen to incorporate pastoral spaces within the settled agrarian order, British officials moved vigorously to map them as village spaces. "Shortly after annexation," wrote Steedman, the Settlement Officer of Jhang in the 1870s, "it became necessary to fix village boundaries and to create private proprietary rights in land where they had never before been recognised, even if, as is very doubtful, they had ever

[63] Smyth and Thuillier, *A Manual of Surveying for India*; Douie, *Panjab Settlement Manual* (1899).

[64] Fascinated by the open spaces of the bār, early surveyors described the tract in detail. See "Observations on Pargana Zaderpoor, District Jhang", by M.F. Luberford, in charge of Camp no. 2, Survey of India, Dehra Dun Records; Report of the Operations of the Jech Doab Revenue Survey for Season 1854–5, by W. Housden, Survey of India, Dehra Dun Records.

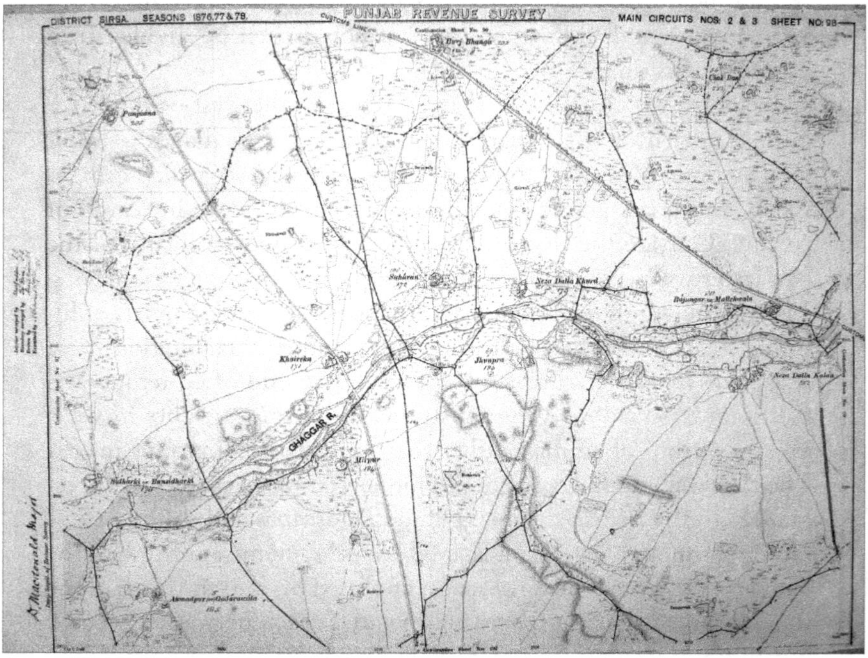

Fig. 7: Cartographic Enclosure.

Land around rivers, irrigated by the water overflow, was usually cultivated; but even here the new cartographic lines demarcating villages enclosed large swathes of the pastoral landscape.

Source: Punjab Revenue Survey, Sirsa, Main Circuits 2 & 3, Sheet no. 98, Season, 1887–9, Survey of India, Dehra Dun Records, 208/6, 09332.

Courtesy: National Archives of India.

existed."[65] For tax liabilities to be decided, all open spaces had to be enclosed, territorial boundaries marked, property rights within them fixed, and titles to land recorded. How could rights to land be enumerated and adjudicated unless the location of the land was clear and the fields within them unambiguously demarcated? Even before the Regular Settlements were made in all the various regions, revenue officials had begun this process of demarcation, of incorporating pastoral settlements within agrarian spaces and bounding the villages. Carrying out the First Regular Settlement in Jhang, Monckton described how pastoral hamlets were reanointed as villages:

> The revenue arrangements of the native Governments in the Multan province, never having recognised the village system, but dealing separately with each well or cluster of wells, there were naturally no well defined estates, and the mauzahs (villages) in Mr. Cocks and the Summary Settlements were merely parcels of land paying revenue under one denomination but with no fixed principle of their union. Generally there would be one principal village by which the name of the mahal would be distinguished, with subordinate hamlets and outlying wells often at a great distance and situated within the boundaries of another estate.[66]

The south-west – around Dera Ismail Khan, Multan, and Muzaffargarh – was also a vast pastoral territory. In this arid tract of scanty rainfall, cultivation was limited once again to riverbanks and depressions, and, as in many other pastoral tracts, small hamlets were to be found around wells located on the uplands, beyond the flood plains. Here too officials preferred to visualise the terrain as an agrarian landscape and divided the country into mauzas, grouping clusters of wells or embankments into villages, slicing up parts of the grazing land as the property of the village, and acquiring the rest as government property.[67]

---

[65] Steedman, *Jhang S.R. 1874–1880*, para 86.

[66] Monckton, *Jhang S.R., Lahore 1860*; E.B. Steedman, the Settlement Officer of Jhang in the 1880s, was categorical: "Neither under the Syals nor under the Sikhs were there village estates with demarcated boundaries as there are now. These are our creations, exotics transplanted from the plains of the North-West Provinces." Steedman, *Jhang S.R., 1874–1880*, para 82.

[67] Settlement manuals recognised this act of official invention: "The village

Elsewhere, in the hills, villages were similarly constituted. Surveying Kangra in the early 1850s, Barnes warned against the use of inappropriate categories to order the landscape, pointing to the "essential difference" between the mauzas of the hills and those of the plains.[68] Sensitive to questions of nomenclature, Alfred Lyall, a settlement officer, said: "It is important that these differences should always be borne in mind, and not overlooked because of the similarity of nomenclature which we have imposed. Words which originated in villages of the plains, or in our revenue circulars, were brought into Kangra by our Settlement officials, and used to describe facts to which they do not in their ordinary meaning, accurately apply."[69] But their awareness of differences did not stop either Barnes or Lyall from regrouping the hamlets of the hills and scattered plots of cultivated lands into new revenue circuits, and calling them mauzas. On the revenue map administrative space had to be homogenised, categories of description had to be uniform. Not recognised as distinct administrative units, hamlets could only be represented as unbounded sub-units of a mauza, their discrete existence informally acknowledged but officially erased. They could not be cartographically demarcated with borders, though Barnes was acutely aware of the existence of hamlet boundaries, and the symbolic significance these had for the inhabitants.[70] Recognising the bureaucratic need for uniformity, he appointed lambardars and

---

is a fortuitous aggregation of independent units. The units in Sind tract are wells, i.e., the well and the lands irrigated by it . . . Several of these wells or embankments as the case may be, are collectively called a village, and are looked upon from an administrative point of view as forming one community; but they are not, properly speaking, sub-divisions of a village, but a series of proprietary units not really in any way knit together but thrown into association either by the necessity for mutual protection, or still more often, by the accident of having been included for administrative purposes within a common village boundary, and now maintaining that association simply as the result of the revenue system of the country." Douie, *Panjab Settlement Manual*, p. 81; see also pp. 88ff., O'Brien, *Muzaffargarh S.R., 1873–80*, pp. 3–8; H.G. Tucker, *Dera Ismail Khan S.R., 1872–79*, pt 1.

[68] Barnes, *Kangra S.R., 1855*, paras 107–10.

[69] Lyall, *Kangra S.R., 1865–72*, para, 13.

[70] Barnes emphasised that independent hamlets brought together to form

patwaris for each mauza, displacing the authority of the moqaddams who earlier headed each separate hamlet.[71]

For a long while the boundaries of mauzas were ambiguous lines whose illusory fixity existed only in maps. When Survey of India officials began their operations in the mid 1850s, they frequently found no trace of the boundary lines given by revenue officials, nor of villages indicated in sketch maps drawn during the summary settlement immediately after annexation. An exasperated Shortrede, carrying out the survey operation of the Jech Doab in 1854–5, wrote: "These sketch maps are very imperfect guides; villages being shown as E & W which were to be found N & S . . . As was to be expected the detached villages in the Bar were found in locations very different from those indicated, and this occasioned a good deal of line setting. In some cases the Survey came upon villages the existence of which was seemingly unknown."[72]

On the bār around "pergunnah" Katowal, twenty-three mauzas had been demarcated. Making his rounds through this area, Housden noted: "Beyond the marks on the ground . . . nothing positive was known as to whether they were actual Mouzahs . . . Some are inhabited and have cultivation, some have cultivation alone, and many are without either."[73] Often, villages had a life only on the sheets of a map, or in signboards hung on trees.[74]

---

a revenue circuit, a mauza, had "their separate boundaries, which are jealously maintained." Barnes, *Kangra S.R., 1862*, para 105.

[71] See Lyall's description of Barnes' effort to introduce uniformity. Lyall, *Kangra S.R., 1865–72*, para 17.

[72] Report of the Operation of the Jech Doab Revenue Survey for Season 1854/55, Survey of India – Dehra Dun Records, 1850s, no. 25, Mss.

[73] Remarks on Pergunna Katowal, by W. Housden, Camp no. 3, Jech Doab Survey for Season 1854/55, Survey of India, Dehra Dun Records, 1850s, no. 25, Mss.

[74] Revenue officials went around demarcating uninhabited open prairies as villages. As Channing, judge in a Punjab court, explained: "A village, according to the sense in which the word is generally used in revenue matters, may contain no houses, it may be a 'mauzah gháirábad'. Thus, the other day, in Hissar I had a case before me in which the owners of an "uninhabited" village in Hissar lived in an adjoining village of Patiala. Would it be sufficient

By the time the decennial census operations began in the 1870s, cartographic truth had become classificatory fact. All ambiguity over boundary lines had by now been erased. Census enumerators went about collecting the demographic data of all villages, classifying them according to population and tracking changes in their numbers. But what were they counting? What was the "village" of the census? From 1891, the census adopted the definition of "village" that was legally encoded in the Punjab Land Revenue Act of 1887. Section 3 (1) of the act stated that for the purposes of the act the village was simply a revenue unit. "Hence the village of our Tables," explained H.A. Rose, the Census Superintendent, in 1901, "is, as before, a fiscal unit and not necessarily a village in the ordinary sense of the term."[75] He was aware, as were later census officials, that the "village" of their enumeration was often no more than an arbitrary category produced by administrative fiat, and that colonial diktat had eroded the difference between villages long established and those created in the late nineteenth century. But Rose still had to count and classify them, so that his questioning of the validity of the category was simultaneously an affirmation of its bureaucratic sanctity.

A half-century later, even after the British had left India, the census meaning of "village" as a category had not changed. "The definition of village," the *Punjab Census Handbook* of 1961 stated, "is identical with that of 'mauza' under Section 3 (1) of the Punjab Land Revenue Act, 1887."[76] This meant that the village of the census continued to be essentially a fiscal category – a bounded space over which revenue

---

to affix the notice to a tree? I understand that it would. The term village here evidently does not mean merely a collection of houses because of the wording 'village in which the land is situate'." F.C. Channing, Judge, Divisional Court Delhi Division, to the Under-secretary to GOP, Rev. Dep., Punjab Rev. and Agr. (Rev.), October 1886, A 33–43.

[75] Rose, *Punjab Census, 1901*, para 24.

[76] *District Census Handbook, Punjab*, vol. I, 1961, p. ii, para 1. It further explained: "The term village, in all Censuses since 1901, has been used for an area for which a separate Record of Rights is maintained, or which has been separately assessed . . . or which the State Government has otherwise declared as an 'estate'."

had been assessed in the past, a space that had been allotted a hadbast number in a list of villages, a place that was required to have its own record of rights. Even villages that had no population continued to be retained in the directory of villages since they had hadbast numbers: they were simply classified as "uninhabited".[77] Transformed into numbers, reckoned as cartographic entities, plotted through hard lines on the map, revenue villages acquired a corporeal existence.

When Gandhi spoke of the country's seven hundred thousand villages, he was referring to census numbers.

Bounding Sovereignty

Towards the end of May 1847 a small conflict over village boundary markings unfolded in the Cis-Sutlej States. Like many such seemingly small events it had a wider story to tell.

The administration of Punjab had been taken over, in effect, just a year earlier. (Annexation of the entire province happened a couple of years later.[78]) British officials were busy enclosing the landscape, mapping villages, and transforming the land into taxable units. The Maharaja of Patiala wrote to Wynyard, Settlement Officer of the Cis-Sutlej States, objecting to the attempts to demarcate villages within territories that were exclusively his, and coparcenary villages in which he had police jurisdiction.[79] Keen to move ahead with the project, Wynyard referred the matter to his superiors, expressing his clear

[77] Ibid. Figures of uninhabited villages in each district were not separately mentioned in census reports before 1961.

[78] The British victory at the Battle of Aliwal on 28 January 1846 was followed by the Treaty of Lahore (9 March 1846) and the Treaty of Bhyrowal (16 December 1846). Through the terms of these treaties the territories south of the River Sutlej were ceded to the British, the "mutinous troops" of Lahore disbanded, a British Resident posted at the court, and British forces stationed in Lahore. The Resident was to "have full authority to direct and control the duties of every department" of the administration.

[79] No. 205, 31 May 1847, Wynyard, Settlement Officer, to Major Mackeson, Commissioner and Superintendent Cis-Sutlej States, Home Misc., IOR/H/761. The subsequent letters in this section, unless otherwise stated, are collated in this file.

opinion that the survey should extend to all villages. Major Mackeson, Commissioner and Superintendent of the Cis-Sutlej States, was circumspect. How could the British move into princely territories, where the raja was sovereign, and begin marking village boundaries? Would this not impinge on the sovereignty of the raja that the British had affirmed? Emphasising the need for caution, Mackeson asked Wynyard to refrain from taking any action that might alarm the princes and subvert their authority. The British government, he felt, ought not to destroy their trust and goodwill.[80]

Deferring to the opinion of his superior, Wynyard stopped the work of village bounding. But he remained unconvinced. By mid June he replied to the commissioner. Village demarcations, he insisted, "will in no way affect the interests of the Chiefs or diminish their authority in their respective possessions, but on the contrary, will supply them with data, on which to rest a better system of revenue."[81] An assertive expansionist, he felt that in any case all these states "sooner or later should escheat to the British Government."[82] Since the villages would then have to be surveyed, measured, and bounded, it would be wise to begin the process when surveys were being conducted in British areas. This would save time and effort, and rationalise expenditure.[83]

Mackeson's reply was firm and categorical.[84] He emphasised the need to distinguish between the different forms of sovereignties within the Cis-Sutlej territories under discussion. The boundaries of villages could be marked off, village by village, only within spaces over which the British had police jurisdiction. Here the British government had a right to mark villages and it was possible to enforce boundaries. In territories where the British had no police jurisdiction – Patiala, Jind, Nabha, Maler Kotla, Faridkot, Mamdot, Chhachhrauli, etc. – village boundaries could not be demarcated. Any attempt to do so would

[80] No. 54, 8 June 1847, Mackeson to Wynyard, Home Misc., IOR/H/761.

[81] Home Misc., IOR/H/761.

[82] Ibid.

[83] No. 224, 17 June 1847, Wynyard to Mackeson; no. 220, 19 June 1847, Wynyard to Mackeson, Home Misc., IOR/H/761.

[84] No. 44, 18 June 1847, Mackeson to Wynyard, Home Misc., IOR/H/761.

undercut the authority of these rulers, and without police jurisdiction the boundaries could not be effectively maintained. In the case of territories that were jointly held by one of the eight sovereign chiefs and a dependent chief, or two sovereign chiefs together, boundaries could be marked to separate the jointly held lands from the territories under the exclusive possession of any one of the chiefs, but not to demarcate villages within the coparcenary estates.

For a while Wynyard was quiet. Irritated with the commissioner's hesitations and unhappy with the restraints imposed on him, he raised the whole issue again in December 1847, requesting in a letter to Mackeson that the earlier orders be reconsidered and village bounding and census operation be allowed within all territories.[85] To reinforce his argument, Wynyard referred to petitions from dependent rajas demanding survey and demarcation of villages within estates held jointly with sovereign rajas. Mackeson was still not persuaded. Dependent chiefs, he said, wanted the demarcation of villages and separation of rights, for this would give them greater autonomy. But precisely because of this, sovereign states like Patiala objected to the demarcation. They felt this would weaken their own sovereignty and undercut their hold over the dependent chiefs.[86] Village boundaries, Mackeson reiterated, should not be drawn where the British had not introduced its police force.[87] To mark village boundaries within sovereign states was to subvert their power and weaken their hold over their dependants,[88] and "The contingency of succession by escheat should not operate to induce us to weaken the feudal tie. If we put up the boundary we must enforce it and interfere between the feudal Chief and his Vassal."[89]

On Wynyard's insistence the papers were sent up to the Board of Administration, Punjab, for its opinion. After mulling over the

[85] No. 44, 13 December 1847, Wynyard to Mackeson; no. 152, 21 December 1847, Wynyard to Mackeson, Home Misc., IOR/H/761.

[86] No. 198, 26 December 1847, Mackeson to Wynyard, Home Misc., IOR/H/761.

[87] No. 106, ibid.

[88] No. 20, 31 January 1948, Wynyard, Home Misc., IOR/H/761.

[89] Ibid.

issue for over a year, the secretary to the Board wrote to the governor general in May 1849, detailing the Board's policy.[90] Persuaded more by Wynyard than Mackeson, the Board declared that village demarcations should be made in all areas under British jurisdiction, within all estates where the British government had any share, and in the territories of all protected chiefs not holding sovereign power. Only in the lands of sovereign chiefs was it necessary to follow a more cautious policy. Playing on the difference between compulsion and persuasion, the Board suggested that the sovereign chiefs should not be compelled but "may be induced to allow" village demarcation.[91] The Raja of Jind and Nihal Singh Ahluwalia of Kapurthala had permitted village markings, and it was possible to persuade others to recognise the advantages of a professional survey and clear demarcation of village boundaries. This would enable a separation of rights, delineation of jurisdiction, and elimination of disputes.

The rhetoric of universal good sought to repress the spatialising logic of expansionist power. The act of bounding could not be so easily dissociated from the question of sovereignty and juridical authority. To demarcate a village was to declare it subject to policing, to a judicial system, to an administration. It was to establish authority within the bounded space and define spaces of sovereignty. Only a sovereign had the right to mark and maintain spatial boundaries within his territories. This meant, conversely, that the marking of village boundaries was an act that affirmed the claim to sovereign power. By the same logic, the attempt to demarcate villages within someone else's territory was to question the sovereignty of the individual who held that territory.

Wynyard's view prevailed in the end – the notion that spatial ordering ought to begin even before formal takeover, for it would ease the process of establishing power within lands not yet entirely under British control. In pronouncing the need to map villages over all territories, the Board reaffirmed an expansionist logic. The

---

[90] 17 May 1849, G.I. Christian, Sec., to the Board of Administration for the Affairs of the Punjab, to H.M. Elliot, Sec. to GOI with the Governor General, Home Misc., IOR/H/761.

[91] Ibid.

project of marking village boundaries was one of constituting colonial sovereignty.

Agrarian Spaces, Village Structures

As the survey and mapping proceeded, colonial officials came to recognise that the structure of the spaces they were categorising as "village" varied. At least three types could be seen. One: villages of the plains with the abadi (habitation) in their centre, these being common in central and eastern Punjab. Two: villages that were constituted for fiscal purposes by incorporating within a bounded space a series of hamlets, as was done in some places in the hills, in arid tracts, and in pastoral zones. Three: villages that were formed, again for revenue purposes, by stringing together scattered individual homesteads located within cultivated fields. We get an idea of these spatial contrasts in Figs 8 and 9.

Tehong was a village in Jullunder – one of the most densely settled and intensively cultivated districts of Central Punjab. As Fig. 8 shows, by the early twentieth century there were only small patches of uncultivated land (banjar) in the village. Possibly the only space not regularly tilled was the swamp in the south that attracted birds in winter and was swollen with river overflow in the monsoon. The density of lines marking the field boundaries reveal a landscape carved into minute fields.

The abadi – village site – was at the centre, with fields all around. The dwellings were located at the edge of the upland (dhaha), beyond the reach of the river that regularly flooded the low-lying riverine tract – the bét. During the sowing and harvest seasons, peasants moved from the abadi to the field, worked through the day, and returned in the evening. In Tehong, as in most of Jullunder, wells were critical for cultivation. With the water table no deeper than thirty feet in most places, digging wells was easy and ensured two crops a year. With wells, the fields could be watered through the winter months for the rabi crop. In 1883 there were forty-one wells, and by 1905 their number had increased to eighty-five – most of them brick lined. But, as is clear from the map, habitations did not come up around the wells.

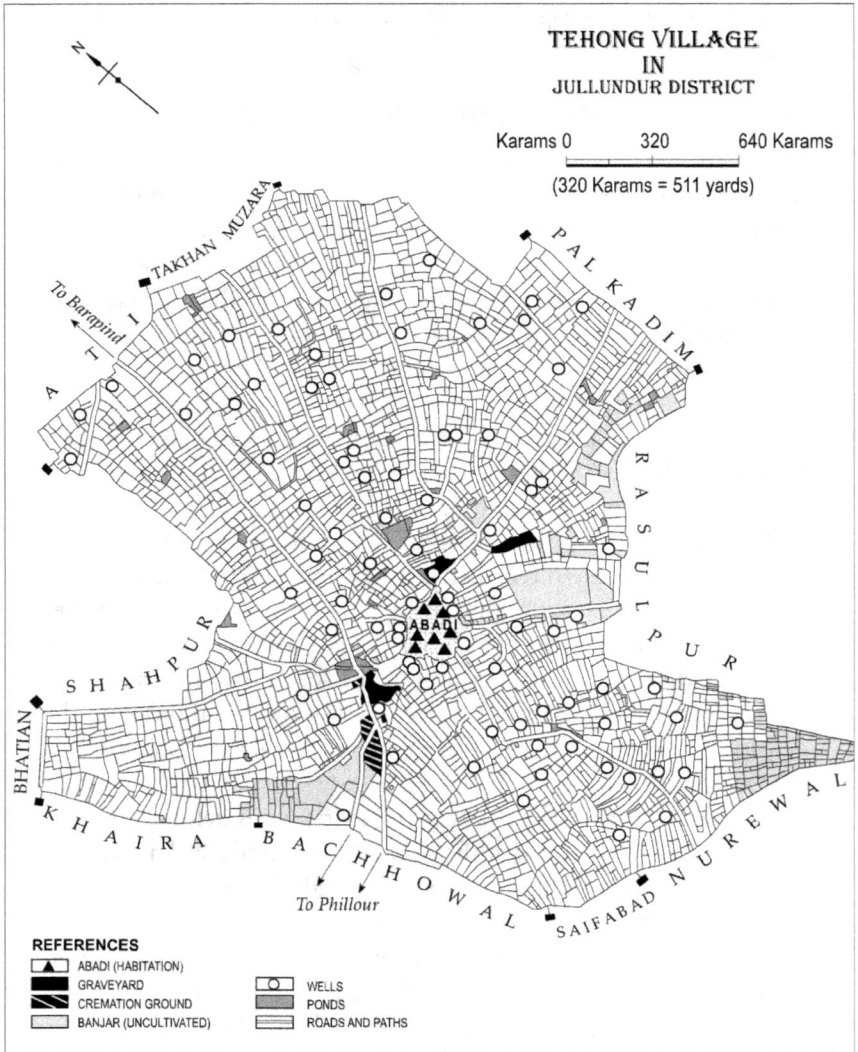

TEHONG VILLAGE
IN
JULLUNDUR DISTRICT

Karams 0   320   640 Karams

(320 Karams = 511 yards)

N

TAKHAN MUZARA

To Barapind

PALKADIM

RASULPUR

SHAHPUR

BHATIAN

KHAIRA

BACHHOWAL

ABADI

To Phillour

SAIFABAD

NUREWAL

REFERENCES

▲	ABADI (HABITATION)			
■	GRAVEYARD			
◨	CREMATION GROUND	◯	WELLS	
▨	BANJAR (UNCULTIVATED)	▨	PONDS	
		▤	ROADS AND PATHS	

Fig. 8: Tehong Village.

This map was prepared for a village survey in the late 1920s on the basis of the rough khasra map of the village. Numerous wells were dug over the landscape but the habitation site was at the centre.

Source: Das and Calvert, *Tehong V.S.*

Examining Fig. 9, we see a different village picture. Bhambu Sandila was located in district Muzaffargarh. There were two broad eco-zones in this district. One was the thal, an arid sandy stretch with little vegetation, except jand or jal, and the occasional date palm. The northern part was particularly desolate, almost devoid of vegetation, but in the south luxuriant grass sprang up with the first shower of rain. This was the land of camel graziers and shepherds, who roamed with their herds and flocks but built their dwellings around wells that were dug as much to cultivate small patches as to get water for animals and humans. Their habitations were located mostly on the thal bank, overlooking river valleys where spring levels were high and wells could be dug. On two sides of the thal, along the rivers, were belts of low-lying land, sandy stretches covered by a thin layer of alluvium brought in annually by river floods. Watered by rivers and irrigated by inundation canals and wells, this tract could sustain cultivation alongside animal rearing. Bhambu Sandila was located within this riverine tract.

The inhabitants of Bhambu Sandila combined animal rearing with cultivation. Everyone kept goats, grazing them on the common land and penning them on the fields after the harvest, for manure. Goat milk was consumed as well as sold, goat hair had a ready market, and old goats were bought for slaughter by butchers. The rainfall being meagre, bārani cultivation was limited, and bajra, cotton, and fodder – the chief kharif crops – were produced in small quantities. Rabi crops could be produced only on lands irrigated by both canals and wells. The water from inundation canals, being irregular, was not dependable. Fed by floods from the Indus and Chenab, its supply depended on the level of winter snowfall in the Himalayas, the time of their melting, and the level of rainfall. To ensure water for the fields when inundation canals dried up, wells had to be dug to irrigate the fields at sowing time. Without wells, the rabi harvest could not be ensured.[92] In this arid tract wells were critical for all forms of life: goats, humans, crops. As Fig. 9 shows, hamlets came up around the wells,

[92] Even in the 1930s, only 60 per cent of the village area was cultivated and only 28 per cent of this area had secure irrigation. *Bhambu Sandila V.S.*, 1935, ch. II.

Fig. 9: Bhambu Sandila Village, 1934–5.

This map was prepared for a village survey in the late 1920s on the basis of the rough khasra map of the village. Note how the habitations came up around the wells scattered over the landscape.

Source: Rahim and Khan, *Bhambu Sandila V.S.*

and nineteen of them were scattered over the mauza. There was no central abadi.

The British idealised the villages of the plains. Many officials, it is true, spoke of the merits of homesteads located within peasant fields. Such a spatial organisation, they felt, saved time and energy. Cultivators did not have to walk long to reach their fields every morning and return home in the evening. Dispersed dwellings also resolved the problems of sanitation, drainage, and sewage that were inevitably associated with centralised abadis. Yet in their mind the village of the plains – with its habitation site at the centre – typified the spatial structure of North Indian villages, the specificities of other village types being inevitably defined by contrast. For these officials, the compact villages of the plains signified order; they were easier to watch and control. Scattered hamlets over the landscape connoted disorder, anxiety, and fear of the unknowable.

The spatial arrangement of dwellings within the abadi of the plains also reflected a sense of order. After surveying all the villages of the plains, the census of 1911 described the principles underlying their spatial organisation:

> The principle borne in mind appears to be to have a bazaar or road somewhere in the middle into which opened the shops that were required for the commercial needs of the inhabitants. The houses were built with their back to the bazaar and opening into the fields or open country where the strength of the population was small, or with courtyards leading onto the bazaar. Where the population to be housed was larger, the houses were built in double rows with a narrow lane between each two lines. The houses opened into these lanes which were duly connected with the main street. This appears usually to be the nucleus of the village homestead . . .[93]

Over the years, as the population increased and the village expanded, dwellings were added, with villagers wanting to live near their relatives. The abadi then extended in odd ways, taking awkward shapes, disrupting the original order.

[93] *Punjab Census Report*, 1911, p. 20.

The spatial organisation of the abadi reproduced the social hierarchies within it. The dwellings of powerful landowners, the headman and the merchants, were usually located at the centre near the bazaar; then came the dwellings of the kamins – the village servants – and finally, situated at the outskirts, segregated from the main habitation, were the hutments of the chuhras. Their resthouses too were pushed out of the bounds of the village. This spatial structure (Fig. 10) reaffirmed the image that colonial officials had of village India and its social organization mediated by caste and pollution taboos.

If the settlement within the village thus spatialised social hierarchies at one level, the relationship between villages reaffirmed power structures at another. In the villages of the plains, the dominant groups usually lived in the biggest villages. These were the oldest villages where lineage proliferation over the centuries had led to a continuous process of expansion, allowing for a congregation of the original settlers in one location. At various times, as the village grew, people from it migrated and settled in other seemingly uninhabited places, founding new villages, which in turn grew over the years. In Rohtak, for instance, 366 villages out of a total of 511 villages were held by Jats in the late nineteenth century.[94] The major Jat clans dominated all the old villages, established twenty to twenty-five generations earlier, that is, they were about 500–600 years old. The villages of the Brahmans – brought in by the Jats – were established fifteen generations earlier. The Gujars of the region continued to be mobile pastoralists till the eighteenth century, and their villages were of more recent origin, no older than 160 years. Within the Jats, the dominant clans controlled the biggest and the oldest villages and the minor clans lived in the smaller villages. Clan power was reaffirmed through narratives of village origin. Claiming the longest ancestry was a way of asserting power. In their village histories the Rathis – one of the powerful Jat clans – for instance, declared that they were the earliest settlers, and had established many of their villages thirty-five generations earlier, much before other clans came into the region.[95]

[94] Purser, *Rohtak S.R., 1882*, para 18.
[95] Ibid.

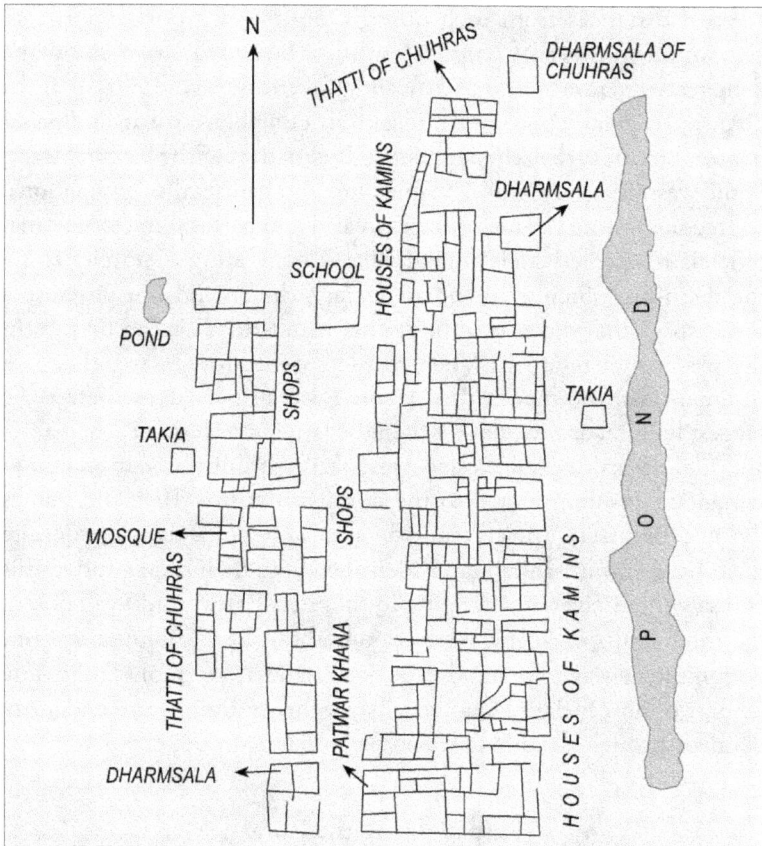

Fig. 10: Spatial Structure of the Plains' Villages of Central Punjab
Source: *Punjab Census, 1911, Report*, p. 20.

In the plains, clan power, lineage depth, and village strength were all connected in complicated ways.

In the pastoral and arid tracts the size of a village had no direct link with its temporal depth. The biggest villages were not necessarily the oldest or the strongest. When the thakbast operations were in progress in such tracts and mauza boundary lines were being decided, revenue officials found it essential to include large areas within each mauza. The landscape appeared uninhabited, and the wells and hamlets were at great distances from each other. Only by incorporating a large area and a number of hamlets within a bounded space could the demarcated mauza appear as a meaningful entity. So the villages of the plains, particularly in central and eastern Punjab, were usually smaller in area, but more densely populated. The mauzas of the pastoral tracts of the west were spread over a larger area and had smaller populations.

In constituting the new villages in arid and pastoral tracts, colonial officials reaffirmed social hierarchies. Considering hierarchy to be the defining principle of Indian society, they could not visualise a social space that did not embody that principle. This can be seen in the practice of naming. When hamlets were brought together as a revenue unit, the mauza thus formed was usually named after the biggest hamlet, or the one in which the lambardar resided. The names and identities of other hamlets were thus administratively as well as semantically subordinated to the dominant entity. Their old names did not disappear. They remained a part of people's daily life despite the official erasure. Inhabitants identified with their dhoks and kothis and saw themselves as belonging to these. As Barnes and Lyall noted, the inhabitants of kothis were zealous about kothi boundaries. But within the new agrarian landscape, kothis, deras, or dhoks could only be part of an officially denoted village, their administrative identity defined through a name that had been mapped onto them.

Respatialising the Rural

Colonisation did not proceed only by taking over the rural landscape through physical conquest. Spaces had to be reconstituted to make them adequate for the purposes of colonisation – the operation of capital and the expansion of the agrarian frontier, revenue extraction and the institution of property rights, the mapping of fields and the separation of clearly judiciable territories, the determination of legal subjects and fiscal citizens. The demarcation of villages was one such act within the wider spatial reconstitution of the rural.

Villages, as I have emphasised, existed earlier, but they were not the *only* structure of rural habitation; nor was the entire rural landscape incorporated within demarcated village boundaries. This happened in slow stages over the colonial period. To understand the complicated ways in which colonial spatialising practices constituted the village as the universal rural, we need to recognise the distinction between different types of villages: between those that came up in the reverine belts and fertile plains, and those in the dry belts, pastoral tracts, scrublands, or rocky hill regions; between villages with long histories and the newer implants that were bureaucratic creations; between villages with deep lineages and dense populations, and those that were agglomerations of scattered hamlets, or simply pieces of land with hadbast boundaries, often without habitation sites, cultivated fields, or inhabitants; between those that were organised around rights to land and those whose constituent social bodies were formed around rights to pastures, wells, and inundation canals.

I am arguing that colonial officials saw the villages of the fertile plains as archetypal – embodying the core characteristics of the Indian rural – and sought to map villages over the entire countryside, reterritorializing the landscape as a village-scape. In this process of universalisation the idea of the village was refigured in several different ways. It became, at one level, a fiscal unit – an "estate" in colonial revenue parlance, the founding unit of revenue administration in North India. If the unit of revenue assessment (the mahal) in Bengal was the zamindari, in North India it was the village. If in Bengal the mahal (the revenue estate) and the mauza (the village) were distinct categories, in North India they tended to be synonymous. Each spatial unit designated as a village was now separately surveyed, its revenue-yielding capacity assessed, and the state fiscal demand fixed. The village in this sense became a fiscal category, and those recorded as landowners within the village became fiscal subjects.

Through the thakbast operation, survey officials sought to constitute the village as a clearly demarcated space with delimited boundaries that were publicly recognised and administratively endorsed. When the maps of all the villages drawn by the revenue survey department (naksha thakbast) were collated by the Survey of India into well-produced revenue maps, the boundaries of these villages became cartographic facts, visually encoded and bureaucratically attested. Through this fiscal cartography, revenue villages acquired a visual as well as administrative reality – plotted and named in the map, its existence encoded in a thakbast number, its size measured, its shape clear to the eye.

These processes were seen by colonial officials as essential to the idea of property in land. Within the colonial legal regime, rights to land could be categorically fixed and made judiciable only if they could be clearly located within a defined space, and the boundaries of each field definitively marked, as it was in the shajra kishtwar – the village maps prepared by patwaris. Within this regime, individuals could become rights-bearing subjects only when their names and the extent of holdings under them within the village were categorically specified in the official record, as they were in the khewat-khataunis. The land records – the jamabandi, khewat-khatauni, wajib-ul-arz, shajra nasb, etc. – were kept separate for each village. The village papers constitut-ed the *village as record*, affirming the legal rights and obligations of all landholders within that spatial entity, and naturalising the idea of the village as the founding unit of rural society. This transformation of the landscape as bounded villages was a silent – at times not so silent – process of enclosing the commons, an act that produced the rural as the agrarian.

For colonial officials, however, the "true village" was more than a fiscal and administrative category. Monckton, as we saw, referred to most of the villages of Jhang as "mere parcels of land paying reve-nue under one denomination, but with no fixed principles of their union."[96] And Lyall spoke of the villages of the Kangra valley as an "aggregation of isolated freeholds, which are distinct from each other and held by men of different castes, who have nothing in common."[97] What exactly is this "principle of union" that Monckton was referring to? What was the "commonness" that Lyall was looking for? Clearly, the "true village" in official thinking was one that had an inner coherence, an inner unity. Which was – what?

This brings me back to the idea of the "estate" in the colonial imagi-nation. The "estate" in Blackstone was a unit of property: it defined the

[96] Monckton, *Jhang S.R., 1860.*
[97] Lyall, *Kangra S.R., 1865–72,* para 27.

specific relationship between co-owners with respect to a thing, most commonly land. Transferred to the colony, transformed into a fiscal category, and translated as "mahal", the estate could not be separated from the idea of property. In official thinking it was the organisational structure of property, the proprietary body that imbued estates with their inner meaning, their logic of existence. In Bengal, the zamindari as mahal was seen both as a revenue estate and a unit of property, with the zamindar as property holder as well as revenue manager.[98] In the North West Provinces and Punjab, the true village was supposed to be one that was united through the collective bond of the landowners to the land. To be true, a village could not be merely a fiscal entity; it had to embody a deeper unity, one that made property relations intelligible and tied the khewatdars (landowners) into a meaningful collectivity. The theory of tenures (as we will see in the next chapter) provided the grid through which the agrarian landscape was made intelligible. It supplied a corpus of categories through which the inner structure of the village was grasped and framed, property established as the universal basis of the collective rural body, and the relationship between the individual and the social specified.[99]

The geo-body of the nation was not formed only by marking its frontier, its outer boundaries, and demarcating the nation-space as a sovereign territory, defining the we-ness and the otherness.[100] It was built through a deeper internal conquest, one that sought to grasp the entire landscape and establish the constituent units upon which the geo-body of the nation was to be founded. Everyday social spaces with multiple forms of living were sought to be recast into regulated spaces, the site for the micro-operation of power at the local level – but

[98] Ray suggested that zamindars were essentially revenue collectors who had proprietary rights over collecting the jama, but no rights of possession. Ray, *Change in Bengal Agrarian Society*. The separation of two forms of rights – revenue collecting and property owning – is useful but too sharply drawn. The two rights were intimately connected.

[99] On the internal organization of village space, the constitution of village panchayats and the effort to consolidate the power of the coparcenary brotherhood and lambardars, see ch. 3 below.

[100] Winichakul, *Siam Mapped*.

a "local" that was visualised as an integral unit of the national. This was not done by erasing ties and institutional structures that were seen as "traditional", and establishing modern identities untainted by inscriptions of the past. It was done by searching for those traces of the past that could be refigured as constitutive elements of the colonial modern.

3

In Search of Tenures

COLONIAL POWER IN THE countryside was built through a new regime of categories. A vocabulary of terms was essential to comprehend reality, schematise knowledge, and classify social relations. Local peculiarities had to be captured through familiar terms that carried meaning beyond the locality, and which had wider, if not universal, applicability. These categories proliferated as colonial rule gained in depth and density: if some withered and faded, others acquired the power to shape imagination and reality, and still others became hypostatised terms which blinkered the perceptions of officials and historians. So significant indeed was this production of categories that it is possible to refer to a process of accumulation of semantic capital as a necessary condition of colonial rule.

The colonial state classified North Indian rural society into three categories: zamindari, pattidari, and bhaiachara. Nineteenth-century revenue manuals defined these categories for the benefit of administrators, and official tables annually enumerated the number of village tenures in each of these classes. As the categories gained currency, their truth was taken for granted and their validity continually affirmed. Post-colonial administrations continued using colonial manuals, and subsequent academic histories of rural India ritually reproduced and thereby authenticated these colonial classifications, providing them with the credence and authority by which terms come to be settled and normalised. Consequently, these categories structure our image of North Indian rural societies and our conception of the internal rules of their social organisation.

Customary law is expected to vary between tenure types. Property claims and inheritance rights in pattidari and bhaiachara villages are supposed to differ. The use of seemingly indigenous terms has given the categories a historical authenticity, the tenures appearing to have a long life stretching back into the pre-colonial past. It is as if a codifying state, propelled by its interest in local institutions, discovered village tenures and faithfully recorded their existence, counting their numbers, noting their mutations, and reaffirming their statistical existence in the annual returns. Indeed, historians too have been persuaded to project these categories back into pre-colonial times, constructing on their basis a picture of eighteenth-century rural society.[1]

Tenure type	Number of villages	Number of holders/shareholders	Gross area (in acres)
Zamindari			
i) held by individuals	1489	4541	2,539,174
ii) held by cultivating communities	3242	47510	2,712,458
Pattidari	1825	701,615	2,772,293
Bhaiachara	8315	774,942	15,706,202
Mixed or imperfect bhaiachara	20186	1,829,779	29,302,245

Fig. 11: Classifying Villages, Spatialising Tenures (Punjab 1883–4). Similar statistics were produced for each district and each tehsil, creating an impression of statistical authenticity.

Source: RLRAP, 1883–84, Statement XXXIII.

[1] Noman Siddiqi, *Land Revenue Administration Under the Mughals*, p. 31. Siddiqi writes: "there were zamindars who were co-sharers in the co-parcenary zamindaris referred to as pattidari and bhaiyyachari and bissadari." The question is: do the terms pattidari and bhaiachara appear as tenurial categories in pre-British sources, not whether there were coparcenary communities earlier. Siddiqi's footnote is ambiguous. He quotes Baden-Powell, *Land Systems*, as one of the sources of his statement and adds: "there is evidence that this type of zamindaris [bhaiachara and pattidari] did exist in the seventeenth century and British records only point to the continuity of the system which operated in the first half of the eighteenth century." Ibid., p. 31. Indu Banga suggests the terms are not to be found in pre-colonial sources (see Banga, *Agrarian System of the Sikhs*), and Cohn (in *An Anthropologist Among the Historians*, pp. 398ff.)

Existing debates on the origins of bhaiachara and pattidari have only confirmed faith in these categories, leaving unquestioned what is in fact their lack of historicity.[2]

It is not difficult to show that these categories, like many others, are colonial constructs. What I wish to emphasise is not their emptiness or their failure to encapsulate reality. They may not have expressed the survival into the colonial period of a pre-existing social reality, but they did become founding categories in the new colonial rural order, encapsulating within themselves the new organising principles of rural society. They redefined the meaning of custom, the shape of social relations, and the nature of property. They refigured the entire landscape as part of an agrarian order. We need therefore to look at the generation and circulation of these categories and at the process by which the colonial regime created its own new regime of classificatory truth. This requires an investigation not only into the etymology and genealogy of the terms, but also into the discourses and practices which invested them with meaning or delimited their significance – an enquiry into the power of words also requires a determination of the limits of that power.

The tenurial terms put revenue officials in a double bind. Settlement officers touring Punjab villages in the mid-nineteenth century searched in vain for realities that fitted the tenurial descriptions. Most agreed that the terms were spurious. Surveying Karnal, Denzil Ibbetson found them "meaningless"; in Ludhiana, Walker described them as "distinctly misleading".[3] Baden-Powell, writing his monumental three volumes, *Land Systems of British India*, lamented the dubious use of these "unfortunate terms"; and Douie's authoritative *Panjab Settlement Manual* informed revenue officials that the classification was "neither complete nor of much practical use."[4] Yet none of these

---

uses the term cautiously. The question, moreover, is not of the lineage of words, but of those words expressing the same meaning and connoting tenurial types.

[2] See Fox, *Kin, Clan, Raja and Rule*, pp. 59ff., 119ff.; Stokes, *The Peasant and the Raj*, p. 77.

[3] Ibbetson, *Karnal S.R., 1872–80*, p. 95; Walker, *Ludhiana S.R., 1878–83*, p. 79.

[4] Baden-Powell, *Land Systems*, vol. I, p. 157. Douie, *Panjab Settlement Manual*, p. 64. Baden-Powell felt that the tenurial terms were "based on a

critics could get away from using the categories they were criticising. They themselves emphasised the need to know the terms, introduced nuances in their definition, entered the tenurial returns, and in the process helped to make the terms seem authentic.

The note of scepticism never disappeared from the official discourse on tenures, but it was increasingly repressed as the nineteenth century wore on. The self-doubts and apprehensions of officials involved in the early enquiries into village tenures were replaced by a certain self-confidence in late-nineteenth-century officials fed on hard data computed and clearly stated in the records. Even the most committed empiricists, sensitive to the mismatch between concepts and observed reality, grew resigned to the use of the classification. Why and how did the categories gain currency despite official awareness of their problematic nature? What was the logic of the classificatory practices that imbued the terms with meaning?

Mapping Tenures

The classification of tenures was part of the larger imperial project of mapping and surveying. The mapping of tenures was, in fact, seen as the "first step necessary to the proper preparation of the records."[5] Tenurial classification provided, as it were, a key to the working of the agrarian system. The entries in the khewat-khataunis made sense only when read in relation to the evidence on tenures. By referring to the tenurial structure, officials believed, it was possible to understand the internal architecture of the village, its constitutive logic, and its generative and organising principle. The nature of rights and obligations, inheritance customs, the mechanisms of land transfer,

---

distinction of no import whatever: it conceals, indeed, the totally different origin which the tenures may have had . . . while what meaning it has is apt to mislead or to obscure distinctions that really are important." *Land Systems*, vol. II, p. 103.

[5] Originally the statement was made by Prinsep. See Prinsep, Asst Settlement Officer, to R. Temple, Settlement Officer Rechna Doab, 9 September 1852, in Barnes, *et al.*, New System of Field Measurement.

claims on common land, and modes of revenue payment were all to be defined by the specificities of the tenurial system and by histories going all the way back to origins.[6]

Within the taxonomic imagination of the nineteenth century, to know something involved referring the visible to the invisible, and moving from surface appearance to underlying determination in order to discover the organic relationship that tied articulating structures to designating structures. This was a mode of knowledge profoundly different from the one prevailing in Europe in the seventeenth and eighteenth centuries.[7] In the taxonomic logic of the eighteenth century, to classify was to bring identical things together: to establish a table of identities and differences, to compare visible structures and correlate elements that were homogeneous, differentiating them from those that were heterogeneous. As the nineteenth-century imagination moved beyond the domain of the visible, the basis of the taxonomies changed. We now see a search not merely for identities and differences between visible elements, but for their internal relationships, their deeper link to a larger organic structure. The meaning and mode of being of all visible elements – their empirical existence – were seen to be defined by the hierarchy of their functions, the history of their succession, and the interior architecture of the organic structure within which they were related. This quest for understanding led colonial officials to the theory of tenures, which explained the links between observable elements in rural society and supplied a history of their coming into being.

Tenurial classification, however, remained a problem. Gathering information on tenures, officials discovered, was difficult. On the basis

[6] The proprietary tenure of the village was noted in the shajra nasab – the genealogical tree of the owners that E.A. Prinsep began, for the first time, including in the record of rights. The shajra nasab recorded the history of the village, the different pattis that constituted it, and the different shares that the proprietors had within them. Narrated by those recorded as proprietors, the village history, like other constituents of the standing records, consolidated the power of the proprietary body. See Prinsep, *Sealkote S.R.*, 1865. See also Prinsep, Settlement Paper No. 11, and No. 33.

[7] Foucault, *The Order of Things*, chs 3–5.

of his experience of the North West Provinces, Thomason warned settlement officers surveying Punjab in the early 1850s: "the process is a laborious one, which the persons employed in the formation of records are apt to slur over. Each peculiarity of the tenure probably has to be elicited by repeated questions and the expressions to be carefully adjusted, so as to exactly to meet the case."[8] The natives of the country being "peculiarly prone to inaccuracy and slovenliness," said Thomason, they were unlikely to collect this evidence meticulously. Writing fifty years later, at the turn of the nineteenth century, Douie shared Thomason's suspicion of the native recording agency. "A settlement officer," he wrote, "must be on his guard against a tendency on the part of his subordinates to label a tenure by some familiar official term instead of carefully describing its actual incident."[9] Native sloth and lack of precision were to be compensated by the white man's exactitude, truth, and objective fact.[10]

Information on tenures could be collected only when tenurial categories were understood by observers and informants. Survey officials who toured the countryside with khatauni registers in their

[8] The task of the settlement officer was seen as particularly significant since he was likely to face native resistance. Thomason was emphatic that "Completeness of records can only be ensured by great vigilance on his part. The villagers are themselves reluctant to lay open to public scrutiny the internal economy of the village. They are distrustful and slow to appreciate the motives that lead to the enquiry. The strong, the crafty and the dishonest wish to avoid a proceeding which will tie their hands and close every door against future encroachment and intrigue . . . Here then all depends upon the Settlement Officer." Thomason, *Directions*, para 149.

[9] Douie, *Panjab Settlement Manual*, para 140.

[10] The good settlement officer was idealised as one who was diligent, meticulous, committed to the search for fact and truth, and the pastoral care of his flock. These ideals were canonised in manuals: "He must understand the subject himself thoroughly, he must accustom his mind to classify and methodise [*sic*] his work, he must learn to detect the weak or incompetent point of a statement, he must call into practice all these powers with unremitting watchfulness and diligence; above all, he must be actuated by a simple desire to promote the interests of the people; and by the uniform and conciliating exhibition of this he must win their confidence and attachment. In proportion as he possesses these qualifications, he will be entitled to the character of being a good Settlement Officer." Thomason, *Directions*, para 149.

hands were often as confused as the villagers about the meaning of tenures. "Much difficulty has been experienced, and much confusion in consequence at first resulted," reported Prinsep in 1852, "owing to the extreme indifference and inability of the people to explain, and the ignorance, or inexperience of the moonsurims in understanding all the local tenures that prevail . . ."[11] Forced to operate with an alien and unfamiliar framework of categories, confused patwaris fumbled and made dubious entries. Unable to accommodate the observed reality within the given terms of reference, they mechanically labelled the agrarian landscape with tenurial stereotypes. Inevitably, colonial officials relied on village elders as local knowledge holders who could guide the patwaris. Survey instructions specified that in the preparation of the khatauni, the patwari was to be accompanied by chaudhris who, as "men of superior intelligence", could help in "unravelling and classifying the many intricate tenures."[12] But village elders could not unravel the meaning of terms whose inner logic they themselves did not understand.

The Logic of Classification

The logic of colonial ethnographic enquiry conflicted with the logic of systematisation, schematisation, and classification. The logic of enquiry led officials to look for differences, peculiarity of instances, and variation in tenures. It shaped Douie's anxiety about the problematic use of "familiar terms" in labelling tenures and emphasised the official rhetoric's emphasis on precision and detail. The logic of classification had on the other hand forced a process of reduction, a condensation of detail within the frame of overarching categories: peculiarities were translated as variations within a type, sub-categories were invented only to affirm the power of meta-categories. Classification through categories is a mode of encapsulation, a process by which

[11] Prinsep, Asst Settlement Officer, to R. Temple, Settlement Officer Rechna Doab, 9 September 1852, para 9, in Barnes, et al., New System of Field Measurement, *SPCAAP*, vol. I, no. 3 (11).

[12] Ibid. See also Translation of the Directions to Putwarees, or Village Accountants, Regarding the Conduct of Field Measurements in the Baree Doab, As Modified to the System Pursued in the Rechna Doab, *SPCAAP*, vol. I, no. 3 (11).

multiformities and conflicting details are captured within the semantic space of a term and ordered into comprehensible subgroups. The tenurial enquiry was shaped by this contradictory logic.

If an understanding of the agrarian landscape required surveys, the survey required categories. So the new colonial power in Punjab, embarking on its first regular survey, looked for guiding principles and framing categories. The first-generation Punjab officials were mostly Thomason's men from the North West Provinces. John Lawrence, a civilian from there, had become, as we saw, the first Lieutenant Governor of Punjab. When he left Punjab in February 1859, Robert Montgomery, another civilian from the North West Provinces, took over the lieutenant governorship. Edward Thornton, Charles Mansel, Robert Cust, George Campbell, Donald McLeod – men who occupied important official positions in Punjab in the 1850s and '60s, had all served in the North West Provinces.[13] Nurtured by Thomason's ideals and impressed by the working of the village system here, these officials were convinced of the need to preserve the village community. The three tenurial categories Thomason had invented – zamindari, pattidari, and bhaiachara – were integral to their thought and structured their conception of village society.[14] Since the Jat villages of Punjab appeared similar to those in the North West Provinces, these officials perceived the newly annexed territories through the classificatory categories with which they were already familiar. Thomason's *Directions for Settlement Officers*, written for the North West Provinces, was accepted as the authoritative textbook for the Punjab revenue department. It was so widely admired that officials were reluctant to deviate from its instructions.[15] A revised

[13] van den Dungen, *The Punjab Tradition*. On the Thomason School, see Penner, *The James Thomason School in North India*; Muir, *The Honourable James Thomason*; Temple, *James Thomason*; Temple, *Men and Events of My Time in India*, ch. III.

[14] Thomason transformed Blackstone's categories (particularly "coparcenary" and "severalty") into terms that appeared indigenous to Indian society. For Blackstone's discussion of these terms, see idem, "Of Estates in Severalty, Joint-tenancy, Coparcenary, and Common", *Commentaries*, vol. 3, ch. 12.

[15] The publication of *Directions* is celebrated in most contemporary

revenue manual, produced by Robert Cust in 1866, and Barkley's *Directions for Revenue Officers* published in the 1870s, borrowed extensively from Thomason's text. So the tenurial categories with which Punjab's landscape was reordered had to bear the burden of their own pre-history.

In the course of travel from the North West Provinces to Punjab the meaning of categories changed. At times the same category acquired confusingly divergent meanings. Around Benaras, in the North West Provinces, British officials had observed villages held by upper castes where control over land was regulated by the customs of brotherhood (bhai-achar).[16] Soil peculiarities were taken into account to distribute claims over land, each person being allocated a mix of good and bad quality soil. Conceptualising such peculiarities, and keen on classificatory categories, officials invented the notion of a bhaiachara tenure as one in which rights were regulated by collective custom, as distinct from pattidari, a tenure in which ancestral shares defined rights and obligations.[17] Transformed into a generic category, the concept of bhaiachara tenure was subsequently expanded to include all village types where rights were regulated by some form of custom other than that of male lineal descent.[18] In some villages of the North West Provinces, the number of ploughs owned by a cultivator determined his share of the land within the estate; in other tracts critically dependent on well irrigation the number of bullocks an individual brought to work such wells defined his share of the crop that was collectively harvested.[19]

---

accounts as a major event within the revenue history of North India. See Muir, "Directions", in *The Honourable James Thomason*.

[16] Baden-Powell, *Land Systems*, vol. I, pp. 162–3; for the early settlement of the region by Jonathan Duncan, see Measures Connected with the Settlement of the Province of Benaras, vol. 1, Selections from Duncan Records, IOR/V/23/132 (BL). For the later settlement, see Porter, *Benaras S.R.*, 1887.

[17] Thomason, *Directions*.

[18] Thornton, Sec. Secretary, Government of NWP, to H.M. Elliot, Secretary to the Sudder Board of Revenue, NWP, 31 July 1845, on Settlement of Delhi, STD, no. 3277 of 1845; also Baden-Powell, *Land Systems*, vol. 1, pp. 161ff.

[19] Whiteway, *Muttra S.R.*, 1879, pp. 44–5. On the problems of classifying

When the concept of bhaiachara made its way to Punjab, it was stretched further. By the 1860s it was being described as a tenure in which the notion of ancestral share had lost its significance and what an individual actually possessed was the measure of his rights and obligations. It was said that, in the course of time, the exercise of power and the operation of market forces allowed some individuals within pattidari villages to acquire land, adding to their ancestral share and nibbling away the shares of others. So the real holdings of individuals no longer corresponded to their notional ancestral shares. The actual size of an individual's holding, rather than his presumed inherited share, became the basis of fixing his revenue obligation. In the course of a few decades the meaning of bhaiachara as a category had been turned upside down. If in the North West Provinces it referred to a world of custom, in Punjab it stood for its inverse, the realm of contract and market, of unconstrained individual right.[20]

Other categories were similarly transformed, defacing their earlier meaning. The term zamindari tenure, as officials admitted, "conveys no suggestion of jointness and common holding".[21] The early

---

bhaiachara in Uttar Pradesh, see Reid, *Etawah S.R.*, 1868–74, pp. 126ff.; *Azamgarh S.R.,* Appendix VII.

[20] Lawrence, *SRGOI*, no. 6, p. 140. Scholars have often overlooked the fact that the same tenurial category came to express different social forms. This confusion is clear in Stokes' critique of Fox's notion of bhaiachara. Fox argued that bhaiachara was the product of mere lineage proliferation of the families of chiefs and revenue grantees, and the steady progress of tenures through a continuum. Stokes differed. Tracing bhaiachara to a tribal past, he wrote: "The hallmark of the true bhaiachara was, indeed, that it was tribal, that practically all cultivators belonged to a single clan or tribe, that all held equal shares and almost all shared in the proprietary management." Stokes, *The Peasant and the Raj*, p. 77. Stokes and Fox are speaking of two different notions of bhaiachara, both part of the revenue vocabulary. Their meanings are different; the histories encoded in the concepts are not the same. Fox and Stokes, of course, see the tenurial categories as objective entities – positivities – pre-figuring British rule, not as colonial discursive constructs. What I am arguing here is that the inner dynamic of such tenurial categories cannot be understood without exploring the logic of their discursivity, and the practices through which they were refigured.

[21] Baden-Powell, *Land Systems*, vol. I, pp. 157–8.

settlements in Bengal had inscribed the term with a meaning that was difficult to erase from the official imagination: it meant individual – not collective – control over an estate.[22] But in Punjab's official revenue terminology, as well as that of the North West Provinces, it referred to the tenure of an undivided joint body, a village collectively held by a tribe or clan. The difference on the one hand between the semantic connotations of a term sedimented by history, and on the other the official meaning in revenue language, created confusion.

The confusion was compounded by the flexible and contradictory interpretations of the meaning of "jointness". The meaning that flowed from the theory of tenures was in conflict with the meaning defined by enumerative practice. In theory, an undivided joint holding, the zamindari tenure, was one collectively held by a tribe or clan. In actual practice, villages held by a single individual were classified as joint holdings, which when divided – after they were partitioned amongst descendants – became pattidari. Where villages were held by individual lambardars, the tenure was again classed as zamindari.[23] The idea of jointness – conceptually associated with the time of a village's origins, or with the original tribal settlement – was extended to describe individual rights usurped, purchased, or acquired in the nineteenth century. By a peculiar play of contrariness, the concept of zamindari, associated by officials in Bengal with individual rights, was first forced to embody the idea of tribalism and jointness – the negation of individual rights – and then in classificatory practice, through another volte-face, the idea of jointness was attached to individual rights over village revenue.

---

[22] Officials of the North West Provinces regularly complained of the way Bengal revenue categories shaped their imagination, leading to a problematic categorisation of rights and tenures: Thornton wrote in 1848: "On first acquiring the country, the local officials fresh from Bengal, with the notions prevalent there under Lord Cornwallis, were strongly possessed with the necessity of finding in all parts of the country large landed estates whom they called Zamindars." J. Thornton, Sec. to Govt. of N.W.P., to W. Muir, Sec. Sudder Revenue Board, 17 February 1848, *SRGNWP*, *Thomason's Despatches*, vol. 1.

[23] Douie, *Panjab Settlement Manual*, Book II: Record of Rights, ch. VIII; Wilson, *Sirsa S.R.*, 1879–83, ch. V.

In this theory of tenure, pattidari emerged as the founding category, in relation to which other categories acquired their meaning, their specificities, their inner coherence. Zamindari and bhaiachara were defined in opposition to, and as different from, pattidari. If pattidari represented severalty – a multiplicity of shareholders and their separateness – zamindari expressed jointness and unity. If pattidari embodied the principle of ancestral shares, bhaiachara signified the death of this share principle. The terms of these oppositions were not violated by the contrary and mutating definitions of zamindari and bhaiachara as tenurial categories. This, in fact, explains the logic that underlies the confusing multiplicity of meanings of tenurial categories.[24] Survey officials who went to the villages in search of tenures, with Thomason's *Directions* in one hand and survey sheets in the other, faced problems. Nowhere could they detect tenures that conformed to their classificatory categories. Nowhere did the measured holdings correspond to the notional share of individual landholders. When revenue officials categorised such villages as bhaiachara, they denied the possible play of the patti principle – the principle of shares – in the life of the surveyed community.[25] This was particularly true in the early decades of British rule in Punjab, when the categories were seen as exclusive and exclusionary. It was as if in a bhaiachara village the share principle could not operate, and in pattidari tenure holdings could not deviate from the notional ancestral shares. Zamindari and pattidari, as defined in theory, proved difficult to discover in practice. In a situation where landholdings changed hands, and the size of holdings mutated, some losing and others gaining land, there was an in-built pressure for tenures to be classified as bhaiachara.

---

[24] Zamindari, for instance, could mean a joint tribal holding, or a tenure held by a landholder, or one under a lambardar. Beneath this variety was a supposed commonality: against the separation of rights within pattidari, each of the diverse meanings of zamindari connoted jointness.

[25] Patti was a term used to define a share of ancestral land – holdings being divided into several pattis (or panna/lot) depending on the number of descendants and claimants. An idea that was used to define shares within a holding was transformed by colonial officials into a classificatory category to define a village type. On patti see also Smith, *Rule by Records*, Ch. 4.

While officials saw pattidari as the founding category of tenure, enumerators tended to record bhaiachara as the dominant form (see Fig. 11). This tendency became embedded in enumerative practice. The notion of shares was difficult to operationalise within a regime wanting land ownership to be associated with fixity, requiring the boundaries of rights to be categorically marked and recorded. Unlike ancestral shares, actual ownership – documented in the khewat-khatauni – was visible, corporeal, and easier to investigate. Tired enumerators preferred to classify a village as bhaiachara than investigate the difference between notional ancestral share and actual possession. "The work is so long and expensive," wrote Henry Davies from Gurdaspur in 1854, "that all parties are anxious to bring it to an end; hence, if the zamindar will only agree to pay according to the area recorded in their names, the muharrir (clerk) at once evades the task of comparing his khataoni (record of rights) with the shares."[26]

A different logic was at work in villages that were recorded as pattidari. In pattidari tenure the assessment was on the basis of the land within a village, but the total assessment was distributed according to ancestral shares. This was to the disadvantage of a patti if the land was actually less than the ancestral share, for the revenue demand was then more than the assessment warranted. Inevitably such a patti would apply "to have its assessment fixed according to its land and no longer according to traditional share."[27] Powerful landowners on the other hand welcomed the move towards bhaiachara. It made their control over a holding that was larger than their ancestral share legitimate and legal. This process of transformation through classification, infinitely reproduced at lower levels, reincarnated pattidari tenures as bhaiachara.

Officials who spoke of preserving custom were disturbed by this internal logic of the classificatory process. Prinsep fumed at the tenurial enumeration, speaking eloquently of the power of the collective

[26] Henry Davies, *Gurdaspur S.R.*, 1859, p. 15.

[27] After observing this enumerative process at work in Gurgaon, Wilson wrote: "The same tendency prevails within a patti; and the process goes on until you have every man owning a defined plot of land and paying the revenue assessed directly on that plot." Channing and Wilson, *Gurgaon S.R., 1872–83.*

principle and the violence wrought by enumerative practices.[28] Almost fanatical in his belief in the coparcenary brotherhood, he sought to reverse the decisions of revenue surveyors and restore to the brother-hood rights annihilated in the survey process.[29] He called in the elders, pointed to the implication of a classification of their tenure as bhaiachara, and persuaded them to reassert their faith in the share principle. He pointed to the injustice of recording as bhaiachara those villages in which possession really was not the measure of rights, and where the working of some share principle had always been admitted:

> I have known as many as 120 villages in pargana Shakargarh where the tenure had to be changed. People could not stand it (classification of the tenure as bhaiachara); disputes were engendered; and even where the record was upheld by the district authorities (so tenacious are the village communities of their old usages), I have seen instances where they have admitted [to Prinsep] to a share and to equalisation of possession with share; and they have gone back to their villages and redressed the injury.
>
> Seeing how property is held universally by tribes, how more readily understood is a share as the expression of a man's liability, and what reverence is paid by the descendants of a common ancestor to old usages, as affecting each others' rights, I am not surprised that there should be this adherence to the pattidari type of tenure.[30]

Prinsep was unambiguous in his views and authoritarian in his practice. He pushed through a massive revision of settlement records, defending ancient usage from the onslaught of "innovations".[31] But

---

[28] Prinsep declared with a rhetorical flourish: "this process of annihilation of existing titles to land in co-parcenary esates is going on under our Government in a most extraordinary degree; and unless an early remedy is applied (for it all arises from our record system at last settlement not being built upwards from customs as they existed) a very serious injury will be sustained by a large mass of landed proprietors . . .": para 94, Report by E.A. Prinsep, Settlement Commissioner, *HOCPP*, 1870 (159), p. 141.

[29] Ibid.

[30] Prinsep, *Sialkot S.R.*, 1865, pp. 98–9.

[31] See Report of E.A. Prinsep, Settlement Commissioner, Amritsar Division, Punjab, no. 12, 12 January 1865; Report of E.A. Prinsep, Punjab, no. 111, 21 March 1865, *HOCPP*, 1870 (159), pp. 104–6, 132–4.

such tenurial reclassification only reproduced the problem. Instead of bhaiachara, these villages now became pattidari. If the earlier classification could recognise no trace of the share principle, the new category erased the evidence of market forces. How could the notion of pattidari be sustained when measurement revealed that landholdings deviated from ancestral shares? How was clear classification possible when none of the enumerative categories captured what was observed, when reality was polymorphous – revealing the operation of apparently opposing principles – and resisted incorporation into neat categories, when the rights and obligations of individuals were regulated neither solely through the principle of ancestral shares nor only through the market, both being present and absent, operating at one level and dysfunctional at another? Officials, torn between model and evidence, sought to reconcile opposing pressures in ambiguous ways. Henry Davies, overseeing the settlement operation in Gurdaspur, pleaded:

> I am not advocating a fanatical adherence to ancestral rights, but the maintenance of a popular custom; for the fractions vary considerably from the original shares . . . I in no way depreciate the value of measurement: it is the only means of testing whether or not men have got the extent of land for which they pay revenue. But having ascertained the agreement of shares and holdings, I would uphold the system intelligible by long use to the coparceners, and not substitute the area for the share as the measure of rights and rule of the apportionment. On the contrary, I would insist on a new fractional detail of shares in preference to giving up the old plan altogether.[32]

Davies tied himself into knots seeking to reconcile the irreconcilable: the opposition between his commitment to the science of measurement and his respect for the share principle. In the end, the idea of pattidari could be sustained only through an assertion of faith, through the conviction that pattidari, embodying the ancient idea of shares, somehow ought to be saved from the threatened collapse. Davies, in fact, recommended its revival wherever possible.[33]

[32] Davies, *Gurdaspur S.R.*, 1859, p. 15.
[33] He said: "if reasserted hereafter by common consent of coparceners, I recommend its revival." Ibid., p. 15.

Classification of the zamindari tenure created similar problems. Failing to discover joint tribal holdings in all regions, officials sought to rescue the term by refiguring its meaning. As mentioned, villages settled with single zamindars or lambardars were classified as zamindari, a form of tenure conceptually meant to embody the idea of tribal jointness. Through what logic was this conceptual turnaround made possible? Baden-Powell explained it:

> A village community settling with government through its "lambardar" is treated as in form, a case of settlement with a landlord, because, though each sharer has his revenue, in a sense, individually fixed, it is as a share of a lump sum with which alone the government is concerned: the middleman is the person who pays the village assessment as a whole – i.e. *the ideal body, the jointly responsible whole, represented by the seal or signature of the headman* [emphasis added]. The headmen themselves are not in any way or sense whatever, the middlemen; the village as a whole is, and this is saved from being an absolute fiction or legal ideality, by the fact (always potentially available but rarely enforced) of joint liability of the whole estate, whether divided into separately enjoyed shares or not.[34]

This is convoluted reasoning, a desperate effort to translate the theory of tenures into operational categories. It acknowledges and denies at the same time that zamindari as a tenurial category was a fiction. The argument proceeds by establishing a formal equivalence of forms. The notion of tribal cohesion, when impossible to discover in the villages, is seen personified in the figure of the landlord or embodied in the person of the lambardar. The lambardar expresses the will of the community, he stands for the whole, and is the concentrated expression of the collectivity. He is not, in fact, an individual: he *is* the whole. The headman collects the revenue, standing between the state and peasant society, but in bureaucratic reckoning he is not the middleman, "the village as a whole is". Within this logic, a settlement with the lambardar could be represented as a settlement with a collective body. To this body is attributed a collective will, and through a rhetorical move the will of the state is transferred to

---

[34] Baden-Powell, *Land Systems*, vol. II, p. 101. Emphasis added.

the village body. Instead of saying "the state settles with the village", Baden-Powell says "the village body settles".

The collectivity embodied in the tenure is affirmed through another conceptual move. In practice, individually fixed revenue demands based on the detailed individual assessment of each holding were aggregated to arrive at a lump sum which the lambardar was to collect and give to the state. Conceptually, however, the lump sum was not presented as an aggregate of individual demands, for the individual was stated to be paying "a share of the whole", asserting thereby the idea of jointness. And for each defaulting individual the village was then made jointly responsible for the payment of the lump sum.[35] But this joint responsibility was then again transferred back to an individual – the lambardar – who had to collect and pay all dues to the state, but who through his signature and seal could represent "the jointly responsible whole". Within the discourse of custom, contracts and obligations appeared legitimate only when expressed in the language of shares and collectivities.

Over time a maximalist and a minimalist notion of jointness emerged. As the embodiment of a tribal collectivity jointness became a maximalist notion, to be discovered only in an assumed past. In the minimalist definition, jointness meant either of two things. First, that one person, a lambardar or a revenue farmer – rather than many individuals – paid the revenue, collecting it from various individuals who had been individually assessed. Second, that the villagers were jointly responsible for the payment of revenue, a responsibility borne on their behalf by a lambardar.

Tenurial terms were thus stretched, emptied, and refilled with new content. They were forced to accommodate contrary meanings: their ideal forms, their original essences, were continuously disrupted by alternative truths revealed in the process of enquiry. Yet, though the officials found them useless, the terms were retained – misleading

---

[35] On the question of joint responsibility in the context of the North West Provinces, see Thomason's Minute on the Joint Responsibility of the Coparcenaries in Putteedaree Estates, *SRGNWP, Thomason's Despatches,* vol. 1, pp. 445–52. For a discussion around the issue of joint responsibility, see no. 47, C. Allen, Officiating Sec. to the Govt of NWP, to Sec. to the Sudder Board of Revenue, NWP & Agra, 30 December 1848. Ibid.

and fictive, but in the end indispensable. Even officials who critiqued the categories continued to use them. This amazing persistence of categories, despite their acknowledged vacuity, reveals the logic of classification – the powerful need for homogenisation, for a sense of order, for the illusion of comprehension. Baden-Powell's massive three volumes on the land systems of British India powerfully express the working of this logic. He warns against any general theory of tenures, pointing to the possibly various ways in which villages were originally founded and their historically individual trajectories.[36] His volumes are packed with details of these particularities and variations, and yet he emphasises the need for classifying categories and proposes modifications to the original scheme of things.

By preparing the khewat-khatauni, the landscape was incorporated into an agrarian map. The khataunis were to show not only fields but also the number of trees, the dung heaps, and sugar mills in the separate possession of each shareholder. A khatauni number was tagged to each tree. Each element of the "interior landscape" acquired meaning as part of an external landscape comprising settled agriculture, structured by the system of village tenure.

Temporalising Space and
Spatialising Time

Tenurial classification was not merely a taxonomic exercise of separating out forms and contrasting tenurial types; it was a method of conceptualising the temporal distance between forms. The tenures did not simply differ from each other, they followed in a sequence.

> The general formula . . . is that the clan originates in the tribe, the village in the clan, and the joint family in the village . . . the subsequent history after the village is established is, first, joint ownership by all the members of the community, just as there was joint ownership by the tribe. Then the area is divided into several taraafs, each held by coparceners, and each group constituting a section of the commune. Lastly, within the taraaf there are defined plots of land; or to look to the idea and not to its concrete expression, the first theory is that of common enjoyment of

---

[36] See in particular Baden-Powell, *Land Systems*, vol. I, pp. 94ff.

the produce without dividing the land; the next that the land may be divided, but it must be held according to shares determined by descent; and the last, that the facts found to exist must be accepted, that if a man has more or less than his ancestral or customary share would give him, it is too late to correct the anomaly: shares are disused, and in course of time forgotten . . . The severalty of clans and villages succeeds the collective property of tribes: the severalty of sections of villages and families follows upon the joint ownership of the village.[37]

Difference is here read as temporal distance, distribution of forms is seen as succession in time. Zamindari was the original form, followed by pattidari, and then bhaiachara. The movement was from joint property to divided property (severalty), from the collective to the individual. Once the historical succession of forms was worked out, the effort to identify the specific tenures in different regions became an exercise in the temporalisation of space. When the khatauni registers specified a village as pattidari or bhaiachara, and the statistical returns classified the tenurial forms of each region, colonial officials mapped time on to spaces. Taxonomic space now came to connote a typological time; synchrony became diachrony. Allocated a position in a pre-ordered theory of evolutionary stages, each space now revealed a specific temporality, a stage in the evolution of agrarian society. Each space pointed to a past and a future; each space was the past and the future of another. Time had to be visualised, just as much as landscapes had to be inscribed with specific temporalities.

This history of village tenures is framed within a larger evolutionary meta-narrative. The movement from zamindari to bhaiachara was a movement from the primitive to the modern, from blood to territory, from a constraining social order controlled by the brotherhood to unregulated individual agency.[38] In the writings of Henry

---

[37] Tupper, *PCL*, vol. II, p. 53. See also the quote from Maine in Baden-Powell, *Land Systems*, vol. I, p. 175. Here the stages in the village system are seen as analogous to the changes in an undivided family, where property passes from the joint holding of the undivided family to the individual holdings of divided households.

[38] On the framing ideas of Victorian evolutionism, see Burrow, *Evolution and Society*; Stocking, *Victorian Anthropology*; Kuper, *The Invention of Primitive Society*. For a recent defence of evolutionism, see Cameiro, *Evolutionism*

Maine these ideas find their simplest and most provocative formu-lation.[39]

The time of tenures, framed within evolutionary meta-narratives, was unilinear. The movement was inevitably from collective to indi-vidual property. "It is almost a natural law," emphasised Roe, the Settlement Officer of Hoshiarpur district in 1874, "that tenure should only change in one direction, from joint holdings to severalty, and from shares to possession."[40] Reflecting on his experience as a settlement officer, James Wilson wrote in a letter to Tupper: "The tendency is all from zamindari to pattidari, from pattidari to bhaiachara; and none the other way round."[41] Tupper himself never tired of referring to this

---

in Cultural Anthropology. Cameiro traces the lineage of his ideas to the evolutionism of Leslie White.

[39] See Diamond, ed., *The Victorian Achievements of Sir Henry Maine*; Mantena, *Alibis of Empire*. In her important book, Mantena tracks the ideo-logical shifts in colonial India in the second half of the nineteenth century: the crisis of liberalism, the consolidation of conservatism, and the powerful in-fluence of Maine in fashioning this shift. I think, however, that Mantena overstates the radicalness of this shift, overdraws the influence of Maine in shaping agrarian policies, and ignores the ambiguities of late-nineteenth-century agrarian conservatism. Conservative rural paternalism appeared in different forms in India and had a lineage dating back to the early nineteenth century. Maine himself drew upon this tradition. His own thoughts on the agrarian were internally fraught: seeking to reconcile the idea of individualism within the frame of collective evolution, criticising the liberal idea of the market as liberating force but believing at the same time that the move towards individuation was both inevitable and necessary for the progress of society. In the decades after the 1850s, the paternalist agrarian vision was articulated in varied ways by different individuals, each an act of figuration, the product of a creative reconstitution of ideas from the intellectual resources of the time. Benthamite ideas jostled with those of Blackstone, Utilitarian inspirations mediated paternalist conservatism, reworked in new forms. Moreover, if we shift our focus from the canonical texts to the way ideas are appropriated and reworked in everyday practice, we discover many more strands and constitutive ambivalences within official thought as expressed on the ground.

[40] Roe, *Una Pargana (Hoshiarpur) S.R., 1869–70*, p. 45.

[41] Quoted in Tupper, *PCL*, vol. II, p. 44.

evolutionary sequence as an "indisputable natural law". In writing the history of tenures, most colonial officials were thus tracking the linear history of modern individual property.[42] Efforts to critique this unilinear transition usually ended up reaffirming the frame.

The theory of tenures thus temporalised the idea of the village community and spatialised the concept of the village as a differentiated structure. Divorced from the theory of tenures, the idea of the village community was developed in colonial discourse around the notion of changelessness and immobility.[43] The theory of tenure underlined the inevitability of change. Tenures could not reproduce themselves at the same state over an extended period of time: embedded in their functioning were the seeds of their transformation. So, time was seen as a constitutive part of a tenure's existence: it was, in fact, immanent within tenurial forms. For colonial officials the crucial issue was whether this change was to be aided or checked, whether the original essence of tenures was to be preserved amidst change.[44]

[42] Maine integrated this idea of the transition from collective to individual property into a civilisational narrative. In opposition to those who were keen to conserve the coparcenary community, apprehensive of the process of individuation of rights, Maine saw the movement towards individuation as inevitable and necessary. No-one who believed in the civilising process, Maine felt, could think of resisting this change. In fact, he said, "civilization is nothing more than a name for the old order of the Aryan world, dissolved but perpetually re-constituting itself under a vast variety of solvent influences, of which infinitely the most powerful have been those which have . . . substituted several property for collective ownership." *Village Communities in the East and West*, p. 230. On Maine's theory of progress, see Burrow, *A Liberal Descent*. On the ambiguities of the Victorian ideas of progress and the inner anxieties of many of the believers, see Burrow, "Henry Maine and the Mid-Victorian Ideas of Progress", in Diamond, ed., *Victorian Achievement*. On Maine's own uncertainties and shifts in ideas, see Cocks, "Maine, Progress and Theory", in Diamond, ed., *Victorian Achievements*.

[43] On the production and circulation of the idea of village community, see Dumont, "The 'Village Community' from Munro to Maine", pp. 67–87; Dewey, "Images of the Village Community", pp. 291–328; Breman, *Shattered Images*; Burrow, "The 'Village Community' and the Uses of History", in McKendrick, ed., *Historical Perspectives*.

[44] This argument is part of a larger debate on the politics of conservation

This temporality of change concealed a continuity. The evolutionary discourse of tenure conceptualised this continuity in two ways. First, the pattern of transformation was seen as repetitive and recurrent, and second the essence of the original form was seen as enduring. Within this meta-narrative, fissioning was presumed to be a universal process of fracture, breaking units into smaller parts that bore the imprint of their origin. In describing the process, Tupper used the analogy of a genealogical tree with many branches, each drawing its initial sustenance from a single main root. "A leading stem is severed; the branches gradually part from this, and the shoots from the branches. But wherever a cutting falls and germinates, the same process is repeated in miniature."[45] This process is endlessly repeated at all levels, breaking up collective property and transforming a tribe into individual peasant households. The process through which a zamindari changed into first pattidari and then bhaiachara was no different from that which broke up each bhaiachara household into smaller units: "The evolution of separate holdings within the village is, stage by stage, analogous to the evolution of villages within the tribe."[46]

Through all stages of change, the original essence of tenures, defined at the time of origin, remained unchanged. Since individual property emerged from a collective, and villages from tribes or clans, the later forms carried the marks of their origin. In fact, the enquiry into evolutionary stages moved from the present to the past. Evolutionists like Tylor and McLennan had suggested that the institutions of one stage survived into the next, not necessarily as material relics but in symbols and rituals.[47] These symbolic forms, like fossils, provided clues to the past; inscribed in them were the characteristics of another

---

and transformation that is discussed in ch. 5. See also Dewey, "Images of the Village Community".

[45] Tupper, *PCL*, vol. II, p. 52.

[46] Ibid. See also Maine, "The Tribe and the Land", *Lectures on the Early History of Institutions,* in particular p. 118.

[47] Tylor, *Primitive Culture*, chs VII and VIII. On Tylor, see Stocking, "Mathew Arnold, E.B. Tylor and the Uses of Invention", pp. 783–99; Kuper, *The Invention of Primitive Society.*

society.[48] These were empty forms with no functional relationship to the present serving only as signifiers of a bygone era, of a time when they were living institutions. Influenced by Tylor and McLennan, colonial officials spoke of relics, survivals, vestiges, and fossils, and discovered a continuity in time that allowed them to move from the present to the past, from the past to the present.

Operating with this evolutionist's master narrative, officials searched everywhere for collective property, coparcenary brotherhoods, and tribal origins.

The Prison-house of Categories

It was difficult in the late nineteenth century to get away from evolutionary meta-narratives and their framing categories. Baden-Powell was one official who tried desperately to distance himself from overarching theories and evolutionist ideas of tenure, but his opposition remained inconsistent and contradictory.

At one level, Baden-Powell seems to oppose Maine and Tupper, assertive evolutionists, critiquing their theory of knowledge and rejecting their ideas of land tenure. Proceeding from deductive theory, Tupper emphasised the importance of conceptual truths that had been already established, the general ideas that comparative jurisdiction had shown to be irrefutable truths.[49] Ridiculing such deductive knowledge, Baden-Powell spoke of the importance of observation and the empirical study of actual factors which had "always been at work in the production of the tenures we actually see around us . . ."[50]

---

[48] The preface of general history, McLennan suggested, is to be found in "materials presented by barbarism". A study of this material provided a clue to modern rituals and symbols: "we can trace everywhere, disguised under a variety of symbolic forms in the higher layers of civilization, the rude modes of life and forms of law with which the examination of the lower makes us familiar." McLennan, *Studies in Ancient History*, p. 4. McLennan's idea of survivals and traces is rearticulated by Maine. See Maine, *Village Communities in the East and West*, pp. 9–12; idem, *Lectures on the Early History of Institutions*, pp. 14, 35, 144, 214–16, 275–6, 388.

[49] Tupper, *PCL*, vol. I, pp. 42–7.

[50] Baden-Powell, *Land Systems*, vol. I, p. 95.

The classification of tenures had suffered because concrete enquiry had been ignored: "Had these been always observed, we should have been spared some strange mistakes."[51] He persistently reinforces his arguments with claims about their facticity, not with reference to theory, as Tupper does: "Every one of these heads is derived from an observation of the recorded facts in Oudh, the North-Western Provinces, Madras, Bombay and the Punjab."[52] But Baden-Powell cannot throw evolutionism overboard. It hides in the text behind a mass of details.

The significance of the comparative method advocated by Baden-Powell was elaborated at the time by social evolutionists who, from Maine to McLennan, felt that Europe's past could be grasped and a general theory of evolution formulated through a comparative study of surviving primitive institutions in other parts of the world.[53] Since patterns of evolution were the same everywhere, each society could be located at different points within the same evolutionary time scale: each society could help reveal the past or future of another.

Baden-Powell appears to critique the evolutionist theory of a universal and uniform development from tribal to individual property. North Indian coparcenary villages, he argues, did not all originate from ancient tribal settlements. They had diverse histories. Some were founded by rajas or chiefs, others by revenue grantees; some were usurped by revenue officials, plunderers, and adventurers,

[51] Ibid., p. 95. While acknowledging Maine's contribution, Baden-Powell attacks Maine for his astonishingly self-confident assertions based on "deficient", "imperfect", and "limited" evidence. See Baden-Powell, *The Origin and Growth of Village Communities in India*, pp. 4–5.

[52] Baden-Powell, *Land Systems*, vol. I, p. 130. In a later book he wrote: "I confess, therefore, to have felt more concerned about marshalling the facts of the case, and setting forth the conditions under which those facts are found, than with elaborating arguments and conclusions." Idem, *The Indian Village Community*, p. vi.

[53] Maine, Tylor, and McLennan were not the only ones to emphasise the significance of this comparative method. See Freeman's *Comparative Politics*. See also Collini, Winch, and Burrow, *That Noble Science of Politics*, in particular ch. VII: "The Clue to the Maze: The Appeal of the Comparative Method", pp. 207–46.

others were purchased in more recent times by revenue farmers, created by government intervention, or settled by clans and pioneer colonists who cleared the land. After the history of original founding, Baden-Powell traces a history of the disintegration and dismemberment of estates. The raja or chief dies, the estate is broken up according to the laws of partible inheritance, or at times internal dissension leads to the break-up of the family and the partitioning of estates. And "we soon find a number of co-sharers, all equally entitled, claiming the whole estate . . . forming what is called a 'joint village community'."[54] From the evidence of such communities, Baden-Powell argues, we cannot inevitably read a past history of tribal settlement. The villages that were seemingly joint had varied origins and diverse histories:

> It is exceedingly important to remember how easily in the course of a few generations a single family multiplies . . . so that when we now see a whole group of villages in one locality having the same origin, we might almost suspect the settlement of the whole tribe, whereas really it is a case of multiplication of descendants and the separation of interests, consequent on the dismemberment of one single family estate.[55]

Baden-Powell thus rejects the flattened, unilinear evolutionism of Maine and Tupper and counters their deductive theory with the evidence of a complex history. He emphasises, one might say, the difference between linear time and evolutionary time, a difference which Maine, Tupper, and many other officials tended to erase.[56] Linear time expressed the multiplication of tenures and fragmentation of holdings through laws of descent, while evolutionary time expressed a deeper transition from one stage of society to the next. Yet many of the metaphors, framing categories, and assumptions that Baden-Powell used were a part of evolutionist discourse. The significance of partible inheritance, the image of the genealogical tree, the idea of

[54] Baden-Powell, *Land Systems*, vol. I, p. 133.

[55] Ibid.

[56] On the notion of time stated from within the evolutionist tradition, see White, "History, Evolutionism, and Functionalism"; for a critical exploration of the evolutionist notion of time, see Fabian, *Time and the Other*; and Thomas, *Out of Time*.

fissioning, all remain important in Baden-Powell's theory of tenures and evolution of property. His suggestion that the present form of every tenure does not reveal a unitary past, a single point of origin, is a critique of the evolutionist theory of traces. But Baden-Powell reintegrates the theory in a modified form. Instead of the traces of a unitary process, he refers to multiple traces: different rights bearing the imprint of different histories are preserved, "layer upon layer", within the tenures.[57] Within joint villages, with their diverse origins, he discovers in the end "the operation of that process which is known by jurists to be a necessary one in the history of property – the transition from *joint* to *several*."[58]

Baden-Powell, in fact, could never reject evolutionism univocally, unambiguously, and publicly, not even in his most mature work, *The Indian Village Community* (1896). Writing in the late nineteenth century, when both evolutionism and positivism were hegemonic in Europe, he totters uncertainly between the two frameworks of knowledge, countering evolutionism with positivism at one point and reaffirming evolutionism at another. He does not question evolutionist theories; he only contests their universalist claims. His typical strategy of argument is to limit the operational field of any generalisation and conclusion, presenting facts to undermine universalist assertions and suggesting the possibility of variations. There was no universal village, he argues, no single origin, no unilinear development. The joint village was not "a primitive, still less a once universal form of land holding."[59]

[57] The original settlement by a raja or a revenue grantee, or a "marauding" clan, was followed by a history of dismemberment of estates, usurpation by revenue officials, and partitioning among descendants. Then come the British: "They perceive that the result of all that has gone before has been not merely to efface old tenures, and substitute new interests in their places, but rather to leave traces of several different rights, and to impose, as it were, layer upon layer of interests, each revealing itself in varying degrees of strength and preservation." Baden-Powell, *Land Systems*, vol. I, p. 101. Through an act of displacement, Baden-Powell transfers on to the British his own perception. Not every British official saw this multiple layering.

[58] Baden-Powell, *A Manual*, p. 61.

[59] Baden-Powell, *The Indian Village Community*, p. vii. He suggests that joint villages were to be found only among the "superior-tenures" of Hindu-

He tries to demonstrate that "the so-called joint villages followed and did not precede, the village of separate holdings." This thesis inverted the evolutionist consensus against Rousseau that collective property pre-dates individual property. Yet Baden-Powell hesitates to push his argument to its logical end, or mount a critique whose implications he is unwilling to acknowledge. As if torn by inner doubt, Baden-Powell reaffirms his loyalty to the evolutionists. Not only does he appreciate the writings of Maine and Laveyele, he seeks to reconcile their mutual oppositions.[60] Having questioned Maine's argument about the originary form of property, he is content to accept the evolutionist sequence once collective property was established.

Landscaping Village Communities

Within the colonial imagination, as we have seen, the countryside was an agrarian landscape, not just of villages but of village communities. As the process of tenurial classification progressed in the various regions, pastoral landscapes were refigured as agrarian. The project of tenurial classification allowed no space for alternative institutional forms of social relations outside the framework of officially recognised tenures. All rural social groups were to be identified as not only living in villages, but as members of village communities; all rural spaces were to be recast as tenurial spaces. In this sense, tenurial classification became a powerful instrument of agrarian conquest.

Aryans and the later tribes who settled in Northern or Upper India, not among the South Indian tribes, where the ryotwari form of individual holdings predominate.

[60] Baden-Powell considered Laveyele's theory of the tribal origin of property "perfectly correct" when the settlements of the frontier were considered, while Maine's idea of the patriarchal family being the originary institution was appropriate in non-tribal areas. Typically, Baden-Powell suggests an empirical explanation for a conceptual difference. The evidence they saw, the facts they referred to, were different; and their theories in turn were relevant for different contexts. He says: "there is no occasion to make any choice between these two opinions or to regard them as in any need of reconciliation. Both contain a good deal of the truth, and they are not opposed . . ." *Indian Village Community*, p. 229.

In the agricultural plains of central Punjab and the agro-pastoral south-east, officials discovered village communities in their "truest form", in different stages of their evolution: though even here sceptical officials periodically ruminated on the meaninglessness of the official classification. As early as 1844, when he was Collector of Delhi, John Lawrence had penned his classic description of the village communities of the region:

> In no part of the North Western Provinces are the tenures so complete and well recognised as here; no districts in which the ancient village communities are in such excellent preservation, or where the practice of our civil courts has done so little harm. They are admirably adapted to resist the evil effects of bad seasons, epidemics and other evils incidental to this country. Bound together by ties of blood connection, and above all, common interest, like the bundle of sticks . . . they are difficult to break. Drought may wither their crops, famine and disease may depopulate their houses, their fields may be deserted for a time, but when the storm blows over, if any survive, they are certain to return.[61]

Most of the core elements constituting the stereotype of the Indian village community appear in these remarks. The idea of an internally cohesive unit, bound together by ties of blood, capable of withstanding external threat, and surviving all crises was central to the notion of the village community that Maine and others elaborated later. Lawrence was Maine's main informant on Indian rural life.[62] Observations about Delhi villages were to become the premises of a universal theory.[63]

---

[61] Frequently quoted, Lawrence's became a foundational statement. See Purser and Fanshawe, *Rohtak S.R.: 1873–79*, p. 27, para 26. Thomason reported in 1848 that coparcenary communities were in a "perfect state" not only in the Delhi territory, but in Bundelkhand, and were common throughout the Doab in the North West Provinces, on the right bank of the Jumna (Yamuna), and in the southern and western parts of Rohilkhand: *SRGNWP, Thomason's Despatches*, vol. 1, p. 447.

[62] Maine recognises this in the Introduction to *Village Communities in the East and West*, 1871, p. vi. Baden-Powell was amazed at the certainty with which Maine elaborated his theories of village communities on the basis of uncertain and inadequate sources.

[63] Lawrence had of course read C.T. Metcalfe's famous – and tirelessly

Outside this zone, beyond the plains of Punjab, the village community was rarely to be found before it was officially created through the settlement process. In the hills of Kangra, there were no compact coparcenary groups tracing their lineage from a common ancestor. But G.C. Barnes, who settled the tract in the early 1850s, identified the tract as bhaiachara, attached the pastoral commons to the villages, and imposed on the village a notion of joint responsibility for the payment of revenue.[64] Only later did revenue officials admit that in the hills no village communities in the proper sense existed. Carrying out the settlement operations of the 1870s, Lyall described at length how Barnes had ignored the differences between the plains and the hills, and forcibly bound together fragmented landholdings into village communities.[65]

On the north-west frontier, tribal groups involved in trading, raiding, and pastoralism inhabited the hills west of Suleimans. Some plied the caravan trade between India, Afghanistan, and beyond, while others guarded the passes, raiding traders who did not pay the tribal tolls.[66] Their life was mobile and fluid and their settlements embodied this fluidity. Tribal territories were not fixed agrarian settlements but areas within which the authority and power of a tribe (wirasat) was exercised and peace between tribal factions negotiated in order to focus raiding and feuding on external targets. Each tribe was subdivided into sections, and its territory divided into tappas under

---

quoted – formulation in Minute on the Settlement in the Western Provinces, 7 November 1830, Minutes of Evidence taken before the Select Committee on the Affairs of the East India Company, III Revenue, *HOCPP*, 1831–2, vol. XI, pp. 331–2.

[64] Barnes, *Kangra S.R., 1850–55*, paras 121–9.

[65] Lyall wrote: "By this imposition of joint responsibility Mr Barnes bound together the landholder of each mauzah into a kind of village community . . . What he did was to apply to the hill circuit, with slight alteration, the terms and forms which are in use for an estate in the plains, of the kind known in Settlement jargon as a bhaiyachara mehal." Lyall, *Kangra S.R., 1865–72*, p. 27. Many years later Douie reaffirmed Lyall's view. See *Panjab Settlement Manual*, p. 74.

[66] Bhattacharya, "Pastoralists in a Colonial World"; idem, "Predicaments of Mobility".

the khels.[67] Viewing the arrangements through their agrarian lenses, revenue officials settling the region saw in this tribal tract evidence of the village community in its primal coparcenary form, the original primitive stage surviving due to the isolation of the region. They hastened to settle the tribes, restricting their mobility, "moulding the tenures into shares with which they were already familiar", encouraging the growth of fixed agrarian property.[68]

Further north – around Rawalpindi, Jhelum, Gujrat, and Hazara – a hybrid village tenure was imposed. At the time of annexation the British found Pathan clans controlling this stony terrain, with cultivators located in the outlying hamlets (dhoks).[69] Subordinated by the Khalsa Raj, the clan chiefs were yet powerful enough to resist a full settlement with the cultivating communities. So officials invented a new tenure, malik kabza, defining the rights of an agrarian community that acquired its control over land through occupation (kabza), and not its patrilineal connection with the original founders of a coparcenary community.[70] Like other village tenures, the joint responsibility for revenue payment was given over to malik kabza holders,

[67] On the complicated process of settling with the Bannuchis, Waziris, Marwats, Khataks, Bhittanis, see Memorandum on the Bhittanis, Punjab For., March 1879, A 12a; Punjab For., June 1879, A 12b; Memorandum on the Waziris, Punjab For., November 1873, A 15; Punjab For., May 1879, A 16; see also Thorburn, *Bannu S.R.*, 1879, ch. VII; Urmston, Notes on the Bunnoo District.

[68] Douie, *Panjab Settlement Manual*, Book II, Record of Rights, ch. VIII, para 164; see also paras 165–6, 174. On the policy of settlement, see chs 9 and 10 below. On the settlement of the different tribes, see Bruce, Notes on the Dera Ghazee Khan District, *SRGPD, NS*, no. 9; Papers Relating to State of Affairs in Swat, *SRGPD,NS*, no. 14; Cavagnari, Report on the Kohat Pass Afridis, 1867, *SRGOPD, NS*, no. 19; Minchin, Memorandum on the Beloch Tribes, *SRGPD, NS*, no. 3, p. 79; Papers Relating to the Gakhar Tribe, *SRGPD, NS*, no. 23. On rights in Dera Ghazi Khan, Punjab Revenue, February 1872, no. 31. For the land settlement of the Bhittanis, see S.T.G. Tucker's note, Punjab For., March 1879, A 5.

[69] James, *Report of the Revised Settlement of the Mommunds*.

[70] On malikan kabza tenure in Gujrat, see Punjab Rev. (Rev.), October 1873, A 4. For Hazara, see Wace, *Hazara S.R.*, pp. 121–3, 117–19, pp. 158–9, 254–6; for Rawalpindi, see Cracroft, *Rawulpindi S.R.* By the 1870s the term

but they were denied ownership of the village commons, which were considered the property of the tribal clans, who were stated to be the original owners (waris).[71] The two defining characteristics of jointness of coparcenary communities were split: one community (malik kabza) had the collective responsibility of paying the revenue, and another (tribal warisans) had the collective right over the village commons. The joint responsibility of paying revenue did not qualify the malikan kabza tenure holders to be seen as members of the coparcenary community. Only those classified as descended from the original owners (waris) were recorded as coparceners.[72]

We can thus identify at least two distinct trajectories within this process of transformation of a pastoral landscape into landscapes of village communities. In some regions, tribes were forced to settle and land revenue was imposed separately on the area of land allocated to each tribe, making each section jointly responsible for the payment of this demand.[73] By official definition, each tribal section was thus transformed into a joint proprietary body, and the land under the control of each section became a mauza – a single revenue estate – and in revenue language, a village.

In a second move, discrete individual holdings were strung together and christened a village community. In the Beloch country around Dera Ghazi Khan, arid expanses of grazing land were studded with scattered wells around which individuals cultivated, their rights being in proportion to their labour input in digging the well.[74] But for revenue settlement the terrain had to be perceived as a conglomeration of villages. "There are no village communities in the district," wrote Fryer. "Every village is made up of separate and independent

---

kabza dari was also being used in the discourse on tenures in the North West Provinces. See, for instance, Evans, *Agra S.R.*, p. 17.

[71] Memo by the Financial Comm. on the Question of Malik Kabzas in Gujrat, Punjab, Agr. Rev. and Commerce, September 1873, no. 7.

[72] Ibid.

[73] On the link between taxation, settlement, and the constitution of a fiscal subject, see ch. 9 below.

[74] See the discussion on adhlapis and chakdars in ch. 5 below.

landowners bound together by no common interest in the land but
only associated together for revenue purposes, and in former times for
mutual protection."[75] Official returns, however, showed that 12,210
out of 13,727 well-estates in this region were held in common.[76] In
the hills of Kangra too, as we saw, individual holdings were knitted
together into a bureaucratically constituted collectivity.

The Limits of Classification

The theory of village tenures was thus the basis for classifying and
ordering rural society, transforming non-agrarian landscapes into
agrarian ones, defining the sources of rural rights, and grading these
rights through a hierarchy based on blood and ancestry. In the process
it consolidated a male brotherhood and patriarchy, marginalising the
rights of women and of those who could not belong to brotherhoods
that were defined by blood and lineage. In empowering the dominant
agrarian community it eroded the rights of "lower" castes and non-
agriculturists.

[75] Fryer, *Dera Ghazi Khan S.R., 1869–74*, para 216. Fryer wrote: "Most Sind
villages, i.e., in the tracts near the Indus, are mere collections of wells grouped
together for revenue purposes, but not really in any way knit together": p. 75. On
the rights around canals and wells in Dera Ghazi Khan and Dera Ismail Khan,
see also Punjab Rev. & Agr. (Rev.), January 1882, A 2/141; Bruce, Notes on
the Dera Ghazee Khan District, p. 132; Minchin, Memorandum on the Beloch
Tribes.

[76] Fryer, *Dera Ghazi Khan S.R., 1869–74*, p. 75. Settlement manuals
recognised this act of official invention: "The village is a fortuitous aggregation of independent units. The units in Sind tract are wells, i.e., the well
and the lands irrigated by it . . . Several of these wells or embankments
as the case may be, are collectively called a village, and are looked upon
from an administrative point of view as forming one community; but
they are not, properly speaking, sub-divisions of a village, but a series
of proprietary units not really in any way knit together but thrown into
association either by the necessity for mutual protection, or still more
often, by the accident of having been included for administrative purposes
within a common village boundary, and now maintaining that association simply as the result of the revenue system of the country." Douie,
Panjab Settlement Manual, p. 81.

But there were limits to the project of classification. The order it seemingly imposed was often ephemeral and illusory. Even in the plains of central and south-east Punjab, the discourse of tenures resulted in enumerated village communities with revenue records, but that revealed very little about the internal constitution of the villages. Exasperated officials found it impossible to classify any particular village through a single category. Different parts of the village seemed to conform to the characteristics of different tenures. It was as if there was a cross-hatched pattern or a patchwork of rights, with the supposed characteristics of various tenures fusing in a way that made it impossible to separate them.[77]

The knowledge produced by tenurial records was often entirely deceptive. Tenurial definitions inform us that the zamindari tenure was the originary joint form of coparcenary communities, embodying the principle of collectivity; in a sense, it was the Other of modern individual property. Yet the evidence shows that the zamindari tenures of revenue records often referred to individuated rights, at times created under British rule. In Karnal, when Ibbetson carried out the settlement operations in the 1870s, 64 out of 336 villages were supposed to be "held in common by the body of owners" and were therefore classified as zamindari. But on enquiry it was found that 44 of these 64 zamindari villages of Karnal were held by the big landowning families of Skinners and Mandals or purchasers from them; 9 were uninhabited plots of land belonging to large villages but with separate boundaries of their own, and 8 were on the river's edge where land was held collectively to overcome the uncertainty created by river action, and in the remaining 3 villages jointness consisted of an imposed joint responsibility to pay the revenue. These zamindari

[77] Ibbetson wrote from Karnal: "The fact is that a village may have four or five pannas with two or three thulas in each; there may be common land of the village of each panna, of each thula, and of two or more thulas jointly, the scale of separate interest in each varying in its nature from one another, and each single family holding by possession and not according to shares; so that it is as a rule, impossible to describe the tenure of a village in a word, or to classify it satisfactorily under the recognised headings." Ibbetson, *Karnal S.R.*, pp. 95–6.

tenures were neither surviving forms of ancient collective property nor reminders of the tribal origins of agrarian community.

Elsewhere in Sirsa, zamindari appeared as the dominant form of tenure when, at the first settlement, village headmen were recognised as the proprietors of the villages, with rights over the uncultivated land and the responsibility to pay revenue. Here again zamindari tenure was an official creation, not an ancient tribal form of joint holding. The transformation of these revenue estates into pattidari and bhaiachara was a result of a simple process of partitioning the headman's rights and did not reflect any deeper process of social transition from communal to individual property. In 1838 all the 650 villages of Sirsa were recorded as "held jointly" by proprietors (zamindari). By the time of the regular settlement (1852–64) 100 villages were partitioned; and by 1880 another 224 villages were partitioned. The enumeration of 1882 shows 258 villages as pattidari, 112 as bhaiachara, and only 270 as undivided.[78]

Empowering the Village Brotherhood

Governance required institutions. The power of village brotherhoods, sanctified by the theory of tenure, was consolidated by empowering panchayats. Within the patriarchal agrarian imaginary, village communities were to be ordered through their own institutions of arbitration. In the early years after the annexation of Punjab, this patriarchal assumption was taken for granted. All three members of the board – the Lawrence brothers and Robert Montgomery – hated the old Regulation System that was in force in most of the provinces then under British control.[79] They dreamt of a system that would be simple, efficient, accessible, quick, and inexpensive. Rural justice had to be dispensed on the spot, with the jurors sitting not in court but amongst people under a banyan tree.[80]

[78] Wilson, *Sirsa S.R., 1879–83*, p. 374.

[79] Regulation System was so called because in the provinces of the three existing presidencies – Calcutta, Bombay, and Madras – governance was to be within the framework of an elaborate system of regulations. This was seen as unnecessary in the newly conquered territories, specially in the frontier.

[80] Gibbon, *The Lawrences*, p. 26 , pp. 119ff. See ch. 1 above.

The village panchayat was discovered as the institution that could ideally perform this function. "Private arbitration is a potent means of popular justice," declared Temple, the second secretary to the Punjab Board, with a patriarchal flourish.[81] "From the first," he wrote in 1850, "the Board have been anxious that public disputes should be referred to that rude tribunal whose voice is all powerful in the regulation of private affairs . . .'[82] Rude and rough justice was perceived as quick, simple, and more authentic: it was local, popular, and sanctioned by tradition. By preserving this cherished institution of the village community, it was felt, imperial authority could root itself in local society and build on inherited traditions; it could ensure true justice, unencumbered by rules and regulations that villagers could not understand.[83] The village elders, it was believed, knew local norms as they operated in practice and so were best equipped to uphold them. Inspired by this patriarchal ideal of self-adjudicating village communities, the Punjab officials of the early 1850s went about formalising the panchayat as the first court for the arbitration of social disputes. Instructions were issued to all district officers to first attempt an amicable resolution, failing which the parties were to be referred to a panchayat. If the disputants refused the mediation of a panchayat, then a panch-sultani, a committee of village notables, was to be appointed ad hoc by the district officer.[84]

[81] *RAP, 1849/50–1850/51*, para 223. The secretary of the Board at the time was P. Melvill, but Richard Temple, who became the second Secretary of the Board, penned most of the final draft of the first report. Much of the report was written in Templetonian language. See Bosworth-Smith, *Life of Lord Lawrence*, vol. I, pp. 275, 386–7.

[82] Ibid.

[83] Reporting in 1850 on their vision of civil justice, the Punjab Board declared: "the aim is to abandon all technicalities, circumlocutions and obscurities, to supply and abridge every rule, procedure and process." *RAP, 1849/50–1850/51*, para 221. The early reports of the Board give us an account of how the Lawrences saw local arbitration as desirable, necessary, and efficient: tribunals that will be easily accessible to the rural population. *RAP, 1851/52–1852/53*, pp. 76–8; *RAP, 1853/54–1854/55*.

[84] See the retrospective recounting of this early history of panchayats in Note by Thornton on the Proposal to Revive the Panchayat, 1878, *SRFCP, N.S.*, no. 65.

Even before this experiment could take off, the patriarchal ideal came under question. Officials in different districts began doubting the morality of the panches and the efficiency of the system. Initially, the complaints were dismissed. When the Deputy Commissioner of Multan reported that the system of arbitration was more "an obstruction to the settlement of disputes than the means of its speedy adjustment", he was officially snubbed.[85] But soon the self-assurance of the paternalists began to waver. Though they could not renounce their commitment to the patriarchal ideal, they began admitting that in practice the institution of the panchayat was probably less popular in the villages than they had imagined. The institution had to be retained but its powers had to be modified.

Faced with widespread criticism of the system, the board yielded. In 1853 the panchayat system was radically altered. Panchayats were no longer to be patriarchal tribunals for the settlement of disputes but committees for investigating issues that were referred to them by the district judge. They had to record evidence and explain their findings. Their decisions had no force of law unless confirmed by the judge, and their suggestions could be rejected or modified. The decision of the judges was then further subject to appeal. Transformed into an adjunct of the court, denied any independent power to adjudicate, the system of local arbitration was first affirmed and then undercut.

This hybrid system continued in force till 1866. Judges appointed arbitrators, asked them questions, and heard their opinion in court. As the working of the system was evaluated, new subjects of debate emerged. When news from the districts suggested the panchayat system was "losing popularity", those critical of patriarchal ideals were relieved. They read into people's minds, interpreted their thoughts, and declared that *the people* had no faith in the panches: they saw them as corrupt, partial, and prejudiced. What *the people* wanted, it was said, was British justice; they trusted the impartiality of British judges. Captain James, the Commissioner of Peshawar Division, said: "I have as little confidence in the award of the arbitrators as the

<hr>

[85] Ibid., para 26.

people themselves."[86] The Commissioner of Hissar wrote: "panchayats are often so corrupt and apparently increasingly so, that unless expressly wished for by the parties, or otherwise deemed essential, it is better perhaps to avoid reference to arbitration."[87] A strong supporter of the panchayat system in 1853, Richard Temple, when Commissioner of Lahore, also admitted that "the manner in which the defeated parties almost invariably impute partiality to their own arbitrators is remarkable."[88]

Not all paternalists were disenchanted. They preferred to read the evidence differently. True, panchayats were not functioning well, they said, but the problem was not intrinsic to the system. The institution did not work because it had been disrupted by British intervention. The Commissioner of Lahore explained in 1861: "Seated round the village tree or in the *chaupal*, they will discuss and decide the dispute entrusted to their judgement with great attention and due regard to substantial justice, but when the arbitrators are taken from their homes to a formal court, how can we be surprised at the too frequent complaint that the panchayat have not perfectly inquired into the case, and have given a partial decision."[89] Every system, he seemed to say, works within a context. Every institution has its inner rationality, its peculiar logic. Taken out of the social context, displaced from the original site of its working, integrated into an alien structure, it could not possibly function properly. Restored to its primordial setting, allowed its own logic of working, panchayat justice could flourish. Patriarchs railed against "innovations" and harped untiringly on the idea of rural innocence, on the notion of fairness appropriate to rural settings, and on the need for speedy rustic justice.

The Code of Civil Procedure enacted in 1866 changed the norms

[86] Report of the Commissioner of Peshawar Division, in *Report on the Administration of Civil Justice, Punjab*, 1860.

[87] Report of the Commissioner of Hissar Division, *Report on the Administration of Civil Justice, Punjab*, 1860.

[88] Quoted in Note by Thornton on the Proposal to Revive the Panchayat, 1878, *SRFCP, NS*, no. 65.

[89] Report of the Commissioner of Lahore Division, *Report on the Administration of Civil Justice, Punjab*, para 117.

of panchayat functioning. The court was no longer to refer disputes to arbitrators for their opinion. Only those involved in the disputes could ask for arbitration. And once a case was referred, the decision of the arbitrators was final; it could not be questioned except on grounds of corruption. After the Code of 1866 was passed, the earlier cycle of debate was repeated. Officials from the districts reported that the popularity of the arbitration process was rapidly declining. Armed with this evidence, critics of the arbitration system mounted an attack that was by now familiar. Disenchanted with a corrupt indigenous system, they said, people were affirming their faith in the impartiality of British judges. The patriarchs, on the other hand, thought – as they did earlier – that the new innovations were killing a "vigorous native institution". Local arbitration by panchayats, they asserted, ought to be the court of first appeal, particularly in all petty cases. Once the dispute reached the higher courts, litigants were unlikely to ask for arbitration by local panches.

By the late 1870s, the debate widened. C.R. Lindsay, who was at the time a judge at the Chief Court of Punjab, circulated a questionnaire in 1878 asking landowners, judges, and other notables for their opinion on the proposal to revive panchayats. Panchayats, most landowners said, would be popular with the people.[90] It was an ancient institution, uncomplicated, convenient, and cheap. Arbitrators usually knew the people involved in the dispute and were aware of the case. Panchayat adjudication would save time and expense.[91] There would be no need to sign stamp papers, no need to spend time investigating the case, no need to meet infrastructural expenses. Landowners would not have to waste money paying lawyers and petition writers. No elaborate rules were required, no detailed manuals and digests were necessary. A simple code was sufficient to guide the panches.[92]

The revival of the panchayats, it was said, was an urgent necessity. With the working of the British judicial and administrative system,

[90] Quoted in Note by Thornton on the Proposal to Revive the Panchayat, 1878, *SRFCP, NS*, 65.

[91] Ibid.

[92] Ibid.

the village elders had lost power. In fact, Amin Chand, Judicial Assistant in Ajmer, dramatically pronounced that "the influence of such men of position has diminished to such an extent that even a sweeper would not obey them if they were to direct him to keep public places clean."[93] By reviving the panchayats the local men of influence would regain their notion of self, and their sense of honour. "Proud of the honour conferred upon them by Government, and prompted by a desire of being respected, the members of the panchayats will act honourably and will be thankful to Government, for it will keep up their respectability and secure their access to authorities."[94] The landowners' sense of honour, said Amin Chand, would guard against prejudice and corruption for they were honour-bound to check village vices, discipline badmashes, and establish order.

From official notes and memos the debate now entered the public domain. On 7 September 1878, Syed Ahmad Khan published an article in the *Aligarh Institute Gazette* rebutting arguments for the revival of panchayats. To him the panchayat was "an institution of the dark ages and quite unsuited to the present state of civic science and arts."[95] His plea was for a system of modern justice based on codified law, adjudicated by educated and trained judges. Within his modernist frame, adjudication through panchayats was an abhorrent and archaic idea.

Twenty days after Khan's article appeared, *Akhbar-i-Anjuman-i-Punjab* published a polemical rejoinder.[96] Syed Ahmad Khan was undoubtedly an educated man, it said, but "his love for Western civilization has produced in him a strong dislike for everything native . . ."[97] He had no capacity to appreciate native ideas, associations, arts or

[93] Amin Chand, Judicial Assistant, Ajmer, in answer to questions put by C.R Lindsay, Judge Chief Court, Punjab regarding the establishment of panchayats in villages. Ibid.

[94] Ibid.

[95] *Aligarh Institute Gazette*, 7 September 1878.

[96] *Akhbar-i-Anjuman-i-Punjab*, 27 September 1878, extracted in *SRFCP, NS*, 65. See also Anjuman-i-Punjab, *Proceedings in Connection with the Proposed Establishment of Village Panchaits*, 1878.

[97] Ibid.

manufacture. Contrary to Syed Ahmad Khan's opinion, *Akhbar-i-Anjuman-i-Punjab* argued that adjudication in village matters did not require Western education or legal training. It required men of intelligence who were aware of village life and could decide matters quickly and fairly. How could a villager file a suit at a distant court when his crop was damaged by a neighbour, or when the path to his field was blocked by another villager, or when someone hurled abuse at him? In all such petty cases, the newspaper stated, village elders could adjudicate more effectively than court judges. The only problem, *Akhbar-i-Anjuman* felt, was that within the British regime the village headmen had lost their authority and influence and were no longer held in honour. Panchayats could flourish only if legal powers were restored to them.[98]

The debate simmered over the subsequent thirty years. Panchayat arbitration was continued in many districts, but the anti-patriarchal voice effectively resisted its universal revival. In 1878 Lindsay and Thornton convinced the provincial authorities that a general revival would be retrogressive; and in 1901, when an enquiry was made as to the feasibility of a wider experiment with the system, the lieutenant governor again accepted the argument of the critics.[99] Mackworth Young summarised the opinion to the Government of India thus:

The weight of opinion in this province is clearly against any system of village courts or village panchayats at the present time. No suitable material is forthcoming for their composition. Arbitration is unsatisfactory already, when disputants can choose their own arbitrators. Matters will not be improved if a standing board in whom litigants have little or no confidence is appointed . . . Corruption, incompetence and partiality would necessitate a right of appeal, and some sort of record would then be indispensable, and the whole advantage of the system would vanish . . . The Lieutenant Governor is unable to recommend that an

[98] Many of the newspapers of the time argued for the revival of panchayats. See the opinion of Hursukh Rai, editor, *Koh-i-noor*; Sayad Nadir Ali Shah, editor, *Rahbar-i-Hind*; Nizar Ali, editor, *Akhbar-i-Anjuman*; Futteh-ud-din, editor, *Lahore Punch*: collected by Lindsay, *SRFCP, NS*, 65.

[99] GOP, Letter no. 37S, 25 May 1901, Home (Judicial), no. 138, May 1901.

attempt should be made to revive a system which derived its vitality from conditions and circumstance which have passed. [100]

In the meantime the nationalist movement was gathering strength and the demand for swaraj growing louder. In 1907 a Royal Commission for Decentralization was set up. The report it submitted in May 1909 proposed the constitution of panchayats in villages as a safe experiment in self-government.[101] A few months later a Draft Bill for the Establishment of Panchayats in the Punjab was circulated for comments, and after three years of debate became an act.[102] Over the next decade panchayat bills were passed in most provinces across India.[103]

The system that was instituted was, therefore, not exactly ancient. Formally established through legislation, the panchayat was now legally recognised as the lowest unit of the colonial judicial hierarchy. Through the late nineteenth century the patriarchs and their critics had battled against each other to define the form and bounds of panchayati power. Every demand for local autonomy had created anxieties about the limits of state sovereignty, and every assertion of state control prompted patriarchal fears about the subversion of local systems that needed to be sustained.

But few colonial officials had ever seriously considered the panchayat as the site of local autonomy. From the early years of colonial rule in Punjab the autonomy of the panchayat was both recognised and

[100] Ibid.

[101] Report of the Royal Commission upon Decentralization in India, vol. 1, *HOCPP*. R.C. Dutt was the Indian member of the commission.

[102] No. 266, M.W. Fenton, Chief Secretary to GP, to Secretary to GOI, Home Department, Punjab Home (Judicial), June 1909, nos 26–32. On the debate, see also Punjab Home (Judicial), July 1910, A 36–72; Punjab Home (Judicial), Dec. 1912, A 1–116.

[103] These panchayat bills were widely discussed in meetings and newspapers. See, for Punjab, *TOI*, July 1927, p. 11; Bombay, *TOI*, 13 March 1930, p. 6; Central Provinces, *TOI*, 17 April 1928, p. 10; Deccan, *TOI*, 23 June 1932, p. 10; Indore, *TOI*, no. 1, 1921, p. 8; Kolhapur, *TOI*, 7 July 1927, p. 13; and *TOI*, 28 October 1927, p. 12; Travancore, *TOI*, 14 September 1914, p. 6; Berar, *TOI*, 6 November 1929, p. 6; Poona, *TOI*, 19 September 1931, p. 13.

denied. When the Board of Administration declared in 1848–9 that public disputes ought to be referred to that "rude tribunal whose voice is all powerful" in village affairs, it was not arguing for radical local autonomy. The working of the panchayat, it emphasised, had to be carefully watched. The selection and appointment of arbitrators, the conduct of their enquiry, the mode of collecting evidence, and recording the award had to be "scrupulously and jealously guarded".[104] The arbitrators in fact had to come to court to deliberate; they were not allowed to take any evidence home, and their opinion was not to be considered final unless the presiding officer, appointed by the government, saw it as just and fair.[105] The system had to work within the overall structure of colonial judicial administration, not outside it.

Notions of sovereignty and autonomy, ideas about procedures and systems, proposals about rules and regulations, continued to be debated with polemical vigour. By the end of the nineteenth century most patriarchs had come to recognise that local adjudication *had* to be subject to checks, its procedures had to be formalised. Panchayats had to conform to some broad rules formulated for their functioning – maintain a register, make an entry of the cases, note the date they were instituted, register the names of the parties, the amount of the claim, and record the order passed. The Panchayat Act of 1912 required that a muharrir be appointed to check and register all panchayat records. He was to ensure that the identifying details of the plaintiff and defendant were entered in the prescribed form, a concise report of the dispute was recorded, and the decision of the panches – along with an explanation of the reasons for the decision – noted in column 10 of something called the Judgement Sheet. Each member of the bench had to sign a Judgement Sheet, a Decree Sheet, and a Certificate of Execution, and maintain a Register of Applications for reference.[106] But there can be no doubt that the

[104] *RAP*, para 223.

[105] Ibid.

[106] Punjab Home (Judicial), December 1912, A 1–116; Punjab Home (Judicial), July 1913, A 72. An annual report of the working of the Act was also maintained for many years. See *Report of the Working of Panchayats in the Punjab*, annual, 1925–6 to 1940–1.

Panchayat Act consolidated the power of male brotherhoods within the villages.

If in the long term the panchayats empowered the village brotherhoods in problematic ways, the nationalists were implicated in this process of patriarchal consolidation. Originating in the mid nineteenth century as a proposal of paternalist officials, the demand for the constitution of panchayats had become, by the early twentieth century, a part of the nationalist agenda. In fact the panchayat bills were ultimately enacted in the various provinces only when the nationalist demand for local self-government resonated with the colonial patriarchal vision, enabling the materialisation of an idea that had long been resisted by modernist voices within the corridors of colonial power.

Anointed by the colonial state and nationalists alike, the panchayats became a critical site for the consolidation of patriarchal power in the villages. Their implications for the working of rural society – not only for women and dalits – are yet to be fully realised seventy years after Independence.

4

The Power of Categories

Having mapped the rural landscape into tenurial types, locating villages in time and space and determining their social constitution, revenue officials proceeded to classify the rural population and define individual rights in land within the villages. Two categories – proprietor and tenant – became critical in this project of understanding, for they were assumed to be the only categories through which agrarian society could be comprehended and ordered. Their validity was taken for granted, their universal applicability never seriously questioned. They became the categories of power, the categories that mattered, the categories that sought to constitute, not simply express, social relations. Enquiries framed through them posed specific types of questions and pushed officials towards certain forms of answers. Indeed, so powerful were these categories and so overwhelming their pressure that officials persistently drew conclusions against the grain of their evidence. Historians' debates on property rights have continued to operate within a terrain defined by such juridical terms, thus reaffirming the assumption of their universal and natural character. "Landlord" and "tenant" have become the master terms through which all agrarian relations are now conceptualised.

My purpose in this chapter, as in those preceding it, is to understand the structure and constitutive power of the conceptual refiguration that resulted from this classificatory process. I seek to probe a cluster of terms through which agrarian society was locally and officially imagined and ordered, and explore the way existing rights were perceived, translated, and reclassified. Semantic changes, I suggest, were symptomatic of profound changes in agrarian relations, for categories not only mediate social relationships, they help constitute them.

Ethnographic Truth and the Question of Rights

Intent on building colonial rule on native institutions, British officials in Punjab were wary of disturbing the existing social fabric. Settlement officers starting off on enquiries into rural rights were repeatedly reminded of Thomason's directive: "The object of the investigation is not to create new rights, but to define those that exist."[1] They were told that "no change should be made in existing rights, or in the mode of their exercise." This, as we shall see, was Mission Impossible. The very act of recording and then translating local rights into legal categories transformed the nature of the rights and their sources of authority.

When the earliest settlements in Punjab were carried out in the 1850s, no detailed enquiries into existing rights were undertaken. By the 1860s, however, officials were asking about the customs of people, preparing a record of rights (wajib-ul-arz), and mapping the social and physical landscape of Punjab. These records offer us a rich official ethnography of notions of local rights in Punjab's various regions. They tell us about the constitutive logic of these rights and the meaning of the categories that embodied them.

It seems that the vast corpus of categories revealed in the official ethnographies had a connotative function. They referred back to a history of lived practices that imbued specific social relations with their particular meaning. Most often they narrated the history of a beginning, of a time when the existing relationships were forged and the founding acts establishing all that was valuable had come into being. In regions covered with low forest and scrub, for instance, the agrarian frontier could expand only by clearing the shrubs. Tribal chiefs in Dera Ghazi Khan and Multan mobilised people to clear,

[1] Thomason, *Directions*, para 76.

plough, and cultivate the land.[2] Elsewhere, in the dry tracts of places like Hissar, migrant groups moved into uncultivated spaces, uprooted the flora, established habitations, tilled the land, and extended the boundaries of cultivation.[3] Those who came together to collectively clear and cultivate were known as butimar or mundemar (buti=shrub/bush, munde=stumps/roots, and mar=clear/uproot/destroy).[4] It was taken for granted that the butimar would cultivate a share of the land he cleared. The actual share of the individual butimar depended on the number of hands each family of butimars contributed to the clearing operation and the number of plough cattle they brought with them. Claims over their share were passed down the generations and reaffirmed by their daily labour on the land.

In many submontane tracts, such as Hoshiarpur and Dera Ghazi Khan, the silt-bearing water of hill torrents had to be harnessed for cultivation. Fields had to be bounded on all sides, and embankments – usually three- to four-foot high mounds – had to be raised to hold water.[5] The embanked field was known as a bund, the mound was called a lath, and those who built the embankments and maintained them were known as lathbunds. Over the months when streams ran dry, zamindars selected sites of cultivation, ploughed them with oxen, and heaped soil into mounds with which they enclosed

[2] Punjab Rev. & Agr. (Rev.), February 1872, A 16; Bruce, Notes on the Dera Ghazee Khan District; Tupper, *PCL*, vol. II, p. 251.

[3] Wilson, *Sirsa S.R., 1879–83*, ch. III.

[4] *PTECR*, Foreign (Rev.), Jan. 1870, A 44–71. See also Foreign (Rev.), 28 April 1868, A 196. *PTECR* was reproduced as part of *HOCPP*, 1870 (159). The different commissioners conducting official enquiries into the nature of rights described the claims and obligations of butimars and mundemars. See the statements of the following: Major S.F. Graham, Deputy Comm., Dera Ismael Khan, *PTECR*, p. 71; Major Mercer, Deputy Comm., Amritsar District, *PTECR*, p. 64; J. Beecher, Comm. and Sup., Derajat Div., *PTECR*, p. 71; Minchin, Offg Deputy Comm., Dera Ghazee Khan, *PTECR*, p. 71; J. Naesmyth, Offg Comm. and Sup., Hissar Div., *PTECR*, p. 68.

[5] Tucker, *Dera Ismail Khan S.R., 1872–79*, paras 14, 203. See also Tupper, *PCL*, III, pp. 176–7, 184–5; Thorburn, *Bannu S.R.*, 1879, pp. 48ff.; Bruce, Notes on the Dera Ghazee Khan District; Diack, *Customary Law of the Dera Ghazi Khan District*.

their fields. Mudbanks upstream were reinforced with brushwood to withstand the fiercer torrents. Shallow channels were dug to evenly distribute the water over the cultivated fields of each lathbund. A torrent would be allowed in through a mouth in the bund which, when filled, was saved from excessive inundation by closing the inflow and opening a side channel that allowed the water to pass into contiguous fields.[6] By this method the upper grounds were watered first, and then the lower. Swollen waters often flooded the country for miles, washing away laths and sweeping away embankments. Such laths could not be rebuilt, nor the enclosed fields (bunds) ploughed until the water had receded and the soil was dry. Cultivation in such regions was possible only through the continuous labour of lathbunds. Their participation in such collective work defined claims and responsibilities. They were under an obligation to build and maintain the laths, which then gave them the right to use silt-bearing water and cultivate specified portions of the embanked fields.

There were, similarly, tracts where the expansion of cultivation was linked to the construction of wells. Those who moved into scrubland and shared in the task of digging wells had a claim to the water as well as to the land so irrigated. Rights to land were linked to such claims to water, the individual shares depending on the contribution each member of the well community had made in sinking the well. Very often an individual landholder who had no well invited someone to help him construct it. The helper got half the share of the well as well as some of the land and paid the landowner revenue (mahsul). Such right-holders were variously designated: chakdars in Multan, mukarraridars in Rawalpindi and Attock, kuhmars and adhlapis in other places.[7] Most of these terms indicated the source of their rights. Chak refers to the woodwork of a well, kuh means a well, and adhlapi points to the half-share (*adh*=half) of the well-sinker. Their

---

[6] Tucker, *Dera Ismail Khan S.R., 1872–79*, paras 13–14, pp. 203ff.

[7] Punjab Rev., Agr. and Com. (Rev.), Feb. 1872, A 16; Baden-Powell, *LSBI*, vol. II, pp. 658, 663; Thorburn, *Bannu S.R.*, para 207; Tupper, *PCL*, III, pp. 134–5; Robertson, *Rawalpindi S.R., 1880–7*; Roe, *Multan S.R.,* 1881, para 72; Roe, *Customary Law of Multan, 1883*, para 36; Steedman, *Chiniot A.R.*, 1880, para 48.

claim to the land and water flowed from the originary act that made life possible – the act of digging the well, the investment of time and effort in its sustenance.

The adhlapi system was common in the construction of canals too. One settlement officer, F.W.R. Fryer, provides a detailed account of the practice in Dera Ghazi Khan in the 1850s. When a new project of excavation had to be undertaken, "the whole canal was divided off into sections, and the labour also was divided."[8] At times, those who controlled the land in the area – he calls them proprietors – dug the canal using family labour, at other times they took the help of outsiders. Digging the canal authenticated a person's claim to the estate irrigated by the canal. Fryer says: "When the canal was dug, the branch canals and cuttings were made by the people themselves, who divided the water by their own committees, each proprietor became the owner of an estate possessing the advantage of canal irrigation, as a return either for his own labour in excavating a portion of the canal, or else as a return for the capital he had sunk in paying someone else to dig his share of the canal."[9] When an outsider was called in to help with the digging, the local landowner had to give the man half his irrigated land in return for the labour.[10] The right of the adhlapi to the land was taken for granted.

Claims and rights were thus constituted through performative acts. These acts – clearing shrubs, digging wells and canals, building laths, harnessing streams – created expectations and claims. Tilling the land over time, and using the well or stream, affirmed the claims, reaffirmed expectations. Collective acts, socially visible, forged a community that recognised each other's entitlements and responsibilities. Rights were understood and taken for granted, not explicitly formulated. Implicit in action, in practice, their recognition was established through repeated performance. Any chief or powerful zamindar who sought to violate the understanding and deny claims that were

[8] No. 29, 11 Feb. 1871, Fryer, Settlement Officer, Dera Ghazi Khan, to the Offg. Comm. and Sup. Derajat Division, Agr. Rev. and Commerce (Rev.), Sept. 1872, A 15.

[9] Ibid.

[10] Ibid.

taken for granted was socially censured. His actions were seen as unjust.[11]

The categories that point to these rights inevitably refer to collectivities. The specific nature of these collectivities was forged through different forms of collective acts and was dependent on norms and ideals fashioned through those acts. Expectations were structured by those ideals, claims and rights were mediated by those ideals.

What was to be done with the evidence on rights collected by official ethnographers? How could that evidence be the basis of the agrarian order envisioned by colonial officials?

Translating Categories

An act of translation was necessary to accommodate an order based on custom within the framework of a colonial regime based on written laws. Customary rights had to be translated into legal rights. Old terms had to be translated into new makeshift equivalents. The local terms were heterogeneous, discrete, non-comparable; each referred back to a specific origin of right and opened up particular histories. The bootimar/butimar, the adhlapi, and the lathbund had distinct histories, and the terms pointed to these different origins. The new legal regime required categories that could move beyond differences and particularities, categories that were homogenous and universal enough to comprehend and order the agrarian zone beyond the local. Moreover, the "ambiguities" and "insecurities" associated with the earlier framework of rights needed to be replaced with the fixities and certainties of the new.

Nineteenth-century political economy provided the two key ordering categories that we have seen: landlord and tenant. Officials debated their respective rights, but not the veracity of the terms. At one level,

---

[11] Local officials repeatedly told the Tenant Enquiry Committee in the mid nineteenth century that those with such customary rights could not be evicted from their holdings. Jaishee Ram, Extra Assistant Comm., Amritsar District, stressed that any such eviction was socially unacceptable: "it was considered an act of injustice in former times, as much as it would be at present." *PTECR* , 1870, p. 82.

the initial definitions seemed clear. The landlord was the proprietor who had the rights to lease out his land to tenants for cultivation, collect rent, sell the land, or mortgage it. Tenants leased in land for cultivation and paid rent to the landlord. From the definitions flowed the questions that were to be asked in the enquiries into land rights. Who paid the rent and to whom? Who had the right to sell and mortgage? The initial clarity of simple definitions disappeared as officials proceeded with their enquiry and sought to fit local terms into juridical moulds. The evidence they confronted appeared contradictory and the answers to their questions were ambiguous.

On the ground, it was often difficult to distinguish the proprietor from the tenant. Who was the proprietor in tracts where cultivators had collectively cleared the forest and settled villages, or dug canals and brought water to parched fields? These acts of particular labour were sources of specific rights that distinguished the butimar from the lathbund. But what distinguished one butimar from another? Settlement operations required that the agrarian population be first slotted into the two primary categories (landlord and tenant) before they could be divided into sub-categories. All the older terms, it was assumed, could be translated into these overarching ones. Inspired by this belief and convinced of the feasibility of the classificatory project, settlement officers pressed local officials and village elders to identify proprietors and tenants and list the local terms through which tenancy relations were established in the past. Even when local officials found past distinctions between proprietor and tenant vague and fuzzy, they had to proceed with the task of classification. Asked to distinguish the terms, Jaishee Ram, Extra-Assistant Commissioner of Amritsar, replied: "In the Sikh times the question did not arise as to the respective rights of the two classes of proprietors and culti-vators. Rights were nowhere clearly defined or established."[12] Did he not know of any form of tenancy? Pushed into giving a more categorical answer, he referred to an agrarian relationship that he thought resembled tenancy. But the enquiry required him to be more specific. What were the terms of this tenancy and its nomenclature?

[12] Ibid., p. 81.

Jaishee Ram was reluctant to specify, certain that any definite answer would be false:

> I am asked what is its name? I don't believe it has any. The fact is, in past times no one took the trouble to search into fine points of right, so no name was necessary. I believe the names now given by the zamindars and others are not genuine names of such classes. In old Sikh Khusrehs in a Rundhawa village, you will find Rundhawa, Goojur, Gill, all entered one after the other, with no distinctive title to show status. I am sure that excepting "Pahees" no other class of cultivator was sufficiently distinct to receive a name. "Zemindar" was a common title for all having anything to do with land.[13]

Yet the pressure to classify more specifically was unrelenting. After persistent protests, Jaishee Ram went on to enumerate the possible categories into which cultivators could be classified, even as he doubted the validity of his classification. He was one of many such.

So, who was the proprietor? How was he to be identified? In the face of evidence that appeared hazy and an observed reality that was difficult to fit into juridical categories, a Procrustean solution seemed unavoidable: officials relied on the founding theory of coparcenary community. "I have thought it quite sufficient," explained the Settlement Officer of Ambala district, "if he is not of the Bhyachara, to record him as a tenant."[14] But who belonged to the bhaiachara? Having first identified the dominant caste/tribe of a village as constituting the coparcenary community and tracing lineage from a common male ancestor, revenue officials reaffirmed the rights of the dominant castes by taking for granted their proprietary rights to cultivated lands and village commons. Gujars and Gills in a Randhawa village were likely to be classed as tenants, while in most villages the names of women and "lower" castes were unlikely to figure as landowners. Non-dominant castes, "lower" castes, non-agriculturists, and women were thus faced with a double exclusion. First denied membership to the male patriarchal coparcenary agrarian community, they were then deprived of their right to be classed as proprietors. New legal contracts

[13] Ibid.
[14] Wynyard, *Ambala S.R.*, 1859, para 310.

were to be built upon colonial assumptions of customary gender and caste contracts.[15] As the male village brotherhoods consolidated their power, these exclusions were strengthened.

The theory of coparcenary village community could not resolve all the problems of categorisation either. There were villages in which cultivators of heterogeneous castes had tilled the land for generations, there were tracts settled by colonists of diverse origin, and there were long-standing cultivators whose rights descended from the female line. They could neither be incorporated into the coparcenary community as the British defined it, nor could officials differentiate their substantive rights in land from those of the proprietors. The problem was tackled by splitting the category of proprietors into superior and inferior (ala malik and adna malik) and the category of tenants into occupancy tenants and tenants at will (mauroosee and ghair-mauroosee). The original settlers who were considered members of the village community were classed as superior proprietors. Up to the late 1860s, a range of other right holders – the butimars who cleared the scrub, the lathbunds who created and maintained embankments, the chakdars of Muzaffargarh and Multan, and the adhlapis in other regions who dug wells and cultivated a share of the land irrigated by the well – were all usually lumped under the generic category "inferior proprietor". One fact linked these diverse groups within the official logic of classification: they had ownership rights to the land they cultivated but they did not belong to the coparcenary community.[16] In some revenue records their right was

[15] On the idea of sexual contract underlying contract theorists, see Pateman, *The Sexual Contract*.

[16] Barkley defined the inferior proprietor in the following words: "There are sometimes also proprietors holding lands within the estates of village communities, and are not entitled to share in the common profits, nor liable to anything other than the revenue of their own lands, the village charges ordinarily paid by the proprietors and the quit rent, if any, payable to the proprietary body of the village." Note reproduced in *RAP, 1872–73*. See also Barkley, *Directions for Revenue Officers*. Cust specified the different classes of "inferior proprietors" thus: (i) descendants of the female side from the original locators of the village; (ii) descendants of those who assisted in the location of the village but were not of the same caste or tribe with the

malikan kabza – a right acquired merely from the occupation and control of land, as distinct from the rights of a shareholder within the village brotherhood.[17] A malik kabza had the right to cultivate, sell, mortgage or lease out his land; but he had no share in the village commons (shamilat-deh), or in the village income (malba); nor did he have a say in the running of village affairs. Allowed a partial access to the status of proprietor, adna maliks were still excluded from entry into the village brotherhood. The categorisation of proprietary rights persistently reaffirmed the power that tenurial classification had invested in the coparcenary community. Dominant groups everywhere, as we will see, began resisting the entry of outsiders in an effort to consolidate the power of the brotherhood.

These sub-categories also regularly broke down. The terms had to be stretched, twisted, and reinterpreted as the project of terminological ordering proceeded in the different regions. Reincarnated as superior and inferior proprietors, a diverse variety of right holders were homogenised into seemingly comparable figures in the annual statistical tables of the land revenue department. But this comparability was an illusion produced by the act of terminological redefinition. In the central and eastern plains, superior and inferior proprietors were both cultivating zamindars whose difference lay in their relation to the village brotherhood. Those included in the brotherhood were seen as superior to those excluded. Revenue, however, was settled with whoever cultivated the land, whether inferior or superior. Further west, around Multan, Rawalpindi, Dera Ismail Khan, and Muzaffargarh, coparcenary communities were weak and local power was in the hands of tomandars, Pathan maliks, and muqaddams. In this vast pastoral zone, peasant colonists brought in by the tribal maliks,

---

locators were not admitted to the village community; (iii) tenants who have acquired proprietary right; (iv) outsiders who have purchased land. Cust, *Revenue Manual,* pp. 33–4.

[17] On the category malikan kabza see Punjab Agr. Rev. and Comm, Sept. 1873, A 7; Punjab Agr. and Rev. (Rev.), Oct. 1873, A 4; Wace, *Hazara S.R. 1868–74,* pp. 121–3, 117–19, 158–9, 254–6; Cracroft, *Rawul Pindee S.R., 1864.*

zamindars, and muqaddams settled land near the rivers and irrigated the dry tracts by digging canals and wells. Here the label of superior proprietor was attached to those who had claims to traditional authority and power but were not necessarily cultivating zamindars.[18] Their "superiority" recognised at one level was denied at another, the revenue settlement being mostly with the "inferior" proprietors of the revenue records – the cultivating zamindars.[19] If in the central plains of Punjab the power of superior proprietors, as cultivating owners, was consolidated by the British, in west Punjab it was undercut, at least till 1857. Thus, beneath the deceptive certainty of official nomenclature was a confusing assortment of meanings. Since the coparcenary community of the official imagination was impossible to discover in all regions, differential rights over uncultivated land emerged as the only feasible common criterion for demarcating forms of proprietorship.

Splitting the category of tenants was similarly a problem. Officials recognised that cultivators classed as tenants could not all be lumped

[18] O'Brien, *Muzaffargarh S.R., 1873–80*, ch. 6; Cracroft, *Rawul Pindee S.R., 1864*, paras 300ff.; Mackenzie, *Goojerat S.R., 1861*, para 177; Talbot, *Jhelum S.R., 1895–1901*, paras 115–17.

[19] O'Brien explained the distinction between the superior and inferior proprietor thus: "The superior proprietors, as such, have no right to interfere in the management or the cultivation of the appropriated lands of a village. The settlement has in no case been made with them, except where they are also inferior proprietors. Their rights are restricted to receiving their fee in grain or cash, and to disposing of the unappropriated, waste in the village . . . The inferior proprietors in a village have usually no common ties of clanship. They are a miscellaneous body, each member of which was originally introduced either by the government or by the superior proprietors. In villages where superior proprietary right exists, the inferior proprietor is usually entitled only to the land occupied by himself or his tenants. The unappropriated land belongs to the superior proprietors." In Rawalpindi, Attock, Jhelum, and Gujrat a considerable body of malikan kabza – "inferior proprietors" – were created "who paid nothing but the revenue assessed on their holdings, but had no share in the village waste." See O'Brien, *Muzaffargarh S.R., 1873–80*, ch. 6; Cracroft, *Rawal Pindee S.R., 1864*, paras 300 ff.; Mackenzie, *Goojerat S.R., 1861,* para 177; Talbot, *Jhelum S.R., 1895–1901*, paras 115–17. In central Punjab, rights to the village commons, of course, became a basis of identifying the coparcenary community itself.

together: some had stronger rights than others. But how were they to be distinguished? What defined the sameness of or difference between cultivators with widely varying sources of rights? Proceeding with the baggage brought from the North West Provinces, settlement officers operated with the twin categories of occupancy tenant and tenant at will. The occupancy tenant was to have security of tenure: his rights were to be protected against the caprice of the proprietor, against possible eviction from his land, and arbitrary rent enhancements. His rights were hereditary and he could sell and mortgage his holding. Tenants at will had no claim to such security nor any right to alienate their land. Their own desire had no meaning, they were subjects of the will of their master, the proprietor. But who was to be classed as an occupancy tenant? What would be the valid source of this right?

In the districts where settlement operations were first launched, officials assumed that settled occupancy of land was the natural basis of a right. Cultivators who had tilled the land over generations acquired a right of occupancy. Such occupation had to be continuous. A framework of thought that saw settlement as the basis of virtue, progress, order, and civilisation could not accept the logic of a life of mobility and fluidity. Settlement officers investigating rights were amazed to discover that peasants in rural India often left their village lands during times of famine, migrating to distant places, but returned sometimes after decades to claim their rights in the village. This past practice was incomprehensible to those who linked security and permanence with continuity of possession.[20]

---

[20] Commenting on the practice, John Lawrence, with all his love for peasants and their customs, could not hide his sarcasm: "The owner may for years or even for generations have deserted his property, which may have since passed through many hands: he may in pursuit of more exciting employment, such as raids and border skirmishes, have thrown up his land in the hope of one day repossessing it, and in the knowledge that the mere fact of titular right gave him weight in the council and the assemblies of the tribe: the present possessor may have held the property as owner, and sustained its credit in times of distress: still the original owner considers himself landlord, and claims to be recorded as such." *RAP*, 1851/52, *SRGOI*, no. 6, p. 123. If occupancy is the source of right, then these claims appear unacceptable. Lawrence questions and ridicules the claims in the act of describing them. The original owner is presented as a figure of suspicion, a deserter, someone fond of raids and

So in the districts from Ambala to Ludhiana the length of uninterrupted occupancy became a measure of tenancy right.[21] In the
summary settlements of the early years after conquest, resident cultivators who had possessed their land continuously for twelve years,
and non-residents who had cultivated them for twenty, were classified as occupancy tenants. By the mid 1850s there was a reaction
against this mode of translating rights. Edward Thornton, Settlement
Commissioner, wrote to settlement officers in 1855 asking them
to carefully enquire into the customary privileges of different rural
groups before categorising them.[22] The twelve-year rule was not to
be the ultimate criterion for determining rights. Subsequently, in tracts
across the Chenab River, rural rights were carefully investigated, and
the diverse premises of various claims and meanings of local terms
examined and recorded. These ethnographic enquiries, in fact, provide historians with the sources of their knowledge about butimars,
lathbunds, adhlapis, mundemars, and chakdars.

Yet in the end these local terms had to be absorbed within the framework of juridical categories, their heterogeneity transcended through
a process of reclassification, the diverse premises of their claims
refigured through the logic of a unifying explanation. Having investigated the nature of customary rights, officials ultimately had to
differentiate between those with authentic claims to stable occupancy
and those with none.

---

skirmishes, not a peaceable citizen. His rights were "titular" and "nominal",
hence illegitimate and unjust. The occupier, on the other hand, was seen as
productive; *he* was the proper and rightful owner of the land.

[21] This is recorded in all the settlement reports of Ambala, Ludhiana, Jullunder, Hoshiarpur, Kangra, Ferozepur, Gurdaspur, Amritsar, Lahore, Sialkot,
Gujranwala. "As a general rule," wrote Wynyard, "uninterrupted possession
for and above 12 years, in succession from father to son, established within
that time, was held to be prima facie sufficient proof that a tenant should be
entered as having a right of possession." Wynyard, *Amballa S.R.*, para 311.

[22] No. 283, 14 Sept. 1855, Thornton to Ouseley, Settlement Officer of
Shapur, *PTECR;* D.F. McLeod, the Financial Commissioner, supported the
move, and the Chief Commissioner repudiated the twelve-year rule. See
no. 1010, 11 Dec. 1855, Temple, Sec. to Chief Commissioner, to D.F.
McLeod, Financial Comm., *PTECR.*

Many officials recognised that this project of translation was impossibly difficult. Fryer, Settlement Officer at Dera Ghazi Khan, was torn between the desire for ethnographic sensitivity and the demands of bureaucratic classification. While proceeding with the settlement operation he was categorical about his preference for local terms and says so in 1871 to his superior: "Hitherto I have recorded tenants as simply 'Butamur' or Lutmar', or by whatever term they have been locally known."[23] He was clearly aware of the task he was expected to execute. "It will be necessary," he wrote, "to declare what status is implied by these terms."[24] But he felt it would be better if the Tenancy Act (Act XXVIII of 1868) was declared inapplicable to the district.[25] The condition in Dera Ghazi Khan district being radically different from that in others, the specificity of local rights could not be accommodated within the categories of the Tenancy Act. Was this plea for exception acceptable within the classificatory project of the colonial state? Was this really an exception at all? Was not difference a constitutive characteristic of the landscape of social relations? Implicit in the idea of exception was the notion of an imagined normal.

Unable to decide on the issue, the Commissioner of Derajat Division forwarded Fryer's proposal to the higher authorities. The financial commissioner was firm in his response: the local terms could not be officially ratified. Any effort to do so, he said, "leads to so much complication, and lands us so entirely in indefiniteness" that the project of tenancy classification would be thrown overboard. The search for fixity, uniformity, and conceptual order could not be so

[23] No. 72, 1 April 1871, F.W.R. Fryer, Settlement Officer, Dera Ghazi Khan, to the Comm. & Sup. Derajat Div., Punjab Agr. Rev. and Com. (Rev.), February 1872, A 16.

[24] Ibid.

[25] Tenancy Act (Act XXVIII of 1868) sought to secure the rights of those classified as occupancy tenants. Occupancy rights were granted to those tenants who resided in the village and cultivated their land continuously for twelve years, while non-resident tenants acquired this right after twenty years. Occupancy tenants were not to be evicted as long as they paid an "equitable rent", and rents could not be enhanced at will – they could be revised only during the revenue settlements when revenue demands increased. Those classified as tenants-at-will were not protected against eviction and enhancement of rent.

easily given up. He recommended that the lathbunds and butimars be now declared tenants at will in terms of the Tenancy Act of 1868. If they were ejected from their holdings, they could claim compensation for the capital and labour they had invested in them. The "limited" rights of occupancy they had, he felt, "could be met equitably by an award of compensation on ejectment."[26] Seen through a grid that valorised continuous occupancy for twelve or twenty years as the basis of occupancy rights, the claims of the butimars appeared no more than "limited". The length and continuity of occupancy had to be the universal qualifying index for rights of occupancy.

Fryer was not persuaded. On receiving the financial commissioner's proposal, he reiterated his conviction. The specific rights of butimars and lathbunds had to be respected. Since they could not be ejected according to custom, it was wrong to classify them as tenants at will. In fact, Fryer argued, none of the categories of the Tenancy Act could effectively capture their rights: "if recorded as tenants with rights of occupancy, 'Butamar' and 'Lutmar' tenants would get more than their rights, and if recorded as tenants-at-will, it appears to me, they will get less than their rights."[27] Unlike the occupancy tenant of the Tenancy Act, argued Fryer, the butimar could not sell the land, and unlike the tenant at will his right to continuous cultivation could not be questioned.

What was the way out of the classificatory conundrum? How was it possible to respect ethnographic difference within a regime of uniform and fixed agrarian categories? In the end, the lieutenant governor sought to resolve the problem by affirming the importance of the record of rights but defining the limits of its juridical validity. He gave special permission to detail the rights of record holders in all the frontier districts – including Dera Ghazi Khan – in the record

[26] Ibid.

[27] No. 155, 13 June 1871, Fryer, Settlement Officer, Dera Ghazi Khan, to the Offg Comm. and Sup., Derajat Division, Punjab Agr. Rev. and Com. (Rev.), February 1872, A 16. The Assistant Settlement Officer similarly argued against the butimar being classed as tenant-at-will: "The Butimar tenure is a permanent one, and to eject a Butimar tenant is not in the landlord's power; compensation would not reconcile a Butimar tenant to ejectment." Ibid.

of rights. These entries on the status of tenants, however, were not to be authorised as final. The record of rights could be questioned in court. The aggrieved could file a suit against the rights stated in the entries. The decree of the court would then have the force of law. This meant that as part of the record of rights the entries in Dera Ghazi Khan would have the same force as those in other frontier districts. The authenticity of past rights was thus to be ethnographically affirmed but judicially questioned. If the wajib-ul-arz (record of rights) was to display the minutiae of particular rights with all their differences, the judicial process was expected to ensure their uniformity. Whether – and to what extent – it could is a different story. Difference was thus to be both recognised and negated.

After the Tenancy Act of 1887, adhlapis, butimars, and lathmars, alongside other similar categories of right holders – mundemar, mukarraridar, taraddadkar – were classified as occupancy tenants of the third class.[28] What the juridical term "occupancy tenant" recognised was not the different histories of rights that the local terms

[28] The Tenancy Act of 1887 – introduced after two decades of conflict between those classified as tenants and landowners – reaffirmed the need to protect occupancy tenants, but modified the terms of classification. The temporal measure for judging rights was qualified. It was declared: "No tenant shall acquire tenancy by mere lapse of time." For the recognition of occupancy rights, the 1868 Act had formulated the twelve-year rule for resident tenants and the twenty-year rule for non-resident tenants. Now the quality and nature of the relationship to the land was emphasised as important. Three classes of such tenants were distinguished. Occupancy tenants of the first class (Section 5 [1] [a]) were those who had occupied the land for two generations in the male line, for a period not less than twenty years, without paying rent beyond the amount of land revenue. Occupancy tenants of the second class (Section 5 [1] [b]) included those who had settled the land with the founder, had cultivated continuously for twenty years, but had paid a rent. Those who could not claim rights under Section 5 (a and b), but had "improved" the land as butimar, lathmar, or adhlapi, were classed as occupancy tenants of the third class. Their claims to secure tenancy were based on whether they had invested in "improving" the land, not on the period of their occupancy. No category of occupancy tenants were to be evicted as long as they paid an "equitable rent", and no eviction could be without a decree of arrears of payment and a legal suit for eviction. In all cases of eviction, compensation had to be paid.

connoted, but its common claim to secure tenures. The identities of adhlapis, abadkars, and butimars were now split. Within the local community they could continue to see themselves, at least for a time, as bearers of rights that flowed from their original role in clearing the land and making it fertile.[29] The ethnographic evidence of these perceptions existed in the record of rights prepared for each village. In relation to the law, however, they became juridical individuals – occupancy tenants – subject to the rules and clauses of the tenancy acts.[30]

By the 1880s this framework of juridical categories was firmly established. Subsequent questionings and modifications, through legislation and adjudication, happened within the framework. Officials were well aware that much within it was pure invention, but it

---

Douie, *Panjab Settlement Manual,* paras 207–16. See also Punjab Tenancy Bill, Punjab Rev. & Agr. (Rev.), October 1886, A 10–32.

[29] See ch. 6 below. After the passing of the Punjab Tenancy Act of 1868, in fact, revenue officials were not even allowed to enquire into the customs regulating the relations between proprietors and tenants, nor enter them in revenue records. Henceforth the subject was to be governed not by custom but by the provisions of the act. That is why Fryer's enquiries into custom, and also why the governor general's permission to enter these customary rights in the record of rights in the frontier acquired significance.

[30] In the enquiries into customary law in the 1870s, questions relating to the issue of tenancy were specifically excluded. It was stated that "no future entries in the settlement record regarding the relations of proprietors and tenants will be deemed to be agreements within the meaning of the Punjab Tenancy Act." By the rules under the Punjab Land Revenue Act (ch. III, 35), it was further specified that care was to be taken in filling up the administration papers so as to exclude all details opposed to any existing law. It was considered unnecessary therefore for the agrarian record to contain entries relating to matters treated in the Punjab Tenancy Act. If such entries coincided with the provisions of the Act they would be superfluous. "If they were to conflict with the provisions of the Act it would be illegal to incorporate them with the village administration paper." So under ch. III, 33, clause 16, the administrations's paper was to contain "the rights of cultivators of all classes not expressly provided by the law." Agr. Rev. and Com. (Rev.), May 1877, A 12.

was a case of having to shrug shoulders and accept what was seen as indispensable to the organisation of a settled agrarian society. Even the terms mauroosee and ghair-mauroosee were only seemingly local. Wynyard reported from Ambala, a district in the east, that people "did not appreciate the difference between the two kinds of tenants the '*mauroosee*' and '*ghair mauroosee*'. These terms were introduced here or elsewhere in the Punjab by the 'Settlement Establishment'." [31] In the far west, settling one of the dry semi-pastoral tracts that were to become part of the Canal Colonies by the turn of the century, Elphinstone searched in vain for mauroosees and ghair-mauroosees. The distinction, he emphasised, "is a creation of our Government. Under native rule in this part of Punjab it was altogether unknown." [32] Even in the Doab plains of central Punjab, settled for centuries, the nomenclature was said to be "novel". "It is not indigenous to this part of the country," reported Temple from Jullunder. "It has been introduced by the settlement." [33] Prinsep mounted a campaign against protective legislation, attacking its categories and the administrative rationale that justified their use. He spoke of preserving local custom against the corrosive power of an alien implant. [34] Yet not even he could get away from translating customary rights into the new juridical

[31] Wynyard, *Amballa S.R.*, 1859, para 363.

[32] Elphinstone, *Googaira S.R.*, 1860, para 49.

[33] Temple, *Jullundur S.R.*, 1852, para 302.

[34] He said: "The terms 'Mauroosee' and 'Ghair Mouroosee' have been introduced with a view to uniformity with other districts: but I regret the distinctions locally known are not kept up." Prinsep, *Sealkote, S.R.,* para 372. In a report explaining the norms he followed in his enquiry into the record of rights, Prinsep said: "My orders are to base the settlement on village custom. I consider it is right that we should go by custom. It is this following out of policies, which we as a rule originate, that has done more to establish the general charge of settlement record being erroneous than anything else. We cannot do wrong if we act in the interest of the people, and base the fabric on what they prove to us exist. Of course if these rights are dormant no one can restore them; but if otherwise, where is there any safety unless we follow existing usage?" Prinsep, Annual Report on the Settlement Operations of the Year 1865–66, 13 Aug. 1866, addressed to the Financial Commissioner, *PTECR* , pp. 60ff.

categories, using the terms proprietor and tenant indiscriminately, without recognising the problems.

Rights vs Practice

Prinsep was not the only one to use the rhetoric of custom. Thomason, against whom Prinsep fumed, had directed revenue officials to observe, record, and define rights as they existed, without altering them. And John Lawrence, Prinsep's arch-antagonist, was known for his paternalist love of peasant custom. Adversaries in the great debate on rural rights referred to custom with equal ease in authorising opposed views. Custom, as we see here and will see later, can be read in different ways.

Behind this struggle to define the meanings of different categories of rights were conflicting notions of property and custom. What constituted a right? What were the sources of its authenticity? How could the past be read to discover the legitimate customary perquisites of a right-holder? In grappling with these questions, colonial officials dipped into the conceptual resources of conflicting traditions, from Blackstone to Bentham, even as they remembered the need to ensure revenue flows and tie the population to fixed property. Within the tangle of individual and differing opinions, expressed with arrogant passion by some and nagging self-doubt by others, we can discern two sets of opposed views.

At one level, there appears to be a clash of two unambiguously asserted contrary opinions. Prinsep personified one. In the pre-British period, he thought, tenants never had any right of occupancy, and proprietors always had the power to eject and evict.[35] In ignoring the customary rights of proprietors and protecting tenants, the first settlement of the late 1840s and early 1850s had done a great injustice. The record of rights prepared at the first settlement without proper enquiry was false and needed to be revised. As Settlement Commissioner of Amritsar Division, Prinsep ordered enquiries into

[35] Settlement Commissioner's Report, no. 196, 28 April 1863, *PTECR*, pp. 60ff.; See also no. 6, Minute by H.T. Prinsep, 5 November 1869, *PTECR*, p. 15.

the recorded rights of 1675 villages with 10,770 occupancy holdings, and declared that over one-fifth of the occupancy tenants had actually no valid right to protection.[36]

Against Prinsep's espousal of the rights of proprietors was the seemingly unambiguous opinion of those who discovered in the past unquestionable evidence of secure tenant rights. E. Lake found the distinction between proprietor and hereditary tenant fuzzy in an earlier time: "in many villages the title of the so-called proprietors is not much better than that of the hereditary cultivators, and originated much in the same way."[37] R.H. Davies, Deputy Commissioner of Shahpur, echoed this opinion: "Under the Sikh Government the most favoured class of cultivators were men who held a status very little inferior to that of the proprietors themselves . . ."[38] Peasants who cleared the land and dug the wells could never be ousted by the proprietor. In Sikh times, it was the kardar, not the proprietor, who had the power to eject; and the kardar could evict proprietor and tenant alike for failing to cultivate land or defaulting on dues.

At a deeper level, the debate moved beyond a bland opposition of opinion. In their less passionate and more reflective moments, officials were willing to shift the discussion to the more complicated issue of unpacking the meaning of rights. Did rights and claims flow from practices in the past, or did they inhere in the very idea of property? Prinsep did not entirely disagree with the fact that cultivators had

---

[36] Ibid. Many officials were similarly emphatic about the absence of secure tenures in the past. H. Elphinstone, Deputy Commissioner of Jullunder, insisted: "No length of possession as tenants entitled any class of cultivators to hold at fixed rates, or prevented the proprietors from ejecting them in favor of others. The power of the proprietor appears in this respect to have been unlimited and unrestrained." *PTECR*, p. 65.

[37] E. Lake, Comm. and Sup., Jullunder Division, *PTECR*, p. 65. For Lake's views, see also Memorandum by Colonel E. Lake, Financial Comm. of the Punjab, on the Status of Cultivators in the Districts of the Umritsar Division, *PTECR*, pp. 41ff. He said: "indeed, very frequently the privileges and rights enjoyed by the two classes were so very similar, that it was exceedingly difficult to determine whether it was right to reduce one to the subordinate position of cultivator . . ." Ibid., para 2.

[38] *PTECR*, p. 69.

in the past often continued to cultivate the same fields over generations without being evicted by proprietors. Yet the prevalence of this
practice could not deny certain natural rights that the idea of property
embodied: "it is universally admitted that the landowner had the
right to evict any tenant, and could do so at any time; that this right
was seldom exercised in case of resident cultivators who held land
from the founding of the village, or from generation to generation:
but still, that a proprietor was in no way barred by local usage from
evicting any tenant whatever the circumstances of his occupancy, and
however long he may have held the land . . ."[39] Practices were not to be
confused with rights. This is an assumption that R.E. Egerton, Major
Mercer, C.P. Elliot, and many other officials shared with Prinsep. All
admitted that butimars, bhaiwals, and adhlapis had not been turfed
out of their villages in the pre-British past. Yet these same officials
were equally vehement that "It was in the power of proprietors to eject
the cultivators, in favour of others without making any concession
whatever. It mattered not how long the cultivator might have been
on the land, he was liable to ejection at any time at the will of the
proprietor."[40]

Prinsep's argument was ultimately internally contradictory. He
used the rhetoric of custom but refused to see customary practice as
the source of valid peasant rights. Against peasant claims to security,
he was a Benthamite Utilitarian Positivist who saw in uncodified
practice nothing but ambiguity and uncertainty. To be valid, rights
had to be embodied in publicly stated, empirically identifiable, legally specified codes; in the absence of these, the claims of peasants
appeared to be "neither clear nor defined".[41] But this Benthamite
scepticism disappeared in relation to the rights of proprietors. They
were assumed to have "an undoubted right to evict, even if they had
never done so in the past." What was the basis of this indubitable
right? If the rights of cultivators were not specified by a public law,
nor were the rights of proprietors. The underlying idea that informed

[39] Settlement Commissioner's Report, No. 196, 28 April 1863, *PTECR*,
p. 60, para 4.
[40] C.P. Elliot, Offg Deputy Comm., Ludhiana, *PTECR*, p. 67.
[41] Ibid.

Prinsep's pronouncements was simple. The rights of proprietors in-hered within property and, in fact, defined the word "property". Prinsep treats absolute and exclusive rights as natural. Even if in practice these rights were not exercised and peasants were never in effect ejected, proprietors *qua* proprietors still had the right to evict tenants, to sell and mortgage rented land. For Prinsep, these rights were inviolable, embedded in the idea of property itself, and always to be taken for granted.[42]

The fact of this proprietary right being almost never exercised was explained through a contextualist argument. In the pre-British period, it was said, when land was abundant and labour scarce, proprietors were keen on retaining cultivators of their land. In times of anarchy, oppression, and poverty it was in the mutual interest of tenants and proprietors to support each other.[43] Land had been of

[42] Officials read Blackstone in opposing ways. If some saw him as elaborating the premises of the common law tradition that sanctified conventions and practices, others drew upon his opening remark in *Commentaries*, book II, ch. 1, that property is "that sole and despotic dominion which one man claims and exercises over the external things of the world, in total exclusion of the right of any other individual in the universe." Blackstone, *Commentaries on the Laws of England*, book II, ch. 1 (1765–9). Blackstone's argument on property was caught in a contradiction: between the exclusion criteria he enunciates at the beginning, and the subsequent elaboration of the history of conventions and customs that refigured that right. The exclusion anxiety implicit in Black-stone was powerfully expressed by Prinsep in the debate over rights. The exclusive right to property, he argued emphatically, was inviolable: it implied sole dominion, complete mastery, and sovereignty; it was not dependent on whether this right was actually exercised in practice. For an exploration of this exclusion anxiety in Blackstone, see Rose, "Canons of Property Talk, or Blackstone's Anxiety".

[43] Colonel G.H. Hamilton, Offg Comm. and Superintendent, Delhi Division, wrote: "In those days of anarchy and misrule, the poorer classes could exist only under the protection of their superiors, and the superior classes derived from their dependants their wealth, influence and position. Each class depended on the other, and each was interested in keeping up the connection. The superior furnished land to cultivate and means of cultivation, and the inferior gave his labour . . . the interests of both were similar, they both wanted to cultivate the land, to secure their crops from plunder, and

little value because the extortionate revenue demands of the Sikhs had absorbed all surpluses and ground proprietors down into deadening poverty. If in such a dismal time proprietors did not exercise their rights, they did not thereby renounce them. Now that the value of property had increased with the coming of security and law, the record of rights could not invalidate the unrealised but indisputable prerogative of proprietorial possession.[44] It was as if the rights that inhered in property – the "natural" qualities that constituted property as property – had been repressed and subverted by adverse past circumstances and now had to be recognised and consolidated by a regime that respected the law and was instituting it formally in the region.

Officials like John Lawrence and William Muir had operated with a different notion of custom, right, and law. For Lawrence the question of the legal rights of cultivators before British rule was unimportant. "The point of enquiry would appear to be," he emphasised, "not whether the landlord had the right of evicting, but whether he used, as a matter of fact, to evict."[45] If on various grounds of self-interest the landlord "refrained as a rule from ejecting his long resident cultivators," then it was "most inadvisable to deny them as a class the same absolute security from eviction which they enjoyed of old."[46]

---

to resist oppression. They were thus mutually bound to each other, and they acted for their mutual benefit." *PTECR*, p. 67.

[44] Prinsep made this argument persuasively. The fear that the tenant code would confiscate pre-existing property rights was expressed even in the statements of Robert Cust who introduced the Tenant Code: "It is not just, because the Sikhs reduced all proprietors and cultivators to one dead level without semblance of law, that we should, with pretence of law, stereotype the state of things. It is one thing to say that proprietary rights are extinct and to make all cultivators proprietors, and another to say, that those who are proprietors, should enjoy nothing worth calling property." *PTECR*, p. 67.

[45] Minute by J. Lawrence, Viceroy and G.G. of India, on Tenant Right in the Punjab, 30 April 1867, Foreign (Rev.), Jan. 1870, A 48.

[46] Ibid. See also Note by Sir John Lawrence, Viceroy and GG of India, 30 August 1866, *PTECR*, p. 32. For Muir's views, see Minute by Muir, 1863, on Act X, 1859, 1859, *PTECR*, p. 155; Note by W. Muir, Sec. to Govt, 15 Oct. 1866, GOP, nos 397–512, Sept. 1866, *PTECR*, pp. 151ff.

Brandreth and Melvill conceded that the terms mauroosee and ghair-mauroosee were coined over the settlement, but these terms, they felt, only sought to verbalise rights that existed in practice. In the pre-British period, there were no settlement manuals or directions for revenue officials, but everyone recognised that cultivators of long standing did not expect to be evicted. In drawing up the record of rights, the British now had to capture the substance of these customary expectations.[47]

This framework of thinking drew upon the common law tradition that saw law as embodied practice; its function was to make explicit what was taken for granted, to discover and reveal what had been happening on the ground.[48] Practice was seen as foundational, the source of all authenticity and meaning, the repository of value. It embodied the shared sense of reasonableness and justice within a society; it structured expectations; it defined the limits of sovereign action and was the measure of public rules. Rules existed in so far as they were used and were publicly recognised as having been in use. Statutes were reasonable and acceptable only to the extent that they conformed to the common law of the kingdom and with the practices of the past. Law could not break from the past: its validity and authority derived from continuity. So, the categories through which the British classified rights needed to establish this continuity in order to provide justice and secure expectations.

Fixity, Security, and Legal Order

Property is nothing but a basis of expectation; the expectation of deriving certain advantages from a thing which we are said to possess, in consequence of the relation in which we stand towards it.

Now this expectation can only be the work of law. I cannot count upon the enjoyment of that which I regard as mine, except through the promise of the law which guarantees it to me. – Bentham, *Principles of the Civil Code*, ch. VIII, p. 137.

[47] Memorandum on the Question of Hereditary Tenants, by P. Melvill, Offg, Comm. Amritsar Div., 16 Sept. 1864, *PTECR*, p. 130; E.L. Brandreth, Statement of Commissioner, Rawalpindi Division, *PTECR*, p. 185.

[48] See Postema, *Bentham and the Common Law Tradition*.

In defining rights, the discourse of custom was overwritten by Utilitarian Positivism. Bentham's critique of common law confusions, his long struggle against Blackstone, influenced even those in the colonies who were intent on preserving custom and respecting the rights of different social groups.[49] Bentham, in any case, did not entirely reject the value of custom; he sought to appropriate it in utilitarian ways.

Most officials agreed that existing pre-colonial social practices and conventions had to be investigated and respected, but the ambiguities associated with past rights were to be replaced with publicly codified, universally known, and categorically stated rights. Utilitarian reason saw this sense of fixity as the crucial basis of secure expectations. Within a rational order, individuals ought to have the capacity to make rational decisions, foresee the future, and act on the basis of their expectations. This was not possible unless their rights were secured through publicly enacted rules, their expectations ensured against arbitrary interference.[50] Expectations, Bentham says, are fundamental to human life. Humans, in contrast to animals, have a capacity to look forward, to expect, to anticipate; they have the power of foresight. This ability to foresee, plan, and shape the future, this power of the imagination, transforms the discrete and disjunct moments of human life into one continuous flow. "Expectation is a chain," wrote Bentham, "that unites our present and our future existence, and passes beyond ourselves to the generations which follow us."[51] So, expectation needs to be secured. Without predictability there can be no plan for future projects, nor the continuity and coherence vital to human happiness.

Security of expectation was in fact seen as essential for humans to be fully human, for them to act rationally. Being a rationalist, Bentham saw the world as logically ordered, and human beings, by virtue of their practical reason, as playing their roles within this ordered universe by thinking and judging, planning and acting. This

[49] For further discussion on Bentham's critique of common law confusions, see ch. 5 below.

[50] Bentham, "On Expectations", *PCC*, ch. VII.

[51] Bentham, "Of Security", *PCC*, p. 136.

then required personal security and the elimination of the constraints (tradition and common law) that forced individuals to submit to the authority of tradition and prevented the exercise of independent judgement. Everyone had a fundamental right to be rational, to be able to judge, and determinate laws secured expectation, making rational judgment possible.[52]

Security of expectation was also the basis of liberty. In order to rationally order life and give it a sense of coherence, it was necessary to feel secure about liberty. By maximising security and stabilising expectation, law creates the basis of meaningful liberty.[53] By codifying rights, powers, duties, and responsibilities, law minimises insecurities.[54] Law, Bentham argues, is neither an instrument of coercion nor the arbitrary command of the sovereign. It lays down a framework of rights within which individual lives can be meaningfully lived, planned, and organised, their expectations formed and realised. These it consolidates by transforming what is indeterminate and notional into what is substantive. In relation to property and law, meaningful utilities were those that derived from expectations: "The idea of property consists in an established expectation . . ."[55] Property has no value without the expectation of a secure right over it.

It followed that expectations shaped by custom were distinct from those secured by law. Customary expectations were not binding; they were not obligatory, secure, or stable. Therefore, common law rules could never become laws. If customary expectations were to be respected, they had to be encoded in legislative acts and authorised by the seal of a sovereign power. Against Prinsep, Lawrence and Brandreth emphasised that cultivators who had cleared the land and

[52] Bentham, "On Expectations", *PCC,* ch. VII; "Rights and Obligations", *PCC,* ch. I; "Ends of Civil Law", *PCC,* ch. II; "Power of the Laws over Expectations", *PCC,* ch. XVII.

[53] Bentham, "Ends of Civil Law", *PCC,* ch. II; Postema, *Bentham and the Common Law Tradition*, pp. 171ff.

[54] Bentham, "Of Security", *PCC,* ch. VII; "Of Property", *PCC,* ch. VIII; "Analysis of Evils which Result from Attacks on Property", *PCC,* ch. X; Postema, *Bentham and the Common Law Tradition*, pp. 187ff.

[55] Ibid., p. 138.

cultivated their fields over generations had a reasonable expectation that their rights would be undisturbed, that they would not be evicted. But in arguing for the need to protect tenant right, Lawrence and other protectionists were operating with the notion of positive law; they were expressing the Benthamite desire to reduce custom to a stable code. Once custom is encoded, it is legislative acts and judicial decisions, not local practices, that become the basis of custom.[56] And once record comes to rule, custom ceases to be the valid source of a right. As Cust put it: "No customary right can be created under a system of record."[57] Only custom authorised by law could possess judicial validity and secure expectation.

Laws could shape as well as undermine expectations. If good laws secured expectations, bad laws disturbed them and violated the basis of social order. Prinsep feared that the protectionist move to secure the rights of occupancy tenants would undermine the very basis of property. Proprietors were gradually discovering that the rights they associated with property were being denied to them by law. They could neither evict tenants nor increase their rent. This confiscation of property by law had to be stopped, declared Prinsep, or else fear and insecurity would spread like a contagion:

> This process of annihilation of existing title to land in co-parcenary estates is going on under our Government in a most extraordinary degree; and unless an early remedy is applied . . . a very serious injury will be sustained by a large mass of landed proprietors, who now are awakening to the fact that property in land is a valuable commodity, and are seeking to maintain what is admitted to be theirs, but that the records (of all things) come in to disturb them.[58]

[56] Introducing the code on tenant rights, Robert Cust, the Officiating Financial Commissioner, emphasised in 1860: "Contract, customary, parole, or written, must be the basis of the relation betwixt land owner and tenant . . ."

[57] *PTECR*, para 24, p. 7.

[58] Prinsep, Annual Report of the Settlement Operations of the Year, 1865–6, 13 Aug. 1866, para 94; see also *PTECR*, para 83, p. 141. Opposing the proposed Tenancy Bill, he repeated the apocalyptic vision of a zamindar member of the Lahore Committee: "Gentlemen, if this clause and the previous regarding new rights are allowed to stand . . . I declare to you there will be

Once a law was instituted and rights recorded, they were not to be disturbed, changed, or violated. When Prinsep proceeded to revise entries made in the records of the first summary settlement, his revisions were declared illegal. Most officials feared revision would create a precedent, threaten the sanctity of records, and undermine the basis of rights. It was more important to sustain the inviolability of records, the stability of law, and the security of expectations than rectify stray errors that may have crept into the records.[59]

Steeped in the language of custom, the discourse of rights was at the same time saturated with Benthamite ideals. The concern with security of expectation and the fixity of law appears obsessively in arguments by all participants in the debates. In codifying custom, classifying categories, and specifying their meaning, officials in the colonies had to negotiate the contrary pulls of opposed traditions – of Blackstone and Bentham. We will return to this in a later chapter.[60]

The Production of Categories

In categorising social relations thus, colonial officials were operating on two interlinked registers: one ethnographic, the other bureaucratic.

---

an insurrection everywhere." Memorandum on the Punjab Tenancy Bill, 18 April 1868, *PTECR*, p. 153. Prinsep was echoing Bentham's fear of bad laws that disturb expectations. "Every attack upon this sentiment (expectation)," wrote Bentham, "produces a distinct and special evil, which may be called a pain of disappointment." Bentham, *PCC*, pp. 136–7. Elsewhere he wrote: "An attack upon the property of an individual excites alarm among other proprietors. This sentiment spreads from neighbour to neighbour, till at last the contagion possesses the entire body of the state." Bentham, *PCC*, p. 143. Such an attack, Bentham argued, deadens industry, nurtures lethargy and prevents people from maximising the productive use of resources. Bentham, "Analysis of Evils which Result from Attacks on Property", *PCC*, ch. X.

[59] On the disturbing effects of makings radical changes in the settlement records, see Note by Sir John Lawrence, Viceroy and Governor General of India, 30 Aug. 1866; Minute by J. Lawrence, Viceroy and Governor General of India, 30 April,1867, on Tenant Right in the Punjab, *PTECR*, p. 160.

[60] See ch. 5, below.

Bureaucratic need and administrative imperative required uniform, comprehensible, and legally recognised categories, these being the motivation for colonial ethnographic investigations. But it also meant framing the enquiries with questions relevant to governance. In effect, this meant that a whole social world, with all its specificities and variations, was being appropriated through juridical categories that drew, as noted, from conflicting legal traditions.

How was this diversity of ethnographically discovered social terms transformed into bureaucratic categories? It is possible to distinguish a set of related operations at work. First, there was the process of *translation*. As we have seen, local terms were translated into new official categories, either one taken from Western political economy (landlord/tenant, occupancy/tenant at will), or one seen as appropriately indigenous (mauroosee/ghair-mauroosee). Second, there was the act of *condensation* and *displacement*, whereby several existing categories were fused and amalgamated into one generic category.[61] This inevitably meant an erasure of the specificities of local terms – the affective ties they expressed, the differing origins they could be traced back to. The condensed version came to express a new classificatory reality, its new definitions having reworked the meanings of the earlier categories. Third: condensing was part of a wider process of *homogenisation*. The bureaucratic needs of a centralising power, as noted, required that varying social relations be expressed as uniform categories. It was as if the chaos of nature had to be ordered and the anarchy of the past brought under control to render the social landscape legible. Fourth, a process of *legal codification*. Administrative categories had to be transformed into others that were publicly specified and legally endorsed. As the bearer of a juridical category, a

---

[61] I deploy the terms "condensation" and "displacement" somewhat in the way Althusser does in his reworking of Freudian notions. Condensation and displacement are used by Freud to express the compression of a number of dream thoughts into one image, or the transference of the physical intensity from one image to another. Althusser refers to condensation as a process through which varying contradictions, developing at an uneven pace, fuse into one in the overdetermined moment of revolutionary crisis, reconstituting the inner essence of each individual contradiction. See Althusser, *For Marx*.

person had legally defined rather than only socially recognised rights. People had now been made legal subjects.

Renaming was an act through which the histories of people were refigured. The constitutive principles that underlined the existing semantic order were displaced. Butimar as a category, for instance, was the bearer of a history. Those who saw themselves as butimars claimed a past and traced their rights back to the origin of social life when forests were cleared, land made productive through collective labour, and the social ties that forged the lived community came into being. This history was erased when the butimar was renamed "inferior proprietor" or "occupancy tenant". His identity was now linked to a different history – of physical possession and occupation. Within the new classification he was no different from the lathmar or adhlapi, or anyone who cultivated a piece of land for twelve or twenty years. They were all uniformly occupancy tenants with rights defined by the tenancy acts. Uninterrupted possession became the index of a temporal continuity, the basis of occupancy rights.

This idea of temporality underlining the new regime of rights was different from the notion of temporal continuity expressed by peasants during the official ethnographic enquiries. The very term butimar, for instance, located a peasant within a time continuous with that of his ancestors, connecting past and present, the time of the ancestors and the time of the descendants. It was not a temporal continuity premised on notions of continuous physical occupation of land. When speaking of the origin of rights, butimars narrativised this idea of temporal continuity, affirming the sanctity of the rights they possessed.

The question that bothered colonial officials was: How could rights be recognised when possession was discontinuous, when the situation was of lands remaining unoccupied for stretches running into many years? While officials asserted continuous possession as the basis of proprietary and occupancy rights, peasants asked how rights could be questioned when they were sanctified at the origin of time. Constituted through the toil of their ancestors, such rights were seen as unquestionable and sacrosanct. As the bearer of the term butimar, the peasant was the living personification of a mythic continuity that could not be displaced by the mere physical fact that his occupation of land was discontinuous.

The ethnographic enquiries had, it is clear, produced evidence that spilled over and beyond the frames of reference that sought to contain them. This surplus tended to disrupt the framework from within, creating problems of interpretation, forcing modifications in categories and keeping judges busy in the courts. The past resists erasure, not always but very often. Embedded institutions are not easily wiped away. Affective ties that define social bonds are rarely dissolved by bureaucratic fiat without murmurs of protests. It takes time for a new regime of categories to acquire constitutive power, for the new categories to be taken for granted. Questionings are part of the history that brings a new habitus into being and defines its form.

Of course, not everyone questions, at least not persistently or forever. Nor do all questionings disrupt the power of the new categorical order. As we have seen and will again in what follows, the meaning of new categories is usually shaped and reworked through a dialogic process that is internally diverse.

5

Codifying Custom

IN LATE-EIGHTEENTH-CENTURY Germany, Herder and the Brothers Grimm set about recording large numbers of folk ballads. Their effort was to capture the collective creativity of people within a specific culture, and, by documenting their stories, to salvage something of the past from oblivion. Samuel Johnson and James Boswell, the eminent English couple, were driven by similar intent to look for primitive custom in the western isles off Scotland, and in fact by the 1850s a serious interest in folklore and music had matured across several countries of Europe.[1] This discovery of popular culture was part of the large sweep of a wide-ranging Romanticism which celebrated the wild and the natural, the primitive and the archaic, the simple and the sublime, the spontaneous and the instinctive. It was an offshoot of the revolt against Reason and Classicism; it was part of the new current in favour of cultural pluralism.

Like many ideas and attitudes, this interest in the ancient, the popular, and the distant made its way into the colonies. Its journey there was attended by all the twists and turns and paradoxes and contortions that such travels usually entail, but all the same within a few decades of the European folklorists colonial officials in many parts of the empire came to be preoccupied with rather similar cultural investigations and were to be found rooting about for folk traditions in far-flung provinces. While travellers to India voyaged in search of the picturesque and the exotic, the more curious among those already stationed to govern India developed an analogous interest in gathering

---

[1] Burke, *Popular Culture in Early Modern Europe*, pt I; Dorson, *The British Folklorists*.

knowledge about the social unfamiliar – in the customs, rituals, and practices of native inhabitants.[2]

Official interest in these matters assumed a specific structure in colonial Punjab. Conquered in 1849, almost ninety years after the British subdued the nawabs of Bengal, this region, as noted in various ways in the earlier chapters, experienced a form of rule very different from the one established in the east. In Bengal the British saw zamindars as key figures in the countryside and the possible basis of Company Raj. In Punjab, cultivating peasants rather than zamindars were identified as the objects of imperial concern. Whereas the wet tracts of Bengal sustained a deeply stratified rural structure and a firmly entrenched caste order, Punjab, a drier tract, was in official discourse the proverbial land of peasant proprietors. If Cornwallis and his zamindari system epitomised British rule in Bengal, Lawrence's dream of Punjab showed a "country thickly cultivated by a fat, contented yeomanry, each riding his own horse, sitting under his own fig tree . . ."[3]

Knowing and recording rural custom became a defining feature of the politics of paternalism in Punjab. After the British conquest, peasants in Punjab's villages became increasingly aware of colonial officials recording their folk-tales, ballads, songs, and proverbs – in addition to investigating their customs and codifying customary law. The nature of property rights, marriage patterns, inheritance customs, and collective rights on village commons – the life-ways of a whole world – were now being enquired into.

During the settlement process that started in 1850, a record of custom was added to the administration papers (wajib-ul-arz). By 1865 Prinsep, the Settlement Commissioner of Amritsar, drew up an alternative plan of recording custom. He insisted that within coparcenary societies, the relevant unit for enquiry into custom was the tribe, not the village. So the mode of enquiry had to shift. Within a few years, riwaj-i-ams, a detailing of the customs of different tribes, were produced for several districts. The records, however, did not acquire

[2] This entanglement of romanticism with imperialism is discussed in chs 1 and 6 herein.

[3] Cust, *Pictures of Indian Life*, p. 255.

an independent identity in print: they were published as appendices to settlement reports, not as separate volumes.[4] Subsequently, in 1873, Tupper was given charge of further systematising the process of recording custom.[5] He wrote a series of influential memorandums on customary law and prepared an elaborate questionnaire on the basis of which the subsequent riwaj-i-ams in Punjab were to be prepared.[6] Individual innovations were to give way to standardised and regulated practice. By the 1880s, five volumes of customary law of separate districts were published, in the 1890s another eleven volumes appeared, and by the second decade of the twentieth century over thirty district volumes flooded administrative offices.

These British ethnographic texts reveal as much about Indian custom as about the official observers – their minds, the conventions of their language, the assumptions implicit in their questions, and their conclusions. It is important to understand the concepts which framed the vision of these official ethnographers and directed their gaze, the processes through which a region's customary practices were codified, and the contexts which mediated this process. In the colonial situation the rhetoric of custom becomes a new language of power and legitimation. My primary interest in this chapter is to move on to some of the specificities – the logic, the ambivalences, and the implications of this rhetoric.[7]

---

[4] By 1865 the riwaj-i-ams of Amritsar, Gurdaspur, and Sialkot were completed and those for Lahore, Gujranwala, Gujrat, and Kangra were under preparation. The finalised records were appended to the settlement reports of these volumes. The customary law volumes of these districts prepared on the basis of Tupper's uniform questionnaire were published only in the 1890s and after.

[5] No. 4375, 21 November 1873, Officiating Under Secretary to GOP, to Secretary to Financial Commissioner, *PCL*, vol. I, p. 197.

[6] See C.L. Tupper, "Memorandum on the Means of Ascertaining Customary Law of the Punjab", 2 June 1973; C.L. Tupper, Memorandum Explanatory of Question on Tribal Custom . . . and of Questions on Agrarian Custom, 2 June 1875, *PCL*, vol. I, section V.

[7] For the process of codification of custom in Africa, see Moore, *Social Facts and Fabrication*; Chanock, *Law, Custom and Social Order*; Benton, *Law and Colonial Cultures*; Comaroff, "Colonialism, Culture and the Law".

From Text to Practice

A Code of Gentoo Laws, the first major colonial digest on Hindu law, was published in 1776.[8] About a hundred years later appeared Tupper's *Punjab Customary Law*.[9] These works represent two different strands of colonial legal discourse. Both are tied in their opposition to Benthamite Utilitarian Positivism, yet are very different from each other. Against the Utilitarian disdain for tradition, they celebrated tradition; against the Utilitarian argument of practical reason and the principle of utility, they invoked the authority of custom; against the Benthamite plea for radical reform by the state, they saw the need to conserve and build on established rules; against the aggressive Utilitarian projection of British rule as an enlightened alien power, they hoped to transcend the alienness by presenting colonial rule as rooted in indigenous society. Both sought to base British rule on custom and tradition, but they were involved in very different imperial projects.

The late-eighteenth-century Orientalist tradition saw ancient texts as the source of authentic knowledge about immemorial custom and tradition.[10] The Sastras and the Koran, it believed, set out the codes of conduct of Hindus and Muslims, and defined the customary laws which mediated social relationships as well as conflicts within communities. Practices were seen as legitimate only when they conformed with the injunctions of ancient texts. So, present practice was no acceptable proof of valid custom: it could represent perversions, distortions, and deformations of the original

[8] Halhed, *A Code of Gentoo Laws*.

[9] Tupper, *PCL*, appeared in 1881.

[10] On the Orientalists, see Majeed, *Ungoverned Imaginings*, chs 1–3. On the late eighteenth-century discovery of Indian tradition by European scholars, see Schwab, *The Oriental Renaissance*; Marshall, *The British Discovery of Hinduism in the Eighteenth Century*; Kejariwal, *The Asiatic Society of Bengal and the Discovery of India's Past*; Halbfass, *India and Europe*. On law, see Derrett, "The Administration of Hindu Law by the British". On a discussion of Orientalism as a wider discursive formation, see Said, *Orientalism*; MacKenzie, *Orientalism: History, Theory and the Arts*; Yeğenoğlu, *Colonial Fantasies*; Lewis, *Rethinking Orientalism*.

principles. Practices became tainted with the passage of time, marked with the imprint of generations; the real principles were buried under the weight of history. To preserve immemorial custom a return to the original form was essential: custom had to be purged of foreign influences and sastric law had to be consolidated where an amalgam of practices had developed. The original authoritative texts had to be identified, translated, and understood, and colonial codes had to be based on and authorised through these texts.[11]

Since the time of Hastings, Orientalist scholars had immersed themselves in the project of discovering and translating sacerdotal texts deemed authentic, and in the preparation of definitive digests.[12] After the acquisition of diwani in Bengal in 1757 there had been, initially, a toleration of the diverse systems of popular justice and a fluid interpretation of the Sastras by pandits. This had created some insecurity about the ambiguous basis of justice and, concomitantly, the need for a stable foundation of legal knowledge. Flexible and conflicting interpretations of sastric injunctions had to be replaced by the certitude of authoritative digests of traditional textual knowledge.

In May 1773 eleven pandits began work on the first major digest. Their work, *Vivadarnava-setu* (A Bridge Across the Ocean of Litigation), was published in 1775 and translated by N.B. Halhed into English as *A Code of Gentoo Laws*. Subsequently, under Jones' supervision, Jagannatha Tarkapancanana produced another digest, *Vivadabhangarnava*, translated into English by H.T. Colebrooke. Jones, whose object was to produce "a complete digest of Hindu and Mussulman law", published *Al Sirajiyyah: Or the Mohamedan Law of Inheritance* in 1792, and the *Institutes of Hindu Law: Or*

[11] Hastings ordered that "the laws of the Koran with respect to Mohamedans and those of the Shaster with respect to the Gentoos shall invariably be adhered to." Derrett, "The Administration of Hindu Law by the British", p. 289.

[12] Kejariwal, *The Asiatic Society of Bengal and the Discovery of India's Past*; Derrett, "The British as Patrons of the Sastras". Jones was obsessed with the question of authenticity: the right texts had to be located and properly translated. See Majeed, *Ungoverned Imaginings*, ch. I; Rocher, "British Orientalism in the Eighteenth Century".

the Ordinances of Manu in 1796. Colebrooke's authoritative work, *The Digest of Hindu Law,* appeared in 1798.

The Orientalist thinking on custom, tradition, and law was relentlessly attacked by Utilitarian Positivists inspired by the ideas of Bentham.[13] Mill, like Bentham, criticised any "obscurantist" reverence for tradition and linked it to the ruling conservative ideology in eighteenth-century Britain which was pathologically opposed to liberal reform. The task of law, for the Utilitarians, was to define the basis of a new social and political order rather than conserve the old regime; the valid concern of the law-maker was not the discovery of past custom – the law as it *is* – but rather the law as it *ought to be*.[14] Laws in this view, as we noted in the previous chapter, did not express a deeper pre-given reality, the inner coherence of a pre-structured community with a collective history; they established that coherence by introducing order into a chaotic world of conflicting individual interests. Laws were exogenous, not endogenous, to a community; they provided a framework of fixed and public rules which made ordered life possible. Individuals needed to be bound not by ties of community but by a commitment to clear, determinate, unambiguous public rules, systematised into a single universal code enacted by a proper legislative authority. The defining principles of this order were Reason and Utility, not shared tradition and custom.

Substantial sections of Punjab's officialdom, as noted, reacted

[13] See Majeed, *Ungoverned Imaginings* for James Mill's critique of Orientalism; and Stokes, *The English Utilitarians and India* for a more general account. On Benthamite Utilitarianism there is now a rich scholarly literature. See Hume, *Bentham and Bureaucracy*; Rosen, *Jeremy Bentham and Representative Democracy*; Harrison, *Bentham*; Postema, *Bentham and the Common Law Tradition.*

[14] The criticism flowed from Bentham's crucial distinction between the "expositor" of the law and its "censor": "To the province of the Expositor it belongs to explain to us what, as he supposes, the Law is: to that of the Censor, to observe to us what he thinks it ought to be. The former, therefore, is principally occupied in stating, or in inquiring after facts; the latter in discussing the reasons . . ." Cited in Postema, *Bentham and the Common Law Tradition,* p. 304. The law-maker, the codifier, had to be the censor, not a mere expositor.

against this Utilitarianism,[15] emphasising the need to preserve the collective life of the community and base law on immemorial custom.[16] But there was no return to the textual Orientalism of Jones and Colebrooke. Drawing on the English common law tradition, Punjab's officials saw custom as embodied in practices rather than ancient texts.[17] Injunctions within the Sastras and the Koran were not self-justifying, they were to be validated by practice.[18] The Punjab Laws Act of 1872 stated that the sacerdotal codes of Hindu and Muslim law were to be followed only to the extent that they coincided with,

[15] This critique, again, had "conservative" roots. On the German sources of a conservative critique of Bentham, see Vinogradoff, *The Teaching of Sir Henry Maine*.

[16] For Tupper, as for Henry Maine, the group historically prefigures the individual: the individual emerges from the group at a specific stage of social development. Maine saw the family as the original form of social organisation, while Tupper, drawing on McLennan, traced the lineage of the individual to the tribe. The principles of tribal society tied the community internally; lineage linked the communities across generations. Custom was the expression of community life and its regulator. Custom had to be preserved; the forces leading to the disintegration of tribes had to be resisted.

[17] The reaction was not limited to Punjab. Maine argued generally that the laws of Manu did not adequately represent local usages, and that "the customary rules, reduced to writing, have been very greatly altered by Brahmanical expositors, constantly in spirit, sometimes in tenor." Maine, *Village-Communities in the East and West*, pp. 53ff. Elsewhere he criticised Jones' assumption that the laws of Manu were "acknowledged by all Hindus to be binding on them". It is probable, Maine felt, "that at the end of the last century large masses of the Hindu population had not so much as heard of Manu, and knew little or nothing of the legal rules supposed to rest ultimately on his authority." It was necessary to conserve the variety of local usages against their absorption by Brahmanical codes: Maine, "The Sacred Law of the Hindus".

[18] In 1854, before issuing the Punjab Civil Code, the Judicial Commissioner M.R. Montgomery discussed "how far those [Hindu and Muslim] codes are affected by, or merged in local custom, and in what places they altogether yield to that unwritten Code which is engraven on the minds of the people." Preface to "The abstract principles of law circulated for the guidance of officers employed in the administration of civil justice in the Punjab", extract appended to Circular No. 37, 16 May 1854, from R. Montgomery, Judicial Comm., Punjab, to All Comms in the Punjab, *PCL*, vol. I, p. 59.

and had been absorbed within, customary practice.[19] When the riwaj-i-ams were prepared in the 1870s and 1880s under Tupper's supervision, official observers were asked to carefully note the distance between actual practices and scriptures. The general tendency now was to repress the affinity between scriptures and practices and play on the differences.

This general conception of custom, reinforced by the contextualist arguments earlier discussed, distinguished Punjab from Bengal in that, so officials argued, Brahmins had no position of power and customary law was "unsacerdotal, unsacremental, secular".[20] Hindu law as developed within the caste society of Bengal was not suited to Punjab, where tribe and clan were the defining features of social order. "Hindu law extravagantly exalts the Brahmans," wrote Tupper, "it gives sacerdotal reasons for secular rules . . ."[21] It derives its principles from caste rather than clan; it sees caste and not tribe as the natural order of society.

This move from text to practice was complicated. It occurred in hesitant and uncertain steps. Dalhousie's declaration in 1849 that British rule in Punjab would be based on native institutions was a statement of intent which conveyed no concrete content. How was custom to be defined and discovered? What were the sources of its authority? Such questions required time for debate. But the task of administration could not wait. On annexation, a set of simple rules of civil procedure – a slightly modified version of what was in operation in the North Western Provinces – was promulgated. Personal rule within the Non-Regulation system, it was believed, was to be based on direct contact with people, unencumbered by complicated and fixed rules. On taking over as Chief Commissioner in 1853, John Lawrence felt the need to place the system on a more uniform and

[19] See Tupper, "Memorandum on the Means of Ascertaining the Customary Law of Punjab", 2 June 1873, *PCL*, vol. I, p. 159.

[20] See "Memorandum on the Customary Law in the Punjab" by C. Boulnois, Judge, Chief Court, Punjab, 28 November 1872, *PCL*, vol. I; "Memorandum on the Means of Ascertaining the Customary Law of Punjab" by Tupper, 2 June 1873, *PCL*, vol. 1.

[21] Tupper, "Memorandum on the Means of Ascertaining the Customary Law of Punjab", *PCL*, vol. I.

secure footing.[22] So a practical manual for officials was quickly put together by Richard Temple, drawing upon diverse textual sources: digests of European jurisprudence, and the great Orientalist texts on sastric law produced by William Jones, T.A. Strange, W. Macnaghten, and H.T. Colebrooke – precisely those texts in opposition to which the specificities of customary practices in Punjab were later defined.[23] The Punjab Laws Act passed in 1872 only authorised the existing manual and gave it a firmer legal status.[24]

Fed on such digests and secure in the authority of their knowledge, officials went about arbitrating on matters of custom. In courts, when judges were called upon to adjudicate disputes over custom even before any serious enquiry had been undertaken, they had to fall back upon their own vague impressions of people's customs, supplemented by cursory enquiries and references to the Punjab Civil Code manual. Court decisions on issues of custom, tainted by such manuals, then became a source of knowledge about custom.[25] Later, in the volumes of the *Punjab Record*, important judicial cases were compiled for ready reference. All customary law manuals quoted case law to prove a point about custom, and customs declared void by the courts

[22] No. 511, 25 July 1853, P. Melvill, Secretary to Chief Comm. Punjab, to the Offg Secretary GOI, *PCL*, I, pp. 51ff. See also Circular no. 37, 16 May 1854, R. Montgomery, Judicial Comm., Punjab, to all Commissioners in the Punjab, *PCL*, vol. I, pp. 58ff.

[23] *Abstract Principles of Law Circulated for the Guidance of Officers Employed in the Administration of Civil Justice in the Punjab to Which is Appended a Proposed form of Procedure*, Lahore: Chronicle Press, 1855; Temple explicitly acknowledges the sources of these borrowings. See Richard Temple Collection, Mss Eur F 86/44 (BL).

[24] See Abstract of the Proceedings of the Council of the Governor General of India for the purpose of making laws and regulations under the provisions of the Act of Parliament, 24 & 25, 5 September 1871 & 26 March 1872, *PCL*, vol. I, pp. 106ff. and pp. 122ff.

[25] Commenting on the action of courts in transforming custom, Tupper wrote: "How far is it probable that under the action of courts, indigenous custom has remained pure? The conjecture does not appear too rash, that if any of those parts of the lexis loci which the Punjab Civil Code treats in any detail were now to be analysed they would be found to be saturated with its influence." Memorandum by Tupper, 2 June 1875, *PCL*, vol. I, p. 207.

could have no legal existence. Textual sources and judicial decisions remained important in the shaping of custom in the period between 1854 and 1872, when the Punjab Civil Code was in operation and the riwaj-i-ams were yet to be codified.

In a sense, textual authority was important even in Tupper's conception of customary law. His theory was not derived from the observation of practices; it was deductive. Drawing from the writings of English common law theorists and nineteenth-century evolutionary anthropologists, he outlined a general theory of the evolution of Punjab society.[26] Indian evidence had no constitutive power in the making of this theory; the theory provided the frame through which the evidence was to be understood and ordered.[27]

The shift from text to practice was thus a problematic one. There was, without doubt, a definite change in the rhetoric of custom. If the late-eighteenth-century Orientalists in Bengal were preoccupied with the discovery of ancient sacred texts, the late-nineteenth-century Punjab officials were busy enquiring into customary practices. But their enquiries into such practices remained implicated within textual processes and were structured by a variety of conceptual assumptions with which these officials operated.

Of Informants and Sovereigns

The enquiry into custom depended perforce upon local informants. This dependence had a peculiar logic. When the Orientalist

[26] Against Maine, Tupper echoed McLennan's theory that the small group emerges from the large, the family from the horde; but against McLennan's view of the matriarchal origins of society, Tupper repeated Maine's patriarchal theory. Maine savaged McLennan but appreciated Tupper. See Maine, "Theories of Primitive Society" and "The Sacred Law of the Hindus".

[27] Tupper wrote: "It cannot be too prominently stated that I pretend to offer nothing but a theory. In an agricultural population, which cannot now be less than ten millions, it is impracticable to exhaust all the facts; and even if I had time to examine vernacular documents in addition to the settlement reports and the *Punjab Record*, it would not have been possible to go beyond a theoretical statement of what the custom possibly would be under given conditions. This is what I mean by a theory of the subject; and I did not see how it could be exhibited in any general view by any other method." Tupper, "The Characteristics of Tribal and Village Custom", *PCL*, vol. II, p. 77.

investigations into Indian tradition began in the 1770s, with ancient texts viewed as the dominant founts of knowledge, pandits were re-cognised as the custodians of that knowledge. Considered as being learned in the Sastras, they knew the language of ancient texts and could help their British masters with them. After the 1793 Cornwallis Code, pandits were attached to the district and provincial courts: to the sadr diwani adalat in Calcutta and to the supreme court. They were to answer questions posed by judges on specific disputes, and inform the court about what the Sastras had to say about the class of dispute in question.[28] Sastric education in the Sanskrit colleges in Calcutta and Banaras sought to produce experts to be consulted during litigation.[29] Pandits were involved in this way in producing colonial digests on sastric law.

This dependence on the power of pandits created a deep imperial anxiety. While a dialogue with native informants was seen as essential to the production of authentic knowledge, such extreme depend-ence was experienced by the British as a form of disempowerment. To assert sovereign power the masters had to transcend their crippling reliance on native knowledge-brokers and claim their own superior right to represent local tradition.

In the process, the authority of pandits was both recognised and denied. The British first persuaded the pandits to prepare the digests and then made disparaging comments about their work. Jones was dissatisfied with the efforts of the eleven pandits who prepared *Viva-darnava-setu*. Arriving in India eight years after the presentation of *A Code of Gentoo Laws* to the East India Company, he set about preparing a more authoritative alternative digest of sastric learning. Jagannatha Tarkapancanana, conversant with both Mitakshara and Dayabhaga legal traditions, prepared the digest *Vivadabhangarnava* to Jones' specifications. Colebrooke translated the work but criticised Jagannatha; and later other official legal experts like Thomas Strange

[28] Lata Mani discusses the structure of the dialogue with the pandits on the question of sati. See Mani, *Contentious Traditions*.

[29] At the Sanskrit colleges the following texts were read: Manu, Mitakshara, Dayabhaga, Dayakarma (Sarigraha), Daya-tattva, Dattaka-candrika, Duttaka-mimansa, Vivadacintamani, Tithi-tattva, Suddhi-tattva, and Prayascitta-tattva. See Derrett, "The British as Patrons of the Sastras", p. 238.

and F.W. Macnaghten even ridiculed him.[30] Colebrooke himself undertook to prepare a work in English which would establish a uniform and accurate basis of judgement and make English judges independent of their Hindu law officers. But he too was dissatisfied with Balam Bhatta and Citrapati, the two local informants who worked with him on the digest.

The question of knowledge became linked to a discourse of morality. The knowledge of the pandits was seen as suspect since their motives and morals were questionable.[31] In Jones' attack on the pandits a feeling of impotent anger fused with a sense of moral outrage: "I can no longer bear to be at the mercy of our Pandits, who deal out Hindu law as they please, and make it at reasonable rates, when they cannot find it ready made."[32] Within official discourse pandits came to be represented as self-seeking, corrupt, and greedy; their works were associated with fraud and forgery.[33] Company intellectuals claimed the moral authority to represent and record Indian tradition even when they recognised the pandits' claim to superior knowledge and their symbolic power in society.[34]

This attitude towards the pandits seems partly rooted in Benthamite ideas. Orientalist traditionalism and Benthamite radical reformism developed in opposition to each other in India, but they also influenced

[30] Macnaghten, *Considerations on the Hindoo Law*, Preface; Strange, *Hindu Law*, vol. II, pp. 175–6. See also Halhed, *A Code of Gentoo Laws*.

[31] *See* Macnaghten's Preface to *Considerations on the Hindoo Law*.

[32] In his "The Sacred Laws of the Hindus", Maine disapprovingly quotes Jones' assessment of the pandits.

[33] See Derrett, "The British as Patrons of the Sastras". The authenticity of important works like Dattaka-candrika was widely questioned by British legal minds in the nineteenth century. Derrett, among others, argues that this was an extremely important late-nineteenth-century work. Raghumani, the probable author of the text, was a highly respectable scholar and was unlikely to "forge" a text: ibid. On juridical fabrication, see Derrett, "A Juridical Fabrication of Early British India".

[34] While Colebrooke set out to work on his project he was aware that the knowledge of the pandits had greater popular legitimacy. "The public have, no doubt, more confidence in the Pandits than in me," he said. Quoted in Derrett, "The British as Patrons of the Sastras", p. 251.

each other.[35] Benthamite prejudices were silently inscribed onto Orientalist legal minds. Bentham reacted against the common law tradition within which common law judges interpreted the spirit of tradition and applied it to new situations; talked of immemorial custom but constantly modified custom; innovated and introduced new rules but pretended – through the use of judicial fiction – that they were old. Such a system, Bentham argued, sustained a regime of despotism, corruption, falsehood, dishonesty, pretence, and deception. When judges innovate, establish rules, and decide law, they become despots. When, through the myth of immemorial custom and through reference to judicial fictions, judges pretend that they have invented nothing, they act with dishonesty, they deceive. Since the "muddle" of uncertain, flexible rules was known only to legal experts and not to the public, these experts could manipulate law and were corruptible.[36] It was necessary to separate judicial and legislative functions, define the proper source of law, and establish that stable and certain legal framework by which public expectations could be made secure and public justification of judicial decisions rendered possible.

Many of these ideas resonate in the writings of Jones and Colebrooke. Their fear of the pandits' corrigibility, their reluctance to accept pandits as interpreters rather than factual reporters of tradition, their search for certainty, are all part of a wider sensibility of those times. Within this tradition, inventiveness in a non-legislative body was suspect: it was the possible basis of arbitrariness, caprice,

[35] Majeed shows how Mill's Utilitarianism can be read as a reaction to the dominant conservative British ideology of the late nineteenth century. Majeed, *Ungoverned Imaginings*.

[36] Bentham saw "judicial fictions" as "lies devised by judges to serve as instruments of, and cloaks to, injustice." Bentham, "Papers Relative to Codification", in John Bowring, ed., *The Works of Jeremy Bentham*, vol. IV, p. 498. The use of judicial fiction by lawyers had pernicious effects: "it has had for its object or effect, or both, to deceive, and, by deception to govern, and by governing, to promote the interest, real or supposed, of the party addressing, at the expense of the party addressed." Bentham, "A Fragment on Ontology", in John Bowring, ed., *The Works of Jeremy Bentham*, vol. VIII, p. 199. For a wider discussion of the notion of judicial fiction, see Postema, *Bentham and the Common Law Tradition*.

dishonesty, and corruption. British scholars, even the Orientalists, were prone to distrust creative informants, ignore the vibrant tradition of contemporary indigenous legal discourse, and freeze sastric learning into old texts.[37] As the British became more and more confident of their knowledge of Indian tradition and custom, consultations with pandit informants became infrequent, and finally in 1864 they were dismissed from the courts altogether, resolving the state's insecurities about the basis of its sovereign power.

The move from text to practice as the source of custom was paralleled by the move from pandits to village elders – the new local informants on custom. In Punjab, village headmen and elders were now seen as "the custodians of village wisdom", the "repositories of local knowledge".[38] They were the anchor around which the community revolved: they held the community together, disciplined its members, preserved order, adjudicated disputes, sorted out conflicts over custom. If customary practices mediated relations within the community, these practices were maintained and reproduced via the mediation of elders.

This conception of the power of elders derived from notions of Indian village communities which became popular after the second quarter of the nineteenth century. It was a conception reinforced

[37] See Derrett, "The British as Patrons of the Sastras", and "The Administration of Hindu Law by the British". He argues that in the pre-British period pandits incorporated local practices into the Dharmasastra and reinterpreted texts. He shows that in sastric learning, a creative seventeenth century was followed by a flourishing, though not assertive or brilliant, eighteenth century. In fact, in the 1820s, a series of learned texts were produced by pandits in response to the scurrilous charges of Strange and Macnaghten; but these genuine sastric works were not relied upon by courts suspicious of recent works. "The pandit as a professor of a living science was rejected for the more or less fossilised treatises which would head the pandit's list of references." Derrett, "The British as Patrons of the Sastras", p. 255.

[38] Wilson wrote: "Like the judges in England, the older men of the tribe are considered to be the repositories of the common law." They were aware of the principles which govern social life and the general spirit behind social practices. Wilson, *General Code of Tribal Custom in the Sirsa District of the Panjab.*

by the theory of the tribal constitution of Punjab's villages. As we have seen, after the 1860s when the theory of tribal origin of primitive society became popular in evolutionary anthropology, Tupper suggested that the family and the village as institutions were preceded by the clan and the tribe; therefore tribal characteristics were inscribed into village institutions as they developed, and tribal elders were refigured as village elders. The consolidation of coparcenary brotherhoods affirmed the power of village patriarchs and sanctified their voice.[39]

Through these elders the British hoped to discover the customs of India's tribes, and at the same time establish power over them.[40] So British officials in Punjab, particularly after the rebellion of 1857, went in search of chaudhris and muqaddams and instituted them where none existed.[41]

Could village elders inform the British about customary practices? How reliable was their knowledge within imperial perception?

[39] See ch. 3 above.

[40] Tupper: "It is through the tribe and clan that Government can gain its firmest hold on the inclinations and motives of the people. The people can be led by their own leaders. It is much easier for a foreign Government to deal with organised bodies of men, through those who can be trusted on both sides, than with miscellaneous hordes of individuals." Tupper, "On the Codification of Customary Law", *PCL*, vol. I, p. 17.

[41] The commissioner of Lahore division wrote: "I do not wish to create the class where it does not exist. I do not wish to maintain an idle and useless class, but . . . to a government of foreigners such as our own, such men are invaluable both in war and peace, for they are the means of communication and explanation to their more ignorant brethren, and they are the depositories of all local traditions and local statistics." No. 535, 16 December 1858, Commissioner of Lahore Division to Financial Commissioner, Punjab, Hissar Division Records, Basta 38, Revenue Case 21, 15 January 1859. From Sirsa the Deputy Commissioner reported: "Hitherto this class of men do not exist, nor can I learn that such ever were recognised in this district by any of the governments preceding ours; but the advantage of such men in every pergunah is too great for me not to advocate its being created at once . . ." Deputy Commissioner Sirsa to Commissioner and Superintendent Hissar Division, Hissar Division Records, Basta 38, Revenue Case 169, 2 April 1859.

The process of enquiry shows that their authority, like that of Bengal's pandits, was both recognised and demeaned; they were represented as knowledgeable as well as ignorant. This contrary assessment was part of the logic of sovereign power as it came to be constituted, and it created a space for imperial intervention in the making of custom.

The Enquiry

The quality of any enquiry depends crucially on the machinery employed to conduct it. The colonial machinery for generating knowledge about custom was, not surprisingly, inadequate for the purpose. Revenue officials had neither the time nor the inclination to carry out exhaustive investigations. Badly paid and overworked, they had little passion for the execution of orders which came from the top.

The village record on customs was frequently stereotyped, the questions difficult, long, and badly formulated. "It has often been merely an elaborate Persian document in the best official language," wrote Brandreth, "drawn up by some learned Hindustani munshi, and copied for every manor of the pargana."[42] The imperfections of the wajib-ul-arz, prepared in the 1850s by revenue officials, were widely recognised, yet the document, being a part of the settlement record, had the same legal force as the settlement and its entries had to be accepted by courts as correct.[43] Things did not radically improve when the first set of riwaj-i-ams were produced in the 1860s. The settlement officer who was responsible for collecting the mass of evidence still had no efficient machinery at his disposal. After attesting the records for Montgomery, Purser cautioned against their reliability,[44] complaining about the incomprehensible language of the questionnaire: "it is incorrect, and is couched in the most

[42] Brandreth, *Jhelum S.R.*, 1865, para 296.

[43] The presumption of correctness was attached to the wajib-ul-arz under Section 44 of the Land Revenue Act. Since the custom recorded on the wajib-ul-arz was considered a "true" custom, the onus of proof in the court was on the party contradicting it. See *PR* no. 54 of 1867; *PR*, no. 87 of 1868; *PR* no. 13 of 1875.

[44] "I think they ought to be received with much caution. In the first place this document is always prepared first by the Superintendent. He is, of

barbarous and unintelligible Hindustani one can imagine." And he added: "when the questions are incorrect, the answers are likely to be the same."[45] Attempts were made to improve records. Every new scheme characteristically traced "anomalies" and "errors" in the past and assured "authoritative" records in the future. But the problems remained.

The nature of codification is defined by its framework of questions. Issues which appear relevant to colonial administrators are likely to be different from those considered important by peasants. The inclusions and exclusions within the enquiry are therefore vital. The wajib-ul-arz, concerned primarily with allocating responsibilities of revenue payment, had restricted its enquiry into village customs to a few questions. When Prinsep prepared the riwaj-i-ams by separating tribal from village custom, the scope of the enquiry was broadened. Yet the focus was still limited, now to a set of issues on which "custom" was deemed to deviate from Hindu and Muslim law. Tupper's scheme, built upon his evolutionary theory of the tribal origins of Punjab agrarian society and the ordering power of the principle of agnatic succession, focused on the questions of transfer of property – through inheritance, adoption, and gift – and on marriage.[46] For colonial officials the importance of understanding rights to property was taken for granted: it was the basis on which the rights and fiscal claims of the state could be clearly defined, the location of people fixed, their rights specified, their mobility restricted. A whole range of other issues important to the lives of the people were marginalised in the enquiry.

The evidence on customary law collected in village meetings with elders was constituted through a colonial ethnographic dialogue. Colonial officials went there not just to hear the wisdom of elders but

---

course, utterly unable to go out of the beaten track, and the track in this case occasionally leads into the slough of downright nonsense." Roe and Purser, *Montgomery S.R.*, 1878, pt III, para 10.

[45] Ibid.

[46] In 1873 Tupper was asked to draw up a series of questions for enquiries into tribal and local customs. The draft questions submitted in 1875 were approved by the provincial government. The third volume of *Punjab Customary Law* is structured around a revised version of these questions.

to question and cross-examine them, sort out ambiguities and contradictions, and then interpret, decide, and attest the truth about custom.
In these investigations there were confrontations between colonial
observers and native informants on the authenticity of practices;
there were also problems of intelligibility and comprehension. When
a superintendent in charge of an enquiry into customary law gathered
the leading men of a village and produced a long questionnaire, many
elders could not understand the implications of the questions, in
part because the questions were drawn up within an alien frame of
reference.[47] Baffled villagers produced answers which interrogators
helped to mould. When community elders were asked to spell out
the generative schemes implicit in their practices, they found the
matter altogether difficult. When generative schemes are immanent
in social practice, people act according to custom without explicitly
formulating the rules of custom. In such a context social practice
occurs in a world taken for granted, within a structure of experience
characterised by silences and languages of familiarity. The discourse
of familiarity, as Bourdieu says, leaves unsaid all that goes without
saying; it cannot express that which has always remained unsaid,

[47] E.L. Brandreth wrote about his experience of such enquiries in Jhelum:
"when they put their seals to the paper, no doubt they thought it very grand,
though they did not know what it was about, as they could little understand
the language . . . the villagers are confused by the long code of rules, and
merely say 'yes, yes', and put their seals to the paper, hoping it is nothing
very dreadful . . ." Brandreth, *Jhelum S.R.*, 1865, para 296. The Settlement
Commissioner of Multan and Derajat Divisions, J.B. Lyall: "If it is grotesque
to propound these questions to a select assembly of headmen, it is much
more so to propound them to the men of one village, most of whom, after
listening to a few questions, will be so bored and stupefied that they will
agree to anything to get away." No. 33 S, 28 September 1875, from Lyall,
Settlement Commissioner, Multan and Derajat divisions, to the Settlement
Secretary to the Divisional Commissioner, *PCL*, vol. I, p. 188. Roe and Purser
reported from Montgomery: "In many cases the people have no custom at all
on the points to which the questions refer." Among the Mohammedan Jats,
for instance, adoption was rare. "Yet the chiefmen, when asked—'Can a man
adopt?'—will be sure to say 'yes' or 'no' . . ." Roe and Purser, *Montgomery S.R.*,
1878, pt III, para 10. To the British, keen on specifying different claims to
the property of a sonless proprietor, adoption was an important issue.

never been articulated.[48] Persuaded to make a reflexive return to their practice, native informants inevitably produced a discourse on custom which could never capture the general sensibility that informed social practice. What appears to the "native mind as familiar, as necessary, as self-evident, as a part of the course of nature" is, as many colonial officials complained at the time, difficult for outsiders to grasp.[49]

Even when the issues were understood by native informants, their answers could still be orchestrated. The oral evidence of village elders had to be verified, and alternative modes of verification employed by different officials defined different truths about custom. Thorburn's account of his investigations into custom in Bannu is revealing. Asked about their inheritance customs, the Bannuchis at first "unanimously" declared that, according to the Shara rule which they followed, a father could gift his property to anyone, even if his male successors were alive. This evidence left Thorburn unconvinced and uncomfortable. He pursued the investigation, cross-questioned the Bannuchis, and was ultimately happy with the answers he helped produce:

> Asked for examples of the exercise of such powers [the right to transfer property to others, in preference to male heirs], not one was forthcoming. Had anyone so alienated half his land? No cases known. As with Bannuchis, so with the Isakhels and others. Thus reasoning from a series of negatives the people were over and over again driven to admit that their first replies were erroneous . . . Here and there I shaped public opinion on most questions in the direction in which I myself and others of experience thought equitable.[50]

What was recorded represented Thorburn's conceptions of equity and justice, which in this case privileged patrilineal over other forms of property devolution – not that of the Bannuchis. Subsequently Arthur Roe, another colonial authority on customary law, discovered that "what took place in Bannu, has taken place in other districts where custom was in its infancy."[51]

---

[48] Bourdieu, *Outline of a Theory of Practice*, pp. 17–18.

[49] Tupper, "Memorandum on the Means of Ascertaining the Customary Law of the Punjab", 2 June 1873, *PCL*, vol. I, p. 160.

[50] Thorburn, *Bannu S.R.*, 1879, para 205.

[51] Roe and Rattigan, *Tribal Law in the Punjab*, p. 18

When the assertions of elders conformed with the ideas of the observer, the authority of precedents could be questioned. Enquiring into Ludhiana's customs, Walker found the method of seeking proof through precedents problematic. Such a method made no distinction between "norm" and "exception". Practices which operated in the past as exceptions could be cited to deny the norm. Moreover, argued Walker, practices which prevailed in an earlier stage of society could not be accepted as the legitimate basis for conditions which were widely different. There was no dearth of evidence that before British rule a daughter's husband was often a co-sharer, and a daughter's son could inherit property.[52] But such practices, existing in a context where land was not in demand, could not be made a rule. They could only be considered "exceptions", however numerous the instances of their practice, because in Walker's logic they "interfered" with and "departed" from "the natural order" of agnatic succession. Walker was certain that, despite past practice, tribal feeling was opposed to any such rule. And in "seeking proof of tribal custom regard should not be had merely to the few precedents . . . but rather to the general expression of tribal opinion. . . ."[53] The leading men were granted a certain power in selecting from a range of past practices what they wanted codified, as long as their ideas did not violate those of the officials.

In these enquiries the administrator-ethnographers were acting in opposed ways, proceeding from different assumptions. Thorburn used the rule of precedents to discount the authority of the elders; Walker cautioned against a slavish submission to the record of past practices. For Thorburn the authority of the elders was questionable, their knowledge of custom dubious. He drove them to admit that their replies were erroneous. For Walker the elders appeared as bearers of wisdom who unconsciously acted in accordance with the principles of custom, who knew the difference between the "norm" and the "exception".

After the enquiry there began another phase in the redefinition of custom. The settlement officer in charge of the enquiry departed

[52] See ch. 7 below.
[53] Walker, *The Customary Law of the Ludhiána District*, p. 37.

with the record of the custom. Back at his office, he was expected to scrutinise the answers, sort out the anomalies and ambiguities, and prepare the final authoritative version of riwaj-i-ams to be kept in the district office and consulted by the courts. This process of the translation of vernacular statements, and the rereading of textualised records and systematisation of evidence, provided a wide space for colonial authorial intervention in the making of custom. Clearly, the enquiry was a process through which the colonial state appropriated custom in specific ways. The nature of this appropriation and the reconstitution of custom was defined by the specific frames of reference through which local reality was perceived, the categories through which it was ordered. As we shall see, this frame was not marked by internal coherence: it was shot through with ambiguities, tensions, and inner contradictions.

The Impossible Task of Preservation

"It is the duty of the Government to improve Native institutions as well as to uphold them. It is possible. . . to domestic[ate] primitive law: you can redeem it from barbarism without killing it down."[54] So said Dalhousie in 1849, and the thought reappears persistently in late-nineteenth-century discussions of customary law in Punjab. It expresses the inner tension between the two contrary impulses which lie behind colonial projects: the will to preserve versus the will to transform indigenous custom and tradition. In the 1840s the terms of this debate were defined by the conservative paternalists, with their romantic concern for village institutions, and the Liberals and Benthamite Utilitarians, with their programme of radical modernist reform. Dalhousie sought to reconcile this opposition. But the reconciliation was not easy. How could traditional institutions and customs be upheld yet improved, redeemed without being killed? How could the Enlightenment ideal of improvement be married to an anti-Enlightenment love of tradition? Such questions continued to frame discussions on customary law in Punjab. Officials continued

[54] No. 418, 31 March 1849, H.M. Elliot, Secretary to GOI, to H.M. Lawrence, C.G. Mansel, and J. Lawrence, *PCL*, vol. I, p. 50.

to grapple with the problem of specifying the nature of the colonial project and the functions and limits of state intervention. The contrary pulls noted in the discussion on rights earlier were rearticulated in a different way within the discourse of custom.

The texture of official conceptions varied. Within one tradition of English common law thinking the object of state intervention was to discover and record existing practices, not to transform them; to systematise but not invent. This language of conservation shaped the rhetoric of Punjab officials. Codification had to be an unprejudiced act based on objective observation, untainted by Western concepts and a priori ideas. Custom had to be presented and codified *as it was*, not *as it ought to be*. It was as if social practices were transparent, they could be seen without conceptual filters. And what was seen could be codified.

This strong demand for some pure objectivity was difficult to sustain. The argument for codification usually ended with a plea for systematisation according to some deliberate plan, a deliberate design guided by principle;[55] and the argument for uncorrupted observation inevitably slipped into a demand for *understanding and explanation*: "the better the people are understood, the better will they be governed. . . Fully to understand a people you must be able to explain its institutions as well as to recount them. . ."[56]

The function of the state was to make the natives aware of the inner coherence and underlying principles of their practices. The customs of the country, it was said, were "by no means mere chance growth," but were "founded on principles susceptible of ascertainment on enquiry and of statement as a fairly consistent whole."[57] These principles could be grasped through modern theories. Observed facts made sense only within such a framework of explanation. Tupper was convinced: "If the facts of rural life in the Punjab be continuously read in the light

[55] "Codification implies the Consolidation of existing law or custom," wrote Tupper. But it was useless to collect the material into a "shapeless mass". The material "must admit of systematic arrangement on a definite plan . . . There must be a deliberate design, and its execution must be guided by principle." Tupper, "On the Codification of Customary Law", *PCL*, vol. I, pp. 15–16.

[56] Tupper, "Some Punjab Survivals", *PCL*, vol. II, p. 98.

[57] Tupper, "Memorandum on Customary Law", *PCL*, vol. I, p. 21.

of modern ideas regarding the origin and progress of society, there is, I think no doubt that their explanation will rapidly proceed."[58] Once the essential principles were understood, ambiguities and confusions could be ironed out and the real practices systematised into codified rules.

The search for this inner principle of customary ordering of society led colonial officials into the hazy history of immemorial custom. Drawing from the writings of English common law theorists and nineteenth-century evolutionist anthropologists, as we have seen, Tupper outlined a general theory of the evolution of Punjab society which he then used to order the evidence on custom.[59] Let me recount the core argument of this evolutionary theory.[60] Tupper suggested that the clan originates in the tribe, the village in the clan, and the joint family in the village (tribe—clan—village—joint family). Once the village is established, property rights pass from joint ownership by all members of the community towards individual ownership. First, a jointly owned village is divided into several tarafs held by coparceners, each group constituting a section of the community; then each share, each taraf, held by the coparceners is further divided into individual plots according to ancestral shares; subsequently the extent of individual ownership changes and begins to deviate from the ancestral customary share; so shares are disused and in course of time forgotten. Underlying the theory is the presupposition of an ever-increasing specialisation within society and a general order of progress from collective to individual property."[61]

Proceeding from such a deductive theory, interrogation only reconfirmed the validity of its initial assumptions. The theory was supposed to provide the only means of ordering an otherwise bewildering mass

[58] Ibid.

[59] See ch. 3 above.

[60] See ch. 3, above, for a discussion of the evolutionary frame of Tupper's thinking.

[61] "The tribe is broken up into different clans, the clans into villages, the villages into lots, the lots into family holdings. The group once simple and homogeneous, becomes complex and diversified. Broadly the theory may be deduced from the general law of evolution." Tupper, "The Village and Severalty", PCL, vol. II, p. 54.

of evidence into a meaningful pattern. The perceived coherence of customary law was thus pre-given. Evidence which did not conform to the expectation of theory was explained in a number of ways. First, a distinction was made between the "norm" and the "exception". All that could not be theoretically accounted for as the "norm" was conveniently accommodated within a spacious term – "exception". Second, a difference was made between the general and the particular. Theory could refer only to general characteristics. Local forms of customs were bound to vary. But within these local forms, the operation of the general principle could still be discerned. Finally, Tupper's theory sought to distinguish between those customs that had the authority of "antiquity" and those which were "innovations" and "novelties". Since each specific social practice conformed to a particular stage of society, it was possible to judge whether a set of rules was logically linked to a particular stage or was a meaningless "survival" from the past.[62] Customs which were in accordance with and tended to conserve the older forms of society were seen to possess immemorial antiquity and had to be preserved. [63] Later innovations which tended to dissolve the original tribal form, premised upon patriarchal lineage and agnatic filiation, had to be repressed as alien intrusions.

This self-image of the officials as codifiers of immemorial custom can be distinguished from their self-image as preservers of a disappearing tradition. Customs, they felt, were changing, and traditions were collapsing, inevitably, naturally. This was an inexorable process, the logic of history. Without enlightened intervention the rot could not be stemmed. Standing amongst the ruins of tradition, the noble Englishman had to salvage the past. Codification could help

[62] Tupper, "The Characteristics of Tribal and Village Custom", *PCL*, vol. II, p. 78.

[63] So it could be said: "The rule whatever it be, that tends to preserve tribal cohesion, community of interest in the village, and the integrity of the family, must if the theory of progress from communal to several rights be sound, always have the weight of past practice in its favour, its converse is by the hypothesis, a novelty; it may be a novelty of long standing, but still an innovation on an older state of things." Tupper, *PCL*, vol. II, p. 78.

preserve the authenticity of tradition, allow officials and judges to spot any attempt at innovation, whether by officials or by the people themselves. And through a theoretical understanding of the inner coherence of practices, the founding practices could be differentiated from "intrusions" which corrupted their original form.

Many colonial officials, however, were troubled by a radical self-doubt. Could the colonial state carry through its project of preservation? Could it really see with clarity a fleeting reality and fix its meaning with any certainty? Could it resist the imprint of a new time into an immemorial structure? In 1873 Tupper was talking of preserving custom against "distortions" through judicial reform.[64] By 1875 he was emphasising the transitional character of Punjab customs and the "impossibility of re-constituting the form it bore immediately before annexation".[65] His voice now carries notes of despair:

> with all the will in the world to preserve amid the transmutation in progress, as much Punjab custom as we can, we must admit that the outline and local colouring, as they existed before the British, cannot be wholly restored. Some portion of the outline, enough of the colouring, we may yet save to show in the new combinations which are appearing, that . . . sufficient account has been taken of the traditions of localities and the peculiar practices of tribes; for more than this it seems vain to hope.[66]

Even this much was difficult to achieve: "What are we, as judicial officers, to do when customs are fading and changing. . . How are we to give to the fleeting forms of custom, as allegedly before us, that precision of outline which would wear a sufficiently definite look under the scrutiny of the courts of appeal? We try to photograph a dissolving view with a bad camera, and no wonder the result is rather blurred."[67] Beneath the audible voice of the preserver was the hidden transcript of the Utilitarian reformer. The aggressive authori-

---

[64] Tupper, "Memorandum on the Means of Ascertaining the Customary Law of Punjab", 2 June 1873, *PCL*, vol. I, pp. 158–74.

[65] Memorandum by Tupper, 2 June 1875, *PCL*, vol. I, p. 207.

[66] Ibid., p. 208.

[67] Ibid.

tarian Benthamite tone of Dalhousie was missing in the discourse of customary law after the 1860s. But the Benthamite spirit did express itself in mellow undertones, in hesitant and surreptitious ways. Officials admitted that it was important for the state to consider "very carefully not merely what the law is but what it ought to be".[68] Tupper, with all his talk of preserving immemorial custom, could still argue that "it is not absolutely unmodified Native usages which are to be upheld, irrespective of their social and political effect, simply because they have existed. We are to maintain native institutions; but the British system must be, and has been, introduced."[69]

Yet the common law mind could not easily accommodate a reforming project. It argued for change, but it cast its argument for reform in the language of continuity. Wilson said, for instance, that customs have always changed, slowly and imperceptibly. Tribal leaders were always devising new solutions to new problems and redefining practices, even while acting according to the spirit of custom.[70] By appropriating the right to reorder custom the British were in fact acting according to tradition. Past practice sanctioned present intervention.

Tradition, Reason, and Time

According to the Punjab Regulation Act (Section 5 of Act IV of 1872), in order to be valid custom had to be "reasonable, continuous, not against public policy or equity, justice and good conscience and not void."[71] This statement reveals the diverse ways in which Punjab officials sought to define the validity of custom. These conflicting

[68] Tupper, Introduction, *PCL*, vol. I, p. 13.

[69] Ibid., p. 11.

[70] Just as common lawyers in England continuously modify custom in accordance with its essential spirit, wrote Wilson, "so the leaders of a tribe are ready, without hesitation, to extend their tribal custom, and to decide in accordance with its principles any new question that comes before them." Wilson, *General Code of Tribal Custom in Sirsa*, pp. 33–4.

[71] For a discussion, see "Memorandum on the Customary Law in the Punjab" by C. Boulnois, Judge, Chief Court, Punjab, 28 November 1872, *PCL*, vol. I, p. 144.

modes of legitimation were implicated in a set of contradictory discourses.

First, there is the obvious opposition between the authority of tradition and the authority of reason. If continuity is the basis of validity, tradition appears self-justifying. Then the validity of a custom lies in the fact that it has been in long use, from time immemorial; it has been an intrinsic part of collective life, a basis of social ordering, an expression of social unity. It is not to be judged through any external criteria of transcendent, universal reason. But the reference to the reasonability of custom and to notions of "equity, justice and good conscience" shifts the grounds of validation. Enlightenment Reason is brought in to judge the validity of tradition and custom. Traditions which violate the principles of justice, equity, and good conscience are unreasonable and hence invalid. Here tradition is not only represented in the language of reason but is appropriated through a framework of Utilitarian, liberal, modernist thought.

But the opposition between tradition and reason is often negotiated in subtler ways within the official discourse of customary law. Village elders were seen as custodians not only of tradition but of "village wisdom": they were aware of the general principles through which social life was to be ordered. Wilson says: "the tribesmen among themselves decide any new case that may arise in accordance with the principles underlying the whole body of their tribal custom, and find no difficulty in applying these principles, though unconsciously, to altogether new sets of circumstances. . ."[72] Custom expressed a collective sense of what was reasonable, just, and fair – of what was seen as the collective good. The persistence and continuity of a custom, its temporal depth, reveal the intrinsic reasonableness of the general principles. Customs develop over time through a process of collective reasoning. Through practice, norms become part of the common sense of a time; and the dispositions shaped in the process define what counts as reasonable. Actions which conform to this sense are therefore reasonable. Reason in such an argument refers not to a unitary concept with a fixed natural Enlightenment essence, but

[72] Wilson, *General Code of Tribal Custom in Sirsa*, p. 33.

to a tradition-shaped sense of reasonableness. The argument of tradition is cast in the language of reason, without being subordinated to it.

All these alternative conceptions of reason were at play in the act of codification and adjudication of customary law. They were the basis of conflicting interpretations of custom and popular questionings of the codified law.

Linked to these differing notions of reason and tradition were shades of difference on conceptions of time. The discourse of custom tended to present custom as timeless, as immemorial. The validity of custom lay in its continuity over time. But how was one to define the pastness of the past, the temporal depth of immemorial custom? Some officials saw the origins of practices as lost in the mists of immeasurable time. It was impossible to specify with certitude the antiquity of a particular practice.[73] If customs are presumed to be timeless and unchanging, then present practice was itself evidence of the antiquity of custom. But in general the time of memory was considered the necessary temporal depth of valid custom: "a custom, to have the force of law, must have existed as long as the memory of the tribe extends, i.e. the memory at least of its oldest members. . ."[74] The memory of the elders, their oral evidence on the practices of the tribe, was therefore important.

Many officials, as we have seen, recognised that customs were not frozen in time. "On all sides transition is in progress," wrote Tupper. In every district "the original social combinations of tribe, clan and village will be found in varying stages of reconstitution."[75]

[73] "There is in this province no rule of law, which prescribes any period during which a custom in order to be valid and enforceable must have been observed. It is sufficient to show that the custom actually prevails and is generally observed in the tribe to which the parties belong and there is no necessity to go further and attempt to prove the impossible, viz. that it has been preserved in the tribe from a period to which the memory of man runneth not to the contrary, the test being the uniformity of practice." *PR*, no. 34 of 1907, p. 151.

[74] Wilkinson, *PR*, 1875, p. 3.

[75] Tupper, *PCL*, vol. II, p. 77.

Customs changed alongside these mutations in the social forms of society. But these changes could not be publicly recognised within the discourse of "immemorial custom"; for this would be to admit a rupture, a discontinuity in time. Since continuity was the basis of authority, temporal breaks were misrecognised in a variety of ways. First: the rule of precedents helped to mask changes. People could always pretend that rules were not new, or that they were implicit in existing norms.[76] Through judicial fictions, a continuity of practices was traced, innovations were hidden. Time transformed was presented as time immemorial, time that knew no rupture. In this conception the collective belief in the continuity of practices was crucial to the myth of immemorial custom, not the actual empirical facts of their immutability. Punjab officials searched for a space within this process of collective myth-making in which they could insert themselves. Through the language of immemorial custom and the rule of precedents, they sought to establish the temporal continuity of their codified laws with the practices of the past.

Second: when precedents were difficult to unearth, the argument of continuity was sustained in other ways. Elders, we are told, knew the spirit which informed customs, the "unthought" which lay within the tradition even though they could not spell out its inner principles. Elders, it was said, confronted new situations and devised new norms but conformed to the general spirit of the tradition. While particular practices changed, the general principles of social order were maintained. In this argument, a reference to precedents was neither an adequate nor a necessary guide to action. Concrete practices of the past were not as important as the *spirit* behind the practices. This sort of common law theory informs Wilson's discussion of the customary law of Sirsa:

> In English common law, by a fiction the judges are supposed to decide each case as it comes up strictly in accordance with precedent, and yet every new decision forms a new precedent, and so modifies the law – in fact, the judges decide each new case which comes before them rather

[76] "When people want a rule they pretend the rule has always existed." Memorandum by Tupper, 2 June 1875, *PCL*, vol. I, p. 205.

in accordance with the principles that underlie precedents than strictly according to any particular set of precedents...

Often when I have put a question to the assembled headmen [in Sirsa] regarding their custom on some particular point, and received an unhesitating answer, a call for instances and precedent has, after much racking of brains, elicited the unanimous reply, "we never heard of such a case, but our custom is as we have said." They were unconsciously deciding the new set of circumstances in accordance with general principles of their custom, familiar to the minds of all.[77]

Wilson felt that the British could intervene in a similar tradition-shaped way to reorder society and maintain the spirit and continuity of customary practices. Again, in this view temporal breaks in custom were denied and time was presented as a continuum.

Custom and Power

The process of codification restructured rural power relations and was also shaped by those relations. The enquiry into custom opened up a space for negotiation and conflict over the truth of practice. If the answers of village elders were framed and directed by the questions they were asked, their perspectives were also inscribed in the records of customary law which were prepared.

Codification of customary law, once again, consolidated the coparcenary community. As we have seen, officials shared a set of assumptions about the relationship between blood and soil. The rights to soil, it was believed, were defined by relationships of blood. Descendants of the original founder of the village constituted the coparcenary proprietary body: they had the first claim to land. Those who failed to assert such a mythical ancestry could not be members of the brotherhood. Records of rights prepared on the basis of such an assumption, as we have noted, inevitably repressed the rights of all those who did not belong to the dominant lineage.

In courts, the claims of lower castes and "non-agricultural" communities to property rights in land were routinely denied. Officials also sought to regulate transfers of land through the assumptions of

[77] Wilson, *General Code of Tribal Custom in Sirsa*, pp. 33–4.

agnatic theory. The myth of common ancestry defined the membership of the coparcenary body and the rights to land, but it also
limited these rights. Since the proprietors held land as co-sharers, they
were not to sell to outsiders. Land had to be held by, and preserved
within, the community of co-sharers – the brotherhood. When land
was up for sale, co-sharers had the first right of purchase, a right of
pre-emption. Judges who mediated conflicts over custom argued from
these assumptions. And their judgments, flowing from theoretical
premises, were recognised as learned observations on practice, and
came to define practice. Consider the famous judgment of 1887 on
the rights of a proprietor to alienate land:

> The land came to him as a member of a village community which at no
> distant period held the whole of their land jointly, recognising in the
> individual members only a right of usufruct, that is a right to enjoy the
> profits of the portion of the common land actually cultivated by him
> and his family, and to share in those of the portion[s] still under joint
> management. In such a community, the proprietary title and the power
> of permanently alienating parts of the common property is vested in
> the whole body. These communities of villages in their turn spring from
> a still more primitive state of society in which the proprietary unit was
> the tribe. . . . It is not unreasonable to presume that the absence of lineal
> male heirs does not confer on a proprietor privileges greatly in excess of
> those enjoyed by his fellows. It should only be natural, that, in such a
> case, the next male collateral . . . shall take the place of the lineal heirs,
> and that his consent to the alienation of land, which by the customary
> rules of inheritance would have descended to him, should also be
> necessary.[78]

This judgment set the pattern for subsequent ones. A picture,
clearly deduced from evolutionary anthropology, is presented here as
an observation of existing reality. The language of judicial discourse
continuously slips from the deductive to the inductive, from the "fictive" to the "real", transcending such oppositions and intermeshing
them inseparably. The imagined reality of the coparcenary community
became part of official and judicial common sense and imposed its

[78] *PR* no. 107 of 1887.

own specific order into the rural world of customary practices.[79] The boundaries of the proprietary community were sharply demarcated, the entry of "outsiders" into it legally restricted. The logic of the argument led to the Land Alienation Act of 1900, when communities classified as "non-agriculturists" were barred entry into the rural land market.

The colonial regime of customary law thus sharpened the opposition between outsiders and insiders, "agriculturists" and "non-agriculturists", the proprietary body and the "lower" castes.[80] This opposition was written into the very definition of customary law, which was applicable only to agriculturists; non-agriculturists were governed by personal law. The argument was that agricultural groups had a tribal past and retained a tribal constitution with all its customary principles, whereas non-agriculturists had no tribal origin and hence no customary law. Even when the existing practices of different groups were similar, they could not be governed by the same customary law. Differences between groups were deepened by narrativising their histories in dissimilar ways. The authenticity of the present was denied by attributing a greater significance to the assumed divergence of past origin.

The process of the codification of custom, as we shall see, also reordered the world of women.[81] Agnatic theory could recognise no rights for women. Patrilineal male inheritance was officially seen as a "natural order of succession": daughters could not succeed, nor could a daughter's or a sister's son. A widow with a male child could not inherit, and one without a child had a life interest: after her death the land reverted to the control of the husband's family, her cognates had no claim. Adoption by a proprietor lacking a biological male heir was necessary to retain community control over land, but adoption had to be from within the male agnates, the co-sharers within the village. Since women could not own land, they could neither sell nor

[79] Justice Plowden observed: "I think we are justified in stating, as a principle consonant with facts, that the mere circumstance that immovable property is ancestral raises a presumption that the individual in possession as owner had not unrestricted power of disposition." Ibid.

[80] See ch. 7 below.

[81] Ibid.

mortgage it. The volumes on customary law for the various districts of Punjab recorded the existence of these customs with the expected monotony.[82]

The structure of customs, derived from the framework of theory, was reaffirmed through a dialogue with informants. Village elders were invariably proprietors speaking at a time when open fields were disappearing behind the expanding agrarian frontier, and when land was becoming scarce and valuable. The village body closed in on itself, strengthened its boundaries, resisted competition, and sought to consolidate control over land. The village elders and lambardars who collected to give evidence on custom agreed over time on an exclusionist policy. Did the "lower" castes and "outsiders" have a right to land? In the initial enquiries answers to such questions were ambivalent. But in the later enquiries the rights of "outsiders" were unambiguously denied. The "outsider", as a category, crystallised in the process.[83]

The customs recorded were male constructs. As many officials and judges recognised, the riwaj-i-am was a document "prepared at the dictates of males only", and was particularly unreliable on questions of women's succession.[84] As the demand for land increased and prices soared, landholders became "more and more anxious to exclude female succession" and were "ready to state the rule against daughters as strongly as possible".[85] Women found it increasingly difficult to come forward to assert their rights.

[82] There were, of course, exceptions. Some volumes of customary law are insightful and record contestatory evidence that allows us to question the dominant picture. See, in particular, the excellent customary law volumes of Sirsa, Ludhiana, Multan, and Gurgaon. On changing rights of women in colonial Punjab, see Chowdhry, *The Veiled Women*; Gilmartin, "Kinship, Women and Politics in Twentieth-Century Punjab"; Oldenburg, *Dowry Murder*. For discussions beyond Punjab, see Sarkar, *Hindu Wife, Hindu Nation*; Arunima, *There Comes Papa*; Majumdar, *Marriage and Modernity*; Sturman, *The Government of Social Life in Colonial India*. For a macro *longue durée* perspective, see Agarwal, *A Field of One's Own*.

[83] See ch. 7 below.

[84] Kureshi, *The Punjab Customs*, p. 43.

[85] *PR* 1908, p. 86. Such observations are repeatedly made in the judicial records. "The record before us shows that the male relations, in many cases

In short, the discourse on custom reveals a dialogue between masters and natives. The native voice was inscribed within imperial discourse, but it was constrained, regulated, and ultimately appropriated. This was a male, patriarchal voice, the voice of the dominant proprietary body, opposed to the rights of non-proprietors, females, and "lower" castes.

At the beginning of British rule rights were ambiguous and practices fluid. In a situation of land abundance, villagers wanted additional hands to work the land and pay the revenue. In practice, non-agriculturists held land, and so did women. As we shall see, there is extensive evidence of a daughter's husband and sons inheriting. Both the agnatic and cognatic principles operated at different levels, and in complicated ways. This complexity could not be accommodated within the dominant official theory, and ambiguities had to be ironed out into coherent, rational codes. Once a "natural order" was defined, conflicting evidence was classed as anomalous.

Naturally, though, the official discourse was not monologic: the dominant voice could not repress all others. Through the cracks opened up by contestation, evidence of alternative practices becomes visible.[86]

The Discourse on Custom

The argument against Anglo-Indian law is often premised upon the assumption that the British ignored customary practices and based their law on an amalgam of sastric learning and Western legal tradition. The gap between custom and law widened when scriptures were privileged within colonial discourse as the source of authentic

---

at least, have been clearly more concerned for their own advantage than for the security of the rights of the widows and other female relatives with rights, or alleged rights . . ." *PLR*, 1901, p. 466. Another judge reflected on the general politics of representation: "Such evidence, in defeasement of the rights of females, recalls to one's mind the remarks attributed in the fable to a tiger when he was shown the picture of a tiger running away from an old woman: 'If a tiger had painted the picture, he would be eating the woman'." *PR* no. 11 of 1901, p. 79. See ch. 7 below.

[86] See ch. 7 below.

tradition.[87] I suggest that the colonial relationship with native tradition was more complex, ambiguous, and varied – spatially and temporally. If, in late-eighteenth-century Bengal, scriptures were seen as synonymous with tradition, in Punjab a century later custom was pitted against sacred texts. But this did not make colonial law any closer to "tradition", it did not preserve the practices of the community uncontaminated. Understanding and codifying custom was as problematic as translating and interpreting ancient texts. Both, in different ways, subjected tradition to transformative processes.

Codification, one could say, hybridised custom: it appropriated indigenous custom through Western categories and mixed heterogeneous traditions. But the concept of the hybrid is both productive as well as problematic, for it suggests an amalgamation of pure essences, hybridity being premised on the notion of something originally pure. The concept seeks to transcend essentialism, only to rehabilitate it.[88]

Tupper, in despair, spoke of the bad camera through which officials took blurred shots. There are two obvious problems with this statement. No camera, we know, can ever capture reality untransformed: the point of focus and the depth of field define the nature of the pictures produced. And is there ever only one camera, one lens, one filter through which the world can be viewed? Different officials, as we have seen, looking through different lenses, saw different

[87] Derrett argues that British intervention fossilised sastric learning, perverted the meaning of texts, and created a "great chasm between custom and law". He feels that Anglo-Indian law would have created fewer problems if it took cognisance of customary practices. Derrett, "The Administration of Hindu Law by the British". Mani suggests that the marginalisation of custom and the sanctity accorded to scriptures defined, in fact, the specificity of colonial discourse. Mani shows with great effect that the entire debate on the abolition of sati was structured within the terms of this discourse: while Liberals pointed to the absence of scriptural sanction for sati, Conservatives produced a scriptural defence of the ritual. Mani, *Contentious Traditions*. In such arguments the specificities of one form of colonial thinking and discourse tend to be projected as a general feature of colonial India. Imperial officials were very well aware of customary practices, but their understandings had their own specific structures.

[88] On hybridity, see Bhabha, *Location of Culture*; Hall, "When was 'the Postcolonial'?", pp. 242–60; Gilroy, *The Black Atlantic*.

realities, interpreted custom in dissimilar ways. Native tradition was not appropriated through any fixed frame of Orientalist discourse which had crystallised and congealed in the West. This frame was not only fractured, it was continuously reconstituted. So we need to look not only at the multiple discourses of tradition and modernity but also at the ways in which the elements of different traditions were incessantly recombined into new forms, new languages of power and domination.

The discourse on custom was not just a textual process, nor simply the fruit of official imagination structured by Western thought. The nature of the dialogues with local informants was crucial to the re-making of custom. While the utterances of the informants were often directed and overwritten by the officials, the natives did not merely cast their answers in the frames provided by imperial officials. They sought to express their perception of tradition and resisted imperial interpretations; they reacted to changing social contexts – to the scarcity of land and its increasing value, the pressure of population, the consolidation of rural power – and then felt the need to redefine customary practices. Etched in the codes which were produced was the patriarchal voice of property-owning elites, a voice neither directly inherited nor entirely borrowed but creatively produced through varied dialogues.

Not all the native voices could be easily accommodated within the imperial discourse on customary law, not all the evidence was always recognised. Codification was also a process of silencing and erasure. Imperial officials defined the terms of validity of custom and the criteria of reasonability and equity; they distinguished between the norm and the exception, between antiquated and living practices. Through their classificatory practices they sought to repress troubling evidence and fix the meanings of customs in the act of encoding them.

But can custom be so easily frozen? Do codes have the power to reorder practices unhindered? Are traditions and customary practices so malleable as to succumb to the transforming power of a codifying state? The common argument that customs are frozen through codi-fication is premised on a simple contrast between the oral and the textual. The oral tradition is seen as fluid, open to a variety of inter-pretations and meanings, a range of appropriations according to the contexts. When the oral tradition is textualised the fluidity disappears, meanings are fixed: put into writing, they become frozen into codes. We now understand that this opposition is problematic. Texts too can convey a variety of meanings; and new meanings are continuously inscribed onto texts in the process of interpretation and elaboration. Codes, like all texts, are open to multiple readings, and the same code can produce different judgments. Codification may seek to fix the meanings of practices, but the original intentions do not always materialise in the same ways. Judicial records reveal how codes were read in conflicting ways, questioned and rewritten. The search for certainty and fixity remained elusive.

Codification does shift the terrain on which conflicts over meaning are played out. While customs remained uncodified, they were embodied in the collective knowledge of the community, remaining as the preserve of the community, interpreted and recorded within the community through its institutions. It remained, at that stage, a process through which the power relations between different castes, sexes, and generations were worked out. Under the colonial regime of codes, the institutions of the state appropriated the right to interpret and rewrite custom. The custom of the community was to be decided by courts; conflicts over understanding were to be resolved through the mediation of courts.

There were, however, limits to the reach of the state. Beneath the regime of codes was the reality of uncodified practices. Inheritance rules, the rights of women, and the norms of marriage did not all change with codification. Rules were violated, norms were publicly flouted, and alternative practices persisted. The official mind could not close itself to the pressure of this subversion. Colonial officials could not continue living in a world of imagined reality, ignorant of native understanding and practice. Subversion and contestation did not simply constitute a private transcript which remained hidden behind the public transcript – a code to which people submitted.[89] The private transcript persistently asserted its presence in public

[89] Scott's major work on hegemony and resistance introduces the useful distinction between the public and the private transcript, but inflates the separation between the two. See Scott, *Domination and the Arts of Resistance.*

spaces, the language and understanding of the rulers felt the strain of contest. Challenged in courts, codified customs were reinterpreted by judges; inundated with conflicting evidence, officials acknowledged the validity of customs unauthenticated by colonial codes.[90] In the process of this cultural confrontation, colonial structures and categories of representation were dislocated and refigured, while the public transcript imprinted itself onto the private in invisible ways.

[90] The codes themselves were continuously modified. Codification of Customary Law, Punjab Home (Judicial), Feb. 1916, A 6–44; Report on the Conference on the Codification of Customary Law, Punjab Home (Judicial), August 1916, A 40–46.

6

Remembered Pasts

Allah mere bar basai	My God peopled the desert.
Char khunt-thon khalkat ai	People came from all quarters
Lambardaran kol bahai	The lambardars settled them beside themselves
Nal pyar de bhuen kadhai	And persuaded them to break up land.
Hun jan de din iman khuhai	They have now lost their good faith
Samidar te arji lai	And brought claims against their partners.
Hakim us di bhuen khuhai	The ruler has taken away their land.
Is kanun di khabar na kai	We knew nothing of this law
Jihra kita hun Sarkar	That the Sarkar has now put in force.
Bedakhli karni nahin darkar	Dispossession is not necessary.

JAMES WILSON, CARRYING OUT the settlement of Sirsa district in the 1870s, heard a poem sung by a peasant poet, Lalu of Dabwali Dhab. Wilson ensured that the poem was carefully recorded and reproduced in an appendix to his settlement report.[1] Writing about the rights of the peasants in the text of the report, he quoted Lalu extensively to substantiate his own argument. The poet's voice authenticated Wilson's.

This seems to pose a paradox, for Lalu's poem is a trenchant critique of the British regime of rights. Powerful and persuasive, it returns to the past to reflect upon the present, censures British laws and the new definitions of rights, and the displacements caused by the new legal structure. For Lalu the present is evil, an abnormal time when strange things happen.

---

[1] Wilson, *Sirsa S.R., 1879–83*, Appendix II.

How are we to look at the poet's words? Or Wilson's appropriation of those words? What can Lalu tell us of peasants' reactions to the colonial regime of rights, of their experience of the violence and pain of colonialism, their notion of the normal and abnormal? What can Wilson tell us about the paradoxes of colonial policies?

Dabwali Dhab

Lalu lived in Dabwali Dhab, a small village in the district of Sirsa. Lying just north of the Bikaner desert, this part of the country was uncultivated scrubland in the early nineteenth century – a parched sandy stretch with scanty rainfall and regular droughts.[2] Here, wells had to be dug to 180 feet to touch water, and tanks ran dry in the blazing summer heat.[3] Travellers on camels carried water in skin bags. Of the 658 villages that could be counted in the 1880s, only 35 had a history going back to the beginning of the century,[4] and of these most were located in the valley of the River Ghaggar – known as the Nali or Sotar. Peasant settlements, as always, began in the river valley and spread outwards.

Dominated by nomadic Bhatti herders, this pastoral tract resisted the frontier expansion of agrarian colonists. The Bhattis had many of their villages in the Ghaggar valley but moved with their cattle over the vast upland prairie that lay between the Ghaggar and Sutlej – locally known as the jangal or rohi. Peasant cultivators daring to settle in this seemingly inhospitable landscape had to survive the raids of pastoral

[2] Even in the twentieth century the tract was described as sandy and arid. With precarious rainfall and less than 5 per cent of the cultivated area under irrigation, it continued to produce only one crop a year. *Sirsa A.R.*, 1925, RFCO 92/44/112.

[3] From J.H. Oliver, Deputy Commissioner Sirsa, to the Commissioner and Superintendent Hissar Division, no. 102, Sirsa, 14 April 1863, *CRSS*; Wilson, *Sirsa S.R., 1879–83*, pp. 6–7. In the tract near the River Sutlej, water could be found within 40 feet, but the depth of the water level increased as one moved south-east away from the river. Near Dabwali it was 160 feet and in some villages more than 200 feet.

[4] On the history of immigration into Gudah taluqa where Dabwali was located, see J.H. Oliver, Deputy Commissioner Sirsa, to the Commissioner and Superintendent Hissar Division, no. 102, Sirsa, 14 April 1863, *CRSS*.

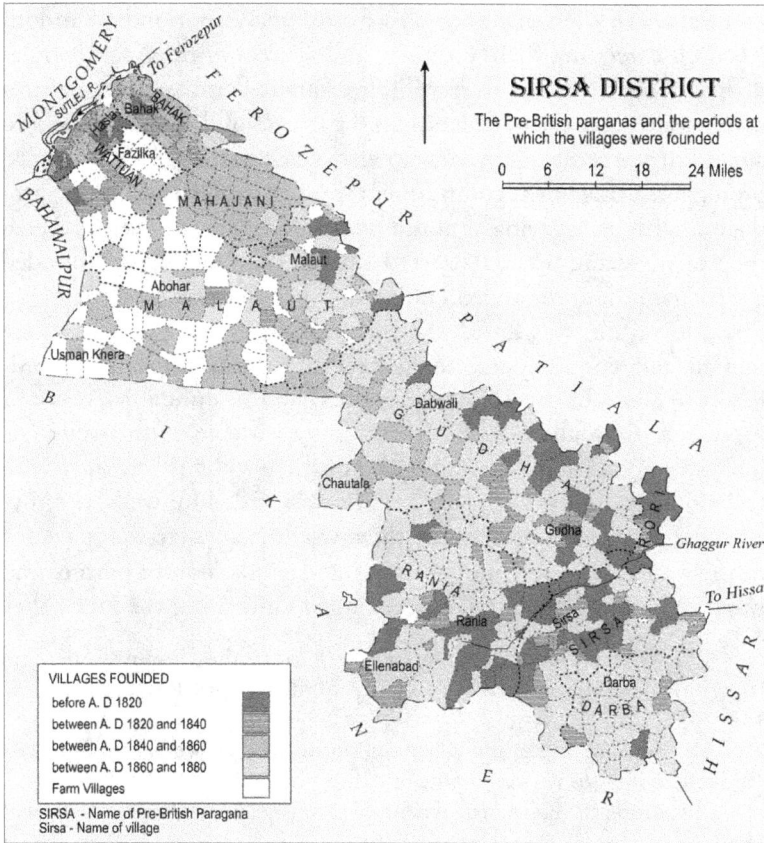

Fig. 12: Chronology of Village Settlement in Sirsa.
Source: Based on a map produced during the settlement operations of
the 1880s.

The earliest settlements came up on both sides of the River Ghaggar. Most
villages were established after the 1820s.

Bhattis who saw the region as *their* territory, *their* grazing ground. Yet
since the late eighteenth century peasants from neighbouring states
had been moving into the area, clearing scrub, breaking up land,
and settling villages.[5] They came mostly from Bikaner in the south

[5] See Papers (MS) Relating to the Settlement of Hissar District, Commissioner's Office to Financial Commissioner, Punjab, 23 April 1863, April
1864.

and Patiala in the north, but also from Bahawalpur and Mamdot.[6] Keen on extending their authority and sources of revenue, the rajas of neighbouring states were willing to grant permission to pioneer colonists to settle the open lands on the fringes of their territories.[7] To all authorised settlers – those who were given pattas – they promised protection against their commitment to pay a certain share of the produce as nazrana.[8] Having obtained permission, the colonisers gathered their relatives and friends, selected a site in the open prairie, founded a settlement, and expanded cultivation. For the early settlers, life in this arid terrain was hard. The brackish water, sandy soil, meagre rainfall, and scorching summer heat meant that nothing but the hardiest crop could be grown and no more than one annual harvest ever produced. Rainfall could be frustratingly variable, with twenty-six inches one year and five inches the next.[9] Droughts returned with tenacious regularity, burnt the prairie grass, dried up wells, destroyed settlements, and re-deserted the area, forcing migrants to return to their villages of origin or simply wander in search of pasture and water.[10] Settlers who survived continued cultivating the lands they

[6] J.H. Oliver, Deputy Commissioner Sirsa, to the Commissioner and Superintendent Hissar Division, No. 102, Sirsa, 14 April 1863, *CRSS*, paras 134–54.

[7] On the founding of the villages in north Bikaner, see Fagan, *Report on the Settlement of the Khalsa Villages of Bikaner State*, 1893, paras 13ff.

[8] "Report on the Position of Tenants in Sirsa" by James Wilson, 15 October 1880, GOI, Rev. & Agr. (Rev.), A 5–6; "Landlord and Tenant Relations in Sirsa District", GOI, Rev. and Agr. (Rev.), May 1882, A 4–6; Wilson, *Sirsa S.R.*, ch. V: "The Growth of Rights".

[9] Wilson, *Sirsa S.R.*, 1879–83, paras 9–10; "Report on the Position of Tenants in Sirsa" by James Wilson, 15 October 1880, GOI, Rev. & Agr. (Rev.), A 5–6. For details of annual rainfall, see statistical statements in *Report on the Season and Crops of the Punjab*, annual volumes, *RLRAP*, annual volumes.

[10] Towards the end of the eighteenth century came the severe chalisa famine of 1783–4. Through the nineteenth century, famines returned with painful regularity every four to eight years, ending with two devastating famines in the closing decade of the century. A chronology of the major famines in the region would include the following: 1803–4, 1812–13, 1817–18, 1824–5, 1833–4, 1837–8, 1843–4, 1850–1, 1860–1, 1868–9, 1877–8, 1888–9, 1896–7, 1899–1900. Wilson, *Sirsa S.R., 1879–83*; GOI, Home Rev. & Agr.

had cleared for as long as they paid the government its dues and performed their share of village duties and obligations.

The Ghaggar valley, where most of the early settlements were located, came under British control in 1818. But the great dry tract that
stretched from this valley to that of the Sutlej further to the north-west
was acquired from the Sikh chiefs only in 1837. Despite the extension of the arable, only about 7 per cent of this area was cultivated
even in 1841. The British, inspired by the vision of agrarian conquest
and committed to the project of sedentarisation, were keen to encourage further colonisation of the "wastes". For this the settlement process
had to be initiated immediately, land rights fixed, revenue burdens
determined, and fiscal obligations defined. Within a year after the
acquisition of the dry tract that later came to constitute Sirsa – at
the time a part of the North West Provinces – there was a summary
settlement in 1838; and in 1852 Thomason, the lieutenant governor
of the North West Provinces, emphasised the urgency of a regular
settlement.[11] Determination of land rights could not await a detailed
enquiry into and understanding of their specific local history.

Looking into peasant rights through the framing categories of
colonial discourse, settlement officials searched for landlords and
tenants. Who was the proprietor in a region where peasants had collectively cleared the forests and made the soil yield, together experi-
encing the joy and pain of settling new land? Intent on differentiating
rights, separating the superior from the inferior, and classifying each

---

(Famine), December 1888, A 12; GOI, Home Rev. & Agr. (Famine), April
1898, A 30–7. Between 1903 and 1921, seven years were abnormally dry;
Sirsa A.R., 1925, RFCO.

[11] On the Bhattiana survey, parganah Darbah, see no. 45, 31 May 1853,
Captain R. Robertson, Superintendent Bhattiana, to Sir Theo Metcalfe, Agent
and Commissioner, Delhi, *CRSS*; also no. 376, 19 August 1853, T. Metcalfe,
Agent and Commissioner Delhi, to the Sadr Board of Revenue, North Western
Provinces, *CRSS*; no. 1121, Agra, 12 October 1855, H.W. Hammond, Secre-
tary, Sadr Board of Revenue, N.W. Provinces, to the Secretary to Government,
N.W. Provinces; no. 353, Agra 19 October 1855, *CRSS*; J. Thomason,
Memorandum Regarding Bhuttee Territory, June 1852, GOI, Rev. & Agr.
(Rev.), June 1882, A 4–6.

individual, officials ended up declaring the headmen of colonising groups the proprietors. The whole area of the district was said to belong to the 5000 people designated owners, while the remaining 25,000 cultivators were classified as tenants with rights of occupancy.[12] Those classified as proprietors were given absolute rights over "forests and wastes". This forced differentiation of rights, entered in the settlement papers, came to signify the nature of the violence that flowed from colonial classificatory practices.

Yet the full meaning of this violence was not immediately understood. What did it imply in practice? Precisely what rights did proprietors have that occupancy tenants did not? How did classification mark a break with the past? Peasants were to learn about rights only through the pain of dispossession. Rights, in fact, were specified and concretised through a battle over meanings.

After the settlement, peasants continued to extend the limits of cultivation and reshape the pastoral landscape. The Bhattis, under pressure from a sedentarist state keen on settling a mobile population, could not resist the march of the arable. They shifted from the banks of the Ghaggar, where they had a few large villages, to the dry tract further west.[13] Pastures shrank as uncultivated lands were enclosed within areas that had been demarcated as villages, or allocated to colonists. The cultivated area of the district, 700,289 acres in 1852, swelled to 1,066,816 acres by 1880, an increase of over 50 per cent. New villages – over eighty of them – were established, even as cultivation expanded within the older villages.[14] Most of the land – over 70 per cent – was cleared by peasants who were categorised as non-proprietors in the settlement papers.[15]

---

[12] GOI, Rev. & Agr. (Rev.), July 1886, A 9.

[13] J.H. Oliver, Deputy Commissioner Sirsa, to the Commissioner and Superintendent Hissar Division, no. 102, Sirsa, 14 April 1863, pp. 42ff, paras 152–3, *CRSS*. The eastern part of the Ghaggar and Sotar valleys were taken from the Bhattis in 1818.

[14] Minute by C.U. Aitchison, Lt. Governor of Punjab, GOI, Rev. and Agr. (Rev.), August 1882; Punjab Rev. & Agr. (Gen.), November 1882, A 1/1347–50.

[15] GOI, Rev. & Agr. (Rev.), June 1882, A 4–6; Wilson, *Sirsa S.R., 1879–1883*.

When clearing the land, peasants expected a right over the soil: it was the custom of the countryside. He who cleared the soil cultivated the land, it was said. The 1852 settlement had, it is true, already declared lambardars as the proprietors, classifying other cultivators as occupancy tenants, but these occupancy tenants had not immediately lost the land they had cleared. Their rights had continued to seem undisturbed, their rents fixed. While the official change of 1852 had stated that the wastes now belonged to the lambardars, the tenants had no means of adequately knowing what this meant, for codified rights were read through the structure of past experience while expectations were nurtured by custom and tradition. Encouraged by the lambardars and the state, peasants had continued to extend cultivation. In the village papers, the patwari distinguished the rights registered in the khewat at the time of the first settlement from the nautor (the new land broken up since the 1852 settlement) held by each cultivator.[16] But to the cultivator who held both lands the distinction was as yet meaningless. Officials, in fact, found it impossible to actually demarcate the line that separated the two types of land.[17] The 1868 Tenancy Act, however, denied to tenants any secure rights on nautor, reaffirming occupancy rights only on khewat land. Returning to the declaration of the First Regular Settlement to the effect that lambardars were the sole proprietors of "wastes", the act granted lambardars proprietary rights over all newly reclaimed land. The dramatic implication of the colonial classificatory process since the 1850s became clear to peasants only when lambardars began dispossessing them of their holdings. Ejectment suits began in the early 1870s, and by the end of the decade nervous administrators began enquiries into the roots of the tenant–landlord struggle.[18]

Yet when the settlement revision proceedings began in the 1870s cultivators still expected a reconsideration of rights and recognition of their claims over lands they had cleared. When the lambardars,

[16] Wilson, *Sirsa S.R., 1879–1883*, p. 374.

[17] Ibid., pp. 374–5.

[18] See "Relations between Landlord and Tenant in North India", Punjab Rev. & Agr. (Gen.), November 1882, A 1/1347–50. See also Punjab Rev. & Agr. (Gen.), March 1882, 2/345.

hoping to further consolidate their position and apprehensive of the possible grant of occupancy rights (as against the rights of tenants at will) to the cultivators, began ejecting them *en masse*, the cultivators contested the suits against them. A trickle in the early 1870s, notices of ejectment had flooded the courts by the end of the decade. In 1870–1 there were 43 notices; by 1880–1 the number had shot up to 1031. Between 1875 and 1880 a total of 2748 notices were served, affecting an area of 51,600 acres.[19] The cultivators contested over 60 per cent of these suits, even when an increasing number were actually decided against them.[20]

The court now became a site for the specification of rights. Peasants began to grasp the meaning of a tenant's rights through the trauma of exile and the violence of the courts. Ejection was not simply something that affected their family earning and levels of economic well-being. It ruptured their relationship to the past, to their ancestors, to their sources of identity and conceptions of self. It upturned the moral world they took for granted and the ideals they valued.

The Remembered Past

If colonialism sought to reorder agrarian society through its own categories, reworking the meaning of customary social relations, peasants too returned to their pasts to judge the present and understand colonial social ordering. If colonial officials liked to see themselves as the preservers of custom, peasant accounts of the colonial present were saturated with the theme of lost rights, lost pasts. But to which past could the peasants return? For there is never any single past waiting to

[19] "Report on the Position of Tenants in Sirsa" by Wilson, 15 October 1880, Rev. & Agr. (Rev.), A 5–6; Punjab Rev. & Agr. (Rev.), September 1882, A 1/1017–18, pp. 439–52; Punjab Rev. & Agr. (Rev.), November 1882, A 3/1377.

[20] The proportion of cases decided in favour of tenants rapidly fell from 41 per cent in 1880–1 to 21 per cent in 1882–3. Wilson, *Sirsa S.R., 1879–1883*, p. 376. See "Working of the Punjab Tenancy Act in Punjab", Punjab Rev. & Agr. (Rev.), March 1874, A 23, pp. 224–78; "Working of the Punjab Tenancy Act in Sirsa", Punjab Rev. and Agr. (Rev.), October 1881, A 8, pp. 624–36; for further discussion, see Appendix to Punjab Rev. & Agr. (Rev.), October 1886, nos 10–13.

be recalled. The act of remembering, we know, is inevitably and always a figurative act through which the past is imagined in light of the present – a present that also acquires specific meaning in this process of discursive dialogue with the past. Lalu's critique of life under the Raj is built upon such an act of figuration. What is important then is to look at the politics of memory, the discourse of lost rights, not to recover an authentic world that existed in the past, not to determine the world as it *really* was in earlier times, prior to British rule, but to understand the nature of Lalu's representation of the past and the present, his understanding of the world and the premises of rights.

∼

The narrative structure of Lalu's poem develops through a series of contrasts between "then" and "now", what happened in "earlier times" and what was happening under the Raj. The past and present of the poem relate to each other as thesis and antithesis, opposing, contradicting, and negating each other. The move from the past to the present is represented as a fall, a tragedy. Everything of value, all that is authentic and natural, resides in the past. So the present, by negating the past, delegitimises itself; the past inauthenticates the present.

In these verses, the line which separates past from present is marked by the British institution of proprietary rights, experienced by the peasants as a cataclysmic event. From the point that the lambardars were recorded as sole proprietors and other cultivators turned into tenants, the world appears transformed. For the peasant, everything seemed to have changed from this moment. A tragic sense of transformation is underlined by a set of oppositions developed in the verses.

First: the past was seen as a time of the making of the community – people came in from various quarters; all sorts of brothers (*bhai*) came together and settled the desert waste. The present was a time of dispersal and fragmentation: having lost their land, people had to flee elsewhere (*bhuin khuha angre nasde*).

Second: the past saw growth, a realisation and generation of the productive potential of land, its fecundity. Deserts were brought under cultivation, scrubland cleared, ponds and wells dug, land broken up, houses built – all through collective acts of peasant labour:

> *Jihriyan samiyan raldi aiyan*
> *Unhan kitiyan bahut kamaiyan*
> *Bute mare te bhuin banaiyan*
> *Muddh kaddhe te vattan paiyan.*[21]

Now the contrary process was in operation: settled villages were being uprooted, cultivated lands being turned into waste (*ujar*). While the butimars had created the world, the angrez and the lambardars were destroying it:

> *Angrejan te nahin si eh bhara*
> *Sannu hukm cha dende mara*
> *"Lambardaro mar lo dhara"*
> *Beiman cha karan mara*
> *Vasdiyan nu ghat den ujara*
> *Unhan pharliya kai kuhara*
> *Pattan lage vasdi bar*
> *Bedakhili karni nahin darkar.*[22]

Third: the experience of the past is represented as collective and homogeneous, the present as fragmented and differentiated. In the past everything had been realised through collective action, co-operation, the pooling of resources. Everyone suffered and lived together, enjoying rights collectively. But now, "of those who live under the Raj, some weep, some laugh." Some have gained while many have lost. "The lambardar eats up the surplus. Peasants come home weeping."[23]

[21] "The peasants who came together/ Performed great labours/ Cleared away bushes and cultivated the land/ Took out the roots and made field boundaries." Wilson, *Sirsa S.R., 1879–1883*, Appendix II.

[22] "We did not expect this ill-treatment from the English/ They gave a bad order/ 'Lambardars make a raid'/ And upon this evil counsel/ Lambardars laid waste inhabited places/ They seized many axes/ Began to uproot the settled land/ Ejectment is not right." Ibid.

[23] "*Jihre lok is raj ich vasde/ Kai ronde kai hasde/ Bhuin khuha agere nasde/ Lambardar sidhi na dasde/ Likhe bajh nahin itbar/ Bedakhili karni nahin darkar.*" Ibid.

Fourth: the social order of honesty, justice, good faith, and honour was disappearing into the past. The lambardars had thrown away their iman (*Lambardar iman kharaya*), the sarkar had done no justice (*niaun na kita koi Sarkar*). It was as if in the upside down world of the present, norms of morality were being inverted: "It is the thirteenth century – be not angry. Things are different though people are the same. People are false and deceitful" (*Sadi terahwin – na ho rohe/ Gallan hor te bande ohe/ Lok ta howen khote drohe*).

Fifth: the new devaluation of the oral encapsulated the breakdown of honesty and trust. In the social economy of good faith which prevailed in the past, the spoken word was honoured, it was the basis of trust and mutuality; social agreements had been often unstated, taken for granted. Now, everything had to be specified and spelt out, and every spelling out recorded on paper. It was as if, tainted by suspicion, speech had lost its symbolic force and sanctity – a loss that could not be compensated by the new power of writing. In a world where nothing is believed without written evidence and oaths (*likhe bajh nahin itbar*), says Lalu, only deceit and dishonesty prevails. "People have sworn on many Qurans, taken oaths and done injury. Honour and good faith have not stood firm. On the Day of Judgment may they be dismayed, those who have told these great lies."

> *Lokan chae bahut Kuran*
> *Chaiyan kasman – karliya jan*
> *Sabit raha na din iman*
> *Roj kiyamat hon hiran*
> *Jinhan baddhe kur eh bhar*
> *Bedakhili karni nahin darkar*

What Lalu was bringing under question was the new belief that writing could ensure truth and accountability, that rights would be secure if publicly proclaimed and officially encoded; that justice could be affirmed through procedures.[24] Relations of trust, he seems to be saying, cannot be ensured by paper, honesty sustained by public

---

[24] On security of expectation and codification, see chs 3 and 5 above. On the significance of writing and record within the Company Raj, see Raman, *Document Raj*; Ogborn, *Indian Ink*; Moir, "Kaghazi Raj"; Hull, "Ruled by Records"; Kafka, "The Demon of Writing"; Smith, *Rule by Records*.

proclamations, truth by legal procedures in court. On the contrary the regime of paper documents yielded a world of deceit and dishonesty, duplicity and fraud.[25] When commitment to truth becomes a ritual performance of formalised oath-swearing, untruth prevails. It was as if the fetish of procedural formality had corroded the inner desire to live by the truth, replacing it with blind conformity to procedure. The arzi (written petition) had for Lalu come to stand for the annihilation of customary claims, expectations, and rights.[26]

Sixth: now under the British Raj rights that cultivators had acquired in the past were being negated. This theme of lost rights is developed through an effort to articulate what was thought to be the natural basis of just rights. The key acts reiterated in the text as the source of cultivating rights were forest clearance, canal and well construction, village settlement, and cultivation. Anyone who had helped settle the desert under difficult conditions ought not to be ejected from the land: "*Dukhan nal basai bar/ Kaure pani karan khuar/ Is kam di koi kare bichar/ bedakhili karni nahi darkar.*"[27] Peasants did not break

[25] The idea that deceit was a metonym for the Angrezi (English) regime of writing, stamps, and legal papers recurs persistently in the poem. And Lalu states over and over again that those who practice deceit will be the objects of divine wrath. In one place he says: "*Kasman cha te jinhan khohe/ Tan oh kiku langhsan par*" (Those who have sworn an oath and snatched away the land, how will they ever get across?) Elsewhere he says: "*Jihre karsan makar phirej/ Unhannu awe Rab di mar*" (Whosoever practices deceit, on him be God's curse); Wilson, *Sirsa S.R., 1879–1883*, Appendix II.

[26] At one level these ideas seem to express the opposition between status and contract that Maine posited, or *Gemeinshaft* (community) and *Gesellshaft* (society) that Ferdinand Tönnies conceptualised. While both Maine and Tönnies, in different ways, speak of the contrast between on the one hand a society mediated by affective relations, traditional rules, and social solidarities, and on the other one characterised by the operation of rational will, self-interest, and contractual relations, they do not unproblematically celebrate the past even in their most pessimistic moments. Both affirm the theory of progress. Lalu's poem is an ode to times past, a trenchant critique of the present. See Tönnies, *Community and Society: Gemeinshaft und Gesellschaft.*

[27] Trans: "People settled the desert through toil and suffering/ The brackish water distressed them/ One should recognise the experience of this hardship/ Ejectment is not right."

up the land by force (*Dhakke nal kisi nahin kaddhi*); they had done so because of the persuasion of lambardars and on an understanding which the lambardars had now violated (*Lambardaran kol bahai/ nal pyar de bhuen kadhai/ Hun jan de din iman khuhai*). Anyone who settled the village and cultivated land could, according to riwaj, continue to hold it: "*Is alake vich sa eh riwaj pachhan/jo koi vahe zamin kabza usda jan.*"

Underlying the argument is a notion of how things are imbued with value, and what constitutes the premises of legitimate rights.[28] The value of land, the poet argues, does not inhere in the land; it is created. If land had been made productive through collective, not individual, effort, then all who contributed to the process had a claim to the fruits of their toil. This creative act was made possible by the coming together of people and the forging of social relations, by the fashioning of a moral world of trust and honesty, duties and obligations. In a sense the creative act not only made the land productive, it constituted the social relationships that sustained the collective act. Collective work meant collective claims – the basis of the bonds that constituted that collectivity. How could the premises of such claims and rights be denied? How could the lambardar be made the proprietor? If productivity was a gift that peasant effort endowed to land, only peasants had a right to the returns of that gift; only those who offered to land their toil had a claim to the fruits of that toil. The British Raj had transformed collective claims into individual rights. Viewed in terms of Lalu's logic, the colonial definition of property rights appeared incomprehensible. His persistent and recurring refrain of was: "We knew nothing of this law that the Sarkar has now imposed" (*Is kanun di khabar na kai/Jihra kita hun sarkar*).

What could be the legitimate grounds for an individual right that excluded the claims of others? A lambardar could claim land as his own, says Lalu, if he had cleared the land and made it yield by dint of

[28] I found the discussion on anthropological notions of value and gift useful in thinking through these ideas. See Sahlins, "The Spirit of Gift", and "On the Sociology of Primitive Exchange"; Bourdieu, "The Work of Time" and "Symbolic Capital", in Bourdieu, *The Logic of Practice*; Strathern, *The Gender of the Gift*; Graeber, *Towards an Anthropological Theory of Value*.

his own sweat, without the help of others: "If the lambardar establishes the village by himself, settling no co-sharer [sami] alongside, if he digs the pond and makes the well, breaks up the land and builds houses, he may then have some claim – if he alone performs all the labour." Had this ever happened? "No-one ever settled a village alone."[29] Within the logic that Lalu elaborates, an individual's claim is only ever valid if by unsupported individual effort he has imbued value within what he claims. Any exclusive individual claim over things produced by collective social effort can have no legitimacy. To deny this logic of claims and rights is to violate all sense of justice.

Here, Lalu seems to be in a dialogue with arguments that are apparently Lockean, turning their assumptions upside down.[30] Locke, like many seventeenth-century philosophers, traced the origin of property in the state of nature, a pre-political state where everyone could do what they wished without the control of political authority. In the state of nature land was held in common: God gave the earth and its fruits in common to men for their use. Men acquire land from the state of nature, where it is held in common, and establish their right and property over it. But within individualistic theories of the seventeenth century – like those of David Hume and Adam Smith – the men who first occupy the land and establish their property over it act as individuals, not as a social collective. When Locke moves from a simple argument of "first occupation" as the basis of just right, to his labour theory of property, he still celebrates the agency of the individual.[31] It is the individual who occupies and works the land, claims it from nature, imbues it with value, stamping it with his personality, "mixing his labour" with it. By transforming the land the individual also constitutes himself as an individual, realises his

---

[29] "*Ikko lambardar basawe/ Sami na kai kol bahawe/ Chhapra kate te khuha lawe/ Bhuin kaddhe te kothe pawe/ Tan usda andaja awe/ Puri dewe kar begar/ Bedakhili karni nahin darkar.*"

[30] For an argument that strongly emphasizes the Lockean resonance in the debate over custom in colonial Bengal, see Sartori, *Liberalism in Empire*.

[31] Locke, "Property". On Locke's theory of property more generally, see Tully, *A Discourse on Property*; Macpherson, *The Political Theory of Possessive Individualism*.

essence, and fashions his personality. Within the Lockean argument, property constituted through individual acts of labour precedes the subsequent formation of civil society and government to protect and regulate individual rights. Lalu's argument, by contrast, centres on the collective social, not the individual; he underlines the importance of collective acts, not individual labour; he speaks of everyone's rights not exclusive individual property. It is the labour of a social collective that transforms the land, makes it productive, creates the premises of legitimate rights; and through this process reaffirms the social basis of its collective existence. The social compact between individuals, and between lambardars and individuals, is made before land is claimed from nature, not after rights and property are established. Individual rights could be legitimately exercised only within the frame of a collective social that acknowledges the rights of every member of the collective, prevents individual exclusionary practices, and specifies everyone's duties and obligations.

Seventh: established norms of power were being subverted in the present. The power of kings and lambardars in the past derived from legitimate sources. Those who performed certain functions and discharged specific duties were vested with power. He who settled the country was the raja: "*Mulk vasawe raja sohi.*" And rajas never took away peasant land; it was the way deserts were peopled (*Badshah, raje kisi na khohi/ is tadbir se basi rohi*). Now, the sarkar was denying the rights of peasants, evicting them, giving the land over to lambardars, and jettisoning all notions of justice (*Niaun na kita Sarkar/Bedakhili karni nahi darkar*). Earlier, relations with the lambardar were sustained through the shared ideal of mutuality. Those who came in to settle the land were all equals: there was no distinction between them, no hierarchy; no-one was the head, no-one the follower. They chose one amongst them as their leader, anointed him "lambardar", put a pagri on his head (*Ralke ae sabbhe bhai/ Suni unhan bar basai/ Ik de sir te pag banhai/ Oh bangaya lambardar*). The authority of the lambardar derived from the people; he had no natural claim to it, no hereditary right over it. In return, the lambardar had borne the obligation of looking after those who cleared the land, and so affirmed his power. Whereas now, under the British Raj, the lambardar had broken the terms of this relationship, renounced honour and good faith, and filed arzis (written notices) against those who had once sanctified his power (*Hun jan de din iman khuhai/ Samidar te arji lai*). What Lalu was describing was not just the breakdown of the moral economy of trust and good faith. He was reflecting on the ethical premises of legitimate power, the moral basis of rightful authority.

The poem, despite its nostalgic critique of the present – infused with a sense of violated justice and insistently returning to the theme of lost rights – invokes the image of the state as the peasant's ma-bāp and pleads for paternal care: "The ruler is our father as well as mother. When children are in trouble, they weep before their parents. If parents do no justice, where can the daughter go?"[32]

In this narrative, time is not conceived of as a continuum, a ceaseless flow from the past to the present. The flow is ruptured. The present represents a negation, a reversal of the natural order of the world. The desired future is a negation of the present, a return to the past. The rupture between the past and the present is total. The past was normal time, the present is abnormal. The past represents the natural order of the world, the present only disorder. The past was a time of harmony, the present of discord. In the past honesty and truth prevailed, in the present deceit and wickedness reign. The past was a time of evolution, the present is a time of dissolution. The past was a process of social becoming – of the coming together of people, of the formation of solidarities and collectivities; the reverse movement of dispersal characterises the present – the desertion of villages, the break-up of families, dissension amongst brothers over property, abnormal suicides. The time of the past is seen as a forward movement; the present has reversed its flow. The time of the poet's memory is thus a flattening of temporal experience – of the past rendered as a homogeneous period of harmony and order, erased of all discordant notes – as well as a seeing of the present as equally flat, a period with no sign or trace of concord.[33] Conflict across time

[32] "*Ta Badshah hunde mai bap/Bete betiya aukhe honde/ Mai bap de agge ronde/ Mai bap na kare nyan/ Beiyanb di phir kihri than.*" Wilson, *Sirsa S.R., 1879–1883*, Appendix II.

[33] This of course is a recurrent feature of peasant memory. See Zonabend,

is magnified, conflict within time eliminated; the significance of the moment of rupture is amplified.[34]

The past and present acquire their meanings not just through this narration of an opposition, they also do so through the sequential ordering of events within the story being recounted: a narrative sequence defines the meaning of what is seen as normal. The sequence runs thus: Pioneer settlers who obtained permission to colonise the wastes brought peasants together and persuaded them to clear the forests. The peasants themselves offered the pagri to the lambardar and accepted him as their head. They then cleared the land, dug the wells, grew crops.

By the above sequential narrative ordering is the position and authority of the lambardar in the past represented as legitimate, the rights of peasants made to seem indisputable. Only by such sequencing can the premises of normality be made credible. Were the sequence changed, the events would lose their symbolic meaning, and the necessary relationship between the different acts established through this specific sequence would not exist.

Framed within the structure of a cosmogenic myth, this narrative of the origin of rights recounts the movement from chaos to cosmos when life was created. This time of origin, like the time of divine creation, was sacred, and its sanctity was evident in everything that originated at this primal moment. The sanctity of this moment is doubly affirmed in Lalu's poetry by fusing and interweaving sacred and secular time within the narrative. The opening sentence announces the divine origin of life and order: it was Allah who peopled the desert, "*Allah mere bār basai.*" Subsequently, cosmogenic time is secularised: collective human action at the moment of creation is seen as a valid source of sanctity, of the constitution of the legitimate social order. The world of peasants came into being – land was settled and made productive – through collective acts which presumed an understanding

---

The Enduring Memory; Scott, *Weapons of the Weak*, pp. 178–83; Vansina, *Oral Traditions as History*.

[34] I borrow the concept of "within timeness" from Ricoeur's use of the Heideggerian notion.

within the collectivity, between the king and the people, between the lambardar and the peasants. It was this understanding that made collective action and the cosmogenic act of creation possible. Notions of rights, powers, duties, and obligations implicit in this understanding were sacrosanct, natural, and normal; and deviations from the normative order established at this cosmogenic time were sacrilegious. From this understanding flowed the critique of the present as the time when the sanctified order was being torn asunder. While peasant claims to rights were authenticated by tracing their roots to the time of origin, the acts of the sarkar and the lambardars were contested as violations of the original understanding.

Recounting the myth of origin is not just a lament at the passing of the old order of justice: the lament revitalises the present. The act of remembering reactualises the events of the time of origin, reanimates the minds of those who remember the memory of the original order. As Eliade puts it, a return to the original time has a therapeutic purpose, which is to begin life once again. The world has to be recreated and its illnesses cured through a symbolic repetition of cosmogony in the act of narrative recall.[35] A recounting of the time of origin – when the land was made fertile and the social order around land brought into being – is also an assertion of a notion of rights. Legitimate rights within the world that Lalu recounts are inscribed with the specific histories of their production, their origin in particular creative collective social acts. To return to that origin is to remember the sources of legitimate rights. It is to express, at the same time, a profound anxiety about the denial of that legitimacy.

There was, of course, no enduring truth residing in memory and waiting to be articulated. Memories, as we know, are always reconfigured in the light of contemporary experience.[36] Traces of the past

---

[35] Eliade likens this regenerative function of a return to the time of origin to the healing function of traditional curative chants which recount the myths of origin of a variety of diseases. A remedy is supposed to become effective only when its origins are rehearsed in the sick person's presence. See Eliade, *The Myth of the Eternal Return*; idem, *The Sacred and the Profane*.

[36] On the politics of memory in the reconstitution of the past, see Appadurai, "The Past as a Scarce Resource"; Rosaldo, *Ilongot Headhunting*; Nora, "Between Memory and History"; Le Goff, *History and Memory*; Lowenthal, *The*

that have been configured in specific ways in collective memory are continuously reinscribed with new meanings. After the various colonial enactments by which the cultural premises of peasant life came under question, notions of justice and rights, duties and obligations earlier taken for granted were sought to be explicitly formulated. Threatened by the new regime of rights, by the new juridical relations, the taken-for-granted peasant world asserted itself in a paranoid defence of its right to exist. The rhetoric of reciprocity expressed a sense of loss, a fear of the passing of the accepted normative order, the breakdown of a sanctified scheme of things.

The Time of Reciprocity

Lalu's longing for paradise, his celebration of the world of reciprocity, I suggest, refer to an ideal state that is often important in the lives of peasants. There can be little doubt that the lives of past cultivators were more complicated and much thornier than Lalu's verses suggest. But if from that past it is the theme of reciprocity, trust, and honour that is remembered, and if the sources of rights are traced back through a narrative of collectivity and mutuality to the primal acts that transformed the land, then that act of recounting tells us something about the ideals that inspired peasant lives, the notions that informed their actions and expectations. We find the same notions canonised in different forms within nineteenth-century folk wisdom around the region, a canonisation that again refers to norms as ideals and models, not norms as practice. Such wisdom, enunciated in proverbs and sayings, internalised as a part of common sense, implicit in action and taken for granted, was usually explicitly recalled, as by Lalu, only at moments of crisis when the implicit ordering principles of life were violated, the taken-for-granted world disturbed.[37]

Past is a Foreign Country; Portelli, *The Order Has been Carried Out*; Ricoeur, *Memory, History, Forgetting*.

[37] On the importance of the performative context in defining the meaning of sayings and folklore, see Hymes, "Introduction: Towards Ethnographies of Communication"; Arewa and Dundes, "Proverbs and the Ethnography of Speaking Folklore"; Ben-Amos and Goldstein, eds, *Folklore: Performance*

The question therefore is not whether relations in the past were actually characterised only by relations of reciprocity and mutuality – they were not – but whether reciprocity was an ideal of value within rural society, a norm in relation to which actions could be judged, mutual expectation formed, and injustice critiqued. Something is missed when the debate on reciprocity is framed around the terms of standard oppositions: when we go on to discover either the existence or non-existence of reciprocity in practice, or a complicated inter-articulation of reciprocal and exploitative relations.[38] The important question is whether reciprocity was considered normative and normal, whether the rhetoric of reciprocity had a shaping power in peasant lives. And if it did, what were the defining elements of that normative order. Lalu's poetic return to the past allows us entry into that imagined order.

In confronting and negotiating the new world, peasants inevit-ably drew upon the resources of tradition; they made sense of new laws through their ideals of the past. The corpus of proverbs and sayings collected by colonial ethnographers in the third quarter of the nineteenth century allows us a glimpse into the structure of dis-positions that defined peasant expectations. These local sayings reveal an enchanted world where self-interest was not acknowledged as such, where everything happened as if the self had to be subordi-nated to the other, as if everyday relations were to be forged only

---

and Communication; Bauman and Sherzer, *Exploration in the Ethnography of Speaking*; Bauman, *et al.*, *Verbal Art as Performance*; Blackburn and Ramanujan, eds, *Another Harmony*. Mir, *The Social Space of Language*.

[38] On the idea of reciprocity as equal exchange, see Wiser, *The Hindu Jajmani System*; and Neal, "Reciprocity and Redistribution in the Indian Village". For an intervention that emphasises the underlying exploitative dimension of seemingly reciprocal relations, see Beidelman, *A Comparative Analysis of the Jajmani System*. For a more complex exploration of the issue, see Breman, *Patronage and Exploitation*. For a wider reflection on the idea of reciprocity, see Gouldner, "Reciprocity and Autonomy in Functional Theory" and "The Norm of Reciprocity". See also Graeber, *Towards an Anthropological Theory of Value*, ch. 6.

[39] We have several sources for nineteenth-century Punjab folklore. Folklore

through gestures of goodwill.[39] When relating to a sanjhi or pahi, many proverbs emphasised, it was important to be generous, kind, and benevolent. The pahi ought to be offered the best land in the village (*Jo awe pah ka buwa, usko dede chalta kua*). Recognise the just rights of a pahi or sanjhi and treat him better than yourself (*sanjhi da tun haqq pahchan, apne nalon changa jan*), ran one proverb; respect them more than your brother or son (*bhai khesh farzand thin, usda wadda man*), said another.

Self-interest, however, was not completely socially repressed and publicly censured. The anticipation of a return was not just implicit in action, it was explicitly articulated within folk wisdom. Acts of generosity and kindness, it was emphasised, were to be reciprocated: "A pahi keeps kindness in mind. If you fulfil their wishes your husbandry will be thoroughly successful" (*pahi bolidar sun man men rakhe prit, unki asa puri de kheti puri jit*); or again: "If the malik shows consideration towards his pahi, the latter will cultivate well" (*malik je kare riayat pahi, tan oh karda changi wahi*). There was the more general dictum: "Give a little and gain much" (*liz warkawa, dher khapulawa*). A zamindar who makes his pahi suffer loses his future livelihood (*pahi nun satawe, ghar aonda rizak ganwawe*).[40] Gestures of generosity, it was recognised, initiate and sustain social relations. Indebted, the recipient of kindness is persuaded to reciprocate with what he can offer – his labour.

In this early-nineteenth-century labour-scarce and land-abundant economy where peasants had to be persuaded into a village, it was a

collected from regional ethnographers was appended to the settlement reports of each district. Maconachie produced a useful volume based on these regional enquiries: *Selected Agricultural Proverbs of the Panjab*. Many others were reported in the pages of *Indian Antiquary*, *Panjab Notes and Queries*, and *North Indian Notes and Queries*. See also Temple, "Some Punjabi and Other Proverbs".

[40] There were many variations on the theme. In the frontier districts of Jhelum, Shahpur, and Rawalpindi it was said: "*Jera sharikan nal khirende, orik fatteh kadhi na painde*" (He who refuses to treat his co-sharers well, will not ultimately succeed), *SAPP*, p. 889; and in Jullunder it was said it would lead to a loss of honour. Ibid., p. 890.

[41] Within the larger corpus of proverbs there are those that survive but rarely

problem to expand and sustain a regular labour supply. Given such
a context, the interests of maliks and the rural community – that is,
the payment of revenue and extension of cultivation – could be most
effectively realised only within a moral universe of generosity, kindness,
benevolence, and a certain spirit of reciprocity. The operation of such
norms was essential for the production and reproduction of social
relations. Structures of exploitation were mediated by such norms.

As a corpus, the proverbs of nineteenth-century Punjab do not
convey an unambiguous message.[41] If the rhetoric of reciprocity
both denied and acknowledged self-interest, it equally recognised
the possibilities of conflict and tension within social relations. The
very language which affirms the values of a good-faith economy also
announces the ever-present threat to those values. While some village
sayings suggest the need to treat sanjhis, pahis, and siris with care and
kindness, others warn of the explosive potential of such relationships.
Form a partnership and have your hair pulled (*Bhaiwali pa, te chunen
pata*), they said in the villages of Muzaffargarh.[42] To work with a
siri was considered as bad as the sun in an overcast sky, the thorn
of a karir tree, and a rivalrous wife.[43] One should resist forming a
partnership, just as one should avoid walking through the middle of
a field, gambling, and jumping over a well.[44] It was as if pain and
suffering, tension and conflict, disaster and death were written into

enter discourse (frozen proverbs), and those which have a more meaningful
presence in social life, mediating social relations, embodying norms and pre-
cepts of social action – "active" proverbs. The latter form a constitutive part of
living discourse. Once textualised, it is perhaps difficult to separate the two,
except by attempting to relate them to the extra-linguistic social context of
which the "active" proverbs are a constitutive part. Within the sub-corpus
of active proverbs, there is a need to distinguish between the sub-corpus as
a whole, which is only potentially meaningful, and "proverbs as utterance",
whose specific meaning is defined by the speech context. For historians, as
we know, it is difficult to recapture the dialogic and performative context in
which "proverbs as utterance" acquire their particular meaning.

[42] *SAPP.*
[43] Ibid.
[44] Ibid.
[45] GOI, Rev. & Agr. (Rev.), June 1882, A 4. On the working of the Ten-

the bonds of such relationships. What gave meaning to the list of seemingly unrelated acts mentioned in each of the folk sayings was their structural similarity. In the proverbs all acts associated with positive values are treated as analogues, and all acts with negative values have the same structural location.

The hidden fear of conflict thus lurked beneath the rhetoric of reciprocity. The evidence of tension in everyday social relations could not be denied, but it was sought to be repressed. The norm of reciprocity was idealised: it provided the model of social practice, enunciated a code of behaviour, defined how a good zamindar and sanjhi ought to act, how they must view and treat each other. It spelt out a structure of expectations and obligations, a frame through which individual actions could be judged, good and bad conduct differentiated. It offered a point of reference for evaluating action, censuring violations, approving conformity. But the idealisation of a world reveals the repressed possibilities of its breakdown, a prospect which it seeks to contain and overcome, but one which is very much part of the social experience of that world. The ideal is tirelessly uttered, not only as a model to be celebrated but as that which is persistently under question.

Within the lived relations of everyday life the rhetoric of goodwill and trust was mediated by the language of interest and calculation. The idea of collectivity incorporated within it an orientation towards the self; the normalising language of harmony also signified its opposite – an anxiety about disharmony. The conflict between these binaries was both acknowledged and denied. This contrariness was constitutive of the habitus, the taken-for-granted world of the peasants.

Lalu's ballad is, in short, an ode to an ideal. But like all nostalgic returns, the past it mourns probably never existed, it was never there to be recovered. What he conjures up as an ideal is a wistfully imagined past.

Through the Native Voice

But there is the paradox we started with. Lalu's story of lost rights, of the pain and violence of colonialism, comes to us inscribed as a colonial text recorded by a colonial official. Lalu's voice is not only embedded in a quintessential text of colonial power – the Settlement Report – it has been appropriated by that power. Wilson speaks through Lalu.

Through Lalu, Wilson carries on his dialogue with other officials, questioning them, critiquing them, establishing the authenticity of his own arguments. Rights, as I have argued earlier, are rarely frozen through acts of encoding. Their terms are elaborated and reworked through conflicts over interpretation, through encounters between codifiers and right holders. Codes emerge through the process of their making.

The flood of ejectment suits that followed the enactment of the Punjab Tenancy Act of 1868 worried officials.[45] As the conflict intensified, the Government of India was forced to ask for a special report on the working of the act. Wilson, the settlement officer, submitted a report in 1880 pointing out that the tenants had "formed a reasonable expectation that they would be protected in the occupation of such land as they had broken up from the prairie."[46] He felt that the wrong done by the arbitrary grant of proprietary rights on cultivated land to headmen at the First Regular Settlement of 1852 could not be set right. But cultivators should not now be subjected to a fresh injustice. The security granted at the first settlement to tenants on the land they had broken should now be extended to all nautor land cleared since the first settlement. Colonel Wace, the settlement commissioner of Punjab at the time, agreed that "the expectations of the tenants were reasonable" and criticised the Punjab Tenancy Act of 1868 for reversing the policy of granting occupancy rights to peasants who reclaimed land.[47] But Wace felt that Wilson's proposal in favour of special legislation for Sirsa granting colonists security of tenure would constitute a second reversal. Lyall, the financial

ancy Act of 1868, see GOI Foreign (Rev.), April 1870, A 2–4; Punjab Agr. & Rev. (Rev.), November 1874, A 5.

[46] Note by Wilson, GOI, Rev. & Agr. (Rev.), June 1882, no. 6.

[47] Note of Major E.G. Wace, Settlement Commissioner, Punjab, no. 227, 3 August 1881, Kausali, GOI, Rev. & Agr. (Rev.), June 1882, nos 4–6.

[48] Note of Lyall, Financial Commissioner, Punjab, 24 August 1881, GOI,

commissioner, supported Wilson's plea for such a special Sirsa-specific legislation – the tenants having formed "a reasonable expectation" which had to be respected – yet Wilson's proposal was ultimately quashed.[48] The lieutenant governor, Egerton, thought that the need for special legislation was unclear, the expectation of tenants uncertain, and the history of tenant struggle a thing of the past. Special legislation would introduce "a great inequality between Sirsa and other districts and rekindle the spark of discontent that had died down."[49] Wilson was disappointed but did not give up his campaign. Through the early 1880s he penned a series of new memos arguing security of tenure for those who had brought waste lands into cultivation, and then returned to the issue in his Settlement Report of the district over a long chapter numbering more than a hundred pages which traced the growth of rights in Sirsa.[50] In support of his argument that colonists expected security of tenure, he now marshalled a vast body of evidence. Lalu's poem became a critical part of Wilson's persuasive text.

Wilson belonged to a tradition of romantic paternal imperialism that was eager to base colonial rule on peasant support, and on the authority of tradition and custom.[51] Keen on hearing peasant voices,

Rev. & Agr. (Rev.), June 1882, nos 4–6.

[49] Letter from Egerton, Lt Governor Punjab, GOI Rev. & Agr. (Rev), June 1882, nos 4–6. See also no. 1126, 24 October 1881, GOP to GOI, Punjab Agr. Rev. & Com. (Rev.), October 1881, A 8.

[50] See in particular no. 132, 26 May 1882, J. Wilson, Settlement Officer, Sirsa, to the Settlement Commissioner, Punjab, Punjab Rev. & Agr. (Rev.), September 1882, A 1. Convinced by Wilson's persuasive memos, the Financial Commissioner and the Lt Governor of Punjab agreed in 1882 that those who had cleared the land and resided in these newly established villages would be granted occupancy rights. See no. 809, 9 August 1882, F.C. Channing, Senior Sec. to the Financial Comm., Punjab, to Sec. to GOP, Punjab Rev. & Agr. (Rev.), September 1882, A 1.

[51] The power of Scottish imagination in shaping Orientalist minds in India is explored in Koditschek, *Liberalism, Imperialism, and the Historical Imagination*. Wilson was from Scotland, like many of his Orientalist predecessors in India: William Erskine, N.B. Edmonstone, Thomas Munroe, John Malcolm, Colin Mackenzie. See also Rendall, "Scottish Orientalism"; McLaren, *British India and British Scotland*; Dirks, *The Autobiography of an Archive*.

[52] Rogers, *Voyage of Columbus*, p. 103, cited in Leask, *British Romantic*

Wilson empathises with the village poet. Lalu's verses nourish his angst. The Romantic image of Arcadian time – the period of conviviality, collectivity, and harmonious mutuality – is rediscovered in Lalu's ballad. For the folklorists, the ballad writer was witness to the passing of the old order, a past surviving only in memory, a dream threatening to disappear. Lines such as "'tis all a dream – Now like a dream 'tis fled", lingered in many folklorist minds.[52]

In the folkloric revival, inspired by romanticism since the eighteenth century, poetry was seen as the language of the people: it was connected with their lives, it encapsulated their collective creativity, it expressed communal wisdom and the essence of their inner being.[53] The folk appeared as bearers of authentic culture, village innocence, simplicity, naivety, and as opposed to learnedness and classicism. The poets were close to the people, bards were the carriers of this authentic folk culture. The quaint world of bards and singers, songs and ballads, threatened by oblivion could be partly salvaged, it was felt, through a heroic act of recovery. In Scotland the great bardic revival that began in the sixteenth century climaxed in the nineteenth, and in the Slavic countries the movement gathered momentum from the late eighteenth century.[54] Stirred by this romanticism, officials in colonial countries too saw themselves as preservers of disappearing cultures. As valiant Englishmen sensitive to the traditions of the people in their care, they had to collect the shreds that survived and preserve them – in texts, archives, and museums.[55]

Writers, p. 31.

[53] On the British folklorists, see Dorson, *The British Folklorists*; idem, *Peasant Customs and Savage Myths*. See also Ben-Amos' assessment of Dorson: "The Historical Folklore of Richard M. Dorson". For the contexualist turn, see Ben-Amos, *Folklore in Context*.

[54] Wood, "Folklore Studies at the Celtic Dawn", pp. 3–12; Davis, "Contexts of Ambivalence".

[55] The *Indian Antiquary* was published from 1872. In 1892 Richard Temple became its editor and continued to edit the journal till his death in 1931. The Pioneer Press, Allahabad, published *Indian Notes and Queries*, 1886–7, as well as *North Indian Notes and Queries*, 1891–6. *Panjab Notes and Queries* came out for some years in the 1880s. On the folkloric tradition in India, see Blackburn and Ramanujan, eds, *Another Harmony*; Blackburn, *Print, Folklore,*

A salvage operation, however, can have many meanings and be implicated in different projects. It is rarely the innocent act of return to a rural idyll, nor simply the expression of some uncomplicated empathy with the folk. In the folkloric movement in nineteenth-century Scotland, the salvage operation was part of a resistance to hegemonic politics. Intimately connected to the constitution of a Scottish identity, it was a metaphor of opposition to English political and cultural domination.[56] Searching for the original Gaelic languages and recording folklore seen as authentically Scottish – distinct from the Irish, uncorrupted by the English – was part of the making of a Scottish self.[57] In the colonies, on the other hand, official ethnographers were inevitably implicated in the politics of domination, acquiring local knowledge for more effective colonial governance. Having grown up in Scotland and been educated at Oxford, nurtured by the folkloric revival but acting as a colonial official in India, Wilson found that his folkloric projects were structured by conflicting pulls. He was sensitive to folk custom, sceptical of any radical Anglicanism, but in charge of carrying through colonial revenue settlements. For him, as for others like him, the salvage operation of an imperial official could never be the same as the folklore projects back in Scotland. In India Wilson stood for a unitary British power. In Scotland, defining the Scottish dialect and marking its distinction from English, he felt, was part of his patriotic duty.[58]

---

and Nationalism in Colonial South India.

[56] Wood, "Folklore Studies at the Celtic Dawn"; Davis, "Contexts of Ambivalence".

[57] For a wider discussion of the nineteenth-century invention of the Scottish tradition, see Trevor Roper, "The Invention of Tradition".

[58] Having spent many years collecting folk wisdom, recording collective custom, and investigating the structure of rural languages in Punjab, Wilson returned to Scotland in the early 1910s to pursue his folklorist interests there. He toured villages around the New Forests of Hampshire, his birthplace Perthshire, and other tracts of Central Scotland, talking to old people and fishermen, recording their speech, collecting their poems, songs, folktales, and sayings. This salvage operation was necessary, he felt, if the authentic Scottish language had to be saved from annihilation – displaced by English,

All the same, if bards were the bearers of an authentic folk culture, such authenticity as they depicted could be preserved, colonial
folklorists inevitably thought, only through heroic imperial acts
of salvage. If Wilson spoke through Lalu's voice, appropriating it
as his own, Lalu could only speak through Wilson. Wilson, like
Temple saw rural poets and bards as the voice of the people. The folk
poem, wrote Temple, is "more valuable than a folktale as a true reflex
of popular notions."[59] As a genre it had a longer history within rural
society. It was more authentic, less variable, and less flexible than
folk tales. Temple went "hunting" for bards, tracking them down
at festivals and fairs, "catching" them at roadsides and persuading them to sing.[60] But like all colonial ethnographers, he could
not acknowledge his dependence on his native informants without
deprecating them at the same time. The bard, he warns us, "is not
always a very reputable personage", he is usually "very ignorant and
often very stupid to boot"; the mirasi is a "disreputable rascal", the
jogis, faqirs, and bhats are all "drunkards", and even the munshis who
record the songs are untrustworthy, sloppy, and lazy.[61] In disparaging
the local informant, Temple establishes the significance of imperial
intervention. The authenticity of the folk voice was restored, the
authority of the recorded text was established, Temple reminds us,
only through his untiring and careful superintendence in checking
and cross-checking, in carefully transliterating and translating each
poem that had been recorded.[62]

---

transformed into a language of the lower classes, seen as an uncouth and vulgar
dialect. Wilson, "Introduction" to *The Dialect of the New Forest in Hampshire*.
See also Wilson, *The Dialects of Central Scotland*; idem, *The Dialect of Robert
Burns*; idem, *Lowland Scotch*. Wilson saw it as his "patriotic duty" to write these
books. Letter, 28 May 1926, to Rev. R.D. Mackenzie, Manse of Kilbarchan,
Milliken Park, Renfrewshire, MS 37766/152b, Special Collection, University
of St Andrews, Scotland.

[59] Temple, *The Legends of the Panjab*, vol. I, p. v.

[60] On Temple as a folklorist, see Naithani, *The Story-time of the British
Empire*; Mir, *The Social Space of Language*, pp. 60–62.

[61] Temple, *The Legends of the Panjab*, vol. I, p. v.

[62] Temple continued to systematise this knowledge of folklore through a
series of essays and books. For the essays, see Temple, "The Science of Folk-

In salvaging Lalu's poem, Wilson was also establishing the authenticity of Lalu's voice, differentiating it from duplicates. When settlement officials went in search of peasant poets and recorded, canonised, and quoted them, mimic versions of the original inevitably appeared. Wilson soon found other rural poets reproducing Lalu's rhymes with variations. Such supposedly mimic versions were considered inferior to the original. Yet they were recorded and referred to as evidence of peasant perceptions.[63] Peasant voices, even when nearly duplicates of those earlier recorded, needed to be mobilised and kept in reserve to reaffirm faith in colonial paternalist ideals, and as ammunition in debates against official adversaries. If imperial recordings silenced some informants, they also encouraged others into creativity. Bards often knew what was required for them to become their masters' voice. Keen on being recorded, they could produce songs that they felt would interest British ethnographers in search of peasant sentiments encoded in bardic lore.

---

lore"; idem, "Agricultural Folk-lore Notes"; idem, "Bibliography of Folk-lore"; idem, "North Indian Proverbs"; idem, "Some Punjabi and Other Proverbs".

[63] See for instance the poem by Balinda, a Muslim Lohar tenant of Inakhera in tahsil Fazilka, not far from Dabwali Dhab. It praises the Angrezi Raj for its efficient settlement operation but bemoans the decision to grant lambardars the right to eject peasants (samis/asamis): "The sarkar ought not to deprive any cultivator of his land/ The cultivators settled the village with the lambardar" (*Qabza kasht kisida na khohe Sarkar/ Pind basaya samiyan lambardaran nal*). "The peasants pay the revenue that the Sarkar fixed in times past/ They have done begar/ drunk brackish water and endured a thousand ills/ lived in the desert through famines and scarcities" (*Hale den kadim te jo akhya Sarkar/ Nale dende eh rahe jo sarkar begar/ Khare pani pike jhali ranj hazar/ Kalan qahtan vich oh baith rahe vich bar*). "After enduring so much hardship they are now helpless/ The sarkar ought not to deprive the cultivator of his land" (*Itni ranj uthake hun hoe lachar/ Qabza kashat kisida na khohe Sarkar*). The ideas that Lalu expresses, the refrains within his poem, recur in the text that Balinda composes. It is not the enunciation of legal property rights but the history of peasant relationship with the land that is seen as the basis of just expectations, claims, and rights. New laws, Balinda warns, ought not violate the premises of this order of normality. See Wilson, *Sirsa S.R., 1879–83*, Appendix II, p. xviii.

[64] See Letter no. 196, 28 April 1863, Prinsep, Settlement Commissioner,

Wilson was not alone in turning to the native voice and referring to tradition to authorise his knowledge. Colonial official
debates over tradition and custom were usually carried on through
the native voice. Prinsep's famous critique of the tenant settlement
in Punjab was the reverse of Wilson's.[64] He had opposed the grant
of occupancy rights to tenants and been keen on consolidating the
rights of proprietors. Wilson suggested that tenants at will should be
reclassified as occupancy tenants; Prinsep proposed the opposite. Yet
he too referred to the voice of the people, carried out enquiries, and
recorded the statements of landlords and tenants to provide backing
for his ideas.[65] Prinsep's disgruntled landlords and Wilson's despairing
and disillusioned tenants all helped officialdom to write their lines and
argue cases that could condradict each other. The opposing world-
views of landlords and tenants were both made vocal in the colonial record.

In speaking through Lalu, however, Wilson does not question the
terms of the dominant discourse; he reaffirms them. He translates Lalu
through categories that all colonial officials shared. Nineteenth-century
political economy provided the language of agrarian colonisation.
When Lalu talked of sami or samidar or samiyan, Wilson translated
the terms as tenant. Sami, as we have seen, comes from the word
sām, which may mean "equal"/"the same", and refers to a partner, a
co-sharer.[66] In the discourse of tenancy, co-sharers become tenants.
Lalu's recounting of custom and practice is refigured by Wilson as a
plea for occupancy rights. When Lalu pointed to the originary acts
of creation and the collective act of clearing the land as the basis of
rights, Wilson emphasised the fact of "continuous possession" as the

Amritsar Division, to Financial Comm. Punjab, *HOCPP*, Appendix I,
pp. 60–3. See also Prinsep's Annual Report on the Settlement Operations
of the Year 1865–6, 13 August 1866, addressed to the Financial Comm.,
Punjab. See ch. 5 above.

[65] See Memorandum by Edward Prinsep, Settlement Commissioner, on
Punjab Tenancy Bill, 18 April 1868, GOI For. (Rev.), Jan. 1870, A 60.

[66] In Hindi sām can also mean "along with" or "together with", suggesting
that the term sāmi could mean working with someone in cultivation.

[67] Reading Blackstone had taught Wilson that continuous possession

defining criterion for supporting peasant claims of occupancy rights.[67]
Lalu's lament for the loss of an entire world premised on the idea of
reciprocity was read as a cry for secure tenancy.

It is also possible to ask if Wilson's predispositions made him hear
Lalu's ballad while filtering out other voices. Lalu's ballad, which
Wilson chose to record, showed him a peasant lamenting the loss of
customary rights as well as the moral and ethical values that the poet
imagined as having governed life in the past. But had the agrarian
imaginary not framed his developmental vision, Wilson may well
have heard another voice, another lament – that of Bhatti and Joiya
pastoralists. Through the late eighteenth century, the Bhattis had
fought a long war against encroaching peasant settlers. They raided
peasant settlements, carried off their crops and cattle, set up large
villages of their own, consolidated political power, and established a
powerful chiefdom which came to be known as Bhattiana. By 1818
the British began taking over Bhatti territories and encouraged a new
phase of agrarian conquest.[68] Peasant settlers now invaded the Ghaggar
valley. They began colonising the great prairie to the west and founded
villages on the bagar – the sandy tract south of the Ghaggar valley.
With the expansion of the agrarian frontier, the luxurious dhaman
grass that flourished on the alluvium of the riverine tract disappeared, the pastures of the upland prairie shrank, and supplies of fodder
for cattle dwindled.[69] The Bhatti pastoralists relocated themselves,
reoriented the paths of their movement, and carried on their war
of attrition. But they too must have spoken of the past – of a time
when their herds could move with ease over the great prairie and their

created the basis of occupancy rights. Blackstone, *Commentaries on the Laws
of England*, book II, ch. XVI.

[68] The eastern part of the Ghaggar and Sotar valleys, as well as the western
part of the Sotar valley around Rania, were taken from the Bhattis in 1818.

[69] On the dramatic disappearance of dhaman grass with the expansion of
the arable, see: From J.H. Oliver, Deputy Commissioner Sirsa to the Commissioner and Superintendent Hissar Division, no. 102, Sirsa, 14 April
1863, *CRSS*, paras 155–6. On the disappearance of barilla and sajji, see
para 158.

[70] In 1839, in fact, the Court of Directors of the East India Company asked

hamlets be set up in the hollows and depressions where rainwater gathered. Wilson, however, had no empathy for the nostalgia of the nomads, for their remembrance of time past. Their laments did not echo in his ears, their displacements found no space in his narrative of lost rights. For Wilson – as for other colonial officials – the dispossession of pastoralism within the colony was a necessary act, part of a great civilisational project.[70] It was inescapably connected to the grand agrarian conquest that they were pioneering.

for a report on "the measures being adopted for the civilization of the wild tribes in the Bhatti Territory". Captain Thoresby, who had been sent to settle Bhattiana, submitted a report detailing the steps planned for sedentarisation of the nomadic population. Wison, *Sirsa S.R.: 1879–1883*, p. 45, paras 38ff. See also J. Thomason, Memorandum Regarding Bhuttee Territory, June 1852, GOI, Rev. & Agr., June 1882, A 4–6.

7

Beyond the Code

OVER THE COLONIAL YEARS a specific form of agrarian regime was consolidated over the countryside. Pastoralists were settled, vast stretches of forests and "wastes" colonised, and the limits of cultivation pushed outwards. The codification of customs, the categorisation of tenures, the legal definition of rights, and the juridical reclassification of agrarian groups created the framework within which an agrarian regime took shape. In the countryside we see a gradual consolidation of patriarchal brotherhoods, a process that signified the displacement of women, "lower" castes, and "outsiders" – those who did not belong to the brotherhood. But the trend line flattens and smoothens the violence of short-term fluctuations, the *longue durée* – to reverse the Braudelian formulation – blinds us to the drama of everyday events, the secular process hides the upheavals of quotidian life. Despite the pressures of the sedentary state and the expansive thrust of the agrarian regime, pastoralists continued to operate, devising new strategies of survival, rethinking their practices, and forcing the state to reformulate its policies. Similarly, women, "lower" castes, and merchant-moneylenders saw their rights erode as the new juridical regime was established and as the village brotherhood forged and strengthened its internal ties. But they too devised strategies of survival, resisted the displacing power of new laws, and created structures within which they could live or operate. Beneath the formal rules we discover informal practices, behind the public affirmation of laws we hear the secret language of subversion, against the new rights we see the assertion of what was seen as riwaj.

Alongside the certitudes of publicly proclaimed law we can uncover the ambiguities in their interpretation and the uncertainties in their implementation. The fixity of what is considered fixed itself comes under question.

In this chapter (as mentioned in the Introduction) I shift from models to strategies, from codes to practices, from discourses of power to the activities of everyday life. I look more closely at the working of the code on the ground – the everyday practices which were both shaped by and which reshaped the regime of rules, codes, laws, and categories. It was through everyday conflicts that the specificity of legal rights was defined and redefined, their meanings clarified and understood; the lived reality was what helped determine which new ideas became part of common sense, how a new habitus gradually came into being.

The habitus, Bourdieu has suggested, is a world that structures common sense, defining what is normal and natural, a world premised on ideals that are not always articulated precisely because they are taken for granted.[1] But this habitus, I wish to emphasise, is not so much a settled state of existence or a fixity but a *process* – and this process is one where what is to be taken for granted is itself under question, where the premises underlying what is considered normal are open to debate. The conflicts around rights and customs that we are exploring in this chapter were all part of such a process which constituted the new sense of normality in the colonial peasant world.

What I am looking at is not how practice deviated from the code, nor how the coherence of the code broke down in practice. All too often, we assume that codes embody coherence and fixity, whereas practices display multiplicity and variation. I am suggesting that the code has a history beyond legislation, beyond the act of its inscription in written words. This history shows how codes are read, received, and reworked, how their seemingly categorical meanings

---

[1] Bourdieu, *The Logic of Practice*, ch. 3. As already mentioned, Bourdieu over-states the incorporative power of the habitus, underestimates the heterogeneity within it, and ignores the constitutive power of practice in shaping differences within the structure of the taken-for-granted world, even though his theoretical oeuvre sets out to conceptualise practice.

are brought under question, revealing layers of ambiguity that constitute uncertainties. When we shift from the terrain of legislation and the procedures of encoding, when we move from the framing visions of officials and codifiers, to the processes of adjudication, as well as to the dialogues between judges and lawyers and the claims of disputants, we are forced to rethink the very idea of fixity. What appeared unambiguous and determinate dissolves into a world of seeming fluidity in which the search for certainty is mediated by its persistent subversion.

The claims of litigants, and the enquiries and debates around them, often reveal a domain of practice that the codes do not sanction. This is a domain difficult to grasp. When litigants refer to past practice, they reinscribe those practices with new meanings, even as they emphasise the authenticity of what they say. Recovered in new social contexts, mobilised as evidence to support new legal claims, practices of the past enter legal discourse recast in a new language and are refigured through the legal process.

The Myth of Patrilineal Descent

Colonial officials assumed that Punjab's agrarian society was built on tribal foundations: while the defining element of order in eastern India was caste, in the north-west it was lineage and ties of blood. Unilineal male agnatic descent, the ordering principle of this society, defined the way property was transmitted, the village community forged, and individual rights specified. If custom had to be protected, this ideal of unilineal male agnatic descent could not be violated.[2]

[2] See ch. 5, above. For much of the twentieth century, anthropologists searched for the defining characteristics of tribal societies in a similar vein, looking for principles that bound the group. The debate over these defining features is framed in terms of a set of oppositions: descent vs residence, patrilineal vs matrilineal, unilineal vs dual. Critiques of evolutionist unilineal descent theory often reaffirm the terms of these oppositions. For a powerful assertion of the unilineal descent theory in the twentieth century, see Radcliffe-Brown, "Patrilineal and Matrilineal Succession"; Fortes, "The Structure of Unilineal Descent Groups"; Evans-Pritchard, *The Nuer*. For a

This patrilineal principle was consecrated in the customary law codified within Punjab: first in the Punjab Civil Code of 1864 and then in the Punjab Laws Act of 1872.[3] In terms of these codes sons, not daughters, inherited property, and in the absence of sons property was to pass to the nearest agnate in preference to female descendants.[4] The son-in-law had no claim to the father-in-law's property, and a widow had a life interest if she did not marry again: her share of her husband's property reverted to the males of the household after her death.

Within the colonial imagination, these rights to property were also linked to the nature of the village community. Structured by the idea of unilineal male descent, the village community was seen as a coparcenary brotherhood of agnates descended from a common ancestor. Within closed exogamous patrilocal communities, the exclusion of women's inheritance was seen as necessary to sustain the cohesion of village society and the premises of its existence. To grant inheritance rights to women who moved out of the village was to threaten the control of the brotherhood over village land; it was to allow the transmission of property to an outsider. The property

---

variety of critiques, see Leach, "On Certain Unconsidered Aspects of Double Descent Systems"; Scheffler, "Descent Concepts and Descent Groups"; Goody, "Marriage Prestations, Inheritance and Descent in Pre-Industrial Societies"; Strathern, "Kinship, Descent and Locality"; Schneider, *Critique of the Study of Kinship*; Kuper, "Lineage Theory: A Critical Retrospect"; Scheffler, "The Descent of Rights and the Descent of Persons". My object here is to explore not the principles that defined the working of the society, but the complex encounter between imagined ideals and practices on the ground, and see how this encounter shapes what people come to see as custom.

[3] See Tremlett, *The Punjab Civil Code*.

[4] This was reiterated in all the local codes of customs. See Roe, *Customary Law of Multan*, 1883, sec. 1 and 2; Kaul, *Customary Law of Muzaffargarh*, 1903, sec. 1 and 2; Douie, *Customary Law of Karnal District*, 1892, sec. 1 and 2; Townsend, *Customary Law of Hissar*, 1903, sec. 1 and 2; Walker, *Customary Law of Ludhiana*, 1894, sec. 1 and 2; Dane, *Customary Law of Gurdaspur*, 1893, sec. 1 and 2; Kensington, *Customary Law of Ambala*, 1893, sec. 1 and 2; Maharaj Krishna, Memorandum on the Tribal Customs of Rohtak; Tupper, *PCL*, vol. II, p. 17f.

of daughters, it was assumed, would inevitably pass on to husbands who belonged to the coparcenary brotherhood of another village.

Officials, however, were aware that practices were infinitely more varied than the code could fully admit. These differences between regions and between communities were to be recorded in the local riwaj-i-ams of each district. But the enquiries into these local and community-specific practices continuously undermined the simple theory of unilineal agnatic descent, even as the customary-law volumes the British produced for various districts re-emphasised the normality of the agnatic principle. As settlement operations proceeded and property disputes ended up in the newly established revenue courts, judges were forced to reinvestigate the question of rights. With each investigation the picture appeared more and more contradictory. In everyday practice, as investigators and judges discovered, the norm of patrilineal descent was never rigidly followed. But what was to be done in a situation where custom as codified was in conflict with custom as practised? Was the authority of the code – and the assumptions on which it was founded – to be reaffirmed without question? Or were the practices that questioned the truth of the code to be legally recognised and validated? Caught in a bind, judges vacillated and differed.

Let us look at a few cases in which the idea of patrilineal descent comes under question. Kishen Singh lived in a village near Amritsar.[5] He had no son. His daughter Achra Devi and son-in-law Mehtab Singh lived with him and looked after his land. When Kishen Singh died in about 1853, his widow Roop Kaur took possession of the property but her daughter and son-in-law continued to reside with her, looking after her, managing the land, and bringing up their own child, Jodh Singh. After Roop Kaur's death in the early 1870s, Achra Devi and Mehtab Singh continued living where they always had and cultivated the same land. But they were soon making the rounds of the courts. For in 1875 Kishen Singh's nephews filed a suit challenging a daughter's right to inherit.[6]

[5] *Mehtab Sing and Another vs Pertab Singh and Others, PR,* February no. 16 of 1877.
[6] Ibid.

Did Achra Devi and her son Jodh Singh have a right to Kishen Singh's land? Officials and judges could not arrive at an unambiguous answer. On the basis of an enquiry into the issue, the assistant commissioner concluded that there was no custom excluding the daughter in preference to male collaterals. Subsequently, however, the commissioner conducted his own enquiry and his two informants, Gunda Singh and Bhagwan Singh, ruled against the daughter's inheritance.[7] Achra Devi appealed. The case went up to the chief court, where the judges again expressed radically opposed views. Justice Lindsay spoke eloquently against the mythic rights of collaterals. He dismissed the ruling of Gunda Singh and Bhagwan Singh as their personal opinion which, he felt, was a belief about "what should be the custom rather than what is the custom."[8] Lindsay claimed to have followed the evidence with care and found "no proof of the alleged custom" which excluded the daughter from inheriting. On the contrary, he could cite many instances of daughters and daughter's sons succeeding to property to the exclusion of collaterals. Justice Campbell, the second judge at the chief court, was not persuaded by Lindsay. Convinced of the validity of the agnatic principle, he decreed that Achra Devi had no right to her father's land.[9]

If Campbell upheld the authenticity of the patrilineal norm, Lindsay pointed to evidence of an alternative practice. In the absence of sons, daughters did inherit, and sons-in-law were brought into the household as ghar-jawai (also called khana damad). When a daughter continued to live with her father after her marriage, the family property had to be kept from being lost to residents of another village. The ghar-jawai was not considered as belonging to his paternal village at all, for he had assimilated himself within the bounds of the community within which he had relocated. This new sense of belonging was cemented through his participation in the collective life of the community to which his wife belonged before

[7] Ibid.
[8] Ibid.
[9] Campbell and Lindsay in this case differed from their own views recorded three years earlier in another case. See *Nihal Singh and Mussammat Rupan vs Kahn Singh and Others*, PR, no. 50 of 1875.

he married.[10] His tie with a mythical descent group was seen as now forged not through common male blood but through residence and ritual sharing. Descent through the female line was thus valid, even if it operated within a framework orientated in favour of male descent. But what operates in everyday practice, taken for granted and rarely questioned, is not necessarily specifically defined as a right.[11] Could a male collateral exclude the daughter of a sonless proprietor, or did a daughter facing disinheritance have a right to resist the claims of the male collateral? Summoned to give evidence, Gunda Singh and Bhagwan Singh admitted that such questions had never earlier been posed to them. Nor could they think of a single instance when the daughter had been excluded.[12] Yet, forced to give a categorical answer, they ruled against the daughter because they found it impossible to translate what the daughter enjoyed in practice into a right that could be positively asserted against the male agnatic inheritance principle. A colonial state that aspired to fix rights unambiguously found it difficult to create space for the fluidity of practice on the ground. What appeared to violate the primary principle of order was difficult to ratify legally.

The theory of agnatic descent was more open to question in the case

[10] How is this to be conceptualised? Was this the operation of a double descent: agnatic descent coexisting with cognatic descent in the female line? Clearly, descent was not univocal. We see evidence of both patrilineal and matrilineal, as well as other forms of succession. But (a) the principle of female descent operated within a framework that had a patrilineal orientation, coming into operation mostly when the principle of male agnatic descent could not operate – in the absence of a son; and (b) to exercise rights over land, women – daughters, sisters, widows – had to live within the village of the property owner: that is, residence had to be patrilocal. Women who left their natal village thus faced a more contested claim to inheritance rights.

[11] It is doubtful whether in the practice of everyday life – as distinct from the codes – in pre-colonial rural India, the rights of women and men were unambiguously defined. Such a determinate idea of rights is part of a new codifying discourse, a new language of rights, that emphasises the importance of legally defined, categorically specified, and publicly pronounced codified law.

[12] *Mehtab Sing and Another vs Pertab Singh and Others*, PR, no. 16 of 1877.

of endogamous communities. Within exogamous communities, so the officials had argued, agnatic descent was necessary to maintain the cohesion of coparcenary brotherhoods. This functional logic could not be extended to endogamous groups. But the effort to accommodate the practice of cognatic descent in the female line as permissible under personal law – as distinct from the codified customary law – of specific exogamous communities did not resolve the problem.[13] The contrary implications of personal law and customary law created an embattled ground on which everyday disputes were fought.

Wazir Khan and Jahangir Khan were two brothers who held land in mauza Riayatput in district Jullunder.[14] Wazir Khan was sonless and Jahangir Khan had two daughters – Mehr-ul-Nissa and Sultan Bibi. When the first daughter died, soon after her father, the widow transferred her husband's property to the second daughter. Being sonless, Wazir Khan also passed on his share of the joint property to his niece. But by the twentieth century agnates were almost routinely contesting women's inheritance. Some distant male collaterals of Jahangir Khan got together to question the right of Sultan Bibi to the land she had inherited.[15]

The chief court felt that women had a right to property amongst an endogamous tribe like the Pathans: "Among exogamous peoples alienation to a female blood relation or her succession to ancestral estate at once introduces a stranger into the community, whereas in an endogamous tribe nothing of the sort occurs."[16] Female inheritance,

[13] The personal law was specific to a section of a community in one place, and could be in conflict with the general principles laid down about the customary law of the wider group.

[14] Mussammat Sultan Bibi and Others vs Ghulam Kaidar Khan and Others, PR, no. 32 of 1915.

[15] The plaintiffs had also questioned the collateral right of the widow. Johnstone cited a number of cases to show that the right of the widow to a life estate – a right over property she could enjoy in her lifetime – had been recognised over time though it was doubted by those who saw this right as a denial of the male agnatic principle. Amongst the twelve cases cited, see in particular PR, no. 146 of 1889; PR, no. 177 of 1889; PR, nos 56 and 111 of 1891; PR, no. 43 of 1905; PR, no. 98 of 1910.

[16] Mussammat Sultan Bibi and Others vs Ghulam Kaidar Khan and Others, PR, no. 32 of 1915.

anomalous within the uniform officially encoded law of the region, was being seen as legitimate according to the personal law of the tribe. To question the right, the plaintiffs had to prove that they now followed customary law rather than personal law. Since they failed in this, the right of Sultan Bibi could not be denied.[17]

But once again the application of the rule was uncertain. In numerous cases we see male collaterals successfully displacing the rights of women within endogamous communities. Afzal Khan held land in Peshawar district. He died in the mid 1870s, leaving a son, a widow, and a daughter.[18] The son succeeded to his father's property, and on his death the property was split into two. One part, in mauza Shewa, was given over to a nephew; another in mauza Asota was entered in the name of the widow. When the widow died, the daughter – Mussammat Wasim – acquired the property. The nephew now filed a suit to dispossess his cousin, arguing that she had a right only to maintenance till she married.

The first court held that by the custom recorded in the riwaj-i-am the daughter had no right to inherit. The daughter appealed to the divisional judge who, after a special enquiry, decided that in spite of the entry in the riwaz-i-am the daughter had a right to hold the property till she married. At the chief court, the judge countered the opinion of the divisional judge, reiterating the general rule that agnates alone were entitled to succeed, not daughters. So the nephew could dispossess Mussammat Wasim as long as he provided her maintenance till she married.[19]

The formalisation of codes of custom and the recognition of the rights of collaterals initiated a process of property litigation, opening up the possibility of collateral rights being asserted, debated, investigated, and judicially reviewed. And since court cases were frequently decided in favour of distant collaterals, displacing female cognates, a new horizon of expectations was legally fashioned.

[17] Ibid.

[18] *Mandas and Another vs. Mussammat Shah Wasim*, PR, no. 44 of 1896.

[19] The judge quoted Rattigan's opinion that daughters could keep land for maintenance till the time of marriage but this was a limited tenure and was rarely exercised because most daughters were married young, and in any case the land was most often managed by agnates.

Collaterals even began questioning practices that were earlier taken for granted. Codified law not only secured expectations, it created them, subverting the legitimacy of past expectations when they conflicted with the codification.

As the scramble for property developed and agnates awoke to the new possibilities, individual peasant households devised strategies to counter the rigid application of new rules. Each strategic move created in turn a new field of conflict over the meaning of rights.

The Politics of Adoption

The practice of adoption seemed to provide one way in which individual peasants could manoeuvre around the law of agnatic descent. But no individual strategy could entirely escape the operation of the law: it had to negotiate a space within it or around it.

Who could the sonless proprietor adopt? Could a sister's or daughter's sons be adopted? Such a practice appeared anomalous within a framework of thought that saw agnatic descent and patrilineal inheritance as the norm. When village communities were assumed to be founded on agnatic ties, suspicion of strangers was considered natural, and resistance to the adoption of a sister's son normal.[20] Inundated with contrary evidence, officials tied themselves up in knots differentiating between the norm and its permissible exceptions, between general custom and local practice, reluctantly accepting the existence of practices in the past that had been invalidated in the process of codifying custom.

[20] "The presumption is entirely against immovable property in a village community devolving through females . . ." Tupper, *PCL*, vol. III, p. 48. All the customary law volumes repeat this view, even in the case of endogamous Muslim communities. As we have seen, officials were initially reluctant to admit to the working of a principle that questioned their theory. In collecting information while codifying custom, officials like Brandreth persuaded informants to say what officials wished to record: that is, that the idea of cognatic female descent recognised in principle in sharia law was not actually followed in practice. See the early customary law volumes of the western tracts of Punjab. Roe, *Customary Law of Multan*, 1883, sec. 1; Kaul, *Customary Law of Muzaffarnagar*, 1903, sec. 5; Saunders, *Lahore S.R., 1865–69*, sec. 1; Purser, *Montgomery S.R.,* 1878, sec. II, p. 196.

The codification of custom created ever-new spaces of legal conflict. Agnates sought to use the code that sanctified and affirmed agnatic rights to question the rights of cognates in the female line. Adoptions along the female line were increasingly contested in the second half of the nineteenth century. Around 1860, in village Qazi Kot of tahsil Tarn Taran in Amritsar, a peasant proprietor, Shama, adopted his sister's son, Sant Singh.[21] When Shama died in 1871, Sant Singh continued to cultivate the 24 ghumaos and 3 kanals that Shama owned. Shama's elder brother filed a suit claiming a right to this land and disputing the adoption. The riwaj-i-am of 1868 had refused to recognise the adoption of a sister's son as valid custom amongst the Sidhu Jats of Amritsar.

When the case came up to the chief court, Campbell – one of the four judges constituting the bench – felt the need for a detailed enquiry. The local riwaj-i-am of 1868 had indeed created a presumption against the rights of a sister's son. But was the book of custom a true record of all the practices of the past? Were such adoptions recognised in Sikh times? The zillah courts had upheld the adoption, arguing that the riwaj-i-am of 1868 could not apply to an act that had happened much earlier, and in the past such adoptions were undoubtedly common.[22] If indeed past practice was different, said Campbell, it was necessary to know when "the custom changed to the non-recognition of sister's son."[23] Justice Lindsay saw no need for any special enquiry, for to him the evidence appeared unambiguous. Enquiries into several cases in the late 1860s had unquestionably established that the adoption of a sister's son was regarded as valid for inheritance throughout the province.[24] Yet new enquiries were again held, past precedents looked into, and village elders reinterrogated. After a review of the evidence the chief court finally ordered that the

[21] *Sawan Singh vs. Sant Singh*, PR, no. 1 of 1875, see appendix I, II, III.

[22] Ibid.

[23] Ibid.

[24] Lindsay felt the need to distinguish between the general right of inheritance and rights related to adoption: "It may be against the custom for a sister's son or daughter to inherit, but even in such case I cannot say there is a general prohibitory rule or custom, but that is very different to adopting a son. If a man may adopt a stranger, it stands to reason he may adopt his

adoption of a sister's son was not contrary to custom. The official book of custom, the riwaj-i-am, was judicially overruled as an authority on past practice.

Codified custom was similarly upturned in numerous other disputes over adoption. Not far from Amritsar, in a village of Moga tahsil of Ferozepur district, three brothers – Kahn Singh, Bhan Singh, and Dharm Singh – joined together in the early 1870s in a bid to reclaim land that had once belonged to their brother. Around 1845 their brother Naurang Singh had adopted his sister's son Nihal Singh.[25] Naurang Singh died and Nihal Singh looked after the land. But then the riwaj-i-am of 1868 declared that the adoption of a sister's/ daughter's son was not recognised among the Bular Jats of the district. Within a few years the courts were flooded with suits questioning such adoptions. Nihal Singh found the rights over the land he had cultivated for decades suddenly threatened.

Caught in the contradiction between code and practice, the courts again produced conflicting judgments. The assistant commissioner found that in the past the adoption of a sister's son was accepted practice, but the commissioner felt that, since this practice violated the general rule of agnatic inheritance, the onus of proving the non-applicability of the norm lay with the defendant. This proof Nihal Singh had failed to provide.[26] At the chief court Lindsay argued that the riwaj-i-am properly reflected the customs of the people and collateral succession should be upheld. Boulnois and Campbell disagreed. Campbell hesitated in delivering judgment, deterred by the relevant entry in the riwaj-i-am of the district. But after hearing the witnesses and looking at the evidence, he decided to put aside the authority of codified custom since it did not really reflect the practices of the people. He said:

> In Sikh times, when the land was of little value and young men of much value, the introduction of a new boy into the community was probably

---

nephew or his grandson, the son of his sister, and the son of his daughter." *Sawan Singh vs. Sant Singh, PR*, no. 1 of 1875.

[25] *Nihal Singh and Mussammat Rupan vs Kahn Singh and Others, PR*, no. 50 of 1875.

[26] Ibid.

looked on with satisfaction, but by the time of our regular settlements the value of land was discovered, and the brotherhood would naturally look to the chances of dividing the land of an heirless co-sharer rather than to the introduction of an extra hand to share in the profits which had begun to be considerable. Hence the main body of a tribe would be inclined to enter as a custom what they wished should be the custom and unless there were men with interests to defend, the general wish for the future was entered without protest. This has not been found uncommon, and I believe it is what took place in the present instance.[27]

Nihal Singh's rights were reaffirmed, the adoption of a sister's son was upheld as part of accepted past practice, and the suit against him dismissed with costs.

In most of these early cases on custom, extensive local enquiries were carried out in advance of any ruling against the riwaj-i-am. Each of these enquiries produced a vast mass of evidence that was difficult to reconcile with custom as codified by the British. Dewa Singh was one of the chaudhris who came to give evidence on the knotty question of adoption. He lived in a village twenty-five miles north of Qazi Kot in Amritsar. A sonless proprietor, he had treated his sister's son Lehna Singh as his own son and given him his property. Why did he do this, he was asked? Was this permissible? Dewa Singh's answer was: "I did this that he might look after me; I had no son, I made him my son; I gave him maliki [ownership]. I had an elder brother, Maggar Sing, who was dead when I made Lehna Sing my heir; but his sons were alive, they were grown up and had children; what objections could they make to the way in which I disposed of my property? Lehna Sing attended to me, and for this reason, I gave him my property."[28] Lehna Singh in turn reaffirmed the expectations of reciprocity implicit in the act of adoption. "Dewa Sing first took care of me," he said, "and now I take care of Dewa Sing."[29] Adoption carried with it obligations as well as claims. Childless proprietors wanted someone to look after the property, cultivate the land, and take care of them when they were old.[30] Within the new language

---

[27] Ibid.
[28] *Sawan Singh vs. Sant Singh*, *PR*, no. 1 of 1875.
[29] Ibid.
[30] This is brought out in Pant, "Speaking in Multiple Registers".

of law, claims taken for granted but only rarely explicitly formulated were translated as "rights".

Official prejudice against the adoption of non-agnates often led to dispossession. The preparation of the record of rights, seemingly an act of objective observation, was a process through which the agrarian world was reordered. Everything depended on the frame of reference through which the recording was done – on whether a practice appeared legitimate, normal, and permissible within this frame. Bakshish Singh in Sirhali – a village in district Amritsar – was lambardar Jodh Singh's sister's son. He cultivated Jodh Singh's land, remained in the village for forty years, and got his sons married in Sirhali. But at the time of the first settlement, British revenue officials, keen on normalising patrilineal inheritance, refused to acknowledge Bakshish Singh as a proprietor. And in the most intensely cultivated regions, where cultivable land was scarce, village opinion had by the 1880s turned against the adoption of non-agnates. Bakshish Singh had no option but to leave the village.

Once written documents became important as evidence, deeds of adoption proliferated. Sonless proprietors began writing them out, often when struck by intimations of demise, so that the household retained control over the property and distant collaterals who might have designs on it were thwarted. Bude Khan, a Naru Rajput of Hoshiarpur district, had five sons. Two of them, Samme Khan and Rode Khan, never married. On 10 October 1890 Samme Khan executed a decree declaring that Alam, one of his brother's sons, had been adopted by him and that the adoption had been ritualised some years back with the usual ceremonies. Within a month of signing the deed, Samme Khan died. Two years later, on 3 October 1892, Rode Khan executed a similar deed claiming Sahib Ali, Alam's brother, was his adopted son. He died twenty days later.[31]

Were these deeds, signed in anticipation of death, formalising past adoptions? We cannot be certain. They declare rituals of adoption had been publicly performed, sweets distributed to the brotherhood, and the boys treated for long as sons. But such declarations were necessary

[31] *Inam Das vs. Rukan Khan and others*, *PR*, no. 25 of 1896.

within the framework of British customary law, which saw these rituals as crucial for validating adoptions. It seems more likely that these were actually gifts being formalised via deeds of adoption. Before they died, Samme Khan and Rode Khan wanted to transfer their property to Sahib Ali and Alam – two sons of a deceased brother whom they were both close to. They executed adoption deeds because the legal validity of transfers through gifts was more easily challenged within the new codified custom. In fact, such strategic adoptions became so common that by the early 1890s the chief court began campaigning against counterfeit adoptions. Suspicious of every adoption deed, it overruled the judgments of lower courts, declaring many such adoptions invalid.[32] In the particular instance above the proclaimed adoption was agnatic; yet it was disallowed.

With the last decade of the nineteenth century we see a gradual hardening of judicial opinion against non-agnatic inheritance. In the case of adoption, the first move was to redefine the onus of proof. In a famous case of 1893 it was decided that the onus of proof lay with the person who claimed that a daughter's or sister's son could be adopted.[33] Until then the onus had lain on those who challenged the adoption of non-agnates.[34]

This change in the burden-of-proof clause transformed the relative power of agnates and female cognates in legal disputes. Up to the 1890s adoption cases were frequently decided in favour of the sister's or daughter's son, or even the wife's sister's son or the brother's daughter's son, despite the initial presumption having been against the transfer of property to cognates.[35] But in the early twentieth

[32] On "counterfeit" adoptions, see *PR*, no. 50 of 1893; *PR*, no. 94 of 1893; *PR*, no. 96 of 1893; *PR*, no. 142 of 1893.

[33] *PR*, no. 50 of 1893.

[34] See *PR*, no. 159 of 1890. This ruling was criticised in *PR*, no. 50 of 1893. It was said that the 1890 ruling was in favour of the adoption of a daughter's son only because the onus was presumed to lie with the party denying the validity of such adoption to prove its point.

[35] See *Hira vs Mussammat Dharmo and Others*, *PR*, no. 26 of 1872; *Sirdar Diwan Singh and Others vs Mussammat Shaubhan*, *PR*, no. 72 of 1878; *Bhupa and Others vs Utam Singh and Another*, *PR*, no. 61 of 1880. See also *PR*,

century most rulings were against such transfers.[36] And every new ruling sought to authenticate itself through a reference back to the 1893 decision. The new orthodoxy was reaffirmed again and again: sonless proprietors must adopt only male collaterals.[37] The myth of patrilineal descent, questioned persistently in courts through the first fifty years of British rule, was finally becoming a part of accepted common sense. Patrilineal male inheritance was thus historically fashioned through colonial legislation and court rulings as these confronted practices on the ground.

The court was undoubtedly a site of negotiation where custom as practice confronted custom as code, entailing a reworking of the code. But such negotiations occurred within a field of force where those in authority tried desperately to fashion the contours of all such changes. The trajectory of these refigurations was never entirely pre-defined, they did not unfold in teleological time; nor was the structure of power that mediated these processes pre-constituted, already formed, inherited from the past. If the colonial remaking of custom consolidated the village brotherhood, affirming male power, the voice of the male coparcenary community became critical to the displacement of women from within the rural property regime.

Against Gifts

Gifts, like adoptions, created space for manoeuvre within the structure of codified custom. The gift of land was a method of transferring land to a recipient who was not defined as a natural heir within the

---

no. 24 of 1867; *PR*, no. 83 of 1867; *PR*, no. 35 of 1874; *PR*, no.13 of 1873; *PR*, no. 50 of 1874; *PR*, no. 23 of 1876. On the rights to inheritance of the brother's daughter, see *Sewa Singh vs Wasawa Singh*, *PLR*, no. 58 of 1901. On the rights of wife's brother, see *Nund Lal and Others vs Lakha*, *PR*, no. 125 of 1880.

[36] See the evidence discussed in *PLR*, no. 10 of 1920.

[37] See *Ralia vs Warim Singh and Others*, *PR*, no. 94 of 1913; *Natha Singh vs Mangal and Others*, *PR*, no. 90 of 1914. *PLR*, no. 10 of 1920, found no case in Jullunder after the 1890s in which the position of a daughter's or sister's son could be legally sustained.

code. It was a means of transcending the constraints imposed by the principle of unilineal agnatic descent as well as a strategy of authenticating female cognatic descent.

Committed to the ideal of agnatic descent, officials were disturbed by a practice that seemed to question the founding principle of order. Yet they were forced to recognise that land was often given as a gift – or what officials saw as a gift. Could the practice be tolerated? If it was to be allowed, then under what conditions was it permissible?

In 1880 Kesar Singh gave his land – 127 kanals 6 marlas – to his cousin Nand Singh. Kesar Singh was an impoverished cultivator living in a village of Hoshiarpur tahsil.[38] His revenue most often remained unpaid, and his debts had accumulated. He had no son and his relationship with his brother, Sahib Singh, was strained. In his time of trouble, it was his cousin Nand Singh who came to his help, paying his revenue and debts, and meeting his subsistence needs. When Kesar Singh died in 1896, his brother challenged the gift and sued for possession of the land that Nand Singh had held for eighteen years. After an investigation, the chief court upheld the gift and affirmed Nand Singh's rights. It had no doubt that Jat customs permitted sonless proprietors to make gifts "on account of services rendered".[39] Recast in the language of commerce, unencumbered by emotion and sentiment, gift here appeared as payment, and hence legitimate because necessary.

Officials recognised that amongst endogamous groups gifts of land to daughters and sisters was common, even if agnates and collaterals increasingly challenged the legitimacy of such gifts. Abid

---

[38] *PLR*, no. 102 of 1901.

[39] In several earlier cases this right had been recognised. See *Sobha vs Gyana*, PR, no. 116 of 1886; *Gopal Singh vs Kheman*, PR, no. 85 of 1889; *Indar vs Luddar Singh*, PR, no. 18 of 1890; *Sher Singh vs Sohail Singh*, PR, no. 19 of 1890; *Narain Singh vs Gurmukh Singh*, PR, no. 116 of 1894; *Rala vs Bauna and Others*, PR, no. 14 of 1901. See also *PR*, no. 62 of 1884. In a judgment of 1894 Plowden had said: "The case seems to show that where there is a sort of moral obligation to compensate for services rendered there is sufficient good consideration to support a gift to one of the heirs, to the exclusion of the rest." *PR*, no. 116 of 1894. This statement of 1894 set the pattern of subsequent rulings.

Ali was a Sayyad living in mauza Chuma of tahsil Gurgaon.[40] He died at the turn of the nineteenth century, leaving a widow and a daughter. Having succeeded to the land as widow's life estate – i.e. for the duration of her life – Mussammat Zainab made a verbal gift in favour of her daughter; and in June 1904, three months after the gift, the mutation of names was formalised.[41] Now, some of Abid Ali's collaterals in the fourth degree of agnatic relationship filed a suit questioning the validity of the gift and the right of the daughter to inherit. After extensive enquiries in the Sayyad villages of the region, the divisional judge, Clifford, declared that among the Sayyads the daughter had the right to inherit in the absence of sons or widows, and that even among the Sheikhs daughters succeeded to the exclusion of male collaterals. As the enquiry was carried through the villages, the patwaris reported case after case where such succession had taken place.[42] When the appeal went up to the chief court, Mussammat Zainab's gift to her daughter was ruled as valid and the claims of the male collaterals were dismissed.[43]

The Sayyad story was replicated amongst the Awans. We see Awan landowners gifting land to non-agnates, and agnates contesting the practice; we see the judges forever vacillating between their commitment to the agnatic principle and their awareness of another reality, between what had to be perforce allowed and what was seen as just. Defined by the play of these contrary pressures, the logic of gifts was both accepted and questioned.

Consider another case. Mawaz lived in Mardwal, a village in the district of Shahpur. Like many other proprietors who had no son,

---

[40] *Muzaffar Ali and Others vs Mussammat Zainab and Others*, PR, no. 58 of 1910.

[41] "Life estate" being the term for "duration of life".

[42] Ibid.

[43] See also *Mussammat Maqsudul Nisa vs Mussammat Kaniz Zohra*, PR, no. 13 of 1908. In this case it was ruled: "The Riwaj-i-am is very clear on this point, and among the Sayyads of Gurgaon a daughter is said to exclude any but sons and grandsons, and several instances are given of such succession, including one in which the daughter gifted part of the estates to her son. The Riwaj-i-am provides in answer to a very explicit and exhaustive question that a daughter succeeds to a full estate."

Mawaz gifted his land, part by part, first to his sister's son, Sher Shah, and then to his wife's brother, Baksha. On each occasion Mawaz's half-brothers contested the gifts. On each occasion the suits were dismissed on the grounds that such gifts were valid, and numerous instances of such gifts exist. But after 1888, and particularly after 1894, a number of judgments were passed against such gifts. This encouraged the half-brothers to sue again against both the gifts. This time the division judge ruled against the gifts and the case went up to the chief court on appeal. Justice C.J. Roe at the chief court declared that the initial presumption was against transfers of land to non-agnates, but admitted that amongst Awans such gifts were in conformity with custom.[44] Yet, bound by his theoretical commitment to the agnatic principle, Roe felt that such a transfer was unjust. So the gifts were endorsed and Baksha's rights were ratified, but he was forced to bear the costs of the case.

Proceeding from the assumptions of evolutionary theories, the general code of agricultural custom had initially pronounced strongly against transfers of land to non-agnates through gifts. When the code was applied to local contexts, and enquiries conducted into local practices, the rule was modified, broadened, and made more flexible. Between the 1860s and 1888 most rulings were in favour of gifts.[45] But in 1888 the burden-of-proof clause was changed in the case of gifts – as was done for adoptions – signalling a trajectory of

[44] Roe was persuaded by the views of James Wilson who had compiled the Riwaj-i-am of Shahpur district. Wilson had found most tribes asserting the general rule that a sonless proprietor cannot give away his ancestral land without the consent of his agnates, but the Awans had categorically stated that land could be given to the daughter, daughter's son, sister's son, son-in-law, or to one of the agnates. "As an Awan girl almost always marries an Awan, and most commonly marries an agnate," said Wilson, "the land is not taken away from the tribe." Operating on the basis of the general codified rule for agriculturists, Wilson had initially disallowed such gifts, but after his enquiries in the cold weather of 1893–4 he spoke of the special norm amongst Awans. See answers to question nos 11 and 12 in Wilson, *General Code of Tribal Custom in Shahpur District*, vol. XV.

[45] See *PR*, no. 43 of 1877; *PR*, no. 62 of 1884; *PR*, no. 136 of 1884; *PR*, no. 49 of 1886; *PR*, no. 116 of 1886; *PR*, no. 178 of 1888.

change that was fortified by the judgment of the chief court passed on 23 May 1894. By the end of the century, the general tendency was to rule against gifts.[46] Transfers through gifts continued, and so did legal rulings in favour of these transfers, but the tide had turned against the practice; and the sanction for such transfers was now seen increasingly as exception rather than norm.[47] Village opinion – that is, the perception of the coparcenary male brotherhood – and legal wisdom fused to assert the power of the agnatic principle, reaffirming male command over rural society.

The Will of the Dead

By the early twentieth century peasants began writing out testamentary wills to formalise the transfer of property after death. Many of these wills were in favour of non-agnates – daughters, daughter's sons, sisters, sister's sons, and sons-in-law. Wills *had* to be recorded, given that this was a regime which devalued the authority of words, doubted the authenticity of oral commitments, and fetishised the legitimacy of written records.[48] And as property transfers to cognates (i.e. along the female line) were increasingly seen as illegitimate – both by the village community and colonial officials – individual peasants had to search for new strategies to counter the power of the prejudice. Writing out wills appeared to be one such possible strategy.

Written testamentary wills were rare within peasant society before British rule. Colonial officials enquiring into custom found little evidence of the practice. Codifying the customary practices of district Hazara, E.G. Wace said "wills are absolutely unknown"; from Shahpur, James Wilson reported that there was "no true custom in any tribe of writing wills"; and Tupper, synthesising general opinion from the various regions, pronounced that wills were definitely

---

[46] *Baksha vs Mir Baz and Another*, PR, no. 79 of 1896.

[47] *Rala vs Bauna and Others*, PR, no. 14 of 1901; *Muzaffar Ali and Others vs Mussammat Zainab and Others*. See also PR, no. 85 of 1889; PR, no. 18 & no. 19 of 1890; PR, no. 116 of 1894.

[48] On writing and recording as strategies of colonial regulation, see Bhabha, "Sly Civility"; Raman, *Document Raj*; Moir, "*Kaghazi Raj*"; Smith, *Rule by Records*.

"foreign to the indigenous system of the country".[49] This in a sense was comforting evidence. Officials were keen to believe that written wills were characteristic of advanced societies – where the autonomous individual was the locus of independent decision-making – and uncommon in archaic cultures regulated by collective norms and untouched by literacy.[50] Individual wills could not be seen as normal in "tribal" formations that idealised patrilineal descent. If wills had the power to transfer property to cognates, the founding principle of customary law would be threatened.[51] When the Awans of Shahpur declared that they recognised the power to bequeath by will, the settlement officer recording the riwaj-i-am reluctantly noted the oral evidence. But he added that "if the true spirit of the tribal custom is to be followed no will should in any circumstances be held binding on the heirs."[52] In his digest of tribal law, Rattigan emphasised that "the devolution of property by will is not only unknown, but it is op- posed to the fundamental principles of the Customary law."[53] Yet with the new practice gaining currency, legal authorities began recognis- ing the need to institutionalise it as custom.[54]

[49] Prinsep's compilation of the tribal codes of Hazara district abstracted by Wace in *Hazara, S.R.*, 1853, para 12; Wilson, *General Code of Tribal Custom in Shahpur*; Tupper, *PCL*, vol. III, p. 94.

[50] In the West, testamentary wills became common with the spread of literacy. In England, testatory wills have been widely analysed to explore the power of kin and family within rural society. Most of the studies show that wills refer only to close kin tied to the testators through strong ties of sentiment and obligation. Writing the will was an act through which the rights of wider kin were legally denied, and the importance of the nuclear group affirmed. See, in particular, Wrightson, "Kinship in an English Village"; and Macfarlane, "The Myth of the Peasantry".

[51] Wills have been difficult to legalise wherever customary law affirms the rights of the wider lineage over property. Customary law restricts the testator's testamentary capacity, whereas testatory wills subvert the logic of customary law. See Sagay, "Customary Law and Freedom of Testamentary Power".

[52] Wilson, *General Code of Tribal Custom in Shahpur District; Ali Moham- mad & Another vs Dulla, PR.*, no. 26 of 1901.

[53] Rattigan, *A Digest of Civil Law for the Punjab*.

[54] In his digest of customary law W.H. Rattigan wrote: "in this province although at the period of our conquest wills were practically unknown the

This process of recognition was difficult. What was to be the norm and how was it to be interpreted? Convinced of the force of the agnatic principle yet apprehensive of obstructing the wheels of progress, judges gave ambiguous verdicts, upholding the legal validity of wills on the one hand,[55] and restraining the limits of their operation on the other.[56] Contrary signals created space for conflicting strategies. If gifts and adoptions were sought to be reaffirmed by written wills – so that the will of the living was not challenged posthumously – official commitment to the agnatic principle nurtured the ambitions of agnates, encouraging them to sue against practices that deprived them of collateral rights. Each dispute that was judged was treated as a special case and each judgment was seen as relevant to a particular instance. At times the judges said the will was valid but not binding.

The Rights of Chastity

Within codified custom the rights of women – widows or daughters – were made dependent on a notion of bodily purity. The codes proclaimed that by custom an "unchaste" widow lost her rights to her husband's property.[57] In everyday life, however, the meaning of chast-

---

subsequent practice has so far sanctioned the power to execute such instruments that it is too late now to deny its existence . . . although the power of testation is a later development than the power of alienation *inter vivos*, yet where the latter is once clearly and fully recognised in a community the introduction of the former is inevitable, and is soon acquiesced in as a necessary element in the law of property." Rattigan, *Digest*, p. 24.

[55] For judgments which deny the validity of wills, see *Muhammad Khan and Others vs Atar Khan and Others*, PR, no. 121 of 1886; *Bahadur and Another vs Mussammat Bholi and Others*, PR, no. 108 of 1893; *Mukarrab vs Fatta and Another*, PR, no. 88 of 1895.

[56] For cases in which the right was upheld despite an awareness that the practice was not common, see *Mansabdar vs Sadar-ud-din*, PR, no. 10 of 1892; *Umar vs Mussammat Sahib Khatum*, PR, no. 76 of 1892. See also *Anokha vs Mohun Lall and Others*, PR, no. 2 of 1870.

[57] Tupper, *PCL*, vol. III, p. 46; Wilson, *The General Code of Tribal Custom*, pt II, section 1 (c); Krishna, *Memorandum on the Tribal Customs of the Rohtak District*, para 21.

ity was less clear and its implication more uncertain than the codes stipulated. And this ambiguity was reflected in judicial practice.

In 1868 Mamraj, a zamindar of a village in Delhi Division, filed a suit for possession of a piece of land that he had bought from Mussammat Soondur.[58] Mamraj complained that a certain Bhola, along with a few other peasants, had refused to let him occupy his land. As the case moved from the court of the assistant commissioner to that of the commissioner and then to the chief court, it was Mussammat Soondur's sexual purity that came up for scrutiny. Mamraj's rights came to hinge on Soondur's chastity.

Mussammat Soondur's husband, Sook Lal, died around 1853. Bhola, who was distantly related to Sook Lal, then cultivated the land that Soondur had inherited. What exactly the terms were on which the land was given out we do not know, but we do know that Bhola raised money to get Soondur's daughter, Nuttia, married in 1857. Some years later, Soondur began living with another man, namely the plaintiff Mamraj, bore him a child, and subsequently around 1866 sold her land to him for Rs 100.[59] Bhola was now unwilling to give up his occupancy of the plot that had been in his possession for many years and which was contiguous to his own land.

Was Soondur's sale to Mamraj valid? Did she in fact have any right over the land she had sold him? When Mamraj filed the suit, Bhola's pleader argued that Soondur had forfeited her right because of her unchastity, and that rights over the land had passed to her daughter, Nuttia. Brought before the deputy commissioner, Nuttia renounced her own claim. Bhola now asserted his right to dispossess the "unchaste" widow and inherit the land as a relative of Sook Lal.

In terms of codified custom, as mentioned, unchastity led to the loss of the widow's rights. Seemingly categorical, this code was yet open to diverse readings. What constituted unchastity? The definition of chastity was clearly linked to control over property as well as over the body of the woman. A widow could have a relationship with other males within her husband's household, and cohabitation with a husband's brother was common: in fact it was not only permissible, it

---

[58] *Mamraj vs Bhola and Others, PR*, no. 78 of 1869.
[59] Ibid.

was even considered desirable. It allowed her husband's family control over her sexuality, her body, and her inheritance. Relationships outside the household threatened this control. And when the widow moved out of the husband's household to live with another man, she entirely repudiated the claims of her marital household over her. It was in such instances of male household property being threatened and collective male right over the wife of the household being questioned that charges of unchastity were made public. Unchastity became the ground on which conflicts over property – land and women – were played out.

In the case of Soondur, everyone accepted that she lived with Mamraj, had deserted her husband's household, and was therefore "unchaste". Had she then any right over her inheritance? The code did specify that an unchaste widow lost her rights over her husband's property. But what did "loss" mean? As pleaders and lawyers debated the concept of "loss", specifying the term, turning its meanings around, we see custom in the process of being legally made. Rattigan argued and the court accepted that unchastity prevented a widow from inheriting her husband's property, but also that the absence of her chastity need not mean loss of right over property that she had already inherited. Sundoor's unchastity was publicly affirmed but her right to sell the land to Mamraj was upheld.

Discussions of a widow's sexual morality became tied in convoluted ways to claims over her property. When Kharak Singh, a Jat peasant of Gurdaspur tahsil, left his village he had no intention of returning. [60] Before leaving he told his wife, Mussammat Chandi, that she could marry any man she liked. Some time later, Chandi went to live with her husband's cousin, Ishar Singh, and bore two children, a son and a daughter. Eight years later Kharak Singh returned to the village. He continued to live in it without however making any move to assert any conjugal rights over Chandi. But when Ishar Singh died, Kharak Singh attempted to claim his property, arguing that he, Kharak Singh, had not actually left his wife, that her relationship with Ishar Singh was therefore both invalid and immoral, and that he Kharak Singh was in fact the real father of Chandi's children. What rights could Kharak

[60] *Lachu vs Dal Singh*, PR, no. 33 of 1896.

Singh have over Ishar Singh's property? To assert this right, Chandi's relationship with Ishar Singh was both accepted – for Chandi was the only link with Ishar Singh – and denied. If Kharak Singh continued to be the husband, Chandi could have no independent right, and the immorality of her relationship with Ishar Singh would deprive her of any possible claim over his property – a double displacement. But was Chandi's action legally immoral? Did she have no right over Ishar Singh's property?

In deciding the case the chief court had to reflect on two issues. First, in what circumstances could a wife live with another man without violating morality, without being unchaste? The judges agreed that it was wrong for a woman to leave her husband and live with another man. But what if her husband left home and did not return, or said that he would not return?[61] Did this not amount to a repudiation of marriage? Second, what ought to be the standard of morality through which local practices were to be judged? Could they be judged through a universal criterion? The first court had denied the charges of immorality, seen Kharak Singh's action in leaving the village as tantamount to divorce, and Chandi's move to Ishar Singh's house as marriage. The divisional judge denied the fact of divorce as well as the remarriage and pronounced Chandi's action immoral, her children illegitimate. The chief court then confirmed the decisions of the first court. Kharak Singh had clearly told Chandi that he would not return, and on his return had demonstrated no evidence of a continued conjugal relationship with her. This showed that he himself considered the marriage dissolved. As for Chandi's relationship with Ishar Singh, the village community had accepted it as legitimate. And such relationships could not be judged through some abstract standard of morality:

> On this subject morality must be taken as equivalent to custom. Some communities, religious or tribal, regard marriage as a sacrament, for which religious ceremonies are necessary; others require no religious ceremonies,

[61] On an earlier occasion the chief court had declared that a custom that allowed a wife to live with another man while her husband was alive, even though absconding, was immoral. *PR*, no. 72 of 1892. See also *PR*, no. 47 of 1890.

but insist on certain legal formalities; and others require no formalities at all, but merely a clear expression of the intention of the parties to live together as man and wife. Some allow a plurality of wives; some only one wife. Some allow no divorce at all; others allow only under special circumstances; others allow it at least to the husband without restriction.

And so the court dismissed Kharak Singh's appeal, and upheld Chandi's rights on Ishar Singh's property.

Let me give another instance to demonstrate this link between charges of unchastity and the politics of property. Ramsukh was a Jat peasant proprietor in Bangraon village of Fatehabad tahsil in the arid plains of Hissar.[62] He had two brothers, Uda and Toda, and two wives, Mussammat Surjan and Mussammat Singari. When Ramsukh died in the 1890s his widows inherited his property and continued to live in the joint household. Some time after Ramsukh's death, Mussammat Surjan gave birth to a boy. It was rumoured that the child was illegitimate. In 1909 Toda and Uda, Ramsukh's brothers, filed a suit asserting their claims over Ramsukh's property. Both the widows had become unchaste, they said, and so had lost their rights. They in fact stated that Bega, Mussammat Surjan's son, was born twenty-one months after the death of Ramsukh. The case was finally settled through a compromise. Ramsukh's property was divided into four equal shares, one each for Uda, Toda, Mussammat Surjan, and Bega. In view of these shares in the property, the charge of unchastity was dropped and Bega was adopted by Uda to cleanse the boy of the taint of illegitimacy and incorporate him formally into the joint household. Four years later Uda adopted again – this time his brother Toda's son Kulasa. The reason for his adoption we do not know: possibly Bega was still seen as a stranger, possibly his uncertain paternity created an anxiety, possibly Toda was keen to strengthen his son's claim over Uda's property. Now Bega filed a suit against this second adoption, arguing that it was invalid and ought not to affect his rights in his adoptive father's property. As the case unfolded, the question of Mussammat Surjan's unchastity and Bega's illegitimate

[62] *PLR*, no. 10 of 1920.

birth reappeared as arguments against Bega's claim to property. The case dragged on. Enquiries were held. The legitimacy of each adoption was debated and rights over the property remained in dispute. In the meantime two generations of males passed away. By 1920, when the case was finally decided, Uda the adoptive father, as well as the two adopted sons – Bega and Kulasa – were all dead.

The court accepted that Mussammat Surjan was unchaste, yet upheld Bega's rights. It was argued that Uda and Toda had lost their right to raise the issue of unchastity and illegitimacy. They had agreed to take shares of their brother's property, they had adopted Bega with the consent of the village brotherhood, formalising the adoption by performing the necessary rituals and ceremonies in public, and subsequently they had got Bega married. Having accepted Bega as an adopted son and integrating him within the village brotherhood, they could not subsequently redesignate him the illegitimate son of an unchaste mother. They could not violate the terms of a compromise from which they had personally gained and through which they had acquired a share of the widow's property. In this particular instance the widow's unchastity had been deemed legally irrelevant.

The court ultimately decreed that an illegitimate son had as much right as any stranger. And since the adoption of a stranger was valid when it was with the consent of collaterals, and sanctified by rituals and ceremonies performed before the brotherhood, the rights of an illegitimate son so adopted could not be denied. Since Bega's adoption had been ratified through public rituals, the rights of his widow Mussammat Dhanni could not be abrogated.

Thus, it seems that public declarations of unchastity within peasant families were not always underpinned by a sense of moral outrage. Behind the rhetoric of morality we see male collaterals struggling to consolidate patriarchal control over property and individual peasants pursuing self-interest. In such struggles women were not always helpless victims. Maligned and targeted, they often managed to retain control over property, and at times also their sense of honour from the slurs of immorality. Immorality, as the courts repeatedly discovered, was difficult to define.

The Community and the Individual

The Punjab Laws Act of 1872 codified the right of "pre-emption".[63] This meant that the first right to purchase a piece of land being sold in the market could now be individually specified, as also the individuals who could be prevented from purchasing it.[64] To colonial officials it seemed natural that this right should be linked to the theory of patrilineal agnatic descent. If the proprietary body of a village was tied through common bonds of descent, and if the codification of customary law was meant to reproduce those bonds, then a right of pre-emption had to be vested in this proprietary body. Land could not be freely transferred to an outsider. Reaffirmed first through rights of inheritance, adoption, and gift as they were codified, the norms of agnatic descent were to be reinforced through rules that regulated rights of sale. The community had to be protected from the unrestrained play of individual desires, the proprietary body had to be sheltered from the corrosive effect of market forces.

In village administration papers written before 1872 there was usually a clause that gave this right of pre-emption to agnates, and after them to members of the village community in general. The Punjab Laws Act of 1872 specified more clearly the hierarchy of claims. In the case of villages held on ancestral shares (pattidari), the first right of pre-emption belonged to co-sharers in order of their lineal relationship to the person selling the land, then to other co-sharers of the village jointly, and if no joint claim was made then to individual landholders of the same village. After 1872, the riwaj-i-ams simply said the custom of pre-emption was regulated by the 1872 Act. Codes of custom that claimed to embody tribal practice were here determined by a legally

[63] *The Punjab Laws Act (IV of 1872): With Introduction, Notes and Rules*, 1897. See also Tupper, *PCL*; Rattigan, *A Digest of Customary Law*. For reformulation of the pre-emption law after 1900, see GOI Rev. & Agr. (Rev.), November 1900, A 3–6; GOI Leg. (Leg.), March 1905, A 59–61.

[64] "Pre-emption right" is the right of an individual or entity to acquire property before it is offered for sale in the market. It specifies the "first right to buy" and the "right of first refusal". In relation to shareholding companies, it refers to the right of shareholders to acquire a share before the share is offered to the public.

invented custom. The right to pre-emption was logically deduced from the myth of patrilineal descent and the fiction of coparcenary agnatic brotherhoods. In the pre-colonial context, when land was abundant – save in the intensive margins of the Doab tracts – and sales rare, pre-emption could not possibly be an effective right.

The clauses of the 1872 act relating to pre-emption were seemingly clear and categorical.[65] They sought to take account of all possible contexts and hierarchise the order of claims. Yet in the actual practice of everyday life the rule allowed space for conflicting claims, opposed readings, ambiguous definitions. And the right of pre-emption became an instrument in the general struggle for control over property.

The key terms of the rule were variously interpreted and endlessly redefined. Sometime in the mid 1870s a village proprietor named Kaka in mauza Mudki of Ferozepur tahsil sold a piece of land – 115 kanals 14 marlas – to some other proprietors of the village.[66] In patti Dogran of mauza Mudki, where this land was located, there were thirty-two proprietors. Sixteen of them combined to file a suit against the sale. Their claim was that, being proprietors of the same patti, they had a right of pre-emption against sale of the land to outsiders. The wajib-ul-arz of the village made no mention of any such right but clause 2, section 14, of Act IV of 1872 did. But this clause, as indeed all clauses of all acts, could be decoded in dissimilar ways. It stated that the right of pre-emption belonged to the landowners of the patti or other subdivisions of the village in which the property was situated *jointly*. What did this really mean? The judicial assistant, Gardiner, felt that the term "jointly" implied that all the pattidars, the proprietors of the patti, had to jointly assert the right and collectively hold the land. No proprietor could individually prevent the sale of land to outsiders; and since the purchaser in this case was also from the same village, he had as much right to buy the land as the pattidars of Dogran who were protesting against the sale. At the chief court, Plowden read the meaning of the term "jointly" differently. For him the term "jointly" referred to the fact that proprietors in a patti – a

[65] On pre-emption, see sec. 9–20 of *The Punjab Laws Act (IV of 1872)*.
[66] *PR*, no. 94 of 1877.

subdivision of a village – were assumed to be joint owners descended from a common ancestor; it did not mean that all of them had to unite to pre-empt the sale of land to outsiders. Every proprietor could exercise this joint right in his individual capacity. Plowden was one of those who believed that the village community had to be preserved, and that the right of pre-emption was essential to prevent the entry of outsiders into the intimate community of a patti bonded by its collective link to a common ancestor. To demand that all co-sharers unite every time to prevent the sale of land to an outsider was in effect to nullify the clause. So the right of an individual to exercise a joint right was upheld and the sale disallowed. The judgment closed the arguments in this particular case but did not resolve the problem of interpretation. Who was the joint holder/co-sharer? What defined the superior claims of one individual co-sharer as against another? As the value of land soared, and landowners monopolised the available land in the fertile tracts, these issues were endlessly reconsidered in the property disputes that swamped the local courts.

The concept of joint rights was always difficult to define. In some regions different forms of co-sharing rights intersected. Multan in the mid nineteenth century was a dry tract. Cultivators who wanted to irrigate their fields had to mobilise capital and labour to sink wells. Those who dug the wells, as we have seen, were known as chakdars, and they had co-sharing rights in the well.[67] At times the holder of the land on which the well was dug was himself a chakdar; but often he merely collected a haq-zamindari from the chakdars who had sunk the well with his permission. By the 1860s we get proliferating evidence of sales of individual shares in these wells. In such sales, who had the right to pre-empt – the landholder collecting haq-zamindari or the chakdars?

Around 1865 Muckdum Ali Mohammad and Sewa Ram bought one-fourth shares in six wells in two villages of Multan. Three years later Sewa Ram sold his shares to Omar Ali, on whose land the wells

---

[67] See ch. 4 above. See Roe, *Multan S.R.*, 1883; *PR*, no. 34 of 1868. The 1868 judgment recognised that the chakdars had a heritable and transferable right in his wells. See also *PR*, no. 5 of 1873.

were situated, and Muckdum Ali bought another one-fourth share in them. Now Muckdum Ali disputed the transfer of Sewa Ram's rights to Omar Ali and asserted the right of chakdars to pre-empt such sales. Omar Ali in turn filed a suit claiming that, as a proprietor of the land on which the wells were situated, he had a right to pre-empt the sales to Muckdum Ali in 1868. A chakdar, he said, was only an asami dumiyanee (intermediate holder), while those who collected haq-zamindari had a superior status. As usual, innumerable enquiries were held, judges differed and dithered, expressed contrary positions, and overturned judgments. Finally the chief court declared that Muckdum Ali as a chakdar had a greater right to pre-empt the sale of shares in the wells than the proprietor who collected haq-zamindari.

This dispute again shows how the right of pre-emption was difficult to define and that it was used by right holders to consolidate their control over land by preventing others from acquiring property. Muckdum Ali and Omar Ali both filed suits claiming the right of pre-emption, hoping to use the law in their mutual struggle to evict the other.[68] To promote individual interest, the language of custom and the sanctity of patrilineal rights were reaffirmed in the conflict over individual rights. The brotherhood as a collective did not struggle against the individual: individuals used the language of brotherhood to further individuated interest. Everything was done in the name of the brotherhood within a regime where this language had been officially legitimated.

As the demand for land intensified and its value increased, landowners used the right of pre-emption to maximise their advantage in the market. The commodity economy did not displace the language of custom, it often operated through it; the limits, constraints, and possibilities within the economy were defined by it.

Ghansham Das, landowner of a village around Delhi, wanted to sell a piece of land.[69] He offered it to Hurdeo and another pattidar for Rs 1200. They procrastinated, showing no eagerness to buy the land,

[68] There were two cross-appeals arising out of cross suits for pre-emptions: (1) *Muckdoom Shah Ali Mohammed vs Oomar Ali*, and (2) *Oomur Ali vs Muckdoom Shah Ali Mohammed*, PR, no. 44 of 1870.

[69] *Mehur Chand and Others vs Hurdeo and Others*, PR, no. 30 of 1870.

demanding that the occupancy tenants on the land be thrown out, and asking that the price of the land be lowered. Then in October 1868 Ghansham sold the land to five pattidars and seven occupancy tenants. Two years after the sale, in April 1870 Hurdeo filed a suit pleading that the sale be cancelled and that he and some other pattidars be allowed a right of pre-emption. The extra-assistant commissioner rejected the appeal after an enquiry, saying that for six years everyone in the village knew of Ghansham's intention to sell the land, and that Ghansham had in fact negotiated with Hurdeo. Since Hurdeo had had adequate opportunity to buy, he had no right of escheat.[70] The commissioner of Delhi later felt that the sale should be annulled, but the higher appellate court refused the right of pre-emption.

Did Ghansham give adequate opportunity to Hurdeo to buy the land? Did Hurdeo have a right of pre-emption? We do not know. But what is clear is that the right of pre-emption was being deployed to consolidate property rights, expel competitors, exclude competition, and threaten sellers. Codified custom was being used as a strategy to prevent a market operation, not to defend tradition. Individuals were mobilising some members of the brotherhoods to fight others. It is through such fights that the language of law became part of the mental world of peasants. The decisions, the changing opinions at different levels, defined the realm of the possible. They shaped the nature of future struggles.

Consider another similar instance of the use of pre-emption rights. In the 1860s a proprietor in a village of Rohtak sold 17 beeghas and 17 biswas.[71] Hashim was keen on buying the land but unwilling to offer more than Rs 400 for it. After a period of fruitless negotiation,

---

[70] At present, escheat generally refers to the power of the state to acquire property for which there is no legal owner. This happens when an individual dies without a valid will, or without relatives who are legally entitled to inherit the property. In feudal England such estates reverted to the crown, a norm that was abolished by the Administration of Estates Act, 1925. In colonial Punjab, since all agnates had a right to claim property after the death of a sonless proprietor, the courts had to often arbitrate on the relative power of these claims, and decide who had the reversionary right.

[71] *Goomanee and Others vs Rahmuddin and Others*, PR, no. 35 of 1870.

the land was sold for Rs 525 in twenty-five small shares. When this sale was finalised, Hashim filed a suit asserting that his land was located next to the plot sold, and so he had a preferential right to buy the land. The purchasers said they had a stronger claim to the land since they resided in the same thok – a subdivision of the village tied, once again, by mythic ties of descent – as the seller. Who in this case had the stronger right? It proved difficult to tell. The assistant commissioner's opinion was different from that of the commissioner, and the chief court differed from both when the appeal came up from the commissioner.

In this conflict, again, the right of pre-emption was being exploited to play the market. Hashim claimed pre-emption rights when negotiations with him fell through. He used the argument of vicinage – his land being in the vicinity of the land sold – to establish his preferential right to the land, and questioned the rights of others to buy it. In stressing that they belonged to the same thok as the seller, the purchasers used the language of law to prove co-sharing as the basis of a right to purchase. These conflicting claims were, in fact, intriguing. According to the assumptions of the wajib-ul-arz the brotherhood that had the right to pre-empt would be related, being lineal descendants of a common ancestor. Here, Hashim was a Malee (a community of gardeners), Rahmuddin and Ala Baksh, who bought the land, were Kassabs (butchers); and both parties claimed proximity to a proprietor who was a Sheikh. All of them actually lived in different thoks and belonged to communities which could not have been related. But they deployed the discourse of custom and referred to the right of pre-emption to operate in a market where land was acquiring a price.

Who was the Outsider?

The customary law codified by colonial officials was premised on the assumption that the village community – particularly of the zamindari and pattidari type – were bonded by lineage ties, that they were agnates descended from a common ancestor. To defend the village proprietary body from outsiders was to protect the rights of agnates against strangers. But officials soon realised that the simplicity of this norm was illusory. On the ground, reality was more complicated. Village and agnatic ties were not always coterminous: village communities were not inevitably tied through common descent.[72] Non-agnates could be co-residents, and distance could separate agnates. The proprietary body and agnates were in fact frequently at war, citing the same rule to fight for their rights. And in the courts of law the initial norm could also produce contrary judgments.

Some years after Mussammat Bholi died, in the early years of the twentieth century one Dasounda Singh appeared to claim his right over the land she left.[73] Who was Dasounda Singh? He said he was the nephew of Albel Singh, who had originally possessed the land. After Albel Singh's death the land had passed to his son, Nathu, and then to Nathu's widow Bholi, who died childless. The proprietors of the village, mauza Mohla Mazra of Ambala – who had taken over the land after Bholi's death – avowed that Dasounda Singh's declarations were fictive, that he was no nephew of Albel Singh and was resident at another village, and that the latter had been granted the land by ancestors of the present proprietors. Since the land originally belonged to a proprietary body, they had a reversionary right on the land. While Dasounda Singh and the proprietors of mauza Mohla Mazra were locked in battle, they were united in their claim that the land should not pass on to strangers.

But who was the outsider – Dasounda Singh or the proprietors of Mohla Mazra? The evidence was uncertain, as was the very idea of an outsider. It was clear that Albel Singh had come to the village in the middle decades of the nineteenth century. The 1856 revenue papers showed him as the owner of the relevant plot of land. But had he purchased the land or had it been gifted to him? We know that he married a woman of the village and settled within it. But there was no documentary proof that his father-in-law Rutal had gifted him the land in question. Equally, on the other side, there was no sale deed to attest that it had been purchased. Could these be significant

---

[72] See ch. 3 above.
[73] *Dasounda Singh vs Mangal and Others, PR*, no. 18 of 1910.

facts when innumerable enquiries by the courts showed that in the mid nineteenth century such written documents were yet to become common? The only evidence that could be legally admitted was the testimony of the village brotherhood. In this case, however, it was a party to the dispute.

How was the evidence to be read? The first court refused to recognise the plaintiff as an agnate and denied him any right to Albel Singh's land. The divisional judge accepted that Dasounda Singh was the nephew but still refused him any right to succeed since he was not a resident of Mohla Mazra and a member of its proprietary body. Even as an agnate he was an outsider. But Dasounda Singh pursued the case, appealing to the chief court, where the earlier judgments had all been overturned. The chief court had no doubt that Dasounda Singh was an agnate and recognised the right of a non-resident agnate to succeed since Albel Singh had no surviving kin – neither agnate nor cognate in the female line – in the village of his residence. The onus was on the proprietary body to prove that the plaintiff had no right as a non-resident.[74] This it had not done. The right of escheat could not be presumed to exist with the proprietary body: it had to be proved.

Similar wars between agnates and the proprietor body were evident in village after village from the late nineteenth century.[75] As landowners increasingly acquired rights in different villages, the myth of homogeneous pattidari brotherhoods tied by blood was severely battered. When officials clung to the theory of male agnatic descent and recognised the rights of non-resident agnates as superior to co-shares within the village, they further subverted their own theory of compact village communities comprising co-residential coparceners.[76]

[74] For cases in which the right of non-resident agnates was clearly recognised, see *PR*, no. 110 of 1906.

[75] See *Shaman and Others vs Sardha and Others*, *PR*, no. 61 of 1898; *Rakam Din, Ghulam and Others vs Mussammat Mariam and Others*, *PR*, no. 68 of 1898; *Chet Singh and Others vs Samad Singh and Others*, *PR*, no. 78 of 1898; *Bishen Singh and Others vs Bhagwan Singh and Others*, *PR*, no. 28 of 1904; *Nihala and Others vs Rahmatullah and Others*, *PR*, no. 137 of 1908.

[76] Tupper declared in his founding work that the tie of blood to the near kinsmen of the tribe was stronger than the civil nexus of joint ownership.

In the process the idea of the insider and the outsider grew more and more confused and complicated. Colonial officials spoke of sustaining the inner coherence of the village community and protecting it from the disruptive clutches of strangers. But the stranger was becoming increasingly difficult to define. The village as a bounded territory provided one marker, kinship as a spatial boundary produced another. Where these two conceptions of space overlapped, the conceptual foundations of the colonial understanding of North Indian agrarian society was not disturbed. When the two spaces diverged, as was more often the case, the officials were thoroughly confused. How could they concretise their patriarchal vision, protect the agrarian community and its customs, if the identity of the community to be protected was uncertain?

The ambiguities involved in the notion of an outsider were sought to be resolved through the enactment of the Punjab Land Alienation Act of 1900, which identified the non-agriculturist as the dangerous outsider from whose acquisitive clutches the land of village communities was to be preserved. Since the 1860s Punjab's officials had voiced concern over land passing from agriculturists to non-agriculturists. Village enquiries had revealed an alarming picture of large-scale land transfers, and the annual figures of mortgages and debt compiled by the land records and registration departments confirmed the fears, providing statistics to authenticate impressions.[77] The extent of area sold annually had boomed after the mid nineteenth century. The average area sold every year shot up from 88 thousand acres between 1866 and 1874 to 340 thousand acres between 1889

PCL, vol. II, p. 363. In subsequent judgments this point was often reiterated. See PLR, no. 118 of 1901; PR, no. 110 of 1906.

[77] GOI Rev. & Agr. (Rev.), October 1895, A 72–3. The overall figures for Punjab show that between 1875 and 1878 about 38 per cent of the total land sales were to those classified as "non-agriculturist", and the corresponding figure for the years 1889–93 was 21 per cent. In many regions the figures were higher. For instance in 1884–5 the proportion sold to non-agriculturists was: Gurgaon 81 per cent, Karnal 54 per cent, Hissar 48 per cent, Jullunder 54 per cent. Based on RLRAP, 1884–5. Identifying the "non-agriculturist" remained a problem that officials could never resolve.

and 1893.[78] In many regions in the 1870s and 1880s, more than 50 per cent of the mortgages were to those classified as non-agriculturists. Thorburn was not the only one to paint an apocalyptic picture of the consequences of these land transfers and peasant indebtedness.[79]

Within the image of an agrarian order founded on the conception of village communities, pattidari tenures, and agnatic brotherhoods, non-agriculturists were inevitably outsiders. If unilineal descent provided the principle of order within such communities, the presence of the moneylender signified the principle of disorder. To protect agrarian society, the customary codes of agriculturists had to be preserved and alienation of land to non-agriculturists stopped. Anxiety over the disintegration of agrarian communities – and with it the colonial sense of rural order – fused with the fear of rural revolt. In the decades after 1857 colonial officials were haunted by terrifying images of rampaging peasants burning the account books (bahi khatas) of moneylenders and destroying all symbols of British power, their anger against the Banias turning into rage against all forms of authority. The stability of British rule could not be built on the foundation of a malcontent peasantry losing its land to non-agriculturists.[80] This political suspicion of the moneylender, reinforced by a long tradition of Christian hostility to the usurer, was embodied in the Land Alienation Act.[81]

Who was the non-agriculturist outsider? The Land Alienation Act sought to define the category without ambiguity, but as usual problems of definition remained. In terms of the act, agriculturists could sell their land only to members of agricultural castes or to others who had held land in the village from the time of the first settlement. In the Punjab Laws Act of 1872 the defining categories had been "collaterals" and "co-sharers" – these had the right to pre-empt sales to strangers.[82] This definition, colonial officials soon discovered, did

[78] *RLRAP*, relevant years.

[79] Ibid.

[80] For a detailed account of the varying opinions on the question of land transfer, see van den Dungen, *The Punjab Tradition*.

[81] See Graeber, *Debt*; Le Goff, *Your Money or Your Life*.

[82] The official memos and notes relating to the passing of the Punjab Laws Act 1872 are reproduced in *PCL*, vol. I, sec. III.

not allow moneylenders to be legally cast as outsiders. Anyone who had possessed land in the village even for a year could claim to be a co-sharer with a right to buy land and pre-empt sales to others. With evidence of land transfers mounting, panicky officials searched for a more certain basis of classifying the outsider. Ultimately, they could think of no criterion more appropriate than caste. The primary order of classification in the Land Alienation Act was between agriculturists and non-agriculturists. Regardless of occupation, all cultivating and pastoral castes were considered agriculturists, and all mercantile and "lower" castes were categorised as non-agriculturists.[83]

Once the Land Alienation Act was passed, the rules of pre-emption had to be revised. A committee had proposed in 1898 that the pre-emption clause as laid down in section 12 of the Punjab Laws Act of 1872 be amended "to exclude strangers who have bought into a village".[84] Tupper introduced the Punjab Laws of Pre-emption Bill in the legislative council in 1902. A select committee revised Tupper's initial suggestions and the Punjab Pre-emption Act was passed in 1905.[85] The stated object of the 1905 act was to bring the pre-emption law in conformity with the Land Alienation Act. All "agriculturists" were now given the right to pre-empt sales to non-agriculturists. Amongst the agriculturists, claims were graded in accordance with the degree of agnatic relationship that the pre-emptor had to the owner of the land being sold. With the Land Alienation Act the defining terms of reference in assessing the authenticity of rights on agricultural land changed. The primary term of differentiation was

[83] The only exception was those individuals of non-agricultural castes who had held land for a very long time, from the time of the first settlement.

[84] See Proposed Amendment of the Existing Law of Pre-emption in the Punjab, Punjab Rev. & Agr. (Rev.), A 3–6, November 1900; The Punjab Pre-emption Bill, Punjab Leg. (Leg.), March 1905, A 59–61.

[85] For draft bill to amend the laws relating to pre-emption in the Punjab Rev. and Agr. (Rev.), A 9–10, November 1904. For Tupper's statement and the Select Committee Report, see Rev. & Agr. (Rev.), November 1903, A 19–20. For the draft of the bill that was finally introduced, see Punjab, Rev. & Agr. (Rev.), A 9–10, November 1904. See also Draft Bill to amend the Pre-emption Act of 1905, Punjab Rev. & Agr. (Rev.), October 1909, A 5 & 6.

no longer co-sharer *vs* non co-sharer, or agnate *vs* non-agnate, but agriculturist *vs* non-agriculturist. The basis of earlier differentiation was legitimated through custom; the new one was statutory. This language of opposition between agriculturists and non-agriculturists in fact came to structure the political discourse of the twentieth century in Punjab.[86]

The Commodity Economy and the Language of Rights

These conflicts over rights occurred within a world where agrarian property was increasingly integrated with circuits of exchange. This integration defined the way land was perceived by peasants and the strategies they deployed to regulate its control and transmission. When the British took over Punjab, land sales were not unknown but land had not acquired a generalised commodity form. Vast stretches were available for cultivation and rights of sale and purchase were not yet of critical concern to peasants; nor were they the defining elements of land rights. Over the second half of the nineteenth century the arable frontier expanded under the pressure of a demographic boom and agrarian commercialisation. Open lands disappeared as the state took over forests and commons, proceeding to establish a regime of rights over cultivated land, mapping landscapes, measuring each field and fixing its ownership, specifying rights of possession and alienation.[87]

[86] Agriculturists and non-agriculturists became founding categories of political and cultural discourse. The Unionist Party claimed to voice the interests of agriculturists, and defined its identity in opposition to the Congress, which was projected as the party of mercantile and urban interests. The opposition between the agriculturists and non-agriculturists was played out on the floor of the legislative assembly, consolidated through a series of anti-moneylender legislations, and expressed in newspapers, journals, and pamphlets. For a discussion of the politics of the Unionist Party, see Chowdhry, *Punjab Politics*; Talbot, *Khizr Tiwana*.

[87] Rates of demographic growth according to the census figures show an upswing after the 1860s, a definite downward movement in the 1890s, a sharp decline in the first decade of the twentieth century followed by a gradual revival in the second decade, and a rapid increase thereafter.

Land could no longer be simply broken up and cultivated. It had to be purchased at a price or leased in. The index figure for land price soared from 40 in the early 1870s to 500 by 1920.[88]

The pressure on land was the most intense in the wet zones.[89] In the Bari Doab and the Bist Jullunder Doab the extensive margin was exhausted by the 1880s, the limits of intensification reached. Unable to sustain families on small plots of land, peasants moved beyond the village in search of alternative sources of living.[90] When land grants in the Canal Colonies opened up new opportunities, hordes left Central Punjab, convinced by the promise of the frontier.[91] While peasants moved to distant lands, money-orders brought money back into the village. And this money was poured into land purchases: peasants made valiant efforts to expand their cultivated holdings, retain their roots in the village, and acquire symbolic capital. Buoyed by this flow, the land market floated upwards.

The consolidation of patriarchal property happened within the context of this desperate scramble for land. In the early enquiries of the 1840s and '50s, village elders, as we saw, had often found it

[88] The increase of the quinquennial index of land price (with 1902 to 1906 as base) was as follows: 40 in 1877–81, 98 in 1897–1901, 206 in 1912–16, 540 in 1926–31, 526 in 1936–41, 1140 in 1942–6. *RLRAP* of the relevant years.

[89] By 1881 the density per square mile of cultivated area was 600 in Amritsar and 700 in Jullunder; while in the arid Hissar tracts it was 181 and in Rohtak about 280. See *Punjab Census*, 1881, Statement I.

[90] See Kessinger, *Vilyatpur: 1848–1968;* Agnihotri, "Agrarian Change in the Canal Colonies"; Kamozawa, "Family, Migration and Punjab Society".

[91] Immigrants from central Punjab to the Canal Colonies far outnumbered those from the south-east. Of the total immigrants to the Chenab Colonies in 1911, about 52 per cent were from central Punjab; in 1921 the proportion had increased to 57 per cent. Few were recorded as having come from the dry belt of Hissar, Rohtak, Gurgaon, or Karnal. Of those enumerated in the *Punjab Census* of 1931 as "born outside the district of enumeration", 59 per cent in Montgomery and 50 per cent in Lyallpur – both Canal Colonies – were from Central Punjab, as opposed to less than 3 per cent from the arid districts of the south-east. *Punjab Census*, 1911, Statement XI A, pt I; *Punjab Census*, 1921, Statement XI A, pt I; *Punjab Census*, 1931, Table VI, pt C.

difficult to give categorical answers on points of custom. Persuaded
by officials to affirm the male agnatic principle, they nevertheless described practices that appeared anomalous within the framework
of custom defined by the British. By the 1880s the male voice had
acquired a new coherence. Anxious to strengthen the bonds of the
coparcenary brotherhood, it spoke against the rights of outsiders,
women, and "lower" castes. Reinforced by codified custom as well as
by the laws of pre-emption and sale of land, this masculine voice of
the brotherhood became increasingly strident, and, by the twentieth
century, politically assertive.

While collectively affirming their commitment to a masculinist
code that displaced the rights of women, individually peasants sought
to manoeuvre around the code, reworking the meaning of its specific clauses, creating some space for the affective ties that bound them
to their daughters and sisters. Within the new regime of law, every
act of negotiation became an arena of conflict and every effort to resolve individual conflict created the space for rethinking public law.
Many village disputes were publicly fought and countless ended up
in courts. As plaintiffs and defendants confronted each other, the
meaning and nature of rights were re-examined: new testimonies were
collected, new informants questioned, and framing legal categories
re-scrutinised.

Publicly pronounced and legally attested, the code of customary law
was not unambiguous in its meaning. The Benthamite ideal of fixity
that informed the process of codification dissolved in judicial practice. Officials and judges, we have seen, rarely sang as a chorus. They
interpreted the rights of different groups – agnates and non-agnates,
village coparcenary brotherhoods and outsiders – in dramatically
different terms, judging the truth of the practice in conflicting ways.
Patriarchal control over land undoubtedly consolidated over time, but
it was persistently questioned and continuously refigured.

Through these negotiations and conflicts a new language of law
entered the peasant world, dislocating the terms of reference earlier
taken for granted. In the early decades of British rule, officials enquiring into custom had been recurrently told: "in the past this
was never done", or "earlier this was so". When queried by officials,

villagers had revealed a sense of what was considered just and proper in a specific context; but they had not been able to define any universal principle that underpinned their judgement, any fixed rule they could mechanically follow. Within the new regime of codified custom, practice had to conform to publicly stated rules. The fantasy of certitude was impossible to realise and the official code continuously reworked, but the terms in which practices were conceptualised were unquestionably transformed. Codified law now provided the frame within which conflicts were to be resolved and the commodity economy negotiated. And through the disputes over interpretations of the code, a new language of rights and a new conception of property became part of the taken-for-granted peasant world.

Within this new legal regime, where claims and obligations had to be categorically stated in the language of contract, even affective ties acquired legal forms. Claims and obligations could not be pressed in the court without being specifically documented. This regime of writing nurtured its own illusions. The very fact of writing, many assumed, made a claim legally binding.

What, in the end, is my argument about this relation between custom and law, between the documented and the undocumented, between affective and legal spaces? Let me state once again the two opposing arguments that I seek to resist. One is the notion of some totalising power of codified modern law that absorbs all spaces within it; the other is the idea of plural legal spaces, each existing at different levels, separate and distinct. To see all affective ties as legal ties is to over-valorise the power of the state and the law. It is to erase the spaces that resisted the incorporative drive of the new legal regime – a resistance that often reworked the terms in which the law was encoded. But to see affective relations as untainted by codified law is to operate with a problematic notion of plural spaces.

8

Fear of the Fragment

PRACTICE, AS WE SAW in the last chapter, cannot be mechanically deduced from the norm. To deduce so is to share the assumptions of the norm and accept its universalist claim. It is to blind oneself to the uncertainties and negotiations of everyday life, and the processes through which norms themselves are reworked and acquire social meaning. The drama of everyday life is enacted within the gap between the norm and the practice, a space opened up by the very nature of confrontation between the two. I will now examine the idea by focusing on the ideology and practice of equitable partible inheritance.

~

The village surveys that were carried out in the 1920s and 1930s all over Punjab reaffirmed a picture of the rural landscape that colonial officials had long noted with concern. Everywhere – from the villages of the Canal Colonies to those in the central Doab tracts, from the dry tracts of the south-east to the hills of the north – the fragmentation of landholdings appeared an unmistakable characteristic. At Suner, a semi-dry village in Ferozepur, only 12 per cent of the proprietary holdings consisted of one single plot, 46 per cent were split into 1 to 10 fragments, and 42 per cent splintered into 11 to 65 pieces. The picture seemed more alarming when the area under these holdings was considered. No more than 17 per cent of the area under proprietary holdings had less than 10 fragments, while 83 per cent was broken up

into 11 to 65 plots.[1] At Tehong, located in the more densely populated, intensively cultivated Jullunder district, the situation appeared
even more frightening. In one tract, Patti Hassan Chakian, where a
detailed enquiry was carried out in the late 1920s, about 95 per cent
of the area was covered by holdings fragmented into 10 to 60 pieces.[2]

Wider enquiries showed a pattern in these variations. When Calvert
calculated the provincial statistics in the 1920s and '30s, parcellisation
appeared to be distinctly more marked in some tracts than others.

Fear of the Fragment

From the turn of the twentieth century, British officials were obsessed with the problem of fragmentation of holdings. Within the
colonial imagination fragmentation was the ultimate sign of agrarian
backwardness, an absolute barrier to progress. Imbued with the ideal
of scientific agriculture, this was an imagination that associated modernity with large-scale farming, technological growth with a regime
of order, and agrarian order with compact, consolidated holdings – a
landscape of square and rectangular blocks amenable to visual grasp
and bureaucratic control.[3] For control and taxation, plots of land had
moreover to be identified with individuals, just as much as individuals
had to be fixed and attached to plots.[4] This identification was difficult
when the holding was splintered into plots strewn over the landscape;
and when tax claims on each plot had to be separately calculated, and
the demand from each landowner was itself in fragments. For colonial officials the consolidation of holdings was necessary to order the
landscape, transform agriculture, and rationalise land administration.

Officials never tired of pointing to the problems of fragmentation.
When holdings were fragmented, good land near the village was
exhausted through overuse and bad land at a distance was neglected.
Peasants wasted time and energy moving from one plot to the other.

[1] Dawar, *Suner V.S.*, see Tables 34–35.
[2] Das and Calvert, *Tehong V.S.*, see Table XXIII, p. 58.
[3] See Scott, *Seeing Like a State*, ch. 1. On the appearance of order being
important to the colonising process, see Mitchell, *Colonising Egypt*.
[4] Kain and Baigent, *The Cadastral Map in the Service of the State*; Price,
Dividing the Land.

Cattle had to work the wells through the night and then be taken from one place to another during the day. This meant night feeding, for which fodder had to be cut and carried over considerable distances. Since the fragmented plots were frequently widely dispersed, peasants had to prepare several threshing floors and storage spaces. Keeping a watch over distant fields was difficult, and boundary disputes common: fragmentation multiplied the number of borders and points of tension, and the daily movement from one plot to another along field boundaries deepened the possibility of conflict. Rights over trees that stood on the borders – the ambiguous spaces between the plots – were always under doubt. Fragmentation, above all, splintered a holding into such small parcels that they could not be effectively cultivated. By creating compact holdings, consolidation could easily resolve all these problems; or so the officials imagined.[5]

The argument for consolidation drew upon an ideology of improvement and a critique of partible inheritance that had been normalised in England by the eighteenth century. The great English debate over inheritance practices had started in the sixteenth century, with advocates of primogeniture railing against partible inheritance, seeing it as the cause of the impoverishment of the nobility and the breakdown of landed families.[6] Critics of primogeniture pointed to the inequity of a practice that deprived younger sons of a living and drove them to beggary, vagabondage, and misery. The ideal of equity underlying the idea of partible inheritance was never fully overthrown, but the big landowners of England had by the sixteenth century adopted the principle of primogeniture. In the seventeenth century yeomen mimicked peers, and by the eighteenth the middle classes followed this trend of imitating the ways of their "superiors".[7] Partible inheritance came to be associated with parcellised holdings, a pauperised peasantry, and backward agriculture – with Ireland and France. The discourse of improvement and the enclosure movement

[5] Calvert, *The Wealth and Welfare of Panjab*, ch. VI; Darling, *The Punjab Peasant in Prosperity and Debt*, pp. 28ff.

[6] See Thirsk, "The European Debate on Customs of Inheritance".

[7] Cooper, "Patterns of Inheritance and Settlement"; Howell, "Peasant Inheritance Customs"; Spufford, *Contrasting Communities*.

reaffirmed the idea that "large is beautiful", equating largeness of scale with growth and progress.

For colonial officials this link between partible inheritance and parcellised holdings was a fact taken for granted. Proceeding from this unquestionable truth, they had no difficulty in comprehending the logic of the fragmentation of holdings in Punjab, which seemed to them to flow inevitably from the customary norms regulating rights over land. The principle of equitable partible male agnatic inheritance meant two things. Over every generation, land was to be equally divided amongst male heirs, and in their absence amongst females. This implied not only the division of a single parental holding into several – in accordance with the number of heirs – but also the splintering of each inherited holding into a number of pieces. For, the norm of equitable inheritance required that different qualities of land – good and bad, chahi (irrigated from wells) and barani (rain-fed), nahri (canal irrigated) and banjar (uncultivated), richly manured land near the village (niain) and land located at the extensive margins – were all to be equally shared by each heir. Each descendant was to get a portion of each of the different types of land that his ancestors had cultivated. The extent of fragmentation in such a situation was thereby in direct proportion to the range of variation in the quality of land in any tract and the number of heirs of a landowner.

Times that Bind

When officials pushed for the consolidation of holdings, they came up against layers of peasant apprehension. While admitting that fragmented holdings created a host of problems, peasants were unwilling to give up the land they had inherited. Everywhere, officials found that "the zamindars, or at least most of them, had a strong partiality for the fields held by their forefathers, and are loath to give these up in exchange for others." They argued that "the original settlers of the village were wise and made a fair distribution of strong and weak lands, which should be retained."[8] With all its problems, it appeared, partible inheritance ensured justice and equity.

[8] Das and Calvert, *Tehong V.S.*, p. 65.

Land, moreover, was not a homogeneous mass that could be equated. Each holding had a history embedded within it, a past that could not be easily erased. The relationship of peasants with their land was forged over generations, through the labour of ancestors, through memories of pain and happiness. It was as if the soil had grown personal by soaking in the energies of those who had worked the land, and by finally absorbing into itself all those who had lived by it and died on it. It was imbued with their presence. In this sense land was a repository of time. Inheriting it was to establish a relationship to a specific personal past, to locate oneself within a flow of family time. Working such land also meant discharging a debt to forefathers who had toiled on it and whose sweat, by seeping into it, had made the inheritance possible in the first place. It was equally to establish a relationship to the future, impose on one's descendants an obligation they in turn had to discharge: an obligation to nurture the land, live on it, work it, impress on it the furrows of a new generation.

The logic of consolidation recognised no history of emotion and sentiment that attached peasants to particular pieces of land; nor did it value the customary consciousness that saw land as a bearer of differential use rights. Peasants moreover were unwilling to give up the radical principle of equity – the equal division of good and bad land – that underlay the idea of partible inheritance in North India, even if it led to fragmentation. Land could not be abstracted from its concreteness, its particularities, and transformed into objective uniform space. Variations defined by soil type, quality of irrigation, proximity or distance from the abadi, and the nature of use rights could not all be flattened into an invariant standard area measurable in bland units and open to the application of universal principles of reordering and control. Equity and justice demanded that varying qualities of land be equally divided, their limits and potential equally shared.

Officials were aware of these peasant perceptions but preferred to read them as signs of backwardness. If consolidation was necessary for the march of progress, they felt, peasant sentiments could not always be respected.[9] All the same, some officials, such as Hubert

---

[9] Darling saw no "reason, except human obstinacy and prejudice" that

Calvert, hoped to carry out the process of consolidation through persuasion and popular participation.[10] The first co-operative society for this purpose was formed in 1921 and within a decade officials claimed to have formed 800 societies with 48,000 members, and to have consolidated 336,000 acres at a cost of Rs 2-5-0 per acre.[11] By 1946 the number of registered societies had swollen to 2003 and their members to 257,913.[12] The story of the movement was recounted as a linear narrative of progress.

This narrative of progress was visually represented in official accounts typically through two maps – one before and the other after consolidation.[13] In the first you see a myriad lines jostling for room, thin strips squeezed together, irregular and contorted shapes cluttering the cartographic space. In the second the proliferating lines disappear and are displaced by large neat blocks. The first map was meant to encapsulate the burden of the past, the primitivism of the east, agrarian life bound by custom; the second signalled the future, the move towards modernity, the dawn of a rational order, and the introduction of scientific agricultural practices. A cadastral map that showed up cross-hatched and cluttered lines was a pain to the official cartographic eye. The mess had to be cleaned to produce neat,

---

prevented the consolidation of holdings. Darling, *The Punjab Peasant*, p. 240. In most village surveys the emotional tie with land was considered a barrier to the consolidation of holdings. "Among other features obstructing consolidation," stated one survey, "are sentimental family attachments to certain plots which have been handed down in the family through generations." Dawar, *Suner V.S.*, p. 58.

[10] Calvert, *Progress of Agricultural Non-credit Co-operation*.

[11] *Report on the Working of Co-operative Societies in the Punjab*, 1923, p. 40.

[12] *Report on the Working of Co-operative Societies in the Punjab*, 1946. See also Darling, Notes on Co-operation in the Punjab 1945–6 and W. Pakistan, Darling Papers, Box XIII (CSAL).

[13] This was a typical visual strategy deployed everywhere to reaffirm the image of progress through consolidation. Touring Europe in the late 1920s to study the co-operative movements in various countries, Darling collected a large numbers of such maps and images. See Darling Papers, Box V (CSAL), which contains images of villages in Switzerland and Syria before and after consolidation.

unambiguous maps.[14] The cadastral survey of irregular fields was a nightmare. When each field had jagged edges, surveying became a slow and tortuous process, consuming time and money. The act of measurement was fraught with uncertainty and problems, the boundaries being always in dispute. For officialdom, consolidation stood for legibility and simplicity; it allowed the land to be easily measured, mapped, and taxed.

In all the village surveys of the 1920s we have maps like these seeking to capture the colonial project of agrarian modernisation. Inscribed in many such maps, however, are little histories of resistance, evidence of the barriers that the project of consolidation confronted.[15] The shaded parts in the "After" map show the areas in which the consolidation of holdings was not possible. Not all the village reports tell us the reasons for this failure, but some do. Landowners could not be persuaded to change their views about their relationship to their land. They were unwilling to rupture the threads of affective ties that linked them through the land to past and future.

Two Histories of Partition

Yet the evidence colonial officials collected actually subverted their assumptions. This evidence shows no operation of a unilinear logic pushing smallholders within a system of partible inheritance towards inexorable doom – i.e. with recurring cycles of fragmentation and subdivision of holdings that end in unsustainable minute morcels. When we observe the operation of the inheritance system in practice rather than deduce the logic from the norm, we get a more differentiated picture of the life cycles of holdings. We then see peasants devising a variety of strategies to sustain their hold over their land, counteracting the possible effects of inheritance customs and the disintegrative impact of the market.

[14] See Scott, *Seeing Like a State*, ch. 1.

[15] Notes on Punjab and Consolidation of Holdings, Darling Papers, Box V. See also Darling's notes made in the latter half of the 1930s while touring India to write special reports on the co-operative movement in each province for the Reserve Bank. Darling Papers, Box V (CSAL).

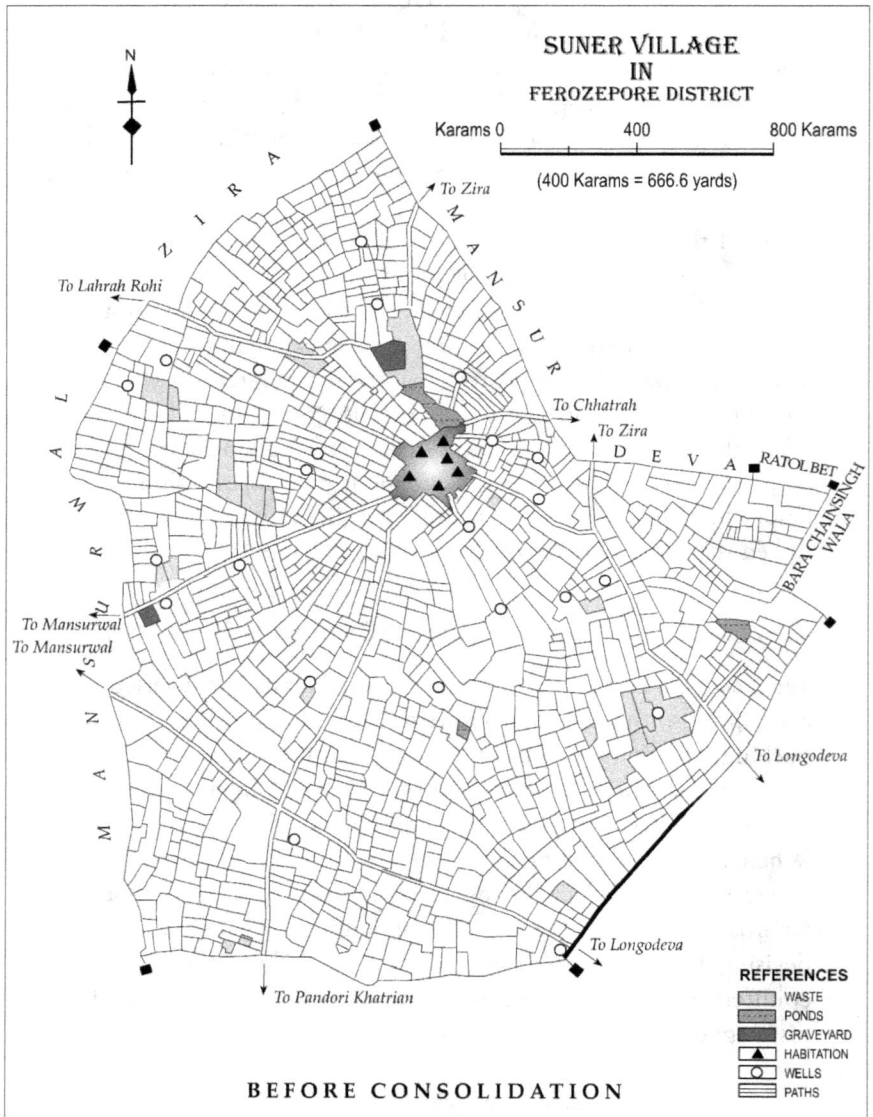

SUNER VILLAGE
IN
FEROZEPORE DISTRICT

Karams 0   400   800 Karams

(400 Karams = 666.6 yards)

N

To Zira

To Lahrah Rohi

To Chhatrah

To Zira

RATOL BET

To Mansurwal
To Mansurwal

To Longodeva

To Longodeva

To Pandori Khatrian

ZIRA AL MANSUR

MANSURWAL

MANSUR

DEVA

BARA CHAINSINGH WALA

BEFORE CONSOLIDATION

REFERENCES
WASTE
PONDS
GRAVEYARD
HABITATION
WELLS
PATHS

Fig. 13a: Before and After – Visualising Consolidation (1936).
Source: Dawar, *Suner V.S.*

Fig. 13b: Before and After – Visualising Consolidation (1936).
Source: Dawar, *Suner V.S.*

Consider the life cycle of a couple of holdings in a Jullunder village. Densely populated and intensively cultivated, Tehong was located on the banks of the River Sutlej. The average size of holdings here was small and the cultivated land splintered into about 13,000 fragments.[16] The Arains, who dominated the village numerically, were traditionally market gardeners known as growers of vegetables. By the twentieth century the limits of agrarian expansion had been reached, with most of the common land cleared and brought under cultivation. As the region became integrated into expanding circuits of commodity production, land under wheat and maize expanded rapidly and cultivators scrambled to add small bits of land to their holdings through lease and mortgage. The everyday history of partitioning unfolded within this context.

Case I: In the year 1848–9 a holding bearing serial no. 121 in Tehong was jointly owned by three brothers.[17] The area of the holding was 315 kanals (29.6 acres) in 48 pieces. The early records of partitioning are not available but at some point between 1850 and 1881 the holding was split among the three brothers, with each of the 48 pieces being equally divided. So at the time of the 1881–5 settlement we find one of the brothers, Kishan, holding 105 kanals, i.e. a third of his father's land, but now split into three holdings (serial nos 384, 385, and 388) in 45 pieces. At the settlement the three holdings were considered to be one and given the serial no. 359. In a single generation partitioning had broken up one holding of 315 kanals into three holdings of 105 kanals, and multiplied the number of fragments almost three times, with each brother getting a share of the original 48 pieces. But if we now follow the life history of serial no. 359 over the next two generations, we find no re-enactment of this dramatic process of subdivision and fragmentation.

When Kishan died not long after the settlement of 1881–5 his two sons, Umda and Arjan, became joint owners of the holding. They purchased 12 kanals 5 marlas in seven pieces and further split one of their pieces into two for cultivation, thus possessing 117 kanals

[16] Das and Calvert, *Tehong V.S.*, ch. 1.
[17] Ibid., pp. 59–60.

10 marlas in 53 pieces. In the jamabandis of 1898–9 their holding became serial no. 457. Soon afterwards Umda died and his two sons became joint owners with their uncle Arjan.

In 1907–8 the holding got a new tag: serial no. 444. The area remained the same but the fragments had increased to 59, six having been split into twice the number for convenience of cultivation. Subsequently the owners exchanged four pieces for four others and in the transaction got 10 marlas extra. They also acquired 7 kanals 5 marlas in four pieces on the partitioning of the shamilat (common land). Some years later they got one more piece of 2 kanals and 16 marlas on another partitioning of common land. And then they amalgamated four pieces into two before re-splitting them back to four. In 1925 the holding bore yet another label, serial no. 536, and was jointly held by two sons of Umda and one son of Arjan.

In the forty years after 1884–5 the holding was not subdivided: its area in fact had increased from 105 kanals to 128 kanals 1 marla. Over two generations the land was held jointly without being partitioned. The fragments did increase from 45 to 64, but not because of partible inheritance. We see a variety of processes at work: five pieces were acquired due to the partitioning of common land, seven pieces were purchased, some pieces were split for the convenience of cultivation, while others were amalgamated or exchanged.

Case II: In 1848–9 a holding, serial no. 102 in Tehong, had an area of 244 kanals in 41 pieces.[18] The land was partitioned in the next generation, but on account of the revolt of 1857 the details of the first partition are again lost. The evidence from 1881 suggests that the holding was probably split into four, and each splintered into over twenty pieces. After this mid-nineteenth-century partitioning and fragmentation the life cycles of the holdings again show a relative stability. Let us look at two of them: serial no. 365 with 36 kanals 16 marlas in 23 pieces and serial no. 367 with 80 kanals 19 marlas in 22 pieces. Between 1881 and 1907 there was no change in the area of these holdings. When the owner of serial no. 365 died his four sons jointly held the land. The owner of serial no. 367 died childless,

[18] Ibid., pp. 61–3.

leaving the holding to his four nephews and a widow, a relative of the owner. After 1907–8, partitioning of the shamilat added to the area of both the holdings, each getting first around 4 kanals and 16 marlas, and then again about 5 to 7 marlas. Once the widow died her share went to the four joint owners of serial no. 365. Finally in 1915–16 both the holdings were amalgamated and entered in the jamabandi as serial no. 442. Some pieces of land within the holding were subsequently consolidated and a few were exchanged. So between 1881 and 1920 the holdings survived without any subdivision: each was jointly held for a time and then in fact amalgamated. The area covered by the holdings – first two and then fused into one – had increased from 117 kanals 13 marlas to 127 kanals 19 marlas, and the fragments had increased from 45 to only 48, despite the fact that six slices of shamilat had been added. Joint ownership, consolidation, exchanges, and amalgamation had counteracted the process of fragmentation. Shares divided between descendants were unified when one line died out, and the widow's share reverted to the males of the household after her death.

The system of partible inheritance did create a tendency towards fragmentation, but it did not operate with an inflexible logic.[19] Peasants negotiated and redefined the implications of the system and the form in which it unfolded. They exchanged plots to unify holdings, leased in fields next to their main plot, and mortgaged out small parcels in distant places; and they resisted the process of partitioning with determined vigour.

Even when the shares of the landowner were minute and spread over the landscape, the plot actually cultivated by him could be in

---

[19] The assumption that partible inheritance inevitably leads to fissioning within households and a subdivision of property is premised on the individualist notion of the person. The underlying idea is simple: driven by the desire for autonomy and independence, individuals break away from the parent household and set up separate units, partitioning the land, nucleating the families. Partitioning here becomes synonymous with fissioning, nucleation, segmentation, and subdivision of holdings. In a sense even Chayanov's model does not get away from the assumptions of this framework. See Chayanov, *On the Theory of Peasant Economy.*

one piece. Consider the following case. In Bhambu Sandila, a village in west Punjab, a man had 14 acres divided over 22 wells. The largest holding was about 3.5 acres, while the rest were all tiny parcels – fractions of acres. He mortgaged all the shares in the different wells and leased in a tenancy of 8 acres. Though the number of the recorded fragments in the khatauni did not decline, this man had a consolidated plot.[20] The hissas that belonged to him, the fragments he owned but mortgaged out, were cultivated by one of the other co-sharers of the wells where the land was located. We are told, "a well which contains such minute shares is in practice cultivated by the owner with the largest shares . . ."[21]

It is in this sense that I refer to two histories of partition. One develops the argument at an abstract level, deduces history from the code. It asks not how the norm of partible-patrilineal inheritance works in different contexts, how it is negotiated, read, defined, and reworked, but what is its logical implication. Assuming an inflexible working of the code, it visualises a world in which the peasant farm is inexorably driven towards self-destruction: the partition of land follows the death of the patriarch, the household breaks up, new households are established, land is equally divided, and consequently fragmented and splintered. This abstract logic produces a deductive history; events are expected to follow the logic of the norm. Anointed as the victim of an inflexible traditional code, the peasant is denied any creativity, any power to refigure the logic of inheritance norms.

The second history descends from the abstract to the concrete, follows the stories of households, and looks at the many trajectories of their lived experiences. It discovers the strategies devised by households to

[20] In the jamabandi record, revised every four years, a separate number is given in the cultivator's column of the annual record to every area of land held by a man under a single title. When a cultivated holding consists not only of land that is owned but also of land that is leased in, taken on mortgage, exchanged, then each of the constituent parts of the holding is given separate khatauni numbers, creating an illusion of many separate cultivators tilling small fragments.

[21] Anderson, *Measures Possible for the Improvement of Economic Conditions of Muzaffargarh District*, p. 7.

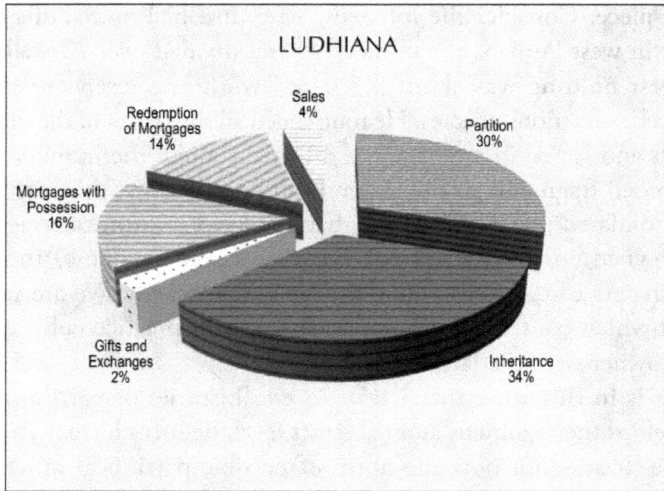

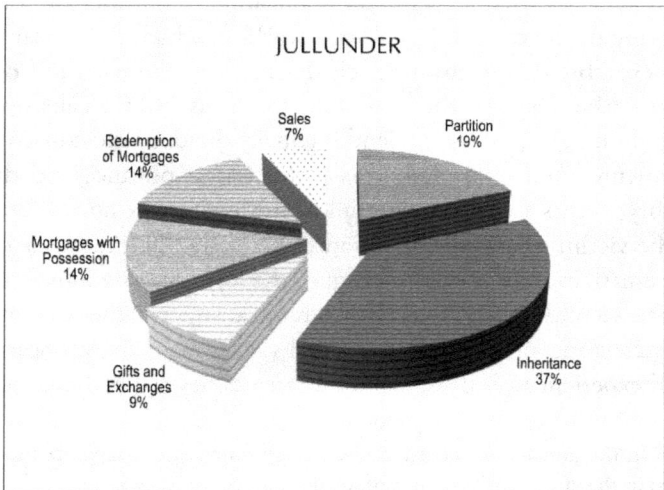

Fig. 14a: Inheritance, Partition, and Other Transfers, Jullunder and Ludhiana, 1893

Source: Based on statements in *RLRAP, 1893*.

The pie charts show the proportional distribution of different modes of annual transfers recorded by the revenue and registration departments.

KARNAL

Mortgages with Possession 4%
Redemption of Mortages 5%
Sales 6%
Partition 9%
Gifts and Exchanges 3%
Inheritance 73%

HISSAR

Mortgages with Possession 3%
Redemption of Mortgages 3%
Gifts and Exchanges 4%
Sales 3%
Inheritance 26%
Partition 61%

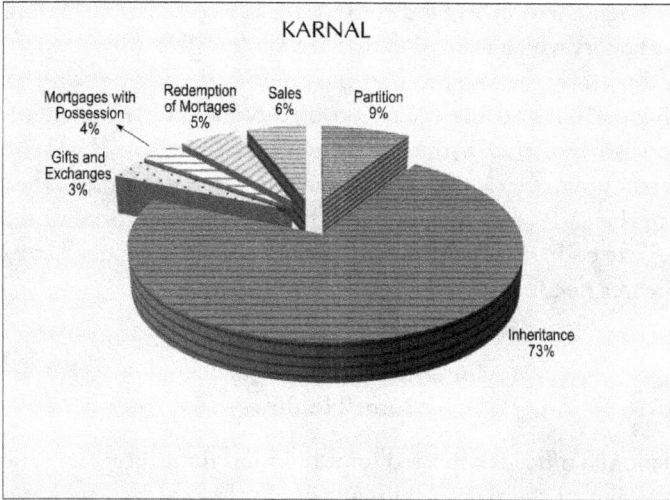

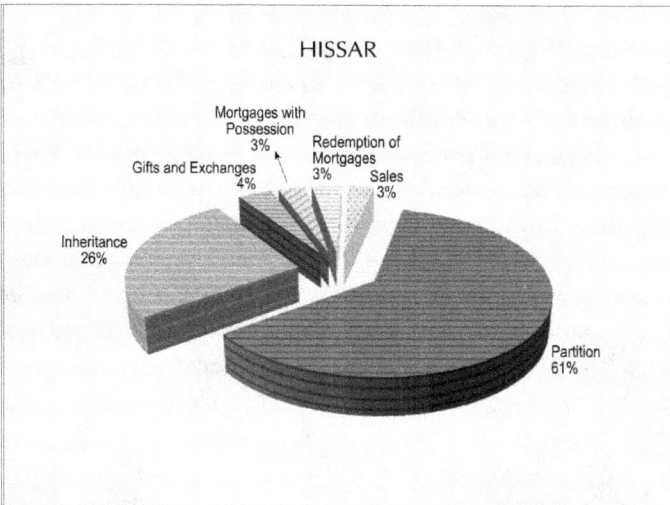

Fig. 14b: Inheritance, Partition and Other Transfers, Karnal and Hissar, 1893.

Source: Based on statements in *RLRAP, 1893.*

The pie charts show the proportional distribution of different modes of annual transfers recorded by the revenue and registration departments.

resist fragmentation, expand cultivation, and consolidate holdings. It is also a history which recognises that joint holdings do not fall apart when confronted by the logic of partible inheritance, the pressure towards individuation, and the operation of the market. The logic of separation is negotiated within the structure of the household in many different ways, even as the principle of jointness is reaffirmed. The meaning of the code is, in fact, defined through these negotiations; and at times the code itself is reworked. This is a history we need to explore in greater detail.

Modernity and the Culture of Joint Holdings

All colonial officials expected joint holdings to disintegrate. They saw it as a sign of the past, a remnant of another time, a marker of primitiveness. Progress within society and the unfolding of modernity, they universally assumed, would be marked by a move from collective to individual rights, from custom to contract. "It is almost a natural law that tenure should only change in one direction," Roe had famously pronounced, "from joint holdings to severalty in shares, and from shares to possession."[22] The dominant paternalist voice in Punjab sought to codify custom and protect coparcenary communities, but it could not get away from the liberal assumption that the desire for individual possession was an innate characteristic in modern society and joint holdings an anomaly. Self-interest, they thought, would ultimately assert itself, individuals would break free of the constraints of the community, and traditional ideas of collectivity would dissolve.

Joint holdings, however, did not disappear. The evidence from village after village, surveyed in the 1920s and 1930s, showed that joint holdings were no relics of the past. In most villages 60 to 80 per cent of the ownership holdings were still jointly held.

The joint holding was, in fact, the anchor around which peasant lives often moved. It allowed some members of the family to migrate in search of work, or in pursuit of dreams of a better life. In

[22] Roe, *Una Parganah, S.R., 1869–70*; see also Tupper, *PCL*, vol. II, p. 45.

large families one or two sons migrated, joined the army, went abroad, or acquired land in the Canal Colonies, while the father and older sons remained back in the village to cultivate the joint holding, with multiple shares (hissas). The wives of migrants stayed behind, looking after their children and working on the family holding. They were to have shelter, food, and not uncommonly sex, within the folds of the joint household.[23] Often a small share of the joint holding was mortgaged to raise the money necessary for migration. The economy of migration was thus intimately connected to the economy of unpartitioned holdings.[24] Migrants were reluctant to part with their share in the joint property even when it was notional. The claim to notional shares eased the migration of single males and gave their families a right to live in the joint household. This link also sustained a sense of belonging, a relation to their village, to their past. When money flowed back, more land was acquired.[25] Each purchase added to the fragments that the household owned, consolidating its patrimonial property and reaffirming the ideal of jointness. The forces of the market did not usher in a world freed from the marks of the past: they unfolded in an enchanted world of affective relations, reconstituting those relations, refigured *by* those relations.

The discourse of the village community and the rhetoric of jointness, as we have seen, allowed landed elites to resist the entry of outsiders and consolidate their hold over landed property by acquiring small fragments through lease, purchase, and mortgage. Not surprisingly, large holdings usually had many more fragments than small ones. The village surveys of the 1920s suggest a clear association between level of fragmentation, size of holding, and household strategy. In Tehong, with its dense population and intensive cultivation, all ownership holdings with less than five fragments were

[23] On widows' resistance to patriarchal claims over her body, see Chowdhry, *The Veiled Women*, p. 88.

[24] Kessinger, *Vilyatpur*; on mortgaging as peasant strategy, see Bhattacharya, "Lenders and Debtors"; on the relationship between mortgaging and migration, see Kamozawa, "Family, Property and Migration in Colonial Punjab".

[25] Anand and Brayne, *Soldiers' Savings and How They Use Them*, BEIP, no. 68.

TEHONG
Ownership Holdings
1924-25

Five and more owners jointly
15%

Three to four owners jointly
23%

A single owner
39%

Two owners jointly
23%

TEHONG
Cultivating Holdings
1924-25

Five and more cultivators jointly
32%

A single cultivator
33%

Three to four cultivators jointly
20%

Two cultivators jointly
15%

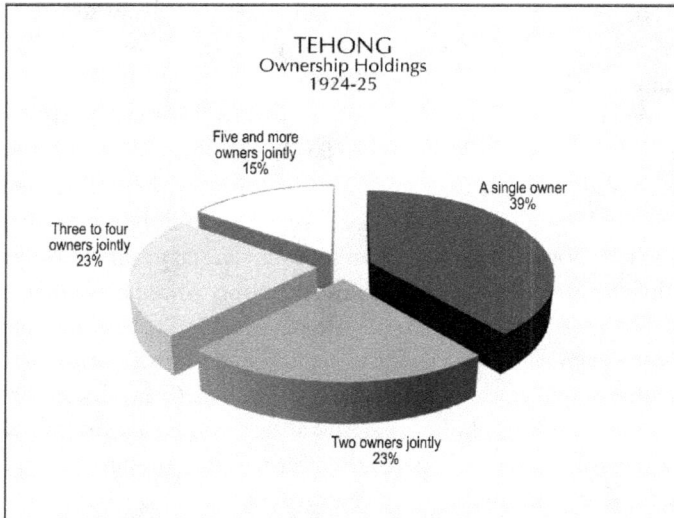

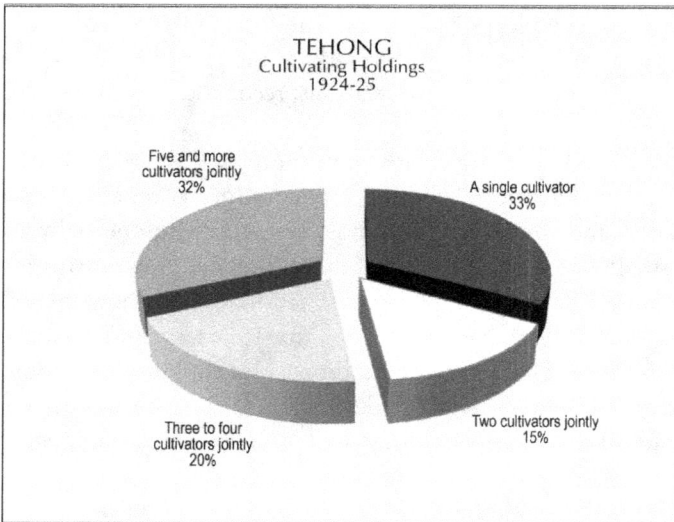

Fig. 15a: How the Land was Held: Tehong Village.
Source: Based on figures in Das and Calvert, *Tehong V.S.*

The pie charts show the limits of individual and joint holdings (ownership and cultivating) in Tehong village of Jullunder district, 1924–5.

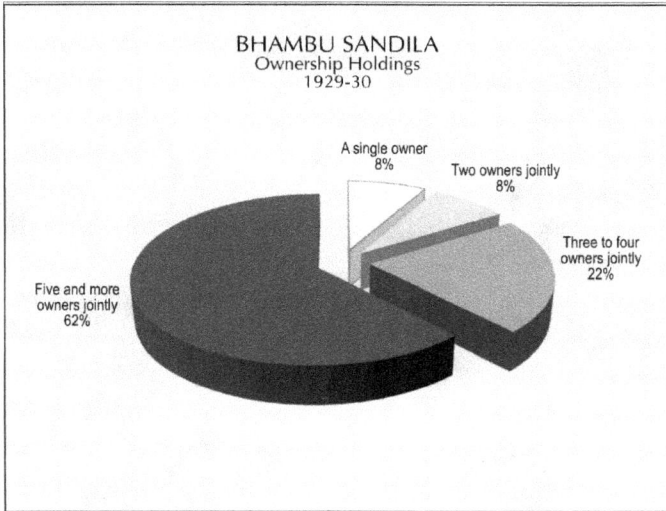

BHAMBU SANDILA
Ownership Holdings
1929-30

A single owner
8%

Two owners jointly
8%

Three to four
owners jointly
22%

Five and more
owners jointly
62%

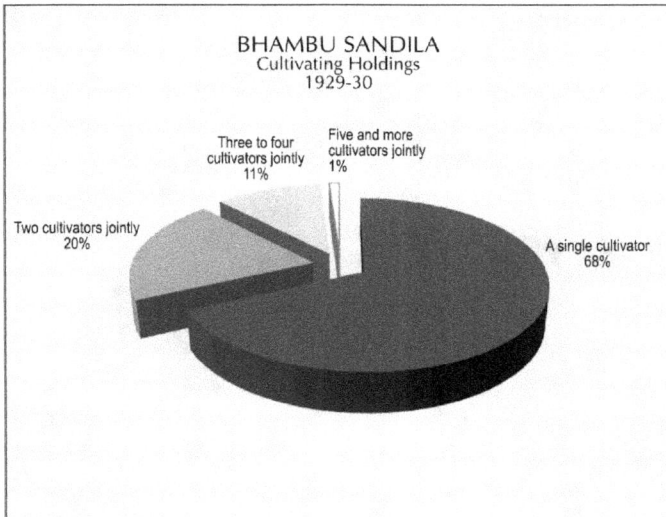

BHAMBU SANDILA
Cultivating Holdings
1929-30

Three to four
cultivators jointly
11%

Five and more
cultivators jointly
1%

Two cultivators jointly
20%

A single cultivator
68%

Fig. 15b: How the Land was Held: Bhambu Sandila Village.
Source: Based on figures in Rahim and Khan, *Bhambu Sandila V.S.*

The pie charts show the limits of individual and joint holdings
(ownership and cultivating) in Bhambu Sandila village of
Muzaffargarh district, 1929–30.

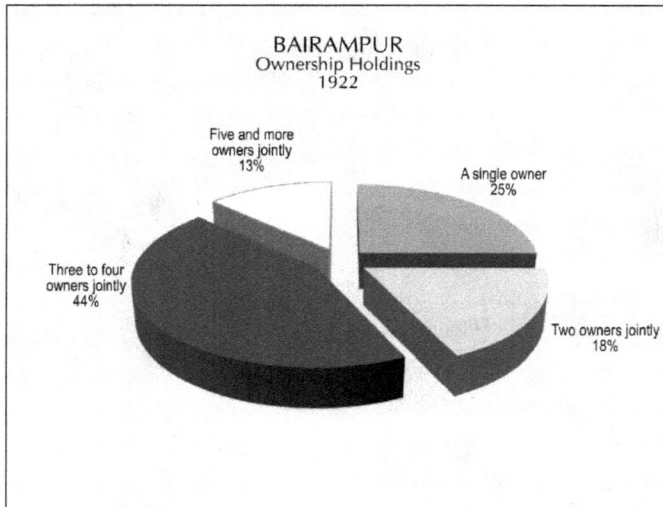

BAIRAMPUR
Ownership Holdings
1922

Five and more owners jointly
13%

A single owner
25%

Three to four owners jointly
44%

Two owners jointly
18%

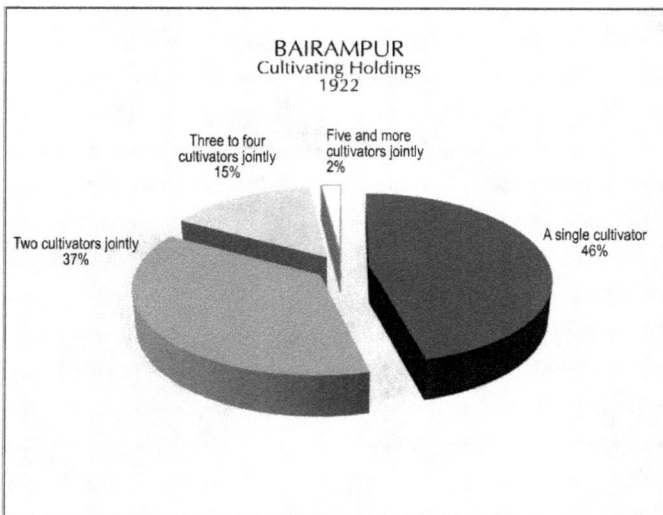

BAIRAMPUR
Cultivating Holdings
1922

Three to four cultivators jointly
15%

Five and more cultivators jointly
2%

Two cultivators jointly
37%

A single cultivator
46%

Fig. 15c: How the Land was Held: Bairampur Village.
Source: Based on figures in Bhalla, *Bairampur V.S.*

The pie charts show the limits of individual and joint holdings (ownership and cultivating) in Bairampur village of Hoshiarpur district, 1922.

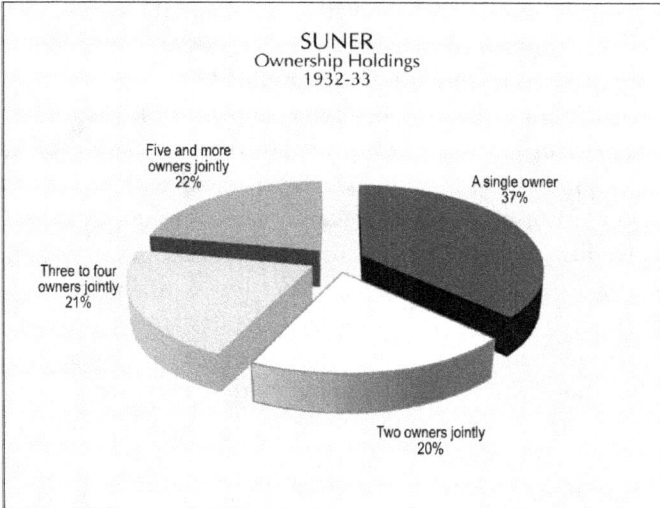

SUNER
Ownership Holdings
1932-33

Five and more
owners jointly
22%

A single owner
37%

Three to four
owners jointly
21%

Two owners jointly
20%

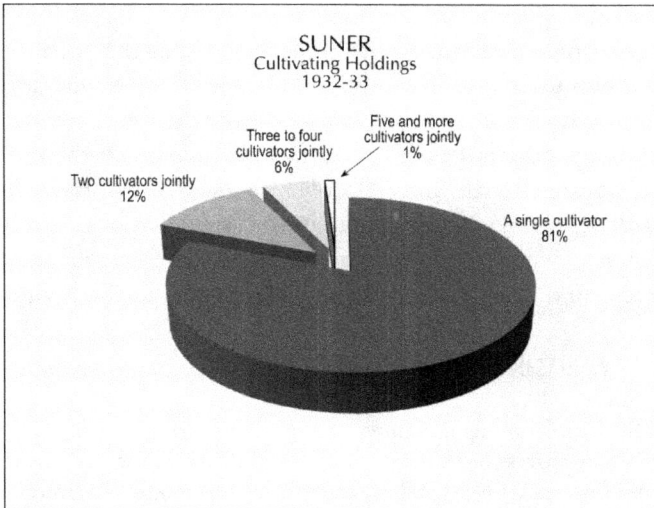

SUNER
Cultivating Holdings
1932-33

Three to four
cultivators jointly
6%

Five and more
cultivators jointly
1%

Two cultivators jointly
12%

A single cultivator
81%

Fig. 5d: How the Land was Held: Suner Village.
Source: Based on figures in Dawar, *Suner V.S.*

Proportional distribution of ownership and cultivating holdings
in Suner village of Ferozepur district, 1932–3.

small parcels of no more than half an acre, and these were not jointly owned. Holdings with over five to six acres were fragmented into ten to sixty pieces but were mostly jointly held.[26]

Large holdings made joint ownership possible, just as much as the strategy of joint ownership made the reproduction of holdings without subdivision feasible. Moreover, those with the resources to expand cultivation could also acquire land through lease and mortgage, reaffirming the possibility of joint cultivation. Conversely, holdings of a small size made joint ownership difficult, for they could not sustain many heads, nor absorb the available family labour; it forced individuals within the family to migrate in search of work and livelihood. Small parcel holders without resources could rarely buy land, though some of them managed to lease in other small parcels to expand cultivation. In Tehong there were 169 owners with less than an acre of land, 38 of whom managed to lease in some land and expand their cultivation within the village. But 36 took to labour to supplement their income, and 63 migrated to the Canal Colonies.[27]

Anthropological studies in India suggest that the partitioning of households usually has a complicated history.[28] Joint cultivation with adult sons does not necessarily break down when sons get married or when the patriarch dies. They continue to live under the same roof, share the same hearth, and collectively manage the land. The first step towards segregation and segmentation is signalled by separating out the kitchen, with the brothers continuing to share the roof and control over the land. In the next stage the dwelling is divided without the

[26] Das and Calvert, *Tehong V.S.* Similar evidence came from other surveys.

[27] Ibid., p. 49.

[28] In discussing this literature, Das and Nicholas emphasise the need to differentiate spaces that are partitioned, and the complex ways in which the idea of jointness is forged and ruptured. United through the common line of birth, male agnates share in property and ritual. The women of a household are bonded through marriage, the sharing of interior spaces, and the daily routine of cooking. Hearth partitions separate the shared space of women, while male agnates continue to manage the property together till the land itself is partitioned. Das and Nicholas, "Family and Household".

land being partitioned, and a sense of jointness is reaffirmed through collective participation in rituals and festivals. Revisionist historical opinion across the world tends to confirm this picture.[29]

Yet we obviously have to make a distinction between joint ownership and joint cultivation. Not all those who hold land jointly, resisting partition, cultivate that land together. Some, as we have seen, migrated in search of work; others looked for good land in newly colonised tracts, leaving the cultivation to someone in the family who remained. At times rich peasants took over the land of others on lease or mortgage, expanding cultivation, consolidating control over cultivated land. Which is why, in all the village surveys to which I referred, we find that the number of holdings jointly cultivated is significantly lower than the number jointly owned. (See Figs 15a, 15b, 15c, and 15d.) Conversely, the number of cultivator's holdings cultivated by a single person is dramatically higher than the number of ownership holding in single possession.

Joint holdings were not fragments of the past, disappearing vestiges anomalous in modern times. Individual will, constituting itself within the framework of jointness, reworked the logic of that jointness, creating the basis of a specific modernity, a particular history of individuation. But operating within the framework of colonial law, joint holdings inevitably had an ambiguous life.

The Market and the Ambiguities of Law

In 1890, the Punjab government circulated a bill for comments. The bill sought to change the law of partition.[30] From the early years of British rule in Punjab the right to partition joint property was both

[29] For discussions of peasant manipulation of partible inheritance systems in Western Europe, see Berkner, "Inheritance, Land Tenure, and Peasant Family Structure"; Sabean, "Aspects of Kinship Behaviour and Property"; Howell, "Peasant Inheritance Customs". Discussions on the strategy of postponing partitions can be found in Czap, "The Perennial Multiple Family Household"; Bohac, "Peasant Inheritance Strategies in Russia". See also Smith, "Families and Their Land".

[30] Punjab Home (Judicial) 1890, May 1890, A 62.

recognised and restricted. What was sanctioned by the Punjab Civil Code of 1872 was a limited right. An individual could demand the partition of a joint property, but he could not enforce it without the consent of the other co-sharers. The idea of individual rights was to be expressed only within the framework of the collective rights of the coparcenary body.[31]

By the 1880s, there was a clamour for change. Frustrated with the ambiguities of these restrictive clauses, many officials demanded that the process of partitioning be made simpler. Within the existing law, they said, creditors who lent money to peasants found it difficult to recover their loans. They could hold the debtors' land on mortgage, but could not possess it as owners even when debtors failed to pay back their debts. Coparceners of joint property were reluctant to allow any part of the property to be sold. Should a protective policy insulate joint property from the natural law of individuation? The new bill sought to foreground the right of the individual to his share of collective property. It was proposed that in cases of partition the court would have the discretion to direct a sale of unpartitioned property on the application of any individual without the sanction of co-sharers.[32]

The move to liberalise the law of partition provoked an immediate reaction. "I am strongly of the opinion," wrote F.W. Egerton, the deputy commissioner of Dera Ismail Khan, "that the law of partition at present prevailing in Punjab had far better be left as it is."[33] He warned of the dangers of interfering with the affairs of the family and destroying the institutional foundation of the village system: "In further tampering with the relations between the joint members of a family *inter se* and substituting a fixed and arbitrary procedure for the flexible village system we run the risk of destroying that unit, and then the village system will be no more, and the village will represent a congeries of individuals with conflicting interests."[34] Influenced

[31] Roe and Rattigan, *Tribal Law in the Punjab*; Tupper, *PCL*, sec. III and IV.

[32] Punjab Home (Judicial) 1890, May 1890, A 63.

[33] No. 35, 4 February 1890, Captain F.W. Egerton, Deputy Comm., Dera Ismail Khan, to the Comm. and Sup. Derajat Div., Punjab Home (Judicial), May 1890, A 62.

[34] Ibid.

by the ideas of Henry Maine, passionate about his own defence of
the village system, Egerton saw the proposed law as both impolitic
and dangerous. If the law was passed, he predicted, the natural laws
of political economy would operate, small holdings would be sold,
rich men would oust the poor, land would slip out of the control of
the family, and the family system would collapse. In mounting this
attack on the new bill, Egerton was expressing a sentiment widely
shared amongst Punjab officials: village custom ought not to be super-
seded by arbitrary enactments; the collective village body should
not be displaced by atomised, self-interested individuals; the village
system had to be protected from the corrosive power of money and
the market.[35]

As the bill circulated, this rhetoric of protection was powerfully
critiqued. The voice of political economy railed against paternalist
sentiments. The same questions were repeatedly asked: How could the
forces of the market be forever constrained? How could the right to
property be both affirmed and denied? To be fully enjoyable, property
had to be commutable into money, it had to be a thing that could
be easily sold and purchased. Even district officials, many of them
Indians, framed their arguments in this language of political economy. Mangal Sain, a tahsildar from Peshawar, emphasised in his
comments on the bill: "The only mode of securing to each coparcener
his full measure of benefits is by converting it into money."[36] Property

[35] In the 1870s, reflecting back on early British intervention on the making
of custom, Tupper wrote: "I trust it is not, even now, too late to suggest that
the Punjab Civil Code went rather too far in the direction of authorising
partition. No doubt its rules were to be subject to local custom; but the tendency was to assert, as a presumption, that every co-partner has a right to
partition, and to throw the onus of proving the contrary on anyone alleging
it. Now, as a matter of theory, the presumption seems to me just the other
way." Proceeding from his evolutionist assumption that collective property precedes individual property, Tupper emphasised: "any rule favouring severalty
(i.e. individual property) is an innovation – it may be one of ancient standing,
but still an innovation." Tupper did not deny that in the long term the family
and the clan would break up, but stressed: "we should do nothing to hasten
the process." Tupper, *PCL*, vol. III, p. 123.
[36] Mangal Sain, Tahsildar, Peshawar on the Draft Bill to Amend the Law
Relating to Partition, Punjab Home (Judicial), May 1890, A 53.

had no meaning, he felt, within the ambiguities of the existing law.

In the intense debate that ensued, land and money came to represent two different worlds, each with its own values and norms. For people like Mangal Sain the idea of property could not be separated from the notion of commutability. It was a notion that saw land as capital, and the easy substitution of one for the other as necessary in modern society. Countering such a vision, Charat Singh, a munsiff, argued: "If cash shares are distributed the respectability of the family will be spoiled, feelings injured, disunion spread."[37] Commutability, he was convinced, would destroy the personal bonds that tied families together and disrupt the norms of mutuality that sustained rural social life.

Colonial law was caught once again between contradictory pressures – the need to transform as well as preserve, institutionalise individual rights as well as sustain joint property, allow the market to operate but contain its disruptive potential. The bill was ultimately passed, hissadars were allowed to sell their shares, but the right to pre-emption remained. The battles for control of land were fought in new ways. While coparceners sought to question any move by a joint owner to sell his share, asserting the right to pre-emption, creditors seeking to acquire shares of joint property devised ingenious ways of operating within the ambiguities of the law.[38]

When Negotiations Fail

The new law, however, did not initiate an era of desperate partitioning. After the experience of the mid-nineteenth-century partitionings, peasants seem to have reaffirmed their faith in joint holdings, with all the males of a household controlling the land collectively instead of

[37] Charat Singh, Munsiff, on the Draft Bill to Amend the Law Relating to Partition, Punjab Home (Judicial), May 1890, A 54.

[38] One standard strategy adopted by creditors was to quote fictitious and inflated purchase prices to pre-empt the possibility of pre-emption. To retain the land as patrimonial property, and exercise the right to pre-emption, joint owners had to pay the co-sharer who was selling his share the price he was getting from the creditor.

dividing it up. The partitioning of land was persistently postponed and it happened ultimately only when all the strategies of joint living were exhausted. Even then, partitioning often meant the breaking away of one of the many co-sharers rather than the complete subdivision of the entire holding.[39]

Conflicts could lead to partition only when partitioning itself was within the realm of the possible – when the idea of partitioning was legally accepted and permitted by social codes. In a world where law begins to mediate all social relations, what is socially imaginable is very often shaped by what is legally permissible. Colonial legal interventions, as we have seen, both encouraged and restrained partitioning. At one level, partitioning was seen as necessary for the individuation of rights: only through partitioning could individual rights be categorically specified, stated publicly, encoded in mutation records, and the individual emancipated from the constraints of the collective. Only through such definite specification could the ambiguities and fuzziness of informal understandings be overcome, the sources of conflict – seen as intimately connected to fuzziness itself – be eliminated.[40] At another level, partitioning was regulated

[39] This is the evidence in the case studies of partitioning that are detailed in the village surveys. The annual figures of the revenue department and the registration department give us estimates of the area affected by partitioning every year. But these refer mostly to the partitioning of shamilat. By the 1870s, as land was increasingly integrated to the commodity economy, the common land was carved into slices. The revenue settlement had attached the shamilat to the village and declared it the collective property of the coparcenary brotherhood. It was, in fact, the shamilat that defined the identifying mark of a pattidari community – their jointness. Peasants, who had been granted rights in the shamilat in proportion to their supposed fractional shares within the village, now began to scramble for possession. As the common land was enclosed and appropriated, the mythic jointness of the pattidari community disappeared and the common rights of the landless vanished, while the figures of partitioning entered in the registration records soared.

[40] This derives in part from the Benthamite tradition that attacked the ambiguities of the common law thinking. See Postema, *Bentham and the Common Law Tradition*, pt II. In part the notion is shaped by the nineteenth-century fetish for precision and exactness. When a political culture of precision

and restricted by limiting clauses to protect patriarchal rights and patrilineal inheritance. Even the liberals within the Punjab tradition could not get away from the idea that male coparcenary brotherhoods ought not to be radically disturbed.

Let me deal with a few cases to show when and how the right to partition was both asserted and limited. I wish to do this by looking at the rights of widows – whose location within the household was possibly the most ambiguous and whose rights legally the most un-certain. Conflicts within the household, as we will see, not only provided the grounds for demanding partition, they were critical to the formulation of the law itself. Legal codes were debated and dis-puted, clarified and reworked, through the legal process that followed familial battles. The law was not simply out there to be enforced and implemented. It was not a fixed frame within which disputes un-folded.

In the 1860s a landowner named Baggoo lived with his wife Mussammat Bhago, cultivating a small plot of twenty-three ghumaos, in a village near Lahore.[41] They had four sons. Upon growing up the sons married and had children, but these sons continued living on the same land and cultivating the same holding. When one of the brothers, Shamir, died young, his widow, Rajjii, continued to live as part of the joint household. In 1872 Baggoo died. Now there was a reorganisation of the household, with the notional share of each hissadar being entered in the mutation record. The land continued to be jointly cultivated but the harvest was to be divided. Rajjii had claim to one-fifth share, her mother-in-law to another one-fifth, and the three brothers one-fifth each. We do not know whether the living sons and their wives continued to share a common hearth, but it is clear that Rajjii cooked her own food and was given one-fifth share of the harvest. As the years passed, relations changed. In 1878 we find Rajjii filing for partition, claiming she was being denied her share of the produce and had been left with no means to survive. The case

---

develops, informal understandings and personal undertakings are no longer seen as trustworthy and reliable. See Wise, *The Values of Precision*; Porter, *Trust in Numbers*.

[41] *PR*, no. 22 of 1878.

was difficult to settle. According to codified custom, a widow could not inherit but had a claim to maintenance, a life interest on the land. Logically, she could not demand a partition. But who was to ensure that claim to "maintenance"? What if she was harassed, humiliated, and denied the pleasure of a dignified existence as well as her notional share of the harvest? On being refused a right to partition by the lower court, Rajjii appealed. The judges at the high court agreed that Rajjii had no customary right to partition, but they still declared that her share be separated. In reviewing the case, the commissioner of Lahore emphasised that Rajjii had been driven to the court by her husband's brothers, and the judges felt that partitioning her share was the only way to ensure justice when her in-laws had persistently failed to do their duty.[42]

By the 1890s the rights of widows to their husband's share were reinterpreted. Custom is nowhere immutable, nor ever born in the mists of time. As we have seen, under nineteenth-century British codification it became subject to judicial reinterpretations and new enactments.[43] The Punjab Land Revenue Act 1887 declared that a widow with a share in joint property was legally a "landowner", and therefore could demand the partitioning of her share.[44] This position was powerfully affirmed in 1895 by Mackworth Young, the financial commissioner of Punjab, in a revenue ruling that marked a critical shift of argumentation seemingly in favour of widows.[45]

[42] Summing up his argument Justice Plowden said: "I think it is quite open to the court to say to the defendants that they have failed in their duty to the widow, and that they must therefore submit to a separation of a portion of the estate which will provide her with proper maintenance and put her beyond reach of their power to injure in future . . ." *PR*, no. 22 of 1878. In most such demands for partition, widows complained of their right to maintenance being denied by their husband's brothers. See *PR*, no. 93 of 1869; *PR*, no. 50 of 1870.

[43] Between 1868 and 1881, widows were not entitled to demand partition before the revenue court, but could only claim the right to "separate possession where it is indispensable to secure her proper enjoyment of her share." *PR*, 1898, p. 286. For the cases from the early decades, see *PR*, no. 93 of 1869; *PR*, no. 50 of 1870.

[44] *PR*, no. 11 of 1895 (Rev.).

[45] See *PR*, no. 82 of 1892.

Embedded orthodoxies are, however, not so easy to dislodge. The language of law creates spaces for contorted argumentation. When in January 1897 Buta, in Hafial village of Rawalpindi, filed a suit against his widowed aunt he was possibly unaware of the new ruling.[46] Buta first asserted his sole ownership of the ancestral land, claiming that his uncle had divorced Jiwani, and so she had no right to the land. When he failed to prove his claim, Jiwani filed for partition. Buta now filed a declaratory suit asserting that widows could not ask for partition. In considering the case, all the judges at the high court were categorical: Buta's effort was to dispossess Jiwani, and according to the new ruling widows were to be seen as rightful "owners" of their share. But did that give them a right to partition? They dithered and debated and finally declared that under the new ruling widows undoubtedly had a right to partition, so that Jiwani's demand was to be considered by the revenue court. But if the ruling of the revenue court was challenged, then the higher courts had to decide whether in fact the custom of the region allowed such claims of widows; and such a questioning then raised an issue regarding the nature of the widow's *title*, not her *right*. In this particular case Jiwani's title as owner was seen as limited, and her claim to partition was denied.

Once again we see judges caught in a bind. On the one hand they saw the movement towards individual holding as a marker of progress – a sign of the passage from the primitive to the modern; on the other they were keen to sustain custom and the founding structures of local society. Every ruling that asserted the legitimacy of widows' right to partition, seeing it as just and necessary, was followed by others that questioned the same right, reinterpreting the meaning of earlier rulings and reasserting the sanctity of patriarchal property.[47] Expressed in the texts of these judgments was a persistent fear: if widows' right to partition was normalised, the male coparcenary brotherhoods – the founding structure of Punjab society – would collapse.

This fear produced new layers of argumentation, new defences of joint property, and new arguments for patrilineal power. If in 1898

[46] Ibid.
[47] See *PR*, no. 63 of 1892; *PR*, no. 82 of 1893; *PR*, no. 6 of 1896.

the argument revolved around the distinction between *right* and *title*, after 1912 the debate shifted to "onus of proof". In 1906, Mussammat Bhag Bhari, a widow living in Mozang village near Lahore, applied for the partition of her share in a joint holding. Bhari said she was allowed no control over the land and no proper share of the produce; and she feared that her husband's nephew, Wazir Khan, was trying to usurp her hissa of the joint holding. When the revenue court decided in favour of Bhari's right, Wazir Khan appealed and the case moved up to higher courts. Adjudicating the case in 1912, two judges were unambiguous in their decision: a widow had unquestionable right to claim partition in such cases, and the onus of proving that she could be restrained from obtaining this right, according to custom, lay with the co-sharer.[48] It was wrong, they emphasised, to invoke the desirability of males controlling and managing the property and to assume that women could not look after land.

Within a few years, however, the logic of this argument was reversed once again. When Mussammat Rabia applied for partition of her share of a joint holding in a village in Jullunder, and the case went up through usual stages to the financial commissioner, Fagan declared that the rights of widows to partition had never been definitively decided in the past.[49] He argued that widows had a right to *apply* for partition but no right to *compel* partition; and the onus of proving the custom in favour of their claim lay on them. This judgment, once again, normalised joint property and patriarchal right within male brotherhoods: the rights of male co-sharers were seen as natural, the widow's right to partition was not.

[48] *PR*, no. 70 of 1912. They said: "The widow has a clear, unequivocal and statutory right in virtue of her possession under the Land Revenue Act to demand partition." Ibid., p. 269.

[49] *PR*, no. 4 of 1917. For other rulings after 1913 that denied the rights of widows to *compel* partition, see *PR*, no. 219 of 1913. Most rulings after 1895 accepted widows' right to separate possession, but not to definite partition. See *PR*, no. 82 of 1898; *PR*, no. 30 of 1905; *PR*, no. 155 of 1909; *PR*, no. 219 of 1913; see also Ellis, *Notes on Punjab Custom*, p. 60. The difference between separate possession and partition was explained at length as early as 1879. See *PR*, no. 116 of 1979 (Civil).

When brothers could no longer operate a joint holding because of the intensity of familial bickering, they could apply for partition. But they could not do so while their father was alive. Custom, as codified in Punjab, generally assumed that sons had no right to ask for partition within the lifetime of their father. Sanctioned in the Hindu Mitakshara law, such a right was not recognised in Punjab agrarian society. Convinced of the hegemonic power of agrarian custom, judges inevitably decided in favour of the right of the patriarch.[50]

Guran Das had agricultural land in Pasianwala village in the district of Sialkot.[51] When he died his son, Shiv Das, managed the land and looked after his widowed mother, Mussammat Radhi. As family conflicts developed over the years, the four sons of Guran Das wanted to separate and filed for partition. As Hindu Aroras, they hoped that their case would be decided according to Mitakshara law. The judges, however, ruled that the customs of Khatris and Aroras living in rural Punjab conformed to the wider customs of the locality. So, sons had no right to demand partition. This was no isolated case. In case after case we see the customs of non-agricultural castes being reinterpreted through the lens of agrarian practice.

So partitioning did not follow naturally from an innate desire for individual landholding and the working of equitable partible inheritance. Individuals do not come into the modern world purged of the inscriptions of the past, desperate to break away from the ties of the joint family, keen to constitute their individuality in opposition to the community. They negotiate their individual space and define their self within collectivities. They break away only when this is not possible – when individual self-interest, constituted in relation to the

---

[50] Justice J. Scott-Smith asserted in 1917: "There is not a single recorded case, or an unrecorded one, so far as I am aware, decided by this Court in which the right of a son to enforce partition during his father's lifetime was recognised. The Punjab Civil Court laid down that a son has not such a right . . . The onus to prove that there was such a right was on the person affirming it." *PR*, no. 105 of 1917, p. 413. See *PR* , no. 113 of 1886; *PR*, no. 112 of 1891; *PR*, no. 90 of 1892; *PR*, no. 105 of 1895; *PR*, no. 5 of 1913; *PR*, no. 85 of 1915.

[51] *PR*, no. 5 of 1913.

community and family, comes in serious conflict with affirmed collective interest, and even then neither always nor inevitably. All the
evidence suggests that the formal partitioning of land happened only
when conflicts within the family made joint living difficult. The way
in which the idea of the self and the community is reconstituted is
defined by the specific ways in which such conflicts are negotiated.

The Logic of Scatter

The resistance to consolidation was not entirely due to issues of sentiment and affect, such as an unwillingness to rupture the bonds
that tied peasants to their forefathers. After all, they did exchange
their fields informally, often leasing in contiguous fields and leasing
out those located at a distance, exchanging fields at times, buying
and selling at other times. When was the exchange of fields seen as
acceptable? When was it resisted? When were peasants willing to
reorder the spatial location of their scattered fields? What defined
their choices, their calculations?

As the Punjab officials found, peasants did not always share their
enthusiasm for the consolidated farm. When Calvert's co-operators
expounded on the benefits of the single field, many peasants in rural
Punjab proceeded to explain the advantages of scattered plots.[52] They
spoke of variations in soils and terrain, and the need to appreciate the
constraints and possibilities offered by different types of land. Once
you understand these variations, they seemed to say, the rationality
of scattered farms is almost self-evident.

Revenue officials were not unaware of soil variations. By the 1830s
the Ricardian theory of rent was part of official common sense. Everyone knew that revenue assessment could not be uniform, for the
quality of soil and the location of the field produced differential
rents from land.[53] Trained by Thomason in the North Western Provinces, many enthusiastic settlement officers proceeded to record soil
differences in minute detail. Surveying Jullunder in the 1870s, Purser

[52] See *Cooperative Society Reports (Punjab) on Consolidation of Holdings*;
Strickland, "Co-operative Consolidation of Holdings in the Punjab".

[53] See Stokes, *The English Utilitarians*; Siddiqi, *Agrarian Change in a North
Indian State*; Gupta, *Agrarian Relations and Early British Rule in India*.

enumerated forty-seven natural soils in Jullunder and Nakodar tahsils, and twenty-one in Nawashahr tahsil.[54] For many officials, discovering local differences became an obsession: a marker of the sincerity of the surveyor and the authenticity of the survey.

The logic of differentiation inevitably came up against the logic of simplification. As Financial Commissioner Wace reminded revenue officials in the 1880s, classification had to be simple; it had to be of practical use.[55] It was useless to record details that had no bearing on revenue assessment. The act of surveying and recording, moreover, had to be manageable, and the task of the patwaris ought not to be made impossibly difficult. Writing the Settlement Officer's Manual for the North Western Provinces, Vincent Smith had emphasised: "(A) Settlement Officer should remember that he is a land valuer, not a mineralogist."[56] Variations had to be recognised, but a proliferation of categories was confusing. Categories of enumeration had to be rationalised, differences had to be abbreviated: one generic term had to stand for a multiplicity of names. The classification had to convey a sense of order, not confusion. Revenue officials were repeatedly told: only what is obvious and visible – that "no one can fail to see" – ought to be recorded. Fine distinctions were difficult to demarcate, and what could not be confidently discerned was likely to be wrongly classified.[57] Certainty alone could be the ground for classificatory knowledge.

[54] Purser, *Jallandhar Tahsil A.R., 1883*; Purser, *Nakodar Tahsil A.R., 1883*; Purser, *Nawashahr Tahsil A.R., 1883*.

[55] Financial Commissioner's Circular, No. 19 of 1889. The specifications were again outlined in Financial Commissioner's Circular, No. 1258, 8 February 1911. This official wisdom was repeated in all instructions to revenue officials. Douie, compiling the settlement manual for Punjab, wrote: "No general rule can be laid down, for everything depends on local circumstances. All that can be said is that the classification should be as simple as possible, and be based on broad differences of fairly permanent character which affect in a marked degree the economic rental of the land. The test to be applied to it is its sufficiency for practical purposes . . ." Douie, *Panjab Settlement Manual*, para 265, p. 140. See also *Punjab Land Records Manual*, paras 7.49–7.53.

[56] Smith, *The Settlement Officer's Manual for the North-Western Provinces*, p. 126

[57] On the changes in the 1880s, see the discussion in *SRFCP, NS*, no. 53,

Once the new rules of revenue survey were formulated in the mid 1880s, settlement officers were reluctant to record local soil names.[58] It was officially notified that all variations had to be reduced to five or six categories – banjar (waste), chahi (irrigated from wells), nahri (canal irrigated), abi (watered by lifts from tanks, or pools, or marshes), sailab (moistened by the river), barani (dependent on rainfall). The different soil types were to be regrouped within these categories.[59] Two criteria of differentiation appeared meaningful to officials: the nature of irrigation and the revenue-yielding capacity of the soil. The quality of irrigation, it was believed, would define the levels of yield and rent, and consequently the revenue assessment.[60] Even good soils, it was emphasised, could not yield much without irrigation, and the natural variation between soils could be compensated through irrigation. The logic of this simplification was to condense the corpus of categories and homogenise even while differentiating. This meant not an elimination of all differences but reclassification through official

---

Proposals for the Systematisation of Future Survey Operations in the Punjab, 1884; SRFCP, NS, no. 55, Recent Papers on Leading Questions Relating to Settlements and Land Revenue Administration, 1885.

[58] By the early twentieth century the ethnographic zeal to discover local taxonomies had waned. All settlement officials spoke of the futility of collecting local terms and the advantages of adopting the simplified classification officially sanctioned. On the changed categories by the early twentieth century, see Rev. & Agr. (Rev.), September 1916, no. 15; Rev. & Agr. (Rev.), March 1916, no. 1.

[59] For instance, barani soils (dependent on rains) in most tahsils were classed into three sub categories: barani-I, barani-II, barani-III. The soils within each of these groups varied in the different districts since the effort was to distinguish three levels of revenue that the barani lands could yield. In Garshankar tahsil of Hoshiarpur district, for instance, barani-I referred to niain – manured land near the village; barani-II to rohi, maira, and sailab; and barani-III to retar, rakkar, rohi-kalrathi (brackish rohi), maira-kalrathi (brackish maira). The connotative power of these distinct soils was lost when they were lumped together under official categories representing different levels of revenue assessment. See GOI Rev. and Agr. (Rev.), September 1914, no. 26, para 5.

[60] On the changed categories by the early twentieth century, see GOI, Rev. & Agr. (Rev.), September 1916, no. 15; GOI Rev. & Agr. (Rev.), March 1916, no. 1.

categories, a process driven by the logic of state fiscality and the enumerative imperatives of a classificatory regime. To be officially useful, variations themselves had to be standardised; differences had to be incorporated within a classificatory grid that was broadly uniform across regions.

Cultivators saw soils with different eyes. To them the official categorisation of barani (unirrigated) into three classes – barani I, barani II, and barani III – made no sense. Within each of these categories were diverse soils, each with its own specific attributes.[61] For cultivators this heterogeneity mattered. Enquiring into folk taxonomies of the past is always difficult, but folk wisdom gives us some clues. [62] Within the local taxa, land was differentiated according to location and terrain, and soils were identified in terms of colour, texture, consistency,

[61] Most ethnopedological studies exploring folk soil taxonomies relate to the ethnographic present. See, for instance, Wilshusen and Stone, "An Ethno-archaeological Perspective on Soils"; Williams and Ortiz-Solorio, "Middle American Folk Soil Taxonomy". On the possibilities of ethnopedology more generally, see Berlin, Breedlove, and Raven, "Folk Taxonomies and Biological Classification"; Berlin, Breedlove, and Raven, "General Principles of Classification and Nomenclature in Folk Biology"; Hunn, "Toward a Perceptual Model of Folk Biological Classification".

[62] During the First Regular Settlement operations that started in the 1850s, some settlement officers gathered local sayings and proverbs and appended them to the Settlement Reports. See Wilson, *Hissar S.R., 1879–83*; Robertson, *Rawalpindi S.R., 1880–87*; Lyall, *Kangra S.R., 1865–72*. Unfortunately not all settlement officers took this task seriously. Then in the mid 1880s the Punjab government asked the financial commissioner, E.G. Wace, to prepare an agricultural primer to be used in village schools. Wace felt he needed to know how far peasants were already aware of the science of agriculture. In a circular letter he instructed all deputy commissioners to collect local proverbs about agrarian life. The collections that flowed in from each district were rearranged and thematised by R. Maconachie and published in 1889. Maconachie emphasised that "these proverbs instead of supplying materials for an Agricultural Primer for the Punjabi can only instruct his rulers." Maconachie, *SAPP*, p. vii. Local knowledge, however, informs rulers in peculiar ways. Wace, who commissioned the collection, saw no need to gather details of local soil names during the revenue settlement, even when the voice encoded in the local proverbs powerfully affirmed the importance of soil variations.

density, capacity to retain moisture, workability, and adaptability. No land was seen as simply good or bad, fertile or barren. Dissimilar soils offered different possibilities, demanded varied inputs, and had to be worked in distinct ways.

One distinction that recurs within folk taxonomy in Punjab is between low-lying land and upland. The upland was commonly known as manjha in Amritsar and Lahore, dhaia in Ludhiana and Jullunder, utar in Ferozepur, and bangar/bagar in the south-east around Karnal, Gurgaon, and Rohtak, whereas low-lying land was hithar and bét in central Punjab and khadir and dahar in the south-east. It was popularly said that those who have low-lying land and high relations can suffer no loss, their enemies can do no harm: *Ohdi dushman kí Karen Jide khet niwan.* It was good to have village settlements on high land and cultivable fields on low land: *Uncha gaon bhala, niche khet bhala.* Watered by rivers and the drainage that flowed down the terrain, low-lying land was naturally moist. When the rivers overflowed during the rains, a thin layer of replenishing alluvium (chhal) was spread over the flood plain. So it was said in Hoshiarpur: *Chhal zamin/ Ki kare amin,*[63] and further north-west, around Hazra: *Jisda dáb, Usda rab* – God is with those who own dáb (land that retains moisture).

But low-lying land was not invariably good for cultivation. Floods could be destructive. In a year of heavy rainfall the kharif (autumn crop) could be ruined even when a bumper rabi (spring harvest) was ensured. In places, devastating floods brought vast amounts of sand and clay, destroying fields, turning banks into enormous stretches of sand. When rivers changed their course – as was common in Punjab – whole villages were washed away, cultivated fields were submerged, and new lands were thrown up elsewhere. Cultivation in such tracts had to adapt to the ecology of the river, take account of the alluvion and de-alluvion.[64]

[63] This meant: If you have good land near the river, fertilised by the chhal (alluvium silt) every year, you need not fear the surveyor.

[64] Over time, officials had to recognise this, since the revenue capacity of the land obviously depended on whether the land existed at all or not, whether it was submerged and therefore not available for ploughing and

The width of the lowland depended in fact on how much the river shifted. In Ludhiana, for instance, it was 5 to 6 miles wide in the eastern part, narrowed to about 1 to 2 miles near Jagraon tahsil, and finally disappeared altogether. In Jullunder, the lowland was a huge expanse of 8 miles width around Nakodar tahsil, but stretched to only 4 miles in Nawashahr tahsil and 1.5 miles in Phillour tahsil. Where the bét was wide, the old bed of the river immediately below the ridge of the upland (dha) was the most fertile, moistened by the river but protected from its destructive action. The ground-water level was high – 10 to 20 feet, in places only 8 feet, below the surface, and well irrigation was easy. The Jullunder bét was dotted with wells surrounded by clumps of trees. Where the bét was narrow, the river could be destructive and peasants longed for land at the edge of the upland. *Dhaha/ beparwah,* it was said in such places in Jullunder.

All soil taxonomies make a distinction between loam and sandy soils. Cultivators, however, recognise a range of differences within these generic categories. In nineteenth-century Punjab, around Delhi, rausuli was a loam that peasants loved. It was fertile and light, required minimal ploughing, and was not labour intensive. Everyone, young or old, could cultivate it: *Rausuli ka kisan, burha ho ya jawan,* it was said. In Jullunder – a doaba with a long history of agricultural settlement, a high density of population, and an agrarian landscape of intensive cultivation – rohi was widely praised. This soil was stiffer than rausuli, required heavier ploughs, and frequent ploughings to make it yield. If it was worked well it yielded much more than the lighter loam. Rohi, in fact, was the metaphor of goodness and distinction, an object of desire: *Bhuin rohi/ Talwar sohi/ Mainh lohi* was a popular saying.[65]

---

sowing. See Papers Relating to Alluvion and De-alluvion Rules, *SRFCP, NS,* no. 19.

[65] This meant: rohi land, a sarohi sword, and a reddish brown she-buffalo are the things of their kind to have. There were variations of this saying in other parts of Punjab. Around Lahore it was said: *Zamin rohi/ Majh lohi/ Jat khrah/ Bauld nahra* (Rohi land, a buffalo with black skin and brown hair, a jat with kharah, and a bullock with upright horns, are things of their kind to have). See Maconachie, *SAPP,* no. 36.

When heavy ploughs, sturdy oxen, and labour were in short supply, peasants looked for lighter loams. Maira was very light, even lighter than the rausuli of Delhi; dosahi was heavier than maira but lighter than rohi. This soil again was widely appreciated. Settle a village where you find dosahi (*Zamin dosahi/ Te mulk vasahi*) was popular wisdom in Sialkot.

Like loam, there were many terms for sandy soils. Maira was a version of sandy loam and retli was pure sand: then there were others – tibba/tibbi, maurat, bhura, dohra. Within popular wisdom these soils were celebrated as well as condemned.[66] On light soils, it was said, crops could be grown with very little effort, no ploughing, and scanty rains. But light soils could not be manured and irrigated, or planted with labour-intensive crops. Suitable for a single crop (ekfasli eksala), they could not sustain double cropping (dofasli eksala). As with other crops their limits and potential had to be recognised.

Clayey soils were similarly differentiated. They were named and classified according to their density, compactness, and workability. Dakar and dabar were terms used in south Punjab for stiff clay that could produce a good crop with intensive cultivation. It required heavy and continuous ploughing to loosen the soil and allow it to breathe. With continuous care and lots of labour it produced a good harvest. Around Delhi it was said that dakar must be well cultivated, just as a Rajput must be well served: *Boe dakar/Sewa Thakar*. But if the soil had too much clay, it was bound to give trouble (*Zamin khakkar/ Sada hai phakkar*). Stiff clay that was difficult to work was known as rakkar or rappar in west Punjab, rarri or rawi around Jullunder, Ludhiana, Hoshiarpur, and Ambala, and khakkar/kakkar

---

[66] Tibba was praised in Jullunder: *Tibba bah te kan ura/ Khan pin un khushka kha* (Plough your sandy tracts, scare your crows and you shall have a dish of rice to eat). Maconachie, *SAPP*, no. 69; and maurat was celebrated in Rawalpindi: *Maurat zamin hai ret/ Hallan bajo hewan khet* (Maurat land is sand, without ploughs crops are produced). Maconachie, *SAPP*, no. 73. But retli and maira were both condemned in Hoshiarpur: *Chhal na lore meghla, ret na jame ghas/ Rohian lahre ladite maire di nahin as* (Alluvial land near the river wants no rain. Sand does not bear grass. Rohi has brought wealth. No hope for maira).

in some regions. Those who cultivate rarri will have neither home nor any roof over their heads, they declared in Jullunder: *Bahar rarri/ Na kothe kari.*[67] But even this soil could be made to yield if the oxen were strong and the soil intensively ploughed and turned over. But on depressions around drainage lines, where the alluvium was deposited over long years and the land perennially dampened by drainage, the soil was most often too compact and stiff, not allowing water to percolate through. On such water-logged clay the salts from the soil rose to the surface, making it difficult to cultivate. Such brackish soil – known as kallar or kalar – was uniformly condemned all over Punjab. Around Delhi, Rohtak, and Gurgaon, where large tracts of brackish soil could be found, it was commonly said: *Kalar ka kya khet/ Kapti ka kya het* (What crop can you expect from kalar land, what friendship can you expect from the deceitful). Kalar was a metaphor for evil. In the analogical discourse of rural life, it was a synonym for all that was troublesome in life. Four things were seen as hell on earth – an unworthy son, a quarrelsome woman at home, going in front of a horse, and kallar soil (*Kallar kheti, kaput ghar, ghar kalaihni nar/ Turyan age chalna, charon narak sansar*). On such land, it was widely believed, roots suffocate, crops dry up even as they grow, and no matter how much you toil to plough the land, you go hungry.[68]

For the cultivator, these fine shades of difference were not superfluous. Each name referred to a discrete experience, an accumulated knowledge of their distinct attributes, an appreciation of their specific requirements and potential. Only an understanding of these differences allowed a cultivator to calculate how much labour was required to cultivate his fields and look after his animal stock, which crops could be grown, and what cropping regime was viable. These choices were shaped by the number of hands within the family, the animal stock, the land and other resources available, and levels of solvency and indebtedness. Since different soils and crops required

[67] Maconachie, *SAPP*, no. 53. Kari refers literally to the beam that supports the structure of a building.

[68] The saying in Hoshiarpur was: *Kallar khet na lage rukh/ Kheti lag lag jandi sukh/ Bhanwan kitni kahian put/ Uthe mul na landi bhukh.* Maconachie, *SAPP*, no. 64.

different inputs of human and animal labour, access to fields with different soils allowed peasants to deploy labour in judicious ways. When a peasant family with a field of maira or dosahi (different types of light loam) had unutilised family labour, it would be keen on a patch of rohi or niain to produce some labour-intensive crops. Conversely, those with rohi or dabar, which required a lot of care and labour for cultivation, were often keen on fields with lighter soils.[69] With very little effort and resource, maira and retli could produce moth and bajra for the household and fodder for the cattle. Even rich peasants who controlled the core areas with good loam wanted the lighter soils to grow fodder crops, diversify their crop regime, and distribute their labour resources. A diversification of the crop regime and cultivation of scattered plots secured the peasant against the vicissitudes of season – delayed rains or failed monsoon, excess rain or destructive floods. When water was in short supply or the rains inadequate, crops on rohi fields could fail, but those on lighter soils still yielded a fair harvest.

Land moreover was not judged by cultivators only in terms of its soil quality. It was often a signifier of many different things. For instance, for many decades revenue officials translated niain as well-manured land. Gradually they came to recognise that this was land near the village that happened to be also well manured.[70] But for peasants niain meant many other things as well. Possession of niain was a signifier of status and privilege – for those who were power-ful and rich most often controlled such land. It allowed access to

[69] Walker, the Settlement Officer of Ludhiana, wrote: "In a village with light soils the people will speak with apparent envy of the 'dakhar' or clay loam of some other village, where the crops are so good, while the owners of this latter sort of soil sigh for the light lands (called *resli*) of their neighbours, which require little ploughing, and where the crops spring in the driest years." Walker, *Ludhiana S.R., 1878–83*, p. 94.

[70] In the early summary settlements of the 1850s and '60s niain land was overestimated since it was generally translated as manured land. Even in the 1890s John Grant, Settlement Collector, Amritsar, stated: "Generally speaking, any land supposed to be regularly manured has been entered as niai, wherever situated." *Tarn Taran A.R.*, para 37.

village wells and enabled the land to be irrigated. When the field was near the village, peasants could properly care for the land and watch the crops, move with ease between the home and the field, and return home for the afternoon meal. It was on niain land that sugarcane, maize, cotton, wheat and other commercially valuable crops were usually grown. So, niain land was a signifier of prosperity, wealth, and good fortune. If you have niain land, it was said, you can have weddings forever: *Bije niain/ Nit byah karain.*

Peasants were thus keen on owning fields at different locations and with different soils rather than one type of soil.[71] Scattered plots did not always create a problem. It allowed them to use different soils with varying requirements and potential, produce different crops, sustain complex crop regimes, and distribute their labour resources in meaningful ways.[72]

When peasants spoke of the wisdom in equally partitioning all

[71] Sensitive officials were aware of this logic of scattering, but saw it as a marker of primitivity – a dependence on nature that could be overcome by technology, simply by ensuring water supply through irrigation. Wilson wrote: "The land is not uniform in character, and from time immemorial, whenever a partition took place, each shareholder endeavored to obtain a bit of land of each different quality, so as to be rendered more secure against the vicissitudes of season, which affects the different blocks of land differently according to their soil or position. The consequence is that the typical peasant's holding consists not of a continuous plot of land all in one place, but of a field here and a field there, scattered over the whole area of the township, often a mile or more apart." Wilson, "Recent Economic Developments in the Punjab".

[72] Several studies show how within a heterogeneous ecological environment, folk perception of soil quality shapes technological choice. The introduction of HYV seeds in many parts of the world had only limited success partly because farmers adopted them only for soils they saw as appropriate to HYV, richer soils that would not easily be depleted of nutrients. On other soils traditional varieties were grown. Farmers thus tried to devise a crop mix that was suitable for the ecological niches within their particular holdings. In a heterogeneous ecological environment, with different soils on scattered plots, any policy that encourages uniform adoption of HYV for all types of soil faces only partial success. Farmers resist the policy and even if HYV were introduced, the crop regime would be "inefficient" and unsustainable. See Bellon and Taylor, "'Folk' Soil Taxonomy and the Partial Adoption of New Seed Varieties".

types of land, and the principle of equity and justice that underlay such division, they were affirming a logic that officials failed to understand. Peasants did not always want consolidated holdings with one kind of soil. Only after three decades of experience did officials and economists come to recognise that exchanges of scattered plots could only be done when soil formations were similar.[73] But scattering through the working of inheritance custom happened precisely because soil types were heterogeneous. Equitable partible inheritance in Punjab by definition implied the division of different types of land, not simply the dispersal of one type of land into scattered plots.

Peasants in Punjab were not alone in showing a predilection for scattered plots. For some time now, historians and economists in various parts of the world have been puzzling over the persistence of this phenomenon and have come to recognise that this persistence has an explicable logic. Some have seen scattering as an insurance against crisis, a protection against shocks;[74] others have argued that it allows the household to distribute labour demand over a longer period of time since the work cycle and the timing of the labour demand for different crops are not the same;[75] still others have shown that the geography of scatter has a connection with the question of access to water, with farmers at the tail of a canal, or at a distance from a well, scrambling for small plots near the source of water supply.[76] I do not think these explanations exclude each other or are in any way opposed to each other, though that is the way the debate has often

---

[73] See Bonner, *Land Consolidation and Economic Development in India*; Agarwal, *Economics of Land Consolidation in India*; Singh, *Consolidation of Holdings*; Joglekar, *Report on Consolidation of Holdings in Madhya Pradesh*; Rizvi, *et al.*, *Consolidation of Holdings*.

[74] McCloskey, "English Open Fields"; Townsend, *Medieval Village Economy*.

[75] Fenoaltea, "Risk, Transaction Costs and the Origin of Medieval Agriculture"; Dahlman, *The Open Field System and Beyond*.

[76] Sengupta, "Fragmented Holdings, Productivity, and Resilience Management", pp. 507–32. For other important essays on scattering, see also Heston and Kumar, "The Persistence of Land Fragmentation in Peasant Agriculture", pp. 199–220; Bentley, "Economic and Ecological Approaches to Land Fragmentation".

developed.[77] Different households, located within varying eco-zones, make their choices for slightly differing reasons and see exchanges of plots, or the consolidation of parts of the holding, necessary in some contexts and unacceptable in others.

The modernist fantasy of an ordered landscape of neat rectangular fields was sought to be realised in the Canal Colonies. Colonisation re-laid the landscape. Forests and grazing lands were cleared on a massive scale, pastoralists and local cultivators were dispossessed, and settlers were given 500 acres on landlord grants and 28 acres on yeoman grants. Consolidated plots, it was hoped, would ensure scientific agriculture. Cleansed of the marks of the past, cleared of the constraints to large-scale farming, the Canal Colony farms were expected to emerge as the locus of future modernisation and progress. "Of all the advantages confirmed by a colony," Darling declared, "it may be doubted whether any is greater than the blessing of the single field."[78] Yet a few decades after the allotments were made, the dream of large-scale capitalist farming on these colony lands slowly began to crumble. Despairing officials saw the history of fragmentation replayed in new settings as the large land grants were split into smaller plots for cultivation and leased out to tenants.[79] To reproduce their households and resist processes of fragmentation and pauperisation, peasants devised their own strategies and were not always willing to enact scripts written by the state.

[77] See, for instance, Fenoaltea, "Risk"; McCloskey, "Fenoaltea on Open Fields".

[78] Darling, *Punjab Peasant*, p. 128.

[79] Agnihotri, "Agrarian Change in the Canal Colonies".

9

Colonising the Commons

Over the century of colonial rule in Punjab, we see a dramatic expansion of the agrarian frontier. In the mid 1870s the cultivated area in Punjab was estimated to be about 22,640 thousand acres.[1] Within the next forty years this acreage had boomed to 28,680 thousand, a 27 per cent increase. In 1875 about 40 per cent of the assessed area was cultivated, by 1915 the proportion was 48 per cent. This dramatic expansion of the agrarian frontier can blind us – as indeed it often has – to the many layers of interrelated histories that lie behind it. To understand these multiple but enmeshed histories we need to go beyond a narrow focus on the internal dynamic of the agrarian zone and estimations of output growth; we must look at what was happening beyond the agrarian frontier. The story of agrarian expansion, I would like to argue, was intimately connected to the histories of scrublands and grass fields.

The turn from agrarian to ecological history has shifted the historian's focus from cultivated fields to forests.[2] This has persuaded historians to explore spaces beyond the agrarian. But scrublands and grasslands have not yet caught the historian's imagination. Instead of indigo, wheat, sugarcane, and cotton, we now look at deodar, sal, and teak; but the frame through which we define our choice of focus, at one level, remains similar. We are looking – whether at cultivated

[1] *RAP*, 1876–7, Table I; *ASBI*, Table II.
[2] Guha, *The Unquiet Woods*; Rangarajan, *Fencing the Forest*; Rajan, *Modernizing Nature*.

field or forest – for the commercially important commodities, for products highly valued by the colonial state and the world market. The criteria of significance defined by the state and reaffirmed through its records continue to structure the limits of our historical vision.[3]

To move to the scrubland is to redirect our focus. But how do we conceptualise this focus? What I am emphasising here is not a radical turnaround that throws the very idea of the agrarian overboard in celebrating the new history of forests and pasturelands. I am arguing – alongside others – against a parochialism that explores different spaces, landscapes, and subsistence systems in their insularity, refusing to recognise the intimate relations that tie them indissolubly. If the history of agrarian spaces cannot be studied in isolation from the history of scrublands, we cannot segregate the latter from the former. This interlacing of histories complicates the very idea of agrarian expansion.[4]

Behind the agrarian expansion was a long history of the takeover of scrublands and grasslands. In the colonial imagination, scrublands were seen as wild open spaces waiting to be appropriated, cultivable but not yet cultivated, burdened by rights in some places but still belonging to nature, unexplored and unexploited. These open spaces had to be surveyed, measured, and mapped; they had to be taken over and controlled, and rights over them had to be defined and asserted. The people who inhabited these spaces needed to be incorporated within village landscapes and settled – their movements regulated, their numbers enumerated. Control over the wilderness was essential before it could be transformed into an ordered agrarian landscape.

[3] A move away from this has been in evidence for some time. See Prasad, "Forests and Subsistence"; Sivaramakrishnan, *Modern Forests*; Agrawal and Sivaramakrishnan, eds, *Social Nature*. In studies on ancient India the shift in focus is more marked. See Ratnagar, ed., *On Pastoralism*; Heredia and Ratnagar, eds, *Mobile and Marginalized Peoples*. For studies on pastoralism, see Singh, *Natural Premises*; Saberwal, *Pastoral Politics*. For an important exploration of the history of "waste lands" and village commons in Punjab see Chakravarty-Kaul, *Common Lands*.

[4] This theme has been developed in Bhattacharya, ed., "Forests, Fields and Farms". See also "Introduction" in Agrawal and Sivaramakrishnan, eds, *Social Nature*.

Nowhere did this process of taking over unfold as dramatically as on the high pasturelands west of the River Sutlej. Here we witness a new experiment in state engineering, the making of a new form of agrarian conquest, different in many ways from the one we have discussed in the earlier chapters. In the next two chapters, therefore, I shift my focus to the way these pasturelands of west Punjab were first taken over and then radically transformed.

In looking at this history I seek to critique two types of teleologies. There is, first, the teleology of power that traces the unilinear unfolding of control by the state, the inexorable logic of its making. The second is the teleology of dispossession and displacement – of specific livelihood patterns and social order, of particular ways of perceiving and relating to landscapes. What these teleologies have in common is a disregard for the dialogic constitution of these historical processes. Both proceed from the assumption that human beings witness history as a spectacle, watch it unfold, and experience its corrosive force: they do not shape its daily routine, navigate its direction in the flow of time, reorient its course. Undoubtedly, the agrarian conquest I am describing comprises stories of displacement – as we have seen all along and shall continue to see in this chapter – and was at the same time a story of the consolidation of a specific form of colonial regime. But we need to move beyond simple narratives of social control as well as uncomplicated stories of loss and despair.

Scrublands, we know, were not open spaces without people, without history, waiting to be appropriated, mapped, measured, and transformed into agrarian landscapes. No space anywhere in the colonial world could be colonised without an encounter with the history of the place and the people who inhabited it – their practices, their ways of life, their customs and norms. These encounters, as they occurred in their micro ways within everyday life, shaped the experience of the colonising process, refiguring at the same time the nature of state practice as well as the experiences of people. In exploring the colonisation of the vast highlands of western Punjab, we cannot erase the history of these encounters. In looking at the grand projects of state engineering we cannot forget the small stories that critically shape the way histories unfold.

Nomads of the Bār

The bārs located in the interfluves of the Sutlej, Ravi, and Chenab rivers were inhabited by a variety of nomadic groups. By the early nineteenth century most parts of this vast pastoral tract were under the control of contending clans. These were not open and empty spaces over which nomads could move at will. Controlled by different tribal groups, parcellised into clan territories, the terrain bore the marks of nomadic politics.

Over the eighteenth century, in the tract between the Sutlej and the Ravi – the Bari Doab – the Kharrals established their dominance. They became the leaders of a coalition of clans – the Great Ravi – who were always at war with the Little (nikki) Ravi. The former, mostly nomadic pastoralists, looked down upon the latter, raiding their cattle, destroying their settlements, and forcing them into submission.[5] Further north, between the Ravi and the Chenab, was the Jhang bār, dominated by the Siyals. From about the seventeenth century, the Siyals consolidated their power by displacing other smaller clans.[6] To the north-east of Jhang was the Gujranwala bār, where the Viraks and the Bhattis struggled for dominance. Under the Mughals, the Bhatti presence was marked all over Punjab, a substantial proportion of the revenue being collected from them in different regions, and most of the Bhatti villages in Gujranwala were established during Mughal times. Through the late eighteenth century they struggled to retain their autonomy, fighting the Sikh Sardars who were consolidating their power, until Ranjit Singh crushed the Bhatti chieftains decisively in 1799.[7] Yet in the 1880s, when the colonial settlements were in progress

[5] On the history of the Kharrals, see Roe and Purser, *Montgomery S.R.*, 1878, paras 27–52; Elphinston, *Googaira S.R.*, 1860; Rose, *Glossary*, vol. III, p. 495f.; Griffin, *The Panjab Chiefs*, vol. I, pp. 259, 509ff.; Ibbetson, *Punjab Castes*, pp. 174–5. On the general history of conflicts amongst the pastoral groups, see also Major, *Return to Empire*, chs 2 and 6.

[6] See Steedman, *Jhang S.R.*, 1885, paras 28–32; Roe and Purser, *Montgomery S.R.*, 1878, paras 27–52; Rose, *Glossary*, vol. II; Griffin, *The Panjab Chiefs*, vol. I, 1885, pp. 504, 511ff.

[7] See Grewal, *The Sikhs of the Punjab*; Grewal and Banga, eds, *Maharaja Ranjit Singh*.

and the region was being mapped, eighty-six villages of Gujranwala were still under the control of the Bhattis.[8]

Recurring cycles of raids and counter-raids were an intimate part of the histories of these nomadic groups. They expressed and shaped the organising principles of their lives. The leader of a nomadic clan was called the rāt, a term that literally meant "powerful man" and "raider". The authority of the rāt depended on his ability to protect his clients and their cattle, and augment the cattle wealth of the community under his protection. The possibility of cattle raids was one of the grounds on which the relationship between the rāt and his followers – the jan – was established. Anyone wanting protection from cattle raids became a client of a rāt, agreeing to pay a tribute – pawanji – in return for protection.[9] To retain his legitimacy, the rāt had to continuously demonstrate his ability to protect the community and raid the enemy. When a hostile clan attacked a jan and carried away camels or buffaloes, the rāt had to identify the raiders and march with his fighting men to recover the cattle. At times the return of cattle was negotiated through the payment of bhunga – a tribute; but when that failed the cattle belonging to the hostile tribe were carried away through counter-raids. Ruling clans regularly lost large numbers of their fighting men in these clashes, but such sacrifice was a signifier of their status, a premise of their symbolic authority, a cost that reaffirmed their power over their clients.

The hierarchy of power between nomadic groups was also established through these raids and counter-raids. To carry away the cattle of a hostile group was to challenge its power and appropriate its wealth. Only through a successful counter-raid could the enemy re-establish its authority and recover lost wealth. Prolonged cycles of raiding and counter-raiding ended only when a negotiated peace was mutually settled, a hierarchy of power established, and a collective tribute paid by the weaker tribe to the stronger one. Throughout the early nineteenth century the small (nikki) Ravi tribes, primarily

[8] Nisbet, *Gujranwala S.R., 1866–7*, p. 5.
[9] Ibbetson, *Punjab Castes*, p. 145; Rose, *Glossary*, vol. II, p. 105; Nisbet, *Gujranwala S.R., 1866–7*, pp. 5–6; Roe and Purser, *Montgomery S.R.*, 1878; Maclagan, *Multan S.R.*, 1901.

agriculturists, were repeatedly raided by the pastoral nomads of the upper Ravi, as the latter tried to assert their superiority and right to collect tribute. A similar story was repeated in the Gujranwala bār, with the Bharwana Siyals of the central highland continually raiding the Jhang Siyals.[10] The raid as a demonstration of power became both ritual and performance, an act that vitalised the community and sapped the strength of the enemy.

As the logic of this politics of raid was played out, smaller lineages attached themselves to the bigger ones, seeking protection against enemy raids, paying their tribute money to the dominant clan. In the early nineteenth century the Waghas and Wasirs grazed their cattle on the central bār under the protection of the Kharrals.[11] Later, in a bid to resist the fiscal demands of the Kharrals, they moved further east, sought the protection of the Viraks, and attempted to expand their power by raiding the Bhattis in the north-east. But when Massan, the Wagha leader, was killed by the Bhattis around 1825, his son Malla returned with his nomad followers to the Kharrals for protection. With the help of Ahmad Shah, the Kharral leader, the Waghas then came to control the central bār before it was taken over by the British.

Raiding was thus a way of territorialising space. By raiding, nomadic groups defined the limits of their mobility, the margins of grazing lands, and the boundaries of their territorial control – boundaries that were porous, fuzzy, and continuously renegotiated through raids, not hard lines that could be plotted on the map.[12] In this sense raids

[10] See Roe and Purser, *Montgomery S.R.*, 1878, pp. 27–52.

[11] This account of their movement was narrated in the local histories of the tribes. See the accounts in Rose, *Glossary*, vol. II, pp. 495ff.

[12] On spatialisation in such zones, see Miggelbrink and Habeck, eds, *Nomadic and Indigenous Spaces*. Deleuze and Guattari see the spatial imagination of sedentary and nomadic societies as radically opposed. The former parcel out "a closed space to people", while the latter "distribute people (or animals) in an open space, one that is indefinite . . ." See Deleuze and Guattari, *A Thousand Plateaus*. Analytically it is possible to make an argument about pure difference in the trajectories of nomadic and sedentary societies, between nomadic space and state space, and posit the idea of opposed essences. In fact nomadic/anti-state and sedentary/state tendencies exist, as Deleuze and Guattari admit, in entangled and mixed forms, held together in tension, battling the other within itself, persistently refiguring the other.

were political: they demarcated the difference between the internal and the external, separating spaces within which raiding was not to be encouraged from those where it was permissible. Raids had to be directed outwards, against the enemy, not inwards, within the community. Between two nomadic territories lay an ambiguous zone subject to negotiation through the raid.[13]

Within this political culture, raiding was also a ritual through which the identity of individuals and their relationship to the community was established.[14] Oral traditions of the bār celebrated the practice of raiding, projecting it as both natural and necessary. From their infancy, children were socialised into the culture of raiding. Boys were urged to join in the practice of the raid without fear of consequences. "Fish swim as soon as they have hatched" (*Macchi sande pungre jamde tarand*) was a common saying in the bār. "My child, if you do not steal you will die of hunger" (*Bachcha chori na karso, ta bhuk na marso*), it was said in Jhang.[15] In most of these nomadic pastoral communities, boys could attain manhood and wear a pag only after they had participated in a cattle raid and demonstrated their ability to lift cattle, contributing to an activity that vitalised the group and regenerated its resources.[16] Outsiders seeking protection

---

But these negotiations happen within frames that have distinct orientations: one defined by the logic of nomadism, the other by the politics of settlement.

[13] Studies show that the in-between zones most vulnerable to raids are usually undergrazed, aggravating the problem of overgrazing in the core pastoral zones. See Hendrickson, Armon, and Mearns, "The Changing Nature of Conflict and Famine Vulnerability".

[14] Innumerable folktales of Punjab revolve around stories of blood vengeance and inter-tribal feuds. Tales of tragic romances across clan boundaries naturalised the idea of the eternal feud. In many of these tales, opposing groups are tied through the antinomies of desire and hate. Love across boundaries is first imagined and experienced before its possibility is denied. See the tale of Mirza Sahiban: Temple, *Legends of Punjab,* vol. I. Also Hir Ranjha: Temple, *Legends*, vol. II.

[15] *Gazetteer of the Chenab Colony*, pp. 21ff., Rose, *Glossary*; Ibbetson, *Punjab Castes.*

[16] In other parts of the world too, oral traditions of nomadic communities often celebrate the culture of raiding. See, for instance, Stetkevych, "Ritual

could become insiders, part of the jan, only after they had joined in a collective raid, forging the ties that bound them to the community. Dependent clans acquired their status as riaya and earned their claim to protection only by agreeing to participate in collective raids.

Within the territories under their control, nomadic graziers moved in search of pastures always in a collective body under their leader, ready to counter cattle raids.[17] Steedman, who investigated the life of these nomads in the 1860s, tells us:

> The Kharral or Sial Rat would move slowly over the portion of the Bar which he claimed to rule, accompanied by the whole of his clan followers and all his *riaya*. These hordes called *jan*, seldom stayed more than one or two months at one spot in even the richest pasture grounds, although they had to sink a fresh well at every grazing station in order to obtain drinking water for man and beast.[18]

The specific relationships that various nomadic groups had to their grazing lands and the temporality of their movement varied. Some, like the Sials of Jhang and the Lakhera Kharrals, with their base in the fertile riverine tract, went up to the bār in the monsoon when it was covered with vegetation, remaining there through the autumn when the kareel (*Capparis decidua*) had its second flowering. Before the end of winter they returned to the riverine and spent the

---

and Sacrificial Elements". In the tales analysed, the mother urges the son to become a man and not be afraid of raiding the enemy, seeking vengeance. Unavenged blood leads to social disintegration. Blood vengeance nourishes the community and devitalises the enemy. We need to be wary, however, of the way such imageries are foregrounded in colonial discourses. Within such representations, the culture of retribution and vengeance comes to stand for the primitivism and barbarism of the nomads. For a discussion of the moral economy of stock theft within a raiding culture, see Anderson, "Stock Theft and Moral Economy in Colonial Kenya".

[17] On the mobility of the nomads on the bār, see No. 468, Captain G.W. Hamilton, Dep. Comm., Jhung, to M.P. Edgeworth, Comm. & Sup., Mooltan Div., 11 October 1851. This report, *On the Tirnee Tax of Jhung,* was reproduced as *SPCAAP*, vol. 1, no. 2, art. 9.

[18] *Gazetteer of the Chenab Colony,* p. 18.

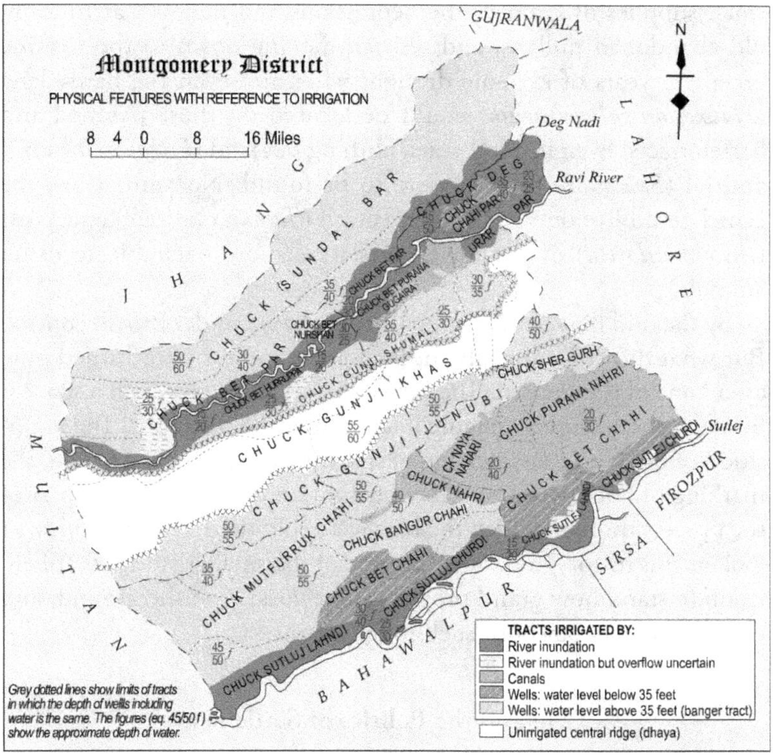

Fig. 16: The Bār Landscape: Montgomery District, 1870s.
Source: Based on "Maps to Accompany the Settlement Report of the Montgomery District, 1878".

summer cultivating grains and pulses, and pasturing their cattle on land inundated by the floods of the previous year. Those living on the lower bār usually had their settlements on the fringes of the bār, near the river, where wells could be dug. They kept their herds on the bār in winter and moved to the river banks in summer, returning to the bār when with the first rains the withered grasses became green once again. Social relationships between the riverine and upland villages were forged to allow this seasonal movement of cattle and people. On the central highlands, however, only camel graziers could survive. They subsisted on camel milk and jungle fruits, produced small supplies of grain in the depressions and hollows, at times in old abandoned nullahs, and resisted moving down to the riverine except in years of extreme drought when not even the hardy lana (*Haloxylon salicornicum*) could be located on these parched and barren tracts. Even in good years, nothing but jand (*Prosopis cineraria*) and jal (*Salvadora presica*) were to be found. No animal but the camel could live on such fodder. Farash (*Tamarix aphylla*) and kikar (*Acacia nilotica*) of the lower bārs were more palatable to other animals.

By the mid nineteenth century the bārs were under British control. But what did control really mean? Spaces are not transformed only after control is exercised. The very practices through which a space is brought under control refigure it and those who inhabit it. The imposition of tax, the reclassification of space, the mapping of a region, the marking of boundaries, and the redefinition of rights were all part of the process through which the bārs were colonised. In what follows I look at this history, focusing on some of the smaller stories that help us understand how grand projects are reworked on the ground, and the constitutive power of such refigurations.

Tirni and the Politics of Settlement

The imposition of tax is one way in which power announces itself. To assert sovereignty is to monopolise the right to tax, to claim the power to authorise taxes. To pay a tax is to accept sovereignty and the authority of those who levy the tax. The right to a tax is always a site where power is negotiated, claims asserted and resisted. Such encounters are most intense in tracts where nomads live.

On the bārs the imposition of a grazing tax – tirni – became critical to the politics of control over the region. Tirni was imposed by the British not simply to earn revenue; as suggested earlier, it had a symbolic significance. By imposing tirni the colonial government asserted its right over open lands, grazing fields, and what appeared to them as wilderness. To pay tirni was to acknowledge that non-agricultural land was neither open space belonging to nature nor common land for collective use: it belonged to the government. I wish to push the argument further and suggest that tirni had other layers of significance. It became a means of asserting power over clan chiefs and transforming nomads into settled pastoralists.

When the British sought to extend their power in the early 1850s over the Jhang bār, they imposed the tirni as a lump-sum tax.[19] The amount was collected from the sadar-tirni-guzar, who contracted to pay the levy, collecting it from members of the jan. All cattle that grazed on the bār were theoretically liable for tirni, but there was as yet no enumeration, nor any demarcated grazing limits. This system came to an end with the Regular Settlement of the late 1850s, when village boundaries were marked and the grazing land within the village given over to village khewatdars – the owners of khewats (numbered fields). Now a distinction had to be made between cattle that grazed within the village shamilat and those that wandered beyond the village and pastured on the bār (tirni-guzar), in the rahnas (clan settlements), jhoks (depressions), and jungles. Sadar-tirni-guzars were given control over villages that desired access to the bār, and the tirni they were contracted to pay was now estimated on the basis of an enumeration. Many villages wanted no access to the bār (naubaramad): these were not under the control of the sadar-tirni-guzar and their cattle were not enumerated. But when naubaramad cattle strayed into pastures outside the village, they were seized by special staff and punitive rates charged, the collection being made directly by the state. With the creation of villages, the demarcation of village boundaries (thakbast), and the new link established between grazing rights and field (khewat) ownership, the power of the sadar-tirni-guzar came to be limited and regulated. Yet the fiscal system still recognised the subordination of the settled village to the pastoral tract.

Within a decade and a half the system was again modified. The process of rationalisation that followed extended the control of

[19] On the development of the system, see Note on Tirni by J.R. Maconachie, Officiating Settlement Sec. to Financial Commissioner, Punjab, *SRFCP, NS*, no. 56; "Memo on Tirni of the Mooltan District", no. 133, 28 August 1878, *SRFCP, NS*, no. 56; Minute by Hamilton, *On the Tirnee Tax of Jhung, SPCAAP*, vol. 1, no. 2, art. 9; "Tirni Tax in Montgomery District", Punjab Agr. Rev. & Com., September 1873, A. 7.

sadar-tirni-guzars but also transformed their identity. It allowed the state to withdraw from direct tirni management while expanding its disciplinary power over the clans. In 1869 the chak system was introduced, and by 1874 the bār scrublands that had been earlier taken over by government were divided into chaks, while all villages, rahnas, and jhoks were assigned to different chaks.[20] Nomadic pastoralists – earlier designated as members of rahnas, jhoks, and villages – were now doubly inscribed with the marks of settlement since they too belonged to the newly demarcated chaks. For tirni-guzar villages, tirni was estimated generally on the basis of an enumeration of animal stock; the tax on cattle that remained unenumerated (naubaramad) was based on a rough estimate. Tirni was thus charged on both enumerated and unenumerated cattle, and the annual contracts for its collection were given over to the old sadar-tirni-guzars, now reanointed as chakdars. As bearers of new territorial boundary markers, chakdars became implicated in the colonial project of the sedentarisation of nomads and the reterritorialisation of pastoral spaces – one of the great projects of the agrarian conquest. Pastoralists were supposed to remain within the chak where they were enumerated. To move beyond meant paying additional tax in the chaks they passed through. They were expected to belong to a locality, restrict their movements, and give up their lives of "wandering about". In talking of the chak system, the financial commissioner of Punjab categorically expressed this rhetoric of settlement. "The advantages of leasing the grazing dues on the chak system are that it affords the means of control over the wandering tribes . . . it tends to localise and settle the people who are thus more likely to take to agriculture; and that the Government rights are better asserted and maintained in the waste lands."[21]

By 1884 the newly established villages of the Sandal bār were emancipated from the control of chakdars.[22] The Multan system

[20] Note on Tirni by J.R. Maconachie, Officiating Settlement Sec. to Financial Comm., Punjab, *SRFCP, NS,* no. 56.

[21] Quoted in ibid., p. 64.

[22] The discussion of the tirni system in the late 1870s and early 1880s is reproduced in *SRFCR, NS,* no. 56. See in particular the detailed memos of Settlement of Officer, Multan (no. 133, 28 August 1878); note by D.G.

Fig. 17: Tirni Mahals in Montgomery.

Source: Based on Maps to Accompany the Settlement Report of the Montgomery District, 1878.

This map shows the "jungle mahals" or blocks into which the nomadic pastures, taken over as "government waste land", were divided and numbered for the collection of tirni (grazing tax). On the cultivated tracts bordering the rivers or irrigated by canals, no tirni was imposed, except on scattered small patches of land.

that was now introduced gave separate contracts for each village and rahna to village lambardars for a period of five years. The process of enumeration was pushed further, village cattle being counted with

Barkley Comm. and Sup. Multan Division (no. 929, 3 October 1881); note by C.A. Roe, Deputy Comm., Multan (no. 325, 8 May 1882).

greater care. Separate tracts were segregated for unenumerated cattle that came in from outside, contracts for these naubaramad tracts being usually given to professional contractors. Spaces were marked with new identities, the boundaries of internal and external being turned around as the colonial state sought to grasp a seemingly fluid pastoral population and subject it to its enumerative and fiscal practices.

Writing in the 1890s, E. Abbot, Settlement Officer, Jhang, captured the trajectory of the tract's fiscal history with a rare deconstructive insight:

> The history of tirni administration shows the gradual narrowing of the unit of assessment from the clan to the chak and from the chak to the individual's village and the simultaneous weakening of the Sadar tirni guzar's power. First, collection from his adherents without enumeration, then collection from adherents after enumeration, followed by the collection in the chak only; and finally the substitution of the lambardars in 1884. Each successive step marks a limitation. First, unlimited grazing and no record; secondly unlimited grazing but a record of tirni paying cattle accompanied by heavy fines for trespass; thirdly, grazing limited to the chak but collection from non-tirni guzar cattle by chakdars themselves; fourthly, grazing limited to the chak and collection of naubaramad tirni by contractors.[23]

Abbot framed his description within an evolutionary teleology that discovers everywhere a shift from collectivity to individuality. But histories never unfold along simple teleologies. Behind the seeming smoothness of the unravelling lie complicated histories of conflicts and negotiations, shifts and reworkings.

Pastoral nomads hated the new fiscal regime. The incidence of demands made on them rose rapidly, the parcellisation of chaks restricted mobility, and the entire system of collection was oppressive.[24]

---

[23] Abbot, *Jhung S.R., 1906*; *Gazetteer of the Chenab Colony*, p. 18.

[24] See Purser's report about the anger of the nomads and desertion of villages, no. 112, 19 April 1873, W.E. Purser, Settlement Officer, Montgomery, to the Officiating Comm. of Settlement, Multan and Derajat Divisions, Punjab Agr. Rev. & Agr. (Rev.), June 1873, A 13. When Lyall passed through the district in February 1872, he was surprised by the violence of people's reaction against the Tirni system: No. 42, 26 May 1873, J.B. Lyall,

They detested the authority of contractors from outside and despised the system of enumerating stock. Behind every action of the state they read calculations hostile to nomads, to their way of life and sense of self. Every move of the British was watched; every action seemed to announce a war against the nomadic way of life. The establishment of the chak system appeared to be a way of enclosing nomadic spaces, restricting movement, and multiplying tax loads: pastoralists now had often to pay tirni at several places when their herds moved through the different chaks. The enumeration of stock was read as a step towards the final takeover of their animals. The farming out of tirni contracts was seen as a plan to bring in outsiders, displace local power, and establish an extortionate system. At many places, pastoralists refused to pay tirni, resisted enumeration, blocked the entry of external contractors, deserted their settlements, and moved to new tracts.[25]

By the early 1870s many officials admitted that the tirni administration was not working well. Alarmed by the desertion of habitation sites in Montgomery, W.E. Purser, the settlement officer, conducted an enquiry in 1873. Reports from all the tracts were unanimous: pastoralists were leaving their settlements to escape the tirni system. T.W. Smyth, deputy commissioner in Montgomery, reported in April 1873: "They are prepared to fight, commit a riot, or do anything rather than allow enumeration to take place."[26] Having traversed the terrain, visiting settlements and talking to the pastoralists, he questioned the logic of the system.[27] He admitted tirni had to be collected and that taxing the pastoralists was legitimate. But he felt that rates had to

---

Off. Settlement Comm., Multan and Derajat Div., to the Sec. to Financial Comm., Punjab, Punjab Rev. & Agr. (Rev.), June 1873, A 13.

[25] On enumeration, see Memorandum by Captain Wace on the "Grazing Tax levied on Sheep and Goats in Hazara", Punjab Rev. & Agr. (Rev.), A 15, May 1873. For the way the policy of enumeration unfolds in later decades, see no. U 270, Major F.J.H. Birch, Enumeration Officer, IV Circle, to Comm. and Sup., Jullunder Division, Punjab Military, December 1901, A 5.

[26] No. 139, 21 April 1873, T.W. Smyth, Dep. Comm. Montgomery, to the Comm. and Sup., Multan Div., Punjab Agr. Rev. & Com., July 1874, A 6.

[27] No. 112, 19 April 1873, W.E. Purser, Settlement Officer, Montgomery,

be fixed with care. An increase of 288 per cent in the thirteen years between 1857 and 1870 was impossible to justify. It seemed to be driven by a perverse logic: "there is a fallacy connected with the Tirni Tax which makes it appear an act of real kindness to the people to raise the tax to the utmost limit. Make cattle breeding unprofitable by a good heavy Tirni Tax, and the people will take to agriculture . . . The Tirni Tax, as a tax, is quite legitimate; as a sort of protection duty in favour of agriculture, it is an absurdity. This district is neither suited for agriculture nor entirely for cattle-breeding."[28]

The inhabitants of Montgomery cultivated land near the river and pastured their cattle on the high land of the bār (see Fig. 16). In such a tract, Purser asserted, the movement of pastoralists ought not to be restricted. They *had* to move in a seasonal cycle to different grazing grounds and combine cultivation with nomadism. The two forms of livelihood were intimately connected: "The more they make by their cattle, the more they are able to extend agriculture; the greater their profits from agriculture, the more cattle they keep."[29] One could not recklessly push ahead with the project of settlement on such a terrain.

After reviewing the practice of giving out tirni leases to contractors, most officials agreed the system was oppressive. The contractors managed to collect the tax but were extortionate. They brought legal suits against defaulters, confiscated animals that "trespassed", and collected dues with ruthless efficiency. On enquiring into the tirni system in Montgomery, it was reported: "We are told that the contractors became so obnoxious that their lives were hardly safe when they ventured among the grazing community to enumerate the cattle."[30] The contractors, officials felt, were bringing a viable system into disrepute. In Montgomery the contractors were dismissed

---

to the Officiating Comm. of Settlement, Multan and Derajat Divisions, Punjab Agr. Rev. & Agr. (Rev.), June 1873, A 13.

[28] Ibid.

[29] Ibid.

[30] See Precis of Correspondence in Montgomery District on Tirni Tax, 16 March 1881, J.M. Douie, *SRFCP, NS,* no. 56. See also "Tirni Tax in Montgomery District", Punjab Agr. Rev. & Com., September 1873, A 7.

in 1879. Colonial officials carried out their own enumeration and collected the fees directly from each village. A few years later the newly appointed tirni zaildars came under attack for failing to assist the state in enforcing the new system. In 1882 these men were also dismissed. When the officials returned to direct management, asking the lambardars to take on the responsibility of collecting tirni, village after village refused to engage with the government.[31] When the Afghan war (1878–80) broke out, thousands of camels were requisitioned. The pastoralists were up in revolt.

Tirni was not a new system. The British had inherited it from the Sikhs. What is inherited as tradition takes on – inevitably and everywhere – new forms. Hamilton, who was asked in 1851 to enquire into the pre-British system of tirni collection, says: "In grazing, the cattle were not restricted to any particular localities within the bār, nor was it divided into separate grazing grounds . . . the whole of the bār was considered common to all cattle feeders of the bordering districts; and when a client had once paid his quota of the tax, he was exempt from further demand, although he might pasture his flocks in the limits of another district."[32]

Here we see two levels of spatialisation. The revenue collection was parcelled out to different tirni-guzars, each with a defined space from which he had to collect tax and give over to the chief controlling the locality. But the pastoralists who paid tax within one of these demarcated spaces had the freedom to move over the entire bār in search of good pasture. The boundaries of the fiscal spatial unit did not define the limits of nomadic movement. The project was not at this point to impose tirni to settle pastoralists, fix them to a location, bound their landscape of mobility. It was to collect revenue and assert the power to do so. Things changed under colonialism. Tirni became an instrument of settling the bār nomads, confining them within demarcated spaces, and colonising the commons. Against this incorporative drive of a

[31] No. 325, 8 May 1882, C.A. Roe, Dep. Comm. Multan, to H.E. Perkins, Comm. and Sup., Multan Division, *SRFCP, NS*, no. 56.

[32] No. 468, Captain G.W. Hamilton, Dep. Comm., Jhung, to M.P. Edgeworth, Comm. & Sup., Mooltan Div., Jhung, 11 October 1851, *SRFCP, NS*, no. 56.

sendentarist state, nomads asserted their right to an alternative notion of space, reorienting the way tirni could be imposed.[33]

In the meantime, the rakhs were being carefully mapped and bounded, transforming the landscape, reshaping lives.

The project of bounding, however, has a troubled history. The will of the state does not unfold over uninscribed spaces, maps are not drawn over blank sheets. On the ground, as it were, the desire to discipline spaces comes up against the will of those who are to be disciplined. The cartographic imagination may seek to produce a geo-body that makes the landscape legible and governable. The state may want to transform "smooth spaces" into "striated spaces", as Deleuze and Guattari suggest, i.e. refigure fluid and open spaces not broken up by hard lines into striped and fragmented spaces, sur-veyed, measured, mapped, and put under state surveillance. But what happens when the inhabitants of a landscape resist the logic of this cartographic domination? I have earlier discussed bounding and mapping as projects of colonial governance, focusing on the vision of the colonial state. Here I look at the everyday life of the project – the negotiations and refigurations through which this history unfolds in one micro-region between the Jhelum and Indus rivers.

The Unpublished Maps

When Wace was urged to demarcate the rakhs of Kahuta and Murree, he discovered that the region had never been properly surveyed.[34] Intermingling with the rakhs were cultivated lands, and the lines of separation between the two were blurred and vague, almost

[33] For a discussion of the relationship between nomadic and sedentary societies, see Barfield, *The Nomadic Alternative*; Khazanov, *Nomads and the Outside World*.

[34] No. 21, 29 April 1875, E.G. Wace, Settlement Officer, Jhelum, to the Comm. and Sup., Rawalpindi Division. *SRFCP, NS*, no. 70. Unless otherwise specified, the revenue files on the waste lands referred to in the next two sections may be found in *SRFCP, NS*, no. 70, pp. 1391–1801. A. Cleghorn, the Conservator of Forests in Madras, was summoned to write a detailed report of the trees and scrubs of the region. See Cleghorn, *Report Upon the Forests of the Punjab*.

non-existent. In 1852, a Captain Robinson had carried out only a topographical survey on a one-inch scale showing the physical features of the region in very general terms. At the time of the settlement in the early 1860s only the cultivated area had been measured, and even that very impressionistically, while nothing was done to define the forest area. Since the settlement the margins of cultivation had extended. What was now necessary was a mauzawar survey on a four-inch scale that would indicate the boundaries of villages and the limits of the cultivated area.[35] Only such a map would allow the project of demarcation to proceed on a firm footing. Wace could of course traverse the area, walk from village to village, and demarcate the tracts to be reserved. But such a demarcation, he emphasised, "would be based on no data, except my personal opinion."[36] The fixity of firm boundaries had to be premised on the foundation of reliable and scientific knowledge.[37]

But who was to produce these maps and what was to ensure their reliability and scientificity? While the Government of Punjab (GOP) dithered, the Government of India (GOI) urged that the Revenue Survey Department be entrusted with the job since the Forest Department was not equipped to carry out such a detailed mauzawar survey. After wavering for a year, in 1876 the GOP asked the Revenue Survey Department to survey and map the hilly tracts of Rawalpindi.[38] Baden-Powell, the conservator of forests, was furious. Upset with this slur on the competence of his department and dismayed at the confidence placed on the Revenue Department, he pleaded for a change in the decision of the government.[39] Always suspicious of the mushy paternalism of Punjab's revenue officials, he now feared

[35] Cracroft, *Rawul Pindee S.R., 1864.*

[36] No. 27, 26 July 1875, E.G. Wace, Settlement Officer, Jhelum, to the Comm. and Sup., Rawalpindi Division.

[37] All officials agreed that demarcation of the rakhs was impossible without proper maps that indicated the details of cultivation.

[38] No. 123c, Simla, 21 June 1876, Lepel Griffin, Off. Secretary to Govt. Punjab, to the Sec. to GOI, Dept of Rev. and Agr. and Com.

[39] No. 332, 22 August 1876, Baden Powell, Conservator of Forests, to the Sec. to Financial Comm., Punjab.

that the war between the departments would be played out on a new site.

H.L. Thuiller, Surveyor General of India, agreed to supervise the survey.[40] H.C. Johnston, Superintendent of the Revenue Survey, Dera Ismail Khan, first carried out the preliminary investigation and then undertook the project of detailed surveying and mapping.[41] As the work proceeded over the subsequent four years, forest officials became increasingly impatient and nervous. Unless the survey was completed speedily, they declared, the rakhs would be sliced up into cultivated patches and no compact area would be left for demarcation as reserve. Foresters had visions of disappearing grasslands, invading peasants, and illegal encroachments.[42] Pressurised by panicky forest officials, the GOP in turn urged the surveyors to make haste and complete their task.[43]

Finally, the maps were produced in 1880. Now the forest officials exploded once again. They questioned the authenticity of the maps and debunked the method of their making. In mapping the area, the surveyors had found the old thakbast in the hilly country utterly useless. The maps did not coincide with the pillars on the ground, and in many places there were neither any pillars nor any village boundaries marked on the map.[44] The only possible source of the surveyors' knowledge was the opinion of villagers who were asked to indicate the limits of their village. The forest officials were astounded. How could the word of villagers possibly be seen as authentic? Wily, crafty, and acquisitive, the villagers – according to the officials – always made

[40] No. 243, Simla 7 August 1876, Col. H.L. Thuiller, Surveyor General of India, to the Sec. to the GOI, Dept. of Agr. Rev. & Comm.

[41] No. 74, Muree, 25 July 1876, H.C. Johnston, Special Sup., Rev. Survey, Rawalpindi, to Sup. of Rev. Survey.

[42] No. 88 CL, Simla, 14 June 1880, Dr W. Schlich, Conservator of Forests, Punjab, to the Sec. to Finance Comm., Punjab.

[43] No. 83 C, Lahore, 27 May 1879, Lepel Griffin, Sec. to Govt. Punjab, to the Surveyor General of India.

[44] This was stated to be the reason for the slow progress of the mapping process. See no. 118, 28 June 1879, Col. H.C. Johnstone, Deputy Sup. of Rev. Survey, Dera Ismail Khan, to the Comm. & Sup., Rawalpindi Div.

fantastic claims which rarely had any basis in reality. If *their* word was to be taken, Baden-Powell had said on one occasion, the entire hillside would have to be considered theirs.

Enraged foresters pleaded with the government not to accept the maps. Underlying their rage was an awareness of the politics of cartographic truth. Maps drawn by the Survey of India carried the seal of authenticity. Once etched into the map, evidence became cartographic fact; it acquired an objectivity and fixity. By transforming villagers' claims into official truths the surveyors had, unknown to themselves, acted in ways prejudicial to the interest of the government. If the government were to accept these maps, the foresters reasoned, they would lose control over property, resources, and revenue which was rightfully theirs; and this loss would also adversely affect the larger interest of forest conservation.

A harried GOP now proceeded to admonish the Survey of India. If the surveyors wanted to mark village boundaries on their maps, why had they not followed the lines of the old 1852 survey? "The boundaries now pointed out by the villagers are absolutely useless," wrote W.M. Young, Secretary to Government, Punjab, "and cannot be followed by the Forest Settlement Officer who must take the lines of the old thakbast maps as far as possible."[45] In 1876, when the Survey of India was first asked to map the region, the GOP had agreed that the old thakbast maps were unreliable and that village boundaries had to be mapped to allow a firm basis for demarcation.[46] Now they had turned around to reaffirm the dependability of the old thakbast and question the very need for mapping village boundaries and the limits of cultivation.

A puzzled and irritated Surveyor General of India was called upon to explain the lapses in the surveying procedures. Lieutenant Colonel J. Sconce, Deputy Surveyor General of the Survey of India, clarified

[45] No. 410 F, Lahore, 9 October 1880, W.M. Young, Secretary to Government Punjab. to the Sec. to Financial Comm., Punjab.

[46] No. 491, Simla, 8 June 1876, A.O. Hume, Sec. to GOI, Department of Agr. Rev. & Comm., to the Off. Sec. to Govt. Punjab; No. 561, 3 July 1876, Lepel Griffin, to the Surveyor General of India.

the method usually adopted in revenue surveys.[47] As a rule the revenue surveys on the four-inch scale followed closely on previously executed settlement and demarcation surveys during which boundary marks were erected and thakbast maps prepared. The revenue surveys were first conducted in terms of the marks that were found on the ground, and subsequently a comparison was made in the office between the revenue survey and the demarcation survey. But the authority of the thakbast maps was never unquestioningly accepted, their lines never mechanically transferred to the revenue maps, for the thakbast maps were usually drawn without rigid verification.[48] The survey of Kahuta and Murree had conformed to these general conventions. But the problem was that in many places the boundary lines on the ground simply did not exist, and in the hilly portions of Kahuta the lines on the map were mostly missing.[49] In such a situation enquiry had to proceed on the basis of information gleaned from village informants. But this information was invariably verified by surveyors before it

[47] No. 188, Calcutta, 29 October 1880, Lt. Col. J. Sconce, Deputy Surveyor General, Survey of India, to the Surveyor General of India.

[48] Sconce wrote: "It has never been the practice in revenue surveys on the 4-inch scale to introduce boundaries on the maps by transfer from the demarcation maps, and as a general rule it would be most unsafe to do so, as the [thakbast] maps are seldom rigidly tested, and in a hilly country the system of survey adopted for the preparation of the demarcation maps is unsuited to ensure accurate results." No. 188, Calcutta, 29 October 1880, Lt. Col. J. Sconce, Deputy Surveyor General, Survey of India, to the Surveyor General of India.

[49] On 4 February 1880, Col. Macdonald, the deputy superintendent in charge of the survey, wrote: "I have been making a comparison of the village boundaries with the thakbast maps in Murree and Kahuta. In what may be termed the plains portion of Kahuta the thakbast maps agree fairly well. The thakbast maps of Muree and the hilly portion of Kahuta are very unsatisfactory. Several are wanting all together. Those we have are all in tatters and are very rough indeed. All that is possible to ascertain from them is an idea of the general shape of the village and the names of adjoining villages. As an effective check on our boundary survey they are, as a rule, quite useless. Boundaries have been transferred from one thakbast to another in the most careless way, the same boundary being shown in one map as stream and in the adjoining one as a ridge of hills." Ibid.

was recorded. Macdonald, the deputy superintendent in charge of the survey, belaboured this point:

> Our boundaries have been surveyed originally by the sub-surveyors, who surveyed the details as pointed out to them by the headmen of the villages. They have been further tested by the surveyors, generally an European Assistant, who sketched the hills. Finally when a sheet surveyed by a Native Agency is checked, the boundary work is tested in parts by the testing officer. The only further test of the accuracy of the boundaries that I can suggest is for a Civil Officer to be deputed to go over each village and satisfy himself by local inquiry whether the correct boundaries have been pointed out to our surveyors.[50]

We can hear the familiar rhetoric of authentication: local information, particularly from native sources, was always checked and cross-checked, carefully and adequately tested, preferably by a European official, before being attested as valid knowledge. The surveyors had no doubt that the maps they had produced through this "scientific" process were reliable.

While the Survey of India was busy authenticating its survey maps of the Kahuta and Murree forests, the GOP, in December 1880, stopped publication of the new maps.[51]

What does this little row over maps reveal? It reveals, first, and most obviously, how fragile were the objectivist claims of cartographic knowledge and how deeply implicated it was in the politics of power. It reveals, second, and more importantly, how this link was itself complicated, for mapping could become a site where a diverse set of conflicts were played out: between different ideals of power, between alternative visions of rule, between diverse notions of appropriating and ordering the landscape. It reveals, third, how instruments of colonisation could seemingly become impediments to that very process of colonisation. Mapping, we know, is an act of possessing; it allows a grasp over unknown landscapes, it brings order to a world of seeming chaos. But what if the act of mapping begins to disturb the eye

[50] Ibid.
[51] No. 518, Lahore, 17 December 1880, W.M. Young, Sec. to Govt. Punjab, to the Surveyor General of India.

of power, provoke the fear of dispossession, and impose an order that resists appropriation? What if the picture of the landscape produced by the map conflicts with the image already firm in the mind of the coloniser? One could never foretell the contours of the story that might unfold in such a situation. For that would depend on the way various conflicts played out, and the ways in which departmental politics (i.e. between the Revenue, Forest, and Survey departments) mediated the colonising project.

In Rawalpindi the new map was suppressed. In 1880 the GOP declared that demarcation of the rakhs was to proceed, as the forest officials now wanted, on the basis of the old thakbast.

The Fraudulent Line

Even before publication of the revenue survey maps was officially stopped, forest officials had begun to demarcate the rakhs. They had waited anxiously for over four years, fearing the implications of a delay in the survey of the region. The process of demarcation, they strongly felt, had to begin whether the maps were ready or not. If the boundaries were not fixed the government's control over the terrain would remain tenuous, the claims of villagers would continue fluid and unconfined. Bounding was an act of internment, of containment. To bound the village was to announce the limits within which the rights of villagers lay. Delays in bounding, the foresters feared, would threaten government control over the grasslands. They would allow villagers to nibble away at rakhs over which the government had asserted rights and surreptitiously extend the frontiers of their villages.

But bounding too was a troubled project. To be meaningful the boundary line had to be fixed, clear, and firm. But how were lines to be fixed? And who was to ensure their sanctity? Having dismissed the authenticity of the map produced by the Survey of India, could the forest officials now rely on the black lines on the old maps that they had earlier dismissed as dubious? In the politics of bounding that proceeded after 1880 the old maps were re-sanctified, becoming in fact the basis on which the forest department distinguished the authentic boundary from the fraudulent.

The fear of fraud had worried forest officials for a long time. Hukum Chand, an extra-assistant commissioner, had originally demarcated the boundaries of the rakhs in Rawalpindi in the 1860s. By the early 1870s doubts were raised about Hukum Chand's boundaries. In 1876 Tara Chand, a naib tahsildar, was appointed to check and correct the demarcations. But the Forest Department continued to be suspicious. It had little faith in the local native officials of the Revenue Department. So when the forest settlement operations began, the boundaries were re-examined by one Anup Rai; and subsequently in 1879 Egerton, an assistant conservator of forests, traversed the terrain yet again. He tallied the demarcations against the lines on the old settlement map and submitted a report that questioned all earlier boundary demarcations. In Khairi Murat, for instance, of the fifteen lines that had been laid, Tara Chand's demarcations were said to be right only in five cases, and of the twelve demarcations where Anup Rai differed from Tara Chand, eight were correct and four wrong.[52] Egerton pointed to the places where the pillars erected did not follow the line of the map, blamed the patwaris and tahsildars of wilful fraud, and accused Tara Chand of being corrupt. Sly villagers and dishonest revenue officials, he suggested, had colluded to extend the boundaries of the villages. Convinced of the truth of the charges, the Forest Department proceeded to relocate the boundaries, pushing them back to the old line, excluding the area over which the villagers had expanded cultivation in the years since the last settlement.[53]

Revenue officials were astounded by this move. In a strongly worded memorandum, E.B. Steedman, Settlement Officer, Rawalpindi, wrote to the Forest Department, dismissing the charges of fraud and protesting against the relocation of the boundaries of the rakhs. He argued that the pillars were put up in 1865 to mark the rakh boundaries. Since then the zamindars had naturally considered that the land up to the pillars belonged to them. Sixteen years after the original demarcation, the Forest Department was now claiming that the pillars originally erected did not accurately follow the line on the thakbast map. It had proceeded to rectify the boundaries,

[52] *SRFCP, NS*, no. 70.
[53] Ibid.

relocate the pillars according to old records, oust the villagers from the land they possessed, and asked them to prove their rights through legal suits. How could this act of dispossession be justified? "I think," said Steedman, "that the proceeding on the part of the Government is decidedly high-handed, unless fraud can be proved against the zamindars, and I do not see how it can be proved."[54] The logic underlying Steedman's argument was straightforward: relocation of the pillars was arbitrary, it would disturb the expectations of zamindars, their sense of security; and security of expectations was the basis of the rational, legal order that the British wished to build.

Steedman was convinced that this act of dispossession was not only high-handed and arbitrary, it was illegal. Boundary pillars erected by tahsildars bore the seal of government authority, and even when wrongly laid they had legal sanctity. Once demarcated, the boundary line could not be relocated without due process. "The Government," he declared, "has no right whatever to summarily, by erecting new pillars, take possession of land in the occupation of another and refer the other to a suit. The Government must sue itself."[55]

The Deputy Commissioner, Rawalpindi, R.T.M. Lang, was equally worried about the legality of new demarcations. Possession, he said, was the basis of occupancy right. Having canonised this principle, how could the government now throw it overboard? The question, he asserted, was not whether the Forest Department was legally the rightful owner of the disputed land according to some old record. The question rather was whether the government had the right, without a legal decree, to oust villagers from land they had possessed for over a decade. In denying villagers the rights that flowed from possession, and in proceeding through executive order rather than a legal route, the government had in fact acted in a way that could not be justified in law.[56] Unless there was definite evidence of fraud, the boundary pillars could not be relocated.

[54] Memorandum, 24 May 1882, E.B. Steedman, Settlement Officer, Rawalpindi, to the Dep. Conservator of Forests, Punjab.

[55] Ibid.

[56] No. 4259 G, 13 October 1882, R.T.M. Lang, Dep. Comm. and Sup., Rawalpindi, to the Comm. & Sup., Rawalpindi Div.

By 1883 villagers began filing suits against the government, questioning the legality of the new demarcations and demanding right of possession.[57] The threat of dispossession had transformed the idea of the boundary into a tangible reality. When the pillars were initially put up in the 1860s, the villagers had only a vague idea of what they meant. No-one really guarded the pillars, no-one maintained them. In a few years, in most places, the pillars had disintegrated into rubble. The lambardars did know of the boundary, but not the full implications of bounding. Only slowly did they learn about the politics of space, the meaning of boundaries. Only gradually did they discover that the vast space beyond the limits of the village boundary, the rakh, was a domain of the state where villagers could not stray without permissions and licences, where village cattle could no longer be grazed without payment of tirni. And the imposition of tirni, they realised, was not just a question of paying money; it signified a loss of sovereignty, the end of freedom. When the lambardars learnt of the tirni tax they told Munshi Hukum Chand: "*Sarkar hamare par zar-i-tirni izad kar lewe to ham ada kia karenge, magar maweshi hamare khule huye tamam pahar par bedastur charte rahen.*"[58] Bounding was being foreseen, even as early as the 1860s, as loss of mobility, a constraint on freedom: it produced a nostalgia for unbounded open spaces: a myth of unregulated access to nature. But its implications for everyday life were learnt only through the everyday experience of small confrontations. As cattle were impounded for trespass and fines imposed for unlicensed entry, the rakh boundary became a site of conflict and negotiation, an ambiguous space around which the drama of colonial encounter was enacted. While the state sent in inspectors to rediscover the old demarcation lines, villagers began pushing the boundaries outwards, breaking old pillars, pressurising tahsildars, questioning the accuracy of new markings, and claiming the sanctity of old rights. Through these encounters the fixity of

---

[57] *SRFCP, NS,* no. 70.

[58] No. 1045, 28 February 1887, F.A. Robertson, Settlement Officer, to the Comm. & Sup. Rawalpindi Div. Translation of the statement: If the sarkar imposes tirni we will discharge our obligation, but till now our cattle have pastured on these open hills without the payment of any tax.

the boundary was both challenged and reaffirmed, and the specific meaning of this concept was worked out.

When by the end of 1882 the villagers of the Rawalpindi rakhs began filing suits against the legitimacy of the new demarcations, the GOP panicked.[59] It had long warned the foresters of the political implications of large-scale dispossession.[60] Having seen the gathering wave of local discontent, the financial commissioner emphasised once again, in 1884, that the alteration of the pillars ought to be minimised. Wherever land had been cultivated for some years without any objection, he said, "such lands should be excluded from the chak and claims of government to the ownership of the land should be resigned, unless strong reason to the contrary, based on gross fraud of the occupiers can be alleged."[61] It became clear that the foresters might possibly win their argument on only one ground: the charge of fraud. It was a charge tirelessly reiterated in the memos and letters of forest officials. They minimised the extent of dispossession, dismissed the fear of social unrest, and claimed that all disputes over boundaries had been resolved without problems.[62] They argued with greater vehemence than ever before that the Forest Department inspections were correct and that villagers and patwaris were undoubtedly implicated in collective fraud. Tara Chand, Egerton avowed, had received "most substantial remuneration for his dishonesty."[63]

[59] Most of the suits were instituted against the Forest Department under Sec. 9 of the Specific Relief Act for re-entry on land from which the villagers had been ousted. No. 335, 2 February 1883, Major R.T.M. Lang, Deputy Comm. Rawalpindi, to the Comm. & Sup. Rawalpindi Div.

[60] As early as 1882, C.H. Hall, the Commissioner and Superintendent of Rawalpindi Division, had warned the GOP: "it will not be politic to oust those in possession and make new arbitrary boundaries although there are records to go upon." No. 354, Rawalpindi, 25 October 1882, C.H. Hall, Comm. & Sup. Rawalpindi Div., to the Senior Sec. to Financial Comm., Punjab.

[61] No. 8720, 27 November 1884, the Senior Sec., to Financial Comm. Punjab, to the Comm. and Sup., Rawalpindi Div.

[62] No. 30, 10 June 1883, B. Ribbentrop, Conservator of Forests, Punjab, to the Junior Sec. to Financial Comm. Punjab.

[63] Completion Report on Khairi Murat Reserve Forest, 22 May 1885, by Captain F.W. Egerton, Assistant Forest Settlement Officer, Rawalpindi.

The GOP, however, preferred caution. Worried over possible social disturbance, they felt the need to carefully monitor the reactions of villagers and "arrive at any reasonable compromise that the owners may desire . . ."[64] If the rakh boundary was not easy to map, it was even more difficult to lay.

What was ultimately fixed was decided by executive fiat after a prolonged and inconclusive debate on what could or could not be seen as the correct boundary line. The certainty of a fixed boundary was asserted by denying the ambiguity of what was declared as fixed. The rhetoric of fixity had to mediate even what could not be fixed with certainty. Fixity, in this sense, embodied power – the decision of those in power to declare the authenticity of what is stated as fixed.

By the late 1870s an area of over ten million acres was classified as part of government rakhs in Punjab.[65] But this exclusion was not easy. The colonial fantasy of uninhabited landscape, unburdened by rights, dissolved as foresters and revenue officials struggled to appropriate the rakhs as the property of government.

To establish a new regime of rights within the governemnt rakhs, the limits of the permissible had to be defined; practices declared unacceptable had to be policed. One such practice that officials tried to regulate was the firing of grass.

Regulating Rights

On 16 May 1872 the foresters in Kahuta tahsil of Rawalpindi detected a fire in rakh Jantrawala.[66] By early June flames were blazing through twenty-two villages of rakh Rajliban. An under-staffed and nervous Forest Department watched in panic as the fire spread from village to village. Stopped in one place, it restarted in another. When it died with the first rains, it had covered, according to the estimates of forest

[64] No. 8720, 27 November 1884, the Senior Sec., to Financial Comm. Punjab, the Comm. and Sup., Rawalpindi Div.

[65] See *RLRAP, 1876–7*, para 92, and statement IX. Over 80 per cent of the area under rakhs was in the Rawalpindi Division (Gujrat, Jhelum, Rawalpindi, and Shahpur districts) and in the Multan Division (Jhang, Montgomery, Multan, and Muzaffargarh districts).

[66] No. 123, 27 June 1872, R.H.M. Ellis, Asst. Conservator, Rawalpindi Subdivision, to the Deputy Conservator, Jhelum Forest Department.

officials, an area of 44,700 acres and destroyed about 1,784,500 trees.

Unable to control the fire and frustrated by their own incapacity, forest officials looked for a believable account of their failure. R.H.M. Ellis, Assistant Conservator, Rawalpindi Division, called for reports, prodded his watchmen to be vigilant, and himself went on inspection tours. His enquiries only confirmed his suspicions. Fires, he was convinced, were fanned by villagers and could not be controlled without the strongest repressive measures. "There seems to be not the slightest doubt," he wrote in his report, "that not only the fires were with intent lit, but also that zamindars . . . did under the cover of night, really feed them and start new ones."[67] How else could one explain the anomalous evidence that he had encountered? How did fires cross rivers, burn against the wind, move from ravines up hills, and spread over spots separated by unburnt vegetation? The forests could not be saved, Ellis emphasised, unless the incendiarism was stopped and the culprits punished.

While Ellis was making his enquiries, an angry Baden-Powell was fine-tuning his own script for a hard-line policy. To him the need for repressive action seemed self-evident. If villagers were fanning fires and rekindling them, and if they were unwilling to help control fires, they had to be brought to trial forthwith.[68] If the villagers protected those involved in forest crime, all ought to be made collectively responsible for conflagrations within the bounds of their village, and all needed to be collectively punished under the Rules of 1855. Baden-Powell's picture, in a sense, was self-assuring. It rescued the forest officials from their own feeling of impotence, their utter failure to do anything about the fires, and transferred all blame to external agencies: the criminality of the villagers and the weakness of the civil administration. To stop the forest fires, the magistrates had to act, *they* had to repress crime, declared Baden-Powell, for the fires had spread mostly in the protected forests under civil administration, not in the reserves controlled by the Forest Department.[69]

[67] Ibid.

[68] No. 233, Camp Barmaor, 23 July 1872, Powell, Offg Comm. of Forests, Punjab, to the Offg Sec., GOP.

[69] No. 225, Camp Barmaor, 29 July 1872, Powell, Off. Comm. of Forests, Punjab, to the Offg Sec., GOP.

Unfazed by Baden-Powell's outburst, H.B. Urmston, Deputy Commissioner, Rawalpindi, took his time to produce his report on the forest fires. He sent the local tahsildar to tour the region, meet villagers, and hear their stories. In the report that he finally wrote in October 1872, Urmston underlined three issues.[70] First: the Forest Department had grossly overestimated the magnitude of the fire. The area affected was not 44,700 acres but 16,200 acres, and the trees within this area were not really "hopelessly injured" as the Forest Department had claimed. The majority of trees were young chir or common fir which gave off new shoots as soon as the rains fell in July. Second: the nature of the seasons explained the scale of the fire. There had been no rains for over a year, forage was scarce, and the dry grass highly inflammable. In such a situation "a few sparks, accidental or otherwise, are enough to set a vast flame in motion, which carries all before it for miles around." Third: a regime of convictions and fines was unlikely to achieve any result.[71] Forest officials, he felt, were insensitive to the feelings of the people, unwilling to listen to their ideas. "A little more consideration of them," suggested Urmston, "would have been highly desirable, specially towards a class of men as inhabit these mountains."[72] What was important was to earn the goodwill of people, not their hostility. Angry people were likely to subvert a system of rules.

Called upon to intervene, the lieutenant governor reaffirmed the need for a policy of conciliation rather than repression. Emphasising the importance of restraint, he wrote to Baden-Powell: "you must on reflection be sensible that the objects you aim at in the matter of forest conservancy are not likely to be attained by mere invocation

[70] No. 2043, 1 October 1872, H.B. Urmston, Deputy Comm., Rawalpindi, to the Comm. & Sup. Rawalpindi Div.

[71] Baden-Powell had claimed that when Plowden was Assistant Commissioner of Murree, fires had been brought under control through firm action. Urmston agreed that Plowden followed a repressive policy, but this had had no positive result. The number of fires under Plowden's assistant commissionership was, in fact, higher than that under his predecessor and successor.

[72] No. 2043, 1 October 1872, H.B. Urmston, Deputy Comm., Rawalpindi, to the Comm. & Sup. Rawalpindi Div.

of magisterial aid."[73] He agreed that the people were opposed to forest conservation and combined "to break the departmental rules and suppress incriminating evidence." Yet, as Conservator of Forests, Baden-Powell was obliged to act with caution and sensitivity: "It is incumbent upon you before appealing to the courts, to show that your measures have been well adapted to conciliate the people."[74]

The confrontation between Ellis and Urmston was replayed over and over again in the subsequent two decades. Foresters were haunted by apocalyptic visions of devastating conflagrations: fires spreading with unstoppable speed, destroying valuable timber, killing every sapling, decimating grasslands, baking the earth. They were equally plagued by the figure of the incendiary villager: they saw him everywhere surreptitiously at work, fanning flames, rekindling fires, subverting every rule of the Forest Department, paralysing its operations. And they all imagined that local revenue officials were abetting the pyromania, refusing to discipline recalcitrant villagers, and being reluctant to punish crime. As the forests continued to burn, exasperated forest officials threw up their hands in despair. If rules were not vigorously enforced and culprits not ruthlessly penalised, forest conservation would have to be given up, they said. When in the summer of 1890 vast areas of Punjab forests were again ablaze, a despairing Conservator of Forests, R.H.C. Whittal, wrote to the GOP:

> I earnestly hope that in this instance the government will take really severe measures, for . . . slight punishments are of no use, and things have now come to such a pass that either these fires must be put a stop to or fire protection abandoned as hopeless. We have enough experience before us now in the fires of 1890 and 1887, to say that it is not the expenditure of money in the form of fire lines, firewatchers, and rewards for assistance which will safeguard our foresters from being burnt. We are practically in the hands of villagers; without their co-operation our measures are futile; every endeavour has been made by means of a liberal Forest Settlement to purchase that co-operation and the result has been a failure. As if

[73] No. 420, 18 November 1872, C.M. Rivaz, Offg Under Sec., GOP, to the Offg Conservator of Forest.
[74] Ibid.

not satisfied with what has been given them under that settlement, they seem determined to force us to abandon all forest conservancy, and to restore them their forests as a thankless and unprofitable investment on the part of Government.[75]

At a time when Whittal was projecting a picture of doom and disaster and foreseeing the collapse of all efforts at forest conservation, the deputy commissioner of Rawalpindi was speaking with the voice of calm, emphasising the need to understand the significance of fire in the lives of local people. "In forest fires there is no malice," he suggested, "the villagers only wish to do what their forefathers have done for ages and in my opinion no penalties however severe will stop them. Their lives depend on the produce of their cattle and in order to get grass they will continue to burn forests whether guards be quadrupled or punishment inflicted."[76] This seeming tranquillity, this plea for understanding, only infuriated forest officials even more.

The unending drama around forest fires revealed many layers of conflict. Fire, we might say, was not the only issue; it provided a context for diverse battles. There was, first of all, a battle to define the limits of the permissible and the legitimate, to specify notions of the normative. For Baden-Powell there was no ambiguity about the rule and the code, no uncertainty about what the villagers could legitimately do, no debate about what constituted crime. The code had already been publicly proclaimed and the rule had been legally attested. All that was required was to implement the norms, enforce the rules, and penalise violations so that the legitimacy and authority of the new normative order could be established beyond question. But the process of normalisation was not that simple. Not everyone looked at the world through Baden-Powell's eyes, not everyone was persuaded by all that he took for granted. What exasperated Baden-Powell and Whittal was the absolute refusal of villagers to submit to the forest codes, their persistence with practices unacceptable to the new regime. And what exacerbated their rage was the attitude of the

[75] *PRFAP, 1889–90*, p. 10.
[76] Ibid., p. 14.

civil administration, its tolerance of practices that subverted what foresters saw as normative

If this dialogue around fire was implicated in a process of normalisation that sought to authorise a new normative order, we need to rethink our conception of the process. Normalisation did not occur through a process of incorporation alone, whereby people were gradually acculturated into a new normative order. The authority of new norms was persistently under question, its premises always under doubt. Normalisation, we could say, was a process through which an acceptable idea of the norm was itself negotiated. It was not a process through which a pre-constituted normal was universalised. And, as the instance of forest fires shows, the idea of the norm could at times remain forever contested. Encoding cannot fix norms and make them stable: it simultaneously opens them up for scrutiny, makes them sites of conflict. The norm does not simply become a site for persistent subversion, one that questions the idea of the fixity of the norm. The norm as code remains forever a space of negotiation and refiguration – a process that refuses to accept the fixity of the code.

Second: the clash between officials revealed the different ways in which they negotiated the conflicting discourses that shaped their arguments. Schooled in the science of forestry that had developed in Germany since the late eighteenth century, forest officials saw themselves as bearers of science and truth, reason and rationality, and the villagers as primitive and irrational, ignorant and unreasonable.[77] The project of conservation was visualised as a war against unreason and the battle against those seen as pyromaniacs was viewed as a struggle for science. Forest officials recognised the need to accept some of the rights of the people but only when they were compatible with the project of conservation. Revenue officials on the other hand appealed to the authority of custom and tradition. They did not deny the logic of conservation or the sanctity of scientific knowledge, but

[77] On German forestry, see Lowood, "The Calculating Forester"; Radkau, "Wood and Forestry in German History". On the link between Indian foresters and German forestry, see Rajan, "Imperial Environmentalism or Environmental Imperialism?".

the rights of villagers and the practices of the past, they felt, could not be ruthlessly erased for the cause of science.

Third: this appeal to the authority of tradition, in opposition to science, inevitably raised the question of governance. Convinced about the truth of science, arrogant about the authenticity of their knowledge, foresters saw themselves engaged in a war that could not be waged through the language of persuasion alone. To establish a regime of order, firm action was necessary, even if this meant coercion and repression. Operating with the language of paternalism, civil officials on the other hand spoke of empathy and understanding, and recognised the need to be sensitive to tradition and custom.

Finally: the clash between forest and revenue officials was also a fight for territorial rights. Through these conflicts the bounds of departmental jurisdiction were negotiated. The foresters were unwilling to allow revenue officials control over non-agrarian spaces – areas that were not under revenue settlements. But in most regions, from the scrublands of Rawalpindi to the forests of Kulu, cultivated and forest lands could not be easily segregated; they were, as many officials discovered, "honeycombed together". If graziers cultivated land, peasants required pastures for their cattle. In most places, rights to graze, or rights to forest produce, went along with rights to cultivate, and the categories – pastoralist and cultivator – were themselves fluid. The problem was particularly acute in those regions where scrublands and grasslands were interspersed with regular patches of cultivation. These areas, where the rights of villagers had to be recognised, were classified as Protected Forests under the jurisdiction of the revenue administration, while the Reserved Forests – where all the commercially valuable timber was located, and from which local right holders were excluded – were given over to the forest administration. This territorialisation of spaces became the focal point of a never-ending fight between departments. Foresters were desperate to extend their control over Protected Forests, and revenue officials were equally passionate about protecting their territorial jurisdiction. The fight over territorial rights, I would suggest, structured their mutual rhetoric, and the way they represented each other. To the foresters, all forests legitimately belonged to them: *they* knew about the science of forestry, *they* had the technical expertise to calculate the sustainable yield, prepare the balance sheets, and ensure regeneration; *they* were committed to the project of conservation. Revenue officials were seen as usurpers who had neither the knowledge nor the will to protect forests. On the other hand, revenue officials were convinced that foresters were insensitive to the imperatives of governance, tactless and abrasive in their relations with villagers, and too aggressive in their denial of local rights. The more the revenue officials and foresters fought over departmental territoriality, the more they magnified the differences that separated them, and the unity that bound them internally.

While memos and minutes circulated in the corridors of power and the war of words persisted, grasslands and forests continued to burn. Forest fires had their temporality, their seasonality. They usually began after March when the grasslands were scorched and the forest undergrowth was dry, and spread rapidly from end May through June as the summer heat soared, evaporating all moisture in the scrublands of North India. The onset of rains had a contradictory impact. While heavy showers soaked all foliage and doused fires, lightning regularly set forests ablaze.[78] After the rains were over the extent of forest areas burnt by fire declined, only to peak again in the pre-monsoon months of the subsequent year.

The association between aridity and fire also determined the annual fluctuations in the areas of forest burnt. When rains failed, fires became more common, and they usually peaked in famine years: for instance, 1886–7 was a bad year, about 49,841 acres of forests in Rawalpindi were destroyed by fire.[79] Mr Shakespear, who enquired into the disastrous fires, reported: "Everything on the ground being like tinder from the excessive drought, it was difficult to make any

[78] Recent studies show that even in the US most of the lightning-set fires occurred during summer and early fall. They were reported in April through September. The majority were in July and August.

[79] *PRFAP, 1886–87*, para 37, p. 12. The forest department report stated: "The year 1886–87 was a disastrous one; the excessive and continued drought having caused a number of forest fires, probably without precedent in the annals of the Punjab Forest Department."

[head]way against the conflagration, and no number of firelines would have sufficed."[80] The next year the monsoon was good and forest fires were under control. The area burnt dropped to only 289 acres.[81] The subsequent year the rains failed, the area burnt by fire increased, and when the monsoons were delayed a year later, in 1889–90, the fires seemed unstoppable.[82] The area of forests destroyed in Rawalpindi soared to 35,064 acres, ten times over the earlier year. Almost 22 per cent of the specially protected area was reportedly decimated. With better rainfall the fires did not spread in 1890–1 but flared again the subsequent year. Drought and scorching heat saw fires spread with phenomenal speed, and 6715 acres of Rawalpindi forests were ruined in 1891–2.[83] Copious rainfall ensured that 1892–3 was "wonderfully free of fires".[84] No forest was recorded as burnt. With shortage of rains the next year the area of Rawalpindi forests burnt increased to 38,097 acres. Such cycles recurred over the subsequent decades. In the drought year of 1898–9, for instance, fires spread with famine, consuming vast areas of forest. In Rawalpindi alone about 8775 acres were burnt, compared to less than 648 acres the year earlier.[85] The area of forests burnt was thus inversely related to the levels of precipitation.

Fires also had their spatial logic. They were more common in the arid belts than in the wet zones, they spread more rapidly in the dry scrublands than in moist forests. In normal years they would be more frequent in the protected forests – in the rakhs where the vast grazing lands were located. Regeneration of grass on these pastures was critically dependent on the practice of firing. Dry grass was fired every year before the monsoon so that new tender shoots could sprout with the rains, offering ideal forage for animals. If there was no prospect of rain, during prolonged scarcities firing was of no use, for without the monsoon showers fresh growth was unlikely.[86]

---

[80] *PRFAP, 1887–88,* para 41.

[81] Ibid.

[82] *PRFAP, 1889–90,* p. 9.

[83] *PRFAP, 1891–92,* p. 10.

[84] *PRFAP, 1892–93,* para 37.

[85] *PRFAP, 1898–99,* para 24; *PRFAP, 1899–1900,* para 23.

[86] After successive bad seasons, in 1899–1900 even forest officials reported:

In such bad years, angry villagers, deprived of entry into Reserved Forests where forage could be found, turned against the regime of protection, setting fire to spaces from which they were excluded. As cattle and humans perished in large numbers, villagers discovered the meaning of reservation through the trauma of death and starvation. Over the decades, fire lines around the reserves were reinforced: wider trenches were dug, grass was uprooted from broader patches of land, and fireguards multiplied. But in times of prolonged drought, fires regularly erupted in the heart of the reserves, in several places at the same time, and often in the dead of night.[87] Thus the logic of fire in different spaces and at different times varied.

By the 1890s the protectionist ideas of the mid nineteenth century faced a crisis. Forest officials doubted the efficacy of a system that in practice failed to stop fires and bemoaned the differences that crippled the efficiency of protection measures.[88] Earlier certitudes began to

---

"The village people were chary of setting fire to the remnants of the old crops of grass in or around the forests, as the prospects of obtaining a new crop were chimeral on account of the drought." *PRFAP, 1899–1900*, para 23, p. 7.

[87] See in particular the report from Kangra on the scarcity year 1897–8. *PRFAP, 1897–98*. Worried about the spread of "incendiarism", foresters reluctantly opened the reserves for grazing. But only parts of the forests were opened and for limited periods. Confronted with angry villagers and continued "incendiarism", forest officials threw up their hands in despair, complained of the ingratitude of the people, and of their desire to disrupt the entire system of conservancy. Officials over the years echoed each other, borrowed from official texts of the past, and framed their arguments in familiar language. What was said in the Forest Reports of the early 1880s reappeared in the subsequent decades. See for instance the following statement: "The facts that fires when extinguished by the Forest establishment broke out again in the same or other parts of the same forest, and that in one or two instances men were actually caught spreading fire about in the reserves, prove conclusively that these disastrous fires are due to incendiarism only. It follows then that all our labour and expenditure are thrown away, as no fire lines or fire guards can contend against person who are determined to fire the forest." *PRFAP, 1893–94*, para 13, p. 7.

[88] When in 1889–90, despite severe strictures, foresters failed to control wildfires, a despairing Officiating Conservator of Forests, Punjab, wrote to the

crumble as old assumptions came under scrutiny. Debunked and criminalised, local practice now came to be re-examined and then, gradually over time, reanointed as science. But in what form?

Regenerating Grasslands: From Practice to Science

In 1978, over a hundred years after the war against fire began in colonial India, a workshop was held in Jamestown in the United States. For three days, 300 resource managers of the National Game Parks were told how to use fire for prairie regeneration. Guidelines for firing were developed, instructions codified, and different techniques of firing specified.[89] In the years that followed, helmeted officials went around with propane gas lighters firing grasslands, setting about 162 fires every year in the USA. Between 1965 and 1984, 902 fires were set and over 69,484 acres burnt through controlled regulation firing. In an ironic twist, a practice that was repressed and criminalised in the West as well as in the colonies, returned with a vengeance – sanctified by conservationists, blessed by science, institutionalised as legitimate – in the most advanced capitalist country of the world. Fire, it is now commonly recognised, is necessary to regenerate grasslands.

Behind this seemingly dramatic turnaround, this shift in attitude to fire, lies a long history of conflict. In the colonies, by the early 1880s foresters in the field were questioning the canonical wisdom of Continental forestry, reflecting mostly on timber regeneration. But canons are not easily dislodged; the doxa does not crumble with the

Punjab government: "On the one hand, forest officers question the law and its administration, on the other, District Officers place little reliance on punitive measures and advise actual firing of the forests under regulation (whatever that may mean) and the opening of a larger area to grazing, admitting at the same time that the necessity of good grazing is the origin of illicit firing. While these differences exist, it is hopeless to expect any amelioration of the evil." *PRFAP, 1890–91*, p. 14.

[89] Higgins, Kruse, and Piehl, *Prescribed Burning Guidelines in the Northern Great Plains.*

first murmur of heretical ideas. When field officers expressed their apprehensions and wrote about the mismatch between inherited theory and field experience, senior foresters reiterated the truth of the science they had learnt in Germany. In 1896, H. Slade, with his experience of forestry in Burma, wrote forcefully against fire protection, arguing that fire in fact created the conditions of teak regeneration, and too much protection was decimating the teak forests of the region.[90] But a year later Ribbentrop, Inspector General of Forests in India, reauthorised Continental wisdom. Fire protection, he declared, was as necessary in Burma as elsewhere.[91] In the years between 1896–7 and 1906–7 the area under fire protection in Burma increased rapidly from 1856 square miles to 8153 square miles.

By the first decade of the twentieth century, the critique of protectionism gathered strength in Burma. In 1905, Troup published an important article comparing two contiguous plots of teak forest in Burma, one protected from fire over nineteen years and the other annually burnt.[92] In the plot subject to firing, saplings were ten times as numerous and the young poles were sound and vigorous. In the protected plot the saplings were suffocated by gregarious undergrowth and teak displaced by bamboo. Rattled by Troup's findings, imperial forest officers everywhere began scrutinising the validity of Continental wisdom. By the winter of 1906 Beadon-Bryant, Inspector General of Forests in Burma, rushed to Tharrawaddy Division where Troup had carried out his study. Beadon-Bryant's investigation, however, reaffirmed Troup's conclusion that fire protection was gradually but certainly extinguishing teak over thousands of miles of moist forests in Burma.[93]

As the critique of protectionism spread, the arguments of the

[90] Slade, "Too Much Fire Protection in Burma".

[91] Stebbing, *The Forests of India*, p. 391.

[92] Troup, "Fire Protection in the Teak Forests of Burma".

[93] See the reports by Beadon-Bryant and George Hart, both inspector generals of forests in Burma. "Note on a Tour of Inspection in Burma", March 1914, quoted in Stebbing, *The Forests of India*, pp. 392–3. For a rich exploration of how this discourse on fire protection develops in the context of forestry in Burma and India, see Sivaramakrishnan, *Modern Forests*, ch. 7.

Burma school were rearticulated by other officials in other places and other contexts. The failure of sal regeneration in Bengal and deodar in the Himalayas was traced back to the accumulation of humus and other organic substances that covered the forest floor, preventing the seeds from reaching ground and interfering with proper aeration and soil drainage. Fire, it was gradually recognised, dehydrated clayey, moist soils, encouraged bacterial activity, increased soil fertility by supplying minerals, salts, and potash, promoted nitrification, cleared debris on the floor – allowing seeds to reach the soil – destroyed weeds and gregarious plant growth that displaced timber trees. Initially, fire protection was seen as harmful only in moist forests. Troup in fact had said that in dry *Pinus longifolia* forests fire protection was critical for regeneration. But by 1915 departmental burning was introduced in the Rawalpindi pine forests as part of silvicultural practice. Early winter fires were considered necessary to prevent wild fires in summer. In winter, trees were felled to create open spaces, logs removed, bushes, grass, needles, and resin deposits cleared from around the trees, and the slash burnt so that in the dry and hot summer months small fires did not turn into conflagrations. Foresters discovered that pine trees over seven inches thick developed a fat bark that protected them from fire; and when the trees did get burnt the stumps gave off new shoots; and if the lower branches caught fire in one year, the upper ones were saved the subsequent year.[94] With controlled winter burning the area of forests burnt through wildfires steadily declined.

Continental wisdom, however, was not easily displaced. In an authoritative manual of silviculture published in 1937, Champion and Griffith, both silviculturists working at the Forest Research Institute at Dehra Dun, wrote:

In a general way, burning the soil destroys most of the raw material which maintains the essential humus content of the soil, and a continued burning regime must be very injurious to its fertility. Burning may however give a temporary impetus to growth by causing an increase in

[94] On regeneration of *Pinus longifolia* in Rawalpindi, see Allah Baksh, "Control Measures"; Mohan, "Controlled Burning and Change in Vegetation"; Stebbing, *The Forests of India*, pp. 403–4.

bacterial activity and hence in available nitrogen. It may also, through its physical effect on the soil and by removing a surface layer, temporarily improve conditions for natural or artificial regeneration, or even be an essential condition for it.[95]

Unwilling to recognise the connection between firing and regeneration, but unable to dismiss it, their *Manual* tottered uncertainly between acceptance and denial. The beneficial effects of fire were acknowledged but presented as superficial, marginal, and temporary; its injurious effects had greater depth and durability. Forest science was too firmly embedded within its Continental heritage to legitimate local knowledge in unequivocal terms. Having defined its identity in opposition to local practice, it was anxious not to destroy the premises of its self-conception.

In any case, the terms of this entire debate amongst foresters lay within the discourse of scientific forestry. For villagers, fire was important for producing good pastures, for foresters the critical question was its link with timber regeneration. Both critics and advocates of fire protection were driven by similar concerns; both were obsessed with teak, sal, and deodar. They took time to reorient their gaze to grass and scrub.

The new science of grassland development in many countries now builds on local knowledge and is based on extensive research into local practices. It is now widely recognised that fire is a necessary part of healthy grassland development and forest ecosystems. We know that in winter, grasses in the prairies dry while their roots stay alive, and new shoots grow with vigour if there is firing in the spring; that fire reduces the build-up of dead and decaying leaves that accumulate on the floor, allowing sun and rain to penetrate the soil and release nutrients, activating the process of photosynthesis, stimulating growth, and promoting seed yields; that fire recycles mineral nutrients from organic to inorganic form by converting litter into ash that dissolves with rainwater, is easily absorbed by the soil, and becomes available for plant intake;[96] that fire in forests also reduces

[95] Champion and Griffith, *Manual of General Silviculture for India*.

[96] Knap, in a 1985 study of long grass prairies of the USA, discovered that an unburnt prairie contained three times the litter found in a burnt prairie,

the overhead canopy, increasing the sunlight that again encourages growth in seeds and roots; that vegetation in many places is in fact so fire-dependent that it needs flames for its renewal; that biomass and inflorescences are increased with burning, and so is the stem density of many grass varieties; that firing is necessary to restore to prairies their natural habitat – after spring fires burn exotic varieties, sun-seeking local varieties begin to grow; that burned grasses respond more efficiently than unburned grasses to nitrogen applications. We know too that the suppression of burning and grazing lead to the displacement of succulent varieties of grass by woody species, and over time promote the growth of a plant cover that is too dense and unattractive for most wildlife.[97]

The "incendiary villager", however, still remains a shadowy figure. His knowledge, criminalised at one time, has now been partly rehabilitated by stages. But transformed as science, this new knowledge is different from the old. It is not tradition and past practice, but "scientific" research that is the basis of its new authority. Through technical experiments and long-term monitoring of observations, biologists and experts in animal science and grassland development are seeking to understand the optimum effects of fire and the conditions that determine the nature of its effects.

Refigured as science, local practice is regulated by rules, regulations, specifications, and prescriptions. Prescribed firing, the manuals and guidelines say, have to be carefully planned and properly timed. Scientific research has attempted to show how firing can have diverse

---

and that the nutrients per unit of this litter were higher. When compared to the burnt prairie, each unit of litter in an unburnt prairie contained over 3.5 times the amount of nitrogen and 2.7 times the amount of phosphorus. This meant that the denser growth in unburnt prairies impoverished the soil of its nutrients, transforming inorganic nutrients into biomass. See Knapp and Hulbert, "Production, Density and Height of Flower Stalks of 3 Grasses"; Knapp and Seastedt, "Detritus Accumulation Limits Productivity of Tallgrass Prairie"; Blair, Seastedt, Rice, and Ramundo, "Terrestrial Nutrient Cycling".

[97] The invasion of woody plants and unpalatable shrubs in grassland and savanna ecosystems has been the subject of much recent research and debate. See Archer, Boutton, and Hibbard, "Trees in Grasslands"; Silva, Zambrano, and Farinas, "Increase in the Woody Component"; Sabiiti, "Fire Behaviour".

effects, not always beneficial; and how the result of firing depends on plant species, and the timing as well as frequency of the fire. A badly timed fire could be harmful for plant growth since fire reduces soil moisture, and firing in dry seasons can be particularly disastrous.[98] Firing in moist areas allows soil aeration, promotes root activity; but regular firing in dry tracts can have long-term detrimental effects on soil by eliminating all moisture and humus. Plant diversity is said to be greatest in intermediate fire frequency rather than regular annual burns. So experts, not laypeople, are to determine the location and the timing of the burn, its frequency and cycles.

Within a regime of prescription, different forms of firing have to be differentiated, their characteristics explained and enumerated, and specific forms have to be prescribed for particular ends. The requirements of each context are to be judged, the cost effectiveness of each form of firing has to be calculated, its optimal efficiency ensured. When in 1872 Ellis saw a fire burn against the wind, he was convinced that it was abnormal, undoubted proof of the malice of villagers, their unquestionable culpability. Now, a hundred years later, backing fire – that burns into the wind, or downwards on a slope – is recognised as one of the most effective forms of burning. Flame lengths are short, the rate of fire-spread is slow, the smoke density is generally lower than in other forms of firing, and control over the fire is easy.[99] Backing fire burns hotter at ground surface and

---

[98] Dense vegetation insulates the soil from sun rays and intercepts rainfall, slows the water movement, and helps infiltration. Burning clears the vegetation cover, increasing the runoff and soil erosion, decreasing infiltration. Sun rays now reach the soil and dry it. Since the soil blackens with burning and warms quickly, evaporation increases and moisture reduces further. With the increase in soil temperature grasses grow quickly, drying the soil further. So a properly timed fire could regenerate grassland, a badly timed one could destroy growth.

[99] By the early twentieth century, this was recognised by colonial foresters. In the dry *Pinus longifolia* forests of Rawalpindi, downhill fires were recommended. Their high intensity on the ground allowed even the moist humas to be burnt effectively; they moved slowly and were easy to control – an important consideration in dry forests; and their low flames did not reach the branches. See Baksh, "Control Measures"; also Stebbing, *The Forests of India*, pp. 403–5.

is more efficient per unit of fuel consumption than flank and head fires. If wage expenses were to be calculated, the overall burn costs for backing fire are higher per acre, for it takes longer to complete the burning.[100] Head fires have greater flame lengths, faster rates of spread, greater smoke volumes, and burn cooler at ground surface than backing or flank fires. Flanking fires burn at an oblique angle and are used to secure the flanks of a head fire. They are said to require expert crew co-ordination and timing.[101]

If, over the colonial years, local practice forced foresters to rethink many of their assumptions and prejudices; scientific forestry in turn refigured local practice, even as it appropriated its wisdom.

Questioned by local voices, resisted by embedded traditions, opposed by nomadic visions, colonisation of the commons happened initially in stumbling steps. Policies had to be rethought, steps retraced, strategies reworked. But in the long term these reworkings became implicated in the project itself. They refashioned its contours but could not halt its march. Some nomads continued their war against the state, devising ever-new strategies of confrontation, even as they negotiated a space within it.[102] Others reoriented their vision, reworked their choices, and became complicit in the project of transformation, even while resisting the changes in their everyday life.

The vision of agrarian conquest had transformed settled agriculture into a universal and normative ideal, to be generalised everywhere. This meant that the agrarian frontier had to be extended beyond the Jullunder Doab, on the vast grazing lands of the bārs. Yet the model of agrarian regime that characterised the central belt of settled agriculture could not be reproduced untransformed. Colonial officials celebrated

---

[100] This cost is to be calculated only when fire personnel are involved in the process of burning. For villagers the longer time required did not imply higher costs. The value of time was not measured in wage hours.

[101] These prescriptions are given in Higgins, Kruse, and Piehl, "Prescribed Burning Guidelines in the Northern Great Plains". See the section on "Methods of Spreading Fire in the Grasslands".

[102] For a strong argument about the hostility of primitive societies to the incorporative drive of the state, see Clastres, *Society Against the State*. In recent years the provocative and suggestive ideas of Clastres have inspired new works on nomadism.

the Jat peasants of central Punjab, admired their carefully cultivated fields of maize and wheat; but they saw everywhere in this region the problems of agrarian expansion: pressure of numbers, fragmentation of holdings, parcellisation of land.[103] Growth, they knew, would come up against these barriers; intensification could not be pushed beyond a limit. The soil exhausts, productivity stagnates, revenue increases become difficult. The scrublands offered a wider field of colonial engineering: they were spaces that could be transformed from above, landscapes that could be made productive. But all this had to be done in ways that transcended the endemic problems of the core agrarian zone. Colonisation of the commons had initially meant taking over the bār, the demarcation of chaks and rakhs, the imposition of tirni, a mapping and bounding of the region, and a redefinition of local rights. Could the landscape become the site of a more ambitious project of agrarian conquest?

[103] See ch. 8 above.

10

The Promise of Modernity, Antinomies of Development

B
Y THE 1880s the colonial state in India embarked on one of its grandest projects of social engineering. It proceeded to concretise its dream of creating an ideal agrarian space within the colony. From the beginning of colonial rule, in Punjab and elsewhere, colonial officials had been driven by the desire to "improve" landscapes and modernise agrarian spaces, even as they sought to maximise revenue returns. But they had found it impossible to put their visions into practice and transform images into reality. Operating in areas with their own histories and traditions, faced with deeply entrenched social structures, and confronted with a maze of customs, practices, and ecological variations, the British had repeatedly to back-track, rework their conceptions, and modify their vision. They had to arrive at policies that were feasible and viable within the given contexts. The imagined ideal was persistently disturbed by the politics of the possible.

Colonisers everywhere search for open spaces that seem to allow unconstrained transformation. The pastoral highlands – the bārs beyond the Sutlej – seemed just such a space. On this vast scrubland there were no valuable trees, no populous villages, no settled peasant cultivating his field, no wheat piled up on threshing floors, no carts carrying local produce to the market. Nomadic pastoralists were the only humans visible, traversing the landscape with their camels

385

and herds, some living on the bārs through the year, others moving between the riverine tracts and the highlands.[1] The highlands were dry, with water levels as much as eighty feet below ground (see Fig. 16). From the earliest days of colonial rule British officials crossing the region had despaired at the desolation of its landscape while fantasising about reordering the "wilderness".[2] By the early 1880s the scrublands had been taken over, reclassified as rakh (waste), mapped, surveyed, and bounded. In the subsequent decades the area came to be subject to an even more dramatic process of change.

The first Canal Colony project was started in Multan in 1886.[3] Over the next fifty years a vast network of perennial canals was spread over the highlands in the interfluves of the Sutlej and Jhelum rivers. The average annual area irrigated through such canals boomed: from around 943,000 acres in the five years ending 1885–6, to 4,123,500 acres by the end of the century.[4] Nine colonies were settled around the canals. In the Chenab Colony, settled between 1892 and 1905,

[1] See the early exploration reports of the different bārs conducted by the Survey of India, Dehradun Records, 1850–60, Serial No. 625, Old No. Rev/5, 1854–7.

[2] In 1841, Henry Lawrence rode through this region, leaving Ferozepur on 16 December and reaching Peshawar on 28 December. His diary and letters give his earliest impressions of the terrain. In one of his letters to a Mr G. Clerk he writes: "From Kussor to Choong and Rungpoor is a wild waste, and on this side of the Ravi the country is covered with coarse grass; and throughout the 70 miles I have travelled during the last two days, I have been struck with the almost entire absence of inhabitants; seeing very few people in or about the thirty scattered villages, and meeting with scarcely a traveller on the road. Road there is none . . ." Letter Books of Henry Lawrence, 1840–1, Henry Lawrence Collection, Eur Mss F 85 (2), BL. Writing about these observations of his hero, Herbert Edwards notes: "Little did Henry think as he marked the desolation through which he marched, that he was only making notes of evils which he himself would have to grapple with in four short years." Edwardes and Merivale, *Life of Sir Henry Lawrence*, vol. 1, pp. 288–9. Within the colonial imagination the pastoral landscape was not only desolate, it was evil. It had to be irrigated, populated, regulated, and reordered.

[3] Punjab Rev. & Agr. (Rev.), July 1880, A 14; Punjab Rev. & Agr. (Rev.), November 1880, A 3.

[4] *Report of the Indian Irrigation Commission, 1901–3*, pt II, ch. XIV, p. 6.

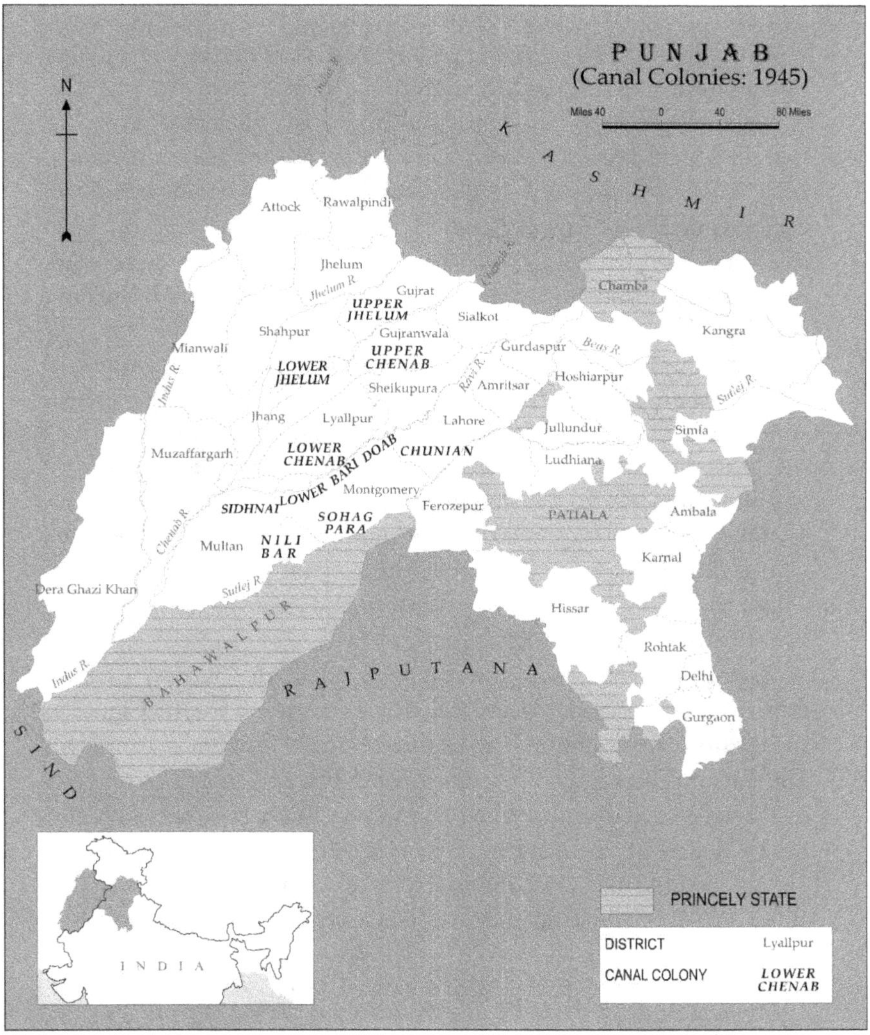

Fig. 18: Map of the Canal Colonies.

over 1.8 million acres were allotted in grants.[5] The area distributed in the other colonies was considerably smaller: in Jhelum Colony about 540,000 acres, in the Lower Bari Doab about 900,000 acres,[6] in the Nili bár 800,000 acres. But together these colonies carved up over four million acres of pastoral land for agrarian settlement.[7]

Colonial officials hoped to mould the space in accordance with their dream and develop it through science, capital, and the imperial imagination. As they saw it, they had been gifted a *tabula rasa*, an empty landscape unencumbered by history and unfettered by social rigidities. The high plateau was dry but the soil was fertile in patches. Once irrigation became available, officials were convinced, the land could be cleared, settled, and ordered via pioneering settlers brought in from the densely populated and intensively cultivated tracts of Punjab where the limits of agrarian expansion had been reached. A new society could be founded with immigrants – the industrious peasants of central Punjab settled in these new colonies – for whom a new regime of customs would be introduced, villages and markets planned, valuable commercial crops produced. A desolate landscape would thus be covered with cultivating fields and made productive. In the Canal Colonies, it was assumed, the limits of the possible could be redefined.

As the process of colonisation proceeded, this fantasy of freedom from constraint, this imperial desire to create a colonial agrarian society from above unhindered by local rigidities, gradually crumbled. The pastoral landscape was transformed but the agrarian conquest could not proceed undisturbed in an exact line with imperial plans. Embedded landscapes are never erased with ease, emptied of people, and reinscribed without problem, for spaces are not as malleable as modernist minds imagine. The nomads were not as docile as

---

[5] *Annual Reports of the Chenab, Jhelum . . . Colonies, 1908*, Statement II.

[6] *Annual Report of the Lower Bari Doab Canal Colony, 1916–17*.

[7] For a discussion of the Canal Colonies from within a developmentalist paradigm, see Ali, *The Punjab Under Imperialism*. For an exploration of some of the ecological implications, see Gilmartin, "Models of the Hydraulic Environment"; Agnihotri , "Ecology, Land Use and Colonisation"; Gilmartin, *Blood and Water*.

colonial officials desired. The colonising projects, as they evolved, were very different from the constitutive elements of the original idea. Here I examine both the vision and the experience of this agrarian colo- nisation and look at the relationship between founding plan and executed project. I explore how spaces become sites of conflict and how the specific mode of their refiguration is defined by conflict. Through this exploration I reflect on the different paths of agrarian conquest and the various modes of colonial domination.

Canals and the Science of Empire

The construction of the canals was, in a sense, the founding act. The Canal Colonies were to develop around canals and derive their very identity from them. By the construction of perennial canals Punjab's officials sought to demonstrate their capacity to tame nature, transform wastes into productive landscapes, and create the basis of a new hydraulic order. The canals would reveal the marvels of Western science, the power of Western reason and rationality. They would signify a transition from the past to the present, from backwardness to progress, from the age of primitive irrigation systems to the birth of the technologically new. They would announce the arrival of modernity and civilisation.

In the early years after annexation, Punjab's officials were reluct- ant to undertake ambitious projects of irrigation. The potential for irrigation was widely recognised and the need for irrigating the Bari Doab – the interfluve between the Sutlej and the Ravi – was greatly emphasised. "No part of the new territory is so important, political- ly and socially," declared the Board of Administration. "In no Doab, is there so much high-land susceptible of culture; so many hands to work; so fine a population to be supported."[8] In the winter of 1849–50 Lieutenant Dyas was deputed to conduct "scientific investigations" so that a working plan for the irrigation of the Bari Doab could be developed. By the end of the season officials claimed that the topo- graphy of the whole of the Doab had been carefully mapped: level

[8] *RAP, 1849–50 to 1851–52, SRGOI*, no. 2, para 351, p. 134.

cross-sections were taken, the nature of the ground – its surface, its drainage, and its undulations – was "precisely ascertained", and the capabilities of the existing canals were all carefully examined.[9] Within a few years, the Punjab administration boasted of having built a canal that was "second in India only to the great Ganges Canal and equal if not superior to the finest irrigation canals of Europe."[10]

Yet the Board of Administration was wary of extending the scale of canal operations. Swamped by new proposals for ambitious irrigation schemes and apprehensive of the excessive enthusiasm of the canal engineers, in 1856 it urged the need for caution:

> the expediency of multiplying permanent Canals of magnitude is doubtful. On the one hand the outlay is vast, on the other the return is uncertain, until the means of exporting the surplus produce shall have been provided. Until this cardinal and crying want, namely, means of exportations shall have been supplied, a number of great Canals would be in advance of the need of the country. Let the new Baree Doab Canal be fairly tried; let effort for a Railway from Umritsar to Mooltan be made (the first measure will hardly be complete without the second); and in the meantime Inundation Canals of small size, but large numbers, will suffice.[11]

Nervous about large outlays and unconvinced about secure returns, Punjab's officials stalled new projects and spoke of the worth of existing inundation systems. They wrote admiringly of the great canals of Multan started by the Pathan rulers and reconstructed under Sawan Mal, and of the value of the Derajat canals that irrigated the parched lands further west.[12] Initiated and supervised by local chiefs and

[9] Ibid., para 354, p. 135.

[10] *RAP, 1851–52* and *1852–53, SRGOI*, no. 6, p. 169, para 424.

[11] *RAP, 1854–55* to *1855–56; SRGOI* , no. 18, p. 61, para 99. On the remodelling of the Bari Doab Canal, see Punjab PWD (Irr.), March 1874, A 17; Punjab PWD (Irr.), July 1894, A 1.

[12] *Canals of the Mooltan District, 1849, SPCAAP*, vol. I, no. 1; Pollock, Memorandum on the Dera Ghazee Khan District; Extension of Canal Irrigation in the Dehra Ismail Khan and Dehra Ghazee Khan Districts, 1868, *SRFCP*, no 18; Punjab Rev. & Agr. (Rev.), July 1880, A 14; Punjab Rev. & Agr. (Rev.), November 1880, A 3; Punjab PWD (Irr.), August 1874, A 26.

power holders, these inundation canals were seemingly constructed without much expense and trouble to the native governments. Local people had combined not only to construct them – digging the channels, raising the embankments, and constructing bunds where necessary – but also to maintain them, contributing their labour every year to clear the silt. So, if the locals could sustain their own irrigation systems, officials reasoned, why should the government intervene? "In such cases, when the community displays so much aptitude for self-government," wrote Melvill in the early 1850s, "the Board consider non-interference the best policy, while they would always be ready to afford any aid which might be solicited."[13]

By the 1870s colonial officials in various districts were actively extending the network of inundation canals.[14] The policy was to initiate projects, minimise government expenditure, cajole and force local inhabitants to build the canal and maintain it with their labour, but take over control of the canal. Colonel Grey, commissioner of Ferozepur, got the cultivators on the left bank of the Sutlej to dig ten inundation canals without pecuniary help from the government.[15] A decade later, while commissioner of Hissar, Grey had three canals constructed. The total length of these canals was 600 miles and the area irrigated annually averaged about 160,000 acres. Initiated by the local government and with no outlay from imperial revenue, the canals were under the supervision of the deputy commissioner. The local government was to regulate the supply of water to the

[13] *RAP*, 1849/50–1851/52, para 348.While Melvill was Secretary to the Board of Administration at the time, Temple drafted most of the report.

[14] Punjab Rev. & Agr. (Irr.), September 1882, A. 2. See in particular no. 3008-I, 13 August 1875, Sup. Engineer Sirhind Canals to Joint Sec. GOP, Irr. Branch; no. 1494-I, 9 June 1875, Sup. Engineer, Upper Bari Doab Canal to Joint Sec. GOP, Irr. Branch; no. 2990-I, 15 November 1875, Sup. Engineer Bari Doab Canal, to Joint Sec. GOP, Irr. Branch. Also Punjab Rev. & Agr., (Irr.), July 1883, A2; Punjab Rev. and Agr. (Irr.), December 1883, A 1.

[15] Punjab Rev. and Agr. (Rev.), December 1880, A 4a, pp. 683–8; Correspondence Relating to the Ferozepur and Fazilka Inundation Canals, *SRFCP, N.S.*, no 61. On the construction and remodelling of inundation canals, see also GOI Rev. & Agr. (Rev.), May 1881, A 33–4; Punjab PWD (Irr.), May 1891.

fields, ensure the labour contributions of each household towards the annual task of clearing silt, and mediate in disputes over water.[16] These canals were not classified in official documents as "state canals": they were said to belong to the community and were to be maintained by it. What this meant was state control without state investment.

By the 1880s, however, the enthusiasm for inundation canals began to fade as perennial canals were increasingly projected as the embodiment of science, modernity, and progress. Even Grey, a great advocate of the inundation system, stated:

> the days of inundation canals have passed. The rivers have been or are being tapped to a degree which much lowers the value of these works by depriving them of the early and later water which is so important to irrigation. The method was after all but a makeshift; it has had its day, and the time has come for arresting the summer floods by weirs, and for distributing them scientifically over the country to afford a duty of 200 acres to the cusac, instead of the 30 to 40 acres which is the average of inundation canals.[17]

The pronouncement was unambiguous: inundation canals had come up against natural barriers to their expansion. A shift to perennial canals would help by enlarging the total irrigable area, reducing wastage, and optimising utilities, with each cusac of water irrigating a bigger area.

The argument for perennial canals was thus framed within a discourse that played on a set of ideas and themes. There was, first, the idea that inundation canals epitomised wastage whereas perennial canals optimised utilities. The deputy commissioner of Dera Ismail Khan recognised that an inadequate supply of river water made the construction of perennial canals in the tract difficult and inundation canals were the only option. "However," he emphasised, "as frequently before urged by officers in charge of this district, very much of the water supply must be wasted, vast labour be year by year rendered fruitless, and the resources of the country remain in a great measure

---

[16] Punjab Rev. & Agr. (Irr.), July 1883, A 1; Punjab Rev. & Agr. (Irr.), July 1884, A 1–3.

[17] Quoted in *Report of the Indian Irrigation Commission, 1901–3*, pt II, p. 15.

undeveloped, until a scientific system of irrigation is applied to the river, and the water supply regulated at pleasure, and distributed as it might be in quality sufficient for the fertilisation of the whole country . . ."[18] This argument, in fact, was official common sense by the late nineteenth century: inundation systems inevitably meant a waste of natural resources, labour, and productive potential. In the monsoon, when the rivers were in full flow, vast quantities of water poured into the sea without being used and the water that did inundate the fields at this time was much in excess of what was necessary. Only Western science could optimise the use of resources by harnessing natural and human potential for the greatest common good.

Second: there was the question of variability, continuity, and stability. Inundation canals were seasonal. They flowed between April and September and were dry in the winter. When the snow in the high mountains began to melt, the water level in the rivers rose and the inundation canals began to flow. In the monsoon, when the rivers swelled, the channels overflowed, the water spilled over the embankments and inundated the fields. The channels continued to flow for a while after the rains, providing valuable late water for the kharif (autumn harvest). But by end October they ran dry as the rivers receded. This seasonality meant excess in one season and shortage in another. Over the monsoon there were frequent floods and breaches in the embankments, in winter there was no water to raise a spring crop (rabi).[19]

Beyond these seasonal fluctuations were the annual variations. The Irrigation Commission of 1901 estimated that in the last two decades of the nineteenth century the average area irrigated from the seven major inundation canals of Punjab increased by about 19 per cent, from 896,296 to 1,069,606 acres. But the annual figures actually varied enormously. In 1899–1900, for instance, it was only 859,981 acres while in the following year it went up to 1,357,699 acres,

[18] Ibid. See also Extension of Canal Irrigation in the Dehra Ismail Khan and Dehra Ghazee Khan Districts, *SRFCP*, no. 18: 3.

[19] On variability and uncertainty of water flow in the inundation canals, see Punjab PWD (Irr.), May 1891, A 1; Punjab PWD (Irr.), June 1894, A 1; Punjab PWD (Irr.), June 1873, A 24.

an increase of 58 per cent.[20] The annual supply was linked to the level of snowfall, the movement of the barometer, the intensity of the summer heat, and the level of precipitation during the monsoon. There was no way, so the officials felt, that this supply could be stabilised, the variations eliminated, and a continuous flow in the irrigation channels ensured.

For colonial officials such instabilities were deeply troubling. Their anxiety derived, first, from an anthropomorphic modernism. To be subject to seasonal rhythms was to be subject to fickle nature, and to be at the mercy of nature was to be primitive. Modernity announced itself by asserting the human capacity to tame and regulate nature. Perennial canals, British officials believed, would enable them to overcome the caprice of nature and allow them to reshape the landscape as they wished. Inundation canals, on the other hand, embodied nature's constraints.

Third: official anxieties about seasonalities revealed a bourgeois concern with broken cycles of production. Capitalism strives everywhere to establish a regime of continuous time that can ensure a stable line of production and a continuous flow of commodities. When the logic of capital gets naturalised, seasonality in general appears intolerable and discontinuities cause worry. The fear of uncertainty also pointed to an obsession with fixity and stability that Utilitarianism had transformed into the doxa of nineteenth-century Britain.[21]

Fourth: there was the question of production efficiency. Within the late-nineteenth-century colonial discourse, inundation canals came to represent a system of inefficient and slack cultivation. Consider the assessment of C.M. King, penned in 1901, about the canal lands of Ferozepur:

> The type of cultivation on lands irrigated from inundation canals is necessarily a low one; the supply is limited to one period of the year, and is very difficult to control; the consequent flooding prevents the proper tilling of

[20] *Report of the Indian Irrigation Commission, 1901–3*, pt II, ch. XIV.

[21] On the Utilitarian idea of fixity, see Postema, *Bentham and the Common Law Tradition*. See also ch. IV supra.

the ground, and if kharif crops are sown at all, they are sown after a very inefficient preparation of the soil. The results of the annual floodings and slack cultivation are very apparent all over the Bet, where all the canal irrigated tracts are burdened with heavy growths of weeds, and all areas subject to percolation are heavily impregnated with kallar . . . Whilst the evils, as far as can be seen, are permanent and progressive, the extra crops raised by canal irrigation diminish year by year as the virgin soil gets worked out, and the position in the Bet is very similar to that of a man living on his capital.[22]

It was as if all problems, all evils, flowed from the intrinsic quality of the inundation canal system. It nurtured a weak form of cultivation, allowed weeds to spread, kallar (salinity) to accumulate, and unhealthy conditions to be reproduced. The introduction of the perennial system, it was repeatedly asserted, would solve all these problems. It would allow the water supply to be controlled, flooding to be regulated, cultivation to be intensive, and productivity to develop. Inscribed with impermanence, associated with a discontinuous temporality, the beneficial effects of the inundation canals were seen as ephemeral and illusory. Only the perennial canals could bring permanent benefits, ensure continuous growth and progress.

Fifth: the issue of control and regulation. Modern perennial canals came to be associated with a regime of precision and regulation, estimation and survey.[23] Before a canal was constructed, precise surveys were to be made to determine soil types, gradients, depth of water, velocity of flow, volume of silting, estimated costs, and projected returns. Cross-sections were cut to decide on the point at which the weir was to be built and the headwork located. Survey reports were to be written up, schemes proposed and reviewed, and then, once the schemes were in operation, regular annual reports were to assess their working. Through the year the level of water was to be gauged and its flow regulated from the headworks. Inundation canals were neither

[22] GOI Land Rev. & Agr. (Rev.), January 1914, A 20, 193.

[23] This rhetoric drew upon a wider discourse of precision and quantification that was naturalised in nineteenth-century Europe. See Wise, *The Values of Precision*; Porter, *The Rise of Statistical Thinking*; idem, *Trust in Numbers*; Hacking, *The Taming of Chance*.

constructed with any such scientific surveys and careful planning, nor was their operation carefully and scientifically regulated.[24]

Within the official mind, inundation canals were in many areas synonymous with poor planning, uncontrolled irrigation, water-logging, kallar, reh, and sickness. In 1867 Adam Taylor, a civil surgeon, was asked to survey the villages around the Western Jumna Canal.[25] In the tracts near the canal he found stagnant swamps with reeds, vegetation in abundance, a spring level near the surface, and widespread sickness. The connection between inundation canals, marsh miasma, and illness was indisputable, he asserted. The canal network and drainage lines were badly aligned. Their intersections caused the high banks of the channels to block the natural drainage of the countryside and create swamps. Percolation from the elevated watercourses raised the groundwater level and made draining the swamps difficult. Stagnant water on clayey tracts brought salts to the surface, destroying the fertility of the soil and causing sickness. Some of these problems could of course be solved by lowering the canal level, realigning the channels, draining the swamps, and filling up hollows and ditches. But could the fundamental engineering flaw of the "native system" be overcome? Taylor was not entirely sceptical but other officials were unconvinced.[26]

Jolted by the devastating famines of 1878–9 and persuaded by the Famine Commission of 1880, Punjab's officials gave up their ambivalence about perennial canals. They had always seen perennial canals as superior to inundation canals but had till now been hesitant about constructing them on a large scale. But from the early 1880s new schemes were widely discussed and a series of ambitious projects undertaken. The earlier fiscal over-caution gave way to large outlays. By 1900 a total of Rs 92 million had been invested on perennial canals

---

[24] The British did build head-works in some of the inundation canals they constructed. But the headworks were not as successful in controlling the working of the canal.

[25] Adam Taylor, Civil Surgeon, Ambala, to T.H. Thornton, Sec., GOP, Sanitary Survey of Villages Watered by the Western Jumna Canal, *SRGOP, NS*, no. 6, para 13.

[26] Ibid. See also Punjab PWD (Irr.), January 1873, no. 15.

in Punjab, and by 1926 over Rs 158,600,000 was spent in just five of the major canal projects.[27] The total outlay on all the irrigation canals in 1926 amounted to about Rs 29.54 million. By the turn of the century it had become clear that the fear of low and uncertain returns from investment that had plagued officials in the 1850s was unfounded. The original capital outlay in most of the canals was recouped with ease. The Lower Chenab Project, started in 1892, proved one of the most remunerative. After the first twenty years it brought in an annual net revenue amounting to 35 to 50 per cent of the capital outlay.[28] This meant that the returns of two to three years paid for the capital costs, estimated in 1927 to be around Rs 35.9 million. In 1917, the accumulated outlay on all the "major works" was Rs 223,305,164 whereas the accumulated net revenue was almost double – Rs 428,026,809.[29] By the twentieth century investment in irrigation had become an appealing financial proposition and the possibility of high fiscal returns began to attract large investments for ambitious projects of perennial irrigation. The logic of imperial science could unfold without burdening the exchequer.

As imperial science marched forward – cutting through the bār, transforming the commons into cultivated fields – the older inundation systems went into decline. While the area irrigated by perennial canals expanded dramatically from the late nineteenth century, the area under inundation canals stagnated, increasing less than 20 per cent in the last two decades of the century.[30] Convinced of the superiority of

---

[27] *RRIDP*, 1926, pt II, p. 8.

[28] The actual returns surpassed all expectations. The original Chenab scheme in 1892 had projected a return of about 12 per cent by 1909–10, and 15 per cent by 1914. The actual net revenue (gross revenue – running expenses), in 1915–16, as a proportion of total outlay was 40 per cent, and net profit (net revenue – interest) was 36 per cent. By 1946, the net revenue had gone up to 50 per cent of the capital outlay. See GOI Rev. & Agr. (Rev.), December 1892, A 16–18; *RRIDP*, 1915–16, 1945–46. For detailed discussion of the outlays and returns, see Ali, *The Punjab Under Imperialism*, ch. 5; Agnihotri, "Agrarian Change in the Canal Colonies".

[29] *RRIDP*, 1917–18.

[30] *Report of the Indian Irrigation Commission, 1901–3*, pt II, ch. XIV, p. 10.

perennial canals and assured of high returns, the imperial government was in the late nineteenth century willing to make large capital outlays on perennial canals. Inundation canals were meanwhile starved of funds: expenses on their construction and maintenance were to be met from whatever could be spared from current revenue, which was rarely adequate even for their maintenance. The construction of perennial canals had, moreover, cut the flow of water in the rivers and squeezed supply to the inundation canals.

The annual maintenance of the inundation canals had in any case become a general problem from the time the Canal Department began to supervise the clearance. Once cher – the collective labour that the community contributed in the pre-British period for the maintenance of collective utilities – was demanded by the state, and the amount of labour to be contributed by each irrigator was specified by the Canal Department rather than regulated by the community, the system began to break down. Cultivators resisted working as cher, saw it as coercive, and refused to clear the silt. The state reacted by threatening to impose water rates wherever the irrigators were seen as obdurate.[31] When in the 1870s an abiana (water rate) was imposed at a uniform rate of Rs 5.5 per acre, in addition to the demand for cher labour, angry zamindars refused to pay and petitioned against the unjust levy.[32] The consequent clashes between local zamindars and the Irrigation Department paralysed the management of inundation systems.

The Irrigation Commission of 1901, meeting after the terrible famine years at the turn of the century, re-emphasised the protective value of inundation canals in the dry tracts of Punjab.[33] But the ideal agrarian order of the British imagination was to be built around the perennial canals that were to stretch through the bār, transforming the pastoral tracts, displacing pastoralists, bringing the wilderness into the fold of "civilisation".

[31] Cher was now defined as water advantage rate paid in the form of labour on the canals. On cher, see App. VI to Fryer, no. 29, 11 February, Punjab Agr. Rev., September 1872, A 15.

[32] On the problem of demanding cher labour, see Punjab Agr. Rev. and Comm. (Rev.), Jan. 1874, A 75–82.

[33] *Report of the Indian Irrigation Commission*, pt II.

A Regime of Squares

Colonial officials had long despaired at the absence of order within the agrarian landscape. Fields were of irregular shape, plots splintered into innumerable fragments, and meandering village boundaries interlocked in complicated ways. In the Canal Colonies they could at last hope to impose their own sense of order.

Over the years, colonisation became associated with a regime of squares. The entire landscape was plotted with a network of straight lines. In most places, before canal construction, the Canal Department carried out a complete survey of the whole bār. A central base line was laid down in the middle of the bār, and from it cross lines were run out at right angles on both sides at distances of 1100 feet. On these cross lines, bricks were laid at intervals of 1100 feet. Watercourses (rajbahas) were designed to run along the sides of the canal squares. Such canal surveys became the basis of subsequent field surveys on the square system. Permanent pillars were laid at the corner of each square of 27.7 acres, and these were subdivided into twenty-five equal squares.[34] The rectangular plot with straight lines – so important in the modernist imagination – was designated a killa. And the act of enclosing the commons, erecting demarcating pillars, and subdividing the land into smaller squares came to be known as killabandi.[35]

[34] For a description of the process of killabandi, see in particular, *Annual Report of the Jhelum Colony 1902–3*, pp. 31–2.

[35] In tracts where killabandi was done, fields were first plotted on maps before they were demarcated on the ground, unlike the cadastral maps of the old districts where fields – of varying sizes and shapes – had to be individually measured before they could be mapped. In 1893–4, while carrying out the killabandi of the Chenab Canal, F.P. Young realised the need to change the earlier system – seemingly troublesome to both the cultivator and the measuring officer – in the tracts under colonisation. "It therefore occurred to me to take advantage of our unique position, and to reverse the usual process by drawing our maps on paper first, and requiring the zamindar to lay his field out on the ground in accordance therewith afterwards." Report on the Colonisation of Government Waste Lands on the Chenab Canal, *RLRAP, 1893–94*, appendix, p. XIV. The zamindars were to relate to the land through the spatial framework provided by the colonisers. Maps were not to

Killabandi was seen as the act of mapping order onto space. The early reports on colonisation describe with great enthusiasm the annual progress of killabandi. We are told of the innumerable obstacles that were faced, and the way each was surmounted as colonising officials set about transforming the imperial vision into reality. Apprehensive of surveys, scared of a further loss of their rights over the bār, and certain that measurement meant taxes, the nomads resisted killabandi. In the existing proprietary villages too, fields had to be remapped, irregular boundaries straightened, ancestral shares transformed into neat rectangular fields, and fragmented plots consolidated into uniform large holdings. The task everywhere proved more difficult than initially visualised. People resented the exchange of lands necessitated by the straightening of village boundaries and holdings, and were reluctant to give up their ancient shares. In many places where killabandi was completed but irrigation yet to reach, people refused to extend cultivation into the "waste".[36] And killa marks usually disappeared wherever land was not brought under the plough. In low-lying chahi lands irrigated by wells, the old field boundaries were well-runnels; when canal officers insisted on demolishing these to construct the new boundaries, the Hithari cultivators refused to oblige.[37] To subdue recalcitrance and counter resistance, canal officers withheld the supply of canal water and threatened to impose high taxes. If killabandi was essential for the agrarian conquest of the landscape and the creation of an ideal order, all barriers to it had to be overcome.

The killabandi regime of squares – a cartographic grid of the ordered society – was an image that drew upon a long Western obsession with straight lines. Within this imagination, the straight

---

record the order that pre-existed on the ground, they were to create the ideal order.

[36] E. Joseph, the colonising officer of Lower Bari Doab Canal Colony, recognised the problem: "you cannot expect people to show much enthusiasm for breaking up the waste area when there are no means of irrigating it or to alter the shapes of their well fields as long as they have to continue using the wells." *RLBDCC*, 1913–14, p. 43.

[37] *RLBDCC*, 1913–14.

line signified clarity, confidence, certainty; it reflected the power of man, the order of science. Squares and rectangles represented uniformity, homogeneity, regularity, symmetry, precision, and neatness – all essential elements of order. This visual imagination defined itself against an alternative aesthetic that celebrated the curved line, the irregularities of nature, the beauty of the unusual, the strange – an aesthetic that had discovered in homogeneity, symmetry, and uniformity only deadening sameness and numbing monotony.[38] Colonial officials sought to reconcile these opposing aesthetic ideals, appreciating at the same time the beauty of nature and the rationality behind symmetry. They searched for the picturesque while recognising the need for precise measurements and the ordering of space. A regime of squares, it was almost universally felt, would make governance easier and more efficient, the landscape more legible, the calculation of revenue demand and crop output simpler. It would affirm the rationality of science and power of the colonisers. The agrarian conquest not only meant extending the arable, but also civilising the nomad and thereby forging the basis of an ideal agrarian order.

The map of the abadi (residential settlement) operated on the same logic. In contrast to traditional villages with irregular boundaries (see Fig. 10), colony settlements were planned within a grid of straight lines, with the chowk in the middle, rows of houses arranged in a series of concentric squares, and the residences of "lower" castes located on the periphery. Unlike the older settlements, which had usually come up around wells, the model colony villages were planned around a marketplace. Two sets of broad roads ran through each abadi at right angles, with narrower parallel lanes connecting the main roads. Each house was numbered and its location predefined.

The village was enclosed and bounded. It had one single entry point, one exit.[39] If this facilitated protection of the village, it equally made possible the easy surveillance and policing of inhabitants.

[38] For an early statement on the aesthetic of the picturesque, see Gilpin, *Three Essays*. For recent discussions, see Marshall, "The Problem of the Picturesque"; Townsend, "The Picturesque".

[39] Young criticised the first plan of the village in which there was more than one entry point. In his own model abadi he enclosed the village within

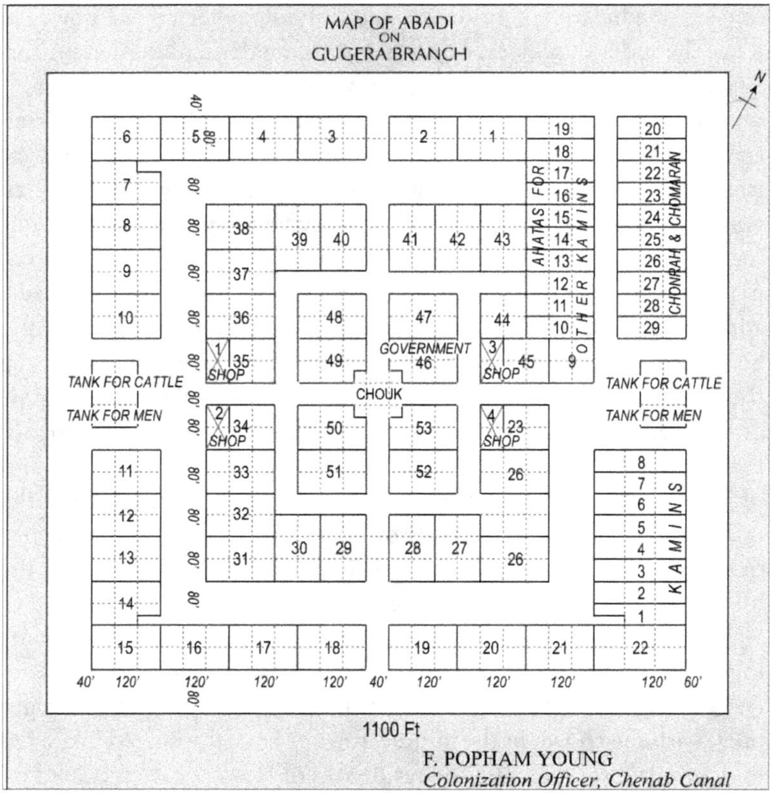

Fig. 19: Vision of Order: The Plan of a Canal Colony Abadi, 1898.
Source: Report on the Colonisation of the Government Waste Lands, *RLRAP, 1898*.

In the long term the order of squares proved an elusive ideal. The killa (1/25th part of a colony square – about 1.1 acres) did become a common measure, but individual fields on the ground could not be demarcated into neat squares. Sales and mortgages of part-holdings made it necessary to re-map field boundaries. In the process the regime of irregular plots reappeared and the lines on the cadastral

---

harder boundary lines. See Report on the Colonisation of the Government Waste Lands Commanded by the Chenab Canal, *RLRAP, 1898*.

maps became messy. As for the model abadis, they were simpler to plan than settle. In most places, grantees claimed their right over the residential sites – extending their control over as much land as they could get – but built their homesteads within their own individual cultivating squares. Locating the house at the centre of their large landholding allowed easier access to the fields and a smoother management of cultivation. Dismayed officials initially fretted at the intransigence of the grantees and threatened punitive measures to enforce compliance with rules. Then, after the plague epidemic of 1907, they persuaded themselves of the virtue of living in isolated houses. Co-residence in compacted settlements, they now declared, increased the possibility of a rapid spread of the epidemic. By 1911 they had conceded to a change in the norm itself.

Enclosing the Fields

From the mid nineteenth century the pastoralists of the bār had, as we have seen, found their movements restricted and their grazing lands converted into government rakhs. Their ideas of territory and sovereignty were under question and the authority of their chiefs was radically restructured. Now, in the closing years of the century, they saw their land being sliced up, reshaped into squares, and given over to people who descended in hordes from the world outside.[40] These outsiders cut down the scrub, grubbed up the roots, and cleared the land; they ploughed the fields and planted crops. Then fences appeared, marking one field from another and barring entry to "outsiders". The pastoralists were told to stop their cattle straying into cultivated fields, trampling crops, and destroying harvests. Suddenly they were outsiders on land they had for long seen as their own. The immigrants swarmed all over, outnumbered the locals, and asserted their monopoly over what till some years earlier had been the land of the nomads.

[40] The massive influx of peasants from the densely populated and intensively cultivated regions of Central Punjab dramatically transformed the demographic profile of the bār. In Lyallpur, one of the major colonies, the population increased from 60,000 in 1891 to 1,167,000 in 1931. This increase of over a million people was largely due to immigration.

Stories of enclosures and displacements, however, rarely unfold without drama. In 1919, an exasperated deputy commissioner of Lyallpur wrote to the Punjab government in despair: "A village of Aklake Khurral aborigines exists here in the centre of a nest of villages of Arain immigrant colonists. This village, 9 headstrong janglis, for 4 to 5 months habitually pastured 3000 cattle on the crops of all neighbouring chaks. They never allowed the cattle to get to the pound, and rescued and rioted whenever the immigrant colonists made any seizures."[41] Every attempt at rescue led to violent confrontations. Many immigrant peasants died. A punitive post was set up in the village, but G.F. Montmorency, the deputy commissioner, was sceptical of its efficacy. A system of roll calls could not tie the Kharrals to a life of innocence and order. Only a heavy communal fine, he believed, would stop such criminal villages from being a nuisance to the settled community.

As reports flowed in from the different regions, it became clear that the story of the Kharral villages was being re-enacted elsewhere in the Canal Colonies. Peasants from central Punjab, who had migrated to the colonies and begun cultivation, found their enclosed fields regularly invaded by cattle from neighbouring nomadic settlements. Cattle rescues led to bloodshed and complaints to officials provoked retribution. The cattle of immigrant peasants were poisoned and harvested crops burnt.[42] The police were as helpless as the peasants. Unable to check the cattle invasions, officials demanded that the

[41] Report of G.F. de Montmorency, Deputy Comm. Lyallpur, Punjab Home (Police), October 1910, A 57.

[42] On cattle poisoning and rick burning in Punjab, see Punjab Home (Police), March 1873, A 11. H. B. Urmstrong, Deputy Commissioner, Rawalpindi, had reported as early as 1873: "To such a pitch has the evil cowardly system now gone that the headmen of the whole country are most anxious to put it down, and have signed a memorial to that effect . . ." Village headmen demanded that in cases of poisoning the offending party should be made to pay for the cattle. But the problem was to identify the offender. In the politics of feuding, revenge and retribution had collective support. Most often, tribal groups were collectively implicated in the act and no-one gave any evidence against the offender.

turbulent nomads be classified as criminal tribes.[43] The severest action had to be taken against those who impeded the progress of colonisation and subverted the foundations of settled agrarian life in the bārs.

Cattle "trespass" as a problem was of course not peculiar to the Canal Colonies. By the mid nineteenth century, worried officials in various Indian regions were debating the need for legislative intervention to stop the evil. The Cattle Trespass Act was passed in 1871, but the clamour for more effective and stringent measures continued for decades. The problem was particularly acute in places where pastoral lands were being taken over for plantations or settled agriculture. In these transitional landscapes, the new order of rights could not be established without the trauma of dispossession and without negotiation and conflict.

In 1883 the tea planters of Wayanad in Calicut demanded a modification of the 1871 act.[44] Trespassing cattle were destroying their plantations, they claimed, and without punitive measures the damage would not be controlled. The existing provisions of the act were too mild and ineffective, the fines too low, and impounding cattle difficult. It was necessary, they felt, to enhance fines, punish attempted cattle rescues, brand all cattle that were more than eighteen months old, and shoot those that strayed into plantations.

---

[43] The nomadic Manes Jats and Vasir tribes residing in village Buddha in Lyallpur were declared criminal tribes in 1918. The charge against the Vasirs read: "The Vasirs, who a generation ago were nomads, own no land but keep large herds of cattle, which are a source of constant annoyance to the neighbouring colonists, in whose fields they trespass with impunity, owing to the dread with which their owners are generally regarded." The Manes Jats, a community of local nomads, had been given canal land, but they refused to settle, saw agriculture as a subsidiary occupation, and grazed their cattle on the cultivated fields of immigrant colonists. Punjab Home (Police), January 1918, A 285, p. 74. The Dhers, Kharrals, and Valana Jats of village Bahuman in Lahore district were notified as criminal tribes in 1907. Gazette Notification, 2 November 1907, Punjab Home (Police), November 1907, A 2. The Biloches in the south were declared criminal tribes.

[44] No. 2211, 11 June 1883, C.A. Galton, Acting District Magistrate of Malabar, to the Chief Sec. to Govt of Madras, GOI, Home (Judicial), December 1883, A 217.

Sensitive to planter interests and keen on establishing the sanctity of the new regime of rights, the GOI began a review of the act.
When in 1886 the planters petitioned once again, the GOI asked
local governments for reports on cattle trespass.[45] The need for some
amendment was widely recognised, but local officials feared the social
implications of harsh measures. With the expansion of the arable
and the contraction of pastures, they conceded, cattle grazing had
become a problem. In many areas, the villages of pastoralists and peasants were honeycombed together. Thoroughfares cut through villages
and the paths that cattle had to take daily to the grazing grounds ran
past cultivated lands. It was difficult to prevent them straying into
the grain fields, particularly when the fields were rarely fenced.[46] In
such a situation punitive action against unintentional straying could
create needless anger against the administration.[47]

Reports from many regions, in fact, suggested that it was the cattle
owners who needed protection from routine harassment.[48] The chief
commissioner of Assam asked for legal power to punish planters
and landholders for the illegitimate seizure and illegal detention of
cattle.[49] They were reportedly seizing any cattle grazing near their land
and holding on to the animals instead of driving them to the official
pound.[50] Graziers could not recover their cattle without paying the arbitrary amounts the planters demanded as compensation. Unless the
planters were restrained, the chief commissioner seemed to say, the
legitimacy of the legal regime itself would be subverted. True, trespass
had to be controlled and legitimate fines imposed, for only then could

[45] Punjab Home (Judicial), September 1886, A 1.

[46] No. 397, 19 October 1886, A. Anderson, Deputy Comm. Hissar, to
the Comm. and Sup., Delhi Div., Punjab Home (Judicial), July 1887, A 8.

[47] No. 347, 22 April 1887, R.E. Younghusband, Senior Sec., to Financial
Comm. Punjab, to the Sec. to GOP., ibid.

[48] For reports from different regions, see in particular GOI, Home (Judicial), January 1888, nos 66–132.

[49] Illegal detention of cattle by landholder and tea planters in Assam, Diary
no. 1041, the Chief Comm. of Assam, no. 2338, 17 August 1888, Home
(Judicial), September 1888, no. 147.

[50] According to rules the impounded cattle was to be driven to the pound
and the fines were to be charged by the pound keeper.

the new rights of property on common land gain legal sanction. But the efficacy of this legal regime would be undermined if publicly pronounced measures were persistently violated by planters and land-holders, if their illegal capture of cattle and extortionate demands to release them went unchecked.

The GOI was now caught in a bind. It was willing to deny the planters the penal powers they were clamouring for, but was reluctant to grant to local officials the power to punish planters under the Indian Penal Code.[51] A legal regime could not appear to be just un-less it disciplined capital, unless it defined the constraints within which everyone had to operate – but could it be so frontally turned against planters? The GOI manoeuvred its way out of the fix by simultaneously refusing the demands of the planters and the Assam chief commissioner. After consultations with the advocate general of Bengal and Madras, and a prolonged debate in the Legislative Department, the Assam chief commissioner was told that his re-quest could have no legal sanction.[52] And in 1888 the planters who had petitioned for greater punitive powers to stop trespass were in-formed by the GOI that their request for the amendment of the Trespass Act could not be accepted.[53]

Trespass was thus a category intimately connected to the new re-gime of rights, particularly in transitional zones. At one level, it ex-pressed the state's desire to settle the population, demarcate fields, and define the spatial limits of mobility. It was a category through

[51] In response to the request by the Assam chief commissioner for an amendment of the Cattle Trespass Act, 1871, ch. V, to allow prosecution of "illegal detention", the Secretary to GOI wrote: "I am directed to say that the Governor General in Council considers it desirable that it should be placed beyond doubt that the practice referred to ('illegal detention') does not render those who adopt it punishable under the Indian Penal Code." No. 1499, 17 September 1888, A.P. MacDonnel, Sec., GOI, to the Chief Comm., Assam, GOI, Home (Judicial), September 1888, no. 148.

[52] See the note titled Detention by Landholders and Tea Planters in Assam of Cattle Trespass on their Land, Diary 1422, Home Department, the Solicitor General to Govt., 19 December 1888, GOI, Home (Judicial), February 1889, no. 50. See also GOI, Home (Judicial), February 1889, A 51.

[53] GOI, Home (Judicial), May 1890, A 89.

which nomadism was to be restricted and criminalised. It signified a new process of territorialisation – a spatialisation of rights, the establishment of a regime in which spaces had to be tied to owners and property made sacrosanct. At another level, the outcry of the planters against trespass revealed the desire of capital to appropriate land as the exclusive sphere of its own operation, its refusal to tolerate other claims on such land.

In the Canal Colonies, however, the problem of cattle trespass had acquired an added dimension. It was the sign of a war between nomads and immigrant colonists. The Kharral cattle did not simply stray into the fields of the Arain cultivators, they were herded in there. It was a deliberate and performative act, flamboyantly executed, in defiance of the new territorialisation. Before British rule, as we have seen, the bār was under the control of different nomadic groups, each with their distinct areas of control. These were spaces within which the sovereignty of each group was exercised, and the hierarchy of power between the rāt and the jan worked out. In the eighteenth century, the Bharwana Sials controlled the Chenab bār in the west, the Kharrals were the masters of the central bār, the Bhattis ruled the Gujranwala bār in the north-east, and the Biloches were dominant in the south. Sial power was in decline by the early nineteenth century, but the Kharrals had pushed further north, helped the Waghas displace the Bhattis, and consolidated their power over the entire central bār. If the territory defined the limits of pasture, the limits of territory – always tenuous and fluid – were continuously negotiated through the politics of grazing and raiding.

With British annexation, the bār was first taken over as government waste, then colonised and settled. Faced with state power, the nomadic chiefs were forced to accept their new position as tirni guzars, and collected the grazing tax (tirni) for the state. But they hated the loss of their power, their territory, their sovereignty, and their grazing lands. In 1857 the great Ravi tribes led by Ahmad Khan, a Kharral chief of Jhamra, rose in rebellion. When this revolt, which became known as the Gugeira revolt, was ultimately crushed by the British army, the rebels were cut to pieces, their villages burnt, their cattle tracked down in the jungles and slaughtered.[54] The civilising state re-enacted in macabre and perverse fashion the logic of tribal feuds.[55]

The rebellion failed but the war continued. It was a daily, unrelenting war against the new rules and new demarcation of spaces, against the new regime of canals and cultivated fields. Within the political culture of the nomads, outsiders could gain entry into a nomadic territory either through war or by submitting to the chief who controlled that space – else the presence of aliens subverted the very idea of territoriality. By the late nineteenth century the cultivated field had appeared as the symbol of the new regime, the visible marks of the radical re-territorialisation. Hemmed in from all sides, surrounded by Arain villages, the Kharrals were now unable to move freely between their summer and winter pastures, from the uplands to the lowlands, or enter the jungles in times of drought when the open pastures withered.[56] The killas that demarcated the fields and the rakhs now marked the lines the nomads could not cross without trespassing. By herding their cattle into cultivated fields and allowing them to pasture

[54] For an account of the Gugeira rebellion, see Cave-Brown, *The Punjab and Delhi in 1857*. The author was a chaplain of the Punjab Movable Column in 1857. See also Andrew Major, *Return to Empire*, ch. VI; *Mutiny Records: Reports*, part 2, pp. 40–64.

[55] A chaplain of the Punjab Movable Column in 1857 tells us that Major Chamberlain, unable to pursue the rebels who retreated across the Ravi, inflicted "the only punishment that was open to him". The rebels had driven off their herds, their main source of wealth, into the jungles. Chamberlain employed professional trackers to trace the herds, rounded up over 2300 cattle and thousands of sheep and goat, and butchered them. To the chaplain, this was undoubtedly the deliberate restaging of a tribal drama: "Thus in the midst of the Punjab was re-enacted on a gigantic scale the old scene so often performed by the rival lairds of the Scottish borders." Cave-Brown, *The Punjab and Delhi in 1857*, vol. II, p. 218. A mimic restaging is, of course, never the same as the original. The violence of a practice within the logic of the feud acquires new meaning when it becomes part of the politics of counter-insurgency.

[56] Classified in British ethnographic records of Punjab as "market gardeners", Arains were seen as good colonists and welcomed to the Canal Colonies.

on crops, the Kharrals were asserting their right over lost space. The Arains were seen as usurpers, outsiders who had to be displaced. The illegitimacy of their claims had to be visibly and overtly challenged.

If cattle trespass emerged as a major crime within the colonial rule of property and signified new territorial rights, its persistence reflected the effort of the nomads to question and renegotiate these new notions of rights, property, and spatiality. The process of negotiation shaped not only the relations of nomads with migrant peasants and the state, it specified the meaning of property. The rights associated with property were not all embedded in the term itself, specified in the grants of land that were given to the colonists.

A New Language of Claims

The war against immigrant colonists continued through the colonial period. Their crops were ruined by invading herds, their harvests burnt by night, their fences demolished, their cattle poisoned with arsenic or carried away in large numbers, their villages regularly raided. Silent resistance, enacted offstage and in the anonymity of darkness, thus combined with collective actions that were theatrically performed and provocatively executed. It was an undeclared war against the new ideas of territoriality and agrarian order, the new notions of normality and legality, the colonisation of the bārs by immigrants, and the new rule of property.

Yet at another level a different process was at work. By the early twentieth century we can hear a different language of negotiation expressed in petitions to officials, articulated in local newspapers, and later by the 1920s asserted on the floor of legislative assemblies. This was a language of rights that accepted the founding premises of the new order and demanded space within it. It narrated painful stories of displacement, suffering, and distress, and asked for justice. At times it defended the right of pastoral groups to live in harmony with times past: to be nomads, retain control over their animals even if not their sovereignty within spaces they saw as their territory. But more often, it claimed the right of the nomads to a life of dignity within the new set-up. It protested not against colonisation as such but against the specific form in which the project was implemented. Here is Sayad Muhammad Khan of Montgomery during a 1929 debate on allotments of grants in the Nili Bār Colony:

> I stick to my old principle that the sons of the soil should get precedence over others in all claims for grants. These are the people who are born and bred there, these are the people who had been earning their bread there and these are the people who have been living there from time immemorial, and now that land is made irrigable, is it fair, is it just and is it equitable that these sons of the soil should be turned out of their holdings, that they should be turned out of their hearths and homes and that they should be sent to some remoter corner, simply because they are not good cultivators? I ask, is that a right principle for the Government to follow. Is it right, Sir, that the sons of the soil should be turned out from this place for facilitating people who are much more advanced educationally, economically, and morally, to receive their share in the colonies.[57]

This is no defence of the nomadic pastoral life. Muhammad Khan sees irrigation as progress, the expansion of cultivation as desirable, and peasants as superior to nomads in every way. He does not celebrate the past against the present, the reason of the nomads against that of a sedentarist state, the trajectory of smooth and open spaces against striated ones. But he questions the principles on which allotments are being granted. Using the language of equity and justice, he pleads for the claims of the "janglis" within the new order, he recounts their anguish and misery. Operating through the discourse of indigeneity, he projects the nomads as sons of the soil, tracing their rights back into the mists of time, to the originary mythic moment of creation when the bārs were supposedly settled. Aware that colonial laws generally recognised the rights of the original settlers, Muhammad Khan transforms the nomads into abadkars (those who settled the land – the original settlers) who, he claims, had cleared the land and settled on it. It was as if nomadism and mobility could not be the basis of any rights over space. The critique of government policy was at the same time an affirmation of the colonial agrarian vision. This dialectic between critique and affirmation has a contradictory logic: it transforms as well as naturalises what it affirms.

[57] *Punjab Legislative Council Debates, 1929.*

Much before this discourse of indigeneity acquired rhetorical power, colonisation had become a site of negotiation. By the end of the nineteenth century, as cattle theft and cattle trespass became endemic, and cattle raids led to riots, it was clear that the policy of colonisation required rethinking. The original colonisation project was based on a radical hostility towards the nomads. They were seen as lazy, rebellious, violent, turbulent, imprudent, and thieving. With their dislike of cultivation, love of mobility, and proclivity for crime, it was said they could not be pioneering colonists. They had to be displaced, watched, and disciplined.

Gradually, it was reluctantly admitted that the refusal to allot land to the "janglis" was unjust and unfair: they had to be given grants even if they were bad cultivators. As the settlement officer of the Chenab Colony said in 1903: "it was only a bare act of justice to acknowledge their claims."[58] But once they were given grants, officials found it difficult to sustain the stereotypes through which they perceived the "janglis". They soon recognised – with a sense of surprise – that the "janglis" were proving to be good colonists.[59] Their lands were carefully cultivated, their villages clean and well kept, their animals properly groomed. After the success of the grants to the "janglis" in the Chenab Colony, officials decided to replicate the experiment in the other colonies that were coming up. But stereotypes are tenacious. And when they become the foundation of a social vision, they acquire amazing resilience. Many officials grudgingly accepted the need to accommodate the demands of the nomads, but saw it only as a pragmatic move necessary for peace and order. The anger of the rebellious nomads could not be controlled without conceding them space within the new order. But could they be seen as either fine cultivators or good subjects?

Caught in a bind, officials both accepted and denied the claims of

[58] *Annual Report of the Chenab Colony, 1903–4.*

[59] Reviewing the developments in the Jhelum Colony, J. Wilson, Settlement Commissioner, noted in a marginal comment that the "janglis" had "in a surprisingly short time, adopted an agricultural mode of life in place of their old wandering pastoral life, and are making very good colonists." *Annual Report of the Jhelum Colony, 1901–2.*

the "janglis". When Muhammad Khan declared that the indigenous population, the sons of the soil, had first claim to colony lands, the financial commissioner sneered at the idea:

> I cannot accept the honourable member's proposition that the local people have the first claim on the Crown waste that becomes available after colonisation. The Government are the trustees of this underdeveloped wealth, which is the property of the province as a whole. The first consideration must be to get the land colonised by the best cultivators in the province. Local people in Montgomery and Multan, are not I am afraid particularly famous as good cultivators. In fact many of them are really not cultivators at all. However, as I have stated, the Government did recognise that it is only fair that the local people should have a certain proportion of land and as long ago as 1913 and 1914.[60]

Craik could not entirely reject the claims of the "janglis" but was unwilling to acknowledge them as ideal colonists. In a familiar move, he deployed the rhetoric of the greatest common good to deny the prerogatives of the indigenous population and justify their displacement as a historically necessary act. If colonisation was a collective good and the peasants of central Punjab the ideal colonists, dispossessing the "janglis" was unavoidable in the general interests of the population.

The developing contradiction within the colonising project was even more evident in the way service grants were allotted. Worried by the shrinking supply of camels, horses, and mules for the army, and the disappearance of pastures with the progress of irrigation, the colonial state had to rework the project of colonisation. But how could the supplies of horses and camels be expanded without encouraging nomadic pastoralism? How could dry lands be irrigated and the animal stock of the region reproduced at the same time? The idea of service grants proposed by the Horse Breeding Commission provided one seeming solution to the contradiction. It dissociated animal breeding from nomadism, tied breeders to land, and linked animal husbandry to cultivation. In the Jhelum colonies 402,000 acres out of a total allocable area of 540,000 acres were originally set aside as peasant

---

[60] *Punjab Legislative Council Debates, 1929.*

grants.[61] At the suggestion of the Horse Breeding Commission of 1901, it was decided that this entire area, 74 per cent of the total, would be given out as service grants for horse breeding.[62] Each grantee would be required to cultivate the land as well as maintain a broodmare for every square (twenty-eight acres) allotted. The prior claim of the government over the animal stock was written into the condition of the grant.[63] Animal breeders just as much as cultivators had to be settled, confined within bounded governable spaces, subject to observation, survey, enumeration, and control.

But who was to get the horse-breeding grant? Was it to be the pastoralist who proclaimed his will to settle and cultivate, or the peasant who agreed to maintain a broodmare? The gathering local anger against the influx of immigrants persuaded the state to create more space within the colony for west Punjab inhabitants. But it was still reluctant to open this space to the pastoral nomads. In the months of March, April, and May 1902 J.H.R. Fraser, acting on behalf of the colonising officer of the Jhelum Colony, selected the first batch of 1000 for horse-breeding grants. The grantees were all peasants from Shahpur, Gujrat, and Gujranwala districts. "The peasant colonists so far selected," reported Fraser later in the year, "are nearly all men of the agricultural class, and care has been exercised in taking as far as possible only men who cultivate with their own hands."[64] Peasants who were willing to buy a mare were given land, though they neither had any experience with breeding nor any real desire to be

[61] No. 56, 11 May 1901, to GOI, in *Annual Report of the Jhelum Colony, 1901–2*.

[62] Financial Commisssioner's Letter no. 7101, 23 November 1901, ibid. See also GOP, no. 145, 4 September 1902, ibid.

[63] Initially the size of the ghorapal abadkar grant was one-and-a-half square (42 acres); this was soon increased to two square (56 acres). See no. 793 S, 14 July 1902, App. A, *Annual Report of the Jhelum Colony, 1901–2*. Also GOP Letter no. 471 S, 14 July 1902, *Annual Report of the Jhelum Colony, 1902–3*, p. 24; GOP, no. 589 S, 23 June 1903; and GOP, no. 1829 S, 9 September 1903, ibid.

[64] *Annual Report of the Jhelum Colony, 1901*, p. 24. See also Fraser to Settlement Commissioner, no. 134, 27 July 1902.

breeders.[65] Yet, a year after the first round of allotment, the colonising officer criticised the laxity with which the grantees had been selected and underlined the need to be even more vigilant about excluding the "janglis" from horse-breeding grants.[66] Within the ideal colony of the colonial imagination, even horse breeding had to be the responsibility of settled peasants. The willingness of nomads to settle was always suspect.[67]

As the clamour for local grants intensified, settlement officers had to reduce the area of colony land that was granted to outsiders. But they still discriminated between landowners and nomads, excluding the "janglis" from the best canal lands and favouring the big landowners of west Punjab for the service grants.[68] Allotments to

[65] The Colonisation Officer of course imagined that peasants could be transformed into breeders, but this hope was marked by a deep uncertainty: "It remains to be seen how this class will prove to be successful horse breeders. As self-cultivating zamindars they are accustomed to dealing with cattle, and know something about live-stock generally, but it will rest with the officers of the Remount Department to teach them the high art of breeding horses." *Annual Report of the Jhelum Colony, 1902–3*, p. 27.

[66] *Annual Report of the Jhelum Colony, 1902–3*, p. 27.

[67] It was as if, inscribed with the marks of a nomadic past, shaped by the culture of mobility, pastoralists lived forever in an enchanted past of mythic freedom. Even when keen on a space within the new order, they were emotively tied to the old. Carrying out the allotment operation in the Lower Bari Doab, E. Joseph, the Colonisation Officer, declared: "the Janglis while eagerly pressing even for such land as we give, and besieging us for inclusion in the lists, look regretfully back on the days when they were free to follow their camels from place to place and obtained from time to time permission to cultivate a few acres below the *dhaya* (raised ground near the river) in some favourably low ground where, if there was any rain at all, a food crop of wheat could be grown with little labour; the reward was great and the revenue light." *RLBDCC, 1913–14*, para 3.

[68] In the Jhelum Colony, when the allotment policy was rethought after 1901, 74 per cent of the total allocable area, reserved initially for peasant grants, was given out as service grants for horse breeding. But the "janglis" received only 15 per cent of this area. The rest went to powerful local Biloch landowning gentry, and influential local men like the zaildars, haqdars, and inamdars. *Report of the Jhelum Colony, 1902–3*. In the Lower Bari Doab, the

"janglis" were usually smaller in size than to landowners.[69] They were mostly located on poor-quality land in marginal areas, at a distance from the perennial canals, or at the end of distributaries, where water supply was erratic. The prime land on the perennial canals, near the head, was reserved for the "ideal colonists" – industrious and enterprising peasants from central Punjab. The explosive implication of this politics of discrimination became apparent as the geography of grants came to overlap with the maps of social conflict.

Promise and Betrayal

Awal sain sachche nun saran	First I will remember the true lord
Ik qissa nawan aj joran	I will tell a new tale today.
Bar agge lut khadi choran	Of the old Bār that was the prey of thieves
Harn, gidar, chuhehan dian ghoran	A tract where deer, jackals, and rats roamed
Sunjan jangal koi nahi raha	Now no barren jungle is left
Young Sahib diya mulk wasa	Young Sahib has peopled the land.
Lyallpur da sun tun hal	Hear the tale of Lyallpur
Ann jal da jithe sokal	Where grain and water abound
Nahr wahundi darwaze nal	The canal runs by gateways
Drakht lawae pal-o-pal	Trees have been planted in rows
Hor pae jamde sawe gha	And green grass comes sprouting up.
Young Sahib diya mulk wasa	Young sahib has peopled the land.

These are lines from a long ballad of forty-three stanzas that a blind poet, Kana, sung when Captain Popham Young, the colonising officer of the Chenab Colony, left Lyallpur in 1899.[70] The ballad tells the

---

"janglis" and Hitharis were allotted only 26 per cent of the 680,000 acres set aside as horse- and mule-breeding areas. *RLBDCC, 1913–14.*

[69] In the Jhelum Colony, for instance, "jangli" grants of cultivated lands were 5 acres of poor quality land as opposed to the usual 28 or 56 acres in the case of all peasant grants. As service grants, the "janglis" and Hitharis received half a square (14 acres) while the Biloch landowning gentry of agricultural castes was given 2 squares (56 acres) each. *Annual Report of the Jhelum Colony, 1902–3.*

[70] We do not know whether the poet was entirely blind as the record claims,

tale of a grand agrarian conquest. In language suffused with a sense of wonder and fascination, it describes how a wild and desolate land was turned into a land of plenty, overflowing with grain, well supplied with water, adorned with trees. This extraordinary transformation was made possible only through the incredible and mythopoeic powers of the British. They created the colony, tamed the wilderness, and peopled the land; they diverted the river, dug a canal that was straight as an arrow (*jin dita darya nun chirae, nahr kadhai siddhi tir ae*), built a weir, dammed the river, cleared the brushwood, mapped the bār, measured the land, connected the place with railways and the telegraph, established markets, and gave land to the Sikhs. They were not only heroic and mighty (*Angrez bahadur bhara bir ae*), they were capable of achieving the impossible. Like saints, they could perform miracles: in a moment they could make the jungle disappear (*Eh Angrez aulia zarur, Sach man ozara na kur, Pal wich jangal kita dur*). They made no empty promises: they fulfilled them. They were true to their word (*ikko waida sachchi bat*).

The words of Kana were reassuring to colonial ears. We see them tirelessly reproduced in official records as evidence of "the impression that the colony made on native minds."[71] The ballad reaffirmed the self-image of the colonisers as aggressive agents of progress, bringing nature into culture and domesticating the landscape through the application of science and reason. It celebrated both the "unbelievable transformation" in the Canal Colonies and the miraculous power of the British. The promise that Kana refers to is the promise of paradise that British officials inevitably made when persuading zamindars from the old districts to migrate to the colonies.

Was Kana capturing the universal experience of those who migrated to the colonies in search of paradise? Barely eight years after Captain Popham Young left, Lyallpur became the centre of an intense social movement that called into question each term of Kana's celebratory

---

and whether he was translating into poetry the experience of the colony as he had heard others narrate. His name, Kana, suggests he was one-eyed.

[71] *Gazetteer of the Chenab Colony, 1904*, pp. 34–5. See also Dobson, *Chenab Colony S.R., 1915.* Penny, *Lyallpur S.R., 1925.*

narrative of colonisation. In December 1906 a Colonisation Bill was introduced and hurriedly passed in the Punjab Legislative Council.[72] It sought to amend the Punjab Colonisation of Land Act 1893. When the Chenab Colony was being settled in the early 1890s, the British were keen to create an ideal agrarian landscape free of absentee land-lordism, minute plots, unirrigated fields, and unsanitary surroundings. Peasant grantees were given large holdings – 28 to 56 acres – but to ensure a measure of control over them they were made crown tenants and denied proprietary rights. They were expected to live in the abadi, not in their farms, and maintain clean surroundings; they could not be absent for long periods or leave the colony without prior per-mission.

Within some years the British discovered the difficulty of pro-ducing the landscape of their imagination. The colonists were building their homesteads within their farms, resisting living in the abadi, disappearing for long periods, and transferring their land in accordance with the customary practices of the old districts. When the colonisation officer began confiscating grants and imposing fines for non-compliance of conditions, angry colonists grumbled and protested, often challenging his actions in court. The Colonisation Act of 1906 was formulated to extend the disciplinary reach of the state, legalise the regime of confiscation and fines, and introduce a set of new terms within the old agreements. The colonists were now required to practice primogeniture, plant trees on their farms, and maintain a broodmare for supply of horses to the government. The patriarchal power of the colonisation officer was consolidated by making his actions sub judice.

As the terms of the bill came to be known, anxious settlers began mobi-lising opinion, organising meetings, drafting memorials, and peti-tioning officials against the bill. Newspapers carried angry letters and articles detailing the complaints of the settlers, narrating their ex-perience – some written by colonists, others speaking on their behalf. Energetic mobilisation was reflected through growing numbers in the

---

[72] For a discussion of the official debate on the bill, see Barrier, "The Punjab Disturbances of 1907".

meetings. On 14 January 1907 about 300 zamindars from 24 villages met in Samundari tahsil and resolved to draft a memorial that was to be submitted to the Legislative Council.[73] Thirteen days later, on 27 January, over 3000 zamindars assembled at Sangla to protest against the bill.[74] At a grand meeting organised in Lyallpur on 3 February, as many as 8000 zamindars of the Chenab Canal collected.[75] The premises of the Arya Samaj, where the meeting was held, overflowed with people sitting on walls and roofs of buildings, clogging the streets and immobilising traffic. Through the month, the Bar Zamindar Association carried on an intense campaign against the bill, appealing to the Jat sense of honour and justice, and stirring them to action. On 22 and 23 March another mammoth meeting was held in Lyallpur in which over 9000 colonists gathered.[76] By the end of March the agitation spread from Chenab to Jhelum, with nationalist leaders like Lala Lajpat Rai and Ajit Singh addressing meetings, touring the rural areas, seeking to integrate the movement in the Canal Colonies into the wider anti-imperialist struggle.[77]

Two different discourses merged and separated in the language of protest that developed around the Colonisation Bill. One was a discourse of morality and ethics. Worried and agitated zamindars repeatedly asked: how could the government dishonour its word, its promises, its assurances? Till now, declared one polemicist, everyone agreed that the British government with all its problems was "sure to stand firm to an agreement that it has once formally made".[78] This conviction was now rudely shaken. The government had subverted the premises of trust and faith. How could zamindars now rely on the word of the government?

[73] *Tribune*, 15 January 1907.

[74] The meeting was announced by Hakim Singh, Joint Secretary of the Bār Zamindars Association, in the pages of the *Zamindar*, 16 January 1907; *Light*, 30 January 1907, *RNNP*, 2 February 1907 (all subsequent references to *Zamindar* and *Light* are from *RNNP*); *Tribune*, 1 February 1907.

[75] *Tribune*, 7 February 1907.

[76] *Zamindar*, 24 March 1907; *Punjabee*, 27 March 1907.

[77] *Zamindar*, 3 May 1907.

[78] *Tribune*, 15 February 1905.

Beyond the moral politics of trust and good faith was the question of law. Drawing upon the legal discourse that colonial officials operated with, pedagogues and publicists, lawyers and zamindars all warned the government against violating assurances that had been not only verbally stated but also formally codified, embodied in agreements that were in fact like contracts.[79] Colonial officials, inspired by Benthamite ideals, had emphasised for long that fixed rules and codified laws were the necessary basis of security, stability, and rational order, and that these allowed the formation of secure expectations and rational calculations. How could such ideas be jettisoned? In a powerful critique of the Colonisation Bill, Harbhajan Singh, a pleader, reminded the government of the meaning of contract: once a contract was made and its conditions specified, no party was entitled "to vary or modify it without the consent of the other party to it".[80] On what basis then could the government arbitrarily and unilaterally change the terms of the colony grants with retrospective effect, modifying the original conditions? The terms could be changed in future, when fresh grants were given on newly colonised lands – though even those ought not to be oppressive – but new clauses could not be written into the conditions of earlier grants.[81] The message was forcefully underlined by the Bar Zamindar Association that met on 27 January:

> In the opinion of this meeting the Government has no justification to alter, amend or add to the conditions of written agreements under which lands were granted in Colonies; and it is unworthy of Government to make even the slightest alteration in formal agreements entered into with the colonists . . . Though the Government is at liberty to make any conditions for future grants of Government lands, yet it is desirable that the rules for future colonies be not stringent.[82]

[79] *Zamindar*, 8 January 1907; *Tribune* 12 January 1907; *Siraj-ul-Akhbar* (Jhelum), *RNNP*, 5 February 1907.

[80] *Tribune*, 15 February 1907.

[81] Ibid.

[82] *Tribune*, 1 February 1907; see also *Zamindar*, 30 January 1907; *Light*, 30 January 1907. The zamindars' meeting at Lyallpur on 3 February 1907 declared in their resolution that the bill was improper, unconstitutional, violated contracts, and unjustly subjected old grantees to new liabilities. It altered

The argument was reiterated with polemical vigour in the *Zamindar*, a newspaper that claimed to represent the opinions of the rural proprietary body. If the Colonisation Bill was to be introduced, declared the *Zamindar*, government assurances would no longer be believed and contracts would lose their sanctity. The promises of the government would be seen as part of a deliberate strategy of deception.[83] It would appear that the government had seduced the people with false promises – persuading them to migrate to an alien land, leave their families and ancestral homes, bear the expenses and rigours of early colonisation, only to then change the terms of settlement once the new colonies had come up and the soil begun to yield.[84] Such deception and breach of faith could only create a popular climate of distrust and suspicion, destroying the authority of the government.[85]

As the theme of deception and bad faith was elaborated, the story of colonisation was recast as a narrative of suffering and heroism, of promise and betrayal. When the Chenab Canal Colony was being developed, 150 families from Batala in Gurdaspur were among the

---

the rules of succession against the provisions of personal and customary law, proposed penal punishments for small offences, provided no check against the offences of officers, and unfairly denied proprietary rights to grantees. *Tribune*, 7 February 1907.

[83] *Zamindar*, 12 January 1907.

[84] Dwelling on this theme of seduction and deception, one poem published in *Zamindar* explained how the cancellation of "all previous contracts had frustrated the hopes entertained by the colonists and created feelings of distrust and suspicion." *Zamindar*, 8 March 1907; see also the wider reporting from other papers in *RNNP*, 16 March 1907.

[85] One writer wrote in the *Tribune*: "The Bill if passed into law is likely to shake the confidence of the people in the integrity and good faith of official transactions which will be disastrous to the good name of and prestige of the Government." *Tribune*, 9 February 1907. Another writer declared that it would rudely destroy the implicit faith in the benevolent intentions of the rulers and provoke a massive social conflagration: "This measure if allowed to stand shall give rise to agitation and irritation through out the whole of Punjab the like of which was never witnessed in this quiet land of the five rivers." *Tribune*, 15 February 1907.

first migrants to reach Jhang. Louise Dane had personally told them "that the land they were going to would be found overflowing with milk and honey."[86] All had been told they would get large fields, plenty of water through the year, and well-connected markets; taxes would be light, harvests secure, and prosperity plentiful. When the migrants reached their destination in 1892 they could see only a vast landscape of aridity, a desolate scrubland covered with wild farash, jand, and lana. Water channels were yet to be dug and for many years the supply of water was erratic and inadequate. The rainfall was good in the first year and large tracts of the land were cleared and broken up; but by July a cholera epidemic had spread and then a malignant fever had prostrated the population. In 1891–2, a total of 7605 peasant grantees received their allotments, 6453 took possession, and of these 914 left never to return.[87] In the subsequent year the story was similar: about 151,865 acres were given out to peasant settlers, but 47,061 acres, or about a third, remained unoccupied.[88] Disappointed migrants enervated by illness and frightened by the wilderness, unwilling to believe the colonising officers, returned to the security of familiar surroundings in their home villages.

If we move from the Chenab to the Jhelum Colony the story is no different. A migrant settler in the Jhelum Colony, recounting in 1910 the experience of the early years of colonisation, replayed the same theme of promise and betrayal. Before the grants were given, we are told, the colonisation officer "so highly eulogised the quality of soil that the colonists thought that it was veritable Eldorado."[89] Only later did the settlers realise that "the so-called fertile land was no better than a series of mounds of sand with patches of land of

---

[86] Many years later, in 1910, inaugurating the Punjab Agricultural College at Lyallpur, Dane recounted with pride how he persuaded the colonists to move. *Khalsa Advocate*, 23 December 1910. For an interesting account of the experiences of a pioneer from Ludhiana, Sunder Shiam Singh, see the oral narrative of his grandson, Pritam Singh Grewal, recorded in Darshan S. Tatla, "Sandal Bar: Memories of a Punjabi Farmer".

[87] *RCGWCC, 1891–92*, in *RLRAP, 1891–92*, App. E.

[88] *RCGWCC, 1892–93*, in *RLRAP, 1892–93*, App. E.

[89] *Zamindar*, 8 March 1910.

worthless quality." Disenchanted but undeterred, the pioneers cleared and ploughed the land, sparing themselves no pain and hardship to bring the land under cultivation, converting the "once barren and desolate country . . . into a luxuriantly verdant field."[90] But the problems of the colonists continued. The water supply was so miserable and unpredictable that even in 1910 the standing wheat crop was drying up. Worst affected were the lands located at the tail end of the canal that rarely got any water. While crops withered and harvests failed, revenue officers refused to remit revenue and the state imposed new water rates, adding to the colonists' burden. In addition to the land revenue and water rates, the colonists were subjected to a range of levies: unpaid labour for digging channels and dredging canals, arbitrary fines for non-conformity with conditions of grants, tips for the patwari and the tahsildar.[91] As the protest against the bill intensified, and the catalogue of suffering grew ever longer, the Canal Colonies were refigured as a place of dire danger. We hear of the constant threat of natural calamities, the fear of wild animals and snakes, unrelenting attacks by "savage janglis", the oppression of sahukars, patwaris, and lambardars.[92]

Narratives of suffering fused with stories of heroism to doubly underline the injustice of British action in altering the terms of the settlement. The pioneer settlers, we are told, faced a hostile environment

[90] Ibid.

[91] *Zamindar* claimed that the settlers had to pay fourteen lakhs as fine and four times that amount as tips to the patwaris. *Zamindar*, 6 December 1907. This probably was an inflated and arbitrary figure. We are not told of the source and basis of the calculation, nor are we informed about the number of years over which this amount was supposed to have been collected. (Who collected information about tips to the patwari?!) But such estimates had a rhetorical function. They were meant to underline the enormity of the fiscal burden, concretise the image of suffering and injustice, and create an image of facticity.

[92] One colonist from the Jhelum Canal wrote: "the poor agriculturists are exposed to all sorts of calamities . . . they have to remain in constant fear of plague, famine, cholera, to say nothing of the pests which ruin crops. The overbearing constable, the meek sahukar, the tahsil orderly, the cringing lambardars and the greedy Zaildar, all vie with one another in putting them to trouble." *Zamindar*, 8 October 1907.

and suffered immense hardship but confronted all problems, worked hard in savage surroundings to transform a wilderness into a productive landscape.[93] Many died, many lost links with their families, but the pioneers went on undaunted to create life in the colonies. It was as if the sacrifices and heroism of the pioneers sanctified their relationship to the land and made the original contracts doubly sacred. To alter those terms now would be an act of horrific betrayal and treachery.

The image of the Canal Colonies that these narratives suggest is radically different from the one offered in Kana's ballad. Kana deifies the British, imbues them with creativity, represents them as the heroic agents of progress, resourcefulness, and ingenuity; in the counter-narrative the settlers are the real heroes, pioneers who tame the wilderness and make it productive with their industry, skill, and courage. In one narrative, the landscape that the early settlers confront in the Canal Colonies is a land of promise, bearing all the marks of progress and development – canals, markets, railways, the telegraph; in the other it is a landscape of savagery and desolation, of danger and death. In one story the British appear as benevolent, selfless, honest, and trustworthy, always honouring their word, caring for the populace; in the other they are seen as violating their promises, dishonouring their commitments, and manipulating poor zamindars. The complicated and contradictory association between these images continued to mediate the relationship between the zamindars and the British in the Canal Colonies.

The contrary voices had one element in common. Both represented the mind of agrarian settlers whose fortunes were linked to the

---

[93] In the pioneering lore of later years, this picture of a hostile landscape recurred, underlining the heroism of the pioneers. In the last years of imperial rule, Malcolm Darling, riding through the Canal Colonies, asked Maharaja Singh, one of the first 140 migrants to Lyallpur, about his initial impressions of the place. Singh said that the country was "all waste but dotted with jand trees, snakes lifting angry heads, enormous scorpions, and not a bird to be seen." In addition to all this was the trouble created by the "janglis". Darling, *At Freedom's Door*, p. 79. These images of danger, fear, poison, death, and desolation appeared in most accounts that Darling heard from the colonists.

expansion of the arable, the colonisation of the pastoral commons. Dispossessed of their pastures and displaced from their fields, most local inhabitants of the region – pastoralists and peasants – experienced the history of this colonisation as a time of violence and repression. Only the power of a small section of the landed aristocracy was reaffirmed.[94]

Antinomies of Development

In the *Canal Colonies Report* of 1933 we read the following account of what colonisation had meant for the bār tracts:

> The year has been one of real progress. The open spaces of the desert have everywhere been portioned out in meticulous rectangles; jungle trees have been felled, and the wandering camel-tracks of the waste have given place to the durable macadam of public roads, running for miles without a curve and without a gradient. The goat-herd's pipe and the quavering love-song of the camel men are mute, and in their place we hear the Klaxon of the motor-lorry and the folding harmonium of the peripatetic preacher. The reed encampments of the nomads, their jhoks and rahnas, open to sun and wind and clean as a dancing-floor, have been replaced by the midden-infested mud-houses of the central Punjab. The nomad himself, once free of the Bār and of his neighbour's cattle, has been pegged out, Prometheus like on his 25 killas, while the vultures of civilisation bury their ravenous beaks in his vitals.[95]

A passage that sets out to recount a story of progress ends up capturing the pathos of development. The official mind, captivated by the idea of settlement, convinced of the need for agrarian conquest, struggles to free itself from the allure of a pastoral imagination. Caught in a bind, it vacillates between two worlds, two visions which refuse to blend into any kind of coherence. Settlement is celebrated and feared, seen as necessary as well as tragic; it is a civilising process, but also signifies disease and death. Nomadism was a thing of the past, part of a world that had to be transformed; but it was equally a metaphor for freedom. The nostalgia for open spaces and the silence

[94] See Ali, *The Punjab Under Imperialism.*

[95] *Canal Colonies Report of the Sutlej Valley, 1933*, quoted in *Montgomery D.G.*, pp. 58–9.

of the desert, the romance of the shepherd's flute and the camelman's love songs contrast with the cacophony of modern urban spaces. The desire for rational ordering clashes with the Romantic's fear of monotony and repetitiveness.

Year after year, the *Colonies Reports* catalogued progress in the colonies. They spoke of the problems of measurement and allotment of land, the hitches in distributing water, the difficulties in persuading colonists to cultivate the crops they were contracted to produce, but they also narrated how these problems were all overcome to ensure development. Yet there were times when these narratives broke down, subverted by evidence that resisted explanation within the terms of these heroic teleologies of colonial achievement, questioned by anxious imperial voices that expressed self-doubt. For every official who congratulated the British for their success in creating the landscape of their imagination, there were others who filed reports on increased salinity in waterlogged canal areas and the steady fragmentation of the land of the colonists.[96]

Optimists had no problem stitching together a story of unmitigated progress. The creation of the Canal Colonies did lead to a dramatic extension of the area under cultivation. Uncultivated pastoral tracts gave way to verdant fields. In Lyallpur district alone over 1.47 million acres were brought under the plough by 1916–17. Almost the entire area, about 99 per cent, was irrigated, most of it watered by the new canals. By 1931, a total of very nearly 10 million irrigated acres were being cultivated in the Canal Colonies. Officials could look around with satisfaction and see irrigated fields covered with wheat in rabi (spring harvest) and cotton in kharif (autumn harvest). Since the 1860s Britain had been keen on reducing its crippling dependence

---

[96] See *Water-logging of the Soil in the Vicinity of Punjab Irrigation*; Lindley, *An Estimate of the Areas Affected By, and Threatened With, Water-Logging*; Taylor, Malhotra, and Mehta, *Investigation of the Rise of Water-Table in the Upper Chenab Canal Area*; Pearson, *Notes on Water-logging in the Punjab*, 2 vols, 3 pts. A Waterlogging Board was set up and from 1928 regular conferences on the problem were held. See *Water-logging Board, Punjab: Proceedings of Meetings, 1928–36*, vols 1–5; *Proceedings of the Water-logging Conference, 1928–38*, annual.

on America for supplies of wheat and cotton. By the late nineteenth century the expansion of acreage under these crops in India had come up against barriers, and officials had been desperately looking for "virgin" lands where these crops could be grown. In the Canal Colonies they hoped to produce American cotton and American wheat without being dependent on America. As Lyallpur developed, wheat came to occupy 77 per cent of the area under foodgrains in 1904–5 and about 80 per cent in 1939–40.[97] By 1920–1 over 250,690 acres in Lyallpur were under cotton, accounting for about 15 per cent of the total cropped area, and by 1937–8 the acreage rose by 50 per cent as cotton came to occupy over 25 per cent of the total area under cultivation. The line on the production graph does not dip even during the Great Depression. At a time when world market prices crashed, landowners and tenants expanded production to meet their cash requirements. And as exports shrank, cotton production was reoriented to meet the demands of a growing internal market.

There were, however, disquieting facts that could not be easily incorporated within this story of progress. It is true that in the Canal Colonies there was a dramatic expansion of total output, and the long-term average rates of growth here were higher than in the central districts, where arable expansion had reached its limits by the end of the nineteenth century.[98] But the figures do not allow us to make a neat contrast between the two zones: the Lyallpur rate is substantially lower than that of other Canal Colony tracts like Montgomery, and not so different from that of some of the older districts like Ludhiana and Gurdaspur. Moreover, when the annual rates of output growth are plotted on a graph we see a recurring picture. In the years immediately after the colonisation of a new tract, there was first a phase of

[97] Estimates based on *RLRAP* and *Reports on the Season and Crops of the Punjab*.

[98] The semi-log rates of growth of agricultural output, between 1906 and 1946, in the Canal Colonies varied from 5.5 in Montgomery, 4.1 in Multan, to 2.0 in Jhang, 1.1 in Shahpur, and 1.2 in Lyallpur. In the central districts the rates were: Ludhiana 1.2, Jullunder 0.35, Ferozepur 0.27, Amritsar 0.20. Prabha, "District-wise Rates of Growth of Agricultural Output in East and West Punjab".

growth, followed by stagnation and decline. In tracts like Lyallpur, colonised in the late nineteenth century, rates of growth plateaued by the second decade of the twentieth century; whereas Montgomery and Multan, colonised between 1915 and 1940, were still showing high growth rates in the 1940s. Clearly, growth in output was driven primarily by an expansion of the arable.[99] Once this reached its limit, output growth slowed and ultimately stopped. In the post-1950 period therefore the rates of output growth in the Canal Colony areas slumped.

This picture is doubly confirmed when we look at the figures of productivity per acre. Yields in Canal Colonies were not unquestionably higher than in the old agricultural districts of central Punjab. In 1916–17 Lyallpur and Montgomery in the Canal Colonies produced 160–175 lbs per acre of cleaned cotton, while in central Punjab Jullunder yielded 240 lbs and Ludhiana 160 lbs. The pattern had not changed in the subsequent decades. By 1937–8 the Lyallpur and Montgomery cotton fields were yielding 220 lbs whereas Ludhiana recorded 300 lbs and Jullunder 220 lbs. Wheat figures were no different. If Lyallpur in 1916–17 produced 1040 lbs of wheat per acre on canal-irrigated land, Jullunder produced 1200 lbs on its chahi (well-irrigated) land.[100] Two decades later the picture was very much the same: Lyallpur was yet to catch up with Jullunder.

A shift of focus from absolute yields to rates of productivity growth offers further insights into the antinomies of development. In most Canal Colonies, after the initial decades, the rates of growth first

[99] This conclusion is widely accepted. See Raj, "Farm Supply Response in India and Pakistan"; Islam, *Bengal Agriculture, 1920–1946.*

[100] Detailed village surveys suggest even higher yields in the Doab – the central districts of Punjab – where smallholders sustained production on intensively cultivated small parcels. Tehong was a village in Jullunder with about 2160 acres of cultivated land, parcellised into small holdings of about 3 acres. Forty per cent of the total area was chahi (well-irrigated). The Director of Land Records suggested in 1930 that chahi lands in Tehong produced on an average 1234 lbs of wheat per acre, and 374 lbs of cotton. These figures are higher than those in the *Season and Crops Reports* and *ASBI*. See Das and Calvert, *Tehong V.S.*, p. 180.

slowed and then turned negative. Not till the 1940s did the lines on the graph turn upwards. Imperial science and capital could not create in the Canal Colonies a developmental regime powered by high levels of productivity.

What explains this seeming paradox? First: these trends in yield reaffirm the proposition I made in an earlier chapter about the relationship between the decline of pastures and agricultural growth. When the permanent pastures of the bār were brought under the plough and converted into permanent fields, the soil contained high reserves of nitrogen, as is usual in all permanent pastures. This reserve could be tapped over long years to sustain fairly high levels of yield. The nitrogen fixed in pastureland, as we saw, has a very slow release rate. Bound up with organic compounds, it is released gradually as the compounds decompose over time. Continuous cultivation of the bār led to declining nitrogen levels and stagnation in yields. The effectiveness of any additional nitrogen supply through farmyard manure depends on the existing stock of nitrogen in the soil. As the nitrogen reserves dropped, larger quantities of manure were required to sustain existing levels of yield. In the Canal Colonies, it would appear, the nitrogen levels were not continuously and adequately replenished. Available manure per unit of land was lower in the Canal Colonies than in the older districts (see Fig. 20 below).

Second: the official dream of high yields on Canal Colony land was based on false assumptions. Officials thought that when industrious peasants were granted large holdings and supplied plenty of water, the problems of growth would disappear. The steady spread of capitalist farming and scientific agriculture would enhance yields and boost rates of productivity. Detailed farm surveys carried out in the late 1920s and the 1930s, however, showed that on small farms in Jullunder and Ludhiana the intensity of cropping and labour use, as well as the levels of yield per unit of land, were higher than on the larger farms of Lyallpur. Generally, peasants with large families living on small holdings sought to utilise all the available family labour to maximise yields and increase their earnings. They double-cropped the land and prepared the fields with care – ploughing, weeding, and manuring as much as possible – and dug wells to irrigate their holdings. The

	Older Districts	Canal Colonies	Jullunder (Central Punjab)	Lyallpur (Canal Colony)
Days of manual labour per cropped acre (in 8 hour days)	27	19	41	20
Days of bullock labour per cropped acre (in 8 hour days)	13	9	17	9
Intensity of cropping on irrigated land	124	99	142	83
Wages paid to permanent hired labourers (in annas)	4.6	5.2		0-4.8
Expenditure on manure per irrigated acre (in Rs.)	1.8	1.06	4.2	1

Fig. 20: How the Farms were Cultivated: A Contrast Between "Older Districts" and the Canal Colonies.

Source: *Farm Accounts in the Punjab, 1937–8.*[101]

number of wells in Jullunder boomed in the early twentieth century. Everyone it seems was digging a well to irrigate their intensively cultivated fields.

Migrant settlers on the larger farms of the Canal Colonies, however, could not maximise yields per acre. Family labour was in short supply, agricultural labourers difficult to find, wages at peak seasons high, and the available manure per unit of land inadequate. Here, migrants expanded production and increased their income by extending the arable rather than by intensifying cultivation. As the arable frontier was pushed outward, fields were prepared without adequate ploughing and manuring.

Third: the expansion of the arable frontier came up against ecological barriers. Driven by conceit and arrogance about their power to reshape all landscapes, colonial officials pushed the frontiers of the arable relentlessly outward. When in 1901–2 allotments in the

---

[101] These estimates were based on accounts kept in a set of individual farms in various districts of Punjab. The investigations were carried out by the Board of Economic Enquiry, Punjab.

Jhelum Colony were being planned, it was initially decided that the "inferior lands" would be given out for "temporary cultivation", for a stable cycle of production was difficult to sustain on such lands. Within a year, calculations changed. The colonising officer reported that there was "no need to revert to temporary cultivation on the Canal in order to avoid loss of revenue, as the supply of grantees has always been in excess of the land available."[102] It was as if all lands could be brought under the plough, turned into wheat or cotton fields, and made to yield revenue. This inexorable drive for arable expansion became characteristic of the very process of colonisation. In the Chenab Colony most of the "culturable" land had been allotted by the end of the nineteenth century. The subsequent opening of the Bhangu Branch created the possibility of another 17,163 acres being allotted. But most of this land was of such poor quality that the colonisation officer found the selected settlers showing "much reluctance in taking it up".[103] This did not deter officials. They blamed the colonists for being greedy and keen only to get the best-quality lands, and for their unwillingness to accept what was being offered to them. "But the land is not as bad as it looks," the colonising officer declared, "and if grantees from outside will not take it, plenty can be found here who will."[104] Settlers continued to complain, but the arable frontier marched on. The official logic was simple: as long as demand exceeded supply, all land could be allotted and taxed, all spaces could be converted into arable. Poor quality of land was not going to be allowed to quench the colonial thirst for expansion; if necessary, the idea of what constituted "culturable" land itself would have to be redefined. This unrestrained extension of the arable created instabilities, leading to crop failures and poor yields on these marginal lands.

Fourth: the dramatic march of wheat and cotton in the Canal Colonies – synonymous with progress in the colonial imagination – created a number of problems. By the 1920s colony officials were despairing at the fact that cotton cultivation was being extended

[102] *Annual Report of the Jhelum Colony, 1902–3*, p. 29.
[103] *Annual Report of the Chenab Colonies, 1902–3*, p. 3.
[104] Ibid.

recklessly without properly preparing the land. Constrained in many regions by the shortage of family labour and high wage costs, farmers of cotton were allowing cotton seeds to be sown broadcast, reducing the seed–yield ratio. The extension of cotton also created a pressure against growing fodder crops that fixed nitrogen in the soil.[105] The decline of pastures and an insufficient supply of fodder inevitably affected animal stock, and this in turn reduced manure supply. Consequently, nitrogen reserves were unreplenished and yields adversely affected. By contrast, fields in Jullunder and Ludhiana – small parcels that had to sustain large families – were heavily manured and intensively cultivated.[106]

The drive towards uniformity and homogeneity characterises modernity's search for order. In the field of agriculture it has inevitably meant – whether in the colonies or in the West – a reduction in crop diversity. In the Canal Colonies, the predominance of wheat and cotton led to declining areas under other crops. Foodgrains like jowar and bajra counted for a very small proportion of the total cropped area. There was no demand for them in Europe, no incentive to encourage their export. Obsessed with whiteness, British officials saw these grains as dark and coarse, and associated them with dry cultivation and backward agriculture. They became in fact markers of primitiveness. The shift from jowar and bajra to wheat was seen as a sign of progress. In Lyallpur, these two crops together covered only about 6 to 7 per cent of the foodgrain area in the first few years of the twentieth century; and by 1940 the proportion had dipped to less than 3 per cent.[107]

This trend towards crop uniformity was paralleled by the move towards genetic homogeneity. From the beginning of the twentieth century, the persistent attempts in Punjab to introduce high-yielding

[105] The Annual Farm Accounts maintained in the selected farms in various districts showed that the proportion of area under fodder crops in the older districts was over 28 per cent, while in the Canal Colonies it was no more than 13 per cent. See Statement IV – A, *Farm Accounts of the Punjab, 1936–37*.

[106] The imputed value of manure used per acre was 80 per cent higher in the older districts: Rs. 1.8 compared to Re. 1 in the Canal Colonies. Ibid., Statement VII A.

[107] *ASBI*, relevant years.

varieties of American wheat and cotton saw the gradual displacement of local desi varieties. In 1930 "improved" strains of wheat were here sown on 2.5 million acres; within a decade and a half wheat covered an area of 8.32 million acres, accounting for 80 per cent of the total area.[108] In response to the Lancashire pressure for long-stapled cotton, the Indian Cotton Association urged Punjab's officials to encourage the cultivation of American varieties. The F-4, introduced in 1908, came to cover 1.13 million acres by 1925.[109] In the 1940s colonial officials in the Canal Colonies were pointing to the areas under improved varieties as a measure of the development under colonisation.[110]

Few, however, could do this without a measure of doubt. In 1919, zamindars who had planted the F-4 discovered a strange disease that was destroying their crop. In September and October the flowers dropped, the bolls did not open properly, the lint was poor, the seed malformed, and the yields low.[111] The yield did not improve the subsequent year, and in 1921 a failure of rain destroyed the cotton crop. Then a few years of good harvest were followed once again by a cycle of poor ones. Such violent fluctuations of yield were not eliminated even in the 1940s. In 1944–5, for instance, on the government farm at Lyallpur the yield of American varieties was no more than 25 per cent of what it had been just two years earlier. The reason: a heavy infestation of jassid, a small wedge-shaped greenish-yellow insect, commonly called the cotton leaf-hopper (kohr or tela in Punjabi), which loved devouring American cottons.[112]

As vast areas of wheat and cotton continued to be regularly destroyed by pests, the Imperial Council of Agricultural Research began

[108] Ibid.

[109] Mohammad, "American Cottons in India: Their Introduction and Development".

[110] Ibid.

[111] Milne, *Report on the Causes of the Failure of Cotton Crop in the Punjab in 1919*; idem, *Report on the Complaints of the Abnormal State of the Cotton Crop in 1921*. See also *Review of Agricultural Operation in British India, 1919–20*; *RLRAP, 1919–20*; *Report of the Season and Crops of Punjab, 1919–20*.

[112] Investigations showed that jassid attacked two varieties of American cotton – 124F and 289F/K-25, and not others like F-4, LSS and 289F/43.

work on resistant varieties. But this did not solve the problems. When immunity was developed against one type of pest, plants still remained susceptible to attack by other varieties of pathogens or insects. The problem lay with the move towards monoculture and uniformity. As recent researches have shown, the displacement of local varieties and the elimination of crop diversity make plant communities particularly vulnerable to recurrent pest invasions.[113] In polycultures, species diversity retards the transfer of viruses by insects and genetic heterogeneity limits the damage by pathogenic organisms – even when they are of virulent strains. In monocultures the hosts are biologically homogeneous, enabling a rapid multiplication and spread of the invading pathogen, transforming every pest attack into a probable epidemic. In the older districts of Punjab, the crop regime that peasants had developed through adaptation with the local environment was genetically more heterogeneous; and the desi varieties of wheat and cotton that they grew were less prone to pest attacks. The yield of the desis was lower than the "amreekan" grown under optimal conditions, but the harvests of the former were more stable.

The British had imagined that in the Canal Colonies these optimal conditions would be ensured. But they were not. By building the perennial canals they had hoped to irrigate the "desolate" bārs, eliminate seasonal fluctuations in supply, regulate the volume of flow in the channels, and optimise water utilisation. Even as officials congratulated themselves on their achievements, there were reports that all was not well with the irrigation system: water shortages were frequent at some points, at others excess water clogged the soil. Confident of their dream and arrogant about their capacity to extend

---

It was, in fact, a pest that usually attacked guara (*Cyamopsis psoralioides*) and damaged cotton only in the absence of guara. This again points to the consequences of species homogeneity. See Mohammad and Ghani, "Cotton Jassid in the Punjab".

[113] See Adams, Ellingboe, and Rossman, " Biological Uniformity and Disease Epidemics"; Matson, Parton, Power, and Swift, "Agricultural Intensification and Ecosystem Properties"; Cleveland, Soleri, and Smith, "Do Folk Varieties Have a Role in Sustainable Agriculture?"

the canals over the entire bār landscape, the canal engineers had proceeded in a hurry. In some regions they had preferred to ignore the compact nature of the clayey soil or the hard rocky substrata that hindered percolation; elsewhere they had disregarded the problem of drainage. By the late 1920s the problem became so acute that a Water-logging Committee had to be appointed to look into the problem.[114]

In waterlogged soils carbon dioxide gets trapped and nitrogen and oxygen supplies are reduced.[115] Since roots require oxygen for effective nutrient uptake, waterlogging inevitably leads to dwindling yields. Compaction and poor soil aeration also retard root growth, suffocate existing roots, and slow nutrient uptake, affecting plant health and leaf activity. Studies have shown that diminished nitrogen uptake restricts cotton growth. Nitrogen from older leaves is translocated to the new leaves, causing chlorosis in the older leaves. The lack of potassium, common in waterlogged soils, affects the cotton fibre and leaf colour, and a build-up of sodium to toxic levels leads to the progressive death of shoots and leaves. The cumulative effect of all this is not only a dramatic decline in levels of yield but also a steady deterioration in the quality of the produce.

Science could not easily sustain the self-arrogance of modernity. The promise of modernity crumbled, afflicted by the antinomies of development.

Two Paths of Agrarian Conquest

I would like to end by arguing that development in the Canal Colonies reveals a pattern different from the shape of things elsewhere in Punjab. Reworking Lenin's famous argument about capitalism, I think it is useful to distinguish two paths to agrarian conquest under

[114] *Proceedings of the Waterlogging Conference, Punjab, 1928–38*, annual. See also *Waterlogging and Rise of Water Level in Chhaj and Rechna Doabs*; Pearson, *Notes on Waterlogging in the Punjab*.

[115] See Kozlowski, "Plant Responses to Flooding of Soil"; Dowdell and Mian, "Fate of Nitrogen Applied to Agricultural Crops with Particular Reference to Denitrification".

colonialism, two ways of visualising the constitution of the agrarian modern within the colonial landscape: one that transformed society from below, and the other that sought to impose a structure from above. The way the contradictory dialectic between these two forms worked itself out defined the specific logic of colonial change.

Agrarian conquest from below proceeded slowly, carefully, almost surreptitiously. From the beginning of British rule in Punjab, officials emphasised that the rural order was to be founded on custom and native institutions. The colonial state remapped the landscape, redefined custom, refigured rights, reorganised social relations, and reordered agrarian regimes. But this transformation was carried through in the name of preservation. The rhetoric of tradition was a defining element of this mode of agrarian conquest and of shaping the agrarian modern. Within it colonisation seemed to work without corroding the social fabric or demolishing existing social structures. This appearance of continuity allowed the violence of colonialism to be misrecognised and historical ruptures to be read as persistences. When an order is built through the language of custom, when law seeks to encode no more than existing practices, the new order does not appear radically alien or severely different. Modernity comes almost surreptitiously, behind the back of tradition.

The language of tradition and custom, however, created constraints. Inhabited landscapes could be reordered, existing practices could be redefined; but there were limits within which this transformation could proceed. Projects of reordering inevitably came up against barriers, social resistance, and the rigidity of embedded structures. Imperialism constantly struggles to emancipate itself from these constraints, to discover spaces where the ideal colonial order of their imagination can be built without hindrance. This is what it sought in the Canal Colonies.

The experiment in the Canal Colonies represented the second path of agrarian conquest. Here the colonial state sought to impose an entire new order from above. It aspired to define everything – the shape of the fields, the lay of the land, the place where the colonist was to reside, the structure of the abadi, the mode of irrigation, the crop regimes, the patterns of inheritance, and even the attributes of the people who could inhabit the land. It wanted to displace the pastoralists and implant a society of industrious and enterprising zamindars. It imagined that the wilderness of the pastoral landscape would allow the possibility of unconstrained transformation.

This simple difference between the two forms of colonisation inevitably broke down. The agrarian conquest from below could not proceed without state initiatives from above. The desire to base British rule on custom and tradition was itself linked to official ideology, a paternalism that was at the same time powerfully influenced by the Benthamite dream of a codifying state.[116] The project of preservation proceeded through processes of enquiry, classification, translation, and codification.[117] The intervention of the master defined the way the customs of the people entered the codes.

Yet there were limits to invention. True, codification did not preserve immemorial custom untainted, nor did the classification of tenures consolidate ancient coparcenary village brotherhoods untouched and unchanged. But the discourse of tradition inevitably meant that the state had to operate with caution, enquire into the practices of the people, listen to their voices, see how practices diverged from the code, and change colonial policies in response to social pressures. It had to operate through the inner logic of an agrarian conquest that sought to reorder society from below.

Developments in the colonies similarly showed that the conquest from above was not as easy as the state had imagined. It could not produce an ideal agrarian space, unhindered and unconstrained. Villagers reacted to the demarcation of the rakhs and angry pastoralists resisted displacement, carrying away the stocks of immigrant peasant settlers and destroying their crops. They asserted their rights to the rakhs and opposed the invasion of outsiders. As 1907 showed, even immigrant peasant settlers were unwilling to accept all the conditions that the state was keen to impose on the grantees. They grumbled about the canal dues and unreliable water supplies, opposed the new laws of primogeniture, demanded security of rights, and objected to state

[116] See chs 1 and 5, *supra*.
[117] See chs 4 and 5, *supra*.

attempts to control their lives, movements, and financial decisions. Once again, the state had to react to these pressures from below, modify the colonisation bill, change the terms in which grants were given, and abolish primogeniture.

This development from above, moreover, was carried through in a language that continued to be paternalist. The development of the Canal Colonies may have been an attempt to realise an imperial dream of a rational reordering of the landscape, establishing a modern agrarian order unconstrained by the heritage of the past, and the rigidities of entrenched social institutions. It may have been inspired by imperial self-conceit: a will to demonstrate that the British could produce in the colonies a model agrarian regime. But colonial officials never tired of emphasising that they were driven primarily by paternalist concerns, by their sympathy for the needs of the people. Colonisation was said to be necessary to relieve the sufferings of central Punjab peasants ground down by demographic pressure, constrained by fragmented, subdivided, minuscule parcels of land. Migration, they repeatedly said, would relieve the pressure on land in the old districts and ensure for the pioneer settlers wealth and prosperity in the colonies.

Within the developmental regime of the colonies, paternalism and rationalism fused into a curious mixture. As paternal masters, colonial officials in Punjab claimed to know their subjects and realise what was best for them. They had recognised the qualities of the central Punjab peasants, glorified their industry and skill in cultivation, and given them large plots of land; but they were equally certain that the development of the colonies could be ensured and the well-being of the settlers guaranteed only if the landscape was rationally ordered, only if colonists followed the rules that had been codified, only if plots were carved out in uniform squares, primogeniture imposed, and the planting of trees and residence in the model village made binding. But what if the colonists thought otherwise, what if they wanted to follow the custom of their home villages, saw partible inheritance as the only basis of equity, and residence requirements as an oppressive control over their private lives? What if they conceived of the new structure of rights through the prism of the old? What if what appeared as rational to official minds appeared irrational to the zamindars?

At such times paternalism turned perverse. Paternal masters lost the language of empathy: they no longer flaunted a desire to listen and understand, sit below the banyan tree and hear peasant complaints. When in 1907 the zamindars of the bār began to campaign against the Colonisation Bill, the paternalists reacted with surprising aggression. Unwilling to believe that the complaints of the zamindars could be genuine, they imagined hidden agents at work churning up trouble: the ever-present Russians, the seditious nationalists, the disloyal lawyers. The police were asked to attend all meetings, track seditious activities, and prepare dossiers on the involvement of nationalist leaders in the movement. Governor General Ibbetson, an old patriarch, drew a picture of impending catastrophe, foresaw the breakdown of British rule in India, and demanded emergency powers to handle the situation – to arrest Lajpat Rai and Ajit Singh, ban all meetings, seal up newspapers. James Wilson, who as Settlement Officer at Sirsa in the early 1870s had empathised with Lalu – the peasant poet we met earlier who recounted the story of lost rights in the countryside – and had discovered in his poem the pain and suffering of dispossessed Sirsa peasants, had become in 1907 the most assertive defender of the Colonisation Bill. On investigating the rights of Sirsa's peasants, Wilson had argued with passion that those who cleared the waste and made it productive always saw the land as their own. A denial of their claim was unjust.[118] Now, thirty-five years later, after three years as Settlement Commissioner in the Canal Colonies, he had forgotten the convictions of his youth. He fumed at the Colonisation Committee proposal that the colonists be made proprietors of the land they reclaimed. There was no custom, Wilson pronounced, that gave the zamindar a right to the land he cleared.[119]

[118] See ch. 6, *supra*.

[119] As Financial Commissioner in 1909, Wilson wrote: "It is not true, so far my experience goes, that in the Punjab the reclamation of waste and unappropriated land is generally recognised as giving a title to proprietary right. Whether this was even the ancient custom in the older settled parts or not, there has certainly been no general idea of his kind in the minds of the people

What accounts for this amnesia, this denial of an idea that Wilson had once so fervently espoused? I can offer two possible arguments. First, within official minds the inner logic of the two forms of colonisation differed. In Sirsa the development was seen as organic, occurring through an evolutionary and natural progression of demographic expansion, pressure on resources, the fissioning and separation of households, the movement to new areas, and the reclamation of waste. It was not a process entirely aided or initiated by the state. The state had to recognise the norms, customs, and expectations that sustained the process. In the Canal Colonies, by contrast, the project of reclamation was organised from above. The state initiated the process, brought the colonists, gave them land and water. The immigrant settlers had no moral or ethical claim to the land, no right to expect any more than what they had already gained through the generosity of the colonial state.[120]

Second: Wilson's paranoia revealed the inner contradictions of paternalism. Kindness and concern for the poor was an intimate part of the rhetoric of paternalism, but this humanist empathy was premised on expectations of deference and obedience. Deeply authoritarian, paternalism could not tolerate any questioning of its

---

for the last two generations." This was an astounding comment from someone who had written the Sirsa Settlement Report and argued so insistently that those who reclaimed the waste expected a permanent right over the land they cleared. In his marginal notes to Wilson's comment Walker, the lieutenant governor, pointed out that the settlers never imagined that their rights over the allotted squares would be similar to tenancies under private landlords: "The idea that they would stand to Government in the relation which they understood to be that of tenants was so alien to them that they were incapable of realizing it . . . they regarded themselves to all intents and purposes proprietors." Punjab Rev. & Agr. (Rev.), April 1909, A1.

[120] Wilson wrote: "the colonists . . . it must be remembered, had, most of them formerly no rights, legal or moral, over their land, and who have been brought from narrow poverty in their old homes and placed, by the beneficence of Government, in a position of prosperity, unimaginable in their fondest dreams." Wilson's minute, 4 May 1907, GOI, Home (Legislative), June 1907, A 4–8.

authority.[121] No doubts could be expressed, no voices raised against the indisputably benign intentions of the filial figure. Every questioning was seen as a possible threat to the bonds of social cohesion that paternalism sought to forge. The benefactors of paternal care were allowed to plead but not protest. In times like 1907 the fears of social breakdown were transformed into visions of apocalypse. When Minto appointed the Canal Colonies Committee, a furious Wilson replayed the images of insurgency that Ibbetson had earlier projected.[122] Plagued by the inner anxieties of his patriarchal ideology, convinced of the illegitimacy of every demand by the colonists, Wilson now had no patience for the language of empathy and concern.

The events that unfolded in the aftermath of 1907 possibly marked the limits of the old paternalistic ideology of Punjab. To survive it had to readapt, become sensitive to a new language of individual rights, and allow some space for rebellion among the subjects. This was a difficult task in turbulent times.

[121] On the multiple strands within paternalism and of its authoritarianism, see Robert, "Tory Paternalism and Social Reform in Early Victorian England"; Roberts, *Paternalism in Early Victorian England*; Thornton, *The Habit of Authority*. On the distinction between the paternalism of the eighteenth century gentry and its mutated, refigured form that became an intimate part of nineteenth-century thought, not just of the Tories, see Mandler, "The Making of the New Poor Law Redivivas"; Brundage and East Wood, "The Making of the New Poor Law Redivivas"; Hall, "Competing Masculinities".

[122] The appointment of the committee, Wilson prophesied, would not only weaken the authority of all civil officials, but "it may prove to be a step towards riot, mutiny and bloodshed, to which troubles in Eastern Bengal are but child's play." Both Ibbetson and Wilson tapped into imperial fears to argue for the need to discipline the colonists with a strong hand. Minute of Wilson, 3 July, 1907, GOI, Rev. & Agr. (Rev.) October 1907, A 13–18.

Epilogue

The Last Ride

"This is the story of a ride across northern India in the winter of
1946–47. The moment was a fateful one – comparable, perhaps,
in historic importance with the summer of 1789 when Arthur
Young set out on the third of his famous rides, across a France on
the eve of revolution."

– Malcolm Darling, *At Freedom's Door*, p. xi.

D ARLING'S RIDE THROUGH THE villages of North India was
charged with a tragic ambivalence. This was possibly his
last ride in India: he had ridden through the Punjab villages
twice before and was unlikely ever to do so again.[1] He knew the
days of the British Raj were numbered – the Interim Government
was already in place. As a gentleman liberal he could not seriously
grudge Indians the right to freedom, but he was troubled by a feeling
of pain and nostalgia. His descriptions of the time are suffused with
a sense of imminent danger and uncertainty: no-one knew what
the future held in store, what sort of government would replace the
British, and how the new dispensation would handle the problems
of the time. Darling could sense an impending civil war; he saw
everywhere "fear, hatred and lawlessness – propaganda's evil brood",

[1] Born in 1880, Malcolm Darling was educated at Eton and Cambridge,
became an Assistant Commissioner in Punjab in 1904, an Assistant Registrar
of the Co-operative Department in 1916, and Financial Commissioner in
1936. He wrote extensively on Punjab rural society and was considered a
leading authority on peasant economy and the co-operative movement. For
an insightful discussion of his early intellectual development, see Dewey,
The Mind of the Indian Civil Service.

and the "constant dread of a sudden stab in the dusk or dark".[2] Yet, like Arthur Young on the eve of the French Revolution, he set out to discover the minds of villagers: What did they think of British rule? How did they compare the present to the past? How were they affected by the war? How did they conceive of azadi? A benevolent paternalist who had spent a lifetime reflecting on the problems of Indian peasants, he was disturbed at the possibility that midnight's children might disinherit their fathers. This ride at freedom's door was as much a tragic last journey – and a nostalgic re-enactment of previous ones – as a voyage to reaffirm faith in his life's vision.

Organising this last ride had not been easy. Having retired in 1940, Darling no longer had the official authority even to secure the horses he needed. He wanted three, since his daughter, April, and her husband were to ride with him. Upon reaching India on 31 October 1946, Darling received a letter from the Directorate of Remount and Veterinary Services that his request for the loan of two Borders could not be granted "owing to a shortage of suitable riding horses".[3] He petitioned officials, met political leaders, and pleaded with the army authorities, impressing upon all the great significance of his projected tour. The ride, he said, would be very difficult even if the horses were found, but he still wished to undertake it for the public good. If carried out successfully it would yield results of value to the government, for the plans of post-war development depended on "an accurate appreciation of village conditions".[4] He also hoped to record for the benefit of future historians "the general conditions of villages on the close of our rule in India."[5] It finally took him over a month

[2] Darling, *At Freedom's Door*, p. xi. The original diary of this ride across North India in 1946–7 is in the Darling Papers, Box LIX 722, which also contains the diary of his daughter April Darling, and correspondence concerning the ride.

[3] Brigadier E.S. Peatt, Director of Remount and Veterinary Services, to Darling, 16 October 1946, Darling Papers, Box LIX 722; Darling to Bhalaji, Sec. in the War Department, 4 November 1946, Darling Papers, Box LIX 722.

[4] Darling to Bhalaji, Sec. in the War Department, 4 November 1946, Darling Papers, Box LIX 722.

[5] Ibid. Darling ended by saying: "In short, I venture to claim that it is to the public advantage that my project should be carried out, and since this

to get two horses – a cold reminder of what loss of colonial power on the ground could mean. All through the subsequent ride Darling reflected on the collapse of British official authority in the rural areas, and its implications. Speaking through seemingly impersonal records, his voice comes through as a valediction on individual and collective loss, a colonial nostalgia for the power the English no longer had.

At Freedom's Door is written as a diary, a literary genre that asserts the immediacy of experience. The words of informants sound as though directly spoken by them, unmediated by the diarist. The text appears to reveal the truth via conversation and dialogue between Darling and a variety of rural informants whom he encounters. In it we hear zamindars, tahsildars, peasants, subedars, and kanungos speaking, interrogating Darling, expressing their nostalgia for the pre-British past, their critique of the colonial present, and their dream of azadi. Yet, *At Freedom's Door*, like all ethnographies in this genre, is only seemingly dialogical, for it is Darling who transcribes the words of his informants and translates their experiences into his own writing. It is he who controls their dialogue, he is the purveyor of their speech. And it is he who chooses the strategies of narration.

∽

As Darling rode through the villages, from Peshawar in the North West Frontier Provinces through the Salt Range and the Canal Colonies down to Jabalpur and beyond the Vindhyas, he was irritated by a recurrent pattern of answers to his queries. Were things better or worse in his youth, Darling asked an eighty-year-old zaildar with a flowing white beard whom he met on the border of Jhelum district near the Salt Range. "Far better. There was then more goodwill and more to eat," was the answer.[6] "And much less litigation," added a dry-faced subedar amongst the horsemen who had joined Darling over this part of the ride. These were echoes of statements

---

cannot be done without horses, I would once more ask for the loan of two Borders, or at least one if two cannot be possibly spared."

[6] Darling, *At Freedom's Door*, p. 49.

Darling had often heard earlier in his horseback days.[7] Referring to the life of his youth, a seventy-year-old villager of Jhang had said in the 1920s: "There was then no borrowing and paying (na lana, na bahana). Now the land revenue swallows up everything, and all are in debt . . . Before there was plenty of milk: now there is not even water, and therefore no fodder for the cattle. Wants too, were few and there was no care (fikr)."[8] Darling could not get away from the pervasive sense of loss the villagers felt at the collapse of a preferred pre-British old order of reciprocity, goodwill, honesty, freedom, and abundance; from their tales of present woes about poverty, debt, hunger, high prices and taxes; from their tales of present slavery and dreams of future well-being.

The horseman appears in the text as a seeker of truth, sifting evidence, differentiating the believable from the unbelievable. If the romantic in Darling acknowledged a rural innocence, his imperial mind suspected all natives of deceit and perjury. He continuously doubts the statements of villagers. "Were they telling the truth? That is the question always in my mind at these meetings . . ." he says.[9] "I don't want to eat lies," he tells a lambardar in a village.[10] Darling had learnt the value of doubt and scepticism from his Socratic teachers in Cambridge, but scepticism can have many lives, it can be deployed in varying – and discriminatory – ways.[11] In the ethnographic encounters he records, the search for truth becomes a strategy for marginalising and repressing troubling evidence. Critical voices are recorded only to be suspected and textually subverted.

Driven by imperial self-belief, Darling's quest for dialogue turns into a refusal to hear. The will to hear is acknowledged and disavowed.

---

[7] He heard similar comments beyond the borders of Punjab. In Pune he was told by a villager in 1939: "In the past there was enough to eat, needs were few: now there are debts, faction is worse, and land revenue is difficult to pay." November 1939, Darling Papers, Box LVI.

[8] Darling, *Rusticus Loquitur*, p. 215.

[9] Darling, *At Freedom's Door*, p. 246.

[10] Ibid., p. 240

[11] On the Socratic teachers, see Dewey, *The Mind of the Indian Civil Service*, ch. 5.

Fig. 21: Wayside Conversation: Darling Questions Villagers.
Courtesy: Centre of South Asian Studies, Cambridge.

As he proceeds on his journey, he begins to dread the tales of pain and suffering, the voices of despair that question his image of British rule as benevolent paternalism.

> They all had the same complaints – the complaint that has run like a telegraph wire all along our road the last sixty or seventy miles. "We have nothing to eat, we are dying of hunger, there is no sugar, no cloth, no matches. Look at our children, how ragged they are. Our lot is unbearable." And so on with every possible variation of these simple but absorbing themes. No one, of course was dying of hunger, and many were tolerably dressed.

What is heard is represented as already known and so not worth hearing: it was the same old story repeated. The complaints appear tiresome, monotonous, almost orchestrated, and above all dubious. When at one point peasants gather and complain about their impoverished state and show Darling the measly half-size chapati they have for their midday meal, he enters their huts to examine the veracity of their claims.[12] He is reluctant to hear the petitions and

---

[12] Darling, *At Freedom's Door*, p. 42.

complaints of the peasants who line up to talk to him and dreads the persuasion of tahsildars and patwaris who seek his audience. He is haunted by the fear of being "waylaid" into dialogues he had no wish to enter.

~

By the 1940s Malcolm Darling had established himself as an eloquent chronicler of the transformation of rural society under British rule. He had with great sensitivity and understanding explored the lives of peasants, looking carefully into the problems they faced and reflecting on possible solutions. Each of the books he published had been full of optimism, expressing confidence in the human ability to control nature and the British capacity to civilise the "primitive". In the diary of his last ride this optimism fades. His effusive celebration of the power of science and human will gives way to a sad recognition of their limits.

In the books he wrote in the 1920s, Darling's descriptions usually develop through a series of contrasts between the primitive and the modern, between the life of the nomad and that of the peasant. "In the western Punjab (i.e. the pastoral tracts not yet irrigated by the canals)," he says, "conditions are dominated by a relentless nature. In the great Canal Colonies . . . we feel everywhere the beneficent hand of man. In the former, life is the immemorial life of India, primitive, isolated, and fatalistic: in the latter, it is the new life brought in by the Pax Britannica, prosperous, progressive, and modern."[13] This description of the mid 1920s, with its boundless optimism in the power of modernity, is repeated in his account of the Canal Colonies some years later. Riding into Lyallpur in January 1929, he had bubbled over with excitement: "Thirty years ago it [i.e. this region] formed part of the great waste tract that stretched almost from Lahore to the Indus, and was the home of shepherd, nomad, and camel. Now it is the most thriving countryside in the Punjab, and the most prosperous in India."[14] For Darling, as for many officials we have seen through

[13] Darling, *The Punjab Peasant in Prosperity and Debt*, p. 111.
[14] Darling, *Rusticus Loquitur*, p. 192. For the diary of this ride, see Darling Papers, Box II.

the earlier chapters, the arid pastoral landscape was desolate and dreary, barren and unproductive; the nomads who inhabited it were lazy, their lives expressed all that was primitive. The Canal Colonies, by contrast, reflect the "fruitful world of human will". Here, through the power of science and reason, a vast "wasteland" where nomads once "roamed" has been turned into a fertile and productive landscape. Passing through the tract, Darling saw beauty everywhere and wrote effusively of "the emerald green of young wheat", the "golden islets of cane", and the "mustard-scented rape riotous in its yellow flowering".[15]

Like most British officials, he saw agrarian colonisation as a civilising act. To develop the countryside it was necessary to clear "wastes", irrigate dry tracts, settle nomads, introduce scientific cropping, popularise new agricultural technology, and augment the productivity of land and labour. In 1929, passing through Nili Bār, a tract recently colonised, Darling met many groups of pastoralists and heard their tales of trouble. The passionate lament of one woman disturbed him in particular:

> We came here before the English, before even the days of Sawan Mal. Seven generation have we lived here. We sank two wells, and cultivated the "jangal" wherever there was water from the rain, and our camels grazed where they pleased. Then were we lords of the "jangal". But now our land has been stolen (here two impassioned arms were flung out in my direction). And we may no longer go here and there with our camels, but must work for a wage and pick cotton, and our men must hire themselves out with their camels. Many have left the village and gone to seek work in the chaks. We used to drink our fill of the milk of our goats and camels; but now our milch camels are few: there is no grazing for them. Some have died, and the others are weak.[16]

Darling hears the voices of the nomads, records them in his diary, but cannot empathise. He sees them as casualties of history, figures from the past who could not survive the forces of change and were destined to be swept away by the unalterable forces of modernity.

[15] Darling, *Rusticus Loquitur*, p. 213; idem, *Wisdom and Waste*, p. 18.
[16] Darling, *Rusticus Loquitur*, p. 229. Sawan Mal was a leading commander of Maharaja Ranjit Singh's army, and governor of Multan.

To extend peasant cultivation and expand the agrarian frontier the nomad had to be pegged, tied to the land, and settled.[17]

By the 1940s Darling came to acknowledge some of the antinomies of modernity. His enchantment with science was severely dented.[18] His euphoric descriptions of change in the Canal Colonies in *The Punjab Peasant in Prosperity and Debt* give way to premonitions of disaster. Darling can now see that the British efforts to transform the dry bārs into a verdant landscape have come up against barriers that colonial science has not been able to handle. In village after village that he rides through, people complain of waterlogging and kallar. The canals have created marshlands, bringing salt to the surface, destroying fertility, congealing the earth, suffocating the crops, and spreading malaria. The effort to drain the water has not resolved problems: in the reclaimed lands the soil has turned into clods. Darling had heard complaints of waterlogging in the early 1930s.[19] But now, in 1946–7, it sounds to him "like leprosy infecting the whole countryside".[20] In the Chenab Colony he is told:

> Vast stretches of fertile land have been turned into arid wastes which grow not even a blade of grass to provide a morsel of fodder to the hungry cattle. The water level has come so high up, that it has literally

[17] Darling writes: "one realises with sadness the inexorable modern law which demands that he who produces little shall give way to him who produces much." Ibid., p. 229.

[18] Talking about the new light that he saw shining in Punjab in the 1920s, Darling wrote: "For man's dependence upon nature it substitutes the conquest of nature by science, and to his dependence upon custom and the village community it opposes the claims of reason and liberty." *Rusticus Loquitur*, p. 342. This reference to the new light disappears in the diary of his last ride. Commenting on the tragic consequence of rechannelling river water into the grand canal network, he now speaks of nature's vengeance: "nature resents interference and will always hit back if she can." Darling, *At Freedom's Door*, p. 66.

[19] Darling wrote: "every blessing finds its devil. The devil that stalks the canal bank is water-logging." *Wisdom and Waste*, p. 9. He went on to say: "Canals may ultimately bring death to the land", p. 24. He was, at the time, expressing a fear he hoped would not prove true.

[20] Darling, *At Freedom's Door*, p. 77.

come under horse's hoof. It oozes by itself . . . Our houses have crumbled to ground and the whole village . . . has been half turned into a big
mound of dust . . .[21]

Numerous villages have been abandoned, the dwellers having
either left or died. Some said they could not even bury their dead,
the water being three feet below the surface. Dismayed by the rapid
spread of the dreaded salt, Darling wonders how long the fertility of
the canal lands can last.[22]

~

When Darling set out on his ride he was aware of what urban-
educated Indians wanted. He had met many of them a year earlier
and heard their talk of freedom. He was now keen to know the minds
of peasants, hoping perhaps to discover a radical difference. After all,
had the British not cared for the peasants, protected them against
usurers and landlords, irrigated parched lands, brought the bārs under
cultivation, introduced ideas of improvement and reconstruction,
built roads and railways, and connected remote tracts to the mandis?
Had he not himself ridden over 1400 miles through Punjab, first in
the winter of 1928 and then again in 1931, only to see for himself
the problems peasants faced, so that British officials might in general
think of ways to address them?[23] Would the villagers not acknowledge all that the rulers had done? Would they not want the British
to stay?

[21] Ibid., p. 77.
[22] Darling, Diary, 1946, p. 487, Darling Papers, Box LIX 722. The war
against the deleterious effect of waterlogging still continues in Pakistan. See
Bhutta and Smedema, "One Hundred Years of Waterlogging and Salinity
Control in the Indus Valley, Pakistan".
[23] See Darling, *Wisdom and Waste*; idem, *Rusticus Loquitur.* For his detailed
diaries as Registrar of Co-operative Societies, see Diary: Punjab Villages
27 July 1934 to 3 March 1935; Diary: Lyallpur 17 November 1936 to 27
November 1936; Diary: Punjab Villages 17 November 1936 to 14 December
1936; Diary: Punjab Villages 20 January 1937 to 3 December 1937; Diary:
Punjab Villages, 9 January 1939 to 31 December 1939, Darling Papers,
Box LVI.

In his earlier rides Darling resisted asking political questions. In 1946–7 this was impossible to resist. All conversation inevitably turned to politics. Passing through Shewa, a large village of 6000 inhabitants in the north-west of Punjab, Darling asked what the villagers wanted most. "We are slaves," said a 75-year-old Pathan, a tall, thin man with an aquiline nose and a red beard. "Under the British we have been walking in the dark," he said, ". . . but now we have come to the door of freedom."[24] Darling interjected: "Surely the Pathan has always been free. In what sense are you not free?" The Pathan explained that in England there were factories, and "men make what they please". Here there were severe restrictions, and "this will be so until the English go," The conversation continued:

"But now you have your own Government," said Darling.

"Yes, but it is only temporary rule," said the old man, "You will not let power go . . . You promise us freedom but don't give it. Have you not been here 120 years and still you do not give it?"

Darling tried reasoning: "The government of forty crores of people can't be handed over in a moment. And until Hindus and Muslims join hands, it is difficult to know to whom to hand over. The English are a law-abiding people and don't like the thought of leaving India to big troubles."

"Leave the country," said a voice to Darling's left; "we will put up with what happens."[25]

Keen to shift the discussion from the present to the future, Darling asked: "What would you do with freedom when you get it?"[26] While he saw himself as a liberal and was sympathetic to the Congress, Darling was sceptical of the rhetoric of "unfreedom" and the slogan of azadi. He was eager to show that no-one actually knew what freedom implied, or what azadi really meant.[27] These were empty slogans

[24] Darling, *At Freedom's Door*, p. 15.

[25] Ibid.

[26] Ibid., p. 16.

[27] This remains Darling's recurrent refrain: "There has been much talk of freedom today. All say they want it, but to few it is more than the latest shibboleth, and for these few it has not always the same meaning." *At Freedom's Door*, p. 104.

circulating from town to country, generating passion and hatred. Villagers repeated them without reflecting on their meaning. They parroted what leaders in the city said: "It's the same at this evil moment throughout the country, and it all derives from Delhi. The 'leaders' have only to say a thing today for all their supporters to say the same thing tomorrow. Years ago I was told by Indian colleagues that *bhedchal* – the way of the sheep – was the way of the peasant, and here it is with a vengeance, and not confined to the peasant."[28]

Darling found it difficult to reconcile his imperial self with his humanist feelings. He set out to discover the mind of the peasants but ended up proclaiming that they had no mind of their own. What they said was not what they thought. They echoed others.

Pushed into concretising their vision of the future, villagers offered answers Darling was reluctant to accept. In Garhi Bazidpur, a village in Gurgaon, he was told: "Now there is bandan – bondage – and there is great difference between freedom and bondage. When we are free, if we sink a well, we shall not pay the well rate."[29] Another said: "Now we can't make guns or aeroplanes. We shall when we are free."[30] In Lyallpur a Sikh peasant asserted: "Now we are slaves. When we are free, we shall serve ourselves, and do as we like. Then we shall gladly pay more taxes."[31] Referring to their state of poverty, an educated peasant-colonist in Lyallpur declared: "When we are free we will have prosperity."[32] In a village in Hoshiarpur Darling heard a villager say: "We will have more industries, we will not let our raw material go to other countries, we will manage things as we like, we will raise the standard of living."[33]

In all such statements the future was visualised as a negation of the present, azadi was imagined as freedom from all suffering. Darling laughs at these dreamt-up futures and counters peasant utopias with dark forebodings, conjuring up images of the breakdown of law

[28] Ibid., p. 18.
[29] Ibid., p. 183.
[30] Ibid.
[31] Ibid., p. 80.
[32] Ibid.
[33] Ibid., p. 101.

and order, the spread of communal violence, the collapse of administration. When Ahir villagers in Gurgaon asked – "the wild beasts
are free should we not be free too?" – Darling quips in his diary, "If
only freedom doesn't make them [the villagers] like wild beasts too!"[34]
Aware though he is that the "unlettered peasants wanted peace, justice,
and enough to eat",[35] he is unwilling to believe that the British had
not tried to provide all this, or that the villagers would get it all with
freedom.[36]

Troubled by the universal cry of azadi, Darling strained to hear
the discordant notes, searching for voices that recognised the gifts of
British rule. He warmed to the wisdom of those who acknowledged
the moral authority of the English, their incorruptibility, their paternal
love for their subjects, their success in establishing law and order. He
had no difficulty being convinced when he heard someone say that
there would be civil war if the English left,[37] or when a Belgian father
in Gurgaon declared that India would explode in the absence of the
English.[38] These, Darling tells us, were the discerning voices of the
wise. His grounding in the liberal Socratic tradition of Cambridge did
not impel him to interrogate *all* statements. He deployed scepticism
with discretion, questioning words that troubled him, and was
reassured by those that were comforting.

~

What Darling desired was an emotive bond between British and
Indians, affective ties that would bind them. He had an innocent

[34] Ibid., p. 183.

[35] Ibid., p. 81.

[36] After listening to the dreams of azadi in an Ahir village in Gurgaon,
Darling remarks: "Poor things – little do they know what they may be in for
with a freedom for which so few are prepared." Ibid., p. 183.

[37] Ibid., p. 79.

[38] *At Freedom's Door*, p. 79. The Belgian father went on to say that in many
villages in Gurgaon the general comments on the coming withdrawal of the
British from India was: "*Afsos! Bara Afsos!* — Alas! Alas, alas!" This statement
about afsos (regret) is not recorded in the typescript of the diary: Darling,
India Diary, 1946, Darling Papers, Box LIX 722, p. 587.

belief in the power of friendship.[39] The teacher he admired over his Cambridge days, Goldsworthy Lowes Dickinson, wrote lyrically about the importance of love and friendship, especially amongst men, and Darling's close associates in the university were all committed to the ideal of friendship.[40] But this was friendship amongst equals, between those who shared their life's vision, possessed similar tastes, and conversed on an equal footing on issues that the community of the select valued. It could not incorporate those who did not belong to such a brotherhood, whose values and ideals were radically different. In the colony, of course, equality was never possible between rulers and subjects. Every relationship was mediated by power, by difference, by hierarchy – a fact that Darling was reluctant to accept.

The Cambridge man's ideal of friendship in the colony fused with his vision of paternal rule – love for those who were not yet mature and who seemed incapable of looking after themselves. Every demand for such paternal care gladdened Darling's heart and affirmed his

[39] For an insightful exploration of the politics of friendship and the problems of dialogue, see Visvanathan, *Friendship, Interiority, Mysticism*. On the cult of friendship in Cambridge, see Dewey, *The Mind of the Indian Civil Service*. My reading of the politics of friendship in the colony is different from that of Dewey's, who suggests that the ideology of friendship could not work in India because Indians and the English operated with radically different notions. For Indians friendship meant total loyalty: real friends had to be absolutely partisan, backing each other against the world, demanding favours from each other, regardless of questions of right and wrong. For Englishmen, he says, "friendship was a more circumscribed affair, a matter of common interests and personal rapport"; it was congenial companionship mediated by "respect for abstract moral principles". In India friendship was a condition of survival, while in England the police and the courts protected persons and property. Dewey, *The Mind of the Indian Civil Service*, pp. 166, 196–8. To me, this contrast seems based on problematic and essentialised binaries: within India and Britain conceptions of friendships could vary. And in the colony friendships between coloniser and colonised, in particular, were inevitably mediated by race and power.

[40] Dewey, *The Mind of the Indian Civil Service*, ch. 5. However, Lowes Dickinson, known for his Sinophilia, was, unlike his other student E.M. Forster, not much enthused by the idea of friendship with India (personal communication, Rukun Advani).

deepest instincts. Recording his experience in a Hoshiarpur village, he says that after a meeting in which everyone seemed anxious to get azadi, he met "a wise old bird of some standing" who said privately: "You should keep a hand on our heads, as a father does with a child who cannot yet look after himself."[41] One lone voice, privately expressed, subverts for Darling the truth of what everyone has publicly asserted at a village meeting.

Darling's friend E.M. Forster was more sensitive to the dilemmas of friendship within an imperial setting. The poignant ending of *A Passage to India* expresses the politics of such friendships with evocative power. As Aziz and Fielding ride together, the latter says: "Away from us, Indians go to seed at once." Aziz cries in mock battle:

> "Down with the English . . . Clear out, you fellows, double quick, I say . . . we shall drive every blasted Englishman into the sea, and then," he concluded, half kissing him, "you and I shall be friends."
>
> "Why can't we be friends now?" said the other, holding him affectionately. "It's what I want. It's what you want."
>
> But the horses didn't want it – they swerved apart; the earth didn't want it . . . the temples, the tank, the jail, the palace, the birds, the carrion . . .; they didn't want it, they said in their hundred voices, "No not yet," and the sky said, "No, not there."[42]

Darling had read Forster. Together they had reflected on life and politics.[43] But writing almost twenty years after *A Passage to India* (1924), Darling was all the same reluctant to give up the convictions of his youth. He recognised, at times, that British and Indians could not be real friends until they were equals. But more often his words appear oblivious of the politics of empire. At a roadside meeting in Garhi, attended by many Sikhs and three communists, he hears a lot about freedom and is assertively told: "We want you to go." Darling listens patiently and then says: "The Sahibs of my race also want to go, and as soon as possible . . . But my worthless opinion

---

[41] *At Freedom's Door*, p. 98.

[42] Forster, *A Passage to India*, pp. 315–16.

[43] On Forster's friendship with Darling, see Dewey, *The Mind of the Indian Civil Service*, chs 6 and 7.

is that neither should you send them away, nor should they choose to go. They should stay, but as brothers and equals. England needs Hindustan in the affairs of the world, and Hindustan needs England in its own affairs."[44]

Equality is read here as mutual need, and the bonds of brotherhood are imagined within the frame of empire. The implications of structured differences – race, power, hierarchy – are ignored. The irony of the framing does not strike Darling: England does not need India in its own affairs; India does!

In the politically charged atmosphere of 1947, at a time when Darling found it difficult to sustain his faith in friendship, walking around a Sikh village he felt one day "a soft little hand" steal into his. Looking down he saw a Sikh boy of five at his side, and they continued hand in hand till he left the village.[45] To Darling the child's gesture was not just heart-warming, it signified a lost possibility, a potential that had not been adequately explored. Writing about the incident in his diary, he laments: "And there is India herself who has never been willing to put her hand in ours. Perhaps the day will come when she will do so, when, as in my case, England is *functus officio*."[46]

That day was yet to come.

~

Darling wrote the diary of his last ride a hundred years after Henry Lawrence published his *Adventures*. The two texts mark two momentous times, they chronicle two rides with contrasting meanings and open up two opposing imaginings. In *Adventures*, Bellasis

[44] Ibid., p. 121. There are many such statements in *At Freedom's Door*. Riding into Gurdaspur, Darling heard a lot of talk of azadi; the man he "felt most in sympathy with" was a little middle-aged peasant with a scrubby red beard who waited on Darling with a deputation of local notables: "Speaking with great earnestness, he said they all wanted freedom, yet they did not want us to go: on the contrary, they were most anxious for us to stay and help them, but as 'brothers and equals'. That seemed to me wisdom itself, for in the futures which of us can do without the other?" *At Freedom's Door*, p. 104.

[45] Ibid.

[46] Ibid.

Fig: 22: The Hand of Friendship.
Courtesy: Centre of South Asian Studies, Cambridge.

rides into Punjab before the region has been conquered; Darling's ride happens on the eve of the British departure from India. *Adventures* – written some years before Lawrence took command of Punjab – looks at the future. It expresses a fantasy of power, a will to dominate, control, and transform a world. In Darling's text the dreams of power dissolve and hopes of friendship are shattered. *Adventures* is about a world to be gained, the empire to be built, and the consequent work to be done. It expresses the self-assurance of imperial authority, its confidence in realising the possibilities that remain hidden from the "natives" in carrying through imperial transformative projects. *At Freedom's Door* is by contrast about the loss of empire.

In *Adventures* the "natives" desire British rule and are willing to be loyal; they love the English, acknowledge their high moral character, sense of justice, intelligence, and dynamism, they recognise their good work. *At Freedom's Door* chronicles the voices of villagers restless for freedom: they question the deeds of the British, refuse to recognise the gifts of British rule, and narrate tales of misery and suffering. Lawrence's imaginary ride into Punjab was an allegory of conquest; Darling's last ride was imbued with colonial nostalgia.

Adventures is about the native's eagerness to be infantalised, to be seen as a child yearning for nurture and in search of a responsible father; it is about the British willingness to be caring and sensitive in discharging their paternal responsibilities. *At Freedom's Door* on the other hand is saturated with the theme of disavowal and rejection: the children, having been looked after by their father, are now repudiating all that their father has done for them. It expresses the imperial angst about being disowned. When the father's right is questioned, his paternal love rejected, his claim to benevolent tutelage doubted, his self-image of being an empathetic guardian mocked, the paterfamilias faces a profound crisis.

Riding in that ambivalent moment of imperial reckoning, Darling sought to gather the splintered pieces of his broken identity. The critical voices that he tried to disrupt in his diary persistently returned to haunt him. Everywhere he heard the cry of azadi; everyone seemed to scream out to him: "We want you to leave." In those unsettling moments the warm memory of the silently confiding hand of the child he met in a Hoshiarpur village could not suffice to reaffirm his self-belief.

Glossary

abadi	habitation; the area where village residents live
abadkar	one who settles a space, clears a tract of land, and brings it under cultivation
abi	land watered by lifts from tanks, or pools, or marshes
adhlapi	one who helps sink a well, thus acquiring rights to land irrigated by the well: the right was usually to a half (*adh*) share of the owner's land
adna malik	classified in colonial revenue records as "inferior proprietor"
ala malik	classified in colonial revenue records as "superior proprietor"
ala-lambardar	chief headman
amin	under colonial revenue administration, a surveyor employed to make village maps and adjudicate boundary disputes
arzi	written petition, application
banjar	uncultivated land, considered barren
bār	uplands – mostly arid pastures – located in the interfluves of the Sutlej, Ravi, and Chenab rivers
barani	cultivated land which is dependent on rainfall
beegha/bigha	a unit of land measure, varying in different parts of India before the British rule. The *beegha* employed in the colonial settlement surveys of eastern Punjab was 5/24ths of an acre. It was

459

	known as the *kachcha beegha*, to distinguish it from the Shahjahani *beegha*, which was exactly three times as large
bét	low-lying land adjoining a river, its soil usually clayey loam, its cultivation dependent on inundation, variously termed in different parts of Punjab as *hithar, khadir, dahar*
bhunga	cess on cattle levied by proprietors (*khewatdars*) on other residents in a village for grazing on the village *shamilat* (land designated by the revenue department as village common)
biswa	a unit of land measure. Twenty *biswas* made a *beegha* (see *beegha*)
butimar/butemar/ bootimar/butamar	lit., those who clear the scrub/shrub (*buti/booti*) or roots (*mund*); individuals who acquired specific rights on the land thus cleared; in some regions called *mundemar*
chaal	alluvium silt
chahi	land irrigated from the well (*chah*)
chak	assessment circle, a block of land on which revenue (land revenue/grazing tax) was assessed at the same rate
chakdar	the term used in Multan for someone who helps in sinking a well and acquires rights to land attached to the well, and irrigated by the well; elsewhere the term used for such right holders was *adhlapi*
chaudhri	rural notable
chaupal	village meeting place
dakhar/dakar	stiff clayey loam
desi	indigenous, local
dhaya	upland, variously termed in different parts of Punjab as *manjha, utar, bangar*

dhok	outlying hamlet
ghair-mauroosee	classified in colonial revenue records as tenants without occupancy rights
ghumao	a unit of land measure: where the *kadam* measure was 66 inches (see *kadam*), a *ghumao* was exactly an acre
hadbast	the village boundary; the list of villages in every tehsil had a *hadbast* number
haq zamindari	also known as *malikana*, this was a fractional charge upon the gross produce of the cultivator, collected by *jagirdars*, *taluqdars*, and zamindars in the Mughal period
hissa	share
jan	people; a community of pastoral nomads, the followers of the clan leader (*rāt*)
jangal	tract covered with scrub, brushwood, and small trees
jangli	those who live in the *jangal*, in lands covered with brushwood and scrub; a term used pejoratively in colonial records, categorising "*janglis*" as the other of settled peasants
jhok	a type of encampment of the nomads
kadam	a unit of land measure. Land in pre-colonial rural India was most commonly measured by pacing. When a man stepped out left foot first, the pace or *kadam* was the distance between the heel of the right foot in its original position and the heel of the same foot after it had been advanced in front of the left foot to take the second step. *Kadams* could vary from 54 to 66 inches
kalar/kallar	brackish soil; soil affected by salinity due to waterlogging; often used more generally to describe land seen as sterile

kanal	a measure of land: twenty *marlas* made a *kanal* (see *marla*), and eight *kanals* made a *ghumao* (see *ghumao*)
kanungo	a revenue official who supervised the work of a number of *patwaris* and co-ordinated the revenue administration of a district
kardar	in pre-British Punjab, an official in charge of a *pargana*, who had fiscal and judicial powers
khasra	a field register in which the field numbers of each field recorded in the village map (*shajra*) are entered, along with the details of the field measurement
khatauni	a list of cultivators' holdings
khewat	in the North Western Provinces and Punjab, a register in which the names of all the share-holders (*khewatdars*) of a coparcenary village were recorded; a record of owners' holdings, the holding on which revenue was charged
khewatdar	one who holds a *khewat*; designated in colonial revenue records of the North Western Provinces and Punjab as proprietor
khewat-khataunis	a combined list of owners' and cultivators' hold-ings, maintained at the revenue record room as a part of village papers
killa	rectangular plots with straight lines (usually of 1.1 acres), the form in which Canal Colony lands were demarcated
killabandi	the act of enclosing and partitioning the com-mons in the Canal Colonies of Punjab, erecting demarcating pillars and subdividing the land into squares – by which method pastoral land was converted into an agrarian landscape
kuhmar	one who helps sink a well (*kuh*) and so acquires rights on land irrigated by the well

lambardar	village headman
lath	mound around an embanked field; embankment
lathbund	those who helped to erect an embankment and who by building and maintaining embankments acquired specific rights in the land so irrigated
mahsul	share of the produce due to the state; under colonial administration it was a share of the produce taken by someone who then paid monetary revenue to the state
maira	a very light loamy soil
malba	officially designated as "village income"
malik	leading man; also, a landowner
malik kabza	those who acquired control over land through occupation (*kabza*), and not patrilineal connection with the original founders of a coparcenary community
manjha	upland, variously termed in the different parts of Punjab as *dhaia, utar, bagar/bangar*
marla	a unit of land measure. Twenty *marlas* made a *kanal* (see *kanal*) and 160 *marlas* made a *ghumao* (see *ghumao*)
mauroosee	revenue term for classifying tenants with rights of occupancy
mauza	a space bounded and designated "village" in colonial revenue surveys; the spatial unit for revenue assessment
muharrir	clerk
mukarraridar	person classified as occupancy tenant in colonial revenue records
mundemar	see *butimar*
muqaddam/ mukaddim	a leading man within the village community, designated in colonial revenue records as "superior proprietor"

nahri	land irrigated by a canal
nazrana	an exaction/cess imposed in addition to the regular revenue demand; a tribute paid by a subordinate landowner to someone more powerful – the *jagirdar* or the state
niai/niain	land near the village, usually well manured
pahi/pahee	in colonial revenue records, a tenant who does not live in the village in which he cultivates land, classified as tenant at will
pana	a subdivision of a revenue estate (*mahal*)
panch-sultani	a committee of village notables
patta	a deed of land grant or lease
patti	subdivison of a *mauza*
patwari	village accountant; the revenue official who maintained village records
pawanji	a form of tribute
rahna	a type of encampment of nomads
rakh	a preserve; pastureland taken over by the colonial state and excluded from "unregulated" nomadic movement
rat	leader of a nomadic clan who offered protection to his followers (*jan*) and led the clan in raids and counter-raids
rausli/rausuli	a fertile, light loamy soil
retli	sandy soil
riwaj-i-am	record of customs maintained by the revenue department
rohi	a loamy soil, stiffer than both *maira* and *rausli*
sailab/sailaba	land moistened by the river
sami	co-sharer, partner (derived from the term *sam*: equal; or "together")

sanjhi	partner in cultivation, sharer: one whose share depended on the amount of labour contributed to cultivation
sajra	map
shajra nasab	record of the history of the village maintained as part of village records
shamilat	land designated by the colonial state as "village common" or "village waste", attached to each village, and over which all *khewatdars* had a right
taraf	a subdivision of a revenue estate (*mauza/mahal*)
thakbast	the process of surveying, measuring, and bounding spaces into villages (*mauzas*)
thok	a subdivision of a revenue estate (*mahal*)
tirni	grazing tax
wajib-ul-arz	record of rights; a village administration paper
waris	owner with rights of inheritance; in the colonial revenue records of North West Provinces and Punjab, those considered original owners were classified as *waris*
wirasat	territory within which the authority and power of the *waris* was asserted

Bibliography

PROCEEDINGS AND CONSULTATIONS OF THE GOVERNMENT OF INDIA

(National Archives of India, New Delhi;
British Library, London)

Foreign 1834–1921
Home (Miscellaneous 1851–1920; Judicial 1851–1936; Legislative 1851–1936; Police 1862–1936; Public 1871–1921; Political 1861–1934)
Public Works 1855–1923
Revenue and Agriculture (Revenue 1859–1921; Famine 1873–1923; Agriculture 1871–1921; Forest 1864–1931; Irrigation 1861–1922)
Surveys and Land Surveys 1881–9

PROCEEDINGS OF THE GOVERNMENT OF PUNJAB

(Punjab State Archives, Chandigarh and Patiala;
Financial Commissioner's Office, Chandigarh;
British Library, London)

Agriculture, Revenue and Commerce, 1871–1881
Foreign 1873–1936
Forest 1871–1932
Home 1871–1936
Irrigation 1873–1923
Police 1870–1903
Public Works 1864–1923
Revenue and Agriculture 1882–1931

DIVISIONAL RECORDS

(The following records were earlier housed in the Haryana Archives, Sector 18, Chandigarh, and have now been transferred to the Haryana Archives, Panchkula, Chandigarh, and to some of the regional repositories in Ambala, Hissar, and Rohtak)

Ambala Division Records (General and Political 1857–80; Judicial Press listed 1857–64; Judicial Non-Press listed 1847–67; Revenue 1846–67)

Delhi Division (Revenue 1857–80; Public Works 1862–73; Judicial 1857–73)
Hissar Division Records (Other matters 1835–1903)

SURVEY OF INDIA RECORDS
(National Archives of India, British Library)

Punjab Revenue Survey Maps, 1870s
Reports of the Revenue Survey Operations in Punjab, Dehra Dun Records, 1850–70s
Reports of Topographical Survey Operations in Punjab, 1850s

NEWSPAPERS AND JOURNALS

Folklore
North Indian Notes and Queries
Panjab Notes and Queries
The Punjabee
Report of the Native News Papers of the Punjab
The Calcutta Review
The Indian Antiquary
The Indian Forester
The Khalsa Advocate
The Tribune
The Times of India

PRIVATE PAPERS

F.L. Brayne Papers (BL)
Dalhousie Papers (NAS)
Henry Lawrence Collection (BL)
John Hobhouse (Broughton) Collection (BL)
John Lawrence Collection (BL)
Malcolm Darling Collection (CSAL)
Richard Temple Collection (BL)
Special Collection, University of St Andrews, Scotland, UK

REPORTS AND MANUALS

Selections from the Public Correspondence of the
Administration for the Affairs of the Punjab

Agnew, Vans, Davies, A., New Method of Fixing and Sketching the Boundaries of Villages (1852), *SPCAAP*, vol. 1, no. 2, art. 6.

Barnes, G.C., Memorandum on the System of Measurement Pursued in the Kangra District Preparatory to the Settlement under Regulation IX of 1833 (1850), *SPCAAP*, vol. 1, no. 1, art. 3.

Barnes, G.C., R. Temple, E.A. Prinsep, and R.H. Davies, New System of Field Measurement in the Punjab – Reports (1852), *SPCAAP*, vol. 1, no. 3, art. 11.

Canals of the Mooltan District [1849], *SPCAAP*, vol. 1, no. 1, art. 1.

Hamilton, G.W., Capt., On the Tirnee Tax of Jhung (1851), *SPCAAP*, vol. 1, no. 2, art. 9.

James, H.R., Report on the Revised Settlement of the Momunds [Hazara], by 1854–5, *SPCAAP*, vol. 2, no. 7, art. 18.

Mozuffurghur Settlement Papers (1850), *SPCAAP*, vol. 1, no. 1, art. 3.

Pollock, F.R., "Memorandum on the Dera Ghazi Khan District, 1860", *SPCAAP*, vol. 4, no. 4.

Selections from the Records of the Government of the
Punjab and its Dependencies: New Series

Bruce, R.B.J., Notes on the Dera Ghazee Khan District, N.W. Frontier, and its Border Tribes, 1870, *SRGPD, NS*, no. 9.

Cavagnari, P.L.N., Report on the Kohat Pass Afridis, 1867, *SRGPD, NS*, no. 19.

Minchin, C., Capt., Memorandum on the Beloch Tribes in the Dera Ghazi Khan District, 1867, *SRGPD, NS*, no. 3.

Papers Relating to the Gakhar Tribe, *SRGPD*, no. 23.

Papers Relating to State of Affairs in Swat, etc., 1877, *SRGPD, NS*, no. 14.

Urmston, H.B., Notes on the Bunnoo District, 1869, *SRGPD, NS*, no. 1.

Selections from the Records of the Office of the
Financial Commissioner, Punjab

Ala Lambardari System (Village Headmen), P.R. 10 (1875), Correspondence 1862–74, *SRFCP*, no. 48.

Extension of Canal Irrigation in the Dehra Ismail Khan and Dehra Ghazee Khan Districts, *SRFCP*, no. 18: 3.

Irrigation Canals, Shahpore District, P.R. 3 (1868), *SRFCP*, no. 10.

Pay of Village Chowkidars and Patwaris, P.R. 4 (1869), *SRFCP*, no. 30.

Proposals for the Systematisation of Future Survey Operations in the Punjab, 1884, *SRFCP*, 54.

Year to be Adopted in the Preparation of Patwaris' Annual Papers and Accounts, *SRFCP*, no. 32.

Selections from the Records of the Financial Commissioner,
Punjab, New Series

Boundaries of Villages and Districts Subject to River Action, 1887, *SRFCP*, *NS*, no. 63.

Correspondence Relating to the Ferozepur and Fazilka Inundation Canals, 1887, *SRFCP*, *NS*, no. 61.

Mr E. Prinsep's Settlements, 1863–1870: Principles of Assessment and Term of Settlement, 1889, *SRFCP*, *NS*, no. 67.

Note on the Systems of Fluctuating Assessment Now Existing in the Punjab, 1884, *SRFCP*, *NS*, no. 53.

Papers Connected with the Rawalpindi Forest Settlement, 1911, *SRFCP*, *NS*, no. 81.

Papers on the Formation of Fuel and Fodder Resources, 1886, *SRFCP*, *NS*, no. 60.

Papers Relating to Canals, 1887, *SRFCP*, *NS*, no. 62.

Papers on the Indebtedness of Agriculturists in the Punjab and Foreclosure of Mortgage, *SRFCP*, *NS*, no. 65.

Papers Relating to the Irrigation Works in the Sialkot District, 1895, *SRFCP*, *NS*, no. 71.

Papers Relating to the Rights of Government in Wastelands in the Rawalpindi District, 1892, *SRFCP*, *NS*, no. 70.

Recent Papers on Leading Questions Relating to Settlements and Land Revenue Administration, 1885, *SRFCP*, *NS*, no. 55.

Revision of Tenancy Entries in Mr E. Prinsep's Settlements Subsequent to the Passing of Act XXVIII of 1868, 1889, *SRFCP*, *NS*, no. 68.

Tirni Administration [Grazing Tax], Lahore: C. & M. Gazette Press, 1885, *SRFCP*, *NS*, no. 56.

Selections from the Records of the Government of the
North-West Provinces

Mr Thomason's Despatches, vol. I: 12 – Despatches and Minutes of the NWP Government, 1844–1850, Selected from a Collection Made by James Thomason for Private Use and Reference while Lieut. Governor.

Customary Law Reports and Digests

Boulnois, Charles, and W.H. Rattigan, *Notes on Customary Law as Administered in the Courts of the Punjab*, London: W. Clowes and Sons, 1878.

Craik, H.D., *Customary Law of the Amritsar District*, Lahore, 1914.

Currie, M.M.L., *Customary Law of the Ferozepore District*, Lahore: Supt., Govt Printing, 1915.

———, *Customary Law of the Hoshiarpur District (Tahsils Dasuya, Hoshiarpur & Garhshankar)*, Lahore, 1914.

Dane, Louis W., *Customary Law of the Main Tribes in the Gurdaspur District*, Lahore, 1893.

Davies, Henry S.P., *Customary Law of the Gujrat District*, Lahore: Civil and Military Gazette Press, 1892.

Diack, A.H., *Customary Law of the Dera Ghazi Khan District*, Lahore, 1898.

Douie, James M.C., *Riwaj-i-am of Tahsil Kaithal of Pargana Indri in the Karnal District*, Lahore: Civil & Military Gazette Press, 1892.

Dunnett, James M., *The Customary Law of the Ludhiana District*, Lahore: Punjab Govt Press, 1911.

Joseph, E.A.A., *The Customary Law of the Rohtak District*, Lahore: Civil and Military Gazette Press, 1911.

Kaul, Hari Kishan, *Customary Law of the Mianwali District*, Lahore: Civil and Military Gazette Press, 1908.

———, *Customary Law of the Muzaffargarh District*, Lahore: Civil and Military Gazette Press, 1903.

Kensington, A., *Customary Law of the Ambala District*, Lahore: Civil and Military Gazette Press, 1893.

Kitchin, A.J.W., *Customary Law of the Attock District*, Lahore: Civil and Military Gazette Press, 1911.

Krishna, Pandit Maharaj, *Memorandum on the Tribal Customs of Rohtak District*, n.d., n.p.

Middleton, L., *Customary Law of the Kangra District (Excluding Kulu)*, Lahore: Supt., Govt Press, 1919.

Punjab District Gazetteers, vol. VIB, 1912, Lahore: Civil and Military Gazette Press.

The Punjab Laws Act (IV of 1872), with Intro., Notes, and Rules (1897).

Rattigan, W.H.A., *Digest of Civil Law for the Punjab: Chiefly Based on the Customary Law As at Present Judicially Ascertained*, Allahabad: Pioneer Press, 1893.

Report on the Punjab Codification of Customary Law Conference, September 1915, Lahore, 1915.

Robertson, Frederick A., *The Customary Law of the Rawalpindi District*, Lahore: Civil and Military Gazette Press, 1887.

Roe, Charles A., *Customary Law of the Multan District*, Lahore: Civil and Military Gazette Press, 1883.

———— and H.A.B. Rattigan, *Tribal Law in the Punjab, So Far as it Relates to Rights in Ancestral Land*, Lahore, 1895.

Rose, H.A., and M.M. Shafi, *A Compendium of the Punjab Customary Law*, Lahore: Civil and Military Gazette Press, 1911.

Rustomji, K.J.A., *Treatise on Customary Law in the Punjab: Being an Exhaustive and Critical Commentary on Punjab Custom*, Lahore: University Book Agency, 1930.

Smith, James R.D., *Customary Law of the Main Tribes of the Sialkot District*, Lahore: Civil and Military Gazette Press, 1895.

Townsend, C.A.H., *The Customary Law of the Hissar District*, Punjab Govt Press, 1913.

Tupper, C.L., *Punjab Customary Law*, vols I–III, Calcutta: Superintendent of Government Printing, 1881.

Walker, G.C., *The Customary Law of the Main Tribes in the Lahore District*, Lahore: Civil and Military Gazette Press, 1894.

Walker, Thomas Gordon, *The Customary Law of the Ludhiana District*, Calcutta, 1885.

Whitehead, R.B., *Customary Law of the Ambala District*, Lahore, Supt, Govt Printing, 1921.

Williamson, Herbert S., *Customary Law of the Gujrat District*, Lahore: Superintendent of Government Printing, 1922.

Wilson, James, *General Code of Tribal Custom in Shahpur District*, vol. XV, Lahore, Civil & Military Gazette Press, 1896.

————, *General Code of Tribal Custom in the Sirsa District of the Panjab*, Calcutta: Government Printing, 1883.

Wilson, William R., *Customary Law of the Dera Ghazi Khan District*, Lahore: Superintendent of Government Printing, 1922.

Settlement Reports and Assessment Reports

Abbot, E.R., *Settlement Report of the Jhang District*, 1906, Lahore: Civil and Military Gazette Press, 1907.

Anderson, A., *Final Report of the Revised Settlement of Kangra Proper, 1897*, Lahore: Civil and Military Gazette Press, 1897.

———, and P.J. Fegan, *Report on the Revised Settlement of the Hissar District, 1887–92*, Lahore: Civil and Military Gazette Press, 1892.

Barnes, George C., *Report on the Settlement in the District of Kangra in the Trans-Sutlej States*, Lahore: Chronicle Press, 1855.

Brandreth, A., *Report on the Settlement of the District of Jhelum in the Rawulpindee Division*, Lahore: Hope Press, 1865.

Brandreth, E.L. *Report on the Revised Settlement of the District of Ferozpur in the Cis-Sutlej States*, Lahore, 1859.

Chand, Munshi Amin, *Report on the Revised Land Revenue Settlement of the Hissar District in the Hissar Division of the Panjab*, Lahore: Victoria Press, 1875.

Channing, F.C., *Land Revenue Settlement of the Gurgaon District*, Lahore: Central Jail Press, 1882.

Correspondence Relating to the Settlement of Sirsa District, Lahore, Central Jail Press, 1873.

Cracroft, J.E., *Report on the Settlement of Rawulpindee*, Lahore, 1864.

Dane, Louis W., *Final Report of the Revised Settlement of the Gurdaspur District, in the Punjab, 1892*, Lahore: Civil and Military Gazette Press, 1892.

Davies, H., *Final Report on the Revision of the Settlement of Gujrat District, 1893*, Lahore: Civil and Military Gazette Press, 1894.

Davies, R.H., *Report on the Revised Settlement of the Greater Part of the District of Gurdaspur in the Amritsar Division*, Lahore: Punjabee Press, 1859.

Diack, A.H., *Final Report on the Revision of Settlement (1893–97), Dera Ghazi Khan District*, Lahore: Civil and Military Gazette Press, 1898.

Dobson, Bernard H., *Final Report on the Chenab Colony Settlement*, Lahore: Superintendent Government Printing, Punjab, 1915.

Dunlop-Smith, J.R., *Final Report of the Revision of the Settlement of the Sialkot District in the Punjab, 1888–1895*, Lahore: Civil and Military Gazette Press, 1895.

Elphinstone, *Report of the Settlement of Googaira District*, Lahore: Koh-i-Noor Press, 1860.

Evans, H.F., *Report on the Settlement of the Agra District, North-western Provinces*, Allahabad: Northwestern Provinces and Oudh Govt Press, 1880.

Fagan, P.J., *Report on the Settlement of the Khalsa Villages of Bikaner State*, n.p., 1893.

Fryer, F.W.R., *Final Report on the First Regular Settlement of the Dera Ghazi Khan District, in the Derajat Division, 1869 to 1874*, Lahore: Central Jail Press, 1876.

Gazetteer of the Chenab Colony, 1904, Lahore: Civil and Military Gazette Press, 1905.

Hastings, E.G.G., *Report of the Regular Settlement of the Peshawar District of the Punjab*, Lahore: Central Jail Press, 1878.

Ibbetson, Denzil, *Report on the Revision of Settlement of the Panipat Tahsil and Karnal Parganah of the Karnal District, 1872– 80*, Allahabad: Pioneer Press, 1883.

James, H.R., *Report of the Revised Settlement of the Mommunds (Hazara)*, n.p., 1853.

Kitchin, A.J.W., *Final Report of the Revision of the Settlement of the Attock District in the Punjab*, Lahore: Civil and Military Gazette Press, 1909.

———, *Final Report of the Revision of the Settlement of the Rawalpindi District in the Punjab*, Lahore: Civil and Military Gazette Press, 1909.

Lyall, J.B., *Report of the Land Revenue Settlement of the Kangra District, Punjab, 1865–72*, Lahore: Central Jail Press, 1874.

Mackenzie, H., *Report on the Revised Settlement of the Goojerat District, in the Rawulpindee Division*, Lahore: Hope Press, 1861.

Maclagan, Edward, *Settlement Report of the Multan District*, Lahore: Civil and Military Gazette Press, 1901.

Maps to Accompany the Revenue Settlement Report of Sirsa District, Calcutta, 1884–91.

Maps to Accompany the Revised Land Revenue Settlement of the Montgomery District, Calcutta, 1878.

Monckton, Henry, *Report on the Revised Settlement of the Jhung District in the Mooltan Division*, Lahore: Hope Press, 1860.

Nisbet, R.P., *Report on the Revision of the Land Revenue Settlement of the Gujranwala District, 1866 & 1867*, Lahore: W.E. Ball, 1874.

O'Brien, Edward, *Report on the Land Revenue Settlement of the Muzaffargarh District of the Punjab, 1873–80*, Lahore: Central Jail Press, 1882.

Penny, J. D., *Final Settlement Report of the Jhang and Gugera Branch Circles of the Lyallpur District*, Lahore: Superintendent of Government Printing, Punjab, 1925.

Porter, F W., *Final Report on the Survey and Revision of Records Recently Completed for the Benares District*, Allahabad: North-Western Provinces and Oudh Govt. Press, 1887.

Prinsep, E.A., *Report on the Revised Settlement of Sealkote District, in the Amritsur Division*, Lahore: Chronicle Press, 1865.

Punjab District Gazetteer, vol. VI B, 1912, Lahore: Civil and Military Gazette Press.

Purser, W.E., *Assessment Report of Nawashahr Tahsil of the Jullundur District*, Lahore: Civil and Military Gazette Press,1883.

———, *Assessment Report of the Jullunder Tahsil of the Jullundur District*, Lahore: Civil and Military Gazette Press, 1883.

———, *Assessment Report of the Nakodar Tahsil of the Jullundur District*, Lahore: Civil and Military Gazette Press, 1883.

———, *Final Report of the Revised Settlement of the Jullundur District in the Punjab, 1880–6*, Lahore: Civil and Military Gazette Press, 1892.

———, and H.C. Fanshawe, *Report on the Revised Land Revenue Settlement of the Rohtak District of the Hissar Division in the Punjab, 1873–79*, Lahore: W. Ball, 1882.

Robertson, F.A., *Final Report of the Revised Settlement of the Rawalpindi District in the Punjab, 1880–87*, Lahore: Civil and Military Gazette Press, 1893.

Roe, C.A., *Report on the Revision of Settlement Records of the U'nah Parganah of the Hoshiarpur District, 1869–70*, Lahore: Victoria Press, 1876.

———, and W.E. Purser, *Report on the Revised Land Revenue Settlement of the Montgomery District in the Mooltan Division of the Punjab*, Lahore: Central Jail Press, 1878.

Roe, Charles A., *Report on the Revised Settlement of the Multan District of the Punjab*, Lahore: W. Ball, 1883.

Reid, J. R., *Report on the District of Azamgarh: Compiled in Connection with the Completion of the Sixth Settlement*, Allahabad: North-western and Oudh Govt. Press, 1877.

Report on the Settlement of the Etawah District, for the Years 1868 to 1874, Allahabad: North-western Provinces Press, 1875.

Saunders, Leslie S., *Report on the Revised Land Revenue Settlement of the Lahore District in the Lahore Division of the Panjab, 1865–69*, Lahore: Central Jail Press, 1873.

Steedman, E.B., *Assessment Report of the Chiniot Tahsil of the Jhang District,* Lahore: Civil and Military Gazette Press, 1880.

Steedman, E.B., *Report on the Revised Settlement of the Jhang District of the Punjab, 1874–80,* Lahore: W. Ball, 1882.

Talbot, W.S., *Final Report of the Revision of the Settlement of the Jhelum District in the Punjab, 1895–1901,* Lahore: Civil and Military Gazette Press.

Temple, R., *Report on the Settlement of the District of Jullundhur, Trans-Sutlej States,* Lahore: Lahore Chronicle Press, 1852.

Thomson, R.G.A., *Report of the Second Regular Settlement of the Land Revenue of the Jhelum District in the Rawalpindi Division of the Punjab,* Lahore: Arya Press, 1883.

Thorburn, S.S., *Report on the First Regular Land Revenue Settlement of the Bannu District in the Derajat Division of the Punjab,* Lahore: Central Jail Press, 1879.

Tucker, H.S.G., *Report of the Land Revenue Settlement of the Dera Ismail Khan District of the Punjab, 1872–79,* Lahore: W. Ball, 1879.

Wace, E.G., *Report of the Land Revenue Settlement of the Hazara District of the Punjab, 1868–74,* Lahore: Central Jail Press, 1876.

Wace, F.B., and F.C. Bourne, *Punjab District Gazetteer: Volume XVIII A, Montgomery District,* Lahore: Superintendent of Government Printing, Punjab, 1935.

Walker, Gordon Thomas, *Final Report on the Revision of Settlement 1878–83 of the Ludhiana District in the Punjab,* Calcutta: Calcutta Central Press, 1884.

Whiteway, R.S., *Report on the Settlement of the Muttra District,* Allahabad: NWP & Oudh Govt Press, 1879.

Wilson, J., *Final Report on the Revision of Settlement of the Sirsa District in the Punjab, 1879–1883,* Calcutta: Calcutta Central Press Company, 1884.

Wynyard, W., *Report on the Revised Settlement of the Southern Pargunahs of the District of Amballa, in the Cis-Satlej States,* Lahore: Chronicle Press, 1859.

Annual Reports, Reports of Commissions/Boards/Special Enquiries (Official/Unofficial)

Anjuman-i-Punjab, *Proceedings in Connection with the Proposed Establishment of Village Panchaits,* Lahore: Albert Press, 1878.

Annual Report of the Lower Bari Doab Canal Colony.

Annual Report on the Punjab Colonies, Lahore: Superintendent, Government Printing, Punjab, n.d.

Annual Reports for the Chenab, Jhelum, Chunian and Sohag Para Colonies (Annual Report on the Punjab Colonies) for the Year Ending 30th September 1902 to 1934, Lahore, 1903.

Farm Accounts in the Punjab, BEIP 1924–45, Lahore: Military Gazette Press, annual.

Lindley, E.S., *An Estimate of the Areas Affected By, and Threatened With, Water-Logging with Their Past History, and of the Extent to Which Remedial Measures Will Be Necessary,* Lahore, 1929.

Mutiny Records, Reports, pts 1 & 2, Lahore: Punjab Govt Press, 1911.

Pearson, H.J., *Notes on Water-logging in the Punjab,* 2 vols, 3 parts.

Proceedings of the Water-logging Conference, Punjab, 1928–38, annual.

Progress Report on Forest Administration in the Punjab, Lahore, annual.

Punjab Legislative Assembly Debates, Lahore: Superintendent of Government Printing, Punjab, from 1936, annual.

Punjab Legislative Council Debates, Lahore: Superintendent of Government Press, Punjab, 1921–36, annual.

Report (General Report) on the Administration of the Punjab for the Years 1849–50 and 1850–51, to 1854–55 to 1855–56, n.p., n.d.

Report of the Indian Famine Commission, London: Eyre & Spottiswoode, 1880.

Report of the Indian Irrigation Commission, 1901–03, Parts I–III, Calcutta: Office of the Superintendent of Government Printing, 1903.

Report of the Royal Commission Upon Decentralization in India, vol. 1, House of Commons Parliamentary Papers.

Report of the Working of Panchayats in the Punjab, Annual, 1925–6 to 1940–1.

Report on Police Administration in the Punjab and Its Dependencies, for the Year, Annual, 1861 to 1937.

Report on the Administration of Civil Justice in the Punjab and Its Dependencies, Lahore: Government Press, annual, 1861 to 1918.

Report on the Administration of Criminal Justice in the Punjab and Its Dependencies, annual, 1853 to 1918.

Report on the Revenue (Land Revenue) Administration of the Panjab and Its Dependencies, 1862–3 to 1934–5.

Report on the Season and Crops of the Punjab, annual, 1901–2 to 1946–7.

Report on the Working of Co-operative Societies in the Punjab, annual 1919–20 to 1948–9.

Revenue Report of the Irrigation Department, Punjab, 1871–1945, Lahore, annual.

Review of Agricultural Operations in British India, 1919–20.

Sanitary Survey of Villages Watered by the Western Jumna Canal (Report by Taylor and Associated Correspondence, 1867–9), *SRGOP, NS,* no. 6.

Taylor, E.M., J.K. Malhotra, and M.L. Mehta, *Investigation of the Rise of Water-Table in the Upper Chenab Canal Area, Punjab,* 1933, Punjab Irrigation Research Publications, vol. 1, part 4.

The Punjab Famine of 1899–1900, 3 vols, Lahore: Punjab Govt Press, 1901.

Water-logging Board, Punjab: Proceedings of Meetings, 1928–36, vols 1–5.

Water-logging of the Soil in the Vicinity of Punjab Irrigation Canals and Measures for the Prevention of Water-logging, Punjab Irrigation Branch Papers, no. A20, 1924.

MANUALS AND LEGAL TEXTS

Baden-Powell, B.H., *A Manual of the Land Revenue Systems and Land Tenures of British India,* Calcutta: Superintendent of Government Printing, 1882.

———, *The Origin and Growth of Village Communities in India,* Oxford, 1899; rpnt Jodhpur: Scientific Publishers, 1985.

Barkley, D.G., *Directions for Revenue Officers in the Punjab: Regarding the Settlement and Collection of the Land Revenue, and the Other Duties Therewith,* Lahore, 1875.

Champion, Harry George, and A.L. Griffith, *Manual of General Silviculture for India,* London: Oxford University Press, 1891, 1938.

Cust, Robert N., *Manual for the Guidance of Revenue Officers in the Punjab,* Lahore: Koh-i-noor Press, 1866.

———, *Pictures of Indian Life: Sketched with the Pen from 1852 to 1881,* London: Trubner & Co., 1881.

Douie, James M.C., *Panjab Settlement Manual,* Lahore: Civil and Military Gazette Press, 1909.

———, *Panjab Land Administration Manual,* Lahore: Civil and Military Gazette Press, 1908.

Ellis, Thomas P., *Notes on Punjab Custom,* Lahore: Civil and Military Gazette Press, 1917.

Halhed, Nathaniel B., *A Code of Gentoo Laws, Or, Ordinations of the Pundits,* London, 1776.

Kureshi, Badr-ud-din, *The Punjab Customs: Containing All the Punjab Rulings up to June 1911,* Lahore: Caxton Press, 1911.

Macnaghten, Francis W., *Considerations on the Hindoo Law, as it is Current in Bengal*, Serampore: Mission Press, 1824.

Maine, Henry Sumner, *Ancient Law*, London: Dent, 1861, rpnt 1972.

————, *On Early Law and Custom: Dissertations on Early Law and Custom: Chiefly Selected from Lectures Delivered at Oxford*, London: Murray, 1883; rpnt. Delhi: B.R. Publishing Corporation, 1985.

————, "The Sacred Law of the Hindus", in idem, *Early Law and Custom: Chiefly Selected from Lectures Delivered at Oxford*, Delhi: B.R. Publishing Corporation, 1985.

————, "Theories of Primitive Society", in idem, *Early Law and Custom: Chiefly Selected from Lectures Delivered at Oxford*, Delhi: B.R. Publishing Corporation, 1985.

Punjab Famine Code, Lahore: Punjab Govt Press, 1888.

Punjab Land Records Manual, Lahore, Superintendent, Government Printing, 1960.

Punjab Law Reporter: Containing Cases determined by the Chief Court, Punjab, and the Financial Commissioner, Punjab, Annual from 1900.

Punjab Record: Containing the Reports of Civil and Criminal Cases Determined by the Chief Court of the Punjab and by the Judicial Committee of the Privy Council on Appeal from that Court, and Decisions by the Financial Commissioner of the Punjab, annual from 1866.

Mooltan Division of the Punjab, Lahore: Central Jail Press, 1878.

Smith, Vincent A., *The Settlement Officer's Manual for the North-Western Provinces*, Allahabad: North-Western Provinces and Oudh Government Press, 1881.

Smyth, Ralph, and Henry E.L. Thuillier, *A Manual of Surveying for India, Detailing the Mode of Operations on the Revenue Surveys in Bengal and the North-Western Provinces*, Calcutta: W. Thacker, 1851.

Strange, Thomas A.L., *Hindu Law: Principally with Reference to Such Portions of it as Concern the Administration of Justice, in the King's Courts, in India*, 2 vols, London: Parbury, Allen, 1830.

Thomason, James, *Directions for Revenue Officers in the North-Western Provinces of the Bengal Presidency Regarding the Settlement and Collection of the Land Revenue, and the Other Duties Connected Therewith*, Calcutta: Baptist Mission Press, 1850.

Censuses

District Census Handbook, Punjab, vol. 1, 1961.

Ibbetson, Denzil Charles, *Report on the Census of the Panjab Taken on 17 February 1881*, Lahore: Central Gaol Press, 1883.

Kaul, Pandit Harikishan, *Punjab Census Report 1911*, Lahore: Civil & Military Gazette Press, 1912.

Maclagan, E.D., *Census of the Punjab and its Feudatories*, Calcutta: Superintendent, Government Printing, 1891.

Middleton, L., and S.M. Jacob, *Census of the Punjab and Delhi 1921*, Lahore: Civil and Military Gazette Press, 1923.

Rose, H.A., *1901 Census of the Punjab, Its Feudatories, and the North West Frontier Province*, Simla: Government Central Printing Office, 1902.

Village Surveys

Abdur Rahim, K., and Bahadur S.N.M. Khan, *An Economic Survey of Bhambu Sandila, a Village in the Muzaffargarh District of the Punjab*, Lahore: Civil and Military Gazette Press, 1935.

Bashir, Ahmad, R.L. Anand, H.K. Trevaskis, and W.S. Read, *An Economic Survey of Jamalpur Sheikhan, a Village in the Hissar District of the Punjab*, Lahore, 1937.

Bhalla, R.L., *An Economic Survey of Bairampur in the Hoshiarpur District*, Lahore: Superintendent of Government Printing, 1922.

Das, Anchal, *An Economic Survey of Gajju Chak, a Village in the Gujranwala District of the Punjab*, Lahore: Civil and Military Gazette, 1934.

———, and Hubert Calvert, *An Economic Survey of Tehong: A Village in the Jullundur District of the Punjab*, Lahore: Civil and Military Gazette Press, 1931.

Dawar, Lajpat R., *An Economic Survey of Suner, a Village in the Ferozepore District of the Punjab: Inquiry*, Lahore: Civil and Military Gazette Press, 1936.

Narain, Raj, and Brij Narain, *An Economic Survey of Gijhi, a Village in the Rohtak District of the Punjab, Inquiry Conducted by Raj Narain, Under the Supervision of Professor Brij Narain*, Lahore: E.A. Smedley, 1932.

Roberts, W., and Randhir Singh, *An Economic Survey of Kala Gaddi Thamman (chak 73 G.b.): A Village in the Lyallpur District of the Punjab*, Lahore: Civil and Military Gazette Press, 1932.

Period Works

Aitchison, C.U., *Lord Lawrence*, Oxford: Clarendon Press, 1892.

Allah Baksh, K.S., "Control Measures for the Protection of the Regeneration of *Pinus longifolia*", *Indian Forester*, July 1932.

Anand, R.L., and F.L. Brayne, *Soldier's Savings and How They Use Them*, The Board of Economic Inquiry Punjab, no. 68.

Baden-Powell, B.H., *The Indian Village Community: Examined with Reference to the Physical, Ethnographic, and Historical Conditions of the Provinces*, 1896; rpnt Delhi: Cosmo Publications, 1972.

————, *The Land-Systems of British India: Being a Manual of the Land-Tenures and of the Systems of Land-Revenue Administration Prevalent in the Several Provinces*, vols 1–3, Oxford: Clarendon Press, 1892.

Baird, J.G.A., ed., *Private Letters of the Marquess of Dalhousie*, Edinburgh & London: William Blackwood & Sons, 1910.

Bentham, Jeremy, *Codification of the Common Law: Letter of Jeremy Bentham, and Report of Judges Story, Metcalf and Others*, 1882.

————, "Papers Relative to Codification", in John Bowring, ed., *The Works of Jeremy Bentham*, vol. IV, Edinburgh: William Tait, 1838–43.

————, *Principles of the Civil Code*, n.p., 1834.

Blackstone, William, *Commentaries on the Laws of England, 1765–1769*, Oxford: Clarendon Press, 1768.

Bosworth-Smith, R., *Life of Lord Lawrence*, London, 2 vols, 1883.

Bowring, John, ed., *The Works of Jeremy Bentham*, vols IV, VIII, Edinburgh: William Tait, 1838–43.

Calvert, Hubert, *The Wealth and Welfare of the Punjab: Being Some Studies in Punjab Rural Economics*, Lahore: Civil and Military Gazette Press, 1922.

————, *Progress of Agricultural Non-credit Co-operation in the Punjab*, Lahore: Punjab Central Press, 1923.

Cave-Brown, J., *The Punjab and Delhi in 1857; Being a Narrative of the Measures by Which the Punjab was Saved and Delhi Recovered During the Indian Mutiny*, Edinburgh and London: William Blackwood, 1861.

Cust, Robert Needham, "Collector of Revenue in the North West Provinces of India", *Calcutta Review*, 1854.

Darling, Malcolm, *At Freedom's Door*, London: Oxford University Press, 1949.

————, *The Punjab Peasant in Prosperity and Debt*, London: Oxford University Press, 1925; rpnt New Delhi: Manohar, 1977.

————, *Rusticus Loquitur: Or, The Old Light and the New in the Punjab Village*, London: Oxford University Press, 1929.

————, *Wisdom and Waste in the Punjab Village*, London: Oxford University Press, 1934.

Diver, Maud, *Honoria Lawrence: A Fragment of Indian History*, London: Murray, 1936.

Douie, James M., "The Punjab Canal Colonies", *Journal of the Royal Society of Arts*, 62.3210 (1914): 611–23.

Eden, Emily, *Up the Country: Letters Written to Her Sister from the Upper Provinces of India*, 1866; rpnt London: Virago, 1983.

Edwardes, Emma, *Memorials of the Life and Letters of Major-General Sir Herbert B. Edwardes*, London: K. Paul, Trench & Co., 1883.

Edwardes, Herbert B., and Herman Merivale, *Life of Sir Henry Lawrence*, 2 vols, London: Smith, Elder, 1872.

Forster, George, *A Journey from Bengal to England, Through the Northern Part of India, Kashmire, Afghanistan, and Persia and into Russia, by the Caspian Sea*, vol. I, 1798; Punjab, Patiala: Languages Dept, 1970.

Gandhi, Mohandas K., *The Collected Works of Mahatma Gandhi: Vol. 96*. New Delhi: Publications Division, Ministry of Information and Broadcasting, Government of India, 2001.

Gibbon, Frederick P., *The Lawrences of the Punjab*, London: Dent, 1908.

Griffin, Lepel, *The Panjab Chiefs: Historical and Biographical Notices of the Principal Families in the Territories Under the Panjab Government*, Lahore: Chronicle Press, 1865.

Henty, G.A., *Through the Sikh War: A Tale of the Conquest of the Punjaub*, 1894; rpnt Punjab, Patiala: Languages Department, 1970.

Hodson, W.S.R., and George H. Hodson, *Twelve Years of a Soldier's Life in India: Being Extracts from the Letters of the Late Major W.S.R. Hodson: Including a Personal Narrative of the Siege of Delhi and Capture of the King and Princes*, London: John W. Parker and Son, 1859.

Ibbetson, Denzil, *Punjab Castes*, Lahore: Civil and Military Gazette Press, 1911.

Jackson, Charles R.M., *A Vindication of the Marquis of Dalhousie's Indian Administration*, London: Smith, Elder and Co., 1865.

Kaye, John W., *A History of the Sepoy War in India, 1857–1858*, vols. 1–3, London: W.H. Allen, 1864; London: Longmans, Green and Co., 1896.

Lawrence, Henry M., *Adventures of an Officer in the Punjaub*, 1846; rpnt Punjab, Patiala: Languages Department, 1970.

Lee-Warner, William, *The Life of the Marquis of Dalhousie*, 2 vols, London: Macmillan, 1904.

Locke, John, "Property", in *Two Treatises on Government*, ed. Peter Laslett, Cambridge: Cambridge University Press, 1988.

Maconachie, R., *Selected Agricultural Proverbs of the Panjab*, Delhi: Imperial Medical Hall Press, 1890.

Maine, Henry Sumner, *Lectures on the Early History of Institutions*, London: John Murray, 1875.

———, "The Tribe and the Land", in idem, *Lectures on the Early History of Institutions*, London: John Murray, 1875.

———, *Village Communities in the East and West: Six Lectures Delivered at Oxford by Henry Sumner Maine*, London: John Murray, 1871.

Markham, Clements R., *A Memoir on the Indian Surveys*, London: Allen & Co., 1871.

Masssy, Charles Francis, *Chiefs and Families of Note in Delhi, Jalandhar, Peshawar and Derajat Divisions of the Punjab*, Allahabad: Pioneer Press, 1890.

McLennan, John F., *Studies in Ancient History: Comprising a Reprint of Primitive Marriage*, London and New York: Macmillan and Co., 1886.

M'Gregor, William Lewis, *The History of the Sikhs: Containing the Lives of the Gooroos; The History of the Independent Sirdars, or Missuls and the Life of the Great Founder of the Sikh Monarchy, Maharajah Runjeet Singh*, London: J. Madden, 1846.

Milne, David, *Report on the Causes of the Failure of Cotton Crop in the Punjab in 1919*, Lahore: Superintendent, Government Press, 1924.

———, *Report on the Complaints of the Abnormal State of the Cotton Crop in 1921*, Lahore: Superintendent, Government Printing, 1922.

Mohammad, Afzal, "American Cottons in India: Their Introduction and Development", *Indian Farming*, VII:10 (October 1946): 457–62.

———, and Abdul Ghani, "Cotton Jassid in the Punjab", *Indian Farming*, VII:9 (September 1946).

Mohan, N.P., "Controlled Burning and Change in Vegetation", *Indian Forester*, LXVII (August 1941).

Muir, William, "The Hon. James Thomason", *Calcutta Review*, July–December 1853, vol. XXI.

———, *The Honourable James Thomason, Lieutenant-Governor N.W.P., India, 1843–1853*, Edinburgh: T. & T. Clark, 1897.

Mutiny Records: Reports, Lahore: Punjab Government Press, 1911.

Phillimore, R.H., *Historical Records of the Survey of India*, vols I–IV, Dehradun: Survey of India, 1945–58.

Prinsep, H.T., *Origin of the Sikh Power in the Punjab, and Political life of Muharaja Runjeet Singh: With An Account of the Present Condition,*

Religion, Laws and Customs of the Sikhs, Calcutta: G.H. Huttmann, 1834.

Rose, H.A., *A Glossary of the Tribes and Castes of the Punjab and North-West Frontier Province*, Lahore: Civil and Military Gazette Press, 1911.

Slade, H., "Too Much Fire Protection in Burma", *Indian Forester*, 22:5 (1896): 172–6.

Stebbing, E.P., *The Forests of India*, 3 vols, London: Oxford University Press, 1923.

Strickland, C.F., "Co-operative Consolidation of Holdings in the Punjab", *Agricultural Journal of India*, vol. XXII: 2, 1927.

Temple, R.C., "Agricultural Folk-lore Notes", *The Folk-lore Record*, vol. 5 (1882): 33–49.

————, "Bibliography of Folklore, Vernacular Publications in the Punjab", *The Folk-Lore Journal*, vol. 4 (1886): 273–307.

————, *James Thomason*, Oxford: Clarendon Press, 1893.

————, *The Legends of the Panjab*, 1884; rpnt Punjab, Patiala: Language Dept, 1988.

————, *Lord Lawrence*, London: Macmillan, 1903.

————, *Men and Events of My Time in India*, London: J. Murray, 1882.

————, "The Science of Folk-lore", *The Folk-Lore Journal*, vol. 4, no. 3 (1886): 193–212.

————, 'Some Punjabi and Other Proverbs", *The Folk-Lore Journal*, vol. 1, no. 6 (1883): 175–84.

————, *The Story of My Life*, 2 vols, London: Cassell & Co, 1896.

Trotter, Lionel J., *A Leader of Light Horse: Life of Hodson of Hodson's Horse*, Edinburgh: W. Blackwood and Sons, 1901.

Troup, R.S., "Fire Protection in the Teak Forests of Burma", *Indian Forester*, 31:3 (1905): 138–46.

Tylor, Edward B., *Primitive Culture: Researches into the Development of Mythology, Philosophy, Religion, Art, and Custom*, 2 vols, London: John Murray, 1871.

Wilson, James, *The Dialect of Robert Burns: As Spoken in Central Ayrshire*, London: Oxford University Press, 1923.

————, *The Dialects of Central Scotland*, London: Oxford University Press, 1926.

————, *Lowland Scotch as Spoken in the Lower Strathearn Districts of Perthshire*, London: Oxford University Press, 1915.

————, "Introduction", in *The Dialect of the New Forest in Hampshire: As Spoken in the Village of Burley*, London: Oxford University Press

(Publications of the Philological Society: IV), 1913.

————, "Recent Economic Developments in the Punjab", *A Paper Read by James Wilson to the Royal Economic Society, 9 February 1910*, London: R. Clay & Sons, 1910.

SECONDARY SOURCES

Books and Essays

Adams, M.W., A.H. Ellingboe, and E.C. Rossman, "Biological Uniformity and Disease Epidemics", *BioScience*, 21:21, 1 November 1971, 1067–70.

Agarwal, Bina, *A Field of One's Own: Gender and Land Rights in South Asia*, Cambridge: Cambridge University Press, 1994.

Agarwal, S.K., *Economics of Land Consolidation in India*, Delhi: S. Chand, 1971.

Agnihotri, Indu, "Ecology, Land Use and Colonization: The Canal Colonies of Punjab", *The Indian Economic and Social History Review*, 33.1 (1996).

Agrawal, Arun, and K. Sivaramakrishnan, eds, *Social Nature: Resources, Representations, and Rule in India*, New Delhi: Oxford University Press, 2001.

Ali, H.A., and T.K. Basu, *Then and Now, 1933–1958: A Study of Socio-economic Structure and Change in Some Villages Near Visva Bharati University, Bengal*, New York: Asia Publishing House, 1960.

————, *Rice and Rural Reconstruction*, n.p., 1932.

Ali, Imran, *The Punjab Under Imperialism, 1885–1947*, Princeton: Princeton University Press, 1988.

Althusser, Louis, *For Marx*, Harmondsworth: Penguin Books, 1969.

Amin, Shahid. *Sugarcane and Sugar in Gorakhpur: An Inquiry into Peasant Production for Capitalist Enterprise in Colonial India*, Delhi: Oxford University Press, 1984.

Anderson, A., *Measures Possible for the Improvement of Economic Conditions of Muzaffargarh District*, n.p., n.d.

Anderson, David, "Stock Theft and Moral Economy in Colonial Kenya", *Africa: Journal of the International African Institute*, 56:4 (1986): 399–416.

Appadurai, Arjun, "The Past as a Scarce Resource", *Man*, 16:2 (1981): 201–19.

————, "Number in the Colonial Imagination", Appadurai, *Modernity at Large*, New Delhi: Oxford University Press, 1996.

Archer, S., T.W. Boutton, and K.A. Hibbard, "Trees in Grasslands: Biogeochemical Consequences of Woody Plant Expansion", in M. Schulze, S. Harrison, E. Heimann, E. Holland, J. Lloyd, I.C. Prentice, and D. Schimel, eds, *Global Biogeochemical Cycles in the Climate System*, San Diego: Academic Press, 2001.

Arewa, E. Ojo, and Alan Dundes, "Proverbs and the Ethnography of Speaking Folklore", in J.J. Gumperz and D.H. Hymes, eds, *The Ethnography of Communication*, New York: Holt, Rinehart and Winston, 1972.

Arnold, David, and Ramachandra Guha, *Nature, Culture, Imperialism*, New Delhi: Oxford University Press, 1995.

Arunima, G., *There Comes Papa: Colonialism and the Transformation of Matriliny in Kerala, Malabar, c. 1850–1940*, New Delhi: Orient Longman, 2003.

Bamford, T.W., *Rise of the Public Schools: A Study of Boys' Public Boarding Schools in England and Wales from 1837 to the Present Day*, London: Nelson, 1967.

————, "Thomas Arnold and the Victorian Ideal of Public Schools", in Brian Simon and Ian Bradley, eds, *The Victorian Public School: Studies in the Development of an Educational Institution*, Dublin: Gill and Macmillan, 1975.

Banaji, Jairus, "Capitalist Domination and the Small Peasantry: Deccan Districts in the Late-Nineteenth Century", *Economic and Political Weekly*, 12: 33/34 (1977), Special Number: 1375–1404.

————, "Mode of Production in Indian Agriculture: A Comment", *Economic and Political Weekly*, 8:14 (1973): 679–83.

Banerjee, Himadri, *Agragian Society of the Punjab: 1849–1901*, New Dehli: Manohar, 1982

Banga, Indu, *Agrarian System of the Sikhs: Late Eighteenth and Early Nineteenth Century*, New Delhi: Manohar, 1978.

Bardhan, Pranab, *The Political Economy of Development in India*, Oxford: Blackwell, 1984.

Barfield, Thomas J., *The Nomadic Alternative*, Englewood Cliffs, NJ: Prentice Hall, 1993.

Barrier, N.G., "The Punjab Disturbances of 1907: The Response of the British Government in India to Agrarian Unrest", *Modern Asian Studies*, I:4 (1967): 353–83.

Bates, Crispin, "The Development of Panchayati Raj in India", in Crispin

Bates and Subho Basu eds, *Rethinking Indian Political Institutions*, London: Anthem Press, 2005.

Bauman, Richard, and Barbara A. Babock, eds, *Verbal Art as Performance*, Prospect Heights, Ill.: Waveland Press, 1984.

———, and Juel Sherzer, *Exploration in the Ethnography of Speaking*, Cambridge: Cambridge University Press, 1989.

Bayly, C.A., *Indian Society and the Making of the British Empire*, Cambridge: Cambridge University Press, 1988.

Beidelman, T.O., *A Comparative Analysis of the Jajmani System*, New York: Monographs of the Association of Asian Studies, VIII, 1959.

Bell, David, and Valentine Gill, *Mapping Desire: Geographies of Sexualities*, London: Routledge, 1995.

Bellon, Mauricio R., and J. Edward Taylor, "'Folk' Soil Taxonomy and the Partial Adoption of New Seed Varieties", *Economic Development and Cultural Change*, 41:4 (July 1993): 763–86.

Ben-Amos, Dan, *Folklore in Context: Essays*, New Delhi: South Asia Publishers, 1982.

———, "The Historical Folklore of Richard M. Dorson", *Journal of Folklore Research*, 26:1, Special Issue: Richard M. Dorson's Views and Works— An Assessment (January–April 1989): 51–60.

———, and K. Goldstein, eds, *Folklore: Performance and Communication*, The Hague, 1974.

Bentley, J.W., "Economic and Ecological Approaches to Land Fragmentation: In Defense of a Much-maligned Phenomenon", *Annual Review of Anthropology*, 16 (1987): 31–67.

Benton, Lauren, *Law and Colonial Cultures: Legal Regimes in World History*, Cambridge: Cambridge University Press, 2002.

———, and Richard Ross, *Legal Pluralism and Empire, 1500–1850*, New York: New York University Press, 2013.

Berkner, Lutz K., "Inheritance, Land Tenure, and Peasant Family Structure: A German Regional Comparison", in Jack Goody, Joan Thirsk, and E.P. Thompson, eds, *Family and Inheritance: Rural Society in Western Europe, 1200 to 1800*, Cambridge: Cambridge University Press, 1976.

Berlin, B., D. Breedlove, and P. Raven, "Folk Taxonomies and Biological Classification", *Science*, 154 (1966): 273–5.

———, "General Principles of Classification and Nomenclature in Folk Biology", *American Anthropologist*, vol. 75 (1973): 214–42.

Béteille, André, "Peasant Studies and their Significance", in idem, *Six Essays in Comparative Sociology*, Delhi: Oxford University Press, 1974.

Bhabha, Homi K., "Of Mimicry and Man; the Ambivalence of Colonial Discourse", in idem, *The Location of Culture,* London: Routledge, 1994.

———, 'Sly Civility", in idem, *The Location of Culture*, London: Routledge, 1994.

Bhaduri, Amit, "Cropsharing as a Labour Process: Size of Farm and Supervision Cost", *Journal of Peasant Studies*, 10: 2–3 (1983): 88–93.

———, *The Economic Structure of Backward Agriculture*, London: Academic Press, 1983.

Bhattacharya, Neeladri, "Lenders and Debtors: Punjab Countryside, 1880–1940", *Studies in History*, NS, I:2 (1985).

———, "Lineages of Capital", *Historical Materialism*, 21:4 (2013), 11–35.

———, "The Logic of Tenancy Cultivation: Central and Southeast Punjab, 1870–1935", *The Indian Economic and Social History Review*, April–June, 20:2 (1983): 121–70.

———, "Pastoralists in a Colonial World", in D. Arnold and R. Guha, eds, *Nature Culture, Imperialism: Essays on the Environmental History of South Asia,* Delhi: Oxford University Press, 1995.

———, "Predicaments of Mobility", in C. Markovits, J. Pouchepadass, and S. Subrahmanyam, eds, *Society and Circulation: Mobile People and Itinerant Cultures in South Asia*, New Delhi: Permanent Black, 2003.

———, "Remaking Custom: The Discourse and Practice of Colonial Codification", in R. Champakalakshmi and S. Gopal, eds, *Tradition, Dissent and Ideology*, New Delhi: Oxford University Press, 1996.

———, "Rethinking Marxist History", *Seminar*, October 1987.

———, ed., *Forests, Fields and Farms: Studies In History*, Special Issue, 14:2 (1999).

Bhutta, Muhammad N., and Lambert K. Smedema, "One Hundred Years of Waterlogging and Salinity Control in the Indus Valley, Pakistan: A Historical Review", *Irrigation and Drainage*, 56:1 (2007): 81–90.

Blackburn, Stuart, *Print, Folklore, and Nationalism in Colonial South India*, Delhi: Permanent Black, 2003.

———, and A.K. Ramanujan, eds, *Another Harmony: New Essays on the Folklore of India*, Delhi: Oxford University Press, 1966.

Blair, J.M., T.R. Seastedt, C.W. Rice, and R.A. Ramundo, "Terrestrial Nutrient Cycling in Tallgrass Prairie", in A.K. Knapp, J.M. Briggs, D.C. Hartnett, and S.L. Collins, eds, *Grassland Dynamics: Long-Term Ecological Research in Tallgrass Prairie*, New York: Oxford University Press, 1998, pp. 222–43.

Bohac, Rodney D., "Peasant Inheritance Strategies in Russia", *The Journal of Interdisciplinary History*, 16:1 (1985): 23–42.

Bonner, Jeffrey P., *Land Consolidation and Economic Development in India: A Study of Two Haryana Villages*, Riverdale: Riverdale Co., 1987.

Bose, Sugata, *Agrarian Bengal: Economy, Social Structure, and Politics, 1919–1947*, Cambridge: Cambridge University Press, 1986.

—————, *Peasant Labour and Colonial Capital: Rural Bengal Since 1770*, Cambridge: Cambridge University Press, 1993.

Bourdieu, Pierre, *Outline of a Theory of Practice*, Cambridge: Cambridge University Press, 1977, revised as idem, *The Logic of Practice*, Cambridge: Polity Press, 1990.

Bouveresse, Jacques, "Rules, Dispositions, and the Habitus", in Richard Shusterman, ed., *Bourdieu: A Critical Reader*, Oxford: Blackwell Publishers, 1999.

Breckenridge, Carol A., and Peter van der Veer, eds, *Orientalism and the Postcolonial Predicament: Perspectives on South Asia*, Philadelphia: University of Pennsylvania Press, 1993.

Breman, Jan, *Patronage and Exploitation: Changing Agrarian Relations in South Gujarat, India*, Berkeley: University of California Press, 1974.

—————, *Shattered Images: Construction and Deconstruction of the Village in Colonial Asia*, Amsterdam: Centre for Asian Studies, 1987.

Brundage, Anthony, and David East Wood, "The Making of the New Poor Law Redivivas: A Debate", *Past and Present*, 127 (May 1990): 183–94.

Burke, Peter, *Popular Culture in Early Modern Europe*, London: T. Smith, 1978.

Burrow, John W., *Evolution and Society: A Study in Victorian Social Theory*, Cambridge: Cambridge University Press, 1986.

—————, "Henry Maine and the Mid-Victorian Ideas of Progress", in Alan Diamond, ed., *The Victorian Achievement of Sir Henry Maine: A Centennial Reappraisal*, Cambridge: Cambridge University Press, 1991.

—————, *A Liberal Descent: Victorian Historians and the English Past*, Cambridge: Cambridge University Press, 1983.

—————, "The "Village Community" and the Uses of History in Late-nineteenth-century England", in Neil McKendrick, ed., *Historical Perspectives: Studies in English Thought and Society in Honour of J.H. Plumb*, London: Europa Publications, 1974.

Cameiro, Robert Leonard, *Evolutionism in Cultural Anthropology: A Critical History*, Boulder: Westview Press, 2003.

Carlyle, Thomas, "The Hero as Man of Letters", in *Selected Writings*, Harmondsworth: Penguin, 1971.

Castoriadis, Cornelius, *The Imaginary Institution of Society*, Cambridge: Polity Press, 1987.

Cederlof, Gunnel, *Landscapes and the Law: Environmental Politics, Regional Histories, and Contests over Nature*, Ranikhet: Permanent Black, 2008.

Chakrabarti, Dilip K., "Beginning of Iron and Social Change in India", *Indian Studies Past and Present*, 14 (1973): 329–38.

Chakrabarty, Dipesh, *Habitations of Modernity: Essays in the Wake of Subaltern Studies*, Chicago: University of Chicago Press, 2002.

———, *Provincializing Europe: Postcolonial Thought and Historical Difference*, Princeton, New Jersey: Princeton University Press, 2000.

Chakravarty-Kaul, Minoti, *Common Lands and Customary Law: Institutional Change in North India over the Past Two Centuries*, Delhi: Oxford University Press, 1996.

Chambers, Iain, and Lidia Curti, eds, *The Post-Colonial Question: Common Skies, Divided Horizons*, London: Routledge, 2001.

Chanock, Martin, *Law, Custom and Social Order: The Colonial Experience in Malawi and Zambia*, Cambridge: Cambridge University Press, 1986.

Charlesworth, Neil, *Peasants and Imperial Rule: Agriculture and Agrarian Society in the Bombay Presidency, 1850–1935*, Cambridge: Cambridge University Press, 1985.

Chattopadhyaya, B.D., *Aspects of Rural Settlements and Rural Society in Early Medieval India*, Calcutta, 1990.

Chayanov, A.V., *On the Theory of Peasant Economy*, Manchester: Manchester University Press, 1966.

Chowdhry, Prem, *Punjab Politics: The Role of Sir Chhotu Ram*, New Delhi: Vikas, 1984.

———, *The Veiled Women: Shifting Gender Equations in Rural Haryana, 1880–1990*, New Delhi: Oxford University Press, 1994.

Chowdhury, Benoy, *Growth of Commercial Agriculture in Bengal (1757–1900)*, Calcutta: Maitra, 1964.

Claeys, Gregory, *Mill and Paternalism*, Cambridge: Cambridge University Press, 2013.

Clastres, Pierre, *Society Against the State: Essays in Political Anthropology*, New York: Zone Books, 1987.

Cleghorn, A., *Report Upon the Forests of the Punjab and the Western Himalayas*, Roorkee: Thomason Civil Engineering College, 1864.

Cleveland, David A., Daniel Soleri, and Steven E. Smith, "Do Folk Varieties Have a Role in Sustainable Agriculture?", *BioScience*, 44:11 (December 1994): 740–51.

Cocks, Raymond, "Maine, Progress and Theory", in Alan Diamond, ed., *The Victorian Achievement of Sir Henry Maine: A Centennial Reappraisal*, Cambridge: Cambridge University Press, 1991.

———, *Sir Henry Maine: A Study in Victorian Jurisprudence*, Cambridge: Cambridge University Press, 1988.

Cohn, Bernard S., *An Anthropologist Among the Historians and Other Essays*, Delhi: Oxford University Press, 1987.

———, *Colonialism and Its Forms of Knowledge*, Princeton: Princeton University Press, 1996.

Collini, Stefan, *Public Moralists: Political Thought and Intellectual Life in Britain 1850–1930*, Oxford: Clarendon Press, 1991.

———, Donald Winch, and John Burrow, *That Noble Science of Politics: A Study in Nineteenth-century Intellectual History*, Cambridge: Cambridge University Press, 1983.

Colls, Robert, and Philip Dodd, eds, *Englishness: Politics and Culture 1880–1920*, London: Croom Helm, 1986.

Comaroff, John, ed., "Colonialism, Culture and the Law", *Law and Social Enquiry*, vol. 26, no. 2, 2001.

Cooper, Frederick, and Ann L. Stoler, eds, *Tensions of Empire*, Berkeley: University of California Press, 1997.

Cooper, J.P., "Patterns of Inheritance and Settlement by Great Landowners from the Fifteenth to the Eighteenth Centuries", in J. Goody, *et al.*, eds, *Family and Inheritance*, Cambridge: Cambridge University Press, 1976.

Coward, R., *Patriarchal Precedents: Sexuality and Social Relations*, London: Routledge & Kegan Paul, 1983.

Cronon, William, *Changes in the Land: Indians, Colonists, and the Ecology of New England*, New York: New York: Hill and Wang, 1983.

Crosby, Alfred W., *Ecological Imperialism: The Biological Expansion of Europe, 900–1900*, Cambridge: Cambridge University Press, 1986.

Czap, Peter, "The Perennial Multiple Family Household: Mishin Russia, 1782–1858", *Journal of Family History*, VII (1982): 5–26.

D'Souza, Rohan, *Drowned and Dammed: Colonial Capitalism and Flood Control in Eastern India*, New Delhi: Oxford University Press, 2006.

Dahlman, C., *The Open Field System and Beyond: A Property Rights Analysis of an Economic Institution*, Cambridge: Cambridge University Press, 1980.

Das, Veena, and Ralph Nicholas, "Family and Household: Difference and Division in South Asian Domestic Life", ACLS-SSRC Joint Committee on South Asia: Sub-Committee on South Asian Political Economy Project II, 1980 (mimeo).

Davies, Damian Walford, *Romanticism, History, Historicism: Essays on an Orthodoxy*, New York: Routledge, 2009.

Davis, Deborah, "Contexts of Ambivalence: The Folkloristic Revival of Nineteenth-century Scottish Highland Ministers", *Folklore*, 103:2 (1992): 207–22.

de Certeau, Michel, "Foucault and Bourdieu", in idem, *The Practice of Everyday Life*, Berkeley: University of California Press, 2011.

———, *Heterologies: Discourse on the Other*, Minneapolis: University of Minnesota Press, 1985.

———, *The Practice of Everyday Life*, Berkeley: University of California Press, 2011.

Deleuze, Gilles, and Felix Guattari, *A Thousand Plateaus: Capitalism and Schizophrenia*, Minneapolis: University of Minnesota Press, 1987.

Derrett, J.D.M., "A Juridical Fabrication of Early British India: The Mahanirvana Tantra", in idem, *Essays in Classical and Modern Hindu Law*, vol. II, Leiden: Brill, 1976.

———, *Essays in Classical and Modern Hindu Law*, vols I–IV, Leiden: Brill, 1976.

———, "The Administration of Hindu Law by the British", in idem, *Religion, Law and the State in India*, New York: Free Press, 1968.

———, "The British as Patrons of the Sastras", in idem, *Religion, Law and the State in India*, New York: Free Press, 1968.

———, *Religion, Law and the State in India*, New York: Free Press, 1968.

Dewey, Clive, "Images of the Village Community: A Study in Anglo-Indian Ideology", *Modern Asian Studies*, 6:3 (1972): 291–328.

———, *The Mind of the Indian Civil Service*, Delhi: Oxford University Press, 1996.

Diamond, Alan, ed., *The Victorian Achievement of Sir Henry Maine: A Centennial Reappraisal*, Cambridge: Cambridge University Press, 1991.

Dirks, Nicholas, *The Autobiography of an Archive: A Scholar's Passage to India*, Columbia: Columbia University Press, 2015.

Divyabhanusinh, *The Lions of India*, Ranikhet: Permanent Black, 2011.

Dorson, Richard D., *The British Folklorists: A History*, Chicago: University of Chicago Press, 1968.

———, *Peasant Customs and Savage Myths: Selections from the British Folklorists*, Chicago: University of Chicago Press, 1968.

Dowdell, R.J., and M.H. Mian, "Fate of Nitrogen Applied to Agricultural Crops with Particular Reference to Denitrification", *Philosophical*

Transactions of the Royal Society of London, Series B, Biological Sciences, 296:1082, *The Nitrogen Cycle* (27 January 1982): 363–73.

Dumont, Louis, "The 'Village Community' from Munro to Maine", *Contributions to Indian Sociology*, 9 (1966): 67–87.

———, and D. Pocock, eds, "Village Studies", *Contributions to Indian Sociology*, I (1957).

Dunkley, Peter, "Paternalism, the Magistracy and Poor Relief in England, 1795–1834", *International Review of Social History*, XXXIV (1979): 317–97.

Evans-Pritchard, E.E., *The Nuer*, Oxford: Clarendon Press, 1940.

Fabian, Johannes, *Time and the Other: How Anthropology Makes Its Objects*, New York: Columbia University Press, 1983.

Fenoaltea, S., "Risk, Transaction Costs and the Origin of Medieval Agriculture", *Explorations in Economic History*, 13 (1976): 129–51.

Forster, E.M., *A Passage to India*, London: Edward Arnold, 1924; rpt Harmondsworth: Penguin, 1979.

Fortes, Meyer, "The Structure of Unilineal Descent Groups", *American Anthropologist*, NS, 55:1 (1953).

Foucault, Michel, *The Order of Things: An Archaeology of the Human Sciences*, London: Tavistock Publications, 1970.

Fox, Richard, *Kin, Clan, Raja and Rule: State–Hinterland Relations in Pre-industrial India*, Berkeley: University of California Press, 1971.

———, *Lions of the Punjab: Culture in the Making*, Berkeley: University of California Press, 1985.

Frängsmyr, Tore, J.L. Heilbron, and Robin E. Rider, eds, *The Quantifying Spirit in the 18th Century*, Berkeley: University of California Press, 1990.

Frasca-Spada, Marina, *Space and the Self in Hume's Treatise*, Cambridge: Cambridge University Press, 1998.

Gadgil, Madhav, and Ramachandra Guha, *This Fissured Land: An Ecological History of India*, Delhi: Oxford University Press, 1992.

Ghose, Indira, *Women Travellers in Colonial India: The Power of the Female Gaze*, New Delhi: Oxford University Press, 1998.

Gidwani, Vinay K., *Capital, Interrupted: Agrarian Development and the Politics of Work in India*, Ranikhet: Permanent Black, 2008.

Gilmartin, David, *Blood and Water: The Indus River Basin in Modern History*, Berkeley: University of California Press, 2015.

———, "Kinship, Women and Politics in Twentieth-Century Punjab", in Gail Minault, ed., *The Extended Family: Women and Political Participation in India and Pakistan*, Delhi: Chanakya Publications, 1981.

———, "Models of the Hydraulic Environment: Colonial Irrigation,

State Power and Community in the Indus Basin", in David Arnold and Ramachandra Guha, *Nature, Culture, Imperialism*, Delhi: Oxford University Press, 1995.

Gilpin, William, *Three Essays: On Picturesque Beauty, on Picturesque Travel, and on Sketching Landscape*, London: R. Blamire, 1792.

Gilroy, Paul, *The Black Atlantic: Modernity and Double Consciousness*, Cambridge, Massachusetts: Harvard University Press, 1993.

Glover, William, *Making Lahore Modern: Constructing and Imagining a Colonial City*, Minneapolis: The University of Minnesota Press, 2008.

Goody, Jack, "Marriage Prestations, Inheritance and Descent in Pre-Industrial Societies", *Journal of Comparative Family Studies*, 1:1 (1970): 37–54.

———, Joan Thirsk, and E.P. Thompson, eds, *Family and Inheritance: Rural Society in Western Europe, 1200 to 1800*, Cambridge: Cambridge University Press, 1976.

Gouldner, A.W., "Reciprocity and Autonomy in Functional Theory", and "The Norm of Reciprocity", in idem, *For Sociology: Renewal and Critique in Sociology Today*, Harmondsworth: Penguin, 1973.

Graeber, David, *Debt: The First 5000 Years*, New York: Melville House Publishing, 2011.

———, *Towards an Anthropological Theory of Value: The False Coin of Our Own Dreams*, New York: Palgrave, 2001.

Gregory, Derek, "Writing Travel, Mapping Sexuality: Richard Burton's Sotadic Zone", in James Duncan and Derek Gregory, eds, *Writes of Passage: Reading Travel Writing*, London, 1999.

Grewal, J.S., *The Sikhs of the Punjab*, Cambridge: Cambridge University Press, 1990.

———, and Indu Banga, eds, *Maharaja Ranjit Singh: The State and Society*, Amritsar: Guru Nanak Dev University, 2001.

———, and S.R. Kohli, eds, *Civil and Military Affairs of Maharaja Ranjit Singh: A Study of 450 Orders in Persian*, Amritsar: Guru Nanak Dev University, 1987.

Grove, Richard H., *Green Imperialism: Colonial Expansion, Tropical Island Edens and the Origins of Environmentalism, 1600–1860*, Cambridge: Cambridge University Press, 1996.

———, Vinita Damodaran, and Satpal Sangwan, *Nature and the Orient: The Environmental History of South and Southeast Asia*, Delhi: Oxford University Press, 1998.

Guha, Ramachandra, *The Unquiet Woods: Ecological Change and Peasant Resistance in the Himalaya*, Delhi: Oxford University Press, 1989.

Guha, Ranajit, *A Rule of Property for Bengal: An Essay on the Idea of Permanent*

Settlement, Paris: Mouton and Co., 1968.

Guha, Sumit, *The Agrarian Economy of the Bombay Deccan, 1818–1941*, Delhi: Oxford University Press, 1985.

———, "Commodity and Credit in Upland Maharashtra, 1800–1950", *Economic and Political Weekly*, 22.52, 1987.

———, *Environment and Ethnicity in India, 1200–1991*, Cambridge: Cambridge University Press, 1999.

———, ed., *Growth, Stagnation, or Decline? Agricultural Productivity in British India*, New Delhi: Oxford University Press, 1992.

Gumperz J.J., and D. Hymes, "The Ethnography of Communication", *American Anthropologist*, 66:6, pt 2 (1964).

———, *The Ethnography of Communication*, New York: Holt, Rinehart and Winston, 1972.

Gupta, Sulekh C., *Agrarian Relations and Early British Rule in India: A Case Study of Ceded and Conquered Provinces, Uttar Pradesh 1819–1833*, Bombay: Asia Publishing House, 1963.

———, "Retreat from Permanent Settlement and Shift towards a New Policy", in Burton Stein, ed., *The Making of Agrarian Policy in British Indian 1770–1900*, New Delhi: Oxford University Press, 1992.

Habib, Irfan, *The Agrarian System of Mughal India 1556–1707*, Second Edition, New Delhi: Oxford University Press, 1999.

———, *An Atlas of the Mughal Empire: Political and Economic Maps with Detailed Notes, Bibliography and Index*, Delhi: Oxford University Press, 1982.

Hacking, Ian, *The Taming of Chance*, Cambridge: Cambridge University Press, 1990.

Halbfass, Wilhelm, *India and Europe: An Essay in Philosophical Understanding*, Albany, N.Y: State University of New York Press, 1988.

Hall, S., "When was 'The Postcolonial'? Thinking at the Limit", in Iain Chambers, and Lidia Curti, eds, *The Post-Colonial Question: Common Skies, Divided Horizons*, London: Routledge, 1996.

Harrison, R., *Bentham*, London, 1983.

Haley, Bruce, *The Healthy Body and Victorian Culture*, Cambridge, Mass.: Harvard University Press, 1978.

Hall, Catherine, "Competing Masculinities: Thomas Carlyle, John Stuart Mill and the Case of Governor Eyre", in Catherine Hall, *White, Male, and Middle-Class: Explorations in Feminism and History*, Cambridge: Polity Press, 1992.

Hall, Donald E., ed., *Muscular Christianity: Embodying the Victorian Age*,

Cambridge: Cambridge University Press, 1994.

Haynes, Douglas, and Gyan Prakash, eds, *Contesting Power: Resistance and Everyday Social Relations in South Asia*, Delhi: Oxford University Press, 1991.

Hendrickson, D., J. Arman, and R. Merns, "The Changing Nature of Conflict and Famine and Vulnerability: The Case of Livestock Raiding in Turkana District, Kenya", *Disasters*, 22.3 (September 1998).

Heredia, Rudolf C., and Shereen Ratnagar, eds, *Mobile and Marginalized Peoples: Perspectives From the Past*, New Delhi: Manohar, 2003.

Heston, A., and D. Kumar, "The Persistence of Land Fragmentation in Peasant Agriculture: An Analysis of South Asian Cases", *Explorations in Economic History*, 20:2 (1883): 199–220.

Higgins, Kenneth F., D. Kruse Arnold, and James L. Piehl, *Prescribed Burning Guidelines in the Northern Great Plains*, U.S. Department of Agriculture EC 760, 1889, Jamestown, ND: Northern Prairie Wildlife Research Center Home Page. http://www.npwrc.usgs.gov/resource/tools/burning/burning.htm (16 July 1997).

Himmelfarb, Gertrude, *The Idea of Poverty: England in the Early Industrial Age*, New York, 1984.

Hobsbawm, E.J., *The Age of Capital, 1848–1875*, London: Weidenfeld & Nicolson, 1975.

———, *The Age of Empire, 1875–1914*, New York: Pantheon Books, 1987.

Holland, J. Lloyd, I. Prentice, and D. Schimel, eds, *Global Biogeochemical Cycles in the Climate System*, San Diego: Academic Press, 2000.

Howell, Cicely, "Peasant Inheritance Customs in the Midlands, 1280–1700", in Jack Goody, *et al.*, eds, *Family and Inheritance: Rural Society in Western Europe, 1200 to 1800*, Cambridge: Cambridge University Press, 1976.

Hull, Mathew, "Ruled by Records: The Expropriation of Land and the Misappropriations of Lists in Islamabad", *American Ethnologist*, 35 4 (2008).

Hulme, Peter, "Polytropic Man: Tropes of Sexuality and Mobility in Early Colonial Discourse", in Francis Barker, *et al.*, eds, *Europe and Its Others*, Colchester: University of Essex, 1984.

Hume, L.J., *Bentham and Bureaucracy*, Cambridge: Cambridge University Press, 1981.

Hunn, Eugene, "Toward a Perceptual Model of Folk Biological Classification", *American Ethnologist*, 3 (1976): 78–86.

Husain, Imtiaz, *Land Revenue Policy in North India: The Ceded & Conquered*

Provinces, 1801–33, Calcutta: New Age Publishers, 1967.

Hutchins, Francis G., *The Illusion of Permanence: British Imperialism in India*, Princeton: Princeton University Press, 1967.

Hymes, Dell, "Introduction: Towards Ethnographies of Communication", in J.J. Gumperz and D. Hymes, eds, *The Ethnography of Communication*, New York, NY: Holt, Rinehart and Winston, 1972.

Irschick, Eugene F., *Dialogue and History: Constructing South India, 1795–1895*, Delhi: Oxford University Press, 1994.

Islam, M.M., *Bengal Agriculture, 1920–1946*, Cambridge: Cambridge University Press, 1978.

Israel, Milton, *Communications and Power: Propaganda and the Press in the Indian National Struggle, 1920–1947*, Cambridge: Cambridge University Press, 1994.

Joglekar, N.M., *Report on Consolidation of Holdings in Madhya Pradesh: (Pilot Survey, 1956–57)*, New Delhi: Planning Commission, 1962.

Jones, Gareth Stedman, *Outcast London: A Study in the Relationship Between Classes in Victorian Society*, Oxford: Clarendon Press, 1971.

Joshi, Chitra, *Lost Worlds: Indian Labour and Its Forgotten Histories*, Delhi: Permanent Black, 2003.

Kabbani, Rana, *Imperial Fictions: Europe's Myths of Orient*, London: Pandora, 1988.

Kafka, Benjamin, "The Demon of Writing: Paperwork, Public Safety, and the Reign of Terror", *Representations*, 98 (Spring 2007): 1–24.

Kain, Roger, J.P. Baigent, and Elizabeth Baigent, *The Cadastral Map in the Service of the State: A History of Property Mapping*, Chicago: University of Chicago Press, 1992.

Kejariwal, O.P., *The Asiatic Society of Bengal and the Discovery of India's Past: 1784–1838*, Delhi: Oxford University Press, 1988.

Kessinger, Tom G., *Vilyatpur: 1848–1968: Social and Economic Changes in a North Indian village*, Berkeley: University of California Press, 1974.

Khazanov, A.M., *Nomads and the Outside World*, Cambridge: Cambridge University Press, 1984.

Knapp, Alan K., and Lloyd C. Hulbert, "Production, Density and Height of Flower Stalks of 3 Grasses in Annually Burned and Unburned Eastern Kansas Tallgrass Prairie: A Four-year Record", *Southwestern Naturalist*, 31:2 (1986): 235–41.

Knapp, Alan K., and T.R. Seastedt, "Detritus Accumulation Limits Productivity of Tallgrass Prairie", *BioScience*, 36:10 (1986): 662–8.

Koditschek, Theodore, *Liberalism, Imperialism, and the Historical Imagination:*

Nineteenth Century Visions of a Greater Britain, Cambridge: Cambridge University Press, 2011.

Kodoth, Praveena, "Framing Custom, Directing Practices: Authority, Property and Matriliny under Colonial Law in Nineteenth-century Malabar", in Shail Mayaram, M.S.S. Pandian, and Ajay Skaria, eds, *Subaltern Studies XII: Muslims, Dalits, and the Fabrications of History*, New Delhi: Permanent Black and Ravi Dayal Publishers, 2005.

Kosambi, D.D., *An Introduction to the Study of Indian History*, Bombay: Popular Book Depot, 1956.

Kozlowski, T.T., "Plant Responses to Flooding of Soil", *BioScience*, 34:3 (March 1984): 162–7.

Krishna, Raj, "Farm Supply Response in India and Pakistan: A Case Study of Punjab Region", *Economic Journal* (September 1963): 477–87.

Kulkarni, A.R., "The Indian Village: With Special Reference to Medieval Deccan", General Presidential Address, Indian History Congress, February 1992.

Kuper, Adam, "Lineage Theory: A Critical Retrospect", *Annual Review of Anthropology*, 11 (1982): 71–95.

———, *The Invention of Primitive Society: The Transformation of an Illusion*, London: Routledge, 1988.

Lawes, Kim, *Paternalism and Politics: The Revival of Paternalism in Early-Nineteenth-Century Britain*, Basingstoke: Macmillan, 2000.

Le Goff, Jacques, *History and Memory*, New York: Columbia University Press, 1992.

———, *Your Money or Your Life: Economy and Religion in the Middle Ages*, New York: Zone Books, 1990.

Leach, Edmund, "On Certain Unconsidered Aspects of Double Descent Systems", *Man*, 62 (1962): 130–4.

Leask, Nigel, *British Romantic Writers and the East: Anxieties of Empire*, Cambridge: Cambridge University Press, 1993.

Letwin, Shirley R., *The Pursuit of Certainty: David Hume, Jeremy Bentham, John Stuart Mill, Beatrice Webb*, Cambridge: Cambridge University Press, 1965.

Lewis, Reina, *Gendering Orientalism: Race, Femininity, and Representation*, New York: Routledge, 1996.

———, *Rethinking Orientalism: Women, Travel and the Ottoman Harem*, New Brunswick, NJ: Rutgers University Press, 2004.

Lowenthal, David, "The Past is a Foreign Country", in Tim Ingold, ed., *Key*

Debates in Anthropology, London: Routledge, 1996.

———, *The Past is a Foreign Country: Revisited*, Cambridge: Cambridge University Press, 2015.

Lowood, Henry, "The Calculating Forester: Quantification, Cameral Science, and the Emergence of Scientific Forestry Management in Germany", in T. Frangsmyr, J.L. Heilbron, and R.E. Rider, eds, *The Quantifying Spirit of the Eighteenth Century*, Berkeley: University of California Press, 1990.

Ludden, David, *An Agrarian History of South Asia*, Cambridge: Cambridge University Press, 1999.

———, *Peasant History in South India*, Princeton, NJ:. Princeton University Press, 1985.

———, ed., *Agricultural Production and Indian History*, Delhi: Oxford University Press, 1994.

Macfarlane, Alan, "The Myth of the Peasantry: Family and Economy in a Northern Parish", in Richard Smith, ed., *Land, Kinship and Life-Cycle*, Cambridge: Cambridge University Press, 1984.

MacKenzie, John M., *Orientalism: History, Theory and the Arts*. Manchester: Manchester University Press, 2007.

Macpherson, C.B., *The Political Theory of Possessive Individualism: Hobbes to Locke*, Oxford: Oxford University Press, 1970.

Majeed, Javed, *Ungoverned Imaginings: James Mill's "The History of British India" and Orientalism*, Oxford: Clarendon Press, 1992.

Major, Andrew, *Return to Empire: Punjab Under the Sikhs and the British in the Mid-Nineteenth Century*, Delhi: Sterling Publishers, 1996.

Majumdar, Rochona, *Marriage and Modernity: Family Values in Colonial Bengal*, Durham: Duke University Press, 2009.

Malhotra, Anshu, *Gender, Caste, and Religious Identities: Restructuring Class in Colonial Punjab*, New Delhi: Oxford University Press, 2004.

Mamdani, Mahmood, *Citizen and Subject: Contemporary Africa and the Legacy of Late Colonialism*, Princeton: Princeton University Press, 1996.

Mandler, Peter, "The Making of the New Poor Law Redivivas", *Past and Present,* 117 (November 1987).

———, *The Strange Birth of Liberal England: Conservative Origins of the Laissez-faire State*, Cambridge, MA: Harvard University Press, 1989.

Mani, Lata, *Contentious Traditions: The Debate on Sati in Colonial India*, Berkeley: University of California Press, 1998.

Mantena, Karuna, *Alibis of Empire: Henry Maine and the Ends of Liberal Imperialism*, Princeton: Princeton University Press, 2010.

Markovits, C., J. Pouchepadass, and S. Subrahmanyam, eds, *Society and*

Circulation: Mobile People and Itinerant Cultures in South Asia, 1750–1950, New Delhi: Permanent Black, 2003.

Marriott, McKim, *et al.*, *Village India: Studies in the Little Community*, Chicago: Chicago University Press, 1955 (also issued by the American Anthropological Association as vol. 57, no. 2, pt 2, Memoir 83, June 1955).

Marshall, David, "The Problem of the Picturesque", *Eighteenth-Century Studies*, 35:3 (Spring 2002): 413–37.

Marshall, P.J., *The British Discovery of Hinduism in the Eighteenth Century*, Cambridge: Cambridge University Press, 1970.

Matson, P.A., W.J. Parton, A.G. Power, and M.J. Swift, "Agricultural Intensification and Ecosystem Properties", *Science*, New Series, 277:5325 (25 July 1997): 504–9.

Mayer, Adrian C., *Caste and Kinship in Central India: A Village and its Region*, Berkeley and Los Angeles: University of California Press, 1960.

McClintock, Anne, *Imperial Leather: Race, Gender, and Sexuality in the Colonial Contest*, New York: Routledge, 1995.

McCloskey, D.N., "English Open Fields as Behavior towards Risk", in P.J. Uselding, ed., *Research in Economic History*, vol. 1, Greenwich, Conn.: J.A.I. Press, 1976.

———, "Fenoaltea on Open Fields: A Comment", *Explorations in Economic History*, 14:4 (1977): 402–4.

McLaren, Diana, *British India and British Scotland, 1780–1830*, Akron, 2001.

Mehta, Uday Singh, *Liberalism and Empire: A Study of Nineteenth-Century British Liberal Thought*, Chicago: University of Chicago Press, 1999.

Metcalf, Thomas R., *Ideologies of the Raj*, Cambridge: Cambridge University Press, 1994.

Miggelbrink, Judith, and Joachim Habeck, eds, *Nomadic and Indigenous Spaces: Productions and Cognitions*, Farnham, Surrey: Ashgate, 2013.

Mills, Sara, *Discourses of Difference: An Analysis of Women's Travel Writing and Colonialism*, London: Routledge, 1991.

Mir, Farina, *The Social Space of Language: Vernacular Culture in British Colonial Punjab*, Berkeley: University of California Press, 2010.

Mircea, Eliade, *The Myth of the Eternal Return: Cosmos and History*, Princeton: Princeton University Press, 1971.

———, *The Sacred and the Profane: The Nature of Religion*, New York, Harcourt, Inc.: 1959.

Mitchell, Timothy, *Colonising Egypt*, Cambridge: Cambridge University Press, 1988.

———, *Rule of Experts: Egypt, Techno-Politics, Modernity*, Berkeley: University of California Press, 2002.

Mohapatra, Prabhu Prasad, "Land and Credit Market in Chota Nagpur, 1880–1950", *Studies in History*, New Series, 6:2 (1990).

Moir, Martin, "Kaghazi Raj: Notes on the Documentary Basis of Company Rule, 1783–1858", *Indo-British Review*, 21:2 (1993): 185–93.

Moore, Sally, F., *Social Facts and Fabrication: "Customary" Law in Kilimanjaro, 1880–1980*, Cambridge: Cambridge University Press, 1986.

Morefield, Jeanne, *Covenants Without Swords: Idealist Liberalism and the Spirit of Empire*, Princeton: Princeton University Press, 2005.

Mukherjee, Mridula, *Colonializing Agriculture: The Myth of Punjab Exceptionalism*, New Delhi: Sage Publications, 2005.

Mukherjee, Ramkrishna, *The Dynamics of a Rural Society: A Study of Economic Structure in Bengal Villages*, Berlin: Akademie-Verlag, 1957.

———, 'Six Villages of Bengal", *Journal of the Asiatic Society of Bengal*, XXIV:1&2.

Muthu, Sankar, *Enlightenment Against Empire*, Princeton: Princeton University Press, 2003.

Naithani, Sadhana, *The Story-time of the British Empire: Colonial and Postcolonial Folkloristics*, Mississippi: University Press of Mississippi, 2010.

Nandy, Ashis, *The Intimate Enemy: Loss and Recovery of Self Under Colonialism*, Delhi: Oxford University Press, 1983.

Neal, Walter, "Reciprocity and Redistribution in the Indian Village: Sequel to Some Notable Discussions", in Karl Polanyi, *et al.*, eds, *Trade and Market in the Early Empires: Economies in History and Theory*, Glencoe, Ill.: Free Press, 1957.

Nichols, Robert, *Settling the Frontier: Land, Law, and Society in the Peshawar Valley, 1500-1900*, Karachi: Oxford University Press, 2001.

Ogborn, Miles, *Indian Ink: Script and Print in the Making of the English East India Company*, Chicago: University of Carolina Press, 2001.

Ojo, Arewa E., and Alan Dundes, "Proverbs and the Ethnography of Speaking Folklore", in J.J. Gumperz and D. Hymes, eds, *The Ethnography of Communication*, New York, N.Y.: Holt, Rinehart and Winston, 1972.

Oldenburg, Veena T., *Dowry Murder: The Imperial Origins of a Cultural Crime*, Oxford: Oxford University Press, 2002.

Pant, Rashmi, "Speaking in Multiple Registers", in Aparna Balachandran, Rashmi Pant, and Bhavani Raman, eds, *Iterations of Law*, New Delhi:

Oxford University Press, 2017.

Paredes, Americo, and Richard Bauman, *Toward New Perspectives in Folklore*, Austin: University of Texas Press, 1972.

Pateman, Carole, *The Sexual Contract*, Oxford: Basil Blackwell, 1988.

Patnaik, Utsa, *Agrarian Relations and Accumulation: The "Mode of Production" Debate in India*, Sameeksha Trust Publication, Delhi: Oxford University Press, 1990.

Penner, Peter, *The James Thomason School in North India, 1822–1853*, Hamilton, Ontario: McMaster University, 1970.

Pitson, A.E., *Hume's Philosophy of the Self*, New York: Routledge, 2002.

Pitts, Jennifer, *A Turn to Empire: The Rise of Imperial Liberalism in Britain and France*, Princeton: Princeton University Press, 2005.

Polanyi, Karl, *The Great Transformation: The Political and Economic Origins of Our Time*, Boston, Mass.: Beacon Press, 1944.

———, et al., eds, *Trade and Market in the Early Empires: Economies in History and Theory*, Glencoe, Ill: Free Press, 1957.

Poovey, Mary, *A History of the Modern Fact: Problems of Knowledge in the Sciences of Wealth and Society*, Chicago: University of Chicago Press, 1998.

Portelli, Alessandro, *The Order Has been Carried Out: History, Memory, and Meaning of a Nazi Massacre in Rome*, New York: Palgrave Macmillan, 2003.

Porter, Theodore M., *The Rise of Statistical Thinking, 1820–1900*, Princeton: Princeton University Press, 1986.

———, *Trust in Numbers: The Pursuit of Objectivity in Science and Public Life*, Princeton: Princeton University Press, 1995.

Postema, Gerald, *Bentham and the Common Law Tradition*, Oxford: Clarendon Press, 1986.

Prabha, Chander, "District-wise Rates of Growth of Agricultural Output in East and West Punjab During the Pre-partition and Post-partition Periods", *The Indian Economic and Social History Review*, 6:4 (1969): 333–50.

Prakash, Gyan, *Bonded Histories: Genealogies of Labor Servitude in Colonial India*, Cambridge: Cambridge University Press, 1990.

———, ed., *The World of the Rural Labourer in Colonial India*, New Delhi: Oxford University Press, 1994.

Prasad, Archana, "The Aitical Ecology of Swidden Cultivation: The Survival Strategies of the Baigas in the Central Provinces of India, 1860–

1890", *Tools and Tillage: A Journal on the History of the Implements of Cultivation and Other Agricultural Processes* (1995).

Pratt, Mary Louise, *Imperial Eyes: Travel Writing and Transculturation*, New York: Routledge, 1992.

Price, Edward, *Dividing the Land: Early American Beginnings of Our Private Property Mosaic*, Chicago: University of Chicago Press, 1995.

Radcliffe-Brown, A.R., "Patrilineal and Matrilineal Succession", *Iowa Law Review*,1935, reproduced in idem, *Structure and Function in Primitive Society*, London: Routledge & Kegan Paul, 1952.

Radkau, Joachim, "Wood and Forestry in German History; In Quest of an Environmental Approach", *Environment and History*, 2:1 (1996): 63–76.

Raj, K.N., "Agrarian Structure and Change in India, *c.* 1750 to 1980", mimeo.

———, "Ownership and Distribution of Land", *Indian Economic Review*, V:1 (April 1970).

Rajan, S. Ravi, "Imperial Environmentalism or Environmental Imperialism? European Forestry, Colonial Foresters and the Agendas of Forest Management in British India 1800–1900", in Richard Grove, Vinita Damodaran, and Satpal Sangwan, eds, *Nature and the Orient: The Environmental History of Southeast Asia*, Delhi: Oxford University Press, 1998.

———, *Modernizing Nature: Forestry and Imperial Eco-Development 1800–1950*, Oxford: Clarendon Press, 2006.

Raman, Bhavani, *Document Raj: Writing and Scribes in Early Colonial South India*, Chicago: The University of Chicago Press, 2012.

Ramaswamy, Sumathi, "Visualising India's Geo-body: Globes, Maps, Bodyscapes", *Contributions to Indian Sociology*, 36: 1–2 (February 2002).

Rangarajan, Mahesh, *Fencing the Forest: Conservation and Ecological Change in India's Central Provinces, 1860–1914*, New Delhi: Oxford University Press, 1996.

———, and K. Sivaramakrishnan, *India's Environmental History*, 2 vols, Ranikhet: Permanent Black, 2012.

Ratnagar, Shereen, "Archaeology and the State", in B.P. Sahu, ed., *Iron and Social Change in India*, New Delhi: Oxford University Press, 2006.

———, ed., *Mobile and Marginalized People*, New Delhi: Manohar, 2003.

———, ed., *On Pastoralism*, Special Issue, *Studies in History*, 7:2 (1991).

Ray, Ratnalekha, *Change in Bengal Agrarian Society: 1760–1850*, New Delhi: Manohar, 1979.

Rendall, Jane, "Scottish Orientalism: From Robertson to James Mill", *The Historical Journal*, 25:1 (1982).

Richards, John F., *The Unending Frontier: An Environmental History of the Early Modern World*, Berkeley: University of California Press, 2001.

Ricoeur, Paul, *Memory, History, Forgetting*, Chicago: The University of Chicago Press, 2004.

Rigney, Ann, *Imperfect Histories: The Elusive Past and the Legacy of Romantic Historicism*, Ithaca and London: Cornell University Press, 2001.

Rizvi, S.M.Z., M.A. Sabzwari, and C.M. Sharif, *Consolidation of Holdings: A Study of the Process of Consolidation of Agricultural Holdings in Selected Villages in Peshawar District*, Peshawar: Pakistan Academy for Rural Development, 1965.

Robb, Peter, *Ancient Rights and Future Comfort: Bihar, the Bengal Tenancy Act of 1885, and British Rule in India*, Richmond, Surrey: Curzon, 1997.

———, ed., *Meanings of Agriculture: Essays in South Asian History and Economics*, New Delhi: Oxford University Press, 1996.

Roberts, David, *Paternalism in Early Victorian England*, London: Croom Helm, 1979.

———, "Tory Paternalism and Social Reform in Early Victorian England", *The American Historical Review*, 63:2 (January 1958): 323–37.

Rosaldo, Renato, *Ilongot Headhunting, 1883–1974: A Study in Society and History*, Stanford: Stanford University Press, 1980.

Rose, Carol M., "Canons of Property Talk, or, Blackstone's Anxiety", *The Yale Law Journal*, 108:3 (December 1998): 601–32.

Rocher, Rosane, "British Orientalism in the Eighteenth Century", in Carol A. Breckenridge and Peter van der Veer, eds, *Orientalism and the Postcolonial Predicament*, Philadelphia: University of Pennsylvania Press, 1993.

Rosen, Frederick, *Jeremy Bentham and Representative Democracy: A Study of the Constitutional Code*, Oxford: Clarendon Press, 1983.

Rubin, I.I., *Essays on Marx's Theory of Value*, Detroit, Michigan: Black and Red, 1972.

Sabean, David, "Aspects of Kinship Behaviour and Property in Rural Western Europe before 1800", in Jack Goody, *et al.*, eds, *Family and Inheritance: Rural Society in Western Europe, 1200 to 1800*, Cambridge: Cambridge University Press, 1976.

Saberwal, Vasant K., *Pastoral Politics: Shepherds, Bureaucrats, and Conservation in the Western Himalaya*, New Delhi: Oxford University Press, 1999.

Sabiiti, E.N., "Fire Behaviour and the Invasion of *Acacia sieberiana* into Savanna Grassland Openings", *African Journal of Ecology*, 26:4 (1988):

301–13.

Sagay, I.E., "Customary Law and Freedom of Testamentary Power", *Journal of African Law*, 39:2 (1995): 173–82.

Sahlins, Marshall D., *Culture and Practical Reason*, Chicago, Ill.: University of Chicago Press, 1988.

———, *Culture in Practice: Selected Essays*, New York: Zone Books, 2005.

———, "The Spirit of Gift", and "On the Sociology of Primitive Exchange", in *Stone Age Economics*, London: Routledge, 1972.

Sangari, Kumkum, and Sudesh Vaid, eds, *Recasting Women: Essays in Colonial History*, New Delhi: Kali for Women, 1989.

Sarkar, Tanika, *Hindu Wife, Hindu Nation: Community, Religion and Cultural Nationalism*, New Delhi: Permanent Black, 2001.

———, *Rebels, Wives, Saints: Designing Selves and Nations in Colonial Times*, Ranikhet, Permanent Black, 2009.

Sartori, Andrew, "A Liberal Discourse of Custom in Colonial Bengal", *Past & Present*, 212: 1 (2011): 163–97.

———, *Liberalism in Empire: An Alternative History*, Oakland: University of California Press, 2014.

Schwab, Raymond, *Oriental Renaissance: Europe's Rediscovery of India and the East, 1680–1880*, New York: Columbia University Press, 1984.

Scheffler, H.W., "Descent Concepts and Descent Groups: The Maori Case", *The Journal of the Polynesian* Society, 73:2 (1964).

———, "The Descent of Rights and the Descent of Persons", *American Anthropologist*, 20 (2001): 339–50.

Schneider, D.M., *Critique of the Study of Kinship*, Ann Arbor: University of Michigan Press, 1982.

Schochet, G.J., *Patriarchalism in Political Thought: The Authoritarian Family and Political Speculation and Attitudes Especially in Seventeenth-Century England*, Oxford: Basil Blackwell, 1975.

Schulze, M., S. Harrison, E. Heimann, E. Holland, J. Lloyd, I.C. Prentice, and D. Schimel, eds, *Global Biogeochemical Cycles in the Climate System*, San Diego: Academic Press, 2001.

Schwerin, Alan, *Hume's Labyrinth: A Search of the Self*, Newcastle upon Tyne: Cambridge Scholars Publishing, 2012.

Scott, James C., *Domination and the Arts of Resistance: Hidden Transcripts*, New Haven: Yale University Press, 1990.

———, *Seeing Like a State: How Certain Schemes to Improve the Human Condition Have Failed*, New Haven: Yale University Press, 1998.

————, *Weapons of the Weak*, New Haven: Yale University Press, 1985.

Seigel, Jerrold, E., *The Idea of the Self: Thought and Experience in Western Europe since the Seventeenth Century*, New York: Cambridge University Press, 2005.

Sengupta, Nirmal, "Fragmented Holdings, Productivity, and Resilience Management", *Environment and Development Economics*, 11 (2006): 507–32.

Sharma, R.S., "Iron and Urbanization on the Gangetic Basin", *The Indian Historical Review*, 1:1 (1974).

————, *Material Culture and Social Formation in Ancient India*, Delhi: Macmillan, 1983.

Siddiqi, Asiya, *Agrarian Change in a North Indian State: Uttar Pradesh 1819–1833*, Oxford: Clarendon Press, 1973.

Siddiqi, Noman Ahmad, *Land Revenue Administration Under the Mughals*, New Delhi: Munshiram Manoharlal Publishers, 1989.

Silva, J.F., A. Zambrano, M.R. Farinas, "Increase in the Woody Component of Seasonal Savannas under Different Fire Regimes in Calabozo, Venezuela", *Journal of Biogeography*, 28 (2001): 977–83.

Simon, Brian, and Ian Bradley, eds, *The Victorian Public School: Studies in the Development of an Educational Institution*, Dublin: Gill and Macmillan, 1975.

Sinha, Mrinalini, *Colonial Masculinity: The "Manly Englishman" and the "Effeminate Bengali"*, New Delhi: Kali for Women, 1997.

Singh, Chetan, *Region and Empire: Panjab in the Seventeenth Century*, Delhi: Oxford University Press, 1991.

————, *Natural Premises: Ecology and Peasant Life in the Western Himalaya, 1800–1950*, Delhi: Oxford University Press, 1998.

Singh, Fauja, *Military System of the Sikhs: During the Period 1799–1849*, Delhi: Motilal Banarasidass, 1964.

Singh, Shrinath, *Consolidation of Holdings: Methods and Problems*, India: Planning Commission, 1957.

Sirajul Islam, *The Permanent Settlement in Bengal: A Study of its Operation, 1790–1819*, Dacca: Bangla Academy, 1979.

Sivaramakrishnan, K., *Modern Forests: Statemaking and Environmental Change in Colonial Eastern India*, Stanford: Stanford University Press, 1999.

Skaria, Ajay, *Hybrid Histories: Forests, Frontiers, and Wildness in Western India*, Delhi: Oxford University Press, 1999.

Smith, Richard Saumarez, *Rule by Records: Land Registration and Village*

Custom in Early British Panjab, New Delhi: Oxford University Press, 1996.

Smith, Richard, "Families and their Land in an Area of Partible Inheritance: Redgrave, Suffolk 1260–1320", in idem, ed., *Land, Kinship and Lifecycle*, Cambridge: Cambridge University Press, 1984.

Spufford, Margaret, *Contrasting Communities: English Villagers in the Sixteenth and Seventeenth Centuries*, Cambridge: Cambridge University Press, 1974.

Srinivas, M.N., ed., *India's Villages*, Bombay: Asia Publishing House, 1960.

Stetkevych, Suzanne P., "Ritual and Sacrificial Elements in the Poetry of Blood Vengeance", *Journal of Near Eastern Studies*, 45:1 (1986): 31–43.

———, *Race Culture and Evolution: Essays in the History of Anthropology, 1883–1911*, Chicago: University of Chicago Press, 1982.

———, *Victorian Anthropology*, New York: Free Press, 1987.

Stokes, Eric, *The English Utilitarians and India*, Oxford: Clarendon Press, 1959.

———, *The Peasant and the Raj: Studies in Agrarian Society and Peasant Rebellion in Colonial India*, Cambridge: Cambridge University Press, 1978.

Strathern, A.J., "Kinship, Descent and Locality: Some New Guinea Examples", in Jack Goody, ed., *The Character of Kinship*, Cambridge: Cambridge University Press, 1973.

Strathern, Marilyn, *The Gender of the Gift: Problems with Women and Problems with Society in Melanesia*, Berkeley: University of California Press, 1988.

Sturman, Rachel L., *The Government of Social Life in Colonial India: Liberalism, Religious Law, and Women's Rights*, New York: Cambridge University Press, 2012.

Sutton, Deborah, *Other Landscapes: Colonialism and the Predicament of Authority in Nineteenth-Century South India*, New Delhi: Orient Blackswan, 2011.

Talbot, Ian, *Khizr Tiwana, the Punjab Unionist Party, and the Partition of India*, Oxford: Oxford University Press, 2002.

Tatla, Darshan S., "Sandal Bar: Memories of a Punjabi Farmer", *Punjab Past and Present*, 29:1 & 2 (1995), pp. 160–75.

Taylor, Charles, "To Follow a Rule", in Richard Shusterman, ed., *Bourdieu: A Critical Reader*, Oxford: Blackwell Publishers, 1999.

Teltscher, Kate, *India Inscribed: European and British Writing on India, 1600–1800*, Delhi: Oxford University Press, 1995.

Thapar, Romila, *From Lineage to State: Social Formations in the Mid-first Millennium B.C. in the Ganga Valley*, New Delhi: Oxford University

Press, 1984.

———, "Perceiving the Forest: Early India", *Studies in History*, 17:1 (2001).

Thirsk, Joan, "The European Debate on Customs of Inheritance, 1500–1700", in Jack Goody, *et al.*, eds, *Family and Inheritance: Rural Society in Western Europe 1200–1800*, Cambridge: Cambridge University Press, 1978.

Thomas, Nicholas, *Out of Time: History and Evolution in Anthropological Discourse*, Cambridge: Cambridge University Press, 1989.

Thompson, E.P., *Customs in Common*, London: Penguin Books, 1993.

———, *The Making of the English Working Class*, Harmondsworth: Penguin Books, 1963.

———, *The Poverty of Theory & Other Essays*, London: Merlin Press, 1978.

Thornton, P., *The Habit of Authority: Paternalism British History*, London: Allen & Unwin, 1966.

Tönnies, Ferdinand, *Community and Society: Gemeinshaft und Gesellschaft*, Michigan: Michigan State University Press, 1957.

Townsend, Dabney, "The Picturesque", *The Journal of Aesthetic and Art Criticism*, 55:4 (Autumn 1997): 365–76.

Townsend, Robert M., *Medieval Village Economy*, Princeton: Princeton University Press, 1993.

Trevor Roper, Hugh, "The Invention of Tradition: The Highland Tradition of Scotland", in E.J. Hobsbawm and T.O. Ranger, eds, *The Invention of Tradition*, Cambridge: Cambridge University Press, 1983.

Tully, James, *A Discourse on Property: John Locke and His Adversaries*, Cambridge: Cambridge University Press, 1980.

Uselding, P.J., ed., *Research in Economic History*, vol. 1, Greenwich, Conn.: J.A.I. Press, 1976.

van den Dungen, P.H.M., *The Punjab Tradition: Influence and Authority in Nineteenth-Century India*, London: Allen & Unwin, 1972.

van der Veer, Peter, *Imperial Encounters: Religion and Modernity in India and Britain*, Princeton: Princeton University Press, 2001.

Vansina, J., *Oral Traditions as History*, London: James Currey, 1985.

Vinogradoff, Paul. *The Teaching of Sir Henry Maine*, London: H. Frowde, 1904.

Visvanathan, Susan, *Friendship, Interiority, Mysticism: Essays in Dialogue*, New Delhi: Orient Longman, 2007.

Viswanathan, Gauri, *Masks of Conquest: Literary Study and British Rule in India*, London: Faber & Faber, 1989.

Washbrook, David, "Economic Development and Social Stratification in Rural Madras: The 'Dry Region', 1878–1929", in Clive Dewey and A.G. Hopkins, eds, *The Imperial Impact: Studies in the Economic History of Africa and India*, London: Athlone Press for the Institute of Commonwealth Studies, 1978.

Whitcombe, Elizabeth, *Agrarian Conditions in Northern India: The United Provinces Under British Rule, 1860–1900*, California: University of California Press, 1971.

White, Leslie A., "History, Evolutionism, and Functionalism: Three Types of Interpretation of Culture", *Southwestern Journal of Anthropology*, 1:2 (1945): 221–48.

Wilkinson, Rupert, *Gentlemanly Power: British Leadership and the Public School Tradition*, London: Oxford University Press, 1964.

Williams, Barbara J., and Carlos A. Ortiz-Solorio, "Middle American Folk Soil Taxonomy", *Annals of the Association of American Geographers*, 71:3 (September 1981): 335–58.

Williams, Raymond, "Thomas Carlyle", in *Culture and Society 1780–1950*, Harmondsworth: Penguin Books, 1975.

Wilshusen Richard H., and Glenn D. Stone, "An Ethno-archaeological Perspective on Soils", *World Archaeology*, 22:1 (June 1990): 104–14.

Wilson, Jon E., *The Domination of Strangers: Modern Governance in Eastern India, 1780–1835*, Basingstoke: Palgrave Macmillan, 2008.

Winichakul, Thongchai, *Siam Mapped: A History of the Geo-body of a Nation*, Hawaii: University of Hawaii Press, 1994.

Wise, M. Norton, ed., *The Values of Precision*, Princeton: Princeton University Press, 1995.

Wiser, W.H., *The Hindu Jajmani System*, Lucknow: Lucknow Publishing House, 1936.

Wood, Juliette, "Folklore Studies at the Celtic Dawn: The Role of Alfred Nutt as Publisher and Scholar", *Folklore*, 110: 2 (1999): 3–12.

Worster, Donald, *Nature's Economy: A History of Ecological Ideas*, Cambridge: Cambridge University Press, 1985.

———, *Rivers of Empire: Water, Aridity, and the Growth of the American West*, New York: Oxford University Press, 1992.

———, *The Ends of the Earth: Perspectives on Modern Environmental History*, Cambridge: Cambridge University Press, 1980.

Wrightson, Keith, "Kinship in an English Village: Terling, Essex 1500–1700", in Richard Smith, ed., *Land, Kinship and Life-Cycle*, Cambridge: Cambridge University Press, 1984.

Yeğenoğlu, Meyda, *Colonial Fantasies: Towards a Feminist Reading of*

Orientalism, Cambridge: Cambridge University Press, 1999.

Yang, Anand A., *The Limited Raj: Agrarian Relations in Colonial India, Saran District, 1793-1920*, Berkeley: University of California Press, 1989.

Zonabend, Francoise, *The Enduring Memory: Time and History in a French Village*, Manchester: Manchester University Press, 1985.

UNPUBLISHED THESES

Agnihotri, Indu, "Agrarian Change in the Canal Colonies, Punjab, 1890–1935", Ph.D. Thesis, Centre for Historical Studies, Jawaharlal Nehru University, 1987.

Goswami, Ritupan, "Rivers and History: Brahmaputra Valley in the Nineteenth Century", M.Phil. Thesis, Centre for Historical Studies, Jawaharlal Nehru University, 2005.

Kamozawa, Maiko, "Family, Property and Migration in Colonial Punjab", Ph.D. Thesis, Centre for Historical Studies, Jawaharlal Nehru University, 2005.

Kar, Bodhisattva, "Framing Assam", Ph.D. Thesis, Centre for Historical Studies, Jawaharlal Nehru University, 2007.

Malik, Bela, "Hill and Forest Economies in Northeast India: Mid-19th Century to Early 20th Century", M.Phil. Thesis, Centre for Historical Studies, Jawaharlal Nehru University, 1991.

Pant, Rashmi, "Peasant Households and Village Communities in Colonial Garhwal, 1815–1950", Ph.D. Thesis, Centre for Historical Studies, Jawaharlal Nehru University, 2011.

Prasad, Archana, "Forests and Subsistence in Colonial India: A Study of the Central Provinces, 1830–1945", Ph.D. Thesis, Centre for Historical Studies, Jawaharlal Nehru University, 1994.

Index

www.ingramcontent.com/pod-product-compliance
Lightning Source LLC
Chambersburg PA
CBHW071822270326
41929CB00013B/1885